Grantees of Arms
Edited by
W. Harry Rylands F.S.A

A facsimile copy produced and privately printed by
The Armorial Register Limited
2016

First Published in 2016
by
The Armorial Register Limited
All rights reserved

ISBN: 978-0-9568157-6-7

British Library Cataloguing-in-Publication Data
A catalogue record of this book is available on request from the
British Library

THE

Publications

OF

The Harleian Society.

ESTABLISHED A.D. MDCCCLXIX.

VIRTVS
EGO FIDE

Volume LXVI.

FOR THE YEAR MDCCCCXV.

Grantees of Arms

NAMED IN

DOCQUETS AND PATENTS

TO THE END OF THE

SEVENTEENTH CENTURY,

IN THE MANUSCRIPTS

PRESERVED IN THE

BRITISH MUSEUM, THE

BODLEIAN LIBRARY, OXFORD,

QUEEN'S COLLEGE, OXFORD,

GONVILLE AND CAIUS COLLEGE,

CAMBRIDGE, AND ELSEWHERE,

ALPHABETICALLY ARRANGED BY

The Late JOSEPH FOSTER, Hon. M.A. Oxon.

AND CONTAINED IN THE ADDITIONAL MS.

No. 37,147, IN THE BRITISH MUSEUM.

EDITED BY

W. Harry Rylands, F.S.A.

LONDON.

1915.

Preface.

IN this Volume will be found the contents of the first of a series of four MS. volumes now in the British Museum, and numbered Add. MS. 37,147, 37,148, 37,149 and 37,150. They were bought after the death of the compiler from Mr. Josslyn Foster on the 14th October 1905, as entered in the first volume of the series.

Joseph Foster did not confine his attention to the manuscripts alone, but has given some references to the printed copies of these old grants, but more particularly when a transcript of the original is given in the various publications mentioned.

In referring to the MSS. preserved at Queen's College, Oxford, he uses two sets of shelf-marks. Wishing to obtain a copy of the Patent to the town of Raleigh in Virginia, I sent the reference given by Foster to Miss E. G. Parker at Oxford, and asked for a copy. She applied to the Librarian and received from him the reply that MS. No. 36 contained nothing heraldic. Later the Librarian very kindly allowed Miss Parker to make a search for the MS. containing this Patent, and after a lengthy examination of Heraldic MSS. she solved the puzzle. Foster, although he gives the proper press marks to other MSS. in Queen's College Library, in the case of these four volumes he uses imperfectly the old numbers, omitting the letter H before the figures. It must be understood in the following pages that the MSS. referred to by Foster should have been entered as follows :—

> [H] 36 should be No. 137.
> [H] 37 „   „ No. 138.
> [H] 38 „   „ No. 139.
> [H] 39 „   „ No. 140.

A full copy of this interesting and unusual form of Patent, granted by William Dethick, Garter, to Raleigh, Virginia, is included in the Additions and Corrections.

Some of these Additions are contained in very rough notes by Mr. Foster, not incorporated by him in the main text. I regret very much that the list of Additions and Corrections is so lengthy, but unfortunate circumstances prevented these, as well as the List of Stray Names, etc., being added to the text of the book as they ought to have been. I trust, however, that the List of Stray Names that I have added will be found useful.

My own additions are always marked by being printed in square brackets; other editorial corrections have been for the most part the correction and extension of the references and other corrections, so as to make them more intelligible. In this I have been very much assisted by the care and trouble Miss Drucker, the transcriber, has given to the work of copying a manuscript often confused with interlineations, imperfect blazons, and wrongly copied words. We must, however, be thankful that Mr. Foster gave so much time and labour to the compilation of this key to the manuscripts containing so many Grants of Arms.

W. HARRY RYLANDS.

STRAY NAMES, ARMS, QUARTERINGS, ETC., BEING CROSS-REFERENCES TO THE MAIN TEXT.

BRADLEY, quartering, *see* Forster (White), Mary.

BRADSHAW, mar., *see* Stanley, Henry.

BRAY, Arms (Longvale), *see* Lownde, Thomas.

BREWES, mar., *see* Wilton, Dame Cecilia.

BRICKLESTON, quartering, *see* Stone, Thomas.

BRID, LE, *see* Bird.

BRIERLEY, *see* Brearley, James.

BRIHYTON ?, quarter⁸, *see* Jekyll, Thomas.

BRIKETT, *see* Birkett *and* Birkhead.

BRITZMAN, *see* Brightman.

BROBREDGE, marriage, *see* Goodchild, Elizabeth.

BROCAS, marriage, *see* More, Nicholas.

BROGRAVE, mar., *see* Billesley, William.

BROTHERS, *see* Kuight, Henry.

BROWNE, mar., *see* Lucas, Margaret.

BROWNE, *see* Bronde, Benjamin.

BRUER, *see* Butman, Henry.

BRYKETT, *see* Birkhead *and* Birkett.

BUCKLAND, quarter⁸, *see* Milles, Thomas.

BUCKLEY, *see* Birkeby, James.

BUDDYER, quartering, *see* White, John.

BUDDYER, Arms, *see* Additions, p. xviii.

BULL, marriage, *see* Branthwaite, Richard (p. 33).

BULLOCK, Grant, *see* Johnson, Rowland.

BULMER, quartering, *see* Beiston, Ralph.

BULMER, marriage, *see* Cooper, Meryall.

BUNCLEY, *see* Boucley.

BURGOYNE, marriage, *see* Bill, Jane.

BUSHELL, Arms, *see* Herd, Richard.

BUTTALL, quartering, *see* Weld, Sir Humphrey.

BUTTELIER, *see* Boteler, Richard.

BUTLER, quartering, *see* White, John.

BUTLER, Arms, *see* Additions, p. xviii.

BYRD, *see also* Bird.

BYRKBIE, *see* Birkbye.

BYRMINGHAM, Arms, *see* Hickman, Henry.

BYRON, quartering, *see* Spence.

BYSSHE, *see* Bishe.

CAERLEON, quartering, *see* Edwards.

CALCHETTI, *see* Culcheth.

CANTRELL, quarter⁸, *see* Wood of Enfield.

CAPLEN, *see* Chaplin, John.

CAREY, marriage, *see* Scroope, Mary.

CARTER, *see* Hasledon, William.

CARY, impalement, *see* Leake, Sir Francis.

CASTELL, marriage, *see* Freear, Thomas.

CAVENDISH, quartering, *see* Spence.

CAWLEY, quarter⁸, *see* Stourton, Edward.

CHAMBERLAYNE, quartering, *see* Faldoe, Robert.

CHAMBERLAYNE, Arms, *see* Smyth.

CHAMPNEYS, mar., *see* Clarke, Edward.

CHARLES, mar., *see* Cartwright, Timothy.

CHARNOCK, quartering, *see* Smith, John, of Walden.

CHEESMAN, mar., *see* Johnson, Edward.

CHEROURICE DE NORMANDIE, *see* Saverey.

CHERRY, mar. and impaled, *see* Merrick.

CHISNOLL, marriage, *see* Bretarge, William (p. 33).

CHOLMLEIGH, mar., *see* Sleigh, Gervase.

CHUDWORTH, quarter⁸, *see* Thomson, John.

CLARK, marriage, *see* Jadwine, Robert.

CLARKE, quartering, *see* Curling, John.

CLARKE, quartering, *see* Arras, Robert.

CLARKE, *see* Norhope.

CLAYTON, quartering, *see* Spence.

CLAZELL, marriage, *see* Fulwer, John.

CLEARKE, *see* Norhope.

CLERVAUX, *see* Chater, William.

CLERVOWE, Thomas de, Grant by, *see* Criketot.

CLEVELAND, Barbara, Duchess of, *see* FitzRoy.

CLIFFORD, quartering, *see* Codrington, Richard.

CLIFFORD, marriage, *see* Malby, Arthur.

COCK, *see* Coke, John.

COCKETT, quartering, *see* Butts, William.

CODINGTON, quarter⁸, *see* Lusher, Nicholas.

CODRINGTON, quartering, *see* Jordan, Edmund.

COKESFORD, *see* Cotesford.

COLE, quartering, *see* Owen, Thomas.

COLEIRE, marriage, *see* Serjeant, Thomas.

COLLIER, *see* Dimocke, William.

COLWICH, quartering, *see* Spence, and Wood of Enfield.

COMBARFORD, quartering, *see* Lusher, Nicholas.

COMPTON, marriage, *see* Weoley, Thomas.

COOKES, marriage, *see* Lewes, Lady.

COOPER, Christopher, Arms, *see* Additions, p. xviii.

COOPER, marriage, *see* Smith, Mary.

COOTES, marriage, *see* Lewes, Lady.

COOTES, *see* Cotes, John.

COPLEY, marriage, *see* Gage, Henry.

CORBETT, Reginald, *see* Hill.

CORDALL, marriage, *see* Webbe, Emma.

CORY, *see also* Cary, John.

COTTLE, marriage, *see* Hall, Sarah.

COTTON, quartering, *see* Venables, Sir Thomas.

COWLEBY, *see* Vincent, Philip.

COWPER, *see* Cooper, John.

CRANTON, *see* Caunton.

CRAWLEY, *see* Shrawley.
CROKE, *see* Blount.
CROMWELL, *see* Williams, Richard.
CUPHOLME, *see* Tupholme.
CURE, marriage, *see* Bennett, Ann.
CURWEN, *see* Kirwin, William.

DACRES, marriage, *see* Brownell, Mary.
DAKYNS, William, forger of grants, *see*
    Rudiard, Thomas.
    Santon, Thomas.
    Sherwood, Sir Rowland.
    Smethwick, William.
DALIN, Alice, mar., *see* Cholwill, Thomas.
DANIEL, *see* Savage, John.
DANVERS, quartering, *see* Davers.
DANVERS, *see* Clarke, William.
DANYERS, *see* Legh, Sir Piers.
DANYERS, Grant and marriage, *see* Savage,
    John.
DARE, Ananias, Arms, *see* Additions, p.
    xviii.
DART, *see* Walles, Lewis.
DAVENPORT, *see* Davenant.
DAWES, marriage, *see* Fynche, Margaret.
DAWNEY, *see* Viscount Downe.
DEANE, marriage, *see* Turner, Sir Thomas.
DE AULA, ? *see* Hawle, Henry.
DE BOYNTON, Arms, *see* Aton.
DE BOYS, Le Sieur de, Dauphin of France,
    see Wood, Thomas.
DE CLERVOWE, Thomas (Grant by), *see*
    Criketot.
DEERING, quartering, *see* Cole, Solomon.
DE HERONYLE, Arms, *see* Wyrley, Roger
    de.
DE LA HULL, *see* Hill.
DE LIGNE, *see* Le Lingne.
DE MORLE, Grant, *see* Corby, Robert de.
DENE, marriage, *see* Vincent, Joane.
DENN, impalement, *see* Gookeine, John.
DEVENISH, impalement, *see* Morley, John.
DICKONSON, *see* Urmeston.
DICKSON, *see* Dixon.
DIGGS, marriage, *see* Rose, Judith, *and*
    Sheldon, Daniel.
DOBBES, marriage, *see* Glasse, Alice.
DODERIDGE, mar., *see* Pyncombe, John.
DOMVILE, Arms, *see* Holes, Thomas de.
DORINGTON, quarterg, *see* Collier, Francis.
DOWNER, marriage, *see* Chamberlayne,
    Robert.
DRAGONER, *see* Drayner.
DREW, quartering, *see* Rowe, John.
DUGDALE, mar., *see* Pidgeon, Elizabeth.
DURLEW, *see* Curlew.
DUTTON, quarterg, *see* Warburton, Peter.

DYER, Arms, *see* Stansfield, Edmund.
DYMOKE, marriage, *see* Sparrow, Ann.

ECCLESTON, quartering, *see* Venables, Sir
    Thomas.
ELDRED, mar., *see* Blaikway, Anne.
ELESTON, quartering, *see* Venables, Sir
    Thomas.
ELKYN, marriage, *see* Wilkes, Alice.
ELSINGTON, *see* Evington, Nicholas.
EMERY, *see* Amery.
ENGHAM, impalement, *see* Nourse, John.
ENGLOSSE, Arms, *see* Hearne, Thomas.
ERNEFORD, quarterg, *see* Lusher, Nicholas.
ERNLES, *see* Holton.
ESME, *see* Hene, William.
EVANS, *see* Ewens, Mathew.
EYNON, *see* Baynham, William.
EYNSHAM, *see* Heynsham.

FALDOE, marriage, *see* Chamberlayne.
FARDINANDO, Symon, Arms, *see* Addi-
    tions, p. xix.
FARENDON, *see* Farndon.
FARMER, *see* Lempster, Lord.
FARMER, *see* Draper.
FARRANT, *see* Ferrand, William.
FAWCETT, *see* Forsett.
FEILDING, marriage, *see* Ellis, Joyce.
FEILDING, mar., *see* Bosworth, Isabel.
FETHERSTON, *see* Parkinson, James.
FINSON, mar., *see* Nutbrowne, Nicholas.
FISHER, *see* Hawkins, Thomas.
FITZHUGH, quartering, *see* Weld, Sir
    Humphrey.
FLEERE, *see* Flyer.
FONSTON, *see* Funstone.
FOX, mar., *see* Whittle, Dame Elizabeth.
FOXLEY, marriage, *see* Haynes, William.
FREAR, marriage, *see* Shaw, Mary.
FULWOOD, William, Arms, *see* Additions,
    p. xviii.

GABBOT, quartering, *see* Lyly (p. 156).
GAKER (or SAKER), quartering, *see* White,
    John.
GAKER (or SAKER), Arms, *see* Additions,
    p. xviii.
GALIARDET, *see* Gallard, Francis.
GARHET, *see* Garset.
GARVES, *see* Gervis.
GARWAY, marriage, *see* Younge, John.
GAYWOOD, quartering, *see* Kytchyn, John.
GHOGAN, *see* Dougan.
GIRDLER, quartering, *see* Stone, Thomas.
GLASSE, *see* Dobbes, Richard.
GLOVER, quartering, *see* Thomson, John.

GODDEN, quartering, *see* Clegat.
GOLBORNE, quartering, *see* Venables, Sir Thomas.
GOLDSMITH, quartering, *see* Hodgson.
GORGES, *see* Warbleton, John.
GORVIES, Arms, *see* Gervies, Arthur.
GOSTON, *see* Gofton.
GOSTRED, *see* Gosfright, George.
GOTLEY, marriage, *see* Treton, Thomas.
GOUGH, marriage, *see* Hubberd, Edward.
GRANDTOFTE, quartering, *see* Clerke, Bartholomew.
GRANTE, quartering, *see* Weld, Sir Humphrey.
GRATEWOOD, marriage, *see* Hill, Jane.
GRAY, marriage and quartering, *see* Tooke, James.
GRAY, Arms, *see* Rotheram, George.
GRAY, marriage, *see* Payton, Anne.
GREEN, quartering, *see* Hamby, John.
GREENFIELD, marriage, *see* Hawthorne, Robert.
GRENDALE, Thomas, Grant, *see* Moigne, Sir William.
GRESHAM, mar., *see* Sampson, Katherine.
GRIMES, impalement, *see* Austen.
GURNARD, *see* Gurney, Richard.
GUYBON, *see* Gibbon.
GUYLEMYN, *see* Gilman.

HABYNGTON, *see* Hannington, William.
HALL, mar., *see* Symmings, John.
HALL, *see* Wall, William.
HAMPDEN, quartering, *see* Parsons, Sir John.
HANCHELL (HANCHETT), *see* Williams, Sir Abraham.
HANSARD, quartering, *see* Hamby, John.
HANSHA, Alice, mar., *see* Lyon, Sir John.
HARBERTS, *see* Roberts, John.
HARDING, marriage and quartering, *see* Randyll, Edward.
HARDOGSON, *see* Harrison, Gilbert.
HARE, marriage, *see* Audley, Thomas.
HARFORD, quartering, *see* Butts, William.
HARGRAVE, coheir, *see* Moulson, John.
HARIOT, quartering, *see* Warner, Mark.
HARLYN, *see* Wilkinson, John.
HARMON, *see* Voysey.
HARPUR, *see* Harper, Richard.
HARRINGTON, marriage and Grant, *see* Rogers, Mary.
HARRIS, *see* Harry, Rowland.
HARVYE, Dyonise, Arms, *see* Additions, p. xviii.
HAULE, quartering, *see* Tooke, James.
HAWTAYNE, ? *see* Hawthen.

HAWTREE, mar., *see* Clinkard, Gabriell.
HAYNES, quarter., *see* Cage, Nicholas.
HAYWOOD, *see* Hayward.
HEARNE, marriage, *see* Hall, Sarah.
HEARNE, *see* Hyrue.
HELER, *see* Helyar.
HENCHMAN, LE, *see* Henxman, Edward.
HERBERT, Arms, *see* Roberts, John.
HERPER, *see* Harper, Richard and William.
HERRIS, *see* Harris, Robert.
HEVER, quartering, *see* Oxburgh, Thomas.
HEYDON, marriage, *see* Rose, Martha.
HEYDON, Crest, *see* Saunderson, Henry.
HEYNSHAM, *see* Hinsham.
HILLS, quartering, *see* Lucas, Margaret.
HINCKSHAWE, *see* Henshaw, Thomas.
HIPPON, marriage, *see* Murgatrod, Michael.
HOBSON, quartering, *see* Roberts, Thomas.
HODGES, marriage, *see* Hall, Sarah.
HOLBEACH, *see* Randes, Thomas.
HOLDEN, marriage, *see* Stevenson, John.
HOLT, *see* Hoult, William.
HOPE, *see* Eyre, Robert.
HORLEY, marriage, *see* Haynes, William.
HORTON, als MORTON, *see* Cowper, John.
HOUGHTON, quartering, *see* Sawyer, and Whitmore, Anne.
HOWARD, change of Arms, *see* Tripp.
HOWE, marriage, *see* Scroope, Anabella.
HOWE, George, Arms, *see* Additions, p. xix.
HOWPER, *see* Hooper, John.
HOWSE, *see* House.
HULL, DE LA, *see* Hill, John.
HULSON, *see* Hudson, John.
HUNGERFORD, *see* Shuger.
HUSSEY, quartering, *see* Jordan, Edmund.
HUSSEY, quartering, *see* Collier, Francis.
HYDE, marriage, *see* Sanders, Helen.
HYDE, marriage, *see* Cater, Margery.

IDEN, quartering, *see* Browne, John.
INGLEDEW, quarter., *see* Lyndsay, Edward.
IRELAND, quartering, *see* Owen, Thomas.
IRTON, marriage, *see* Boorne, Elizabeth.

JENKENS, *see* Jones, Roger.
JENKYN, David ap William, *see* Rawlins, John.
JENYNS, mar., *see* Nychelle, John (p. 182).
JENYNS, William, *see* Gedding.
JOHNS, *see* Jones.
JOHNSON, marriage, *see* Gourney, Anne.
JOHNSON, mar., *see* Mordaunt, Elizabeth.
JOHNSON, *see* Crookhey.
JONES, marriage, *see* Greenhill, Thomas.
JOYCE, quartering, *see* Butts, William.

JUDE, marriage, *see* Mathew, Mary.

KARKIKE, marriage, *see* Smyth, John, of Walden.
KEDERMINSTER, marriage and quartering, *see* Parsons, Sir John.
KEYNSHAM, *see* Heynsham, John.
KILLYOWE, quartering, *see* White, John.
KILLYOWE, Arms, *see* Additions, p. xviii.
KIRKLE, quartering, *see* Butts, William.
KIRKHOVEN, *see* Wotton, Lord.
KNEVETT, *see* Kevett, Thomas.

LACOCK, *see* Laycock.
LAMBERT, *see also* Lambard.
LAMBORNE, quarter⁸, *see* Boiland, Richard.
LANGFOLD, marriage, *see* Flemynge, John.
LASHER, *see* Lussher.
LATHOM, quartering, *see* Stanley.
LAUNDER, *see* Landor.
LAUNDES, *see* Lownde, John.
LAXTON, marriage, *see* Kirkeby, Jane.
LE BRID, *see* Bird.
LE CHAT, Lewis, Arms, *see* Rudd, John.
LEE, marriage, *see* Lyon, Sir John.
LEE, Joan, confirms Arms, *see* Peshale, Robert.
LEEKE, *see* Leake.
LEEKE, *see* Deincourt.
LEIGH, Sir Peirs, Arms, *see* Ashton.
LEIGH, of Cheshire, Crest, *see* Bennollis.
LEVESON, *see* Fowler, Francis Leveson.
LEWKENOR, marriage, *see* Cowper, John.
LEWYS, marriage, *see* Fayrechylde, Joan.
LISTER, marriage, *see* Snode, Mary.
LITTLETON, marriage, *see* Ivatt, Thomas.
LLOYD, quartering, *see* Pennant, Peires.
LLOYD, *see* Fludd.
LOBENHAM, marriage, *see* Atslow, Edward.
LOCKE, marriage, *see* Wappam, Elizabeth.
LODGE, marriage, *see* Ivatt, Thomas.
LONGFORD, impaled, *see* Mills, Thomas.
LOVELL, *see* Vincent.
LOVETT, marriage, *see* Symmings, John.
LOWE, *see* Love, Robert.
LOWEN, marriage, *see* Plumer, Jone.
LUCY, marriage, *see* Meadows, Sir Philip.
LUFKIN, quartering, *see* Stone, Thomas.
LUGG, quartering, *see* Stevens, Thomas.
LUSON, marriage, *see* Bodeley, Denys.
LUTESTRINGES, Patentees of, *see* Patentees.
LYON, marriage, *see* Lee, Elizabeth.
LYON, marriage, *see* Hansha, Alice.

MACCARTHY, *see* Carthy.
MACKWITH, *see* Maycote.

MALBIE } confirmation of Arms, *see*
MALBISSE } Beckwith, Hamon.
MALIFANT, quartering, *see* Butts.
MALISHE, marriage, *see* Key, Anne.
MALVERNE, *see* Parker, William.
MAN, quartering, *see* Stanley.
MANNERS, mar., *see* Constable, Henry.
MARDEN, impaled, *see* Brabourne, Henry.
MARKHAM, mar., *see* Harrington, John.
MARLAY, Sir Roger de, Arms, *see* Morpeth Town.
MARSHALL, *see* Locksmith.
MARTIN, quartering, *see* Treton, Thomas.
MASON, *see* Waltham.
MASTERES, *see* Master, Richard.
MATHEW, marriage, *see* Judde, Andrew.
MATTANY, *see* Buttrie.
MAUNDER, *see* Maundy, Thomas.
MAY, mar., *see* Snelling, Sir George.
MAY, *see* Waye, Thomas.
MAYFIELD, quartering, *see* Kychin, John.
MEARS, marriage, *see* Welby, Robert.
MEENE, *see* Mynne.
MELLISH, marriage, *see* Allott, Alice.
MELTON, *see* Mitton.
MERETON, quartering, *see* Tatton.
MERKAUNT, *see* Markaunt.
MIDDLETON, mar., *see* Cooke, Marmaduke.
MILBORNE, quarter⁸, *see* Butts, William.
MILO, Earl of Hereford, quartering, *see* Jones, of London.
MOLINS, marriage, *see* Florio, Celia.
MONDAY, *see* Mundye.
MONK, marriage, *see* Clarges, Anne.
MONTALT, quartering, *see* Stanley.
MORDEN, *see* Murden.
MORES, *see* Morrise, Thomas.
MORESKINS, quarter⁸, *see* James, Roger.
MORGAN, quartering, *see* Edwards.
MORGAN, *see* Pawlett.
MORLEY, Lord, *see* Cranfield, Edward.
MORLEY, impaled, *see* Hill, Richard.
MORLEY, Arms, *see* Roberts, John.
MORTHEN, impalement, *see* Bayninge.
MORTIMER, quartering, *see* Slannyng, Nicholas.
MORTON, *see* Cowper, John.
MORVILLE, Lord, *see* Condon, Thomas.
MOSELEY, mar., *see* Whitmore, Anne.
MOWSS, *see* Mewsse, Arthur.
MULLYNER, *see* Mollyner.
MUMBRAY, quarter⁸, *see* Lade, Robert.
MURRAY, mar., *see* Baynham, Anne.
MYTTON, MITTON, *see* Mylton.

NEFFEILE, or NEFFIELD, quartering, *see* Jordan, Edmund.

NEWMARCH, quartering, *see* Jones, of London.
NICHOLLS, John, Arms, *see* Additions, p. xviii.
NORRIS, mar., *see* Lane, Sir Richard.
NORTH, mar., *see* Butler, Lady Margaret.
NORTH, mar., *see* Squire, Dame Alice.
NOURSE, *see also* Nurse.
NUTBROWNE, mar., *see* Finsen, Anne.
NUTCOMBE, *see* Natcombe, John.

OGWELL, *see* Coppull, Andrew.
O'HELEY, quartering, *see* Owen, Thomas.
ONSLOW, impalement, *see* Hill, Richard.
ORREBY, coheir, *see* Moulson, John.
OSBORNE, marriage, *see* Pratt.
OSNEY, marriage, *see* Newdyke, Robert.
OSYE, quartering, *see* Wilson, Thomas.
OWEN, marriage, *see* Long, Mary.
OWEN, marriage, *see* Wilkes, Alice.
OWGAN, quartering, *see* Butts, William.
OWNERLEY, marriage, *see* Swann, Anne.
OXENBRIDGE, quarter⁸, *see* Harlakenden.

PANNELLY, quartering, *see* Brownlow, Richard.
PARKE, Arms, etc., *see* Wythens, Robert.
PATEMER, *see* Bryggs, Henry (p. 33).
PAWLETT, marriage, *see* Codnam.
PAYN, marriage, *see* Webb, William.
PAYNELL, quarter⁸, *see* Lucas, Margaret.
PAYNTER, *see* Camborne.
PAYTON, marriage, *see* Grey, Anne.
PAYTON, marriage, *see* Gray, Sir Richard.
PAYTON, marriage, *see* Bright, Thomas.
PECOK, *see* Ridgway, John.
PEERS, *see* Piers, John.
PEIRSE, *see* Pearse, Thomas.
PEMBRIDGE, quartering, *see* Lusher, Nicholas.
PENNE, marriage and quartering, *see* Lucas, Margaret.
PENNINGTON, marriage and quartering, *see* Crule, John.
PERCY, *see also* Persse, Thomas.
PETRUS, *see* Peter.
PHILIPS, mar., *see* Harpham, Alice.
PHITHEAN, quarter⁸, *see* Pennant, Peirs.
PHOGAN, *see* Dongan.
PICKMAN, quartering, *see* Burwell.
PIERS, *see* Edgecombe.
PIGION, marriage, *see* Hope, Ralph.
PIGOTT, marriage, *see* More, John.
PIGOTT, marriage, *see* Clinkard, Gabriell.
PLACE, mar., *see* Brandlyn, Sir Robert.
PLATT, marriage, *see* Knight, Michael.
POOLE, *see also* Powle.

POYNTELL, *see* Poynter, Richard.
PRATT, Roger, Arms, *see* Additions, p. xviii.
PRESSER, Arms, *see* Allott, Alice.
PYNDAR, Arms, *see* Pinner, Thomas.
PYPART, marriage, *see* Thruxton, Thomas.

QUAPLADE, marriage, *see* Bacon.

RADCLIFF, Earl of Sussex, *see* Sydney Coll., Camb.
RALEIGH IN VIRGINIA, Arms, *see* Additions, p. xviii.
RAMSEY, quartering, *see* Dix, John.
RANDES, *see* Holbeche.
RAVEN, quartering, *see* Bloys.
REGINALE, *see* Reynolds, Henry.
REIGNOLDS, *see* Payne, Elizabeth and Henry.
RESKE, *see* Rede, Robert.
RICHARDSON, *see* Hepburn.
RICHMOND, mar., *see* Harbord, Charles.
RICKE, marriage, *see* Senkes, Elizabeth.
RIDLEY, marriage, *see* More, John.
RIDLEY, marriage, *see* Blomer, John.
RIGGES, marriage, *see* Blake, Mary.
ROBERTS, quarter⁸, *see* Chilton, Leonard.
ROCHE, quartering, *see* Butts, William.
ROGERS, quartering, *see* Langford, John.
ROMNEY, marriage, *see* Clarke, William.
ROSE, marriage, *see* Heydon, John.
ROSENGRAVE, *see* Moulson, John.
ROWLAND, *see* Pentecost.
RYDLE, marriage, *see* Blomer, John.
RYTHER, marriage, *see* Wright, Robert.
RYWALLON, *see* Jeffrey, John.
RUSSELL, Earl of Bedford, Crest, *see* Stausfield, Edmund.
RUSSELL, claim of Arms, *see* Warbleton, John.

SACKFORD, *see* Seckford.
SACKVILLE, marriage, *see* Baker, Cicelle.
ST. AMORYE, *see* Amory.
ST. LOWE, Arms, *see* Harding, Henry.
ST. LYSE, quartering, *see* Durant.
SAKER, *see* Gaker.
SALTMAN, quarter⁸, *see* Jordan, Edmund.
SAMPSON, marriage, *see* Gresham, John.
SANDBACH, quarter⁸, *see* Milles, Thomas.
SANDERS, quarter⁸, *see* Chilton, Leonard.
SANDYE, *see* Naper, Alexander.
SARE, *see also* Syer.
SAVIL, quartering, *see* Treton, Thomas.
SAWYER, marriage, *see* Whitmore, Anne.
SCARELL, *see* Searell.
SCHETHER, marriage, *see* Forth, Robert.

SCOTT, quartering, *see* Mewsse, Arthur.
SEGAR, mar., *see* Cartwright, Timothy.
SELEY, quartering, *see* Taylor, John.
SERLE, quartering, *see* Gervies, Arthur.
SEXTON, quartering, *see* Archdale, Martin.
SHAKESPEARE, mar., *see* Arden, Mary.
SHAW, marriage, *see* Freear, Thomas.
SHELDON, marriage, *see* Rose, Judith.
SHELDON, marriage, *see* Rose, Margaret.
SHELDRAKE, marriage, *see* Seabrok.
SHELLEY, marriage and quartering, *see* Randyll, Edward.
SHENSALL or SHERSALL, marriage, *see* Cotesford, John.
SHIRLEY, *see* Ferrers, Lord.
SHUCKBURGH, marriage, *see* Platt, John.
SINGLETON, claims Arms, *see* Bande, Thomas.
SKILLICORNE, mar., *see* Jadwyne, Robert.
SLYGHT, quartering, *see* Hamby, John.
SMETHWICK, release of Arms, *see* Atwood, John.
SMITH, impalement, *see* Guevara, Francis.
SMITH, impalement, *see* Harper, John.
SMITH, quartering, *see* Stourton, Edward.
SMITH, marriage, *see* Cowper, Mary.
SMYTHE, quartering, *see* Thomson, John.
SMYTH, *see* Hares, William.
SNODE, marriage, *see* Farmarey, John.
SOMERS, mar., *see* Cartwright, Timothy.
SOMERSET, Edward, Marg., of Worcester. Crest, *see* Baylye, Thomas.
SONDS, *see* Feversham.
STANDISH, marriage, *see* Platt, John.
STANLEY, marriage, *see* Bradshaw, Anne.
STAPLETON, marriage, *see* Bassett, Jane.
STAUNTON, quartering, *see* Butts, William.
STOCKER, quartering, *see* Jekyll, Thomas.
STORY, quartering, *see* Wood of Enfield.
STOVER, *see* STONER.
STRATTON, quartering, *see* Spence.
SULLOCK, *see* Sellecke, William.
SUNBISHE, *see* Sandbache, Francis.
SUNNING, *see* Gouning, John.
SURTEES, mar., *see* Brandlyn, Sir Robert.
SUTTON, quartering, *see* Beiston, Ralph.
SWANN, impalement, *see* Wilcockes, Roger.
SWETTENHAM, mar., *see* Weoley, Thomas.
SYDENHAM, marriage, *see* Rogers, Mary.
SYTSYLT, about Arms, *see* Feckenham.

TALBOT, Arms, *see* Roberts, John.
TASKER, *see* Adam, Roger.
TAWYERS, *see* Grey Tawyers.
TEDCASTLE, marriage, *see* May, Elizabeth.
TEST, quarter., *see* Codrington, Richard.
THERWALL, *see* Phillipson, Rowland.

THOGAN, *see* Dongan.
THOMAS, *see* Boddie, John.
THOMAS, marriage, *see* Jones, Walter.
THOMAS, *see* Scale, Robert.
THOMPSON, mar., *see* Gilbert, Dorathie.
THOMPSON, *see* Haversham, Baron.
THORNEHOLME, *see* Chorley.
THROCKMORTON, mar., *see* Cony, Henry.
THURGARTON, *see* Cowper, William.
THURSTON, mar., *see* Hearne, Thomas.
THURSTON, mar., *see* Tenacre, Elizabeth.
THYNNE, *see* Weymouth, Viscount.
TILLESWORTH, mar., *see* Browne, Robert.
TOFTE, marriage, *see* Smith, Mary.
TOUCHET, Lord Audley, Arms, *see* Mackworth.
TOURNEY, mar., *see* Webb, William.
TRAPPS, marriage, *see* Crispe, Joan.
TRELAKE, *see* Davy, Joan.
TROTT, mar., *see* Cartwright, Rose.
TROYTE, *see* Guylemyn.
TUDER, impalement, *see* Diman.
TURNER, marriage and quartering, *see* Codd, William.

VAUGHAN, *see* Carbery, Earl of.
VAVASOUR, quartering, *see* Warner, Mark.
VEHAN, Robert, *see* Jeffrey, John.
VENABLES, Arms, *see* Norreys, Lord.
VEYSEY, *see* Voysey.
VINAL, quartering, *see* Treton, Thomas.

WALKER, marriage, *see* Greenfield, John.
WALKER, marriage, *see* Reeve, Agnes.
WALTERS, *see* Stockdale, Christopher.
WARBURTON, Arms, *see* Bennett, Richard.
WARDNAM, *see* Wirdnam.
WARNER, marriage, *see* Lee, John.
WARNER, quarter., *see* Humfrey, Richard.
WARREN, marriage, *see* Davy, Joan.
WARREN, quartering, *see* Stanley.
WARRINGTON, *see* Warmington, Francis.
WASHINGLE, *see* Washington, Laurence.
WAY, *see* May, Thomas.
WEBBE, marriage, *see* Cordell, Emma.
WEEKES, *see* Wickes, Henry.
WELD, *see* Wylde, Thomas.
WELLESBOROUGH, John de, Grant, *see* Purefoy, Thomas.
WEST, marriage, *see* Collens, Jane.
WEST, impalement, *see* Morar, Robert.
WETHERALL, *see* Wyrrall, Gervase.
WEYNMAN, *see* Wenman, Richard.
WHEELER, marriage, *see* Parry, Edith.
WHETLEY, quartering, *see* Whitfield, Thomas.
WHETTELL, *see* Whyttell, William.

c

ADDITIONS AND CORRECTIONS.

P. 4. *For* Allett *read* Abbott, John, and insert on p. 1.

P. 4. Altham, James, *for* Cot. Her. *read* (before) Cat. Heral. Exhib. Soc. of Antiq.

P. 9. *For* Avenon *read* Avenoy in Q's Coll. Oxf. MS.

P. 13. Bande, Thomas, *after* 18 R. II., pt. 2, *read* m[embrane] 4.

„ *For* favor *read* favour.

P. 19. Beckwith, Hamon, *for* Malolaan *read* Malolacn.

Bedell, Capell, *add* after quartering 2 and 3 [Wolleston and Lane].

Bee, *after* Bowyer *add* [quartering Swettenham].

P. 20. Belson, Thomas, *for* 9 H. 8 *read* 9 H. VIII.

P. 21. Line 1, *for* K. H. 7 and 8 *read* K. H. VII. and VIII.

P. 23. Bingley, Richard, *read* of Blythe, Notts.

P. 24. Birkhead, John, *read* of Crouton.

P. 24. *Add.* Bis (or Bix), John, of Babchild Court, co. Kent. Arms, vair on an inescutcheon gules, a chevron charged with a roundle. Crest, a demi-wolf rampant or, collared vair, by W. Segar, Gart. Harl. MS. 1106, fo. 223. (Note by Foster.)

P. 27. Bodeley, Denys, *read* d. of Thomas.

„ Bonnatree, *see* Misc. Gen. et Her., 4th S., vol. v., p. 27, about the date of this grant.

P. 28. Borden, Arnold de, *read* 22 H. VI.

P. 30. Bowerman, James, *read* of Hemyock, Devon.

„ *Add* Branthwaite, Richard, *from* p. 33, *after* Brandreth.

„ *Add* Bretarge, William, *from* p. 33, *after* Breres.

P. 34. Broderick, *should be before* Brodway.

„ Broke, Alice, *for* [1555-6] *read* [155 . .—156 . .].

„ *Add* Bronrick, Henry, *from* p. 35, *after* Bronde.

P. 37. Bubb, Thomas, *for* 1563 *read* 1653.

P. 40. Burgess, John, *for* Catle Bilham *read* Castle Bitham.

P. 43. *Add to* Cademan, Thomas. Harl. MS. 1466, fo. 27b.

P. 43. *For* Carnebell *read* Cambell, *and add on* p. 44 *after* Calvert.

P. 45. Candish. No name is given to the Arms in Harl. MS. 1441, fo. 103 ; in Harl. MS. 5847, fo. 53b, the arms and crest are marked "quere Candish.

P. 46. Carr, Sir John. The entry should read : Genealogist, New Series, vol. viii., frontispiece. In the Brit. Mus. this frontispiece is preserved in the Guard Book, 1856, d. 1, No. 114.

P. 48. Castillion, Geneal., N. S., *for* vol. xix. *read* vol. xvii.

P. 58. Collingborne, *add to* Harl. MS. 1115, fo. 5b.

P. 59. Compton, John, of London, gent., *add* Arms, Arg., a fesse undée betw. three mascles gu. on chief sa. a helmet of the field betw. to eagles' heads erased or. MS. Rawl., B. 102, fo. 110b. (Note by Foster.)

P. 60. Conyares, *for* Add. MS. 4964 [6 ?], fo. 100, *read* 4966, fo. 100.

P. 67. Crosse, Robert, of Charlinch, Somerset, gent., s. of William of the same, 23 Jan. 1584, confirmation of arms and grant of Crest, by R. Cooke, Clar. MS. Rawl. 102, fo. 110 ; Bodleian Lib. (Note by Foster.)

P. 73. De Bonettis, " Rochi, filij Alusij de Bonettis, de Baresis ultra Laguchiam
        de Valle Brembanij in dominio Bergamensi, sub reip. Venetie ditione,"
        Grant of Arms on the commendation of Robert, Earl of Leicester, at
        Kenilworth 14 Aug. 1568, exemplified 30 Jan. 1570-71, by Flower,
        Norr., MS. Ashm. 858, fo. 13—15, copy of grant, Bodleian Lib.

  „   De Cuslin, Nicholas, a Venetian, letters patent 23 Jan., 3 Jas.
        [1605—1606], addition, on a canton ar. a demi-rose gu. and a Scotch
        thistle vert, dimidiated, trick of arms and canton. MS. Rawl., B. 102.
        fo. 11, Bodleian Lib. (Note by Foster.)

  „   De Granata, *should be after* Degge.

P. 83. *Add to* Epes, Allen. Arms, Per fess gules and Or, a pale counterchanged,
        three eagles displayed, 2 and 1, of the field. Crest and motto, MS.
        Rawl. B. 87, fo. 18. (Note by Foster.)

P. 87. Ferrers of Badesley, *read* Harl. MS. 1100, Harl. MS. 1167, and Harl. MS.
        1563. These are copies of the Visitations of Warwick.

P. 89. Fitzwilliam, *for* 15[6]⅝ *read* 155 . .—156 . .

P. 100. Gilbert, Edward, *for* 15[6]⅝ *read* 155 . .—156 . .

P. 101. Giustiniani, George, augmentation, on a chief a lion of England holding
        in his paws a thistle, trick of arms. MS. Rawl. B. 102, fo. 102ᵇ,
        Bodleian Lib., Oxford. (Note by Foster.)

P. 108. Guidot, Sir Anthony, augmentation, on a chief a lion of England betw.
        three fleurs-de-lis or, and a crest, exemplified by Barker, Garter,
        Ambassador to the French King from K. Edw. VI., who concluded a
        peace betweene the saide Kings, trick of arms and crest. MS. Rawl.
        102, fo. 53. (Note by Foster.)

P. 127. Holynshed, Hugh, *for* Candetor *read* Candelor.

P. 135. Isaacson, *for* [William], I.D.D., *read* Isaacson, Henry, of London, and
        . . . . Isaacson, D.D.

P. 141. Jordan, Edmund, *for* Nesscile *read* Neffeile or Neffeild.

P. 154. Leveson, John, the blazon should read : " Crest, a demi hound cuppe ar.
        gouted thereon the necke a fesse oundy ar. & s. & betweene ii gemelles
        v. . . . . p. fesse armed & langued g. sett in a wrethe ar. & b." Stowe
        MS. 692, fo. 65.

P. 157. Longland, John, *for* H. 8 [Her. Coll.?] *read* Hen. VIII.

P. 190. Parkes, Margaret, *read* Parke.
        Saffin, John, of Wolfhereston, Somerset, s. of George, of the same,
        17 Sept., 10 K. Jas. [1612], by W. Segar. [Arms, Az. three
        crescents, 2 and 1, arg. jessant as many estoiles of eight rays or.
        Crest, on a mural crown (ppr. ?) an estoile as in the arms, or.] Harl.
        MS. 1466, fo. 26ᵇ. (Note by Foster.)

P. 208. Raleigh, the Governor and Assistants in the City of Raleigh in Virginia.
        See a copy of the Patent on the pages following.

P. 221. *For* Sames, John, *read* Sammes, John.

P. 247. Swinoke, Thomas, the elder, of Maydstone, co. Kent, exemplified, ratified
        and confirmed to him and his posterity for ever, by R. St. George,
        Clar., Sa., three boars passant arg., Crest, a demi-griffin segreant
        reguardant sable, armed and beaked ar. (Note by Foster.)

P. 260. Tyson, Richard, gent., 3 s. of Samuel, late of Woodland Green, co. Glouc.,
        and of Kingston Seymour, co. Somerset, decd., 2 s. of Edward,
        sometime Sheriff and Alderman, as also Mayor of Bristol, 1659 and
        1660, Colonel of the Train'd bands in the said city, which Edward, 1 s.
        of Edward of Bristol, after of Clevedon, co. Somerset, s. of Nicholas, of
        Birket in Cumberland, etc., Arms painted and attested by Robert
        Dale, Suffolk Her. Vert, three lyons rampant regardant arg., crowned
        gules (? or). (Note by Foster.)

P. 276. White, John, of London, *for* Buddyen *read* Buddyer.

The following is a copy of the Patent from Queen's College, Oxford, MS. 137 (old press-mark H. 36). The arms are painted in the margin, beginning with those of Raleigh in Virginia, with the motto beneath ; this is followed by the quartered arms and crest of John White, the other arms following one another in the order of the grant. The words printed in small capital letters are in the MS. written in larger letters.

Raleigh Ciuitas Virginea.

To all and singuler nobles & gentlemen and others vniuersally, to whome theis presents shall be seene or knowne : William Dethick alias Garter Principall King of Armes, & cheifest officer of Armes, of the most noble order of the Garter, with due Commendations and greetings : For as much as it is expedient and by auncient Custome of honour obserued, that the vertuous worthy and valiant Acts, of excellent men imploied in the most honourable service of God their Prince or Country in peace or Warr, together with the persons, might in all tymes and throwgh all ages, be honoured, rewarded, and their remembrance by sundry Monuments preserued, wherein, wherein [sic in MS.] the cheifest & most vsuall means hath bin, the bearing of Ensignes & tokens of honour in sheilds of Armes (That is to say) Persons soe meriting may flowrish, dureing their lines & their fame encrease, & continue in their ofspring and posterity for euer : &a : We are therefore respectiuely to take notice in this behalfe, That wheras the Queens Matie Elizabeth by the grace of God, Queene of England France & Ireland defender of the Faith, &c: by her hignes lettres Patents vnder the great Seale of England, bearing date at Westminster the 25th day of March in the 26th yeare of her Maties raigne, hath in most roiall Manner giuen and granted, to the Hono^ble Sr Walter Raleigh Knight, Lo^d of the Stannery in the Countyes of Devon & Cornwall, and to heires & Assignes free liberty and lycense to discouer, search find out, & veiwe such remoted, heathen & barbarous lands, Countryes & terretoryes not actually possessed of any Christian Prince, nor inhabited by Christian people as to himselfe heires and Assignes shall seemme good : And the same to hould & enioy, to him his heirs and Assignes for euer, with all prerogatiues, Commoditye⁣s, Jurisdictions, Roialtyes, priuiledges Franchenses & preheminenses, therto or therabouts, both by sea and land, as the said lettres Patents, amongst diuerse guifts grants, & Confirmations, therin Conteined more at large may appeare : And wheras since the granting or makeing of the said lettres Patents, by the means & industry & experience of the said Sr Walter Rawley and other his Associates Company or Assigners ther hath bin and now is a barbarous and heathen land or Country, found out and discouered, called or now termed, OSSOMO COMUC alias WINGUNDACOIA alias VIRGINEA neuer before that tyme actually possessed or inhabited by any Christian Prince or Christian people, And wher[as] alsoe the said Sr Walter Raleigh Knight, for that the inhabiting of the said Country by Christian people, may be greatly to the glory of God the encrease of Christian faith and Religion, thenlargement of the Queens Maties Dominions the l etter execution of her hignes said grant the Common vtility of the whole Realme of England, And aswell the particuler benefit of euery particuler, Adventurer, and traueller, thether thencefrom or therin, as for other diuerse good causes and Considerations, And for vertuous Acts done and to be done, hath by his Indenture bearing date the day of theis presents Amongst diuerse and sundry guifts, grants freely nominated elected, chosen, constituted made and appointed JOHN WHITE OF LONDON GENT, to be the cheifest governour, there and Roger Raylye : [1] Ananias Darr : Christopher Cooper : . . . . [2] William Fulwood, Roger Pratt, Dyonise Harvye, John Nicholls. George Howe . . . . [3] and Symon Fardinando of London Gent. to be the twelue assistants there, And from the said gouernor and twelue Assistants, and their successors, hath for euer confirmed made incorporated and accepted one body Pollitique & Corporate, by the name title and Authority of THE GOUERNOUR AND ASSISTANTS OF THE CITTIE OF RALEIGH IN

---

1. Later on in grant, Baylie and Baily.   2 and 3. Blanks, sufficient for a name.

VIRGINEA WITH THAPPERTENANCES, As by the same Indenture amongst other things therin sett downe, more at large may appeare. In Consideration wherof, and for sundry vertuous and renowned Acts, the enterprizes of the worshipfull, the said gouernour & Assistants, And to the end they and their Companie may be better assembled, knowne & vnited by names, Armes, Seales, Banners & Ensignes, necessary and to be vsed, in all their affaires & enterprizes of honour, loueing & assured Society: And for a further declaration and demonstration, of the premisses, being most willing & desirous, to second and accompanie all vertuous & honourable Acts and renowned Enterprizes, with the Cerimonies and remembrances, due and accustomed, such as to the Authority of my office, doth principally appertaine, haue Assigned giuen granted, Confirmed by blazon and exemplified, vnto the same originall & renowned Cittie of RALEIGH IN VIRGINEA WITH APPERTENANCES: And to the worshipfull the said GOUERNOUR and Assistants, the first founders therof, And to the Cittizens and Communalty of the same, and to their successors for euer, theis Armes or Ensignes of honour in manner and forme following: viz: ON A FEILD ARGENT, A PLAINE CROSSE GULES, WITH A ROBUCK proper in the first quarter: and this symbole or Poesie: CONCORDIA: PARVA CRESCUNT And to the said John White his heires ofspring and posterity, theis Armes or Ensignes of honour following: viz: In the first field for a reward, ERMIN ON A CANTON GULES, A FUZELL ARGENT In the second (for his owne auncient Cote, by the name of White) A CHEUERON BETWEEN THREE GOATES HEADS AND RAZED SABLES, The third (for Wymarke) ON A BEND COTIZED AZURE THREE INCHUCHIONS OF THE FEILD, In the fourth (for Wyat) GULES TWO BARRS, GEMWEYS BETWEE[N] 3 MARTELLETTS, ARGENT. In the fift (for Killyowe) OR A CHEUERON BETWEENE TWO CINQUE FOILES, AND A MULETT SABLES: In the sixt for Gaker, ERMIN ON A BEND SABLES, THREE PHŒNIX HEADS, RAZED OR, In the 7th (for Buddyer) GULES A CHEUERON ARGENT BETWEEN THREE CINQUEFOILES OR, In the eighteth (for Butler) GULES ON [sic] A FESSE COMPOUND ARGENT, AND SABLES BETWEENE THREE CROSSES FORME FIXE OF THE SECOND [1] And his Creast or Cognizance, ON A HEALME ON A WREATH ARGENT: & GULES [2], AN ERMIN SEANT PROPER, MANTELLED GULES, DOBLED ARGENT, And to the said Roger Baily his heires ofspring and posterity for euer, theis Armes or Ensignes of honour following: viz: A FEILD GULES, A CROSSE PATTEE BETWEENE FOWER FUZELLS ARGENT, And to the said Ananias Dare his heires ofspring & posterity for euer, theis Armes or Ensignes of honor followeing: viz: A FEILD GULES, A CROSSE ENGRAILD BETWEENE FOWER FUZELLS ARGENT: And to the said Christopher Cooper, his heires ofspring and posterity for euer, theis Armes or Ensignes of honour followeing, viz: A FEILD GULES ON A CHEUERON ARGENT, A FUZELL GULES, BETWEENE THREE LYONS PASSANT GARDANT OF THE SECOND, And to the said .... [3] his heires ofspring and posterity for euer theis Armes or Ensignes of honour followeing: viz: A FEILD ERMIN ON A BEND COTIZED GULES FIUE FUZELLS ARGENT, And to the said .... [4] his heires ofspring & posterity for euer theis Armes or Ensignes of honor following viz: A FEELD ARGENT, TWO BARRES GULES, ON A CHEFFE OF THE SECOND, FIUE FUZELLS OF THE FIRST, And to the said William Fullwood, his heires: viz: A FEILD ERMIN ON A PLAINE CROSSE GULES A FUZELL ARGENT & OR PER PALE IN A CHEEFE AZURE, THREE FLOWER DE LUCES OF THE THIRD: And to the said Roger Pratt his heires ofspring and posterity for euer, Theis Armes or Ensignes of honour followeing viz: A FEELD ERMIN ON A CHEEFE GULES THREE FUZELLS ARGENT, And to the said Dionise Haruye, his heires ofspring & posterity for euer, theis Armes or Ensignes of honour followeing: viz: A FEELD GULES, A BEARE RAMPANT, BETWEEN THREE FUZELS ARGENT, And to the said John Nicholes his heires ofspring & posterity theis Armes or Ensignes of honour followeing: viz: A FEILD PER BEND ARGENT AND GULES, FIUE FUZELS

1. The painting of this quarter shews: *Gules, a fesse componée Argent and Sable between three crosses formy* (not *filchée*) *Argent.*

2. The wreath is *Argent* and *Sable* in the painted copy in the margin.

3 and 4. Blank spaces left for the names.

COUNTERCHANGED, And to the said George Howe, his heires ofspring & posterity for euer, theis Armes or Ensignes of honour followeing: viz. A FEILD ARGENT, A FESSE BETWEENE THREE FUZELLS, GULES : [1] And to ye said Fardinando his ofspring & posterity for euer theis Armes or Ensignes of hono^r followeing viz : A FEILD ARGENT TWO BARRES WAVEE AZURE, ON A CANTON GULES THREE FUZELLS OF THE FIRST : As in these presents depicted more plainly appeareth : Together with their seuerall Creasts, or Cognizance as in the Margents [2] hereof are plainly & senerally depicted, & sett forthe : TO HAUE AND TO HOULD all and singuler the seuerall named Armes Ensignes of hono^r Creasts in VIRGINEA WITH Y^E APPER-TENANCES, And to the worshipfull the said Gouernour, and Assistants, Cittizens and Communallity of the same, & to their successo^rs And to the heires ofspring & posterityes of the said gouernour, & Assistants, & euery of them for euer : And they to vse, beare enioy and shew forthe the same, with his & their & euery of their liberty and pleasure, at all tymes for euer, and in all places vniuersally, through all Regions, Kingdomes, Countryes & Dominions whatsoeuer, christian or heathen by sea or by land : which seuerall Armes Ensignes of honour, Creasts and Cognizance, & euery part and parcell therof, I the said : WILLIAM DETHICK ALIAS GARTER PRINCIPALL KING OF ARMES, doe by theise presents ratifie confirme giue and grant vnto the said Cittye, and to the said JOHN WHITE, ROGER BAYLIE, ANNANIAS DARRE, CHRISTOPHER COOPER, ... [3] WILLIAM FULLWOOD, ROGER PRATT, DIONISE HARVIE, JOHN NICHOLLS, GEORGE HOWE, ... [4] and Symon Fardinando & to euery of them in seuerallity, & to the heires ofsprings, and posterityes of them, & euery of them for euer, without lett impediment or interrup-tion of any person or persons, And to the intent the premisses may be divulged, & the remembrance therof had in perpetuity, doe reqnire all Princes Nobles & gentiles, to take notice hereof, & to permit the same to passe with the priuiledges and fauours of honour, In Witnesse whereof : &a [5].

1. The arms of George Howe are given in the margin, not as blazoned in the text: *Argent, on a chevron gules between three wolves'* [?] *heads couped Sable, as many fusils lying fesseways Argent.*

2. No crests are given in the margin of this copy, except to the quarterly arms of John White.

3 and 4. Spaces left blank for names.

5. A copy of this Grant preserved in Heralds' College is dated 1586.

Grantees of Arms

NAMED IN

Docquets and Patents
to the end of the 17th Century

IN THE MSS. OF

The British Museum.

ADDITIONAL MS. 37,147.

By J. FOSTER, Hon. M.A., Oxon., 1898.

It is recorded by W. Segar, Somerset, afterwards Garter, that "Cooke, Clar., made many profitable Visitations, both by hymself and his deputyes, whoe, notwithstanding they were well entertayned, feasted and richly rewarded by the gent of ye cuntrey, hath left no memory of them in the Generall office. These were upon decease attached by arrests, alienated and sould. Two Norroys Kinges of Armes, two Windesors, Richmond, Lancaster, Somersett and Yorke, deceased, have done the like to the great sclaunder and decaye of the office and officers present." (Cott. MS. Faustina F. 1, fo. 263.) [printed.]

A

ABBOT, Robert, of London, gent., 9 Aug. 1654, by Sir E. Bysshe, Gart. Guil. 117.

ABDYE, Roger, of London, merch^t taylor & used at his buriall : on Thursday 26 Jan. 1595 (corrected from Jan. to June). Crest 30 June 1595, by Lee, Clar. Add. MS. 14,295, fo. 17^b. 26 Jan. 1595-6, Stowe MS. 670, fo. 58^b; Harl. MS. 1430, fo. 108^b.

ABELL, John, of West Bergholt, Essex, 16 April 1573, by Cooke, Clar. Harl. MS. 1085, fo. 9.

ABINGDON, John, Hindlippe, co. Worc., clerk of the green cloth, 5 Jan. 1577-8; by Ro. Cooke, Clar. MS. Ashm. 834, fo. 6^b, copy of Grant, Bodleian Lib. Guil. p. 213.

ABINGTON, Anthony, of Dedeswell, co. Glouc., one of the gent. ushers to Q. Eliz. 1595, by R. Lee, Clar. Add. MS. 14,295, fo. 39, and Harl. MS. 1359, fo. 104; Harl. MS. 1069, fo. 8; Stowe MS. 670, fo. 65^b; Add. MS. 4966, fo, 92.

„ Eustace, of Calleys and Herts, 1 July 1546 (? by Hawley). Add. MS. 16,940, fo. 201.

ABNEY, of Notts and of London, linen draper. Harl. MS. 6179, fo. 66.

ABORROWGH, John, of Callys, 1 Jan. 1548-9 (? by Hawley). Add. MS. 16,940, fo. 203.

ABRAHAM, William, Wingrave, Bucks, 1669 (? by Bysshe, Clar.). Harl. MS. 1405, fo. 7; Harl. MS. 1105, fo. 16.

ACHESON, Sir Archibald, Knt. and Bart., 1 Feb. 1631-2, by Lyon, Grtr. [K. of Arms?]. Add. MS. 2,689.

ACKLAN, Hugh, of Acklan (co Devon), 1588, by Cooke's deputy. Stowe MS. 670, fo. 22 ; Harl. MS. 5887, fo. 41^c.

ACRES, George, s. of Robert, Acres Hall, co. Lanc., gent., grant 16 Mar. 1576-7, by (Ulster K. of Arms), for services in Ireland, France, Flanders, and elsewhere. Harl. MS. 1507, fo. 420, 2. Grants II., 680, Her. Coll. ; copy of patent Q's Coll. Oxf. MS. 38, fo. 95 ; Hist. Soc. Lanc. and Chesh., xxxiii., 257 ; Le Neve's MS. 420.

ACTON, John, Cheapside, the King's goldsmith certif., by Sir J. Borough, Gart. Grants I., 431 ; Harl. MS. 1105, fo. 56 ; Add. MS. 26,702, fo. 91 ; 35,336, fo. 145 ; Harl. MS. 6140, fo. 41.

„ Sir Robert [of co. Worcester], and his nephew Robert, petty Captain augm : for taking [Mons. Honingcourt] a prisoner at siege of Bulleyne, by C. Barker, Gart. Harl. MS. 5846, fo. 4^b.

ADAM, Richard, London, Quar. of 6, 1590, by Cooke. Harl. MS. 1359, fo. 95^b ; 1598 in Harl. MS. 1422, fo. 121^b.

„ Thomas, Saffron Walden, Essex, Esq., 30 Sept. 1614, by Camden. Harl. MS. 1422, fo. 39 ; 6095, fo. 31 ; Guil. 87.

„ William, Tydd St. Mary, co. Linc., 15 Feb. 1558-9, by Dalton & conf^d 12 Oct. 1562, by Hervey. Harl. MS. 1359, fo. 45^b ; Add. MS. 16,940, fo. 59 ; Harl. MS. 1116, fo. 48.

„ Philip, Owston, Yorks, 11 Aug. 1612, by St. George, Norr. Harl. MS. 1422, fo. 49^b ; Harl. MS. 6140, fo. 72^b.

„ Roger (als. Tasker), London, grant 1584 : alterⁿ 1590, by Cooke. Harl. MS. 1359, fo. 103^b ; 1422, fo. 119^b ; Guil. 197.

„ William, of the Middle Temple, 14 Mar. 1639-40, by Borough. Harl. MS. 1105, fo. 56^b ; Guil. 363.

ADDINGTON, Thomas, London, skinner, by Barker. Harl. MS. 5846, fo. 3 ; Stowe MS. 692, fo. 9^b.

ADLER, Thomas, of Harvard Stoke [? Haverstoke] ? 16 . ., by Ro. Browne, Blue-mantle [?]. Harl. MS. 1085, fo. 8.

ADLYN, John, London, 1590, by Cooke. Harl. MS. 1359, fo. 101.

ADYE, John (or ADE), of Dodington, Kent, gent., s. and h. John of Sitting-bourne, gent., dec^d, s. and h. John of Greete in Dodington, whose youngest bro. was Nich^s, who beareth, az : a fesse indented betw : 3 cherubims or: their faces silver, crest grt^d to John and to Nicholas his bro., and the posterity of John of Greete, 20 May 1613, by Segar. Harl. MS. 1359, fo. 57^b, and 1470, fo. 169 : copy of grant Brit. Mus. Add. MS. 12,225, fo. 2, and Guil. 83 ; Add. MS. 4966, fo. 100 ; Harl. MS. 6140, fo. 63.

AGARD, Francis, of co. Derby, 1 Aug. 1566, by Harvey. Add. MS. 16,940, fo. 8. Grants I., 406 ; Add. MS. 35,336, fo. 137.

AGBROWE, Edward and Robert, sons of Wm., 1656, by Bysshe, Garter. Add. MS. 26,758, fo. 16^b ; per fess undée azure and gules three saltorelles argent.

AGBOROUGH, Sir Robert (als. Townesend, Kt., etc.) ; name and arms of Towusend 29 May 1663 ; by Walker, with consent of Horatio, Lord Townesend. Add. MS. 14,293, fo. 46 ; 14,294, fo. 17^b ; Harl. MS. 1172, fo. 56 (and Guil. 245). Copy of grants.

AGMONDISHAM, John, Rough Barnes, Surrey, by Cooke. Stowe MS. 670, fo. 26.

AISLABY, George, principal registrar of the Archbishoprick of York (s. of Robt. Osgodby, Yorks), 25 Oct. 1663, by Walker. Add. MS. 14,293, fo. 61 ; 14,294, fo. 15^b ; Harl. MS. 1172, fo. 63. (Guil. 370) copy of grant.

AKEYROD, Henry, Folkesthorpe, Yorks, 1 June 1614, by Ri. St. George. Caius Coll. Camb. MS. 528, fo. 3. Copy of grant, Add. MS. 14,295, fo. 61 ; Harl. MS. 6179, fo. 37^b ; Stowe MS. 703, fo. 71.

ALBERYE, Thomas, Wokingham, Berks, 9 Nov. 1590, by Cooke. (Harl. MS. 1441, fo. 13^b, copy of grant Brit. Mus.), 1359, fo. 103 (10th Nov. in Harl. MS. 6140, fo. 52^b) ; four stockdoves.

ALDEN, John, of [Hertfordshire] the Middle Temple, assigned 8 Sept. 1607, by Camden. Harl. MS. 1422, fo. 40 ; Guil. 95.

ALDENN, Gawen van, born in Cologne, Stowe MS. 706, fo. 60, by G. Dethick, Gart. in Latin ; Grants I., 95. Add. MS. 35,336, fo. 126, 99 ; V. O. Grants 150.

ALDHAM, John, Shymplynge, Norfolk, 1563, by Harvey. Add. MS. 16,940, fo. 44.

ALDRED, John, Lyons in France, 1585, by Cooke's deputy. Stowe MS. 670, fo. 11ᵇ.

ALDRYDGE, Robert, Doctor, register of the order of the Garter, 25 Jan. 1536-7, by Barker. Stowe MS. 692, fo. 9ᵇ ; Cott. MS. Faustina E. 1, 13.

ALDERSEY, Lawrence, son of Thos., of Chester, confirmed 1597, by W. Dethick, Gart. Add. MS. 35,336, fo. 31 ; V. O. Grants 174.

ALEXANDER, ..., by Segar. Add. MS. 12,225, fo. 2ᵇ ; arg. 5 barrulets gu. over all a lyon rampᵗ holding a battle axe or.

„   Richard, of Herts, gent. Add. MS. 35,336, fo. 70 ; V. O. Grants 494.

„   Thomas, Framlingham, Suff: (married, etc.), 6 July 1664, by Bysshe (?). Harl. MS. 1105, fo. 38.

ALFREY, ..., Sussex, crest by Barker. Stowe MS. 692, fo. 10ᵇ ; Harl. MS. 5846, fo. 3ᵇ ; two demi swans indorsed, their necks, the one closed with the other, the first sa. the 2ⁿᵈ arg., etc.

„   John, 1 Mar. 1459-60, by John Smert, Gart. (quartering Bruggs), attested by Cooke, 1595. Harl. MS. 4900, fo. 16ᵇ, copy of Grant, Brit. Mus.

ALFRAY, Thomas, Battle, Sussex, 1591, by Cooke. Harl. MS. 1359, fo. 95ᵇ.

ALICOCK, Thomas, Silvertoft, Northamptonsh. Crest 8 June 1616, by Segar and R. St. George. Add. MS. 12,225, fo. 2 ; Guil. 233.

ALISON, Robert, Hastinglee, Kent, 1587, by Cooke. Harl. MS. 1359, fo. 88ᵇ ; Add. MS. 4966, fo. 53.

AL[L]AN, ..., Stamford, by W. Dethick. Harl. MS. 1453, fo. 33ᵇ ; entered by R. Brooke, York Herald.

ALLEN, ..., Essex, by Cooke, Clar. Stowe MS. 670, fo. 34. Giles of Haseleigh, 31 Eliz. 1589 ; Vis. London 1634 ; Harl. MS. 1441, fo. 143ᵇ.

ALLEN (ALEYN), Christʳ, Yorks, 1550, by ? Hervey. Add. MS. 16,940, fo. 11.

„   Christʳ, Borden, Kent. Crest, 17 Feb. 1615-16, by Segar. Add. MS. 8932, fo. 4 ; Add. MS. 12,225, fo. 3 ; Guil. 196 ; Le Neve's MS. 254.

„   Edward (see Thomas), Sheriff, London. Crest, 17 Aug. 1620, by Camden. Harl. MS. 6095, fo. 37 ; Grants II., 578 ; Guil. 389.

„   Francis, of Chelsey, Esq., one of the clerks of the Q's Majesties privy Council, 2 July 1563, by Sir G. Dethick, Gart. Q's Coll. Ox. MS. 145, fo. 7 ; Harl. MS. 1441, fo. 64ᵇ ; (Grants II., 652) ; Harl. MS. 1116, fo. 80ᵇ.

„   George (s. of George), Stanton Woodhouse, par. of Youlgreave, co. Derby : confᵈ 6 June 1586, by Flower. MS. Ashm. 844, fo. 64, copy of grant Bodleian Lib. ; 16ᵗʰ June in Guil. 116 ; Reliquary, xxi., 240.

„   Sir John, Thaxted, Essex, temp. H. 8. Add. MS. 26,702, fo. 14 ; 45,887, fo. 5.

„   Thos. (Alleyne), Northants, 9 Dec. 1458, 37 Hen. VI., by Guyan, K. of Arms ; Grants II., 578 and 684. Stowe MS. 676, fo. 2 ; Q's Coll. Oxf. MS. 37, fo. 3, and 146, fo. 16ᵇ. Copy of grant also in Harl. MS. 1172, fo. 1ᵇ.

„   Thos. (Aleyn), of the Court, Porter, by Barker. Harl. MS. 5846, fo. 2ᵇ.

„   Thomas and Edward, of city of London, (sons of Thomas). Crest, 17 Aug. 1620, by Camden ; Grants II., 578. (See Edward above.)

„   Wm. (Alyn), of Railey, Essex, gent., by Barker. Harl. MS. 5846, fo. 2ᵇ ; Stowe MS. 692, fo. 9.

„   William, Alderm. of London, 1561, by Harvey. Add. MS. 16,940, fo. 25ᵇ.

„   William, Brindley, Cheshire, 22 Aug. 1613, by R. St. George. Harl. MS. 1422, fo. 81 ; 1441, fo. 153.

„   Capt. William, then Comanding a Company of foot and drum major at Oxford, 11 March 1644, by Walker, Gart. Her. Coll., 25.

ALLENSON, Sir William, Kt., late Lord mayor, and now Alderm. city of York, 29 May 1635, by Sir W^m Le Neve, Norr. Surtees Soc., xli., p. 52. Copy of grant, Brit. Mus., Harl. MS. 6179, fo. 20.

ALLETT, John, of Imber, co. Linc., and now of city of London, and Sheriff, 27 Aug. 1580, by Sir G. Dethick, Gart. Harl. MS. 1441, fo. 100^b, and Q's Coll. Oxf. MS. 145, fo. 50 (in both erroneously written Abbott). *See* his wife, next entry. Add. MS. 4966, fo. 53, 70.

ALLOTT, Alice or Anne, of London, dau. of Edmund Key, and widow of Hy. Melishe of London, and wife of John Allett last named, by Wm Dethick, Gart. Harl. MS. 1453, fo. 35^b; 3526, fo. 143^b; Add. MS. 26,753, fo. 122^b. The coat is antiently borne by the name of Presser, a coat fitte for any nobleman; entered by Brooke. *See* Key.

ALSOPP, John, of London, Aug. 1597, by Rhee [Lee], Clar. Harl. MS. 1537, fo. 108^b.

ALSTON, Sir Edward, D. Med. presid. and fell. Leyden in Holland, 4 Feb. 1643-4. Harl. MS. 1172. fo. 11^b. Licence to practice in England, 20 June 1665.

ALTHAM, James, London, alderm., 5 Sept. 1559, by Harvey. Add. MS. 16,940, fo. 28^b; Cot., Her.; Harl. MS. 5887, fo. 67^b; Exhib. Socy. Antiq., 64.

ALVERSTON, *see* JENOURE.

ALWARDE, *see* AWFORD, John, Ipswich, Surrey [*sic*], by Barker. Coat, Harl. MS. 5846, fo. 2 and 3; Stowe MS. 692, fo. 10^b and 9. Crest, Add. MS. 26,702, fo. 55, and coat.

ALWORTH, Giles, of Meighing, par. of Wroughton, Wilts, gent., a loyal person, 12 Oct. 1662, by E. Walker, Gart. Her. Coll., fo. 48.

AMCOTES, Alex^r, of Stropp, co. Linc., Quarterly of 6, and crest conf^d 5 Oct. 1548, by Barker. Harl. MS. 1359, fo. 14; 1422, fo. 11^b; Add. MS. 26,702, fo. 60.

AMERIDETH, Edward, Quar. of 4 and crest, by W. Dethick, Gart., Camden and Segar. Add. MS. 12,225, fo. 5^b.

AMERY, or EMERY, Thomas, of Little Badow, Essex (son of Thos. son of Thos.); conf^d 20 May 1628, by Segar. C. 21, fo. 78, Her. Coll.; Guil. 358; Add. MS. 12,225, fo. 39^b; Harl. MS. 6179, fo. 43.

AMHERST (Richard), Kent, May 1607, by Camden. Harl. MS. 1422, fo. 20; 6095, fo. 9^b; Berry and Guil., 339.

AMORYE, or ST. AMORYE, Giles, Cotherington, co. Glouc., 1592, by Cooke. Harl. MS. 1359, fo. 112; Add. MS. 4966, fo. 93.

AMY, John, London, D.C.L., Master in Chancery and Advocate in the Court of Arches; son of John, son of Robert of Abington, co. Camb.; son of Symon, etc., 10 April 1593, by W. Dethick, Gart. Q's Coll. Oxf. MS. 37, fo. 84; copy of grant; Stowe MS. 676, fo. 61; Add. MS. 35,336, fo. 62; V. O. Grants 423; Harl. MS. 5887, fo. 49^b; 1105, fo. 3.

AMYAS, Thomas, Depham, Norfolk, 1576, by Cooke. Harl. MS. 1359, fo. 123.

AMYDAS, Robert, London, gent., by Barker. Harl. MS. 5846, fo. 2; Stowe MS. 692, fo. 9; Add. MS. 26,702, fo. 53.

ANDERSON, Edmond, Erbury, co. Warwick, 4 July 1572, by Cooke. Harl. MS. 1359, fo. 122^b; MS. Ashm. 844, fo. 17, copy of grant, Bodleian Lib.; Grants II., 526, and Guil. 86.

„ Henry, of the towne of Newcastle upon Tyne, gent., 3 Nov. 1547, by G. Dethick, Norr. Harl. MS. 1359, fo. 5^b; 1507, fo. 422, copy of grant Brit. Museum; Q's Coll. Oxf. MS. 37, fo. 12; 39, fo. 9, and Guil. 230; Add. MS. 35,336, fo. 7, and V. O. Grants 45; Le Neve's MS. 432.

ANDREW, Thomas, and his brethren, Randolf, Richard, W^m, and James; coat conf^d and crest granted 1334, 8 Ed. III., by Guyan, K. of Arms; a forgery; copy of patent, Harl. MS. 1507, fo. 99, 431, and Q's Coll. Oxf. MS. 38, fo. 1, and 146, fo. 19; Le Neve's MS. 431.

„ Thomas, s. and h. of Richard, co. Warwick, gent., conf^d 1476, by Thomas [Holme], Clar. Harl. MS. 1359, fo. 28^b.

ANDREWES, ..., crest, a greyhound's head, etc., by Barker. Harl. MS. 5846, fo. 5ᵇ; Stowe MS. 692, fo. 10ᵇ.

ANDREWS, John, Little Lever, Lanc., gent., 16 Mar. 1664-5, by W. Dugdale, Norr.; entered at Visitⁿ (Her. Coll.) C. 37, 72ᵇ.

ANDREWES, Sir Matthew, Kt., Hearsham and Ashley, Surrey, President East India Co., 9 Dec. 1675, by W. Dugdale. Harl. MS. 6834, fo. 178; Grants III., 22, and Add. MS. 35,336, fo. 148.

„ Anthony, Bisbrooke, Rutland, gent., 28 Oct. 1583, by Sir G. Dethick, Gart. Q's Coll. Oxf. MS. 145, fo. 13ᵇ; Harl. MS. 1441, fo. 69; Grants I., p. 228; Add. MS. 35,336, fo. 121.

„ John. *See above.*

„ Richard, Lynton, co. Worc., grant 27 March 1529, by T. Wriothesley, Gart. Copy of grant in French, Brit. Mus., Harl. MS. 1507, fo. 376, and Q's Coll. Oxf. MS. 38, fo. 21; 25 May in Harl. MS. 7025, fo. 199; Le Neve's MS. 376.

„ Thomas, Bury Sᵗ Edmund's, Suff., 1560, by Harvey. Add. MS. 16,940, fo. 11ᵇ; Harl. MS. 1116, fo. 57.

ANGELL, William, of London, son of Thos. of Pecarke, Northts., gent., son of Robert; confirmed by Camden. Harl. MS. 1422, fo. 40ᵇ; 6095, fo. 33.

„ William, of London, son of Thos., son of Robt. of Pekark, Northts.; crest 1 May 1614, by Segar. Add. MS. 12,225, fo. 5ᵇ; Grants II., fo. 483.

ANGEVIN, Bernard, letters patent 11 Mar. 1445-6, dated from palace Westmʳ. Harl. MS. 1470, fo. 59; MS. Ashm. 840, fo. 109; 858, fo. 62, copy of grant, Bodleian Lib.; Rymer's Fœdera, xi., 81.

ANGUISH, ..., Norwich, by Segar. Add. MS. 12,225, fo. 5; (Harl. MS. 1055, fo. 39).

ANNESLEY, Sir Francis, Knt. and Bart., Vice treasʳ and Chief Sec. Ireland and of the King's Privy Council there, and Viscᵗ Valentia, and by reason of that dignity Vice treasʳ; supporters granted 6 March 1627-8, by Segar. Add. MS. 12,225, fo. 5.

ANSCELL, ..., by Cooke, Clar. Stowe MS. 670, fo. 54ᵇ.

ANSTRUTHER, Sir James, of Ardric, clerk to the bills; 2ⁿᵈ son of Sir Philip of that ilk; matriculated 15 May 1682, by Erskine, Lyon K. of Arms. Stowe MS. 714, fo. 92ᵇ.

ANTROBUS, Thomas, one of the six clerks [in Chancery], Sept. 1604, by Camden. Harl. MS. 1422, fo. 18, and 6095, fo. 2.

ANWICK, John, London (by Sir G. Dethick). Q's Coll. Oxf. MS. 145, fo. 30ᵇ; Harl. MS. 1441, fo. 79ᵇ; 6179, fo. 19ᵇ; 6140, fo. 39; Stowe MS. 703, fo. 33ᵇ.

APLEGARTH, Robert, Ropley, Southants; crest granted 31 May 1569, by Sir G. Dethick, Gart., Cooke and Flower. Q's Coll. Oxf. MS. 39, fo. 156 (MS. 145, fo. 23); Harl. MS. 1359, fo. 55; 1441, fo. 75ᵇ; MS. Ashm. 844, fo. 22, copy of grant, Bodleian Lib.; of Copley, Surrey, in Guil. 222.

APOTHECARIES' COMPANY, arms, crest and supporters, 12 Dec. 1619, by Camden. Harl. MS. 1359, fo. 77; Her. and Geneal. i., 124.

APPENRETH, Griffith, of the towne of Callais, by Barker. Harl. MS. 5846, fo. 4; Stowe MS. 692, fo. 9ᵇ; Harl. MS. 5887, fo. 8.

ARCHDALE, Martin, London, 29 Oct. 1578, by Ro. Cooke, Clar. Harl. MS. 1405, fo. 8ᵇ; 6140, fo. 32ᵇ. Quartering Sexton, confirmed by Wm. Dethick. Harl. MS. 1453, fo. 35ᵇ; entered by R. Brooke.

ARCHER, Andrew, Tamworth, co. Warwick, Esq.; crest 1597, by R. Lee, Clar. Harl. MS. 1359, fo. 39; 1422, fo. 94; Add. MS. 14,295, fo. 121.

„ Henry, Theydon Gernon, Essex, son of Wᵐ, 2 son of Richᵈ, son of John, son of Symonde Boys of Theydon Gernon; crest 2 Apr. 1575, by Cooke. Harl. MS. 1359, fo. 7, and Morgan's Sphere, ii., 74; Grants II., 493, 515; copy of grant Brit. Mus., Add. MS. 12,474, fo. 116.

ARCHER, John, London, gent., son of John, late of Kent, son of Thos. of Theydon Gernon, Essex, gent., son of John, son of Simon de Boys; confirmed 2 Apr. 1575, by Cooke. Stowe MS. 677, fo. 13^b ; Grants II., 493, 515, ermine on a cross sable, a crescent in Bannerman's MS. 9, fo. 447.

  ,, Robert, Wainfleet, co. Linc., and Tamworth, co. Warw., 24 Mar. 1684-5, by Sir Wm Dugdale and Clar. Harl. MS. 6834, fo. 178; Grants III., fo. 268; Lansd. MS. 867, fo. 52 ; Add. MS. 35,336, fo. 173.

ARDEN, Mary, d. and h. Robt. of Wellingcote, co. Warw.; wife of John Shakespeare of Stratford on Avon, 1599, by W. Dethick, Gart., and Camden. Miscel. Geneal. et Heral., 2 Series, vol. i., p. 109 ; Grants II., 508.

ARDERNE, William, of Stretton (Biggleswade), Beds, Clerk of the Market of the King's most honourable household, by Barker. Harl. Soc. 5846, fo. 2^b ; Stowe MS. 692, fo. 9^b; Grants I., 286.

ARDREN, William, of Beds, son of Thos. of Cheshire, gent.; grant 20 Nov. 1550. Q's Coll. Oxf. MS. 37, fo. 28, and 39, fol. 30, copy of grant; Harl. MS. 1359, fo. 81 ; Add. MS. 35,336 and V. O. Grants, fo. 4.

ARGALL, Thomas, crest confirmed 1562, by Harvey. Add. MS. 16,940, fo. 59^b, by Barker ; Stowe MS. 692, fo. 6, as Argoyll, then of Surrey.

ARMAR, or ARMOURER, Francis, Belford, Northbld., gent.; crest 10 Dec. 1547, by G. Dethick, Norr. Harl. MS. 1507, fo. 438, copy of grant, Brit. Mus., and Q's Coll. Oxf. MSS. 37, fo. 15 ; 39, fol. 6 ; Harl. MS. 1359, fo. 4 ; Grants I., 332; V. O. Grants, fo. 48, and Add. MS. 35,336, fo. 8 ; Le Neve's MS. 438.

ARMITAGE (Robert), London, from Doncaster, by Segar. Harl. MS. 6140, fo. 76 ; Add. MS. 12,225, fo. 3 ; C. 24, Her. Coll., and Guil. 74 ; Add. MS. 4966, fo. 54.

ARMORER, Sir William, first equerry of the Great Horse to the King ; Augm. 8 July 1662, by Walker. MS. Ashm. 840, pp. 423-4 ; 858, pp. 226-7, copy of grant, Bodleian Lib. (equerry to K. Jas. and K. Chas. I.; Major and Lt.-Col. of horse ; followed the King into the Low Country, and returned with him to England. Copy of grant Harl. MS. 1172, fo. 9 ; Add. MS. 14,293, fo. 31 ; 14,294, fo. 4^b).

ARMORERS' COMPANY, 15 Oct. 1556, by T. Hawley. MS. Ashm. 858, p. 18, copy of grant, Bodleian Lib.; Her. and Geneal., i., 122 ; Proc. Soc. of Antiq., 2nd. Series, vol. i., 1860, p. 197 ; 10 Oct. in Add. MS. 16,940, fo. 208^b ; Cat. Her. Exhib. Soc. Antiq., 64.

ARNOLD, Edmund, of Gt. and Little Leesthorp, co. Leic., Esq., LL.B., Dec. 1663. Harl. MS. 1107, fo. 17 ; 1470, fo. 127 ; g. D. [gives Date ?] patent [Dec.] a^o 1653 in Guil. 334 ; Bysshe's Grants, fo. 4. in Her. Coll., and Grants I., 178.

  ,, Richard, citizen and Haberdasher of London ; crest granted 31 Dec. 1611, by Segar. Harl. MS. 1507, fo. 117, copy of grant, Brit. Mus., and Q's Coll. Oxf. MS. 38, fo. 121, and Harl. MS. 1172, fo. 17 ; Add. MS. 12,225, fo. 3^b ; Guil. 334; Add. MS. 4966, fo. 26^b; Harl. MS. 6140, fo. 26^b.

  ,, Roger, Middx., gent., grant 20 Feb. 1564-5, by Sir G. Dethick, Gart. Harl. MS. 1359, fo. 70^b ; Q's Coll. Oxf. MS. 39, fo. 125, copy of grant ; Grants I., 178 ; Add. MS. 35,336, fo. 111 ; Harl. MS. 6140, fo. 7.

ARPE, Peter, Chertsey, Surrey, 30 June 1631, by R. St. George. Add. MS. 14,295, fo. 67^b, and I. 23, fo. 67^b. Her. Coll.

ARRAS als. HITCHCOCK, Robert, Caversfield, Bucks, gent.; Arras quartering Clarke, 30 Nov. 1560, by Dalton. Harl. MS. 1359, fo. 44^b; Add. MS. 16,940, fo. 22 ; Harl. MS. 1422, fo. 107^b.

ARTHUR, ..., Springfield, Essex, ..., by Segar. Add. MS. 12,225, fo. 3^b; C. 21, fo. 203^b, Her. Coll., and Guil. 295.

  ,, John, of Dorset, Esq., 4 Feb. 1646-7, by Bysshe, Gart. Harl. MS. 6140, fo. 18.

ARTIFICERS' COMPANY. *See* TRADESMEN. Harl. MS. 1410, fo. 11.

ARTILLERY COMPANY, The Honourable. *See* MILITARY.

ARUNDEL, Earl of (Philip), Achvm^t 28 May 1580, by Cooke.   MS. Ashm. 844, fo. 38, copy of grant, Bodleian Lib.

„   Col. Richd., of Trerise, Baron Arundel of Trerise 17 Chas. II. ; supporters 20 April 1665, by Sir Edward Walker, Gart.   Harl. MS. 6079, fo. 79 ; R. C. Families, iii., 162.

ASHAWE, Leonard, of Shawe, co. Lanc., son of Leonard, son of Roger, Esquire, of the Hill ; Quar. of 6 ; crest granted 6 May 1599, by Segar, Somerset, Norroy nominate.   Q's Coll. Oxf. MS. 146, fo. 44 ; Harl. MS. 1359, fo. 36^b ; 1422, fo. 114^h ; Add. MS. 12,225, fo. 4 ; 14,295, fo. 115^b, and Guil. 230.

ASHBURNHAM, Lord, supporters 24 June 1689, by T. St. George, Gart.   Harl. MS. 6834, fo. 68 ; Grants IV., 45.

ASHBY, ..., Quenby, co. Leic., Quarterly, crest granted 1602, by Camden.   Harl. MS. 6095, fo. 22^b.

ASHE als ESSE, ..., Devon, confirmed Dec. 1613, by Camden.   Harl. MS. 6095, fo. 28 ; Harl. MS. 1422, fo. 38^b.

ASHMOLE, Elias, Windsor Herald, crest, etc., 13 Aug. 1660, by W. Dugdale, Norr. (Her. Coll.), and 16 May 1661 (Berry).   See also Harl. MS. 1105, fo. 20^b ; Bysshe's Grants, fo. 19, Her. Coll., original grant in Bodleian Lib.

ASHTON, Christopher, Croston, co. Lanc., gent., crest 17 May 1548, by G. Dethick, Norr.   Harl. MS. 1359, fo. 3 ; 1507, fo. 448, copy of grant, Brit. Mus., and Q's Coll. Oxf. MSS. 37, fo. 21 ; 39, fo. 16, and 38, fo. 51 ; Stowe MS. 676, fo. 17^b ; Cott. MS. Faustina E. 1, 59 ; (confirmed by Camden to Ashton of Hampton Ct. in Hants, Guil. 352) ; Grants I., 332 ; V. O. Grants 53 ; Add. MS. 35,336, fo. 10 ; Le Neve's MS. 448.

„   Henry, Colonel to Emperor of all the Russias, confirmed 16 Aug. 1632, by Segar.   Add. MS. 12,225, fo. 2^b ; Harl. MS. 6140, fo. 79^b.

„   Richard, Whalley, co. Lanc., gent. (2. s. Raufe of Gt. Laver), receiver of the revenues for co. Lanc. and Northbld., Cumbld., Westmld. and the Bpk. of Durham ; Quarterly, confirmed 1 Dec. 1561, by Dalton.   Harl. MS. 1359, fo. 52, crest granted.

„   Sir Thos. and Sir Piers à Leigh, Holyroode Day, May, 11 Hen. VII., 1496, determined in the King's Chamber at Westminster, by the Earl of Derby, before Garter and Norroy, for each of the above.   Harl. MS. 1424, fo. 86^b.

ASHWORTH, Gervais, Eton, Windsor, attested March 1585, by Flower, Norr., and his son, Somerset.   MS. Ashm. 844, fo. 17, copy of grant, Bodleian Lib., and Guil. 130.

ASKETYNE, James, als Astyne, of Morrant's Court, Kent, Esq., crest 6 June 1578, by Sir Gilb. Dethicke, Gart.   Harl. MS. 1359, fo. 59 ; Grants I., 131 ; Q's Coll. Oxf. MS. 39, fo. 163, copy of grant ; Add. MS. 35,336, fo. 104 ; Harl. MS. 5887, fo. 27^b.

„   Richard, als Astyn, of par. of West Peckham, Kent, 4 Oct. 1572, by Sir G. Dethick.   Harl. MS. 1441, fo. 79 ; Q's Coll. Oxf. MS. 145, fo. 29^b.

ASKEW (Alan), of Gray's Inn (son Christopher of Richmond, Yorks), crest (Stowe MS. 706, fo. 15^b) 15 March 1615-16, by St. George, Norroy.

„   Christopher, mayor of London 1533.   Harl. MS. 1116, fo. 38^b, by Richmond, Clarencieux.

ASPIN, Rev. Wm., rector of Emberton, Bucks, 20 Feb. 1667-8, by Sir T. St. George, Gart. and Clar.   Harl. MS. 6179, fo. 63 ; Harl. MS. 6834, fo. 17 ; Grants III., fo. 342 ; Lansd. MS. 867, fo. 52 ; Add. MS. 35,336, fo. 180.

ASTELL, Henry, of Knaptoft, co. Leic., augm. and crest 1581, by Cooke, Clar. Bannerman's MS. No. 9, fo. 445.

ASTEN, Thomas, gent., confirmed at Amsterdam 27 Dec. 1653, by Sir E. Walker,
Gart. Her. Coll., fo. 45.

ASTLEY, Jacob, Lord, supporters 28 Mar. 1648, by Sir E. Walker, Gart. Her.
Coll., fo. 12 ; Le Neve's MS. 4.

ASTRY, Sir Raufe, L. Mayor London (1493-94) 12 Sep. 2 [Rich. III., 1484 ?],
(1480—86), per T. Holme, Clar., Kt. Harl. Soc. Bedfordshire [p. 77 n]
temp. E. IV. ; Add. MS. 26,702, fo. 28.

ATCHELEY, Robert, Draper, Aldern. of Barnards Castle Ward, senr. Sheriff, London,
1504 ; coat on crest temp. H. 7. Add. MS. 26,702, fo. 34b.

ATCHEQUER. See HARFLEAT.

ATHOWE, John, Breseley, Norfolk, 1586, by Cooke. Harl. MS. 1359, fo. 91, and
1422, fo. 93 ; Add. MS. 4966, fo. 64b.

ATKINS (Henry), D. phys., by Cooke. Harl. MS. 1422, fo. 17b ; 2275, fo. 90 ;
1115, fo. 8 ; and 5839, fo. 2 ; Morgan's Sphere, 107.

„ Thomas, of ye county and city of Gloucester, by Barker. Harl. MS. 5846,
fo. 4b ; Stowe MS. 692, fo. 11.
Probably the same—
Thomas, of Hempsted, co. and city of Glouc. ; crest 26 Nov. 1548, by
Barker. Stowe MS. 677, fo. 48 ; copy of grant 606, fo. 60.

ATKINSON, ..., co. Camb., 1624 ; sa. a cross flory az. betw. 4 escallop shells or ;
crest, a lion sejant arg. holding in the dexter paw an escallop shell or, by
Segar. Berry.

„ Robert, Newark, Notts, Capt. of a troop of horse under the command of the
Rt. Hon. the Marquis of Newcastle for safeguard of the Northern parts of
the realm 28 Nov. 1663, by W. Dugdale, Norr. (Her. Coll.).

ATON, William de, challenged the arms borne by Robert de Bointon, and was
upheld on submission to Lord Percy, 5 April 1375. Harl. MS. 1178,
fo, 44.

ATTLEE, Will, of Lee, Sussex, gent., C.C. and C.G. 15 Nov. 1567, by G. Dethick,
Gart., Cooke and Flower. Le Neve's MS. 495.

ATSLOW, Edward, of London, D. phys., son of Wm. of Everseale, Beds, gent., by
his wife Ann, d. and h. of John Lobenham of Brikelsworth, Norfolk,
gent. ; crest 27 June 1579, by Cooke. Harl. MS. 1052, fo. 192b, copy of
grant Brit. Mus., Harl. MS. 5887, fo, 62b.

ATTERBURY, ..., Atterbury, Northants, by Cooke. Stowe MS. 670,
fo. 33b.

ATTYE, Arthur, of Newington, Secy. to Robt. Dudley, Earl of Leicester, 1583, by
Cooke. Harl. MS. 1359, fo. 98b ; Atye in Add. MS. 14,295, fo. 35b ;
Guil. 182 ; Add. MS. 4966, fo. 63.

ATWATER, William, D.D., Dean of H. M's Chapel, grant 13 April 1509, by
Wriothesley, Gart., and R. Machado ats. Richmont, Clar. Stowe MS. 676,
fo. 8 ; MS. Ashm. 858, p. 17, copy of grant, Bodleian Lib. ; V.O. Grants
97 ; Add MS. 35,336, fo. 19.

„ William, S.T.D., Cannington, Somt, dean of H. M's chapel ; crest 28 June
1513, by Wriothesley, Gart., and Benolte, Clar. Stowe MS. 676, fo. 10 ;
MS. Ashm. 858, pp. 9—10, copy of grant, Bodleian Lib., and in French,
Q's Coll. Oxf. MS. 38, fo. 27 ; V. O. Grants 97, etc.

ATWELL, John, Mamhead, Devon, gent., 7 or 17 Feb. 1614-15, by Camden.
Add. MS. 14,295, fo. 63b ; 9th Feb., in Harl. MS. 1422, fo. 39b, and 6095,
fo. 32 ; C. 2, fo. 153, Devon, Her. Coll.; H. St. George, 9 Feb. 1614, in
Le Neve's MS. 332.

ATWOOD, John, Worcester, release (in French) of arms to him by Humphrey
Smethwick, patent 6 H. 6, 1428. MS. Ashm. 35, fo. 366, copy of grant,
Bodleian Lib.

AUBREY, William, of co. Brecon, D.C.L., 10 June 1572, by Cooke. MS. Ashm.
844, fo. 35, 36, copy of grant, Bodleian Lib. ; Q's Coll. Oxf. MS. 37,
fo. 52 ; V. O. Grants 429 ; Add. MS. 35,336, fo. 63.

AUDLEY, ..., Essex, crest, by Barker (1536—50); Harl. MS. 5846, fo. 4 ; Stowe MS. 692, fo. 10ᵇ.

„ Robert, of Beerchurch, Essex, Esq., confirmation 15 Feb. 1578-9, by Cooke, Clar. Q's Coll. Oxf. MS. 38, fo. 96, copy of confirmation.

„ Thomas, London, son of John, of Sutton, Kent, gent., and Maudlin his wife, dau. of John Hare of London ; confirmed 7 Oct. 1608, by Camden. Stowe MS. 677, fo. 12ᵇ ; Guil. 199.

AUDYN, Laurence, Dorchester, by Segar. Add. MSS. 12,225, fo. 4ᵇ, and 4966, fo. 55ᵇ ; Harl. MS. 6146, fo. 77ᵇ.

AUNEBY, John, of Sherwood Hall, within the township of Eyronod (? Ewood), Yorks, 11 Aug. 1612, by R. St. George, Norr. Stowe MS. 706, fo. 14ᵇ ; Harl. MS. 6140, fo. 72ᵇ.

AUNGER, Richard, Cambridge, esq., s. of John (and Elinor his wife, d. and co-h. of John Baron, gent.), s. of Richard, lineally descended of the ancient house of Aunger, of Essex ; Quarterly coat, crest given 28 Nov. 1581, by Cooke. Harl. MS. 1359, fo. 121 ; Q's Coll. Oxf. MS. 38, fo. 105, copy of grant.

AUSTEN, ..., London, exemplified 1603, by W. Dethick, Gart. ; a patent Jan. 1606, by Camden. Harl. MS. 1422, fo. 19ᵇ ; 6095, fo. 6 ; Harl. MS. 1441, fo. 122ᵇ.

„ . . . ., London, ? impaling Grimes, May 1611, by Camden. Harl. MS. 1422, fo. 36, No. 1, and 6095, fo. 15, No. 1 ; entered in Visit. Surrey, 1662, to Sir James Austin of Southwark ; Add. MS. 5533, fo. 158.

„ Edward, Tenterden, Kent, crest 12 April 1603, by Camden. Harl. MS. 1470, fo. 166, copy of grant, Brit. Mus. ; May 1611 in Harl. MS. 1422, fo. 36, No. 2, and 6095, fo. 15, No. 2 ; Grants I., 30 ; Guil. 189 ; Add. MS. 35,336, fo. 89 ; Le Neve's MS. 457.

„ John, s. of Richard, of Walpole, Norfolk, confirmed or testified 20 Nov. 1625, by R. St. George, Clar. Grants II., 651.

AVELIN. See EVELYN.

AVENON, Alexander, Alderm. of London (fr. Cornwall), 21 Jan. 1566-7, by Sir G. Dethick, Gart. Q's Coll. Oxf. MS. 145, fo. 11 ; Harl. MS. 1441, fo. 67ᵇ. Avenoy in Stowe MS. 703, fo. 14.

AVERY, William, Fillongley, co. Warwick, 25 June 1579, by Cooke. Misc. Gen. et Her., i., 230, copy of grant, Brit. Mus.

AWFORD, John (see ALVARD), coat, by Barker (1526—50). Harl. MS. 5846, fo. 2 ; Stowe MS. 692, fo. 9. For crest see Alvard v. Alward. Add. MS. 26,702, fo. 55.

AYDE, John, Lincoln's Inn, studt.-at-law (s. of Thos. of Ketteringham, Norfk., gent., s. of Thos. of co. Dublin), 7 June 1664, by Walker. Harl. MS. 1172, fo. 37 ; Add. MS. 14,293, fo. 42 ; 14,294, fo. 10ᵇ, and Guil. 259.

AYLETT, John, of Magdalen Laver, Essex, capt. of a troop of horse in the regᵗ of the Rt. Hon. Lord Lucas, did with much courage behave himself in several encounters on Hilton Hills and in Sunderland against the Scottish army then invading this Kingdom, and since served at the battail of Listithiell, Newbury, etc. ; at Oxford 20 Nov. 1645, by Walker. Harl. MS. 1172, fo. 70ᵇ ; Add. MS. 14,293, fo. 94, and 14,294, fo. 32 ; Her. Coll., fo. 28. See Harl. MS. 1397, fo. 258ᵇ.

AYLYFFE (ALEIFFE), ..., of Colvell, Kent, by Barker. Harl. MS. 5846, fo. 3 ; Stowe MS. 692, fo. 10ᵇ.

„ Sir John, Sheriff of London (fr. Wilts), 5 March 1548-9, by Hawley. Add. MS. 16,940, fo. 203, and Harl. MSS. 1165, fo. 27ᵇ, and 6140, fo. 125.

AYLMER, Sir John, confirmed June 1607, by Camden. Harl. MS. 6095, fo. 9ᵇ (this patent was given to Samuel A. of Mogelinton Hall als Mowden Hall, Essex, Esq.).

AYLMER, Samuel, 10 Nov. 1597, by Wm. Dethick, Gart., a bird called an "Aley."
Harl. MS. 1422, fo. 19; Q's Coll. Oxf. MSS. 36, fo. 59, and 38, fo. 114,
copy of grant; Stowe MS. 676, fo. 119ᵇ; V. O. Grants 298; Add. MS.
35,336, fo. 44.

AYLOFF, William, Braxted, Essex, 1588, by Cooke. Harl. MS. 1359, fo. 113;
Add. MS. 4966, fo. 61.

AYLWORTH, John, Somerset, by Barker (1536—50). Harl. MS. 5846, fo. 3ᵇ;
Stowe MS. 692, fo. 10ᵇ; Add. MS. 26,702, fo. 8.

AYLWIN, William (Capt.), of Treeford, Sussex, confirmation crest granted 22 May
1634, by R. St. George, Clar. Harl. MS. 6140, fo. 24; Harl. MS. 1566,
fo. 170; Harl. MS. 6134, fo. 49.

AYSHCOMB, John, Lyford, Berks, Esq., crest 14 May 1613, by Segar. Add. MS.
12,225, fo. 4; Grants II., 492; Le Neve's MS. 464.

AYSON, Richard, Sheering, Essex, and bar.-at-law Inner Temple; s. of Nicholas,
s. of John, s. of John Ayson or Ashton; by Segar, Gart., Camden, Clar.,
and R. St. George, Norr. Add. MS. 12,225, fo. 4ᵇ, and Guil. 100; Harl.
MS. 6140, fo. 78ᵇ.

B

BABER, Edward, Regelbery, Somerset, Esq. (and to the posterity of John, his
father), crest given Jan. 1574-5, by Cooke. Harl. MS. 1359, fo. 27;
Add. MS. 4966, fo. 91, and 37,147, fo. 9ᵇ.

   „   Sir John, Kt., physician in ordinary, crest 30 April 1663, by Sir E. Walker,
Gart. Fo. 50, Her. Coll.

BABTHORPE, Robert, of London; at this present gent. chirurgeon to the Queens
Majestie, crest 20 May 1563, by Harvey. Harl. MS. 1359, fo. 59ᵇ; Add.
MS. 16,940, fo. 12ᵇ; Q's Coll. Oxf. MS. 39, fo. 97, copy of grant, and
Grants II., 557.

BACHE, Raphael, Stanton in the Peak, co. Derby, 10 Dec. 1634, by St. George,
Clar. MS. Ashm. 858, p. 162, copy of grant, Bodleian Lib.; Reliquary
XXII., 52.

BACHELOR, Daniel, Aston Clinton, Berks [Bucks], and of the privy chamber,
Feb. 1606-7, by Camden. Harl. MS. 6095, fo. 6ᵇ; 1422, fo. 19ᵇ; and
Guil. 290; another coat, or, a fesse sa., 3 elephants' heads erased sa.,
12 Nov. 1604; Harl. MS. 6095, fo. 2ᵇ; 1422, fo. 18ᵇ, struck out.

BACKHOUSE, Nicholas, London, grocer (after Alderm.), s. of Thos., of Whitrige,
Cumbld., crest 27 Mar. 1574, by Cooke. MS. Ashm. 840, fo. 405, and 858,
pp. 185-6, copy of grant, Bodleian Lib.

BACKSHELL, John, Beeding, Essex, 13 Jan. 1666-7, by Sir E. Walker, Gart. Her.
Coll., fo. 63.

BACKWELL, Edward, citizen and Goldsmith, of London, 24 Dec. 1681, by Sir
Wᵐ Dugdale, Gart. and Clar. Add. MS. 14,830, fo. 170, and Grants III.,
fo. 140.

BACON VEL BARONN, crest, a bloodhound's head sa. erased and eared arg., having
a hog's foot in his mouth, by Barker. Harl. MS. 5846, fo. 19ᵇ and 5;
Stowe MS. 692, fo. 20, 23; see Thos., of Hessel, below.

   „   Nicholas, 1ˢᵗ grant, az. on a fesse betw. 3 fleurs de lis or, as many griffins'
heads erased of the field, langued gu.; crest, a bore's head couped and
tusked gu., having in his mouth a griffin's head erased arg., by Barker,
1536—49. Harl. MS. 5846, fo. 9ᵇ; Add. MS. 26,702, fo. 71ᵇ; and Stowe
MS. 692, fo. 22ᵇ; Legh's Accedens, 1568, 2 or 3 edn., p. 101. This is the
only proper coat and crest of the premier baronet of England. Second or
spurious confirmation.

   „   Thomas, Northam, Herts, now of Linsted, Kent,   ⎫ sons of Robert,
   „   Sir Nicholas, Kt., Ld. Keeper of the Gt. Seal of England, and ⎬ late of Drinks-
   „   James, Alderm. and Sheriff of London,   ⎭ ton, Suff. gent.

Add. MS. 5523, fo. 98 [on scrap of paper stuck in] :—

This Sir Nicholas Bacon, lord Keeper, brought up by his father yᵉ Abbotts sheep Reeve at schoole at length beinge sent to be made a prieste and perceivinge that his Crowne must be shaven rather than that he wonld abide yᵗ wʰ he soe much misliked, he ran away and after he had hid himselfe a greate while at ye lengthe by an uncle of his yᵗ was a riche tailor he was sente and mayneteyned at ye Innes of Coorte from whence he was admitted to yᵉ dignity which after he came unto.

The statements which follow are false : s. of John, s. of John, s. of Walter of Drinkston, s. of Robert, *temp.* H. IV. and H. VIII., high sheriff Norf. and Suff., *temp.* H. IV., s. of Hy., s. of Adam, s. of Sir John, Kt., s. of 2. Sir Edmond, Kt. and heir to Dame Margaret his wife, d. and h. of Robert Quaplade, esq., which son Edmᵈ was s. & h. of Wᵐ, esq., *temp.* E. II., and therefore the coat and quartering was illicitly confirmed. Crest 28 Feb. 1568-9, granted by Sir G. Dethick, Gart., Cooke and Flower. Harl. MS. 1359, fo. 56ᵇ, etc.; 1441, 5823, and 5847 ; Legh's Accedens, 2ⁿᵈ ed., 1568, and 3ʳᵈ ed., 1576, fo. 58, etc.; Her. and Geneal., vol. i., pp. 59, 60 ; vol. ii., p. 540 ; MS. Ashm. 844, p. 44 (copy of grant Bodleian Lib.), and Q's Coll. Oxf. MS. 145, fo. 17ᵇ and 22 *bis. See* pedigree Add. MS. 5523, fo. 98, and 19,116, fo. 63, vice Comites Norfolciæ 1843, 4to.

BACON, Thomas, of Hessel. Suff., 9 May 1514, by T. Wriothesley, Gart., and Benolt, Clar. Le Neve's MS. 253.

BADBROKE. *See* BOULBROKE.

BADD, ..., Farham, Hants, 2 Jan. 1626-7, by Segar. Add. MS. 12,225, fo. 6 ; Hants Visit., C. 19, 120ᵇ, Her. Coll., and Guil. 127.

BAESHE (*see also* BASHE), Edward, London and Herts, 10 Dec. 1550 (by T. Hawley) and 3 Feb. 1571-2, by Cooke and Flower. MS. Ashm. 844, fo. 33, 38, copy of grant, Bodleian Lib., and Q's Coll. Oxf. MSS. 37, fo. 50, and 39, fo. 143—145 : Add. MS. 16,940, fo. 204ᵇ. *See* T. Baker, his wife, and Guil. 382 ; Her. Exhib. Soc. Antiq. Catalogue, 63 ; Harl. MS. 5887, fo. 105.

BAGENAL, Rauffe, Staffs, by Barker. Harl. MS. 5846, fo. 10 ; Stowe MS. 692, fo. 22ᵇ ; Harl. MS. 6179, fo. 16.

BAGGE, ..., of Lanc., July 1656, by Sir E. Bysshe, Gart. Harl. MS. 1441, fo. 151ᵇ ; 6179, fo. 54ᵇ ; Harl. MS. 1466, fo. 24ᵃ.

 „ Sir James, Plymouth, Apr. 1607, by Camden. Harl. MS. 1422, fo. 19ᵇ ; 6095, fo. 7, and Guil. 406.

 „ William [of Shipdam, Norfolk, by Edward Bysshe, Gart., 1566 (*sic* 5th June 1656)]. Burke's Armory.

BAILDON. *See* BALIDON.

BAILLIES, Bryan, Cottingley, co. York, 5 Jan. or Feb. 1578-9, by Flower. Cains Coll. Camb. MS. 528, fo. 9, copy of grant ; MS. Ashm. 834, fo. 16ᵇ, copy of grant, Bodleian Lib., and Guil. 172 ; Harl. MS. 6179, fo. 37ᵇ.

BAKER, William, New Windsor, Berks, 14 July 1655, by Bysshe. Grant, MSS. Ashm. 810, fo. 404 ; 858, fo. 206-7, copy of grant, Bodleian Lib., and Guil. 206, who adds "declared void soon after the restoration."

 „ . . . ., of Mayfield, Sussex, by R. St. George, Clar. Harl. MS. 1105, fo. 5.

 „ . . . ., London, draper, by Sir E. Bysshe, Gart. Harl. MS. 1441, fo. 148ᵇ.

 „ Christopher, Dartford, Kent, by Cooke [1573]. Harl. MS. 1359, fo. 87 ; 1422, fo. 45 ; Add. MS. 4966, fo. 58.

 „ Cicelle, dau. of Sir John, Kt., ux. Sir Thos. Sackville, Baron of Buckhurst, Lord high treasurer of Exchequer ; ? a grant of supporters to her Apr. 1602, by W. Dethick, Gart. Q's Coll. Oxf. MS. 36, fo. 92 ; Stowe MS. 676, fo. 136ᵇ.

 „ Daniel, Hatton Garden, par. of St. Andrew, Holborn, 21 July 1680. Stowe MS. 714, fo. 158 ; Grants III., fo. 105.

BAKER, Edmund, Calais, 14 Feb. 1545-6, by Barker. Stowe MS. 692, fo. 23ᵇ ;
  Harl. MS. 5846, fo. 11ᵇ.

  „   George, London, surgeon to Q. Eliz., by Cooke. Harl. MS. 1359, fo. 87 ;
       1422, fo. 45 : Add. MS. 4966, fo. 66.

  „   George, same coat, London, gent., s. of Christopher of Tenterden, Kent, s. of
       John of same, s. of Symond of Feversham ; confirmed 10 May 1573 to the
       posterity of Christopher, his father ; another, with slight alteration in
       crest, 1 Apr. 1579, by Cooke. MS. Ashm. 840, fo. 403 ; 858, fo. 196—99,
       copies of grants, Bodleian Lib. ; Genealogist, N. S., vol. vi., p. 242, and
       Misc. Gen. et Her., ii., p. 1 ; MS. Ashm. 840, fo. 424-5, copy of grant,
       Bodleian Lib.

  „   George, s. of Thomas of West Peckham, Kent, exemplified by Segar. Add.
       MS. 12,225, fo. 7.

  „   Sir Henry, of Sissinghurst, Kent, Kt. and Bart., alteration by Segar. Add.
       MS. 12,225, fo. 6ᵇ.

  „   Henry.

  „   James, Bures Gifford, Essex, gift 1559 (Harvey's Grants). Add. MS. 16,940,
       fo. 17. See Henry. Stowe MS. 670, by Cooke, Clar.

  „   John, London, by Barker. Harl. MS. 5846, fo. 9 ; Stowe MS. 692, fo. 22ᵇ.

  „   John, Morpeth, Northumbld., gent., 6 Apr. 1548, by G. Dethick, Norr.
       Harl. MS. 1507, fo. 444, copy of grant, Brit. Mus., and Harl. MS. 1359,
       fo. 3ᵇ ; Q's Coll. Oxf. MSS. 37, fo. 18 ; 39, fo. 14, and 38, fo. 50 ; Grants I.,
       330 ; Le Neve's MS. 444.

  „   John, of Cambridge, 1577, by Cooke, Clar. Harl. MS. 1422, fo. 45 ; 6179,
       fo. 10ᵇ.

  „   John, Shrewsbury, by Segar : sa., a gryphon rampt. segreant and ducally
       gorged or. Add. MS. 12,225, fo. 6 ; Guil. 266.

  „   Sir Richard, Sissinghurst, Kent, by Segar. Add. MS. 12,225, fo. 9.

  „   Thomas, Chester, confirmed 1629, by Segar. Add. MS. 12,225, fo. 6 ; Stowe
       MS. 677, fo. 7ᵇ, of Nantwich, "procured by me R. Mundy," and Guil. 266 ;
       Add. MS. 12,474, fo. 108 ; Harl. MS. 6140, fo. 64.

  „   Thomas, Battell, Sussex, May 1615, by Camden. Harl. MS. 6095, fo. 32ᵇ ;
       Harl. MS. 1422, fo. 39ᵇ ; Guil. 307.

  „   Thomas, Swaney, High Sheriff Salop, confirmed 14 Oct. 1649, by Ryley,
       Norr. MS. Ashm. 858, pp. 136-7, copy of grant, Bodleian Lib.

  „   Tomasyn, wife to Edward Baeshe of London, 15 Nov. 1553 (by Hawley).
       Add. MS. 16,940, fo. 206ᵇ ; Harl. MS. 1115, fo. 66ᵇ.

BALDWIN, Edward, Wiltons, par. of Beaconsfield, Bucks, and Thomas, his brother,
       19 Dec. 1662, by Sir E. Bysshe. Grant : Harl. MS. 1470, fo. 81, grant of
       arms, Brit. Mus. ; Harl. MS. 1105, fo. 18ᵇ, 20 ; Bysshe's Grants, fo. 18,
       Her. Coll. ; November in Guil. 114.

  „   . . . ., of Beds, by Sir E. Walker ? Harl. MS. 6179, fo. 109ᵇ.

  „   Henry, Dunridge, Bucks, 13 Feb. 1656-7, by Sir E. Bysshe, Gart. Harl. MS.
       2275, fo. 40.

  „   Richard, Diddlebury, Salop, crest 10 June 1580, by Cooke. MS. Ashm. 858,
       fo. 130, copy of grant, Bodleian Lib.

BALAY, Richard, of Leicester and York, 14 Sept. 1643, by H. St. George, Norr.
       Harl. MS. 1105, fo. 13.

BALE, Sir John, of Carleton Curlieu, co. Leic., Knt. (s. of John), Quarterly coat,
       by Segar. Add. MS. 12,225, fo. 9, and Guil. 385.

BALES, Robert, Norton, Northts., by Segar. Add. MS. 12,225, fo. 11ᵇ.

  „   John, Wilby, Sussex or Suffolk, 10 Dec. 1576, by Cooke. Stowe MS.
       670, fo. 80 ; Harl. MS. 1085, fo. 27ᵇ ; Add. MS. 4966, fo. 53ᵇ.

BALFOUR, James, Kt., of Pittendreich, 6 Feb. 1566-7, by Sir Robt. Forman, Lyon
       K. of Arms. Grants II., 672.

BALIDON, Peter, of the boro' of Derby, gent., 4 Dec. 1663, by W. Dugdale, Norr.
       Her. Coll.

BALL, William, s. of Thomas, of the Privy Chamber to Philip and Mary, Cheshire, arg., a lyon rampt. sa. holding a grenade fired [a bale of wildfire], ppr., 20 June 1572 (by Segar, Add. MS. 12,225, fo. 9b), by Cooke, Clar., confirmed by Segar. Proc. Soc. Antiq., 1897, 2nd S., xvi., 351.

„ Edward, of town of Cambridge, gent., grant 8 July 1575, by Cooke. Stowe MS. 677, fo. 16b, pedigree, p. 17.

„ Richard, D.D., s. of Lawrence of Northampton, crest, by Segar. 22 Dec. 1613 in Guil. 171 ; Add. MS. 12,225, fo. 7.

„ Robert, of London, s. of Robert of Wencester, Suff., 27 June 1576, by Cooke. Le Neve's MS. 498.

„ Robert, of Scottow, Norfolk, s. of John, s. of Ralph of Parham, Suffolk, Esq., s. of Sir Hy., co. Derby, Kt., confirmed 25 Oct. 1576, by Cooke. Harl. MS. 1359, fo. 24 ; 27 Aug. in Add. MS. 14,295, fo. 50.

„ Thomas, of the town and co. of Newcastle-on-Tyne, esq., comptroller of H.M.'s Customs for the porte of the said towne, confirmed 24 Oct. 1633, by Segar. Stowe MS. 677, fo. 16b, see pedigree, p. 17, and grant to Ed. Ball.

BALLARD, John, Much Dewchurch, co. Hereford, 1 Jan. 1557-8, by Sir G. Dethick, Gart. Q's Coll. Oxf. MS. 145, fo. 53 ; Harl. MS. 1441, fo. 102 ; 5887, fo. 18.

BALLETT, John, London, Goldsmith, 24 Eliz. 1582, by Cooke. Guil. 181 ; Harl. MS. 6140, fo. 38.

BAMBURGH, Capt. Thos., of Howsam, Yorks, s. of Wm, crest 7 May 1583, by Cooke. Harl. MS. 1359, fo. 93b ; 1422, fo. 95b, and Add. MS. 14,295, fo. 37b ; 4966, fo. 63b.

„ Robert, of Stickforth, co. Leic., crest 1561, by Harvey, Clar. Add. MS. 16,940.

„ William, Rendlesham, Suff., gent., s. of Robert of Stickforth, co. Leic., confirmed 1561, by Harvey. Harl. MS. 1422, fo. 95b ; Robt. in Add. MS. 16,940, fo. 25 ; Harl. MS. 6140, fo. 68.

BAMFIELD als BARNEFIELD, Robert, Edgmond, Salop, akin to Sir Amias Bamfield of Poltimore, Devon, Sheriff of the county, as per letter 17 Apr. 1604, that he is descended from Walter, a younger son of the said family ; confirmed with due difference 18 May 1604, by Camden. Harl. MS. 1422, fo. 17b ; 2275, fo. 90 ; 1115, fo. 8b ; 5839, fo. 2b ; Cott. MS. Faustina E. 1, 45 ; Guil. 102.

BAMFORD, John, Puly Hill, Yorks, crest 28 May 1625, by Borough. Harl. MS. 1422, fo. 12 ; 1441, fo. 46 ; 1105, fo. 9b. John, s. of John, s. of Thurston of B., co. Derby. Add. MS. 14,295, fo. 106 ; Add. MS. 26,702, fo. 91.

„ Lionel, s. of John, s. of John, s. of John, s. of John of Bamford, co. Derby, 28 May 1625, by Borough. Harl. MS. 1422, fo. 41.

BANCROFT, Richard, Archbp. of Canterbury, Nov. 1604, by Camden. Harl. MS. 1422, fo. 18b ; 6095, fo. 2b, and Guil. 126.

BANDE, Thomas, his arms claimed by Nicholas de Singleton, given in favor of T. B., 24 Jan., 18 R. II., 1394-5. Patent Roll, 18 R. II., pt. 2 ; Stowe MS. 840, fo. 61b.

BANESTER, Lawrence, Easington, Yorks, out of Lanc. ; confirmed 10 Mar. 1578-9, by Flower. MS. Ashm. 834, fo. 20b, copy of grant, Bodleian Lib. ; Guil. 74.

BANGOR, John, confirmation of arms 18 Nov. 1456, by Guyan, King of A. Harl. MS. 1509, fo. 15 ; 1359, fo. 28 ; Q's Coll. Oxf. MSS. 37, fo. 2 ; 146, fo. 30, copy of grant ; Add. MS. 14,295, fo. 15 ; Stowe MS. 677, fo. 12 ; Misc. Gen. et Her., i., p. 54 ; Harl. MS. 5887, fo. 72b ; 1172, fo. 1, copy of grant.

BANKES, Edward, London, gent., crest granted 1 June 1566, by Sir G. Dethick, Gart. Stowe MS. 676, fo. 142 ; Cott. MS. Faustina E. 1, 21 ; Q's Coll. Oxf. MS. 36, fo. 107, copy of grant ; Guil. 364.

BANKES, John, Little Shelford, co. Camb., 21 Nov. 1589, by Cooke. Harl. MS. 1422, fo. 94ᵇ; 1359, fo. 97ᵇ; Add. MS. 4966, fo. 89.

BARBADOS, Island of, Seal, 11 April 1663, by Sir E. Walker, Gart. Her. Coll., fo. 5.

BARBARO, Daniel, a patrician of Venice, augmentation 12 Feb. 1550-1, 5 Ed. VI. MS. Ashm. 858, fo. 19, 20, copy of grant, Bodleian Lib.

BARBER, ..., London, or, two chevrons, and in chief 3 fleurs de lis gu., by Camden. Morgan's Sphere of Gentry, 118.

  ,, Gabriel, London, gent., 1627, by H. St. George, Clar. Grants II., 653, same as preceding, a cinquefoil ? for diff.

  ,, Edward, als. Bannock, of Denver, Norfolk, Esq., and to the several descendants of Robert, his father, decᵈ, testified, by John Withie. Harl. MS. 1105, fo. 21, and Bysshe's Grants, fo. 23, Her. Coll.

  ,, Robert, Ashmore, Dorset, crest 1 April 1670, by Walker. Harl. MS. 1172, fo. 69; Add. MS. 14,293, fo. 78; 14,294, fo. 23.

BARBERY and SURGERY, the craft of, copy of original grant 29 Sep. 30 H. VI., 1451, perhaps by Roger Legh, Clar. Harl. MS. 1470, fo. 245, copy of grant, Brit. Mus., Misc. Gen. et Her., i., p. 11, etc.; see Add. MS. 16,940, fo. 42ᵇ, for Surgeons' Co., by Harvey.

BARBER CHIRURGEONS, the mystery and community of the Corporation, arms, crest and supporters 2 June 1569, by G. Dethick, Gart., Cooke and Flower. Harl. MS. 5847, fo. 21; Q's Coll. Oxf. MS. 39, fo. 157; copy of grant (MS. 145, fo. 20ᵇ), 1562, in Harl. MS. 1116, fo. 67; Cat. Her. Exhib. Soc. Antiq. 66, in lieu of arms granted 1561 ?

BARD, Henry, Visct. de Bellomonte, augmentation at Oxford 10 March 1646-7, 21 Chas. I., by Walker. MS. Ashm. 858, fo. 49, 51, copy of grants, Bodleian Lib., supporters 20 March 1645-6; Her. Coll., fo. 11.

  ,, William, North Kelsey, co. Linc., confirmed 16 March 1562-3, by Harvey. Add. MS. 17,506, fo. 27ᵇ; Guil. 365; Add. MS. 4966, fo. 46.

BARGRAVE, John, als. Barger, Patricksbourne, Kent, pat. Sep. 1611, by Camden. Harl. MS. 1422, fo. 35ᵇ; 6095, fo. 16; Her. and Geneal., ii., p. 429; Guil. 359.

BARKELEY, Thomas, Okenburie, Cornwall, 1583, by Cooke, Clar. Harl. MS. 1079, fo. 155; crest differs in Stowe MS. 670, fo. 46.

BARKER, Christopher, printer to Q. Eliz., 13 Feb. 1578-9, by Cooke. Harl. MS. 1422, fo. 63.

  ,, George, s. of Randle, of Over, Cheshire, s. of Thos., of Vale Royall, etc., confirmed July 1638, by H. St. George, Norr. Misc. Gen. et Her., i., p. 279, copy of grant, Brit. Mus.

  ,, Henry, Bures Giffard, Essex, by Cooke. Harl. MS. 1359, fo. 102ᵇ.

  ,, James, Haughmond, Salop, 22 April 1562, by Harvey. Q's Coll. Oxf. MS. 37, fo. 42, copy of grant; Harl. MS. 1422, fo. 12; Add. MS. 16,940, fo. 39ᵇ; Grants II., 558-9; Harl. MS. 1441, fo. 46; 6140, fo. 69ᵇ; Proc. Soc. Antiq., N. S., xvi., 350.

  ,, John, see TAYLOR.

  ,, Robert, of Inner Temple, s. of John, of Bildesdon, Suff., s. of John, s. of Robert of same, crest 5 May 1585, and to the posterity of his grandfather, by Cooke. Harl. MS. 1172, fo. 6, copy of grant, Brit. Mus.; Harl. MS. 1359, fo. 99ᵇ; 1422, fo. 63; Add. MS. 4966, fo. 53ᵇ.

  ,, Rowland, Wollerton, Salop, s. of Edward, s. of John and Elizabeth, sister and coh. of Sir Rowland Hill, confirmed 17 Dec. 1582, by Cooke. MS. Ashm. 844, fo. 55, copy of grant, Bodleian Lib.; Guil. 248; Proc. Soc. Antiq., 1897, 2nd S., xvi., p. 352; Le Neve's MS. 467.

  ,, Thomas, Linden, Rutland, 7 Feb. 1664-5, by Sir E. Bysshe, Clar. Harl. MS. 1470, fo. 119, copy of grant, Brit. Mus.; Bysshe's Grants, fo. 8, Her. Coll.; and Guil. 394; Harl. MS. 1105, fo. 17ᵇ.

BARKER, William, s. of Thos., s. of W^m, s. of Thos., s. of Henry, sometime of
Northumberland, gent., 10 Jan. 1560-1, by Dalton. Harl. MS. 1359,
fo. 48, and Guil. 359.

BARKEHAM, Edward, of London, Alderman, Oct. 1611, by Camden. Harl. MS.
1422, fo. 35 ; 6095, fo. 16 ; Guil. 68.

BARKLEY. See BIRKBY.

BARKSTEAD, Sir John, Kt., lieutenant of the Tower, by Sir E. Bysshe, Gart.
Harl. MS. 1105, fo. 15^b.

BARLOWE, Roger, Slebech, co. Pembroke, crest 1559. (Harvey's Grant) ; Add.
MS. 16,940, fo. 38^b.

„   Thomas, Sheffield, Yorks, 20 Aug. 1691, by T. St. George, Gart., and
J. Dugdale, Norr. Stowe MS. 714, fo. 175, and Grants IV., 88, Her.
Coll. ; Harl. MS. 1085, fo. 56 ; 6179, fo. 73.

„   William, Bp. of Rochester, March 1607-8, by Camden. Harl. MS. 1422,
fo. 20 ; 6095, fo. 9.

BARNABYE, Thomas, Salop, Quarterly coat, crest 1562, by W. Harvey. Add. MS.
16,940, fo. 19^b, of Hull and Acton, co. Worcester. Add. MS. 19,816,
fo. 103^b, same crest in each. Harl. MS. 1116, fo. 55^b.

BARNABY, John, Colchester, Essex, 10 March 1554-5 (? by Hawley). Add. MS.
16,940, fo. 207^b ; Harl. MS. 1432, fo. 32^b.

BARNARD, ..., Yorks, by Wm Dethick, Gart. Harl. MS. 1422, fo. 16^b ;
1069, fo. 1.

„   Abell, Pirton, Oxon, gent., whose ancestor descended from the worshipful
family of the Barnards of Enderby, Yorks, allowed by Camden. Harl. MS.
1359, fo. 38^b ; Add. MS. 14,295, fo. 120 ; Quarterly arms, Harl. MS.
6140, fo. 31.

„   Archibald, a Gascoigne, a free denison, a lord of manor of Hagneby, co.
Linc., 24 Dec. 1580, by G. Dethick. Harl. MS. 1115, fo. 2 ; Add. MS.
17,506, fo. 39 ; Q's Coll. Oxf. MS. 146, fo. 42.

„   Francis, of Venice, augmentation 3 Aug. 1546, by Barker, letters pat.
Stowe MS. 912, fo. 12^b, and MS. Ashm. 858, fo. 10—12, copy of grant,
Bodleian Lib.

BARNE, Sir George, Maior of London, 15 Sept. 1552. (? Hawley's Grants) ; Add.
MS. 16,940, fo. 205. See his wife, Alice Broke.

„   George, of London, confirmed 1559. (Harvey's Grants) ; Add. MS. 16,940,
fo. 18.

„   George, Alderm. of London, and to John, his brother, and the heirs of
Sir George, their father, confirmed 15 Feb. 1580-1, by Cooke. Guil.
258.

BARNEBY (see BARNABY), Hull, co. Worcester, Quarterly, by Cooke's deputy.
Stowe MS. 670, fo. 40 ; Le Neve's MS. 255.

BARNES, Edward, London, crest 1614, by Camden. Harl. MS. 6095, fo. 30^b ;
Guil. 172, s. of Richard Barnes vel Baron, of London, mercer, who died
24 Apr. 1598 ; Harl. MS. 1422, fo. 39.

„   Elizabeth (wife of Henry Billingsley of London, gent.), dau. and coh. of Hy.
Barnes by Mary, dau. and coh. of . . . . Boyse, 13 Nov. 1570, by Cooke or
Dethick. Harl. MS. 1422, fo. 117^b.

„   Richard, Bishop of Carlisle, 23 Apr. 1571, by Sir G. Dethick, Gart. Stowe
MS. 703, Cooke and Flower ; Q's Coll. Oxf. MS. 145, fo. 26^b ; Harl. MS.
1441, fo. 77 ; Harl. MSS. 5823, 5847 ; Add. MS. 18,582.

„   Richard, S.T.D., Bp. Suff. of Nottingham, Bp. of Carlisle and now of
Durham ; s. of John, s. of Edward, s. of James, s. of Edwin, s. of Edmund, all
of co. Lanc., s. of Oliver of Suffolk. Quarterly : 1 and 4, Barnes ; 2 and 3,
az., on a bend arg. a bear sa., on a chief of the second 3 roses gu., radiated
(or en soleil) or. 4 Apr. 1580, by Flower. MS. Ashm. 834, fo. 35, copy
of grant, Bodleian Lib., in Latin.

BARNESLEY, ... (Staff. and Surrey), 15 Feb. 1597-8, by W. Dethick, Camden and Segar. Add. MS. 12,225, fo. 7ᵇ; Staff. Visit. 123, Her. Coll., and Guil. 121.

BARNET, *see* HODDESDON.

BARNEWELL, Edward, Cransley, Northts., 1566, by Harvey, confirmed by Camden. Harl. MS. 1422, fo. 37ᵇ; 6095, fo. 23.

BARNEY, ..., Norfolk, by Cooke. Stowe MS. 670, fo. 76ᵇ; Add. MS. 4966, fo. 37ᵇ.

BARN[H]AM, Francis, London, confirmed 1561. (Harvey's Grants); Add. MS. 16,940, fo. 26ᵇ.

„ Thomas, of Horsham St. Faiths, Norfolk, and

„ John, of Norwich, and Thomas his brother, by Sir E. Bysshe, Clar., 1 Aug. 1667. Harl. MS. 1105, fo. 22; Bysshe's Grants 27.

BARONSDALE, William, D. phys., 25 June 1604, by Camden. Harl. MS. 1422, fo. 18; 2275, fo. 91ᵇ; 1115, fo. 9; 5839, fo. 3, and Guil. 383.

BARONN als BACON, a bloodhound's head erased sa., etc., by Barker. Harl. MS. 5846, fo. 5, 19ᵇ; Stowe MS. 692, fo. 20, 23. *See* BACON.

BARON, Edward, of London, sergeant of ye lawe, s. of Richard of London, s. of Peter of Saffron Walden, Essex, Esq., Sergeant-at-law, exemplified by Camden. Harl. MS. 1359, fo. 38; Add. MS. 14,295, fo. 119ᵇ; Quarterly in Harl. MS. 5887, fo. 52ᵇ.

BARRELL, Francis, Rochester, 3 Feb. 1664-5. Bysshe's Grants, fo. 25, Her. Coll.; Harl. MS. 1105, fo. 21ᵇ.

„ William, Bownshill, co. Hereford, 1586, by Cooke. Harl. MS. 1359, fo. 89; 1422, fo. 51ᵇ, father of Gilbert of Isleworth, Middx.; Add. MS. 4966, fo. 34ᵇ.

BARRETT, John, Herts, 13 July 1465, by Walter Bellengier, Ireland K. of Arms. Copy of grant in French, Q's Coll. Oxf. MS. 38, fo. 8, and Brit. Mus. (Harl. MS. 1507, fo. 393); Harl. MS. 1171, fo. 19; Le Neve's MS. 392.

„ Leonard, Fordham, co. Camb., 4 Sept. 1575, by Cooke. Eastern Counties Collectanea, p. 65, copy of grant, Brit. Mus.

„ Thomas, Richard of London, and Robert, sons of Thomas (or William) of Kingswood, Wilts, crest 6 Feb. 1590-91, by Wᵐ Dethick. Grant, Q's Coll. Oxf. MS. 36, fo. 1, copy of grant; Stowe MS. 676, fo. 83, 92.

BARRETT, Thomas, of Thoroton, Notts, and to brothers Richard, George and John, 12 May 1663, by W. Dugdale, Norr. (Her. Coll.)

„ William, of the Devizes, Wilts, 20 Nov. 1577, by Cooke. Stowe MS. 670, fo. 61ᵇ.

BARROWE, ..., crest, by Barker. Harl. MS. 5846, fo. 5, and Stowe MS. 692, fo. 23.

„ Isaac, doctor in physick in Cambridge, 1589, by Cooke. Harl. MS. 1359, fo. 97ᵇ; 1422, fo. 86ᵇ, and Guil. 185; Add. MS. 4966, fo. 87ᵇ.

BARROW, Thomas, clerk, 6 Jan. 1476-7, by Walter Bellingham, Yrlaude K. of Arms. Harl. MS. 1820, fo. 71ᵇ; (many years in the service of Richard, Duke of Gloucester) Proc. Soc. of Antiq., 1897, 2nd S., xvi., p. 344 (original grant).

„ Thomas, clerk, 22 October, 11 H. VII., 1495, and Richard (his brother) of Wynthorpe, merchᵗ of the Staple, 22 Oct. 1495, by John Writhe, Gart. Surtees Soc. xli., 38; Add. MS. 14,298, fo. 35, copy of grant, Brit. Mus.; Proc. Soc. Antiq., 1879; 2nd S., xvi., p. 347, 1897.

BARSHAM, ..., Norfolk, parti per pale gu. and arg., a chief or, by Segar. Add. MS. 12,225, fo. 10.

BARTHROP, Jonathan, barrister of Gray's Inn, and Henry his brother, sons of Henry of Retford, 28 Feb. 1661-2, by Sir E. Walker, Gart. Her. Coll., fo. 45.

BARTELLOT, Walter (Bartlet), s. of Richard, Stopham, Sussex, confirmed quarterly of 8 and grant of crest 27 Nov. 1616, by Segar. Add. MS. 12,225, fo. 7ᵇ; Quarterly of 6, by Cooke; Stowe MS. 670, fo. 47; Harl. MS. 6140, fo. 77. *See also* BERTHELOT. Harl. MS. 6140, fo. 77ᵇ.

BARTLETT, Ellis, Branscomb, Devon, 12 March 1661-2, by Sir E. Bysshe, Clar. Bysshe's Grants, 38.

BARTON, Thomas de, 30 Sept. 1403. Local Gleanings Mag., by J. P. Earwaker, 23.
„ Thomas, ... crest, by Dalton. Harl. MS. 1359, fo. 45b.

BARWICK, John, D.D., dean of St Paul's, and to his brother Peter, D. phys., arms and augmentation 20 Nov. 1661, by Sir G. Walker, Gart. Her. Coll., fo. 43.

BARWYCKE, Thomas, Brightlingsea, Essex, gent., crest 6 May 1592, by Cooke. Add. MS. 14,295, fo. 26 ; Harl. MS. 6179, fo. 14b.

BASHE (see also BAESHE), Edward, Stansted, Herts, 3 Feb. 1571-2, by Cooke and Flower. MS. Ashm. 844, fo. 33, 38, copy of grant, Bodleian Lib. ; Guil. 382 ; Harl. MS. 5887, fo. 105.

BASSILL, Symon, Comptroller of H.M.'s Works, 10 Aug. 1599, by W. Dethick, Gart., and Camden. Stowe MS. 676, fo. 129 ; Q's Coll. Oxf. MS. 36, fo. 78, copy of grant.
„ William (Basylle), Bastington, Wilts, 15 May 1548. (? Hawley's Grants) ; Add. MS. 16,940, fo. 202b.

BASSANO, ..., musitian to Q. Eliz., by Segar. Add. MS. 12,225, fo. 8.

BASSE, ..., London, gu., a chevron arg. betw. three plates, by Segar. Add. MS. 12,225, fo. 9b ; Harl. MS. 6140, fo. 27. See also BAESHE.

BASSET ? . . . ., Arg., three piles meeting in base az. within a bordure pellettée sa. : crest, a (griffin's ?) head pellettée sa., by Bysshe, Clar. Harl. MS. 1105, fo. 38, as Bryan, and Bysshe's Grants 32.

BASSET, Jane, s. of Thos. (s. of John of North Luffenham), nx. Brian Stapleton of Carlton and Burton, Notts, chr 14 May 1527, and pedigree of four generations, by T. Wriothesley, Gart., and Tonge, Norr. Stowe MS. 676, fo. 13, and MS. Ashm. 858, fo. 3, 4, copy of grant, Bodleian Lib.

BATE, Leonard, Lupset, Yorks, gent., gift 8 Feb. 1565-6, by Flower. Harl. MS. 1395, fo. 35 ; Add. MS. 14,295, fo. 40.

BATEMAN, ..., or, three crescents surmounted with as many estoiles gu., 1613, by Segar. Add. MS. 12,225, fo. 8 ; Stowe MS. 712, fo. 71.

BATES, John, of Norton, Suffolk, 20 Dec., 3 K. Jac., 1605, by Segar, Gart. Harl. MS. 1085, fo. 21b.

BATHURST, ... of the Isle of Wight, confirmed July 1616, by Camden. Harl. MSS. 1422, fo. 40b, and 6095, fo. 34b.
„ Lancelot, London, by Cooke. Harl. MS. 1359, fo. 98 ; Add. MS. 4966, fo. 63b.

BATT, Nicholas, Fordingbridge, Hants. Cooke's Gifts ; Stowe MS. 670, fo. 83b.

BATTERSBY (Nicholas, Harl. MS. 1079, fo. 60), patent June 1605, by Camden. Harl. MS. 1422, fo. 219 ; 6095, fo. 4b ; or, a saltire [paly of 12] erm. and gu. ; crest, a ram passant erm. armed and unguled or, confirmed by Camden.
„ John, Bowland, Yorks, coat altered 25 Mar. 1605-6, by R. St. George, Norr. Add. MS. 14,295, fo. 80, i.e., removal of chief gu. thereon three escallops arg. ; Harl. MS. 1142, fo. 7, as Nicholas ; N. and Q., 2nd S., vol. xi., 171 ; Le Neve's MS. 487.

BAUGHE, Rowland, Twyninge, co. Glouc., gent., crest, 11 Nov. 1574, by Cooke. Harl. MS. 1441, fo. 51 ; (1359, fo. 95) copy of grant.

BAVAND, Thomas and Robert, sons of John of Chester, July 1638, by H. St. George, Norr. Misc. Gen. et Her., i., 278, copy of grant, Brit. Mus.

BAWNE, John, of Kyrne, Yorks, by R. St. George, Norr. Le Neve's MS. 254.

BAXSTER, Thomas, als Shipden, Cromer, Norfolk, 28 Aug. 1576, by Cooke. Add. MS. 4966, fo. 60b ; Harl. MSS. 1359, fo. 113b, 1085, fo. 51b, and 1422, fo. 95 ; Stowe MS. 670, fo. 66.

BAYLIFFE, William, Clement's Inn, by Cooke's deputy. Stowe MS. 670, fo. 29 ; Harl. MS. 1441, fo. 136.

BAYLY, ..., of Middle Temple, treasurer, sa., a chev. between three human hearts or, by Segar. Add. MS. 12,225, fo. 8b ; Harl. MSS. 6140, fo. 64b, and 1105, fo. 7b.

BAYLY, Roger, Assist. Gov' Raleigh, Virginia, by W. Dethick.   Q's Coll. Oxf. MS.
    36, fo. 120.
BAYLYE (or BAILYE), John, Hoddesdon, Herts, 16 Feb. 1634-5, by St. George,
    Clar.   Harl. MS. 1470, fo. 8 ; copies of grant Brit. Mus. and Q's Coll. Oxf.
    MS. 38, fo. 145 ; Harl. MS. 1441, fo. 50 (and Guil. 355), copy of grant,
    Brit. Mus.
  ,,   Thomas, license from Edward Somerset, Marquis of Worcester, to bear his
    crest, the portcullis under the Coronet of a Marquis in an escocheon,
    26 Feb. 1654-5.   Harl. MS. 1470, fo. 246.
BAYLYE, Thomas, of the city of Coventry, 17 July 1677, by Sir W. Dugdale, Gart.
    and Norr.   Stowe MS. 714, fo. 119 ; Grants III., fo. 62 ; Harl. MS. 6832,
    fo. 371ᵇ.
  ,,   Walter, M.D. (Oxon) to the Queen, s. of Hy. of Warmwell, Dorset, grant
    23 Apr. 1594, by W. Dethick, Gart.   Stowe MS. 676, fo. 109 ; Q's Coll.
    Oxf. MS. 36, fo. 39, copy of grant.
  ,,   William, London, at the feast of the B. V. M., 1524, by T. Wriothesley,
    Gart.   Harl. MS. 5846, fo. 8, and Stowe MS. 692, fo. 22.
BAYNBRIGGE, William, Derby, 20 Nov. 1582, by Flower.   MS. Ashm. 844, fo. 55ᵇ,
    copy of grant, Bodleian Lib. ; Guil. 342 ; 55ᵇ, crest, an arm holding a
    battle-axe ; 56ᵇ, crest, a bloodhound ; Grants II., 649 ; Reliquary, xxi.,
    240.
  ,,   William, of Lockington, Leics., confirmed 14 Feb. 1583-4, by Flower.   MS.
    Ashm. 844, fo. 56ᵇ, crest, a goat, etc., copy of grant, Bodleian Lib. ; Guil.
    342 ; Reliquary, xxi., 240.
BAYNE, Ralph, Bp. of Coventry and Lichfield, arms 20 Nov. 1554, by (? Hawley).
    Add. MS. 16,940, fo. 207.
  ,,   Roger, Woodhall in Netherhall, Yorks, 2 Oct. 1612, by R. St. George, Norr.
    Add. MS. 14,295, fo. 60.
BAYNES, Capt. Adam, of Knowstrop, Yorks, 10 Aug. 1650, by Ryley, Norr.
    Surtees Soc., xli., 54, copy of grant, Brit. Mus.
BAYNHAM, Robert, s. of Richᵈ, s. of Chrisʳ of co. Glouc', 2 Nov. 1631, by Segar.
    Add. MS. 12,225, fo. 8ᵇ ; Guil. 151.
  ,, {William, Grove, co. Hereford, 1588, by Cooke.   Harl. MSS. 1359, fo. 113, and
        6146, fo. 44.
        BAYNHAM, VEL EYNON.   Harl. MS. 1422, fo. 95 ; Add. MS. 4966, fo. 85 ;
        Harl. MS. 5887, fo. 24.
BAYNINGE, Anne, Visctess., née [widow of] Murray, supporters 17 May 1674, by
    Walker.   Harl. MS. 6834, fo. 178 ; Grants III., fo. 6.
  ,,   Pawle, London and . . . ., 1588, by Cooke, ? impaling Morthen of Essex,
    Quarterly.   Harl. MSS. 1395, fo. 104, and 1422, fo. 95 ; Add. MS. 4966,
    fo. 84ᵇ bis.
  ,,   His wife Susan, d. and h. of Richard Morthen of Mistley, Essex.   Stowe MS.
    670, fo. 23 ; Add. MS. 14,297, fo. 23ᵇ.
BEALE, ..., sa., on a chev. or between three gryphons' heads erased arg., as many
    mullets of six points gu., by Segar.   Add. MS. 12,225, fo. 10.
BEARDE, William, North Kelsey, co. Linc., confirmed 16 March 1562-3 (Harvey's
    Grants).   Add. MS. 16,940, fo. 12 ; Le Neve's MS. 251 ; Add. MS.
    17,506.
BEAUCHAMP, John, Powick, co. Glouc., 1586, by Cooke.   Harl. MSS. 1359, fo. 91,
    and 1422, fo. 93 ; Add. MS. 4966, fo. 64ᵇ.
BEAUPRÉ, Dorothy, wife of Robert Bell of Beaupré Hall, Norfolk, confirmed with
    quartering 19 June 1571, by Cooke.   Harl. MSS. 1422, fo. 7ᵇ, and 1470,
    fo. 165.
BECHAR, Henry, Bishops Morchard, Devon, confirmed 1564 (Harvey's Grants).
    Add. MS. 16,940, fo. 46, and Harl. MS. 1390, fo. 32ᵈ, and a later crest by
    Cooke 11 Eliz., 1569.
BECKFORD, William (s. of Sir Thos., late Alderm. city of London, Kt., decd.),

2 Feb. 1685-6, by Sir W. Dugdale, Gart. and Clar. Add. MSS. 14,293, fo. 24, and 14,931, fo. 128 ; Grants III., fo. 282 ; Lansd. MS. 867, fo. 52.

BECKHAM (Richard ?), of Narfold, Norfolk, 1576, by Ro. Cooke. Harl. MS. 1085, fo. 38.

BECKINGHAM, Thomas, Tolleshunt Major als Tolleshunt Beckingham, Essex, and to Stephen, Tolleshunt Darcy, Essex, gent., 2nd bro. of Thomas, crest 12 May 1596, by Lee, Clar. Add. MS. 14,295, fo. 44b ; Harl. MS. 1359, fo. 35b.

BECKWITH, ..., crest . . . ., by Barker. Harl. MS. 5846, fo. 5 ; Stowe MS. 692, fo. 23, "a demi bustard."

„ Hamon, s. of Nicholas, confirmation of the coat of Malbie or Malbisse 14 Oct. 1340 at the Mansion House and manor of "Saymour," by Peter de Malolaan, lord de Mauley, Earl Marshal and lord Chancellor, Chamberlain to Ed. III., supported by Henry, Lord Percy, Sir Robert Boynton and Sir Wm Aton or de Acton. Extinct Baronetcies.

„ Sir Leonard, Yorkshire, augmentation. Harl. MS. 5846, fo. 11 ; 4, fo. 22b ; Harl. MSS. 6179, fo. 16, and 5887, fo. 2.

BECQUET, Bartholomew (a Fleming), Comptroller to her most Catholic majesty and Cabinet Secy. to the Duchess of Bavaria, 23 Apr. 1696, by T. St. George, Gart. and Clar. Add. MS. 14,831, fo. 86 ; Grants IV., fo. 208.

BEDELL, Capell, Hunts, 1 and 4, gu., a chev. betw. three escallops arg., quartering 2 and 3, by Segar. Add. MS. 12,225, fo. 10b ; Harl. MS. 6140, fo. 78b.

„ Sir John, Hammerton, Hunts, Kt., 1 and 4, gu., a chev. engr., etc., by Segar. Add. MS. 12,225, fo. 10b.

„ Mathew, London, Alderm. (out of Beds), alteration 20 Jan. 1632-3, by St. George, Clar. Harl. MS. 1370, fo. 35, 67 ; Guil. 246 ; Harl. MS. 1085, fo. 1.

„ William, Writtle, Essex, ... by Barker. Harl. MS. 5846, fo. 7 ; Stowe MS. 692, fo. 22.

BEDYLL, John, of the Manor of Randes, Weybridge, Essex, gift 1563. (Harvey's Grants) ; Add. MS. 16,940, fo. 48b.

BEDFORD, Thomas, Doctors' Commons, London, gent., dep. registrar, examiner, translator and interpreter of foreign languages in the high court of Admiralty for this realm of England (s. of John, late rector of Heyford, Northts.), 8 Feb. 1677-8, by Sir Wm Dugdale, Gart., and St. George, Norr. Add. MS. 14,831, fo. 200 ; Grants III., fo. 75.

BEDWELL, William, B.D., Essex, per saltire lozengy or and gu. and erm., by Camden. Harl. MS. 6095, fo. 35 ; Stowe MS. 712, fo. 71.

BEE, see DEE, LEE, REE.

BEE or BEY, Gilbert, Basingstoke, Hants, gent., crest granted 29 Nov. 1567, 10 Eliz., by G. Dethick, Gart., and Cooke. Q's Coll. Oxf. MS. 39, fo. 131, copy of grant ; see Harl. MS. 5887, fo. 68, 111.

BEE, John, Basingstoke, s. of Gilbert, s. of John, etc. (quartering Bowyer), crest 18 Jan. 1573-4, by Cooke. Copy of grant Brit. Mus. ; Misc. Gen. et Her. N. S., iv., 386.

BEECHER, James, Shorne, Kent, confirmed 6 Oct. 1574, by Cooke. Guil. 160.

BEERE, John, Kent, 1586, by Cooke. Harl. MS. 1359, fo. 91b ; Add. MS. 4966, fo. 65.

BEIGHTON, Thomas, Wirksworth, co. Derby, 1 June 1675, by Walker, Bysshe and Dugdale. Harl. MS. 6834, fo. 178 ; Grants III., fo. 13.

BEISTON, Ralph, ... 1578-9, by Sir G. Dethick. Harl. MSS. 1441, fo. 89b, and 5847, fo. 46 ; quartering Sutton, Berkeley and Bulmer, see Add. MS. 18,582, fo. 49.

BELCHER, William, Guilsborough, Northts., by Cooke. Stowe MS. 670, fo. 6.

BELFALD, Thomas, of Gray's Inn, certifd 5 Nov. 1637, by Borough. Grants I., 429 ; of Thorpe, Northts., by Borough, Harl. MS. 1105, fo. 55 ; Add. MS. 26,702, fo. 89b ; Harl. MSS. 1441, fo. 57, and 4966, fo. 22.

BELL, Edward, Newland, co. Glouc., s. of W^m, s. of Edward of the same, s. of Edward of Newcastle, Northumberland, 1571, by Cooke. Harl. MS. 1422, fo. 47 ; Edm. in Harl. MS. 6140, fo. 70^b.

„ John, Bp. of Worcester (1539—43). ? Hawley's Grants ; Add. MS. 26,702, fo. 54.

„ Richard, of Gray's Inn, Counsellor-at-law, and residing in the city of York (17 Nov.) 1612, by St. George, Norr. Harl. MSS. 1359, fo. 9^b, and 1422, fo. 13^b, adds 17 Nov. and Sec. to the Earl of Rutland, lord president of York ; Harl. MS. 6140, fo. 73.

„ Robert, s. of William, of Yorks, now one of the Temple, gift 13 Nov. 1560, by Dalton. Harl. MSS. 1359, fo. 46^b, and 6140, fo. 70.

„ Sir Thomas, of Gloucester, ... by Barker. Stowe MS. 692, fo. 12^b ; Harl. MS. 5887, fo. 27.

BELLAMIE, Joane, dau. and sole heir of William, s. of W^m of Hadley, Middx., confirmed 1567, by Sir G. Dethick. Stowe MS. 676, fo. 32 ; Q's Coll. Oxf. MS. 37, fo. 47, copy of confirmation ; Grants I., 166.

BELLAMY, Thomas, Datchett, Bucks, quarterly coat, crest 17 Sept. 1571, by Cooke. MSS. Ashm. 840, fo. 395-6, and 858, fo. 199, 201, copy of grant, Bodleian Lib. ; Harl. MS. 5887, fo. 57^b.

BELLASYSE, Sir Thos., Kt. and Bart., supporters, by Segar. Add. MS. 12,225, fo. 11^b.

BELLIN [BELYN], Thomas, Alderm. of Chester, 1581, by Flower. Add. MS. 14,295, fo. 76 ; Randolph, now of London, with two quarterings, Harl. MS. 5887, fo, 88^b.

BELLMAN als BELLMANOIRE, John, of the privy chamber to Ed. VI., grant 20 Nov. 1552, 6 Ed. VI., by Sir G. Dethick. Grants I., 27 ; Q's Coll. Oxf. MS. 39, fo. 38, copy of grant ; Harl. MS. 1359, fo. 77^b.

BELLOMONT, see BARD, Henry, Viscount.

BELLOWE, John, Misted upon Aukeholme, co. Linc., by Barker. Harl. MS. 5846, fo. 12^b ; Stowe MS. 692, fo. 12^b.

BELLY, John (Gt. Paxton, Hunts), D.C., Chancellor of dioc. of London, Provost Oriel Coll. Oxford and a master of the high court of Chancery, grant 23 Oct. 1602, by Camden, confirmed 10 Nov. following by W. Dethick, Gart. Q's Coll. Oxf. MS. 36, fo. 93, copy of grant ; Stowe MS. 676, fo. 137 ; Guil. 355.

BELLAY, Sir Thos., Gt. Paxton, Hunts, by Camden. Harl. MS. 1422, fo. 42^b ; knighted at Bagshott 22 July 1615.

BELSON, Thomas, Aston, Oxon, gent., grant 20 Nov. 1517, 9 H. 8, by T. Wriothesley, Gart., and Benolte. Harl. MS. 1359, fo. 29.

BELVIN, see HELYAR.

BELWOOD, Roger, Leathley, Yorks, and a student of the Middle Temple, 3 June 1667, by W. Dugdale. (Her. Coll.)

BENCE, John, Kingsfield, Suffolk, and Edmund, his bro., sons of John, of Benhall, Suff., dec^d, and to their uncle Alexander, of London, merch^t, who fined for alderm., bro. of John, of Benhall afores^d, who was son of Alex^r, of Aldersbury, Suff., 1 June 1661, by Sir E. Bysshe, Clar. Add. MS. 14,293, fo. 8^b ; Harl. MS. 1105, fo. 16^b ; Bysshe's Grants, fo. 1, Her. Coll. ; and Guil. 320.

BENDALL, Hopefor, Mile End, Middx., 8 Feb. 1692-3, by St. George, Gart. and Clar. Stowe MS. 714, fo. 133 ; Grants IV., 130, and Guil. 404 ; Harl. MS. 1085, fo. 57.

BENDLOWE, Christopher, Much Bardfeld, Essex, by Barker. Harl. MS. 5846, fo. 12; Stowe MS. 692, fo. 12^b.

BENGER, Thomas, Gt. Milton, Oxon, gent., crest 1 Oct. 1553, by Sir G. Dethick, Gart. Harl. MS. 1359, fo. 63 ; Q's Coll. Oxf. MS. 39, fo. 48, copy of grant ; Grants I., 240.

BENNE, Robert, London, of the Temple, confirmed 23 Oct. 1573, by Cooke, Clar.

Harl. MS. 6086, fo. 91ᵇ, s. of John, of Walden, Essex, servant to K. H. 7 and 8 ; Le Neve's MS. 486.

BENE, John, ..., arg., on a bend counter embattled, etc., by Segar. Add. MS. 12,225, fo. 11.

BENNETT, Ann, d. of Humphrey, of Salop, ux. Thomas Cure of Southwark, 1588, by Cooke. Harl. MS. 1359, fo. 108 ; Stowe MS. 702, fo. 115.

„ George, Wilby, co. Leic., [certified] by Browne, Bluemantle. Stowe MS. 703, fo. 72.

„ Rt. Hon. Sir Henry (after Earl of Arlington), a principal Sec. of State, augmentation 12 Oct. 1663, by Sir E. Walker, Gart. Her. Coll., fo. 58.

„ John, Newcastle-upon-Tyne, Queen's Master of the Ordnance of the North parts of England, augmentation and crest 6 Dec. 1560, by Dalton. Harl. MS. 1359, fo. 47 ; Harl. MS. 6140, fo. 70 ; Her. and Geneal. IV., 95 ; Misc. Gen. et Her., i., 48.

„ John, London, vintner, ..., by Cooke. Harl. MSS. 1359, fo. 88, and 1422, fo. 46ᵇ ; Add. MS. 4966, fo. 19ᵇ.

„ Nicholas, citizen and haberdasher of London, s. of Nichˢ of Medingleigh, co. Camb., crest 24 June 1633, by St. George. Clar. Harl. MS. 1470, fo. 130, copy of grant, Brit. Mus. ; Guil. 185.

„ Richard, Lubbenham, co. Leic., by Barker. Harl. MS. 5846, fo. 9ᵇ ; Stowe MS. 692, fo. 22ᵇ.

„ Richard, High Sheriff city of Chester, confirmed 1626, by Segar, being the arms of Warburton. See Visitn. 1666, Harl. MS. 2119, fo. 6.

„ Robert, Bp. of Hereford, confirmed 20 Feb. 1602-3, by W. Dethick and Camden. Stowe MS. 676, fo. 123ᵇ ; Q's Coll. Oxf. MS. 36, fo. 95 ; Harl. MS. 6140, fo. 54ᵇ.

„ Thomas, citizen, late Sheriff and Alderm. of London, grant 17 Nov. 1600, by W. Dethick and Camden. Stowe MS. 676, fo. 123ᵇ ; Harl. MS. 5887, fo. 83.

„ Sir Thomas, Kt., lord Mayor London, "patten," by Camden. Harl. MS. 6095, fo. 21ᵇ ; Q's Coll. Oxf. MS. 36, fo. 67, copy of grant ; Harl. MS. 5887, fo. 83.

BEN[N]ETT, William, of High Rooding, Essex, 1 April, 1 Chas. I., grant by R. St. George. Harl. MS. 1052, fo. 207, copy of grant, Brit. Mus.

BENNOLLIS, Jeronime, arms and crest, by W. Dethick, Gart., who buried him at Barking Ch. in London 17 Mar. 1594-5, with the said arms and crest wearing Her Maᵗˢ coate of armes and before him to the church. The said Bennollis not being the Queen's subject nor denizen, a praesident never known before. The crest is Leighes of Cheshire without any difference, entered by R. Brooke, York Hᵈ. Harl. MS. 1453, fo. 33.

BENTHAM, Thomas, Bp. of Coventry and Lichfield, 6 April 1560, 2 Eliz., by Harvey. Grants I., 42.

BENTLEY, John, of Bentley, co. Derby, s. of Humphrey, s. of William, of Ashes, co. Staff., 16 Apr. 1589, by Ed. Knight, Norr. Stowe MS. 706, fo. 12ᵇ ; Harl. MSS. 6179, fo. 14, 1486, fo. 27, and 6140, fo. 29ᵇ, 71ᵇ.

BENYON, George, Essex, by Cooke. Harl. MS. 1359, fo. 92 ; Add. MS. 4966, fo. 58.

„ George, of Allingborne, Sussex, gent., s. of Wᵐ, s. of Roger, crest 17 Aug. 1582, by Cooke. Harl. MS. 1115, fo. 20ᵇ.

BERBLOCK, John, an Englishman, citizen and sometime a Judge in Italy, etc., Certif. of arms 1585, by ? Sir G. Dethick. Q's Coll. Oxf. MS. 36, fo. 112 ; Grants I., 37 ; Wᵐ in Harl. MS. 1105, fo. 3 ; Harl. MS. 6179, fo. 52ᵇ.

BERENGER, Thomas, of Iver, Bucks, 5 April 1610, by Segar. Add. MS. 12,225, fo. 11 ; C. 26, fo. 14, Her. Coll. ; Guil. 129.

BERESFORD, George, London, quarterly, confirmed 1560. (Harvey's Grants) ; Add. MS. 16,940, fo. 20.

BERGAIGNE, Henry de, Col. of a regt. of Horse in the service of the United
Provinces, confirmed 10 Feb. 1631-2, by Segar. Add. MS. 12,225, fo. 12.
BARKELEY, Thos., Oxenburie, Devon, 1583, by Cooke's Deputy Drury. Stowe
MS. 670, fo. 46; Harl. MS. 1079, fo. 15.
BERKELEY, John, Lord, Supporters at Brussels May 1658, by Sir E. Walker, Gart.
Her. Coll., fo. 12.
BERKHAMSTEAD, town, by Camden. Harl. MSS. 6095, fo. 37^d, and 1441, fo. 147^b.
BERNARD, Archibald, see BARNARD.
BERNESLEY, William, Bernesley Hall, co. Worc., 1588, by Cooke. Stowe MS.
670, fo. 26^b, proved from evidences temp. E. 3. See also BARNESLEY.
BERRY, Richard, London, D. phys., June 1626, by R. St. George. Harl. MS.
1422, fo. 14; Add. MS. 14,295, fo. 65^b.
BERTHELOT, Thomas, London (King's printer), 1 Sept. 1549, by Hawley. Add.
MS. 16,940, fo. 203.
BERTIE, Thomas, Bersted, Kent, gent., Capt. of Hurst Castle for the King's
Majesty, 10 July 1550, by Hawley. Harl. MS. 245, fo. 107, copy of
grant, Brit. Mus.; Add. MS. 16,940, fo. 203; MS. Ashm. 858, pp. 232-3,
copy of grant, Bodleian Lib.
BERYFF, William, Colchester, Essex, 5 May 1555 (? by Hawley). Add. MS.
16,940, fo. 207^b.
„ ...., Colchester, Essex, 11 May 1614, by Camden. Caius Coll. Camb. MS.
551, fo. 31^b.
BESTE, Thos., s. of Hy., Middleton, Quernhow in Richmondshire, 19 Feb. 1624-5,
by Segar. Add. MS. 12,225, fo. 12.
BEST, DE, James, London, merch^t, free denison, s. of James of Flanders, 9 July
1617, by Camden. Harl. MS. 6095, fo. 36; Guil. 270.
BEST, John, Bp. of Carlisle, by Dalton. Harl. MS. 1359, fo. 49, 10 Feb. 1560-1,
by G. Dethick, Gart., in Grants I., 61; 5 Mar., Harl. MS. 1115,
fo. 65.
BESTE, John, citizen and haberdasher, of London, descended of a family at Horton
Conrt, Kent, 2 Feb. 1578-9, by Sir G. Dethick. Harl. MSS. 1441, fo. 84^b,
and 5847, fo. 39; Q's Coll. Oxf. MS. 145, fo. 40.
BESTNEY, Robert, London, gent., dep. treasurer of the Q. Majesties Chambre, wh.
Robt. is right heire and lineally descended from Bestney, sometime of the
city of Chester, gent., confirmed 20 March 1559-60, by Dalton. Harl. MSS.
1359, fo. 50^b, and 5887, fo. 10^b; 5 quarters and impaling 3 quarters, Harl.
MS. 5887, fo. 11^b; with 13 quarters, Harl. MS. 5887, fo. 11^b.
BESWICKE, Roger, London, by Cooke. Harl. MSS. 1422, fo. 94^b, and 1359, fo. 100^b,
as Boswyke; Add. MS. 4966, fo. 88^b.
„ William, Spelmonden, Kent, by Barker. Add. MS. 26,702, fo. 1.
„ William, London, gift, 1564 (Harvey's Grants). Add. MS. 16,940, fo. 21.
BETHELL, Richard, Hyde, Hants, crest 1559, W. Harvey's Grants. Add. MS.
16,940, fo. 41^b; Harl. MS. 1544, fo. 69^b.
BETTISWORTH, Thomas, of co. Southants [certificate], by W. Ryley, Lanc. Herald.
Stowe MS. 703, fo. 63.
BEVAN, William, Pen-y-coed, co. Carmarthen, High Sheriff, 1 June 1695, by
St. George, Gart. and Clar. Grants IV., 198, and Guil. 288.
„ Theophilus, student at law, ⎫ brothers.
„ Thomas, D.D.,   ⎭
BEVERIDGE, Thomas, Chief Searcher of the City of Chichester, and all the Havens,
towns, ports, and creekes in Sussex, Esq., and to William, his bro., now
resident in Dnfranille in the county of Valloyne in the province of
Normaudy, gent., s. of W^m, s. of John, s. of Thos., s. of W^m, s. of Thos.,
sometime of Sevenoaks, Kent, esq., arms and crest 30 May 1595, by
Lee, Clar. Harl. MSS. 1507, fo. 391, copy of grant, Brit. Mus.; 1359,
fo. 16; Add. MS. 14,295, fo. 17; Q's Coll. Oxf. MSS. 38, fo. 113, and 146,
fo. 35, 40; Le Neve's MS., fo. 49, 391.

BEVERLEY, Sir George, Dublin, Kt., new coat and crest 20 Jan. 1605-6, by
D. Molyneux, Ulster K. of A. Harl. MS. 2153, fo. 126ᵇ ; Misc. Gen. et
Her., ii., 95, former coat, by Ro. Cooke, Clar., Arg. on a chev. sa. before
[between] three pellets a crescent or, then surveyor of victualls in Ireland.
Stowe MS, 670, fo. 37ᵇ, and Harl. MS. 2153, fo. 126.

BAY, *see* BEE.

BIDDULPH, Francis, Biddulph, co. Staff, confirmed 4 May 1584, by Flower.
MS. Ashm. 844, fo. 57, copy of grant, Bodleian Lib.; Guil. 209.

,,   John, of Exeter, D. phys., and his kinsman.

BIDGOOD, Humphrey, of Fulford, Devon, merchᵗ, 3 July 1690, by T. St. George,
Gart. and Clar. Harl. MS. 6834, fo. 178 ; Grants IV., 62.

BIEST, John Atcham, Salop, confirmed 6 June 1586, by Cooke. Harl. MSS. 1359,
fo. 89, and 1422, fo. 51ᵇ ; MS. Ashm. 834, fo. 59ᵇ, copy of grant, Bodleian
Lib. ; Guil. 332 ; Add. MS. 4966, fo. 34.

BIGGS, John, Saudish, co. Glouc., and of Lenchwike, co. Worc., exemplification 19
May 15 Ed. IV., by W. Hawkesloe. Harl. MSS. 1507, fo. 126, 1043, fo. 32,
and 1566, fo. 115 ; Le Neve's MS. 255.

BILL, Jane. d. of John, of Ashwell, Herts, ux. John Burgoyne of Sutton, Beds,
2 May 1528, by T. Wriothesley, Gart., and Benolte. Harl. MS. 4900,
fo. 22ᵇ.

BILLESBY, William, who marᵈ Anne Brograve. Stowe MS. 670, fo. 81, by Cooke.

BILLESDON, als WILLIAMS, John, gent., 25 Sep. 13 Ed. IV. 1473, by W. Hawkeslowe, Clar. Add. MS. 17,506, fo. 37. Erm., a pile gu. and a chev. sa., all
within a bordure engrailed or.

,,   Robert, gent., 19 Sep. 10 Ed. IV. 1470, by W. Hawkeslowe, Clar. Add. MS.
17,506, fo. 37, Lord Mayor of Lond. 1483 ; Le Neve's MS. 259.

BILLINGHURST, John, Newport, I. of W., 6 July 1654, by Sir E. Bysshe, Clar.
Harl. MS. 1172, fo. 14ᵇ, copy of grant.

BILLINGSLEY, William, London, confirmed 1562 (Harvey's Grants). Add. MS.
16,940, fo. 29.

BILSON, Arnald, borne in highe Germanye, etc., 10 Oct. 1582, by Sir G. Dethicke.
Q's Coll. Oxf. MS. 145, fo. 28ᵇ ; Harl. MS. 1441, fo. 78, refer to this, and
Harl. MS. 6140, fo. 46.

BINGHAM, Capt. ...., by Cooke. Harl. MS. 1359, fo. 92ᵇ ; Add. MS. 4966,
fo. 58ᵇ.

BINGLEY, John, Boughton, Flints, and to ,, John, of Chester,	testified by R. St. George, Norr., 13 April 1605. Harl. MS. 1359, fo. 25ᵇ ; Add. MS. 14,295, fo. 112.

,,   Sir Ralph, by St. George, Norr. Add. MS. 14,295, fo. 79ᵇ ; Harl. MS. 6140,
fo. 73ᵇ.

,,   Richard Blythe, Notts, exemplified 13 Dec. 1605, on certif. of kinship from
Sir Raulf Bingley. Harl. MS. 1359, fo. 25ᵇ ; Add. MS. 14,295, fo. 79ᵇ and
112 ; Q's Coll. Oxf. MS. 146, fo. 137.

BINLOSSE, Robert, Bonvick, [?] co. Lanc., akin to Sergᵗ Binlosse, crest 27 Nov.
1587. Q's Coll. Oxf. MS. 37, fo. 110, copy of grant ; Stowe MS. 676,
fo. 75ᵇ.

BIRCH (John), Baron of the Exchequer, by Barker. Harl. MS. 5846, fo. 4ᵇ ;
(Stydolph, his wife, *see*) Harl. MS. 5887, fo. 87.

BIRCHETT, Joseph, Rye, Sussex, Quarterly, 3 July 1589, by Cooke. Harl. MSS.
1359, fo. 100, and 1422, fo. 120ᵇ ; Jasper in Stowe MS. 670, fo. 34 ; Stowe
MS. 618, fo. 220.

BIRD, James, Brougham, Westmoreland, 31 Oct. 1668, by Dugdale, Norr. Harl.
MS. 1105, fo. 13.

,,   (als BRID), Robert le, Broxton, Cheshire, 20 Feb. 1575-6, by Flower. Guil.
230.

,,   (BYRDE), Thomas, of Overlockshaw, s. of Robt., s. of Thomas, crest 1611, by
R. St. George, Norr. Harl. MSS. 1422, fo. 48ᵇ, and 6140, fo. 72.

BIRD, William, London, gent., confirmed 20 Mar. 1560-1, by Sir G. Dethick. Harl. MS. 1441, fo. 64ᵇ, and Q's Coll. Oxf. MS. 145, fo. 6ᵇ.

BYRD, William, Doctor of the Civil law, s. of Wᵐ (and Mary, d. and h. of James Woodhal of Walden), s. of Thos., s. of Wᵐ, etc., exemplified Mar. 1606, by Camden. Harl. MSS. 1422, fo. 20ᵇ, and 6095, fo. 8ᵇ; Guil. 383.

BIRKBECK, ..., by Sir C. Barker, Gart. Harl. MS. 6179, fo. 13.

BIRKEBY, James, Dewsbury, Yorks, 20 Oct. 1590, by Cooke. Harl. MS. 1422, fo. 23; Add. MS. 16,940, fo. 209; Backley in Stowe MS. (670, fo. 49), or, three garbs sable; Harl. MS. 6140, fo. 73ᵇ.

BIRKBIE (BYRKBIE), Thomas, York (or, three garbs sa.), by Sir G. Dethick, Gart. Add. MS. 26,753, fo. 124 (? 122ᵇ).

BIRKENHEAD, Sir John, D.C.L., at the Castle of Sᵗ Germains, 22 Aug. 1649, by Walker. Harl. MS. 1172, fo. 72ᵇ; Add. MSS. 14,293, fo. 111, and 14,294, fo. 37; Her. Coll., fo. 29.

BIRKHEAD (BRYKETT), Edmund, Bp. of St. Asaph 1513—18. Add. MS. 26,702, fo. 73ᵇ.

„ John, Crouton, Cheshire, by Barker. Harl. MS. 5846, fo. 11ᵇ; Stowe MS. 692, fo. 23ᵇ, and Harl. MS. 6179, fo. 16.

BIRKETT VEL BRIKETT (*temp.* II. 6). Add. MS. 26,702, fo. 22.

BIRTWESELL, (James) John, of Honycot Hall, co. Lanc., by Harvey. Add. MS. 14,295, fo. 76ᵇ; called John of Huncott Hall, co. Lanc., Harl. MSS. 1441, fo. 45ᵇ, and 1116, fo. 68.

„ Oliver, Huncote Hall, co. Lanc., 1560. Add. MS. 16,940, fo. 14ᵇ; John in Harl. MS. 1422, fo. 12, all the same coat.

BISCHOFF, ..., Basle, Switzerland, 6 July 1501, by Maximilian, Emperor; 27 Nov. 1546, by Chas. V., Emperor, and 5 May 1581, by Eudolph of Prague. Berry's Supplement.

BISHE, Edward, Smalfield, par. of Burstow, Surrey, s. of John, s. of Wm., s. of John, s. of John, etc., crest 1 Oct. 1617, by Camden. Harl. MS. 1507, fo. 388, copy of grant, Brit. Mus., and Q's Coll. Oxf. MS. 38, fo. 131; Quarterly of 6 in Add. MS. 5533, fo. 257ᵇ; 40 quarterings in Harl. MS. 1076, fo. 83; Stowe MS. 697, fo. 119ᵇ; Le Neve's MS. 388.

BISHOPP, Edward, of the Mid. Temple, Esq. (s. of Edward of Evesham, co. Worc.), 30 Nov. 1628, by Segar. Add. MS. 12,225, fo. 12ᵇ; Guil. 358; Harl. MS. 6140, fo. 80.

„ Sir Richard, Alveston als Aston, co. Warwick, Esq., 30 years sergeant-at-arms to K. Jas. and K. Chas. at Oxford, 25 May 1645, by Walker. Add. MS. 14,294, fo. 30ᵇ; Stowe MS. 714, fo. 126, and Harl. MS. 611, fo. 25.

„ Thomas, Henfield, Sussex [*sic*], by R. Cooke. Stowe MS. 670, fo. 15; Harl. MS. 1562, fo. 54ᵇ.

„ William, Dorset, gent., etc., crest 10 Aug. 1627, by Segar. Add. MSS. 12,225, fo. 12ᵇ, and 14,295, fo. 83ᵇ; Guil. 358; Harl. MS. 6140, fo. 79ᵇ; *see* Harl. MS. 1441, fo. 159.

„ William, Selscombe, Sussex, 2 Sept. 1662, by Sir E. Bysshe, Clar. Harl. MS. 1105, fo. 42.

BISPHAM, Samuel, s. of Wᵐ, Billing and Bispham, co. Lanc., alteration 1 Dec. 1640, by Sir H. St. George, Norr. Harl. MS. 1470, fo. 215, and Guil. 187.

„ William, of Bispham, grant 30 June 1613, by R. St. George, Norr. Harl. MS. 1470, fo. 58, 87, copy of grant, Brit. Mus.; Add. MS. 14,295, fo. 80; C. 28, fo. 37ᵇ, Her. Coll., and Guil. 162 (father of Samuel), *see* Bispham Memoranda, 314; Quarterly, Harl. MS. 6140, fo. 31ᵇ.

BLACHFORD, Richard, Dorchester and London, merchᵗ, s. of Wᵐ of Holway (by W. Segar, 1629). 10 Aug. 1627 (or 1629) Add. MSS. 12,225, fo. 13, and 14,295, fo. 83ᵇ; C. 24, Her. Coll., and Guil. 405; Harl. MS. 6140, fo. 26, 80ᵇ.

BLACKALL, Richard, lineally descended from family of (? Surrey), searcher of the ports and creeks of the co. of Devon ; crest to Richard and Christopher his son and heir 28 July 1599, by (? W. Dethick, Gart.,) and Camden. Cott. MS. Faustina E. 1, 51ᵇ ; Harl. MS. 6095, fo. 25, and Guil. 403.

BLACKDEN, *see* BLAGDEN, of Surrey, by Cooke. Stowe MS. 670, fo. 45ᵇ.

BLACKAMORE. George, Over, Cheshire, s. of Ralphe, s. of Wᵐ, 22 Apr. 1606 (Nor. in Bannerman MS., No. 9), by R. St. George, Norr. Harl. MS. 6140, fo. 36ᵇ ; Add. MS. 14,295, fo. 59ᵇ, and in a little booke of grants marked 679 Her. Coll.

BLACKBURN (Henry), of Wymondham, Suff., 4 April 1597, 39 Eliz., by R. Lee, Clar. Harl. MSS. 1540, fo. 158, and 1085, fo. 37.

BLACKBURNE, ..., of the Bishoprick of Durham, 4 Apr. 1597, by Camden, Clar. Stowe MS. 697, fo. 121.

BLACKERBY, James, of London, and | 10 June 1664, by Sir E.
  „ Thomas, of Shakerland Hall, Suff., who fined | Bysshe, Clar., and to the for Alderm. and Sheriff of London, and Middx. | descendants of their 1666, and after High Sheriff Suffolk 1669, | grandfather John, of Worlingham, Suff. Harl. MS. 1470, fo. 103, copy of grant, Brit. Mus. ; Harl. MS. 1105, fo. 19ᵇ ; Bysshe's Grants, fo. 16, Her. Coll., and Guil. 384.

BLACKMORE, John, London, granted 18 Nov. 1651 (in Edmondson), confirmed 25 Apr. 1661, by Sir E. Bysshe, Clar. Stowe MS. 703, fo. 70, copy of grant, Brit. Mus. ; Misc. Gen. et Her., 2nd S., vol. iii., p. 269, plate ; Arthur, Harl. MS. 6140, fo. 36ᵇ.

  „ Arthur, of London, by R. St. George, Norr. Harl. MS. 6140, fo. 36ᵇ.

BLACKSHAW, Thomas, of Adlington, Cheshire, s. of Wᵐ, s. of Robert, 1613, by R. St. George, Norr. Stowe MS. 706, fo. 19ᵇ ; Harl. MSS. 6179, fo. 14, and 6140, fo. 74ᵇ.

BLACKSMITHS' GUILD, or COMPANY, alteration of crest from what it was under the hand of Sir Thos. Holme, Clar., 24 June 1610, by Segar. Add. MS. 12,225, fo. 13.

BLACKWALL, Richard, Blackwall, co. Derby, 8 Aug. 1494, by Carlisle, Norr. Harl. MS. 1507, fo. 176ᵇ, 374, copy of grant, Brit. Mus., and Q's Coll. Oxf. MS. 38, fo. 18 ; Grants II., 668 ; Add. MS. 6670, fo. 215 ; Le Neve's MS. 374.

BLACKWELL, William, London, confirmed 1560 (Harvey's Grants). Add. MS. 16,940, fo. 38ᵇ ; Harl. MS. 6140, fo. 54.

BLAGE, Thomas, one of Her Majesties Chaplains, quarterly, by Cooke. Harl. MSS. 1359, fo. 90ᵇ, and 5887, fo. 20 ; Add. MS. 4966, fo. 69.

BLAGRAVE, Thomas, Wilts, confirmed grant 1567, by Sir G. Dethick, Gart. Grants I., 53 ; Stowe MS. 676, fo. 31ᵇ ; Q's Coll. Oxf. MS. 37, fo. 46, copy of grant in Latin.

BLAIKWAY, Anne, dau. of John, of Hornidge, Salop, relict of Sir Revett Eldred, late of Gt. Saxham, Suff., decᵈ, 6 Dec. 1652, by Sir E. Bysshe, Gart., and to her posterity lawfullie begotten. Harl. MS. 1172, fo. 18 ; for grant in Brit. Mus. Stowe MS. 703, fo. 71.

BLAKE, Mary, dau. of William, nʳ Andover, Wilts, ux. Ralph Rigges of Farnham, Surrey, by Segar (Add. MS. 12,225, fo. 13ᵇ), testified by Wᵐ Le Neve 23 Oct. 1610. Grants I., fo. 419, 421.

BLAKER, Edward, Portslade, Sussex (s. of Edward), 19 Feb. 1616-17, by Segar. Add. MS. 12,225, fo. 14 ; Guil. 251.

  „ William, city of Salisbury (s. of William), grant 12 Feb. 1613-14, by Segar. Add. MS. 12,225, fo. 13ᵇ ; C. 22, fo. 19ᵇ ; Her. Coll. and Guil. 248, as BLACKER.

BLAKEY, Simon, Blakey, co. Lanc., 1589, by Cooke. Harl. MSS. 1359, fo. 100ᵇ, and 1422, fo. 94ᵇ ; Add. MS. 4966, fo. 89ᵃ.

BLANCHBASTON, ..., descended out of Normandy, 15 Nov. 1556, by Sir G. Dethick, Gart. Harl. MS. 1359, fo. 68ᵇ ; Q's Coll. Oxf. MS. 39, fo. 80, copy of certificate.

E

BLAND, Adam, London, skinner to Q. Eliz., 10 May 1563, by Flower.   Guil. 137 ;
     sergeant pelter of Westmorland, Harl. MS. 5887, fo. 32.
BLANDFORD, Walter, D.D., Bishop of Oxford, and his brothers, 30 Dec. 1665, by
     Sir E. Walker, Gart.   Her. Coll., fo. 62.
BLANK, Thomas, citizen and Alderm. of London, 10 Oct. 1574, by Sir G. Dethick,
     Gart.   Harl. MS. 1441, fo. 81 ; 1573 in Q's Coll. Oxf. MS. 145, fo. 33.
BLINKARNE, Thomas, Chislehurst, Kent (s. of George, of Holbeck, co. Linc., s. of
     George, servant to Q. Eliz.), "royalist, condemned to dye," 3 March
     1663-4, by Walker.   Harl. MS. 1172, fo. 35, 61, copy of grant ; Add. MSS.
     14,293, fo. 57, and 14,294, fo. 12ᵇ ; Surrey Arch. Soc., iii., p. 323 ; Harl.
     MSS. 1507, fo. 1ᵇ, and 1105, fo. 13.
BLOBHALL, William, Mendham, Suff., gent., confirmed 27 May 1614, by Camden,
     arms, or, on a chief indented gu. two gauntlets of the first ; crest, etc.
     Harl. MS. 1172, fo. 10, copy of grant, Brit. Mus., and 1172, fo. 10.
BLOER, ..., London, arg., a chev. vert. betw. three pomeis, by Segar.   Add. MS.
     12,225, fo. 14ᵇ.
BLOMER, John, Hawkswell, Cumbld., and now of London, who marᵈ the dau. of
     Rydle of Durham (gu., an inescocheon arg. a lion rampt. gu. a border or,
     impaling Ridley, by Sir G. Dethick, Gart.   Add. MS. 26,753, fo. 122ᵇ.
BLOUNT als CROKE, John le, ..., by Barker.   Harl. MS. 5846, fo. 13 ; Stowe
     MS. 692, fo. 30.
   „   William, a mercer in Cheapside, London, s. of John, s. of Morris, 2nd s. of
       Edmond, s. of John, of Mangotsfield, co. Glouc., by Wilma, d. and h. of
       Thos. à Barle, crest 16 Nov. 1572, by Cooke, to the posterity of Morris
       his grandfather.   Harl. MS. 1507, fo. 95ᵇ, copy of grant, Brit. Mus. (Harl.
       MSS. 1359, fo. 10, and 1422, fo. 115), and Q's Coll. Oxf. MSS. 38, fo. 57,
       and 146, fo. 45 ; Add. MS. 4966, fo. 94ᵇ, quartering Barker and
       Lathbroke.
BLOWER, Peter, s. of William, s. of Robert, of Suff., 1 June 1597, by Lee.   Stowe
     MS. 696, fo. 120ᵇ ; copy of grant in Latin Q's Coll. Oxf. MS. 36, fo. 62.
BLOYS, ..., Ipswich, Suff., gu., three dragons passant, etc., by Segar.   Add. MS.
     12,225, fo. 14.
   „   . . . ., Ipswich, Suff., sa., a bend a fesse, quartering Raven and Bladbold.
       Add. MS. 12,225, fo. 14ᵇ ; field altered to gu. in Harl. MS. 1422, fo. 18 ;
       Guil. 127 ; Harl. MS. 1105, fo. 11ᵇ.
BLYTHE, ..., ermine, on a fesse gu. three lions rampant or, 1632, by Segar.   Add.
     MS. 12,225, fo. 15.
   „   George, of Lincoln's Inn, s. of John, s. of Gregory, co. Derby, crest 19 April
       1575, by Cooke.   Harl. MSS. 1069, fo. 8ᵇ, and 1359, fo. 14 ; Caius Coll.
       Camb. MS. 552, copy of grant ; Add. MS. 4966, fo. 66ᵇ.
BLITHE, William, Norton, co. Derby, 1 H. 7, by S. More, Norr., and ratified
     11 Dec. 1566 by Flower.   Harl. MS. 1537, fo. 47 ; Egerton MS. 996,
     fo. 65 ; Harl. MS. 6140, fo. 69.
BLYTHE, William, Lincolnshire, Quarterly, 1590, by Cooke.   Harl. MSS. 1359,
     fo. 94, and 1422, fo. 115ᵇ.
BLUDDER, Thomas, s. of Henry, of Grantham, co. Linc., grant April 1593, by
     W. Dethick, Gart.   Stowe MS. 676, fo. 89ᵇ, 103ᵇ ; Q's Coll. Oxf. MS. 36,
     fo. 25, copy of grant ; Guil. 157.
   „   Thomas, "preferred to a worshipful place of charge in the service of his
       majesties navy Royal"; the above coat exemplified with alteration 2 April
       1600, by Camden.   Harl. MS. 1422, fo. 17ᵇ, and Cott. MS. Faustina E. 1,
       fo. 67ᵇ, a Knight of Mile End Green, Middx., and of Lincolnshire ; also in
       Harl. MSS. 6095, fo. 1ᵇ, 1433, fo. 69, and 1046, fo. 34.
BODDY, John, gent. and one of the Shewers of the Chamber to the Queen's Majesty,
     grant 4 Aug. 1552, by Sir G. Dethick, Gart.   Harl. MS. 1359, fo. 70, copy
     of grant ; Q's Coll. Oxf. MS. 39, fo. 86 ; Grants I., 210.
BODDIE als THOMAS, John, London, Admiral of the North Fleet, crest and

augmentation for services against Her Majesties enemies of the North fleet in Ireland, 16 July 1589, by Cooke. Harl. MS. 1359, fo. 22 ; Add. MS. 14,295, fo. 46 ; Q's Coll. Oxf. MS. 146, fo. 41.

BODENHAM, Roger, co. Hereford, ... 1552, by Sir G. Dethick, az., a fesse betw. two chessrooks or. Stowe MS. 676, fo. 22 ; confirmation in Latin, Q's Coll. Oxf. MSS. 37, fo. 31, and 39, fo. 39 ; crest and exemplification, quarterly of 4, 19 Jan. 1579-80, by G. D[ethick], Harl. MSS. 1441, fo. 90^b (a label of three in 1359, fo. 62), 5825, fo. 49, and 5847, fo. 48 ; Q's Coll. Oxf. MS. 145, fo. 49 ; Grants I., 39 ; Harl. MS. 5887, fo. 38.

BODELEY, Denys, s. of Thomas, of Cornwall, ux. William Luson, Alderm. of London, gift 1558 (Harvey's Grants). Add. MS. 16,940, fo. 41 ; Harl. MS. 1116, fo. 64.

„ John, Streatham, Surrey, crest 1 Oct. or Dec. 1609, by Camden. Harl. MSS. 1052, fo. 206^b, copy of grant, Brit. Mus., and 1433, fo. 97 ; Le Neve's MS. 494.

BODYAM, ..., by Barker, Gart. Harl. MS. 5846, fo. 14^b ; Add. MS. 26,702, fo. 65^b.

BOCUC, William, of London, 7 June 1661, by Sir E. Walker, Gart. Her. Coll., 40.

BOGG or BUGG, Humphrey, Sutterton, co. Linc., 10 March 1602-3, by Camden. Guil. 352 ; Harl. MS. 6179, fo. 14^b.

BOLLES, George, London, Alderm., after Lord Mayor [1617-18], confirmed by Segar. Add. MS. 12,225, fo. 16.

BOLLE als BOLLES, Robert, of co. Linc., Quarterly of 10, crest granted 12 Nov. 1560, by G. Dethick, Gart. Harl. MS. 1359, fo. 80 ; Grants I., 292 ; Richard in copy of grant, Q's Coll. Oxf. MS. 39, fo. 111.

„ William, Worthen, Suffolk, 28 Feb. 1528-9, by T. Wriothesley, Gart., and Benolte. MS. Ashm. 834, fo. 8, copy of grant, Bodleian Lib. ; Guil. 373.

„ William, Osbarton, Notts (s. of W^m of Wortham, Suff.), confirmed 16 July 1575, by Flower. MS. Ashm. 844, fo. 8, copy of grant, Bodleian Lib. ; Harl. MS. 1422, fo. 108^b, and Guil. 311.

BOLNEY, John, Bolney, Sussex, crest 5 Nov. 1541, by Hawley. Misc. Gen. et Her., i., p. 304 ; 10th Nov. in Her. and Geneal., i., p. 80, copy of grant, Brit. Mus. ; Bannerman MS. 9, fo. 450.

BOLTON, John, Bolton Hill, co. Pemb., 5 July 1555, by Sir G. Dethick. Misc. Gen. et Her., N. S., ii., p. 163, copy of grant, Brit. Mus.

„ Thos., Woodbridge, Suff., Esq., descended from Bolton of Bolton, co. Lanc., Quarterly, 26 Aug. 1615, by Camden. Harl. MSS. 1422, fo. 111, and 6095, fo. 35^b ; Guil. 218.

„ William, Prior St. Bartholomew, West Smithfield, juxta London, 22 May 1529, by Benolte, Clar. Arundel MS. 26 (S. xvi.), fo. 172^b, patent in French, Brit. Mus.

BONCLE or BUNCLEY, Sir George, Col. of Horse, late lieut.-gov^r city of Oxford, 1 April 1645, by Walker. Add. MS. 14,294, fo. 31^b ; Her. Coll., fo. 28.

BOND, Dennis, Dorset, alteration by the appointment of Mr Bysshe, Gart. Harl. MS. 1441, fo. 151.

„ William, Captain of Chester, by Cooke. Stowe MS. 670, fo. 16^b.

BONEST, Thomas, Putney, grocer, fined for Alderman, 31 July 1654, by E. Bysshe, Gart. Harl. MSS. 1422, fo. 74^b, and 6179, fo. 29^b.

BONFOY, ..., 1657, by E. Bysshe, Gart. Harl. MS. 1441, fo. 151.

BONHAM, see NORTON.

BONNATRE, John, gent., 1 April 1442, 20 H. 6, by Hawkeslow. Harl. MSS. 1077, fo. 52^b, and 1162, fo. 68 ; Harl. Soc. IX., 275 ; copy of grant, Brit. Mus., in Harl. MS. 1142, fo. 23 ; MS. Rawl. Cod. B. 119, fo. 2, Bodleian Lib.

BONNELL, John, London, merch^t, 5 June 1691, by T. St. George, Gart. and Clar. [Stowe MS.] 716, fo. 51 ; Grants IV., 82, Her. Coll. ; Stowe MS. 714, fo. 132^b ; Harl. MS. 1085, fo. 56, 16 May.

BONNER, D[r] Edmund, Bishop of Hereford, and now of London, by Barker. Harl. MSS. 5846, fo. 19[b], and 6179, fo. 16.

BONWICKE, John, of Mickleham, Surrey, B.D., s. of Benj[n] of Reigate, 3 Feb. 1671-2, by Sir E. Bysshe, Clar. Bysshe's Grants 30 ; Harl. MS. 1105, fo. 39.

„   Benjamin, of Reigate, one of the captains of the trayned bands.

BOOKER, ..., London, out of Notts, or, an eagle displayed vert, crowned of the first, a bordure az. charged with 8 fleurs de lis gold, by Segar. Add. MS. 12,225, fo. 15 ; C. 24, fo. 268[a], Her. Coll. ; Guil. 212.

BOORNE, Elizabeth (wife of Hy. Billingsley, Esq., of London), dau. and co-h. of Henry, by Marg[t], d. and h. of . . . . Irtou, who mar[d] d. and h. of Boyse, 13 Nov. 1570, by Cooke. Add. MS. 14,295, fo. 50.

BOOTH, John, s. of Thomas, of Barton, after Earls of Warrington, grant by Charter or deed of Thomas Booth of Barton, 3 boars' heads erased and erected sa., 5 H. IV. 1404 in Guill. Introd., p. 8.

„   John, residing at Seville in Spain, born in co. Notts (s. of William), testified by Segar. Add. MS. 12,225, fo. 15[b].

BORASTON, Philip, Aldenham, Herts, gent., s. of Henry, s. of Thomas, of the Rock, co. Worc., exemplified Jan. 1606, by Camden. Harl. MSS. 1422, fo. 20, and 6095, fo. 7[b] ; Guil. 390.

BORDEN, Arnold de, of Bordeaux, and his son ⎱ letters patent 28 March 1444, 22
„   Grimond de, of Bordeaux,   ⎰ H. 6. Harl. MS. 1507, fo. 398, for copy ; Rymer V., 132, and Q's Coll. Oxf. MS. 38, fo. 33 ; Cott. MS. Jul. C. VII., fo. 243 ; Stowe MS. 840; Genealogist, iii., 502 ; Lawrence's Nobility of the British Gentry, 8 ; for trick, see Le Neve's MS. 398.

BOREEL, John, "ordinum Zelandiæ secretaris," etc., diploma 20 April 1622, examined by Segar. MS. Ashm. 858, fo. 47, copy in Bodleian Lib.

BORLEY, William Deverel, Longbridge, Wilts, crest 1 May 1546, by Hawley. Add. MSS. 16,940, fo. 200[b], and 7098, fo. 77[b] (fo. 34) ; Harl. MS. 1544, fo. 83[b]. See BURLEY.

BORNE, Gilbert, Bp. of Bath and Wells, arms 21 May 1554, ? by Hawley. Add. MS. 16,940, fo. 206[b].

BOROUGH, John, s. of William, Sandwich, Kent, by Segar. Add. MS. 12,225, fo. 19[b].

„   Thomas, see BURROUGH.

„   William (s. of Walter), Clerk and comptroller of the Queen's Navy, 27 Jan. 1586, by Cooke. MS. Ashm. 844, fo. 67, copy of grant, Bodleian Lib. ; Harl. MSS. 1359, fo. 110[b], and 1422, fo. 93[b], and Guil. 127 ; Add. MS. 4966, fo. 68 ; Harl. MS. 5887, fo. 26[b], Quarterly.

BOROWE, Richard, Cheshire, ..., by Barker. Harl. MS. 5846, fo. 13.

BORRELL, John, Wormley, Herts, ..., by Barker. Harl. MS. 5846, fo. 7[b] ; Stowe MS. 692, fo. 22 ; Harl. MS. 6140, fo. 53[b].

BOSEVILE, Sir Ralph, Bradborne, Kent, achievement of 20 quarterings, 20 Sept. 1620, by Camden. Harl. MS. 1359, fo. 42, copy of grant, Brit. Mus. ; Harl. MS. 5887, fo. 17[b].

BOSVILE, D[r] William, and his bro. ⎱ sons of Wm. B., Alderm. of Oxford, s. of Thos.
„   Edward,   ⎰ of Yorks, 10 June 1638, by Borough. Harl. MS. 1105, fo. 56 ; Add. MS. 26,702, fo. 90[b] ; Guil. 372.

BOSWYKE, Roger, London, ..., by Cooke. Harl. MS. 1359, fo. 100[b] ; Beswick in Harl. MS. 1422, fo. 74[b].

BOSWORTH, Isabel, wife to Sir W[m] Feilding, Kt., co. Warwick, 1 Feb. 1549-50, by Hawley. Add. MS. 16,940, fo. 203[b].

BOTELER, see also BUTLER.

BOTELER (BUTTELIER), Richard, Native of Kents, arms (? and crest) temp. E. IV., by T. Holme, Norr., confirmed 20 Nov. 1567 by Cooke, Clar., Flower, Norr., Turpyn, Windsor Herald, and Cotgrave, Richmond Herald : arg. and sa., gyronny of 24 pieces, three dogs' heads erased collared gu. ; crest, a cup or betw. two wings, one arg. tne other azure. Her. and Geneal., i., p. 80.

BOTELER, Richard, of Kent, two coats: No. 1, arg., three escocheons az. each charged with a covered cup d'or, as procured by Drury ; since altered to this : No. 2, sa., three covered cups within a bordure or. Crest altered (and allowed at the Visitⁿ to Richd B. of Heronden, Kent, Harl. MSS. 1106, fo. 48^b, and 1432, fo. 206). Harl. MSS. 1359, fo. 97, and 1422, fo. 12^b, two coats ; Add. MS. 4966, fo. 87.

„ Richard, of Eastry, of Heronden, Kent, s. of Hen., s. of John, s. of Richard, confirmed 6 July 1599, by W. Dethick and Camden. Stowe MS. 676, fo. 129^b ; Q's Coll. Oxf. MS. 36, fo. 79, copy of grant.

„ Richard, South Creake, Norfolk, ... by Camden. Harl. MS. 1422, fo. 14^b.

„ William, Kirton, Beds, 8 May 1585, by Cooke. MS. Ashm. 844, fo. 60, copy of grant, Bodleian Lib. ; Guil. 78.

BOTHOLMBY, John, of York, 15 March 1666-7, by Sir E. Walker, Gart. Her. Coll., fo. 63.

BOUGHTELL, Sir David, Bodmin, Cornwall, Feb. 1606-7, by Camden. Guil. 385 ; Le Neve's MS. 350.

BOUGHTON, ... crest . . . . by Barker. Harl. MS. 5846, fo. 6, and Stowe MS. 692, fo. 23.

„ Edward, Woolwich, Kent, gent., 11 Feb. 1518-19, by T. Wriothesley, Gart., and Benolte. Add. MS. 14,295, fo. 83 (1518), copy of grant in French, Brit. Mus.

„ William, of Little Lalleford, co. Warwick, Esquire of the body to the King, grant of arms and crest 17 Feb. 1516-17, by T. Wriothesley, Gart., and Benolte. Q's Coll. Oxf. MS. 38, fo. 28, copy of grant in French ; 1516 in Harl. MS. 1507, fo. 422, 430 ; Le Neve's MSS. 422, 429.

BOULBROKE, John, Drinkeston, Suff., grant 25 March 1594, by W. Dethick, Gart. Stowe MS. 676, fo. 91^b, and Badbroke in fo. 107 ; Q's Coll. Oxf. MS. 36, fo. 35, copy of grant.

BOURCHIER, Anthony, Bedesley, co. Glouc., gent., 1 Dec. 1548, by Hawley. Harl. MS. 1507, fo. 437, copy of grant, Brit. Mus. ; Harl. MSS. 1359, fo. 4, and 1422, fo. 71 ; Add. MS. 16,940, fo. 203 ; Q's Coll. Oxf. MSS. 38, fo. 53, and 39, fo. 11 ; Grants II., 483^b ; Le Neve's MS. 437.

„ James, Little Stanbridge, Essex, 12 Jan. 1599-1600, by Camden. Harl. MS. 1422, fo. 22.

„ Sir James, ... Oct. 1610, by Camden. Harl. MSS. 1422, fo. 21^b, and 6095, fo. 21^b.

„ Thomas, London, s. of Richard, s. of Thomas, of Ponkistone, co. Worc., crest 23 Sept. 1587, by Cooke. Harl. MSS. 1359, fo. 110, and 1422, fo. 52 ; Add. MSS. 14,295, fo. 24, and 4966, fo. 51^b.

BOURGES, ... Somerset . . . . March 1614, by Camden. Harl. MSS. 1422, fo. 38^b, and 6095, fo. 29^b.

BOURNE, Richard, Wells, Somerset, Esq., sometime of London and Master of the Merchant Taylors' Co. (brother of Gilbert, Bp. of Bath and Wells, and lord president of the Marches of Wales, temp. Q. Mary, and was also cousin german to Sir John Bourne, secry. to the sd. queen), crest 17 Nov. 1592, by W. Dethick, Gart. Harl. MS. 1359, fo. 22 ; Stowe MS. 676, fo. 82^b; Add. MS. 14,295, fo. 45^b; 1591 in copy of grant, Q's Coll. Oxf. MS. 37, fo. 124.

DES BOUVERIE, William and „ Jacob } merchants, of London, s. of Sir Edward, 26 Jan. 1694-5, by T. St. George, Gart. and Clar. Grants IV., fo. 178.

BOWATER, Thomas, of London (s. of Thos., s. of Thos., of Coventry), by Cooke, confirmed 1627 by Segar. Harl. MS. 1422, fo. 16 ; Add. MS. 12,225, fo. 15^b.

BOWDON, ... Quarterly, sa. and or, in the first quarter a lion passant arg., by Camden. Morgan's Sphere, 117.

BOWELL, Nicholas, Bury Court, Southants, Esq., 13 Dec. 1662, by Sir E. Bysshe. Harl. MS. 1105, fo. 17 ; Bysshe's Grants, fo. 2, Her. Coll., and Guil. 397 ; Add. MS. 14,293, fo. 14.

BOWERMAN, James, Hemyock, Devon, Esq., crest 20 June 1563, by Harvey. Stowe MS. 677, fo. 10ᵇ ; Add. MS. 16,940, fo. 46.

BOWES, Elizabeth, see HARROWE.

„ Of Stretham, co. Durham. Le Neve's MS. 403.

BOWES, Francis, Thornton, co. Durham, confirmed with difference 18 May 1639, by Borough, on certif. of Kinship from Sir G. Bowes of Bradley, Kt. Durham Visitn., ed. Foster.

„ Sir Martin, of London, Alderm. . . . . by Barker. Harl. MS. 5846, fo. 8ᵇ, and Stowe MS. 692, fo. 22ᵇ ; Harl. MS. 5857, fo. 16ᵇ, 17, and three wives, etc.

BOWKER, Francis, Barton, co. Lanc., Quarterly coat 10 Jan. 1574-5, by Sir G. Dethick, Gart. Harl. MS. 1359, fo. 69ᵇ ; Grants I., 89, since in Spain.

BOWMAN, Seymour, Sarum, Wilts, arms and crest and an inescocheon of pretence, 16 Feb. 1669-70, by Sir E. Bysshe. Harl. MSS. 1105, fo. 21, and 1470, fo. 271 ; Bysshe's Grants, fo. 23, Her. Coll.

BOWSCER, Thomas, Stone, co. Glouc., 1606, by Camden. Harl. MS. 6095, fo. 21, and Guil. 413 ; Harl. MS. 5887, fo. 40ᵇ, 148.

BOWYERS, of London, the fellows and masters " consanguines et majores," certificate by Camden. Harl. MS. 1441, fo. 32.

BOWYER (? Thomas, 1570, Harl. MS. 1562, fo. 44), Sussex, Quarterly of 4 and crest. Caius Coll. Camb. MS. 551, fo. 19ᵇ ; (among Camden's guifts) Harl. MS. 1441, fo. 148, and Bannerman's MS., No. 9 (455), crest by Cooke, Clar.

„ Francis, London, grocer . . . . by Ro. Cooke. Harl. MS. 1422, fo. 123, Quarterly, 1 and 4, 2 and 3 : 2 and 3, Sa., three spades, etc.

„ Ralph, 1 and 4, 2, 3, co. Linc., Esq., descended from Bowyer of Knypersley, co. Staff., by Flower, Norr., 13 June 1574 ; Gilb. Dethick, Gart., 9 April 1576 : exemplified 9 April 1576, by Sir G. Dethick, Gart. MS. Ashm. 858, fo. 70, 71, copy of grant, Bodleian Lib.; Harl. MS. 1441, fo. 85, copy of grant; also Harl. MS. 6832, fo. 136 ; Q's Coll. Oxf. MS. 145, fo. 40ᵇ.

„ William, London, Alderm., by Barker. Harl. MS. 5846, fo. 7 ; Add. MS. 26,702, fo. 24ᵇ ; Stowe MS. 692, fo. 22, vert, on a chevron betw. three lions' heads erased or, langued gules, as many trefoils of the field, on a chief barry wavy (of 6) argt. and azure an anchor between two frets of the 2nd.

„ William, " Canserne," ? Sussex, confirmed 1558 (Harvey's Grants). Add. MS. 16,940, fo. 36ᵇ, originally a chevron fleurty vert betw. three bulls' heads erased sable, horned and maned or ; crest, an arm, etc.

„ William, of Knypersley, co. Staff., confirmed 6 June 1574, by Flower. Guil. 179 ; MS. Ashm. 834, fo. 62, copy of grant, Bodleian Lib.

BOYARE, John, servant to Richard Bancroft, Archbp. of Canterbury, circa 1602, by Camden. (Called Sir John, Harl. MS. 5887, fo. 7ᵇ.) Harl. MS. 6095, fo. 19.

BOYCOTT, Silvanus, of Hinton, Salop, and Francis, of Buildwas, s. of Wᵐ, decᵈ, late of Buildwas, etc., 21 March 1663-4, by Bysshe. Harl. MS. 1105, fo. 18ᵇ ; Bysshe's Grants, Her. Coll. ; Misc. Gen. et Her., N. S., ii., p. 162 (copy of grant, Brit. Mus.).

BOYLAND, Richard, of Margettyne, Essex, gent., grant 2 July, 1 Eliz., 1559, by G. Dethick. Harl. MS. 1359, fo. 77ᵇ, and Misc. Gen. et Her., 3rd S., iii., p. 128 ; copy of grant, Q's Coll. Oxf. MS. 39, fo. 96 ; Grants I., 304.

BOILAND, Richard, Esq., Keeper of the Stores within the Tower of London ; with tenor to the posterity of his father Edwd of Margetting, Essex ; crest 28 Feb. 1573-4, by Cooke. Bowland quartering Lamborn. Harl. MSS. 1359, fo. 40^b, and 1422, fo. 116^b; Add. MS. 14,295, fo. 20 ; Harl. MS. 5887, fo. 69.

BOYLE, Stephen, of Kentish Towne, Middx., s. and h. of Alex^r of Yorks, crest granted 24 Jan. 1569-70, by G. Dethick, Cooke, and Flower. Guil. 379 ; Harl. MSS. 1441, fo. 71^b, and 1359, fo. 55^b ; copy of grant, Q's Coll. Oxf. MSS. 39, fo. 159, and 145, fo. 23^b.

BOYNTON, Robert (5 April 1375), arms disallowed 5 April 1375. Harl. MS. 1178, fo. 44. *See* ATON.

BOYSE, Edward, Fredville, Kent, Esq., 1589, by Cooke's deputy. Stowe MS. 670, fo. 37^b.

BRABANTINE, ... 1670. Burke's Armory.

BRABOURNE, Henry, als BRABON, of London, descended from John, Keeper of the mew'd [*i.e.*, moulting] Hawks to Ed. III., arms and crest confirmed, impaling Marden, Guil. 259, 2 May 1629, by Segar. Add. MS. 12,225 fo. 16 ; Harl. MSS. 6140, fo. 65, and 1441, fo. 160^b.

BRADBRIDGE, BREDBRIDGE, or BRODBRIDGE, az., a pheon argent garnished or, by Sir G. Dethick, Gart. Q's Coll. Oxf. MS. 145, fo. 44 ; Harl. MS. 5847, fo. 42^b.

BRADBURY, ..., crest . . . ., by Barker. Harl. MS. 5816, fo. 5^b ; Stowe MS. 692, fo. 23.

BRADSHAW, Anne, dau. of Richard, late of Bonny, ux. Hy. Stanley of Sutton, Bonnington, Notts, 18 March 1576-7, by Ro. Cooke, Clar. Grants II., 510.

   ,,   James, of the Haghe, co. Lanc., by Dalton. Add. MS. 14,295, fo. 76^b.

   ,,   John, of Presteign, Radnor, gift 1561. Add. MS. 16,940, fo. 27 (Harvey's Grants).

   ,,   John (Windsor Herald 1626—33). Caius Coll. Camb. MS. 551, fo. 30^b (among Camden's gifts) ; Harl. MSS. 1105, fo. 7, and 1411, fo. 148.

   ,,   John, of the Exchequer, *temp.* Jac. I., difference, and crest, Jan. 1624-5, by R. St. George. Harl. MS. 1470, fo. 220, copy of grant (in Latin), by R. St. George, Clar.

BRADY, Thomas, of Cambridge, ..., 1586, by Cooke. Harl. MSS. 1359, fo. 90, 117, and 1422, fo. 51^b ; Add. MS. 4966, fo. 28, 69^b.

BRAGG, ..., of Somerset, Arg^t, a chevron v^t betw. three bulls passant gu., 1626, by Segar. Add. MS. 12,225, fo. 17 ; Harl. MS. 6140, fo. 81.

BRAHAM, Sir Richard, for his services in the grand rebellion, augmentation and crest 10 June 1646, at Oxford, by Walker. Guil. 54 ; Harl. MS. 1470, fo. 4 ; Add. MSS. 14,293, fo. 107, and 14,294, fo. 35^b ; Harl. MS. 1172, fo. 73 ; MSS. Ashm. 840, fo. 401-2, and 858, fo. 191-2, copy of grant, Bodleian Lib. ; Her. Coll., fo. 27.

BRAITHWAITE, Thos, of Warcop, Westm^d, gu., on a chev. arg. 3 cross crosslets fitchée sa., alteration in crest 1601, by Segar. Add. MS. 12,225, fo. 16^b ; Harl. MS. 1359, fo. 40, by Knight. *See* BRATHWAITE.

BRAKYN, Thomas, of Cambridgeshire. Add. MS. 26,702, fo. 76^b ; Harl. MS. 5887, fo. 65^b.

BRAMHALL, William, of London, gent., 2nd s. Peter, s. and h. of John, late of Pontefract, Yorks, out of Cheshire (1602, by Segar, in Burke's Armory), confirmed 21 Nov. 1628, by Segar. Add. MS. 12,225, fo. 17 ; Guil. 175.

BRAUNDE, Benjamin, ..., Suff., 10 March 1610-11. *See* BRONDE.

BRAND, John, of Gray's Inn, esq., s. of Rich^d, descended from Sir Thomas, of Hadham, Herts, crest 7 Sept. 1616, by Segar. Add. MS. 12,225, fo. 17^b ; Guil. 337, and 21, fo. 155, Her. Coll. ; Harl. MSS. 1055, fo. 18^b, and 1422, fo. 71.

BRANDE, Thomas, of West Moulsey, Surrey, 1592, by Cooke. Harl. MS. 1359, fo. 103[b].

BRANDLYN, Sir Robert, of Newcastle-upon Tyne, Northumb., Kt., who married Ann, d. of John Place of Halnaby, Yorks, by . . . ., dau. and one of the co-heirs of Tho[s] Surtees, of Dimsdale, co. Durham, arms confirmed ; 2 coats quarterly, and crest confirmed to Thos. and Henry, his bros., 4 Dec. 1561, by Dalton (over all on an escocheon of pretence, quarterly). Harl. MS. 1359, fo. 52[b].

BRANDON, Gregory, of London, and ye executioner of the County of Middx., confirmed, or, four pallets ar., on a canton sable a lyon rampant of the first, by Segar.   Concerning these arms and the malice and contrivance of Brooksmouth, vulgo Brooke, York Herald, see Smith's L. P. of Camden, Add. MS. 12,225, fo. 16[b].

BRANDRETH, John, of Weeford, co. Staff., patent 10 Nov. 1623, by Segar.   Add. MS. 12,225, fo. 17[b] : MS. Ashm. 858, p. 111, copy of grant, Bodleian Lib. ; Guil. 375 ; Harl. MSS. 6179, fo. 53[b], and 1411, fo. 160[b].

BRATHWAYTE, Thomas, of Warcop, Westmd, geat., s. and h. of Rob[t], of Ambleside, s. and h. of Rich[d] of same county, gift 22 Nov. 1591, by Knight, Norr., alteration in crest, by Segar, Norr., 1601, the line was taken away from the greyhound.   Harl. MSS. 1359, fo. 40, and 5887, fo. 7 ; Q's Coll. Oxf. MS. 146, fo. 137 ; Add. MS. 14,295, fo. 122[b] ; Le Neve's MS. 74, 367.

BRAWNE, Sir Hugh, Vintner, atte ye Greyhound in Fleet St., 26 June 1604, by Camden.   Harl. MSS. 1422, fo. 17[b], 2275, fo. 91[b], 1115, fo. 9, and 5839, fo. 3 ; Guil. 269.

BRAXTON, William, see BREXTON.

BRAYBROOK, James, of Suffolk, gent., given by Roger Machado als Richmont Clar., 7 March (copy of grant, Brit. Mus.) 1504-5, 20 Hy. VII. Harl. MS. 1359, fo. 12, and Q's Coll. Oxf. MS. 38, fo. 20 ; Grants II., 637.

  „   Robert, of Norfolk, gent., 4 March, 15 Ed. IV., 1474-5, in Harl. MS. 69, fo. 56[b], by Hawkeslow.   Harl. MS. 69, fo. 56[b] ; Add. MS. 6297, fo. 140 (or 72[b]), 25 Ed. IV. ; MS. Ashm. 857, fo. 522, as John, 4 March, 14 Ed. IV., 1474-5 (15 Ed. IV.), copy of grant, Bodleian Lib.

BREARLEY, James, of London, and Richard, of Marland, co. Lancs., s. of James, 19 March 1615-16, by Camden.   Brierley in Harl. MS. 1422, fo. 40 ; Harl. MS. 6095, fo. 33.

BREDEMAN, George, ... Beds.   Add. MS. 16,940, fo. 10 (Harvey's Grants).

BREEDON, Zaccheus, of Croton, Northants, B.D., and Capt. Thos. Breedon his son, Gov[r] of Nova Scotia and Acadie in America, 11 Feb. 1661-2, by Sir E. Walker, Gart.   Harl. MS. 6179, fo. 40 ; Her. Coll., fo. 45.

BRENDE, Sir John, ... 1559, by Harvey ?, by Barker ? Stowe MS. 692, fo. 12[b] ; Add. MS. 16,940, fo. 36.

BRENT, Sir Nathaniel, of Oxford, a patent Jan. 1613-14, by Camden.   Harl. MS. 6095, fo. 25[b].

BRENTFORD AND FORTH, Patrick, Earl of, augmentation 26 March and supporters 1 April 1645 at Oxford.

BRERETON, John, of Norwich, confirmed 1576, by Cooke, ... by Walker, Gart. Her. Coll., fo. 1—11.

BRERES, Edmond, of Brockhall, Esq., and John, of Marton, gent., crest Sept. 1613, by R. St. George, Norr.   Add. MS. 14,295, fo. 61.

BREWER, Robert, of Boxley, Kent, 2nd s. of Richard of West Farley, Kent, confirmed 7 Aug. 1590, by Cooke.   Stowe MS. 670, fo. 62[b] ; Harl. MS. 1548, fo. 87.

  „   . . . . of London, out of Somerset, confirmed gu., two bends undée or, a chief vair, martlet for difference, by Segar.   Add. MS. 12,225, fo. 18 ; Guil. 70 ; H[er]. C[oll]., 24.

BREWERS, Company of, 23 July 1468, by W. Hawkeslowe, Clar.   Grants II., 539.

BREWSTER, Humphrey, of Rushmere, Suffolk, s. of Robert, s. of Wm., exemplified 3 July 1561, by Hervey. Harl. MS. 1422, fo. 22 ; Add. MS. 16,940, fo. 46 ; Misc. Gen. et Her., N. S., ii., 325, ; Harl. MS. 5887, fo. 54ᵇ.

BREXTON, Wᵐ, of Hants, gent., exemplified by Segar. Add. MS. 14,295, fo. 88ᵇ ; Harl. MS. 1544, fo. 2, 3.

BRICE, ... Dunnington, Somerset, 1573, by R. Cooke, sa., a griffin passant or. Crest : a lion's head erased. Berry's Armory, erm., pierced thro' with an arrow or, feathered and headed argt.

BRIDGE, William, of Bosbury, co. Hereford, by R. St. George. Harl. MS. 6179, fo. 19ᵇ.

BRIDGES, John, of Chillingford and Badowey, Essex, exemplified 10 July 1562, by G. Dethick. Add. MS. 14,293, fo. 23 ; Harl. MS. 5823, fo. 55ᵇ.

„ Noah, Sec. to the Lords of the P. Council at Oxford and clerk to the Commons at Oxf., etc. ; attended his late Majesty at Newcastle, I. of W. ; augmentation 10 April 1661, by Walker, Gart., fo. 43. Add. MS. 14,294, fo. 8ᵇ.

BRIDGMANN, Edward, of Livesley, co. Lanc., gent., 3rd s. of Thomas, of Greenway, Devon, crest 20 Jan. 1620-21, by R. St. George. Add. MS. 14,295, fo. 81ᵇ, copy of grant, Brit. Mus.

BRIGGS (BRIGES), ... of the North, "a salljer," 1646, by W. Ryly, Lancs. Herald.

BRIGGS, Augustine, of the city of Norwich, 3 Jan. 1664-5, by Bysshe, Clar. Harl. MS. 1105, fo. 38*, 39, by Bysshe ; Grants, 29, and Le Neve's MS. 50ᵇ.

BRANTHWAITE, Richard, of Lincoln's Inn, 21 July 1582, by Cooke, Clar. Stowe MS. 670, fo. 7ᵇ, 30ᵇ ; Add. MS. 14,297, fo. 7ᵇ, 28. He married Margaret, dau. of John Bull (1558). See under BRAITHWAITE, Harl. MS. 5887, fo. 7.

BRETARGHE, William, of Bretarghe Hall, co. Lancs., s. of Wᵐ, s. of Wᵐ and Margᵗ Chisnoll, confirmation of arms and crest 20 Jan. 1595, by W. Dethick, Gart. Q's Coll. Oxf. MS. 36, fo. 124, 137.

BRIGGS, David, of London, gent., and of Old Towne, Halifax, Yorks, s. of Richard, s. of Wᵐ, altered and allowed arms borne by Hy. Briggs of Halifax, 22 Dec. 1624, by R. St. George. Add. MS. 14,295, fo. 52ᵇ.

BRYGGS, Henry, als Patemer, of Halifax, Yorks, temp. H. 7. Add. MS. 26,702, fo. 51ᵇ ; Harl. MS. 1820, fo. 56ᵇ.

BRIGGS, Sir Humphrey, Bt. . . . , Houghton, Salop, 12 March 1682-3, by Sir H. Sᵗ George, Clar. Harl. MS. 6834, fo. 78 ; Grants III., fo. 192.

BRIGHOUSE, Martyn, of Colbye, co. Linc., gent., s. of Richᵈ, s. of Richᵈ, s. of John, of Brighouse, Yorks, gent., 1 Dec. 1590, by Cooke. Harl. MS. 1359, fo. 112 ; Add. MSS. 17,506, fo. 26, 4966, fo. 25 ; Grants II., fo. 481.

BRIGHT, Stephen, of Carbrook, Yorks, 2 Dec. 1641, by Borough. Harl. MSS. 1105, fo. 58, and 1069, fo. 110ᵇ ; Guil. 386 ; Harl. MS. 5857, fo. 136ᵇ.

„ Thomas, of Bury St. Edmunds, and Robert, of Nether Hall, both Suffolk, sons of Thoˢ Bright and Margaret Payton, a patent 10 May 1615, by Camden. Harl. MSS. 1422, fo. 39ᵇ, 6095, fo. 32ᵇ ; Her. and Geneal., iii., 328 (20 May) ; Guil. 245 ; Caius Coll. Camb. MS. 551.

„ Thomas, of Netherhall, Suff., "nephew of above named Thomas," 29 July 1641, by Sir J. Borough, Gart. Harl. MSS. 1085, fo. 25, and 1105, fo. 57ᵇ ; Guil. 245.

BRIGHTMAN, als Britzman, William, of Paris Garden, Surrey, gent., s. of John, of Herald House, in Stebbing, Essex, gent., 16 Feb. 1574-5, by G. Dethick. Harl. MSS. 1441, fo. 140ᵇ, and 5823, fo. 35ᵇ ; Q's Coll. Oxf. MS. 145, fo. 35ᵇ.

BRINDSLEY, or BRINSLEY, ..., of Brinsley, Notts, grant . . . . 1569, fo. 16, Burke's Armory.

BRISTOWE, Nicholas, of Ayott St. Lawrence, Herts (Clerk of the Jewels to H. VIII.), coat and crest by Barker, and confirmed by Sir G. Dethick.

F

Harl. MS. 5846, fo. 10[b] ; Stowe MSS. 692, fo. 23[b], 703, fo. 4. Harl. MS. 1116, fo. 82, exemplified 3 Oct. 1544 ; Harl. MS. 1441, fo. 61 ; Misc. Gen. et Her., 2 S., iv., p. 257 ; *see* Q's Coll. Oxf. MS. 145, fo. 1.

BROAD (BRODE), George, Brodhall, par. of Cokested, Sussex, by Sir G. Dethick, Gart. Add. MS. 26,753, fo. 122[b].

BROAD, Henry, of Chiswick, Middx., Esq., s. of Arthur, of Caldwell, Yorks, 12 March 1654-5, by Bysshe, Gart., and 27 June 1661 as Clar. Harl. MS. 1105, fo. 19[b] ; Misc. Gen. et Her., N. S., ii., 311 ; Bysshe's Grants, 15, Her. Coll. ; Harl. MS. 1172, fo. 16 and 26, copy of grant. Harl. MS. 6179, fo. 54[b].

BROCK, Robert, city of Chester, granted 3 Sept. 1580, by Flower. MS. Ashm. 834, p. 25, copy of grant, Bodleian Lib. ; Guil. 191.

„   William, of the Inner Temple, s. of Robert, etc., exemplified 10 Feb. 1602-3, by Camden. MS. Ashm. 858, p. 141 ; Misc. Gen. et Her., ii., 17, copy of grant, Brit. Mus.

BROCKMAN, William, of Beechborough, Kent., gent., by Cooke. Harl. MS. 1359, fo. 115[b], new crest June 1606, by Camden. Harl. MSS. 1422, fo. 19, 5887, fo. 35[b], and 6095, fo. 5[b] ; Guil. 132 ; Stowe MS. 670, fo. 69 ; Add. MSS. 4966, fo. 96, and 5887, fo. 35[b].

BRODBENT, John, Stapleford, Notts, 1601, by Camden, per pale erm. and az., a fesse wavy, gu. ; crest, a pheon, the staff broken embrued at the point, all ppr.

BRODE, Geo., *see* BROAD.

BRODERERS, Company of, 17 Aug. 1558, by Harvey. Misc. Gen. et Her., i., 183, copy of grant, Brit. Mus. (Cott. MS. Faustina E. I., fo. 22).

BRODWAY, Capt. John, of Portslip, co. Glouc., eminent for his sufferings and service to Chas. I., granted 9 Jan. 1661-2, by Bysshe. Copy of grant, Brit. Mus. ; Harl. MSS. 1470, fo. 135, and 1105, fo. 17 ; Bysshe's Grants, fo. 13, Her. Coll.

BRODERICK, William, ye King's Embroder. Harl. MS. 6179, fo. 42[b] ; *see* Misc. Gen. et Her., ii., 359.

BROKE, Alice, wife to Sir George Barne, Lord Mayor [of Lond. 1552-3], gift 155-6 [1555-6 ?]. Add. MS. 16,940, fo. 37[b] (Harvey's Grants).

„   James, Bp. of Glouc., arms 2 May 1554, by Hawley (?). Add. MS. 16,940, fo. 206[b].

„   Sir Rob[t], Lord C. J. of Com. Pleas (of Salop), 2 July 1556, by Hawley (?). Add. MS. 16,940, fo. 208.

„   Robert, of Madeley, Salop, ... 1587, by Cooke, Quarterly of 4. Harl. MSS. 1359, fo. 109[b], 1422, fo. 119[b], 108[b], and 5887, fo. 17[b] ; Add. MS. 4966, fo. 56[b].

BROKESBY, John, of Bradley, Suff., s. of Barthol., grant 23 Sept. 1584, by G. Dethick. Stowe MS. 676, fo. 62[b], copy of grant ; Grants I., 73 ; Q's Coll. Oxf. MS. 37, fo. 86.

BROMAGE, Capt. Thos., of co. Worc., 1647, by Roberts, Ulster [K. of Arms]. Burke's Armory.

BROME, Thomas, Winchester, 3rd s. of Edward, Forest Hill, Oxon, 2nd s. of Sir Christopher of Haulton, Quarterly of 4, 17 June 1640, certified (or testified, *i.e.*, "under his hand") by W. Le Neve, Clar. Grants II., 610.

BROMFIELD, ..., descended out of Wales, Quarterly of 9, confirmed by Segar. Add. MS. 12,225, fo. 18.

BROMFILDE, William, Lieut. of the Ordnance, 10 Jan. 1552-3, by Hawley. Add. MS. 16,940, fo. 206 ; Grants I., 285 ; of South Raynham, Norfolk, gent., in Add. MS. 14,295, fo. 91[b].

BROMHALL, ... Evington, Beds, ... by Sir G. Dethick, Gart. Add. MS. 26,753, fo. 122[b].

BRONDE, Benjamin, of Edwardstone, Suffolk, patent 10 March 1610-11, by Camden. Guil. 265 ; Harl. MS. 6095, fo. 26[b], 1422, fo. 38, as Browne ?

s. of John, of Boxford, confirmed 10 March 1612-13, and to Jacob, Sam[l] and James, his bro[s], in Harl. MS. 1441, fo. 52[b], copy of grant, Brit. Mus.; Grants II., 626 [?].

BRONSOP, W[m], of Berkshire (Quarterly coat in Harl. MS. 1533, fo. 115), crest, by C. Barker, Gart. Stowe MS. 692, fo. 12.

BRONRICK, or BRONCKER, } Henry, of Melksham, Wilts, coat and crest, by Barker.
BROUNCKER rightly, } Harl. MS. 5846, fo. 10 ; Stowe MS. 692, fo. 23 ; Harl. MS. 6179, fo. 16.

BROOKE, John, of Weston, Bucks, s. of Thomas and Alice his wife, d. and h. of Alex. Acton, Quarterly coat and crest 10 Oct. 1582, by Cooke. Add. MS. 14,293, fo. 19 ; Guil. 244.

„ Ralph, York Herald of Arms, "said to be a great lye," s. of Geoffrey, of Wigan, co. Lanc., s. of W[m], s. of Tho[s], Steward to Thomas, Earl of Derby, 1473, and 4 s. of Thomas, of Leighton, esq., living 1 Ed. IV., 8 Aug. 1593, by Knight. Harl. MS. 5805, fo. 103[b], copy of grant ; Harl. MS. 5887, fo. 57[b] ; Le Neve's MS. 224 and 253.

„ (. . . .), of Gateforth, Yorks, ... 1608, by Sir R. St. George. Stowe MS. 716, fo. 55.

„ Tho[s], Whitechurch, Hants, crest 20 Jan., 18 Jac., 1620-21, by Camden. Harl. MSS. 6140, fo. 63[b], 1422, fo. 41[b], and 6095, fo. 37[b] ; Caius Coll. Camb. MS. 552 [?], fo. 15 ; Le Neve's MS. 345.

„ see BROCK, Wm., 1603.

„ W[m], or Leonard, of Buckingham, confirmed 1605, by Camden. Pedigree, Leonard, s. of Wm., s. of Robt., s. of Robert, of Buckingham. Harl. MSS. 1422, fo. 41[b], 6095, fo. 21, and 5887, fo. 32[b] ; Guil. 317.

BROOKER, Arthur, of Rochester, Kent, 12 Feb. 1664-5. Harl. MS. 1105, fo. 40, by Bysshe, Clar. ; Bysshe's Grants, 34.

BROOKS, ... Whalley Ho., co. Lanc., ... by W. Camden, Clar. Harl. MSS. 1115, fo. 9, 2275, fo. 91[b], and 5839, fo. 3, and Caius Coll. Camb. MS. 551, fo. 2[b].

BROOME, George, sub-prothonotary or Secondary of the King's Bench, crest 12 July, 2 Chas. II., 1626, by Segar. Add. MS. 12,225, fo. 18[b] ; Guil. 254.

„ George, of Ashford, Kent, out of Salop, az., a sinister hand cooped and erected in pale arg., confirmed May 1627. Harl. MS. 1422, fo. 14 ; Guil. 254 ; Harl. MSS. 6140, fo. 82, and 1105, fo. 12.

„ Thomas, see BROME.

„ William, ⎰ sons of John, of Ewithington, co. Hereford ; for assisting Chas. II.
„ John, ⎱ with money in foreign parts ; assigned 16 Nov. 1670, by Walker, Gart. Add. MSS. 14,293, fo. 80, and 14,294, fo. 23 ; Harl. MS. 1172, fo. 69 ; Guil. 114.

BROUNCKER, Henry, see BRONRICK and BRUNCKARD.

BROWKER, Hugh, of the Inner Temple, one of the prothonotaries of the Com. Pleas, 3 June 1589, 31 Eliz., by Cooke. Harl. MSS. 1359, fo. 118, and 1433, fo. 84 ; Add. MS. 4966, fo. 96[b] ; Harl. MS. 5887, fo. 51[b].

BROWNE, ... of Essex, 11 June 1592, arg., on a chev. gu. three cinquefoils [roses ?] of the field, a crescent for diff., crest, out of a breastplate three feathers. Harl. MS. 1422, fo. 16[b], by ? Cooke or W. Dethick.

„ Confirmed 1614, by Camden, erm., on a fesse embattled counter embattled sa., three escallops arg., crest, out of a mural crown gu. a stork's head and neck erm., beaked az. Harl. MSS. 6095, fo. 29[b], and 1422, fo. 39 ; Guil. 244, as of Ludlow, May 1614.

„ Anthony, of Hounslow, Middx., esq., confirmed 15 March 1560-61, by G. Dethick. Harl. MS. 1441, fo. 64 ; Q's Coll. Oxf. MS. 145, fo. 6.

„ Christopher, of co. Lincs., 20 July 1480, by J. More, Norr. Grants II., 627 and 633.

„ Humphrey, s. of Humfrey, of London, descended out of the North, 28 Feb. 1615-16, by Segar. Add. MS. 12,225, fo. 19 ; 18th Feb. in Guil. 263 ; Harl. MSS. 5887, fo. 113[b], and 6140, fo. 62[b].

BROWNE, John, of Portland, Norfolk, 8 Oct. 1612, by Camden.   Harl. MS. 6095, fo. 40^b.   Archibald in Le Neve's MS. 352.

„   John, of Brenchley, Kent, patent, quarterly with Iden, 7 Dec. 1626, by Segar. Add. MS. 12,225, fo. 19 ; Guil. 264 ; 12th Dec. in Misc. Gen. et Her., 2nd S., vol. i., p. 126^b.   Sworne servant to K. Charles, sole officer for founding and casting great ordnance.   Copy of grant of patent, Brit. Mus., Harl. MS. 6140, fo. 63^b.

„   John, Spexall, Suff., ... by Cooke.   Stowe MS. 670, fo. 48^b.

„   John Baptist, of Millayne in Italy, gent., crest 15 Sept. 1551, 5 Ed. VI., by Hawley.   Harl. MS. 1422, fo. 38 ; Add. MS. 14,295, fo. 28^b.

„   Leonard, of Pinchbeck in Holland, co. Linc., confirmed 10 June 1632, by R. St. George.   Harl. MS. 1470, fo. 13, 200 ; Edward in Guil. 206, etc.

„   Nich^s, of Snelston, co. Derby, exemplified 15 Aug., 5 Ed. VI., 1551, by G. Dethick.   Harl. MS. 1441, fo. 63^b; Thos in Harl. MS. 1422, fo. 38 ; Q's Coll. Oxf. MS. 145, fo. 55 ; Harl. MS. 1093, fo. 49.

„   Nicholas, of Marshall, co. Derby, confirmed 4 Nov. 1582, by Flower.   MS. Ashm. 844, fo. 53, copy of grant, Bodleian Lib. ; Guil. 121 ; Reliquary, xxii., 50.

„   Nicholas, of Delphe in Holland, Serg^t-at-law, dated at Brussels 1 Feb. 1658-9, by Walker.   Harl. MS. 1172, fo. 72; Add. MSS. 14,293, fo. 99, and 14,924, fo. 33^b ; Her. Coll., fo. 31.

„   Sir Rich., of Lancashire, Kt., 6 July 1583, by G. Dethick.   Harl. MS. 1441, fo. 61^b; Q's Coll. Oxf. MS. 145, fo. 2.

„   Rich^d, of London, s. of John, of Browne Hall, co. Lanc., given at London 7 July, 26 Eliz., 1584, by G. Dethick.   Harl. MS. 1359, fo. 26 ; Add. MS. 14,295, fo. 16, or to his father, see preceding entry ; Harl. MS. 1422, fo. 38.

„   Richard, s. of Thomas, of Upton, Cheshire, crest 4 June 1605, by R. St. George. MS. Ashm. 858, fo. 142, copy of grant, Bodleian Lib. ; Add. MS. 14,295, fo. 79^b.

„   Sir Rich^d, Kt. and Bart., a clerk of the privy Council resident in the court of France; alteration of arms 24 July 1663, by Walker (letters patent 14 Feb. 1649-50 at Castle Elizabeth in the island of Jersey).   Harl. MS. 1172, fo. 64, 65 ; Add. MSS. 14,293, fo. 64, and 14,294, fo. 18^b ; Her. Coll., fo. 2, copy of grant, etc. ; Harl. MS. 6140, fo. 23.

„   Richard, of Mousley, Norfolk, 5 Aug. 1668.   Harl. MS. 1105, fo. 20^b ; Bysshe's Grants, 20, Her. Coll.

„   Robert, of Buckinghamshire, gent., granted 4 Oct., 4 Ed. VI., 1550, by G. Dethick.   Harl. MS. 1359, fo. 81 ; copy of grant, Q's Coll. Oxf. MSS. 37, fo. 27, and 39, fo. 24 ; Grants I., 290.

„   Robert, of London, gent., goldsmith, s. of John, of Bekensfield, Bucks, and of Alice his wife, d. and h. of Andrew Tillesworth of the same place, s. of Robt of B., 6 Feb. 1564-5, by Harvey, allowed at Visitn. 1574 by Cooke. Harl. MS. 1422, fo. 118^b and 113, Quarterly ; Harl. MS. 1359, fo. 11 ; Add. MS. 16,940, fo. 13^b ; Harl. MS. 5887, fo. 56.

„   Robert, ... 20 Oct. 1581, by Cooke.   Burke's Armory.

„   Thomas, of Thysthe (Osythe ?), Norfolk, coat and crest 20 Nov. 1544, by Barker, party per chevron or and az. a wyvern.   Harl. MS. 5846, fo. 10^b; Stowe MS. 692, fo. 23^b.   Add. MS. 14,298, fo. 37: volant or, langued gu., in the chief three estoyles az.   Crest: a hand charmeaux holding a fetter lock gu., the sleeve bendy or and az., undée, the cuff argt.   Harl. MS. 5887, fo. 9.   [See Burke's Armory, Browne of Diss.]

„   Thomas, of Harewode, Herts, gift 1559, 2 Q. Eliz. (Harvey's Grants).   Add. MS. 16,940, fo. 16^b.

„   Thomas, of London, gift 1561 (Harvey's Grants).   Add. MS. 16,940, fo. 33^b.

BROWNE, Thomas, of Browne's (*alias* East) Illersh, Devon, gift 1564, by Harvey, Clar. Add. MS. 16,940, fo. 35ᵇ.

„   Thomas, of Walsingham, Norfolk, 1632, by St. George. Burke's Armory.

„   Thomas, of Boston, s. of Thomas Gamaliel, s. of Thomas, s. of Thomas, of Fishtoft, s. of Alan, of Boston, all co. Linc., who died 1503, confirmed 16 June 1642, by Sir Wm. Le Neve, Clar. Grants II., 530ᵇ, 687.

„   ⎧Valentine, of Totteridge, Herts, Treasʳ of Ireland. 26 Sept. 1559, 1 Eliz.,
      ⎪   by Barthy. Butler, Ulster [K. of Arms]. Harl. MS. 1507, fo. 440,
      ⎪   copy of grant, Brit. Mus., confirmed 5 Dec. 1560, by G. Dethick,
      ⎪   Harl. MS. 1441, fo. 63, and of Croft in the Marsh, co. Linc., one of the
      ⎨   Auditors of the Exchequer *temp.* Q. Mary, and Treasʳ of H.M.'s town of
      ⎪   Berwick *temp.* Q. Eliz. Harl. MS. 1359, fo. 49ᵇ, for copy of grant, *see*
      ⎪   Q's Coll. Oxf. MSS. 38, fo. 72, and 39, fo. 94 and 122 ; another coat
      ⎪   (145, fo. 4ᵇ) : Grants I., 59 ; Le Neve's MS. 440.
      ⎪Valentine, of Totteridge, also 24 April 1561, by L. Dalton, Norr. Add.
      ⎩   MS. 17,506, fo. 38ᵇ ; Harl. MS. 1359, fo. 49ᵇ.

„   William, London, s. and h. of John, also of London, Kt. Harl. MS. 5846, fo. 8ᵇ, arms, per pale gu. and sa., on a chev. engrailed arg. between 3 leopards' faces or, as many escallops az., for Browne, *temp.* H. VIII. ; Add. MS. 26,702, fo. 77, crest, a crane az., winged and collared gemel gu. ; Harl. MS. 1422, fo. 38 ; Add. MS. 26,702, fo. 77, No. 1 ; Stowe MS. 692, fo. 21ᵇ ; Barker's Grants.

„   (William, of London, Stowe MS. 692), arms, arg., on a chev. gu. between 3 cranes az., membered of the 2ⁿᵈ, as many trefoils slipped argt. ; crest in Add MS. 26,702, fo. 77, No. 2, a crane's head and neck per pale az. and gu. between 2 sprigs of broom stalked vert. Harl. MS. 5846, fo. 5ᵇ ; Stowe MS. 692, fo. 23 ; Add. MS. 26,702, fo. 77, 2 ; Barker's Grants.

„   William, per pale indented arg. and or, over all a chev. between iii escallops gu., impaling gu., a chev. between three luces ayrantz [haurient] argt. Stowe MS. 692, fo. 21ᵇ ; Barker's Grants.

„   Wistan, Knt. (in Spain ?), augmentation (?) 15 Sept. 1511, at Burgae, by letter from Ferdinand, King of Aragan. MSS. Ashm. 858, fo. 41, and 834, i., fo. 30ᵇ ; Wolstan in Harl. MS. 4900, fo. 29, copy of grant, Bodleian Lib., by T. Wriothesley, Gart., and Benolte.

„   Sir William, Bt., 1699, came from Dantzic. Harl. MS. 6179, fo. 170ᶜ, " Isopose a pattnt."

BROWN BAKERS of the City of London, confirmed to the Wardens, assistants and commonalties of the Misterey and Company of . . . ., 28 June 1569, by G. Dethick. Harl. MS. 1441, fo. 78ᵇ ; 1572 in Q's Coll. Oxf. MS. 145, fo. 29.

BROWNELL, Mary, d. and h. of John, of Derby, by Sir Wm. Dugdale and St. George, Clar. Harl. MS. 6834, fo. 178 ; Grants III., fo. 185, and Dugdale's Grants, fo. 20 ; wife of Sir Robt Dacres of Clerkenweil, Kt., 8 Feb. 1682-3 ; *see* H. Dacres' grant, Le Neve's MS. 459.

BROWNHILL, ..., of London, merchᵗ, 6 Dec. 1662, by . . . . Add. MS. 14,293, fo. 12.

BROWNLOWE, ⎧Richard, of Kirkby Underwood, co. Linc., and of the Inner Temple,
            ⎪   prothonotary Court of Com. Pleas, crest 20 June 1593, by Cooke,
            ⎪   Clar., Quarterly, a patent of the first coat and crest. Harl. MS.
            ⎪   1359, fo. 121 ; Grants II., 504 ; Cat. Her. Exhib. Soc. Antiq.,
            ⎨   p. 70.
BROWNLOW,   ⎪Richard, of the Inner Temple, confirmation 12 Oct. 1602. Add.
            ⎪   MS. 12,225, fo. 19ᵇ, or, an inescocheon with an orle of 8 martlets
            ⎪   sa., by Segar, Norr. ; Harl. MS. 6140, fo. 77ᵇ ; Cat. Her. Exhib.
            ⎩   Soc. Antiq., p. 71 ; Grants II., 508, Quarterly, with Panelly.

BROXHOLME, John, now of the city of London, s. of John, of Oresby, co. Linc., crest 23 Jan. 1580-1, by G. Dethick. Harl. MSS. 1441, fo. 101, and 1442,

fo. 22 ; Le Neve's MS. 258ᵃ ; Add. MS. 17,506, fo. 33ᵇ, and Q's Coll. Oxf.
MS. 145, fo. 51.

BRUDENELL, Edmond, of Deane, Northts., gent., crest 5 May 1553, by T. Hawley.
Add. MS. 16,940, fo. 15 ; for copy of grant, see·Q's Coll. Oxf. MS. 38,
fo. 59 ; Harl. MS. 5887, fo. 15ᵇ.

BRUGE, John, of Dymmock, co. Glouc., 19 Dec. 1520, by T. Wriothesley, Gart.,
and Benolt, Clar. Add. MS. 6297, fo. 139.

BRUDGES, or BRUGES, ..., crest . . . ., by Barker. Harl. MS. 5846, fo. 6ᵇ ; Stowe
MS. 694, fo. 23.

BRUGES, ..., of London, Quarterly coat, patent 1612, by Camden. Harl. MSS.
1422, fo. 110, and 6095, fo. 26.

BRUGGES, Ludovic de, of Gruthuse, Prince of Steenhuse, etc., cr. Earl of Winchester, arms by letters patent, 23 Nov. 1472, 12 Ed. IV., P. R. 12 Ed. IV.,
Pt. I., m. 11, copy of grant, Brit. Mus. Stowe MS. 840, fo. 61 ; Harl. MS.
980, fo. 170.

BRUGGFORD, John, grant in French 29 Aug. 1415 (3 Hen. V.) at Harfleur, by
Edward, Duke of York, Staffordsh. Visitation 1614, fo. 76 ; MS. Ashm.
858, fo. 94, copy of grant, Bodleian Lib.

BRUNCKARD, Sir William, of Westminster, 7 Oct. 1576, by Cooke, Clar. Add. MS.
4966, fo. 45.

BRUMSTEAD, Thomas, Middx., and Clements Inn, gent., grant Nov. 1666, by Sir
E. Walker, Gart. Harl. MS. 1441, fo. 132, bd. [buried ?] 15 Jan. 1666-7.

BRUNSELL, ⎰ Henry, D.C.L., rector of Claworth, Notts, preb. of Ely and Southwell,
⎪ and . . . . Reliquary, xxii., 244,
⎨ Samuel, D.D., sons of Oliver Brunsell, grant 10 March, 13 Chas. II.,
⎪ 1660-1, by Walker. MS. Ashm. 858, fo. 155, 156, copy of grant,
⎱ Bodleian Lib. ; Harl. MS. 6179, fo. 80ᵇ.

BRUNSKILL, Ambrose, of London, 1645, by Browne, Bluemantle [?]. Stowe MS.
703, fo. 71.

BRUTON, William, of Exeter, Devon, confirmed Feb. 1639-40, by Borough. Harl.
MSS. 1105, fo. 56ᵇ, and 1441, fo. 57 ; Add. MS. 26,702, fo. 92ᵇ ; Guil. 384.

BRYAN, ... Harl. MS. 1105, fo. 38 and 39ᵇ, ? by Bysshe (see Basset), argt.,
three piles meeting in base argt. within a bordure pellettée sa. ; crest, a
griffin's head pellettée sa.

  ,,   William, of Bullingbroke, co. Linc., crest 10 April 1561, by W. Harvey, Clar.
Add. MSS. 17,506, fo. 38, and 16,940, fo. 39.

BRYDALL, John, batchʳ-at-law and sec. to Sir Harbottle Grimston, Knt. and Bart.,
Mʳ of the Rolls, and late Sec. to Rt. Hon. Sir Chaˢ Cæsar and ye
Lᵈ Colepeper, former Masters of the Rolls ; Capt. and Capt.-lieut. of ye Co.
of foote comᵈ by Edward, Lord Littleton, Ld. Keeper, etc. ; arms and
augmentation 1 Aug. 1661, by Walker. Harl. MS. 1172, fo. 50 ; Add.
MSS. 14,293, fo. 29, and 14,294, fo. 3.

  ,,   Walter, Clerk and yeoman of H.M.'s Jewel House, late Lieut. of a troop of
horse in Duke of York's regᵗ comᵈ by Col. Chas. Cavendish, 21 June
1669, by Walker. Harl. MS. 1172, fo. 68 ; Add. MSS. 14,293, fo. 77,
and 14,294, fo. 23 ; Guil. 88, copy of grant.

BRYDGE, John, of Salop . . . . 2 Nov. 1552, by Hawley (?). Add. MS. 16,940,
fo. 206.

BRYGANTYNE, John, of Portsmouth, Hants, coat and crest, by Barker. Harl. MS.
5846, fo. 12ᵇ ; Stowe MS. 692, fo. 12, 12ᵇ ; Harl. MS. 6179, fo. 16.

BRYGANTINE, John, of Tenterden, Kent, 1 Jan. 1550-51. Add. MS. 16,940,
fo. 204ᵇ. (? These two the same.)

BUBB, Thomas, of Bristol, Sheriff of the city 1653, 5 Nov. 1563, by Bysshe. Harl.
MS. 6832, fo. 413 ; Add. MS. 26,758, fo. 16.

BUCK (Thomas and John), esqnire bedells of the Univ. of Cambridge, 2 Oct. 1639,
by Borough, Gart. Harl. MSS. 1105, fo. 56ᵇ, and 1441, fo. 58 ; Add.
MSS. 26,702, fo. 92, and 5822, fo. 23.

BUCKE, James, s. of Matthew, late of Winterborne, co. Glouc., Esq., augmentation 17 July 1685, by W. Roberts, Ulster [K. of A.]. Harl. MS. 4108, fo. 56ᵇ, copy of grant, Brit. Mus. ; Guil. 394 ; 1680 in Add. MS. 14,293, fo. 15ᵇ.

BUCK, John, of Hawlish or Hawbeck, als Hanby Grange, co. Linc., 1592, by Cooke. Harl. MS. 1359, fo. 106 ; Add. MS. 4966, fo. 93.

BUCKE, Thomas, of Hamshey, etc., Hants, gent., crest 26 Aug. 1583, 25 Eliz., by G. Dethick. Harl. MS. 1441, fo. 67ᵇ, and Q's Coll. Oxf. MS. 145, fo. 11ᵇ.

BUCKE, Thomas, of Hants, granted, ? confirmed, Oct. 1586, by W. Dethick. Stowe MS. 676, fo. 65, copy of grant, and Q's Coll. Oxf. MS. 37, fo. 90, 91.

BUCKERIDGE, John, Bp. of Worcester (1611), by Camden. Harl. MSS. 1422, fo. 35ᵇ, and 6095, fo. 14ᵇ.

BUCKLAND, Richard, of Shepton Mallet, Som¹, coat and crest, by Barker. Harl. MS. 5846, fo. 8 ; Stowe MS. 692, fo. 22 ; Harl. MS. 6179, fo. 16.

BUCKLANDE, Richard, of London, gift . . . . 1560. Harvey's Grants ; Add. MS. 16,940, fo. 22ᵇ.

BUCKLE, Sir Cuthbert, Lord Mayor of London, s. of Christopher, of Brough, Westmorland, gent., confirmed 29 Jan. 1579-80, by Cooke. Harl. MS. 1359, fo. 121, and Grants I., 221 ; Harl. MS. 1561, fo. 243.

„ Isabel, of co. Warwick, wife of Sir John Ayliffe of Brinkworth, Wilts, Knt., Sheriff of London, 1556-7, by Hawley. Add. MS. 16,940, fo. 208ᵇ ; Harl. MS. 1443, fo. 16ᵇ.

BUCLER (BUCKLER), Walter, of Cawswey, Dorset, Esq., coat and crest, by Barker. Harl. MS. 5846, fo. 11 ; Stowe MS. 692, fo. 23ᵇ ; Harl. MS. 6179, fo. 16.

BUCKLEY, Henry, of Barling's Abbey, granted 4 Dec. 1564, by G. Dethick, Gart. Stowe MS. 676, fo. 29, copy of grant, Q's Coll. Oxf. MS. 37, fo. 43 ; Grants I., 288.

BUCKMINSTER, William, of Peterborough (s. of Richᵈ, s. of John, of Peterborough), and to Thomas, of London, clerk, eld. s. (or 2nd s.) of said John ; crest 24 March 1578-9, by G. Dethick. 8 May in Harl. MS. 1441, fo. 89ᵇ. Guil. 276 ; MS. Ashm. 834, fo. 20, copy of grant, Bodleian Lib. Confirmed to (in Harl. MS. 1441, fo. 89ᵇ) Wᵐ Buckminster, eld. s. of John, of Peterborough, gent., and to Thomas, of London, clerk, 2nd s. of said John, of P., 24 March 1578-9. Harl. MS. 5823, fo. 47ᵇ: Wm., eld. s. of Richard, eld. s. of John, and Thomas, as above. Q's Coll. Oxf. MS. 145, fo. 47, 47ᵇ; Harl. MS. 5887, fo. 39 ; copy of grant, Harl. MS. 1116, fo. 49.

BUDDEN, see BUTTON, 1690.

BUFKIN, Leven, of Goore Court, par. of Ottham, Kent, Esq., s. of Ralph, of the same, arms confirmed and crest given 22 Feb. 1576, 19 Eliz., by Cooke. Harl. MS. 1359, fo. 120ᵇ.

„ Henry, Otham, Kent, certif. 3 April, 1644. Berry's Armory.

BUGGEN or BUGGIN, Edward, of London, gent., o. s. of William, late of co. Staff., confirmed under the hand and seale of Dalton, Norr., 4 July 1559, 1 Eliz. Harl. MS. 1359, fo. 50, confirmed 10 April 1562, by (Harvey) ; Add. MS. 16,490, fo. 27ᵇ; Grants II., 511.

BUGGINS, Edward, M.P., etc. (s. of William, of co. Staff., gent.), one of the cursitors of the High Court of Chancery, and principal of the Company of Cursitors ; a clerk of the Exchequer ; clerk controller of her Majesties pastimes and revelles, and also of Tents and pavilions ; one of H.M. Commissioners for the Sewers in the co. of Middx., and one of the burgesses in the presᵗ parliament ; grant by Dalton and confirmed by Harvey ; confirmed 20 April 1578, by Cooke. Guil. 270 ; MSS. Ashm. 834, fo. 19, and 844, fo. 61 ; copy of grant, Bodleian Lib.

BUKFOLDE, Hy., of Bukfolde, Sussex, crest . . . . 1562. Add. MS. 16,940, fo. 39 ; (Harvey's Grants).

BULBECK, John, of Kingston, sen^r . . . . confirmed 24 April 1559, by Harvey. Guil. 180 ; Add. MS. 16,940, fo. 46^b.

BULL, Edward, ... Norfolk, confirmed 1553. Add. MS. 16,940, fo. 10^b; (Harvey's Grants).

,,   John, of London, gift 1561. Add. MS. 16,940, fo. 18 : (Harvey's Grants).

,,   { John, of London, ... 1588, by Cooke. Harl. MSS. 1359, fo. 95, and 1422, fo. 88^b.

,,   { Margaret, dau. of J. Bull, in Stowe MS. 670, fo. 30^b, with crest.

,,   Randall, of London, clockmaker to Q. Eliz. and K. Jas., 17 July 1615, by Segar. Add. MS. 12,225, fo. 20 ; Guil. 152 ; Harl. MS. 6140, fo. 61^b; Grants I., 375.

,,   Stephen, of Gillingham, Kent, Master Gunner of England, 20 Aug. 1601, by W. Camden. Grants II., 580, sable, a chevron betw. 3 Cannon erect, or, given by Wm Segar, Norroy King of Arms. Harl. MS. 5887, fo. 64^b.

BULLEYN, Dominick, of Venice, coat and crest . . . . by Barker. Harl. MS. 5846, fo. 4^b.

BULLOCK, Edward, of Loftes in Much Totham, Essex, s. of Edward, s. of John, of Wyborough, Essex, confirmed 9 Feb. 1602-3, by Camden. Harl. MS. 1359, fo. 24^b ; Add. MS. 14,259, fo. 111 ; Grants I., 295 ; Le Neve's MS. 458.

,,   George, has arms granted to Rowland Johnson, whom see. (Add. Ch. 19,882.)

,,   Hugh, of London, s. of Gilbert, of co. Lanc., 20 Aug. (42 Q. Eliz.) 1600, by Camden. Stowe MS. 677, fo. 15 ; Cott. MS. Faust. E. I., fo. 7^b, for copy of grant, Brit. Mus. ; Gilbert in Harl. MSS. 1422, fo. 17^b, and 6095, fo. 1^b; Guil. 381.

,,   John, of Derby, co. Derby, crest 20 June 1609, by R. St. George. MS. Ashm. 858, fo. 155, copy of grant, Bodleian Lib. ; Add. MS. 14,295, fo. 80^b; Reliquary, xxii., 49.

BULMER, W^m, of Uppislaud (? Hoppyland), Yorks, gent., s. of Rauff, of Wilton, Yorks, Kt., 22 March 1520-1, by T. Wriothesley and Wall, Norr. Harl. MS. 1052, ult. (212), copy of grant, Brit. Mus.

BULTEEL, John, sec. to the Lord High Chancellor, crest 10 Jan. 1660-1, by Walker. Misc. Gen. et Her., N. S., iv., 421, copy of grant, Brit. Mus. ; Quarterly, with Visitation coat or singly.

BULTON, John, of Bulton, co. Pemb., gent., granted 1 July, 2 and 3 Ph. and M., 1556, by G. Dethick. Harl. MS. 1359, fo. 67^b ; copy of grant, Q's Coll. Oxf. MS. 39, fo. 66.

BUNBURY, Henry (of Bunbury, Cheshire), confirmed 24 June 1602, by Segar. MS. Ashm. 858, fo. 140, copy of grant, Bodleian Lib.

BUNCE, James, of Otterden, Kent, s. of John, s. of John, 1589, by Cooke. Harl. MS. 1115, fo. 18 ; Q's Coll. Oxf. MS. 146, fo. 469.

BUNCLEY, Sir Geo., a Col. of Horse, late Lieut. Gov. City of Oxford, at Oxford, 1 April 1645, by Walker, Gart. Add. MS. 14,294, fo. 31^b ; Her. Coll., fo. 28.

BUNGEY, John, of Mystole, Kent, 14 Oct. 1589, by Cooke. Harl. MSS. 1359, fo. 104^b, 1422, fo. 95, and 1561, fo. 161 ; Add. MS. 4966, fo. 84.

BUNNING, Richard, Denton, Norfolk, 24 Jan. 1664-5, by Bysshe, Clar. Bysshe's Grants, Her. Coll., 33 ; called Dunning in Harl. MS. 1105, fo. 40.

BURDETT, Francis, of Burthwait, Yorks, at London, 20 Nov. 1599, by W. Dethick and Camden. Surtees Soc., xli., 44, copy of grant, Brit. Mus.

,,   George, London, Quarterly, etc., by Cooke. Stowe MS. 670, fo. 8.

BURGESS, John, of Crendon, co. Linc., s. of John, of Catle Bilham, etc., Jan. 1631-2, by Segar. Add. MS. 12,225, fo. 20 ; Guil. 76 ; Harl. MS. 1441, fo. 154.

,,   William and John, of Westport, Dorset, s. of John, s. of John, of Stamford, Berks, confirmed or granted 11 April 1614, by Camden. Guil. 413 ; Harl. MS. 1441, fo. 113.

BURGHILL, Francis, Mowbray Herald, augmentation 6 Oct. 1679, by Sir Wm. Dugdale and H. St. George, Norr. Stowe MS. 714, fo. 157 ; Grants III., 114[b], copy of grant, Brit. Mus.

BURGOYNE, John, of Sutton, Beds, coat .... by Barker. Harl. MS. 5846, fo. 7[b] ; Stowe MS. 692, fo. 22.

BURLEY, William, Deverell, Longbridge, Wilts, crest 1 May 1546, by W. Hawley, Clar. Harl. MS. 1544, fo. 83[b] ; Add. MSS. 16,940, fo. 200[b], and 7098, fo. 77[b]. See BORLEY.

BURLTON, Humphrey, of Wribnall, co. Worc., at Oxford, augmentation 5 June 1646, by Walker, Gart. MS. Ashm. 858, fo. 52, 53, copy of grant, Bodleian Lib.

„ Humphrey, of Ribenhall [Wribbenhall ?], co. Worc., royalist, dated at London, 30 June 1660, by Walker. Harl. MS. 1172, fo. 71[b] ; Add. MSS. 14,293, fo. 101, and 14,294, fo. 34[b] ; Caius Coll. Camb. MS. 528, fo. 1 ; copy of grant, Her. Coll., fo. 31.

BURLZ, Thomas, of Depedene, Suffolk, gent., given 4 April 1597, 39 Q. Eliz., by R. Lee. Harl. MS. 1359, fo. 18[b], 21[h] ; Add. MS. 14,295, fo. 11[b].

BURNABY, Richard, of Watford, Northants, crest 27 Oct. 1554, by Hawley. Harl. MS. 1115, fo. 33 ; Hills, J. R., Market Harbro', p. 333 ; 21st Oct. in Add. MS. 16,940, fo. 207 ; original in the possession of R. A. Dyott, 28 Goldington Road, Bedford, in 1902.

BURNEBY, W[m], of Gt. Saxham, Essex, gift .... 1559 (Harvey's Grants). Add. MS. 16,940, fo. 45[b].

BURNELL, ..., of Norfolk, ..., by Segar. Add. MS. 12,225, fo. 20[b], parti per fess .... in chief a barque, sailes trussed up and hoisted to the main top : in base a syren.

BURNETT, Thomas, Wood Dalling, Kent, s. of Duncan, late of Norwich, D[r] of phys., 5th s. of Alex[r], of Leys, Scotland, certified 30 June 1640, by W. Le Neve, Clar. Visitn. Norfk.

BURRELL, ..., Herts, by T. Wriothesley, Gart., and Benolte, Clar. Harl. MS. 6086, fo. 91[b].

BURRINGTON, John, co. Devon, ..., by Wriothesley, Gart. Harl. MS. 1422, fo. 14.

BURROUGH, Thomas, Wyckham Crook, Suff., 20 June 1586 (20 Eliz.), by Ro. Cooke. Le Neve's MS. 256 ; Add. MS. 4966, fo. 53 ; Stowe MS. 670, fo. 58 ; Grants I., 50.

BURSTON, Richard, of Shorne, Kent, 19 June 1573, by Cooke. Harl. MS. 1359, fo. 122.

BURTHOGGE, Richard, of Bowdon, Devon, J.P., 6 April 1688, by [Sir] T. [St. George], Gart., and H. St. George, Clar. Harl. MS. 6834, fo. 49* and 60[b] ; Grants, 415 [? 465].

BURTON, ⎰ Bartholomew, rec[r] of Excise duties, Westminster, and his bro[r]
⎱ William, also of Westminster, 22 July 1696, by T. St. George, Gart. and Clar. Grants IV., fo. 228.

„ Francis, Capt. of a horse compy. of the auxiliary forces in the City of London, 26 Jan. 1660-1, by Walker, Gart. Her. Coll., 37.

„ Humphrey, Lindley, co. Leic., and Kingsbury and Coventry, co. Warwick, 27 Nov. 1683, by Sir W. Dugdale, Gart., and St. G[eorge], Clar. Harl. MS. 6834, fo. 178 ; Grants III., fo. 171-3.

„ John, of Castell Bourne, Sussex, 31 Aug. 1570, 12 Q. Eliz., by Cooke, Quarterly coat. Harl. MSS. 1359, fo. 115[b], of Essex in 1422, fo. 121 ; Stowe MS. 670, fo. 69 ; Harl. MS. 5887, fo. 26[b] ; Add. MS. 4966, fo. 96.

„ Nicholas, of Ingelsthorpe, co. Derby, Esq., 6 March 1581-2, by G. Dethick. Harl. MS. 1441, fo. 102[b], and Q's Coll. Oxf. MS. 145, fo. 53[b] ; Stowe MS. 703, fo. 57.

„ Sir Robert, of "the Courte" (City) of Yorke, 22 May 1478, by John Writhe, Norr. Harl. MS. 6140, fo. 74 ; Stowe MS. 677, fo. 50 ; Add. MS. 14,293, fo. 123 ; Burke's Commoners, iv., 265, copy of grant, Brit. Mus.

BURWELL, ... of Woodbridge, Suff.; Quarterly: 1 and 4, or, a chev. erm. betw. three burdock leaves erect ppr., a cresc[t] for diff.; quartering 2, Alvert, and 3, Pickman, by Segar. Add. MS. 12,225, fo. 20[b]; Harl. MSS. 1085, fo. 22[b], and 6140, fo. 78.

  ,,   William, of Sutton, Suff., gent., grant March 1587, by W. Dethick. Stowe MS. 676, fo. 70[b], copy of grant: Q's Coll. Oxf. MS. 37, fo. 101.

BURY, Gilbert, of Ashmell, Rutland, confirmed 1564 (Harvey's Grants). Add. MS. 16,940, fo. 21[b].

BURYE, Humfrey, of Hearne, Beds, gent., quarterly coat subscribed in 1555, by Harvey. Harl. MSS. 1422, fo. 117, and 1359, fo. 31[b]; 1566 in Add. MS. 14,295, fo. 27.

BURY ST. EDMUND'S, Suffolk, the town of, 29 Nov. 1606, by Camden. Harl. MS. 1422, fo. 19[b], and 6095, fo. 6; Cat. Her. Exhib. Soc. of Antiq.

BUSBRIDGE, ... Kent, attested . . . . 1588, by Cooke, Clar. Harl. MS. 6164, fo. 8.

BUSBY, John, of Addington, Bucks, by R. St. George, Clar. Harl. MS. 6140, fo. 23[b].

BUSHE ⎰ John, of Dulton, Wilts, coat and crest . . . . by Barker. Harl. MS. 5846, fo. 12; Stowe MS. 692, fo. 23[b].
  ,, ⎱ John, of Dawlton, Wilts, confirmed ? Aug. 1560 (Harvey's Grants). Add. MS. 16,940, fo. 20[b], no blason.

  ,,   Paul, Bp. of Bristol (1542—53). MS. Ashm. 858, fo. 17, 7 July 1542, by Barker. Copy of grant, Bodleian Lib.; Stowe MS. 692, fo. 23[b]; Memo. in Le Neve's MS., fo. 428.

BUSHORE, John Michael, s. of Michael, "burghermaster of Lyndas," Germany, confirmed 18 May 1588, by W. Dethick. Stowe MS. 676, fo. 73[b]; copy of grant in Latin, Q's Coll. Oxf. MS. 37, fo. 106.

BUTLER, Anthony, Colt or Coates, co. Linc., confirmed . . . . (Harvey's Grants). Add. MS. 16,940, fo. 12 . . . .; Harl. MS. 1116, fo. 56[b].

  ,, ... wife of John Tindall, whom see.

BUTTELER, George, of Fen Drayton, co. Cambr., gent., Quarterly, arms and crest allowed at the Visitation of Cambr. 1575, by Cooke. Harl. MSS. 1359, fo. 86, and 1422, fo. 119; Stowe MS. 670, fo. 73; Add. MS. 4966, fo. 94.

BUTTLER (of London), Henry, s. of Thomas, s. of John, of Wheldrakes, Yorks, Esq., s. of Thomas, s. of John, s. of John, in co. York, Esq., 20 Oct. 1591, 33 Q. Eliz., by Cooke. (2nd s. in) Harl. MSS. 1422, fo. 12[b], and 1359, fo. 94; Add. MS. 14,295, fo. 45.

BUTLER, John, of Kirkland, co. Lanc., gent., crest granted Dec. 1560 (3 Eliz.), by Dalton, Norr. Harl. MS. 1359, fo. 49; Gregson's Fragments, 3rd ed., p. 267.

  ,,   John, of Hanley . . . . Aug. 1606, by Camden. Harl. MSS. 1422, fo. 19[b], and 6095, fo. 6.

BUTTLER, John, Mayor of Exeter, J.P. and Alderm. of same city, dep. lieut. of the militia for the city and county, etc., for royalist services, 1 March 1663-4, by Walker. Harl. MS. 1172, fo. 58; Add. MSS. 14,293, fo. 53, and 14,294, fo. 13, copy of grant.

BUTLER, Lady Margaret, dau. of Richard, of London, grocer, wife to the late Sir Edward North of Sartelage, co. Cambr., 1 Feb. 1564-5, by G. Dethick. Harl. MS. 1441, fo. 66[b]; Misc. Gen. et Her., 3rd S., vol. ii., p. 193, copy of grant, Brit. Mus.; Q's Coll. Oxf. MS. 145, fo. 9[b], and Grants II., 652; Stowe MS. 692, fo. 71.

  ,,   Thomas, of Beansay [Bewsey], co. Lanc. (called Baron of Warrington), s. and h., etc., crest 20 May 1561, by Dalton, Norr. Harl. MS. 1359, fo. 50; Add. MS. 14,295, fo. 77, a knight, and grant of crest: quarterly coat.

BUTMAN, Henry als Bruer, of Scoolencis, France, confirmed 20 Jan. 1583-4, by G. Dethick. Stowe MS. 676, fo. 63[b], copy of grant, and Q's Coll. Oxf. MS. 37, fo. 88, in Latin.

BUTTES, Edmond, of Fulham, Middx., confirmed 1561 (Harvey's Grants). Add. MS. 16,940, fo. 49.

BUTTON, John, *see* BULTON.

,, W^m, of Alton, Wilts, 10 Oct. 1553, ? Hawley, confirmed by Cooke, Clar. Harl. MS. 1422, fo. 123^b; Add. MS. 16,940, fo. 207.

BUTTON or BUDDEN, ..., 10 Dec. 1690. Edmondson and Berry's Armory, ? not an English grant; not ? Grants IV., 67 : ermine, a fesse gu. betw. three crosses bottonnée az.

BUTTRIE, Clement, a!s Matanye, of Lawrence Marston, Northants, 27 Nov. 1580, by Cooke, Clar. Harl. MS. 1359, fo. 122.

BUTTS, William, achievement certified by W. Camden, Clar. Grants II., 598, Quarterly : Butts, Cockett, Walden, Owgan, Kirkle, Staunton, Harford, Malyfant, Roche, Milborne, Joyce and Butts.

BYDE, Edwd, of Lincoln's Inn, 2nd s. of John, Alderm. of London, 1 April 1666. Harl. MS. 1105, fo. 42, by Bysshe, Clar.; Harl. MS. 6179, fo. 25^b.

,, John, of London, Alderm., confirmed .... 1648, by Bysshe. Add. MS. 26,758, fo. 16 ; Stowe MS. 677, fo. 27^b ; Harl. MS. 6832, fo. 413.

BYDE, Col. Sir Thomas, of Ware Park, Herts, and a Justice of peace (s. of John, late Alderm. of City of London), confirmation of coat borne by his father; grant of new coat 3 May 1669, by Walker. Add. MS. 14,294, fo. 30.

BYERLEY, William, of Gray's Inn, 1634, by R. St. George, Clar. Harl. MSS. 1105, fo. 8^b, and 1105, fo. 13.

BYNG, Robert, of Wrotham, Kent, 11 June 1574, by Cooke. Harl. MSS. 1359, fo. 89, and 1422, fo. 51^b ; Add. MS. 4966, fo. 34 ; Grants I., 112. *See also* HILL for Quartering.

BYRDE, Thos., of Over Lockshow, s. of Robert, s. of Thos.; crest 1611, by R. St. George, Norr. Harl. MS. 1422, fo. 48^b.

BYRKBYE, *see* BIRKBY.

BYSSE, James, of Batcombe, Som^t, 1591, by Cooke. Harl. MSS. 1422, fo. 23^b, and 1359, fo. 121.

BUXTON, Robert, Tybenham, Esq., s. of John, s. of Robert, s. of John, 13 May 1574, by Ro. Cooke. Grants II., 530.

C

CARNBELL, Thomas, citizen and alderm. of London (sheriff 1619-20), grant 20 Sept. 1600, by W. Dethick, Gart., and W. Camden, Clar. Q's Coll. Oxf. MS. 38, fo. 85 ; copy of grant, Add. MS. 24,753, fo. 124 ; Stowe MS. 676, fo. 133 ; Caius Coll. Camb. MS. 551, fo. 30^b ; Harl. MS. 1441, fo. 148^b.

CADE, W^m, of Wylesden, Middx., gift 1559 (Harvey's Grants). Add. MS. 16,940, fo. 14^b.

CADELL (*see* CORDELL), John, of Long Melford, patent 20 Feb., 2 Ed. VI., by Hawley, Clar. Harl. MS. 6140, fo. 60.

CADIMAN, Thomas, D^r of Physick to the Queen, s. of Thomas of Rygate, Norfolk, exemplification 16 Dec. 1633, by Segar. Add. MS. 12,225, fo. 21 ; Guil. 132 ; Harl. MS. 6140, fo. 78^b.

CADY, John, Gt. Ellingham, Norfolk, 1 Oct. 1575, by Cooke. Harl. MS. 1085, fo. 50^b.

CAERLION, Louis, Kt. and M.D., (on St Sampson's Day) 28 July 1491, by J. Writhe, Gart. Harl. MS. 1507, fo. 401 ; copy of grant in French, Q's Coll. Oxf. MS. 38 ; for trick see Le Neve's MS. 401, 416.

CÆSAR, Julins, 1587. *See* DALMARIUS.

CAGE, Nicholas, gent., confirmation of Cage, Quartering Haynes, *circa* 1605, by Camden. Harl. MSS. 1422, fo. 109, 6095, fo. 19^b, and 5887, fo. 16^b.

,, William, an outer barrister of Lincoln's Inn, and to the sons of his father Robert of Cambridge and London, s. of Richard of Pakenham, Suff., altered 1 March 1624-5, by R. St. George. Harl. MSS. 1470, fo. 43, 162, and 1507, fo. 413 ; Guil. 384 ; copy of grant, Q's Coll. Oxf. MS. 38, fo. 139 ; Le Neve's MS. 413.

CAIUS, John, doctor of physick, s. of Robert of Yorkshire, founder of Gonville and Caius Coll. in Cambridge, 2 Jan. 1560-1, by Dalton, Norr. Harl. MS. 1359, fo. 48 ; Her. and Geneal., i., 81 ; copy of grant, Brit. Mus. ; Cat. Her. Exhib. Soc. Antiq. 65.

CAIUS COLLEGE, CAMBRIDGE, 1560-1, by Dalton. *See* grant to D'r Caius ; *see also* Gonville and Caius MS. Her. and Geneal., i., 81 and 120 ; copy of grant, Brit. Mus.

CALDICOT, Clement, s. of W'm of Melbourne, co. Camb., confirmed by Segar and R. S'.t George. Add. MS. 12,225, fo. 21 ; Guil. 386 and C. 27, fo. 129'b ; Harl. MS. 1406, fo. 11'b, copy of grant ; Stowe MS. 716, fo. 55 ; Her. Coll.

    ,,   Mathias, of co. Camb., certif. by R. St. George, Norr., Stowe MS. 716, fo. 55 (neither date nor king, Add. MS. 14,295, fo. 55), and Segar, Gart. Harl. MS. 6164, fo. 83, copy of grant, Brit. Mus., and in Harl. MS. 1406, fo. 11'b.

CALDWALL (Robert), of London, haberdasher, by Segar. [Harl. MS.] 1422, fo. 16'b, az., a cross pattée fitché between 8 stars in orle, or ; Add. MS. 12,225, fo. 21'b (? the arms of Mr. Talbot of Grafton, co. Worc., Harl. MS. 1422, fo. 16'b) ; Robert in Harl. MS. 1422, fo. 16'b, and 2 alterations.

    ,,   Ralph, of Alston, co. Staff., by Wriothesley, Gart., and Benolt, Clar. Harl. MS. 1422, fo. 16'b.

CALLEY, Ralph, of Highway, Wilts, gent., 13 Nov. 1579, by G. Dethick, Gart. Harl. MS. 1441, fo. 90'b, and Q's Coll. Oxf. MS. 145, fo. 48'b ; Harl. MS. 5887, fo. 38.

CALLOWE, Anth'y, of Micheldean, co. Glouc., ..., by R. St. George, Clar. Add. MS. 14,295, fo. 93.

CALTON, John, deputie warden of the Mint, 1586, by Cooke. Stowe MS. 670, fo. 20.

    ,,   Henry, of Babraham, co. Cambr., granted 25 Jan. 1567-8, by G. Dethick, Gart., and Cooke and Flower. Add. MS. 17,506, fo. 376, " passed by the whole office "; Guil. 299.

CALVERT, ..., of Lancashire, by W. Dethicke, Camden, and Segar, sa., on an inescocheon between 8 owls in orle, 3 guttés (or drops) sable. Add. MS. 12,225, fo. 21'b.

    ,,   Sir George, Knt., one of H.M. principal Secretaries of State, 1621, by R. St. George. fo. 62 ; C. 13 [Visit. Yorksh., 1612], fo. 37.

    ,,   Sir George, Baron Baltimore, of Baltimore in Ireland, and of the Privy Council to K. James there, 1624, grant of supporters, by Segar. Add. MS. 12,225, fo. 22.

CAMBORNE, als PAYNTER, Wm., of Deverell, Wilts, in the par. of Gwinion, Cornw., gent., confirmed 22 July 1569, by G. Dethick, Cooke and Flower. Harl. MS. 1441, fo. 73'h ; Stowe MS. 676, fo. 33, copy of grant, see Q's Coll. Oxf. MS. 37, fo. 49, and MS. 143, fo. 20 ; Harl. MS. 1105, fo. 8'b ; Genealogical Mag., ii., 125.

CAMBRIDGE, Regius professors, Physic, Law, Divinity, Hebrew and Greek, 13 Nov. 1590, by Ro. Cooke, Clar. *See* Harl. Soc., vol. xli., Visit'n Camb., and Archæol. Journal, vol. 51.

CAMBRIDGE UNIVERSITY, 9 June 1573, Soc. of Antiq. Cat. Her. Exhib., by Cooke, Clar.

CAMBRIDGE TOWN, 7 June 1575, by Cooke, Clar. Add. MS. 5822.

CAMPE, ..., London, assigned 2 July 1604, by Camden. Guil. 268 ; Stowe MS. 606, fo. 25'b.

CAMPION, Henry, of London, s. and h. of Rich'd, of Heny, Essex, gent., quarters reversed in Harl. MS. 5887, fo. 90, crest 19 Nov. 1573, by Cooke. Stowe MS. 714, fo. 124'b ; Harl. MSS. 1359, fo. 95'b, and 1422, fo. 122.

CANARY ISLANDS, arms, crest and supporters 1 June 1665, by Sir E. Walker, Gart. Her. Coll., fo. 61.

CANDELOR, Richard, of Walsingham, Norfolk, gent., crest ("a bonocon's head") 22 June, 2 Eliz., 1560, by G. Dethick.   Harl. MS. 1359, fo. 70 ; copy of grant, *see* Q's Coll. Oxf. MS. 39, fo. 113 ; Grants I., 172 ; Candler in Harl. MS. 5887, fo. 52.

CANDISH ? Quarterly 1 and 4, three cross crosslets, 2 and 3, three fleurs de lis, crest, *see* slip [no slip inserted], by G. Dethick.   Harl. MSS. 5847, fo. 54, 1441, fo. 103, and Q's Coll. Oxf. MS. 145, fo. 45ᵇ.

CANHAM, John, of Milden, Suff., 12 Jan. 1662-3.   Harl. MS. 1105, fo. 18ᵇ ; Bysshe's Grants, 12, Her. Coll.

CANN, Sir Robert, Knt. and Bart., Royalist, Mayor of Bristol (s. of Wᵐ, also Mayor, killed by the rebels 1643), *see* altered and assigned 8 March 1663-4, by Walker.   Add. MSS. 14,293, fo. 56, and 14,294, fo. 12 ; Harl. MS. 1172, fo. 61 ; Guil. 320, copy of grant.

  „   Wᵐ, of city of Bristol, esq., ... Dec. 1652, by Bysshe, added in another hand " not delivered."   Harl. MS. 1105, fo. 10ᵇ.

CANNOCK, of Lincolnshire, ..., by Segar.   Add. MS. 12,225, fo. 24, erm. a fret, and on a chief gu. 3 annulets arg.

CANNON, Sir Thomas (? co. Pembroke), Feb. 1614-15, by Camden.   Harl. MSS. 1422, fo. 38ᵇ, and 6095, fo. 28ᵇ.

CANTERBURY, College of, B.V.M. and Sᵗ Nicholas, 1 Jan., 27 H. VI., 1448-9, copy of grant, Brit. Mus. ? Carta 27, H[er.] C[oll.], No. 40 ; Stowe MS. 840, fo. 60.

CANTON, ..., crest, a camel sa. bezantée, about his neck two gemelles the type of his tayle and his feet from the knees downw. or and gu., by Barker.   Harl. MS. 5846, fo. 26 ; Stowe MS. 692, fo. 30ᵇ.

CAPELEN, *see* CHAPLIN, John, of Stonham, Hants, 1592, by Cooke.   Harl. MS. 1359, fo. 111ᵇ ; Add. MS. 4966, fo. 24ᵇ, Berry under Chaplin ; Stowe MS. 670, fo. 49ᵇ.

CAPELLO, Vincent, Venetian patrician, augm. by H. 7, letters patent dated at Richmond 1 July, 6 Hy. VII., 1491.   Ashm. MS. 858, fo. 61, 62, copy of grant, Bodleian Lib.

CAPPER, or CUPPER, John, of Oxon, gift (Harvey's Grants).   Add. MS. 16,940, fo. 7ᵇ.

CAPPES, William, of Arlo and Long Stratton, Norfolk, 7 Aug. 1576, by Cooke, Clar. Bannerman's MS., No. 9, 454.

CARBERY, Richard Vaughan, Earl of, arms in 1st quarter of Blethyn ap Enyon, Prince of Powis, as his paternal coat, 20 Aug. 1664, by Walker.   Copy of grant, Harl. MS. 1172, fo. 67 ; Add. MSS. 14,293, fo. 51, and 14,294, fo. 9ᵇ.

CARBONEL, Wᵐ, of London, crest 21 March 1693-4, by Thos. St. George, Gart., and Hy. St. George, Clar.   Grants IV., 154-6 ; Guil. 380 ; Harl. MSS. 1085, fo. 57, and 6179, fo. 87.

CARD, Andrew, of Gray's Inn, barr. at law, and to the descendants of Wᵐ, his father, 31 May 1695, by Thos. and Hy. St. George, Gart. and Clar.   Add. MS. 14,831, fo. 149 ; Grants IV., fo. 194 ; Stowe MS. 714, fo. 104 ; Guil. 184 ; Harl. MS. 6179, fo. 96.

CARDALL, Wᵐ, of Middx., coat and crest ...., by Barker.   Harl. MS. 5846, fo. 22 ; Stowe MS. 692, fo. 29ᵇ, as CORDALL.

CARDINAL COLLEGE, Oxford, 4 Aug. 1525, 17 Hy. VIII., by Wriothesley and Benolte.   Harl. MS. 4900, fo. 18, pᵗᵉ in Dʳ Fiddes.

CARDYNALL, Wᵐ, of Much Bromley, Essex, 10 June 1556, by Thos. Hawley, Clar. Add. MSS. 16,940, fo. 208, and 7098, fo. 79 (fo. 127).

CARELL, John, sergᵗ at law, crest ...., Barker's Grants.   Harl. MS. 5846, fo. 25ᵇ.

CARKAREDGE, Thomas, of Maidstone, Kent, by ? St. George.   Add. MS. 14,295, fo. 70.

CARKIKE, Ralph, of London, gent., s. of W^m, of Annington, Devon, crest 18 or 23 Dec. 1578, to the posterity of his father, by Cooke. Guil. 68 ; copy of grant, Q's Coll. Oxf. MS. 38, fo. 99, 100 ; Grants II., 509.

CARLETON, Anthony, of Baldwin Brightwell, Oxon, confirmed 1558 (Harvey's Grants). Add. MS. 16,940, fo. 43 ; Harl. MS. 1116, fo. 62.

CARLOSSE, Col. W^m, of Broomhall, co. Staff, at Brussels, 21 May 1658, by Sir E. Walker, Gart. Harl. MS. 1105, fo. 12^b ; Her. Coll., fo. 3.

CARLYLE, Alexander, of London, gift .... 1560 (Harvey's Grants). Add. MS. 16,940, fo. 34.

CARLYLE, or CARLIELL, Christopher, of Cumberland, gent., s. of Alex^r, s. of Lawrence, s. of Robert, etc., a valiant captain, crest 10 Oct. 1593, by E. Knight, Norr. Harl. MS. 1359, fo. 31^b ; Add. MS. 14,295, fo. 27 ; copy of grant, see Q's Coll. Oxf. MS. 36, fo. 21, in Latin.

CARNABY, Sir Reginald, Kt., augmentation and crest 1534 at request of Hy., Earl of Northumb^d, by Hawley. Harl. MS. 1470, fo. 195—198, copy of grant, and in Q's Coll. Oxf. MS. 38, fo. 36 (see also Stowe MS. 670, fo. 23, without the augmentation), by Cooke (?).

CAROLINA, arms, crest and supporters of the province of Carolina (1 June 1705, by Laur. Cromp, York Herald [?]). Le Neve's MS. 259.

CARONGES, ... temp. Hy. VIII., by Benolt, Clar. Add. MS. 26,702, fo. 68^b ; Harl. MS. 1422, fo. 32^b.

CARPENDEN, Gabriel, of London, descended out of Kent: Paly of 6, arg. and gu., on a chev. sa. three cross crosslets or, by Segar. Add. MS. 12,225, fo. 23^b.

CARPENTER, Richard (and William), of Coleford, par. of Newland, co. Glouc., gent., Quarterly coat and crest, ? a grant, May 1600, by W. Dethick, Gart., and W. Camden, Clar. Copy of grant, Q's Coll. Oxf. MS. 36, fo. 86.

„   W^m., of Cobham, Surrey, gent., of the Privy Chamber extraord. to Ch. II., 4 March 1663-4. Copy of grant, Brit. Mus., Harl. MS. 1470, fo. 165 ; Harl. MS. 1105, fo. 17^b ; Add. MS. 14,293, fo. 5 ; Harl. MS. 1422, fo. 8 ; Bysshe's Grants, 5, Her. Coll.; Guil. 194.

CARPENTERS' COMPANY. Cat. Her. Exhib. Soc. of Antiq., 24 Nov. 1466, 6 Ed. IV., by W. Hawkesloe. Harl. MSS. 472 and 6860 ; Her. and Geneal., i., 120, copy of grant, Brit. Mus. See History of Carpenters' Company, by E. B. Jupp, 1848, p. 10.

CARR, Edward, of Twickenham, Middx., gent., descended from Carr of Latham, co. Lanc., certified by W. Camden (no date). Grants II., 586.

„   Sir John, of Hart, co. Durham, at London, grant of a standard 4 March 1515-16, by Wriothesley and Yonge. Her. and Geneal., i., 79 ; copy of grant, Brit. Mus., facsimile in Genealogist, vol. viii., frontispiece ; Cat. Her. Exhib. Soc. of Antiq., 62.

„   Robert, Earl of Rochester, arms confirmed and supporters granted ; ye warrant from K. James, for " a lyon of England " for a mark of honour to his arms and to the banner at Windsor, to Sir Wm Segar is dated 9 May, 9 Jac. I., 1611. See Cott. MS. Faustina E. I. 30 ; MS. Ashm. 858, fo. 53, copy of grant, Bodleian Lib., and Add. MS. 12,225, fo. 24 ; Harl. MS. 588, fo. 193 ; Le Neve's MS. 393 ; Q's Coll. Oxf. MS. 38, fo. 120.

„   (Sir Robt, K.B.), Viscount Rochester, R. Warrant, one of our lyons passant gardant gold as augm. in dexter part of coat of arms, and banner at Windsor, 8 June 1611, and supporters 9 May 1611. Cott. MS. Faustina E. I. 38 ; Harl. MS. 1507, fo. 393 ; MS. Ashm. 858, fo. 45, 46, copy of grant, Bodleian Lib., and Q's Coll. Oxf. MS. 38, fo. 120, and of supporters.

CARRE, Edward, of Bristol, out of Cumberland, ... 1574-5 ? by G. Dethick. Harl. MS. 1441, fo. 83 ; Q's Coll. Oxf. MS. 145, fo. 37^b ; Harl. MS. 5823, fo. 37^b.

CARRELL, John, of Warneham, Sussex, ... 1588, by Cooke. Harl. MSS. 1359, fo. 113^b, 1422, fo. 95, and 5887, fo. 85 ; Add. MS. 4966, fo. 61^b.

CARRIQUE, Richard, of Borton on the Hill, co. Glouc. (Quarterly of 4), s. of Richard, of Tewkesbury, 25 Jan. 1588-9, 31 Eliz., by Cooke. Harl. MS. 1359, fo. 97 ; Add. MS. 4966, fo. 89ᵇ ; Harl. MS. 1430, fo. 97.

CARSEY, Thomas, of Southbarow, Norfolk, gift . . . . 1563 (Harvey's Grants). Add. MS. 16,940, fo. 49.

CARTER, ..., of London, descended out of Herts, arg., a chev. betw. 3 cart wheels vert, 1612, by Segar. Add. MS. 12,225, fo. 22 ; C. 24, fo. 316ᵃ [Visit. Lond., 1634], Her. Coll., and Guil. 298.

„ Thomas, Kempton, Beds, by Sir H. St. George, Kt. Harl. MS. 1390, fo. 31.

„ Goddard, of Alverscot, Oxford, 22 Nov. 1670, ? by Sir E. Bysshe. Harl. MS. 1105, fo. 42ᵇ.

„ William, Rowton, Norfolk, 24 Feb. 1610-11, by Camden or Segar. Stowe MS. 712, fo. 70ᵇ ; compare Le Neve's MS. 357.

CARTHEY, Visct of Muskery, Charles MacCarthy, 21 Sept. 1639, by T. Preston, Ulster K. of A., arms confirmed and supporters granted. Harl. MS. 1470, fo. 32 ; Grants II., 678.

CARTWRIGHT, Rose, dau. of John, of co. Derby, wife of John Trott of London, confirmed . . . . 1574, by Flower. MS. Ashm. 844, fo. 75, copy of grant, Bodleian Lib. ; Guil. 395 ; Reliquary, xxii., 245.

„ Richard, of Aynho, Northants, Esq., 2nd s. of Hugh, and bro. of Edmond, of Ossington, Notts, confirmed 25 Nov. 1633, by R. St. George. Add. MS. 14,295, fo. 57ᵇ ; C. 34, fo. 25ᵇ [Visit. Nottingham, 1662], Her. Coll.

„ Thomas, of Syon, certified 1634, by Hy. St. George, Richmond. Harl. MS. 1422, fo. 124ᵈ.

„ Timothy, who marᵈ Penelope, relict of Nichˢ Charles, Lancaster Herald, and dau. of Sir W. Segar by his 1ˢᵗ wife Eleanor Sommers, wh. Timothy was son of Wᵐ. of Washbourne, co. Glouc., gent., confirmed 20 May 1617, 15 Jac., by Segar. Add. MS. 12,225, fo. 22ᵇ ; Guil. 298 ; Harl. MS. 6140, fo. 81ᵇ.

„ Wᵐ, of Assington [Ossington], Notts, given . . . ., by Cooke. Harl. MS. 1359, fo. 120ᵇ ; Add. MS. 14,295, fo. 45ᵇ.

„ Wᵐ, of Newland, Yorks, 12 Aug. 1612, by R. St. George, Norr. Berry's Suppᵗ, Her. Coll. 140, fo. 72.

CARUS, of Kendal, Westmorland, ..., by Dalton, Norr. Add. MS. 14,295, fo. 76ᵇ (98ᵃ).

„ Thomas, Esthwaite, Westmorland, ... ? by Harvey. Add. MS. 16,940, fo. 10ᵇ.

CARVILL, John, of Nun Monkton, Yorks, by R. St. George. Add. MS. 14,295, fo. 60 ; B. 21, 225 ; C. 13, 225 [Visit. Yorks, 1612], Her. Coll.

CARY, see CORY.

„ John, of London, merchant, confirmed 25 Sept. 1699, by T. St. George, Gart., and kinsman to

„ John, of Bristol, merchant, and Richard, his brother, confirmed 25 Sept. 1699, by H. St. George, Clar. Harl. MS. 14,831, fo. 85, and Grants IV., fo. 326.

See pedigree 3 D. 14 [Her. Coll.].

CARYER, Benjamin, D.D. and Prebʸ of Canterbury, chaplain to K. James, 20 June, 10 Jac., 1612, by Segar. Add. MS. 12,225, fo. 22ᵇ ; Guil. 224 ; Add. MS. 4966, fo. 98 ; H. C. [Her. Coll. ?], 140, fo. 37ᵇ.

CASE, John, of Berwick, s. of Cornelius, s. of Thomas, 9 Dec. 1581, by Cooke. Harl. MSS. 1422, fo. 12, 1441, fo. 46, and 1116, fo. 29.

CASSELL, ..., by W. Ryley, Lanc. Her. [?]. Stowe MS. 703, fo. 64.

CASTLELOCK, John, of Feversham, gent., whose ancestor inhabited there by reason of John, their uncle, who was lord Abbot of that Monastery before the Suppᵐ, crest 10 Aug. 1614, by Segar. Add. MS. 12,225, fo. 23 ; Guil. 276.

CASS, John, of Hackney, Middx., J.P. for the Tower and liberty, Lt. Col. of the
Tower hamlets, and a D.L. there (s. and h. of Tho⁵, late of Hackney,
Middx., J.P., decᵈ), 20 Sept. 1699, by T. St. George, Gart., and H. St.
George, Clar. Add. MS. 14,831, fo. 164; Grants IV., fo. 311; Stowe
MS. 714, fo. 93ᵇ; Harl. MS. 6179, fo. 56ᵇ, 2 cotises added.

CASSILIS, Gilbert, Lord Kaudie (Kennedy), Earl of Cassilis, coat. C. Barker's
Grants; Harl. MS. 5846, fo. 62; Stowe MS. 692, fo. 60.

CASTELL, Robert, of Yorkshire, one of the clerks of the King's Excheqner, 10 June
1479, 19 Ed. IV., by J. More, Norr. Stowe MS. 714, fo. 173, Pedigree,
172ᵇ; Add. MS. 14,295, fo. 58ᵇ; G. 18, fo. 12, Her. Coll.; Grants II.,
635.

CASTELTON, William, of Lincolnshire, 12 May 1482, by T. Holme als Norr. Harl.
MS. 1116, fo. 39.

CASTILLION, Jean Baptista, from near Turin, now of Benham Valence, co. Berks,
esq., etc., s. of Peter, testimonial of arms 10 May 1562, by Sir G. Dethick;
served in the wars *temp.* H. VIII., and for 53 years one of the grooms of
the Privy Chamber to Q. Eliz.; augmentation and crest, by W. Dethick,
Gart. Harl. MS. 1441, fo. 61ᵇ; Stowe MSS. 676, fo. 140, and 697,
fo. 112—114; Q's Coll. Oxf. MS. 36, fo. 100, copy of grant, etc.;
Genealogist, N. S., vol. xix., p. 199.

CASTLEMAN, Paul, of Bedington, Surrey, Esq., 18 Aug. 1662. Bysshe's Grants,
fo. 22, Her. Coll.; Harl. MS. 1105, fo. 21.

CATCHER, John, of London, sheriff . . . . 1587, by Cooke. Harl. MSS. 1359,
fo. 110, and 1422, fo. 93ᵇ; Add. MS. 4966, fo. 56.

CATER, Cornelius, s. of John, of London, assigned 1584, by Cooke. Harl. MS.
1359, fo. 116ᵇ; Add. MS. 14,295, fo. 37; Guil. 241; Grants II., 495;
Add. MS. 4966, fo. 29ᵇ.

„   Margery, d. and h. of John, of Letcombe Regis, Berks; wife of William
Hyde, of South Denchworth; exemplified 20 April 1559, by Hervey.
Add. MS. 16,940, fo. 23; MSS. Ashm. 858, fo. 209-10, and 840, fo. 412-13,
copy of grant, Bodleian Lib.; Geneal., ii., 355; Grants II., 528; Harl.
MS. 1116, fo. 48; Le Neve's MS. 474.

CATERALL, ..., az., a lion passant betw. three mascles or, by Segar. Add. MS.
12,225, fo. 23.

CATHERYNS, Humphrey, s. of Thomas, of Clifton, co. Warwick, now of New Inn,
crest (15 Nov.) 1572, by Cooke. Harl. MS. 1359, fo. 88ᵇ, 91; Cooke's
Grants, fo. 10, Her. Coll.; Guil. 211; Harl. MS. 1052, fo. 13; Add. MS.
4966, fo. 52ᵇ.

CATHORNE, Thomas, Prendergast, co. Pembroke, gent., arms and crest 5 Dec. 1553,
by T. Hawley, Clar. Q's Coll. Oxf. MS. 38, fo. 60, copy of grant, and
Grants I., p. 10.

CATLYN, Richard, of Hatford Hall, Norfolk, testified grant ? 1 Dec. or 1 June 1555
temp. Q. Mary, by G. Dethick. Harl. MS. 1359, fo. 62ᵇ; copy, Q's Coll.
Oxf. MS. 39, fo. 46, in Latin; Grants I., 45.

„   Sir Robert, Lord Chief Justice, confirmed . . . . 1559 (Harvey's Grants).
Add. MS. 16,940, fo. 18ᵇ.

„   Robert, of Rawndes, Northts., confirmed . . . . 1564 (Harvey's Grants).
Add. MS. 16,940, fo. 43.

„   William, of Leyborne, Kent, gent., arms and crest granted 27 Nov. 1460
(probably an error for a later year), by Tho. Holme, Norr. An alteration
in the crest 1 Dec., 9 Ed. IV., 1469. Harl. MS. 1359, fo. 5, also
by T. Holme, Norr.; copy of grant, etc., Q's Coll. Oxf. MS. 38, fo. 5—7,
in French; Grants II., 645, 647; Harl. MS. 1116, fo. 39.

CATZIUS, Sir Jacobus, Dʳ of yᵉ laws, Syndic of the city of Dort, and Knighted by
K. Jas.; arms Quarterly, by Segar. Add. MS. 12,225, fo. 23ᵈ.

CAUNTON, Thomas, and bro. ⎫ of Kilvington, Yorks, crest 1613, by R. St. George,
„   William   ⎭ Norr. Harl. MS. 6140, fo. 73; Stowe MS. 706, fo. 16ᵇ.

CAUNTON or CRANTON, John, of Warwickshire (and Wm. in Burke), coat and crest. Barker's Grants; Harl. MS. 5846, fo. 21, 26; Stowe MS. 692, fo. 29.

CAUSON, John, London .... by Cooke. Stowe MS. 670, fo. 61ᵇ.

CAVALCANTI, John, a Florentine merchᵗ, gent. usher to H. VIII., augmentation 5 Feb. 1520-21. Harl. MS. 1507, fo. 179, and MS. Ashm. 834, fo. 74, copy of grant, Bodleian Lib., and Q's Coll. Oxf. MS. 38, fo. 31, in Latin.

CAVALER, Anthony, of London, gent., gift 20 June 1534, by Wriothesley, Gart., and Benolte, Clar. Harl. MSS. 1394, fo. 320, and 1359, fo. 41; Add. MS. 26,702, fo. 59; Harl. MS. 6140, fo. 67ᵇ.

CAVE, ... of Staunfield (Stanford), coat and crest. Barker's Grants; Harl. MS. 5846, fo. 25 bis; Stowe MS. 692, fo. 31.

CAVENDISH, Henry, of Dovebridge, co. Derby, and his brother
  „ Charles, s. of Francis, decᵈ, Natl. sons of Henry, late of Tutbury, co. Staff., 20 May 1664, by W. Dugdale, Norr. (Her. Coll.)

CAWOOD, John, gent., 10 May, 3 and 4 Phil. and Mary, 1557, by G. Dethick. Grants I., 205; Harl. MS. 1115, fo. 37, copy of grant, Brit. Mus., and Q's Coll. Oxf. MS. 39, fo. 73; Harl. MS. 1359, fo. 69.

CAWTHORNE, William, of Little Bartholomew's, London, gent., 24 Aug. 1648, by W. Ryley, Norr. Harl. MS. 6179, fo. 54ᵇ.

CECIL, see SITSILT.
  „ Dr Powell in his History of Wales, dated 1584, there styles Wm. Sitsyll or Cecil, esq., cousin German to the Lord Burghley removed by one degree only. See Works of Armorie, by John Bossewell, gent., 1572, pp. 81—105.

CHABNOR, Thomas, of Mowsley in Herefordshire .... 1586, by Cooke. Harl. MSS. 1359, fo. 91, and 1422, fo. 93; Add. MS. 4966, fo. 69ᵇ; Harl. MS. 6140, fo. 55.

CHAFFIN, John, or SAFFIN, of Wolf Kerston, co. Som., s. of George, 17 Sept., 10 Jac., 1612, by Segar. Add. MS. 12,225, fo. 24ᵇ; Harl. MS. 6140, fo. 36ᵇ.

CHALKHILL, John, of Kingsbury, Middx., ..., by Cooke. Harl. MS. 1359, fo. 122.

CHALONER, David, of Denbigh, crest 4—15 [? Grants IV., 15], by W. Flower, Norr. Copy of grant, Harl. MS. 1972, fo. 69.
  „ Sir Thomas, of Wales, 1 June 1548, by Hawley (?). Add. MS. 16,940, fo. 202ᵇ.

CHAMBRE, ..., of Essex, crest ...., Barker's Grants. Harl. MS. 5846, fo. 25ᵇ.
  „ ...., crest ...., Barker's Grants. Harl. MS. 5846, fo. 26ᶜ; Stowe MS. 692, fo. 30ᵇ; Add. MS. 26,702, fo. 54.

CHAMBER, Geoffrey, confirmed 26 Aug. 1528, 20 H. 8, by Wriothesley and Benolte. Copy of letters patent, Brit. Mus., Harl. MS. 4900, fo. 20ᵇ, 21. Stowe MS. 671, fo. 75ᵇ; Harl. MS. 5887, fo. 1.
  „ Thomas, of Barkway, Herts; authority from his 3ʳᵈ cousin William Chamber of Wolstie Castle, Cumberland, esq., that Thomas having proved relationship should use his arms and crest with the difference of a second house, 1 March 1623. Harl. MS. 2147, fo. 106.

CHAMBERLAYNE, ..., wife of Robert Faldoe of Maldon, Bucks, esq. Add. MS. 14,295, fo. 25 (? by R. St. George), Quarterly of 9 tricked.

CHAMBERLEYN, Richard, of London, alderm., gift .... 1551 (Harvey's Grants). Add. MS. 16,940, fo. 43ᵇ; see Harl. MS. 5887, fo. 90.

CHAMBERLAYNE, Robert, of Sherborne, ⎫ assigned or allowed 1585, by
  „ George, of St. Omers,   ⎬ Cooke. Guil. 245.
  „ John, brother of Robᵗ,   ⎭
  „ Robert, gent., s. and h. of Richᵈ, late Alderm. and Sheriff of London, and Anne his wife, d. and h. of Robert Downer of Yalling, Kent, gent., 1588, by Cooke. Stowe MS. 677, fo. 8ᵇ; ? Guil. 245.

CHAMBERLAYNE, Thomas, of London, coat and crest (Barker's Grants). Harl. MS. 5846, fo. 23[b]; Stowe MS. 692, fo. 31[b]; crest in margin, Harl. MS. 5887, fo. 8.

CHAMBERLAINE, Sir Thomas, of Coleman St., London, crest confirmed 15 Feb. 1661-2, by Walker, Gart. Guil. 232; Her. Coll., fo. 46.

CHAMBERS, Geo., of Longford, co. Glouc., a servant to Thomas, Lord Windsor [Grants IV. ?], 4 fo. 67, and Grants II., 660, 1 fo. 104, March 1629-30, by R. St. George. Add. MS. 14,295, fo. 67, 104; Grants II., fo. 661[b].

„ John, of Gaddesby, co. Leic., confirmed 3 March 1581-2, by Cooke. Guil. 137; MS. Ashm. 844, fo. 28, copy of grant, Bodleian Lib.

CHAMPYON, Walter, grants 20 March 1527-8 by letters from Chas. V., Emperor, testified by Gabriel, Count of Ostenburg, Sub-Advocate of the Bpk. of Crurcew (Cracow ?). Harl. MS. 1499, fo. 112[b], in Latin.

CHAPLAIN, Sir Francis, Knt., Lord Mayor of London, granted by Bysshe, and confirmed 24 March 1682-3 (Ailesbury, D.E.M.) [Deputy Earl Marshal ?]. Grants 111., fo. 195; Harl. MS. 5861, fo. 38[b] [Certif. July 1683].

CHAPLIN, or CAPELIN, John, Hants.

CHAPMAN, Alexander, of Bourdon (Borden), Kent, coat and crest 38 Hy. VIII., 1546 (Barker's Grants). Harl. MS. 5846, fo. 24; Stowe MS. 692, fo. 32; Allen in Harl. MS. 1422, fo. 73[b], and in Add. MS. 26,702.

„ Henry, of Bowerth, or Baverch, co. Camb., coat and crest, Barker's Grants. Harl. MS. 5846, fo. 24[b].

„ James, now in Spain (s. of Alex., s. and h. of John, of Yorks), testified 10 Aug., 14 Jac., 1616, by Segar. Add. MS. 12,225, fo. 24[b].

„ {John, Quarterly, by Cooke. Harl. MS. 1359, fo. 118; Stowe MS. 670, fo. 69; ? bur. at Clerkenwell 24 Aug. 1603. Harl. MS. 5887, fo. 42; Add. MS. 4966, fo. 96.   } diff. coat.
„ {John, of London, grant 1 May 1573 (Berry's Appendix). Bannerman MS., No. 9, 451.   }

CHAPPELL, Bartholomew, a sergeant bailiff of London, by Segar, or, an anchor in pale sa. Add. MS. 12,225, fo. 25.

CHARD, ..., co. Leic., by Cooke, Quarterly, a label [. . . .], 73, no colours. Stowe MS. 670, fo. 82[b].

CHARK, William, of London, gent., for his great piety and learning, granted and assigned 21 Jan. 1604-5, by Camden, Clar. Cott. MS. Faust. E. I., fo. 48; Harl. MS. 6095, fo. 3; Guil. 294.

CHARLES, John, of Tavistock, Devon, confirmed 1564 (Harvey's Grants). Add. MS. 16,940, fo. 13[b].

„ Richard, of London, ..., by Cooke. Stowe MS. 670, fo. 42.

CHARLETON, Thomas, of Sandiacre, co. Derby, exemplified 23 May 1612, by R. St. George. MS. Ashm. 858, fo. 157-8, copy of grant, Bodleian Lib.; Misc. Gen. et Her., N. S., iv., 109; Grants II., 617[b]; Harl. MSS. 6179, fo. 13[b], and 6140, fo. 72; Reliq., xxii., 49.

CHARNOCK, Richard, Holcott, Beds, 1566, by Harvey, Clar. Harl. MS. 1390, fo. 20.

CHATTERTON, John, of Portsmouth, crest confirmed 22 March 15⅔ [1556-7] (Hawley's Grants). Harl. MS. 1562, fo. 48[b]; Add. MS. 16,940, fo. 50[b].

CHAUCER (Thomas), temp. H. VI., ... Add. MS. 26,702, fo. 28[b].

CHAUNCY, William, of Edgecott, Norfolk, 23 Nov. 1545, Barker's Grants. Harl. MSS. 5846, fo. 24, and 1115, fo. 32[b]; Stowe MS. 692, fo. 32; see Harl. MS. 1410, fo. 47.

CHAUNDLER, William, } s. of Thomas, of Hyde Barton, co. Southampton, dec[d] and George,   } (also descendants of George and William Chaundler, the sonnes of his brother), crest 30 Dec. 1612, 10 Jac., by P. [Will.] Segar, Gart. Copy of grant, Brit. Mus., and Harl. MS. 1172, fo. 9[b]; see Harl. MS. 1441, fo. 121[b].

CHEYTOR, or CHAYTOR, Christopher, of the Bpk. of Durham, ... 1575, by Flower. Harl. MSS. 1453, fo. 74, 1422, fo. 23, and 6140, fo. 70[b].

CHATER, W[m], of Crofts Hall, co. Yorks, s. of Anthy., s. of Christopher, of Butterby, in the Bpk., which Chr[r] married Edyth [? Elizabeth], d. and h. of W[m] [Clervaux] of Crofts Hall, 12 July 1612, by R. St. George. Harl. MS. 1422, fo. 109[b], Quarterly coat and different crest.

CHEALE, John, of Findon, Sussex, and to Philip his brother, and to John and Philip, of the par. of Shermanbury, 20 May 1672. Harl. MS. 1105, fo. 37[b], by Sir E. Bysshe; Bysshe's Grants, 35.

CHEFFINCH, Thomas, one of the pages of H.M.'s Bedchamber from the King's infancy and during his exile in foreign parts and return to England, 14 Dec. 1664, by Walker. Add. MSS. 14,293, fo. 37, and 14,294, fo. 7[b]; Guil. 259, Comptroller of the Excise and Keeper of the private closet to Chas. II.

,,   William, one of the pages of the bedchamber and Keeper of the (King's rarities in Harl. MS. 1441, fo. 132) private Closet (succeeded his bro. Thomas, dec[d]), confirmation 6 July 1670 of the arms granted to Thomas, by Walker. Harl. MS. 1172, fo. 50; Add. MSS. 14,293, fo. 28, and 14,294, fo. 3, a crescent for difference; Guil. 258.

CHELMICK, W[m], of Ragdon, Salop, crest ? 1 June 1582, 25 Q. Eliz., by Cooke. Harl. MS. 1359, fo. 121[b].

CHEQUER, see HARFLEET, of Moland, Kent, 9 May 1564. Harl. MS. 1153, fo. 3.

CHERRY (Sir Francis), of London, arg., a fesse engrailed between three annulets gu., by Segar. Add. MS. 12,225, fo. 25[b]; Sir Francis in Add. MS. 14,295, fo. 75, and Harl. MS. 6140, fo. 48[b]; Harl. MS. 5887, fo. 33[b].

CHERTH, Richard, s. of Rich[d] . . . ., by Cooke. Stowe MS. 670, fo. 52.

CHESLIN, ..., of London, Alderm., by Browne, Bluemantle [?]. Stowe MS. 703, fo. 72.

CHESTER CITY, 3 Sept. 1580, by Flower. MS. Ashm. 844, fo. 51, copy of grant, Bodleian Lib.

CHESTER (. . . .), of Glouc., Quarterly: 1 and 4, gu., a lion passant ermine between three hawks' lures or ; 2 and 3, sa., a chev. betw. three fleurs-de-lis arg. ; crest, a lion's paw erased ermines, by Camden. Harl. MS. 6095, fo. 1[b]; Le Neve's MS. 270.

,,   Robert, of Lee, Essex, granted Feb. 1639-40, by J. Borough, Gart. Harl. MSS. 1441, fo. 57[b], and 1105, fo. 56 ; Add. MS. 26,702, fo. 91[b] ; Guil. 338.

,,   William, gent., 22 May 1467, by W. Hawkslow. Stowe MS. 608, fo. 19 ; R. E. Waters, Hist. of Chester Family, 169 ; Misc. Gen. et Her., 3rd S., iv., 117, copy of grant, Brit. Mus., and Grants II., 537.

CHESTERFIELD, Catherine, Countess of, supporters at the Hague 29 May 1660, by Walker, Gart. Her. Coll., fo. 12.

CHESTON, Thomas, of Mydelhall in Suff., 1587, by Cooke. Harl. MSS. 1359, fo. 109[b], and 1422, fo. 94 ; Add. MS. 4966, fo. 31[b].

CHESYLDYNE, George, of Uppingham, Rutland, gent., s. of Edward, s. of John, s. of John, late of Alaxton, co. Leic., confirmed 31 Jan. 1560-61, by L. Dalton, Norr. Harl. MS. 1359, fo. 48[b], and Rutland Visit[n], Harl. Soc., 50 ; Grants I., fo. 40.

CHEVENING or CHAWNING, Reginald, of Chevening, Kent, confirmed by Segar. Add. MS. 12,225, fo. 25 ; Harl. MS. 6179, fo. 57.

CHIBNALL, Richard, of Astwood, Bucks, 1562 (Harvey's Grants). Add. MS. 16,940, fo. 49[b].

CHILCOTT, William, of Lovelinch, Somerset, s. of William, s. of John, both of Preston, ..., 6 Oct. 1633, by R. St. George, Clar. Harl. MS. 1105, fo. 2[b].

CHILDBORNE, Alexander, of London, 1 Dec. 1539, granted by Hawley, Clar. Le Neve's MS. 501 ; Harl. MS. 7025, fo. 203 (Harl. MS. 1359, fo. 1) ; Stowe MS. 677, fo. 14, copy of grant in Brit. Mus.

CHILDE, John, of Shelley, co. Worcester, 10 March 1575-6, 17 Eliz., by (Cooke ?). Harl. MS. 1507, fo. 256 ; Le Neve's MS. 256.

CHILDERS, Hugh, of Doncaster, J.P., by H. St. George, Norr. Harl. MS. 1105, fo. 12ᵇ.

CHILTON, Leonard, of Cadiz in Spain, gent., s. and h. of John, of Rye, Kent, gent., 24 Oct. 1576, by Cooke. Quarterly of 4: Chilton, Barrowe, Roberts and Sanders. Harl. MSS. 1359, fo. 118, and 1422, fo. 121 ; Stowe MS. 670, fo. 69ᵇ ; Add. MS. 4966, fo. 96ᵇ ; Harl. MS. 5887, fo. 42ᵇ.

CHISNALL, Edward, of Chisnall, co. Lanc., s. of Thomas, confirmed 15 Feb. 1596-7, by W. Dethick. Stowe MS. 676, fo. 115, copy of grant, and Q's Coll. Oxf. MS. 36, fo. 50.

CHOKE, Richard, of Avington, Berks, crest granted 4 July 1576, by Cooke. MS. Ashm. 858, fo. 216, 218, copy of grant, Bodleian Lib.

CHOLMELEY, Sir Hugh, grant of crest 20 Dec. 1547, 1 Ed. VI. (by Hawley), in French, confirmed . . . . 1566, by Flower. Add. MS. 16,940, fo. 202 ; MSS. Ashm. 840, fo. 381, and 858, fo. 179, 180, copy of grant, Bodleian Lib.

CHOLMLEY, Richard, Ryple, co. Worc., s. of Miles and bro. of Jasper, of Highgate, Midd., 1590, by Cooke, Clar. Stowe MS. 670, fo. 39ᵇ ; Add. MS. 14,297, fo. 39ᵇ.

CHOLMONDELEY, Thomas, of Holford, Cheshire, nat. s. of Thomas, Visct. Cholmondeley, 29 Oct. 1663, by Sir Wᵐ Dugdale, Norr. (Her. Coll.)

,, Robert, Visct., supporters 10 June 1661, by Walker. MSS. Ashm. 840, fo. 421-3, and 858, fo. 173-4, copy of grant, Bodleian Lib.

CHOLWICH, William, of Cholwich, Devon, crest 6 June 1657, by Ryley. Harl. MS. 1470, fo. 147, and 1105, fo. 11 ; " made void " Guil. 384.

CHOLWILL, Thomas, of Lodesford in par. of Hartland, Devon (s. of John, s. of Thomas and Alice, d. and coh. of Dalin of Lodesford aforesd.), Cholwill quartering Dalin. Harl. MSS. 1422, fo. 111, and 6095, fo. 28 ; Guil. 332.

CHOPPING, Richard, Alderm. of London, coat and crest. Add. MS. 26,702, fo. 76ᵇ.

CHORLEY or THORNEHOLME, 1594, by W. Dethick, Gart. Harl. MSS. 1453, fo. 33, and 3526, fo. 142ᵇ.

CHOWNE, Nicholas, of Fairlawn, Kent, confirmed (Harvey's Grants). Add. MS. 16,940, fo. 36ᵇ ; Harl. MS. 1076, fo. 112ᵇ, 6 Q. Eliz., 1564-5.

CHRISTEMAS, ..., Essex, crest . . . . Barker's Grants ; Harl. MS. 5846, fo. 27ᵇ ; Stowe MS. 692, fo. 30ᵇ ; Harl. MS. 6179, fo. 22.

CHRISTOPHER, Ro., secondary of the Counter of London, gent., 22 March 1587-8, by Cooke. Add. MS. 14,295, fo. 62ᵇ ; Vincent's Coats and Crests, Nᵒ 175, fo. 13 ; L. 6, Quartered coats and crests, fo. 46 ; Index 1ˢᵗ, Office of Arms : Harl. MS. 5887, fo. 79.

CRYSTMAS, Robert, of Lavnam, Suff., crest confirmed by the Earl of Leicester (Harvey's Grants). Add. MS. 16,940, fo. 33.

CRISTOFORSON, John, Bp. of Chichester, 4 April 1557, by ? Hawley. Add. MS. 16,940, fo. 208ᵇ.

CHUBBE, ..., of Dorset, ..., by Segar, az., a cross or betw. 4 bezants. Add. MS. 12,225, fo. 27ᵇ.

CHURCH, Bartholomew, of Erles Colne, Essex, ob. in the Low Countries, 1613, by Camden, Clar. Le Neve's MS. 355.

,, John, Malden, Essex, grant 20 May 1557, by Harvey, ? Hawley, Clar. Harl. MS. 1115, fo. 35, grant ; copy of grant, Q's Coll. Oxf. MS. 38, fo. 70 ; Grants I., 401.

CHURCHAR, Thomas, Chittingley, Sussex, gent., 10 Oct. 1570, by Ro. Cooke, Clar. Grants I., 96 ; Harl. MS. 1562, fo. 156ᵇ.

CHURCHILL, John, lord of Sundridge, supporters 27 July 1685, by W. Dugdale, Garter. Stowe MS. 714, fo. 143 ; Grants III., 284 ; Lansd. MS. 867, fo. 52.

,, Winston, of Minterne, Dorset, M.P., crest and augmentation by royal command, 20 Jan. 1661-2, by Sir E. Walker, Gart. Her. Coll., fo. 44 ; Harl. MS. 6179, fo. 38.

CHURCHMAN, John, of London, by Cooke. Add. MS. 4966, fo. 52ᵇ ; Stowe MS. 670, fo. 22ᵇ.

CLAPHAM, John, of London, one of the six clerks in Chancery, confirmed .... 1599, by W. Dethick, Gart., Camden, Clar., and Segar, Norr. Add. MS. 12,225, fo. 25ᵇ ; Harl. MS. 6095, fo. 24ᵇ ; Guil. 131.

CLARE, Simon, of Croome, D'Abitot, co. Worc., ... 1562, by Harvey. Harl. MS. 1422, fo. 12 ; Add. MS. 16,940, fo. 43ᵇ ; Burke's Armory.

CLARGES, Anne, ux. George Monk, after Duke of Albemarle, arms and augmentation 20 Aug. 1660, by Sir E. Walker, Gart. Her. Coll., 4, Berry's Supplᵗ.

CLARK (. . . .), a showmaker's son, of Saffron Walden, grant 1596, by W. Dethick, arms not tricked, crest, out of a tower a demi lion rampant, entered by R. Brooke, York Herald. Harl. MS. 1453, fo. 35.

„ . . . ., or, on a bend engrailed az., 3 Lozenges of the first, by Segar. Add. MS. 12,225, fo. 26.

CLARKE, ..., of Herefordshire, exemplification, argᵗ, a chev. betw. 3 lions rampant vert, with 3 quarterings, by Segar, ... Add. MS. 12,225, fo. 26.

„ Andrew, of Wroxham, Norfolk, by Camden. Harl. MS. 6095, fo. 38ᵇ.

„ Edmond, of Kettlebaston, Suff., gent., grant 20 June, 1 Q. Eliz., 1559, by G. Dethick. Harl. MS. 1359, fo. 78 ; copy of grant, Q's Coll. Oxf. MSS. 39, fo. 95, and 145, fo. 2ᵇ ; Grants II., 407.

„ Edward, of the Manor of Ketelbastone, Suff., gent., grant 2 May 1556, by Hawley. Harl. MSS. 1509, fo. 404-5, and 1669, fo. 39 ; Add. MS. 16,940, fo. 208 ; copy of grant, Q's Coll. Oxf. MS. 38, fo. 64 ; Grants I., 300 ; Le Neve's MS. 404.

„ Samuel, of Ashegate, co. Derby, and his brother Cornelius, of Cubthorpe, s. of Ralph, of Ashegate, decᵈ, 12 May 1663, by W. Dugdale, Norr., Her. Coll. Harl. MS. 6179, fo. 22ᵇ.

„ Edward, of Ardington, Beds [Berks], s. of John [s. of John], s. of Angustine, s. of John, of Basildon, Berks, and E[lizabeth], dau. and h. of . . . . Champneys. Clarke quartering Champneys allowed and crest confirmed 21 Oct. 1600, by W. Dethick, Gart., and Camden. Harl. MSS. 1359, fo. 36, and 1422, fo. 114ᵇ, etc.; Add. MS. 14,259, fo. 114ᵇ ; Cott. MS. Faustina E. I., fo. 53ᵇ ; Guil. 251 ; copy of grant, Q's Coll. Oxf. MSS. 36, fo. 114, and 146, fo. 44.

„ Godfrey, s. of Nicholas, of Somersal in Brampton, co. Derby, 19 April 1608, 1611, by R. St. George. Harl. MS. 1422, fo. 43ᵇ (see Wᵐ Clerke [same Arms, p. 54], Add. MS. 14,295, fo. 78ᵇ) ; Harl. MS. 6140, fo. 71ᵇ ; Le Neve's MS. 497.

CLARK, James, Serjeant of H.M.'s "chandry" at Whitehall, and Constable of H.M.'s Castle of Dublin, 26 Jan. 1688-9, by T. St. George, Gart., and H. St. George, Clar. Harl. MS. 14,831, fo. 80, and Grants IV., fo. 30.

„ John, of Kent, 1 Jan. 1500 [sic], ? 1550, by Hawley. Harl. MS. 1422, fo. 43ᵇ.

„ Robert, the elder, of St. Ives, Hunts, 10 Oct. 1671, by Walker. Harl. MS. 1172, fo. 70 ; Add. MSS. 14,293, fo. 86, and 14,294, fo. 25ᵇ ; Guil. 134.

CLARKE (Mathew), King's Lynn, ..., by W. Camden. Cains Coll. Camb. MS. 551, fo. 30ᵇ, and Harl. MS. 4756, fo. 52ᵇ.

„ Sir Thomas, of Plumstead, Kent, Knt., 27 April 1621, by Camden. Harl. MSS. 1422, fo. 43ᵇ, and 6095, fo. 38.

„ William, of Hallywellcombe, Devon, confirmed 1561 (Harvey's Grants). Add. MS. 16,940, fo. 17.

„ William, London, gent., 25 Jan. 1605, by Camden, at the request and charge of his 2 bros. in law Sir Wᵐ Romney and W. Jeremy Danvers. Harl. MS. 1422, fo. 18ᵇ.

CLARKSON, ..., Arg., on a bend betw. 2 trefoils slipped sa. 3 lozenges of the
first, ..., by Segar. Add. MSS. 12,225, fo. 26ᵇ, and 14,295, fo. 114ᵇ;
Harl. MSS. 1359, fo. 25ᵇ, and 1422, fo. 114ᵇ; Q's Coll. Oxf. MS. 146,
fo. 44.

„   . . . ., of Nottingham, different coat (arg., on a bend engrailed sa. three
annulets or), but different crest, by Cooke. Stowe MS. 670, fo. 63.
CLAY, Thomas, of Reigate, ... 1613, by Camden. Morgan's Sphere, 117.
„   William, see CLEY.
CLAYTON, Sir Robert, Knt., Alderm. and Sheriff of London. 1671, by Bysshe.
Harl. MS. 1105, fo. 39; Bysshe's Grants, 30.

„   Thomas, Dr in physic, and Regius Profr, Oxford, Master of Pembroke Coll.,
and his brother James, sons of Wm, of Yorks, gent., alteration 20 March
1627-8, by R. St. George, transd by A. Wood, Oxon, 28 Jan. 1687. Add.
MS. 14,295, fo. 65ᵇ, 66; 2 March 1624-5 in Harl. MS. 1422, fo. 14.
CLEAVER, Sir Charles, of Bygrave, Herts, 10 April 1661 (by Bysshe). Harl. MSS.
1105, fo. 40ᵇ, and 6179, fo. 49; Bysshe's Grants, 36.
CLEGAT, ..., of Kent . . . ., by Segar, erm., on a fesse sa. 3 pheons or, quarter-
ing Godden. Add. MS. 12,225, fo. 26.
CLEMENT, ... crest . . . . (Barker's Grants), (1526—49). Harl. MS. 5846, fo. 27;
Stowe MS. 692, fo. 30ᵇ.
CLENT, John, of Knightwick, co. Worc., certificate by R. St. George, Clar. Harl.
MS. 1105, fo. 3ᵇ.
CLEPOLE, James, of Norborough, Northts., father of Sir John, granted 17 June
1583, by Cooke. Harl. MSS. 1359, fo. 107ᵇ, and 1422, fo. 93ᵇ; Guil.
357; Add. MS. 4966, fo. 31ᵇ.
CLERGIEMENS SONS, WIDOWS AND CHILDREN [a Society or Corporation], 29 Nov.
1684, by Sir Wm. Dugdale and T. St. George, Clar. Harl. MS. 6834,
fo. 178; Grants III., fo. 250; Lansd. MS. 867, fo. 52. [Now the
Corporation of the Sons of the Clergy?]
CLERKE, Bartholomew, D.C.L., of London, Judge (Dean) of the Arches and
a Master in Chancery, and to the descendants of his father John, of Wells,
Somerset, etc., s. of Richard, of Levermere, Suff., gent., etc., confirmed
25 Jan. 1580-81, by Ro. Cooke: Clerke quartering Grandtofte. MS.
Ashm. 844, fo. 171, copy of grant, Bodleian Lib.; Guil. 246; Harl. MSS.
1422, fo. 43ᵇ, and 6179, fo. 22ᵇ.

„   Humph., of Edmonton, Middx., gent., testified 29 Nov. 1633, by R. St. George;
"entered 19 Oct. 1686, by H. St. George." Add. MS. 14,295, fo. 71ᵇ;
Cat. Her. Exhib. Soc. of Antiq., 71.

„   Thomas, of Wirke, Northumberland, 14 Dec. 1560, by Dalton. Harl. MS.
1359, fo. 47ᵇ.

„   Wm (same coat as Godfrey Clarke on p. 53), of Somersall, co. Derby, 14 April
1608, by R. St. George (? Galfridus, Harl. MS. 1093, fo. 26). Add. MS.
14,295, fo. 78ᵇ (fo. 137), an alteration from the original?
CLETCHER, Henry, late of Stockholm, Sweden, etc., exemplified 20 April 1669, by
Walker. Harl. MS. 1172, fo. 68; Add. MSS. 14,293, fo. 72, and 14,294,
fo. 21; Harl. MS. 6179, fo. 78, copy of grant.
CLEY, William, Crych and Chappell, co. Derby, ... 1588, by W. Dethick, Gart.
John in Harl. MS. 6140, fo. 72; 1588 in Harl. MS. 6179, fo. 13; Berry's
Supplement.
CLEYBROOK, Stephen, of Fulham, Middx., 1574, by Cooke. Harl. MS. 1359,
fo. 119; Add. MS. 4966, fo. 94ᵇ.
CLIFTON, John, of London, clothworker, s. of Roger, of London, clothworker, s. of
Richard, of London, skinner to H. VIII., Ed. VI. and Q. Mary, by Segar.
Add. MS. 12,225, fo. 27; C. 28, Her. Coll., and Guil. 102.

„   William, of Clifton and Hodsoke, Notts, gent. (? arm.), crest 15 Nov.,
3 Ed. VI., 1549, by G. Dethick. Harl. MS. 1359, fo. 59ᵇ; copy of grant,
Q's Coll. Oxf. MS. 39, fo. 23; Harl. MS. 1116, fo. 40ᵇ; Grants I., 328.

CLINKARD, Gabriell (s. of Edmund, M.A. Oxon, allied to the family of Pigotts and Hawtrey), head bailiff of the City of Westm. *temp.* Chas. I., royalist, was plundered and tryed for his life, etc., a prisoner at Worcester battle, etc. 2 March 1664-5, by Walker. Harl. MS. 1172, fo. 60 ; Add. MSS. 14,293, fo. 55, and 14,294, fo. 12 ; Guil. 216, copy of grant.

CLOCKMAKERS' COMPY., arms, crest and supporters 31 Jan. 1671-2, by Walker. Harl. MS. 1172, fo. 69b ; Add. MSS. 14,293, fo. 82, and 14,294, fo. 24 ; Harl. MS. 1052, fo. 209, copy of grant, Brit. Mus.

CLOOS, Nicholas, clerk, for services in building Eton College, letters patent 30 Jan. (1448-9), copy Brit. Mus. Excerp. Hist., 364 ; Her. and Geneal., i., 135, after Bp. of Carlisle and of Lichfield.

CLOTHWORKERS' COMPY., arms, no other date, 1530, 22nd Hen. VIII., by Benolt ; crest and supporters 25 March 1587, by Cooke. Misc. Gen. et Her., ii., 173—175 ; Her. and Geneal., i., 123 ; copy of grant, Brit. Mus.

CLOUDESLEY, Capt. Richard, Citizen and Vintner, 13 April 1663, by Sir E. Walker, Gart. Her. Coll., fo. 50 ; Harl. MS. 6179, fo. 24b.

CLOUGHE, Edmond, of Thorpe Stapleton, Yorks, 26 June 1612, by R. St. George. Harl. MS. 6179, fo. 14 ; Surtees Soc., XLI., xlvi., copy of grant, Brit. Mus., s. of Robt, s. of John ; Harl. MS. 6140, fo. 14.

CLOWES, William, of London, gent., s. of Thomas, of Kingsbery, co. Warwick, s. of Nicholas, s. of Jeffrey, of Tutbery, co. Staff., granted 28 Oct. 1576 or 1567, by G. Dethick. Harl. MSS. 1441, fo. 85b and 88, 5847, fo. 49b, and 1422, fo. 22b. Confirmed 27 Oct. 1595, by W. Dethick, Gart. Copy of patent, Q's Coll. Oxf. MSS. 36, fo. 53, and 145, fo. 41b, 45b.

CLUTTERBUCK, ..., co. Glouc., confirmed 9 May 1622, by Camden. Stowe MSS. 706, fo. 54b, and 707, fo. 9, 27b ; Guil. 246.

COACHE, Sir Thomas, of London, 2 June 1606, by W. Camden, Clar. Harl. MSS. 1422, fo. 19b, and 6095, fo. 6 ; 2 Jany 1606-7 in Guil. 203.

COACHMAKERS AND COACH HARNESSMAKERS, Company of, 17 July 1677, by Sir Wm Dugdale and H. St. George, Norr. Harl. MS. 6834, fo. 178 ; Grants III., fo. 58 ; Harl. MS. 6832, fo. 372.

COBBETT, Major John, ... Jan. 1656-7, by Sir E. Bysshe, Gart. Harl. MSS. 1441, fo. 150b, and 1466, fo. 24.

COBLEGHE, John, of Burghtley, Devon, coat and crest. Barker's Grants ; Harl. MS. 5846, fo. 28b ; Stowe MS. 692, fo. 28b.

COCKE, George, of Kingston, Surrey, ... 1639, by Borough. Harl. MS. 1105, fo. 55b ; Add. MS. 26,702, fo. 90b.

COCK, John, of Pryttelwell, Essex, and to Richard his brother, 1 June 1587, by W. Dethick. Harl. MSS. 1470, fo. 274, and 1507, fo. 385 ; Stowe MS. 676, fo. 68 ; by G[ilbert] D[ethick] 20 Feb., 6 E. VI., Harl. MS. 1359, fo. 44, an earlier grant by Cooke ; copy of grant, Brit. Mus., and Q's Coll. Oxf. MS. 37, fo. 96 ; Le Neve's MS. 385.

„ John, of Little Sawbridge, Essex, crest 11 Nov. 1558, by Cooke, Clar. Stowe MS. 670, fo. 29, Lanc. Herald, ob. 1590 ; Le Neve's MS. 386, as Coke.

COCKAYNE, *see* COKAYNE.

COCKBRYEN or COCKBURN, Mr Robert, Bishop of Dunkell, coat . . . . Barker's Grants ; Harl. MS. 5846, fo. 21b ; Stowe MS. 692, fo. 29.

COCKER, Christopher, of Croft, co. Linc., s. of Thomas, s. of Chr, s. of Hugh, of Streythill, Chesh., crest 20 May (10 Eliz.) 1568, by G. Dethick, Gart., Cooke, Clar., and Flower, Norr., and all other heralds. Harl. MS. 1052, fo. 44.

COKERAM [COCKERAM], Philip, of Wigmore, co. Hereford, gent., 10 July, 3 Ed. VI., 1549, by G. Dethick. Harl. MS. 1359, fo. 76b ; Grants I., 147.

COKERELL, Edmond, of the Isle of Wight, coat (Barker's Grants). Add. MS. 26,702, fo. 4b.

COCKERELL, Richard, Peter and Hugh, s. of Richard, of Grimston, Norfolk, by Segar. Harl. MS. 1422, fo. 15.

COCKS, *see also* COX.

  ,, (different coat from John Cocks, gent.), of London, by G. Dethick. Harl. MS. 1422, fo. 16ᵇ. *See also* COX.

  ,, John, gent., granted 20 Feb., 6 Ed. VI., 1551-2, by G. Dethick. Harl. MS. 1359, fo. 60ᵇ; copy of grant, Q's Coll. Oxf. MS. 39, fo. 41, and Grants I., 264, as Cooke, which *see* for blazon.

  ,, John, Arms, Quarterly and crest, 1552, by Dethick, *see* Cooke.

COCKSHUTT, John, M.A. and Minister of God's word, now at Sarratt, Herts, 2nd s. of Wᵐ, 1st s. of Edmond, of Symonston, co. Lanc., out of Cockshutt in Salop, confirmed by Segar, ... Add. MS. 12,225, fo. 28; Stowe MS. 677, fo. 14ᵇ.

CODD, Wᵐ, of Pelicans, par. of Wateringbury, Kent, s. and h. of Wᵐ, s. and h. of George, by Agnes, d. and co-h. of Turner, gent. (Quartering Turner), 17 Feb. 1631-2, by Segar. Add. MS. 12,225, fo. 28ᵇ; Stowe MS. 677, fo. 21; Grants I., 408.

  ,, Wᵐ, of Pellicans, par. of Wateringbury, Kent, s. of George (and Agnes Turner), s. of Richard, s. of Robert, s. of Robert, s. of 3 Robert, s. of Wᵐ, s. of Wᵐ, of Pellicans, confirmed by Wᵐ Le Neve, Clar., 11 June 1640. Grants I., 393 to 400, Her. Coll.

CODDNAM, ..., wife of .... Pawlett, buried at Sᵗ Bartholomew's, Smithfield. Stowe MS. 670, fo. 4ᵇ, etc. [trick of Arms].

CODRINGTON, John, of Codrington, co. Glouc., 1 July 1442, by R. Leigh, Clar. Add. MS. 6297, fo. 139; Harl. MS. 1359, fo. 24 of second part; alteration 23 May, 23 H. VI., 1445, to the same, certifying arms (differing from the above) as worne by him in the service of Henry V., "in battaile, watch and warde," 1 July 1441, 19 H. VI. MS. Ashm. 857, fo. 520-1, copy of confirmation, Bodleian Lib.; in Grants II., 533, the dates are 5 July, 19 H. VI., 1441, and 23 May, 23 H. VI., 1445.

  ,, Richard, of Codrington, co. Glouc., descended from Thomas, 2nd s. of John Codrington of C., *temp.* H. VI., and from an heir general of Clifford, of Frampton upon Severn, by an heir general of Test of the same, confirmed, Quarterly of 6, *circa* 1604, by Camden. Harl. MSS. 1422, fo. 110, 6095, fo. 22, and 5887, fo. 89; Le Neve's MS. 313.

COFFYN, William, of Haddon, co. Derby, crest 24 Aug. 1522, by T. Wriothesley, Gart. Harl. MS. 1507, fo. 10ᵇ and 8ᵇ; copy of grant in French, Q's Coll. Oxf. MSS. 38, fo. 32, and 146, fo. 43.

COGAN, ..., gu., 3 laurel leaves erect arg., in the centre chief point a mullet of 6 points or, Quartering Hamersley, 13 Nov. 1632, by Segar. Add. MS. 12,225, fo. 28ᵇ.

COGGESHALL (John), Melton, Suffolk, 1576, by Cooke, Clar. Harl. MS. 1085, fo. 15ᵇ.

COGHILL, Thomas, of Knaresbrough, and John, of London, his uncle, } erm., a chev. betw. three cocks gu., 1616, by R. St. George, Norr. Stowe MS. 706, fo. 17.

  ,, sons of John, late of London, Henry, of Aldenham, Herts, Thomas, of Bletchington, Oxon, } merchᵗ, lineally descended from Coghill, of Coghill Hall, Knaresborough, by St. George. Le Neve's MS. 500; Add. MS. 14,295, fo. 57; C. 29, 107ᵇ [Visit.] Oxon. [1634]; Add. MS. 4966, fo. 46; Harl. MSS. 1105, fo. 5, and 1441, fo. 152ᵇ.

COKAYNE, William, the eldest, now citizen and skinner, of London, s. of Roger, of Badesley, etc., arms (Quarterly of 7) and crest exemplified 10 Oct. 1597, by W. Dethick, Gart. Copy Q's Coll. Oxf. MS. 36, fo. 61; Misc. Gen. et Her., 3 S., iii., 261.

COKE, John, Master and Fellow Trin. Coll., Cambr., Sec. to Sir Wᵐ Morice, Sec. of State, 18 Feb. 1662-3, by W. Dugdale, Norr. Her. Coll.; Harl. MS. 6179, fo. 67. *See also* COCK.

COKESEY, John, of Eversham, Yorks, *sic* .... Add. MS. 26,702, fo. 76.

COKEYNE, *see* [COKAYNE and] GOOKEINE.

COKSON, John, of co. Lanc., gift by the Earl of Warwick, 1562 (Harvey's Grants). Add. MS. 16,940, fo. 11 ; Harl. MS. 5887, fo. 101^b.

COLBARNE (W^m, York Herald, died 13 Sept. 1567), (? by Barker, very doubtful), arg., a chev. betw. 3 bugle horns sa. stringed or, Crest, out of a Coronet or, a stag's head erased sa., attired or. Harl. MS. 5846, fo. 29^b ; [Harl. MS. 1394, fo. 29^b].

COLBOURNE, W^m, of Bruton, Som^t, ..., by Segar. Add. MS. 12,225, fo. 29 ; C. 22, fo. 378^b, Her. Coll., and Guil. 316 ; [another coat, Harl. MS. 1394, fo. 29].

COLBRAND, Thomas, esq., s. of Ralph, s. of Thomas, s. of John, who beareth, az., three levels gold, which was given in respect of his even and just service done to his prince and country. Quarterly, by Ro. Cooke, Clar. Stowe MS. 670, fo. 4 ; Add. MSS. 12,474, fo. 53^b, and 14,297, fo. 4.

  ,, James, of Chichester, Harl. MS. 1453, fo. 6, same coat and crest as above, by Sir G. Dethick, Gart. Add. MS. 26,753, fo. 118.

COLEBRANDE, James, of Chichester, Quarterly, ..., by R. St. George. Harl. MS. 1359, fo. 116^b ; Add. MS. 4966, fo. 62.

COLCHESTER, Richard, of Gray's Inn, gent., and cursitor of the Court of Chancery for London, s. of Rich^d, s. of Richard, of Honington, co. Warw., gent., crest 20 Dec. 1626, by Segar. Add. MS. 12,225, fo. 29^b ; Harl. MS. 6140, fo. 76 ; Guil. 88.

COLDEWELL, John, D^r of Med., arms, 18 Feb. 1578-9, by Flower. MS. Ashm. 834, fo. 19^b, copy of grant, Bodleian Lib.

COLDHAM, ..., of Midhurst, Sussex, az., a mullet arg^t charged with a torteaux ....., by Segar. Add. MS. 12,225, fo. 29.

COLE, ..., of Kent, crest ...., Barker's Grants. Harl. MS. 5846, fo. 29^b.

  ,, John, Malldon, Essex, Esq., 10 Aug. 1561, by G. Dethick. Harl. MSS. 1441, fo. 70, 1359, fo. 23^b, and 1422, fo. 86 ; Add. MS. 14,295, fo. 51 ; Q's Coll. Oxf. MS. 145, fo. 15.

  ,, John, of Oxford, D.D. *See* William.

  ,, Ralph, Mayor of Newcastle-upon-Tyne, Northumberland, by Segar. Add. MS. 12,225, fo. 29^b ; Harl. MS. 6140, fo. 86^b.

  ,, Ralph, and his son, Sir Nicholas, Knt. and Bart., of Newcastle-upon-Tyne, 3 Dec. 1641, by Borough. Harl. MS. 1105, fo. 57^b ; Guil. 202.

  ,, Richard, of Nailsea, Somerset, Justice of the Peace and Capt of a troop of Horse in the sayd co. (descended from Cole, of Colchester, Harl. MS. 1422), crest 1623, by R. St. George. Add. MS. 14,295, fo. 70 ; Harl. MS. 1422, fo. 86.

  ,, Richard, of Shenley Hall, Herts, High Sheriff, 27 Nov. 1640, by Borough. Harl. MSS. 1105, fo. 57^b, and 1069, fo. 110 : Guil. 387 ; copy of grant, Harl. MS. 5857, fo. 133.

  ,, Solomon, of Lysle, Hants, Quartering Deering, or on escocheon of pretence, ..., by Segar. Add. MS. 12,225, fo. 30.

  ,, Thomas, s. of W^m, s. of Thos, all of London, descend. out of Slade, Devon, confirmed by Segar. Add. MS. 12,225, fo. 30.

  ,, W^m, of Oxford, esq., 20 Nov. 1589, by Cooke. Harl. MSS. 1359, fo. 97^b, and 1422, fo. 86 ; Grants II., 484 ; Add. MS. 4966, fo. 87^b ; Harl. MS. 1412 (Stowe MS. 670, fo. 36, as John, D.D., Dean of Lincoln at Oxford).

  ,, Sir William, Sheriff of London and Middx., 1694-5, and a patent, by Sir H. St. George, 1694, a quiver. Harl. MS. 6197, fo. 86^b (?).

COLEPEPER, Lord, supporters at Oxford, 1 March 1644-5, by Sir E. Walker, Gart. Her. Coll., fo. 11.

COLES, Humphrey, of North Tawton, and now of Croke Burnell, co. Devon, coat

I

and crest, Barker's Grants.   Harl. MS. 5846, fo. 23 ; Stowe MS. 692, fo. 31[b] ; Harl. MS. 5887, fo. 8.

COLING, Richard, Sec. to Lord Chamberlains, Edward, Earl of March, and to Henry, Earl of St. Albans, 10 Dec. 1671 or 1672, 23 Chas. II., by Walker. Add. MS. 14,293, fo. 70 ; Harl. MS. 1172, fo. 39 (Guil. 385), copy of grant.

COLLAR, John, of London, gent., 2 June 1569, by G. Dethick.   Harl. MS. 1441, fo. 102, and Q's Coll. Oxf. MS. 145, fo. 52[b].

COLLARD, John, of Spaxton, Somerset, 24 Nov. 1666, by Sir E. Walker, Gart. Her. Coll., fo. 63.

„   William, of Bramston, Essex (15 or) 16 June 1640, by Borough.   Harl. MSS. 1105, fo. 57, 1069, fo. 110, and 1441, fo. 58[b] ; Add. MS. 14,293, fo. 17[b], 124 ; copy of grant in Harl. MS. 5857, fo. 132 : Add. MS. 26,702, fo. 93[b] ; Guil. 380.

COLLENS, John, of Barnes Hill (or Collenswell), Devon, ..., by Cooke.   Stowe MS. 670, fo. 32.

COLLEN, John, of High Laver, Essex, ..., by Cooke.   Harl. MSS. 1359, fo. 97[b], and 1422, fo. 85 ; Grants II., 614 ; Stowe MS. 670, fo. 36[b] ; Add. MSS. 14,297, fo. 34[b], and 4966, fo. 89.

COLLENS, Jane, d. and coh. of Nycholas, of Broxhed, Essex, wife of Edmond West of Darly Abbey, co. Derby, grant 6 Nov. 1560, by Harvey.   Copy of grant, Harl. MS. 1116, fo. 54, 69[b] ; Add. MS. 16,940, fo. 17[b] ; Proc. Soc. Antiq., 1897, fo. 349 (6th).

COLLETT, Anthony, of Westerfield, Suff., and to Samuel, s. of Philologus, 2nd bro. of Anthony and dec[d], 14 Aug. 1664.   Harl. MS. 1105, fo. 38 and 39[b] ; Crispe's Frag. Gen., i., 57 ; Bysshe's Grants, 32, by Bysshe, Clar. (as Collet).

COLLIER, Francis, of Darlaston, Staff., descended from Robert, who came out of France into England temp. H. VI., confirmed 10 Oct. 1629, by Segar. Add. MS. 12,225, fo. 30[b] ; MS. Ashm. 858, fo. 95, copy of grant, Bodleian Lib. ; Grants II., fo. 686 (Guil. 53), Collier quartering 2, Dorington, and 3 [Hussey], erm., two bars gules ; exemplified, Harl. MS. 6140, fo. 64[b].

COLLYER, Richard, of Puddletrent-hyde, Dorset, gent., s. of John (s. of Henry), and other his brethren, confirmed 20 Oct. 1586, 28 Eliz., by W. Dethick. Stowe MS. 676, fo. 64, and copy of grant, Q's Coll. Oxf. MS. 37, fo. 89.

„   Robert, of Darlaston, Staff., gift 1559 (by Harvey).   Add. MS. 16,940, fo. 34.

COLLINGBORNE, William, of Wiltshire, gent., given by Mr Hawkeslow, King of the south marches of England, 12 March, 13 Ed. IV., 1472-3.   Add. MS. 14,295, fo. 5 ; Harl. MSS. 1115, fo.   , and 1359, fo. 12.

COLLIN, Joshua, of London, consin german of John, of Lincoln's Inn, certified or testified 21 Jan. 1639-40, by W. Le Neve, Clar.   Grants II., 614 ; Misc. Gen. et Her., 3rd S., vol. v., 121.

COLTHURST, Edmund, of Hinton, Somt., 24 Sept. 1573, by Cooke, Clar.   Harl. MS. 1441, fo. 151 ; Cains Coll. Camb. MS. 551, fo. 30[b] (among Camden's gifts) ; Harl. MS. 1385, fo. 42.

„   Mathew, "haberdasher of hattes," London.   Harl. MS. 1441, fo. 151.

COLLINS, Henry, of Budes or Budby, Kent, 10 May 1570, by G. Dethick.   Harl. MS. 1441, fo. 102[b] ; Q's Coll. Oxf. MS. 145, fo. 53[b].

„   John, of Betterton, Berks, 6 May 1672, by Sir E. Bysshe.   Harl. MS. 1105, fo. 42.

„   Joshua, see COLLIN.

„   Richard, of Upton, co. Hereford (one of the officers (ushers) of H.M.'s Chamber), s. of Henry, of King's Stanford in said co., descended from Collins of Shropshire, confirmed Oct. 1612, by Camden.   Harl. MSS. 1422, fo. 37[b], and 6095, fo. 24 ; Guil. 266, Robert.

COLLINS, Thomas (Collyns), prior of Tywardreth, Cornwall, 16 March 1522-3, by Writhe, Gart., and Benolte, Clar. Add. MS. 14,315, fo. 45.

„ Thomas, of Brightling, Sussex, testified . . . ., by Segar. Add. MS. 12,225, fo. 30ᵇ; C. 27, fo. 130, Sussex [1633], Her. Coll.; Harl. MS. 5887, fo. 114ᵇ; Guil. 229; Harl. MS. 1562, fo. 109.

„ Wᵐ, of Rotterdam, Holland, ..., Burke's Armory.

COLSTON, John, of London, s. of Henry, s. of John, and of Linc., by Nich. Charles, Lancʳ Herald, 1603—17. Add. MS. 4966, fo. 45ᵇ.

COLTE, ..., of Suffolk, Quarterly, ..., by Cooke. Harl. MS. 1359, fo. 92ᵇ; Add. MS. 4966, fo. 37ᵇ.

COLVILE (Sir Thomas), Isle of Ely, ..., by Cooke. Stowe MS. 670, fo. 47; Quarterly, Harl. MS. 6140, fo. 52.

COLWALL, Thomas, and Daniel, of London, } sons of Arnold, of the city of Glouc., 20 Jan. 1670-1. Harl. MS. 1105, fo. 22; Bysshe's Grants, fo. 26, Her. Coll.

COLYARE (see COLLIER), Robert, of Darlaston, Staff., gift . . . . 1559 (Harvey's Grants). Add. MS. 16,940, fo. 34.

COMBE, John, of Stratford-upon-Avon (father of the usurer, the friend of Shakespeare), 4 Nov. 1584, by Cooke. Harl. MS. 1359, fo. 117ᵇ; Add. MSS. 12,474, fo. 55, 4966, fo. 20; Harl. MS. 1563, fo. 124; Stowe MS. 670.

COMB, John, of London, July 1603, by Camden. Morgan's Sphere, 117.

COMPTON, John, of London, gent., 14 Oct., 8 H. VIII., 1516, by Wriothesley, Gart., and Benolte, Clar. Copy of grant, MS. Rawl. B. 102, fo. 110ᵇ, Bodleian Lib.

„ William, of Compton Wyniates als Compton in the Hole, co. Warwick, s. of Edmund, s. of Robert, s. of William, augmentation (by letters patent of Nov.), exemplified 14 Dec., 4 Hy. VIII., 1512, and crest by Wriothesley, by warrant under the King's sign manual 7 Nov., 14 H. VIII. Harl. MS. 6073, fo. 2, for copy of grant, Brit. Mus.; Add. MSS. 14,294, fo. 55ᵇ, and 29,785, fo. 13.

COMPAIGNE, Bartholomew, 14 Aug. 1562 temp. Eliz., by G. Dethick. Harl. MS. 1359, fo. 70ᵇ; copy of grant, Q's Coll. Oxf. MS. 39, fo. 123; Grants I., 93.

COMPORT, Christopher, of Eltham, gent., 1 Dec. 1663, by Walker. Harl. MS. 1172, fo. 44, 65, copy of grant; Add. MSS. 14,293, fo. 45, and 14,294, fo. 16; Her. and Geneal. i., 83; Guil. 361.

CONDE, John, Newark, Notts, Clerk of the peace (for the County), 13 July 1663, by W. Dugdale, Norr., Her. Coll. Harl. MS. 6179, fo. 71ᵇ.

CONDON, Thoˢ, of Wellerby, Yorks, and heir to the lord Morville, crest 22 June 1627, by Borough. Harl. MS. 1422, fo. 14ᵇ; Guil. 227.

CONNOCK, John, Liscard, gent., 27 March 1577, by Ro. Cooke, Clar. Grants II., 514.

CONRADUS, Wm., of London, s. of Fredᵏ, of Lubeck in Germany, 10 April, 15 Jac., 1617, by Segar. Add. MS. 12,225, fo. 27ᵇ.

CONSTABLE, Henry, s. and h. of Sir Robᵗ, Knt., s. of Sir Robert by Cath. Manners, etc., Quarterly, confirmed . . . ., by Segar and Camden. Add. MS. 12,225, fo. 31.

CONSTANTINE, Richard, of London, s. of Philip of Gloucester (Chester in Add. MS.), 2ⁿᵈ s. of Wᵐ of Whitchurch, Salop, gent., confirmation of arms 12 July 1575 (22 July in Add. MS.), 17 Q. Eliz., by Cooke. Harl. MSS. 1359, fo. 20, and 1422, fo. 51; Add. MS. 14,295, fo. 49.

CONTARANUS, Sir Aloysius, liege Ambassʳ from Venice, augmentation 20 July 1629 at Westminster, with remainder to his brother Jasper. MS. Ashm. 858, fo. 84—86, copy of letters patent, Bodleian Lib.

CONTREY (see CUNTREY), Thomas, s. of Thomas of Reculver, Kent, 14 Aug. 1612, by Segar, Gart. Harl. MS. 6140, fo. 25ᵇ.

CONY, Henry, of Yaxley, Hunts, s. of Wᵐ and Katherine, dau. of Robᵗ Throckmorton

of Brampton in same co., 1 April 1609, by Camden. Harl. MSS. 1422,
fo. 21, and 6095, fo. 11ᵇ; Guil. 199.

COONNY or CONY, Richard, of Moreton, co. Linc., coat and crest (Barker's Grants).
Harl. MSS. 5846, fo. 30, and 6179, fo. 12ᵇ.

CONEY, Sir Thomas, of Bassingthorp, Knt., and John of Whissendine, Rutland,
2 June 1612, by Segar. Add. MS. 12,225, fo. 31; Guil. 358; Harl. MS.
6140, fo. 80, crest 12 June 1614 : a talbot couped gules.

CONY, William, of Walpole, Norfolk, 11 Feb. 1634-5, by R. Sᵗ George, Clar. Harl.
MS. 1105, fo. 8ᵇ.

CONYARES, ..., of Bagdell Hall, Yorks, and Conyers of the Temple ? by Cooke . . . .
Harl. MS. 1359, fo. 114ᵇ; Add. MS. 4964 [? 6], fo. 100.

CONYERS, Sir George, Knt., crest granted 18 May, 2 Edw. VI., 1548, by G. Dethick.
Harl. MS. 1507, fo. 450, copy of grant, Brit. Mus. ; Harl. MS. 1359, fo. 3 ;
Grants I., 320 ; Stowe MS. 676, fo. 17ᵇ ; Q's Coll. Oxf. MSS. 39, fo. 22,
and 39, fo. 17 ; Le Neve's MS. 450.

COODE, Edward, Posthumous, M.A. and fellow Brasenose Coll., Oxf., s. of John, of
Collington, co. Hereford, etc., 24 July 1660, by Walker. Add. MS. 14,294,
fo. 28ᵇ, crest, a demi-heron volant arg., beaked or, etc. ; Barker's Grants ;
Harl. MS. 5846, fo. 27 ; Stowe MS. 692, fo. 30ᵇ, "burnt and never
delivered."

COOKE, Bryan, of Doncaster, confirmed 27 Aug. 1635, by H. St. George, Norr.
Harl. MS. 1470, fo. 198. 252 ; Guil. 172 ; Harl. MS. 1105, fo. 9 ; The
Seize Quarters of family of Bryan Cooke, 1857, p. 109.

   „   Edmond, of Lozenes in Kent, s. and h. of Henry of Broadwater, Sussex, and
to the posterity of them both, 6 Sept. 1574, 16 Q. Eliz., by Cooke. Harl.
MS. 1359, fo. 123.

   „   Edward, Mildham, Suff., ..., by Cooke. Stowe MS. 670, fo. 31, Quarterly
of 4 and two crests ; there is also an achievement Quarterly of 6 to his son
John on the next page (fo. 31ᵇ).

   „   (Sir George, 1ˢᵗ Bart.), Wheatley, Yorks, Bart., 27 Jan. 1679-1680 (?), by
W. Dugdale. Grants III., fo. 100.

COOK, John, Exeter, Devon, 19 Nov. 1677, by Dugdale, Gart., and H. St. George,
Norr. Harl. MS. 6834, fo. 178 ; Grants III., fo. 67.

COOKE, John, s. of Geo., of Giggleswick, Yorks, 6 June 1653, by Ryley, Clar. (?),
confirmed 1662. Bysshe's Grants, fo. 12, Her. Coll. ; Harl. MS. 1105,
fo. 19 ; copy of grant, Proc. Soc. Antiq., 2nd S., xvi., fo. 354 ; Harl. MS.
1105, fo. 19.

   „   John, of Fulwell Hatch, Essex, Esquire, of the body to Hen. VIII., by
T. Wriothesley, Gart., and Benolte, Clar. MS. Ashm. 858, fo. 23ᵇ, transcribed
from an 8vo MS. of Sir Hy. St. George, now (25 Feb. 1661-2) in the
Custody of Sylvanus Morgan, fo. 208 ? D. 4, Her. Coll. Harl. MS. 1541,
fo. 4 ; crest in Harl. MS. 1432, fo. 6.

   „   John, gent., 20 Feb., 6 Ed. VI., 1551-2, by G. Dethick, Gart. Grants I.,
264, see Cock's Quarterly : 1 and 4, gu., fretty ar., on a fesse sa. three
coaks [cocks] of the 2ᵈ; 2 and 3, sa., on a chevron engrailed arg. three
ermines of the field between three pheons or, all within a border or. Crest,
a demi-lion couped gu., langued and armed az., holding a gilly
flower gu., stalked and leaved vert, around his neck a collar with a
chain argt.

COKE, John, of Upper Sommer, Hants, coat and crest. Barker's Grants ; Cock in
Harl. MS. 1422, fo. 61 ; Harl. MS. 5846, fo. 22ᵇ ; Stowe MS. 692, fo. 31,
as Cooke.

COOKE, John, of Little Staybridge, Essex, 11 Nov. 1585, by Cooke, Clar. Harl.
MSS. 1359, fo. 102ᵇ, and 1422, fo. 83ᵇ; (as Cock in Stowe MS. 670, fo. 29,
and Add. MS. 14,297, fo. 27, but without the label of three).

   „   John, of Shafton, now of Westminster, confirmed by R. St. George (entered
9 March 1685-6, by H. St. George). Add. MS. 14,295, fo. 71.

COOKE, John, 1663, *see* COKE.

COOK, John, of the Inner Temple, 27 Jan. 1679-80, by Sir W. Dugdale and H. St. George, Norr. Add. MS. 14,831, fo. 17, and Grants III., fo. 102; Misc. Gen. et Her., 2nd S., vol. iv., p. 136; Harl. MS. 6179, fo. 60.

COOKE, Nycholas, of Lynstead, Suff., gift 1561. Harvey's Grants; Add. MS. 16,940, fo. 17^b; (confirmed 15 July 1560, by Cooke, in Eastern Counties Collectanea, i., 43, copy of grant, Brit. Mus.; there is an error here as Cooke was not at this date even a member of the College) Eastern Counties Collectanea, i., 43.

„ Sir Philip, of Essex, H. VI..... Add. MS. 26,702, fo. 30^b.

„ Ralphe, of Bristow, Surrey, D.D. and rector there, 12 Aug. 1662. Harl. MS. 1105, fo. 19, copy of grant, Brit. Mus.; Harl. MS. 1470, fo. 104; Bysshe's Grants, fo. 14, Her. Coll.; Barstow in Guil. 386.

„ Sir Rich^d, princ. Sec^y of State for Ireland and Chanc. of the Excheq. there (s. and h. of Wm. of G^t Linford, Bucks, out of Lincolnsh.), confirmed 20 July 1612, by Camden. Guil. 289. (*See* Robert?)

„ Marmaduke, Preb. of York, ⎫ sons of Robert, of Campsal, s. of Hugh, of
William, L.L.D., chancellor ⎬ Campsal, by Alice, daughter of John
to Bishop of Ely, ⎭ Middleton of Norton, Yorks, 26 Sept.
1683, by Sir W. Dugdale, Gart., and
St. Geo., Norr. Harl. MS. 6834, fo. 78; Grants III., fo. 198.

„ Richard, Broomhall, Suff., a person well descended and allied, and a loyal subject, 26 July 1662, by Sir E. Walker, Gart. Her. Coll., fo. 48.

„ Robert, of Mildham, Norfolk, gent., granted 9 or 10 June 1556, 2 and 3 Ph. and Mary, by Hawley. Harl. MSS. 1470, fo. 254, and 1507, fo. 107; copies of grant, Brit. Mus.; Guil. 190; 10th June in Add. MS. 16,940, fo. 208; copy of grant, Q's Coll. Oxf. MS. 38, fo. 63; Le Neve's MS. 407; 10 July in Add. MS. 7098, fo. 79 (fo. 126).

„ Robert, Clar. King of Arms, grant 4 March 1597-8, by Flower. MS. Ashm. 834, i., fo. 17; copy of grant, Bodleian Lib.; Harl. MS. 6140, fo. 33.

„ Robert, of Langham, Suffolk, 1 May 1612, by Camden. Morgan's Sphere, 117. Harl. MSS. 1441, fo. 151, and 1172, fo. 8, copy of grant, Brit. Mus.

„ Thomas, Redmarley Oliver, co. Worc., 4th s. of Thomas, 2nd s. of John, of Norfolk, by Cooke, confirmed or testified by Segar. Add. MS. 14,295, fo. 82^b.

COOK, Thomas, Haberdasher, of London, arg., a lion passant on bend betw. 2 cotises gu., on a chief az. two stars or, by Segar. Add. MS. 12,225, fo. 31^b; Vinc. MS. 154, Her. Coll., and Guil. 171.

„ W^m, of Middx., 15 Nov. 1550, by Hawley (?). Add. MS. 16,940, fo. 204.

COKE, W^m, Milton, Kent, 15 or 25 Aug. 1551, by Hawley. Add. MSS. 16,940, fo. 204^b, and 14,295, fo. 93.

COOKE, W^m, of Cotton, Suff., gift 1561 (Harvey's Grants). Add. MS. 16,940, fo. 43.

„ W^m, London, 1587, by Cooke. Harl. MS. 1122, fo. 83^b; Add. MS. 4966, fo. 56^b.

COOKES, Sir Thos, Bart. (2nd and last), Nor- ⎫ 4 Dec. 1683, by Sir Wm Dugdale and
grove, co. Worc., s. of ⎬ St. Geo., Clar. Harl. MS. 6834,
Sir W^m (1st), High Slip, Worc., ⎭ fo. 78; Grants III., fo. 216.

COOKEINE, *see* GOOKEINE.

COOLINGE, *see* COLINGE.

COOPE, ..., crest ...., Barker's Grants. Harl. MS. 5846, fo. 28; Stowe MS. 692, fo. 30^b.

COOPER, Christopher, an assist.-gov^r city of Raleigh, Va., by W. Dethick, Gart. Copy of grant, Q's Coll. Oxf. MS. 36, fo. 170.

COOPER, Hector, Risegarth, in Walkinton, Yorks, 1 (or 24) Sept. 1612, by R. St. George, Clar. Stowe MS. 706, fo. 15 ; Harl. MS. 6197, fo. 12.

„   James, Hackesworth, Notts, brother to Barbara, by Cooke, Clar. Stowe MS. 670, fo. 38ᵇ.

„   Richard, s. of Richard, of Walthamstow, Essex, by R. St. George. Add. MS. 14,295, fo. 65 ; I. 23, fo. 34.

„   { Robert, s. and h. of Robert Seneschall or Steward of co. pal. of Durham.
    { George, 2ⁿᵈ s. by 1ˢᵗ wife.
    John, and   ] . . . ., 9 June, 7 Jac., 1609, by R. St. George.
    Christopher, and | Cowper in Harl. MS. 1359, fo. 29ᵇ ; see
    Meryall, wife of Thomas } Le Neve's MS. 498 ; Harl. MS. 1105,
    Bulmer of Wilton, gent., | fo. 59 ; Add. MS. 14,295, fo. 78, 59 ;
    by 2ⁿᵈ wife.   ] Harl. MS. 6940, fo. 34ᵇ.

„   Thomas, Bp. of Lincoln, 6 May 1572, by G. Dethick. Harl. MS. 1441, fo. 78ᵇ, and Q's Coll. Oxf. MS. 145, fo. 29.

„   Thomas, of Dowbiggin, Yorks, arms and crest granted by Segar. Add. MS. 12,225, fo. 31ᵇ ; M. 2, fo. 2ᵇ, Her. Coll. ; and Guil. 375.

„   Thomas, St. James Garlickhithe, London, 24 Nov. 1693, by T. St. George, Gart. and Clar. Grants IV., 150.

COOPERS' COMPANY, 27 Sept. 1509, by T. Wriothesley, Gart. Coopers Co., London, by James F. Frith, 1848, p. 34. Her. and Geneal., i., 121 ; Add. MS. 26,702, fo. 75.

COPLEY, Thomas, of Gatam (Gatton ?), Surrey, alteration of crest 16 Feb. 1568-9, by G. Dethick, Cooke and Flower. Harl. MS. 1441, fo. 70 ; MS. Ashm. 844, fo. 2, copy of grant ; Q's Coll. Oxf. MS. 39, fo. 146 (145, fo. 15) ; Sir Roger, Harl. MS. 5887, fo. 51.

COPPEN, Sir George, Clarke of the Crowne, Oct. 1608, by Camden. Harl. MSS. 1422, fo. 20ᵇ, and 6095, fo. 10.

„   Thomas, of London, ... 1640, by Borough. Harl. MS. 1105, fo. 1ᵇ and 57 ; Guil. 386.

COPPULL, Andrew, als Ogwell, of Ogwell Hall, co. Lanc., s. of Lawrence, 19 Feb. 1569-70, by G. Dethick. Harl. MS. 1441, fo. 82 ; Q's Coll. Oxf. MS. 145, fo. 36.

CORBET, Sarah, Viscountˢˢ, supporters 1 June 1680, by Dugdale, Gart. Harl. MS. 6834, fo. 178 ; Grants III., fo. 132.

„   John, Brodishe, Norfolk, confirmed by Harvey, Clar. Bannerman's MS. No. 9, 454.

CORBY, Robert de, granted 6 Jan. 1348-9, 22 Ed. III., by Robt. de Morle, Marshal of Ireland. Guil. Intro., p. 8 ; Camden's Remains, 219, 1ˢᵗ Ed.

CORDALL, Thomas, of London, Mercer, confirmed June 1612, by Camden. Harl. MSS. 1422, fo. 37ᵇ, and 6095, fo. 37ᵇ.

„   William, of Middlesex, see CARDALL, Barker's Grants. Stowe MS. 692. fo. 29ᵇ.

„   Wᵐ, master cooke to Q. Eliz., ... 1592, by Cooke. Harl. MS. 1359, fo. 94ᵇ.

CORDELL, John, of Long Melford, Suff., by T. Hawley,]
    Clar., 20 Feb., 2 Ed. VI., 1547-8. Harl. MS. |
    6140, fo. 60 ; copy, Brit. Mus., no date, bᵈ | Copies of grants, Visit.
    [buried ?] 7 Jan. 1563.   } Suff., 1561, Howard,
„   William, of Long Melford, 10 or 20 Oct. 1549, { i., 246 ; copy of grant,
    3 Edw. VI., by Hawley ; also signed by Cooke. | Brit. Mus.
    Hawley died 21 Aug. 1557. Master of the |
    Rolls, burᵈ 19 June 1581.   ]

„   Emma, wife of John, 1554, dau. of Hy. Webbe of Kimbolton.

CORDWAINERS' COMPANY, 25 June 1579, by Cooke. Misc. Gen. et Her., i., 242, copy of grant, Brit. Mus.

COREN (COREY ?), Richard, D.D., Archdeacon of Oxford and of Colchester,

Barker's Grants, coat and ? crest, "the sun shining or."   Harl. MS. 5846, fo. 30 ; Add. MS. 26,702, fo. 10b.

CORNWALL, ..., of Dorset, ... Dec. 1608, by Camden. Harl. MSS. 1422, fo. 20b, and 6095, fo. 10 ; Guil. 367.

CORPUS CHRISTI COLL., Camb., 23 Dec. 1570, by Cooke, Clar. Cat. Her. Exhib. Soc. Antiq., 66.

CORRANCE, see URREN.

CORREY, Christopher, s. and h. of Thomas, of Northumberland, grant 23 Nov. 1579, by G. Dethick. Stowe MS. 676, fo. 53, copy of grant, and Q's Coll. Oxf. MS. 37, fo. 72, in Latin ; Grants I., 297.

CORSON, Sir Robert de, Baron Holy Roman Empire, 30 Aug. 1500, letters testimonial by Maximilian, Emperor. MS. Ashm. 834, fo. 72, copy of letters patent, Bodleian Lib. ; Harl. MS. 4900, fo. 27b.

CORY, John, of London, gent., sonne of Robert of Tibenham, Norfolk, s. of Thomas, of Norwich, 1st s. of Wm of Bramerton in said Co., confirmed Feb. 1612, by Camden. Grants II., 667 ; Harl. MS. 6095, fo. 26 ; Guil. 269 ; erroneously called Cary in Morgan's Sphere, p. 113.

„   Thos, bencher of the Inner Temple, prothonotary of the court of Com. pleas (18 March) 1639, by Borough. Harl. MS. 1105, fo. 57 ; Guil. 269 ; Stowe MS. 670, fo. 10.

COSEN, Gerard, of Hernunghall or Hernninghall, Norfolk, ..., by Cooke. Harl. MSS. 1359, fo. 88, and 5887, fo. 18 ; Add. MS. 4966, fo. 52.

„   Robert, of Dorset, 15 April 1454 ? by Leigh. Harl. MS. 1116, fo. 38b.

COSSEN, ..., Raveningham, Norfolk, ... 1585. Burke's Armory.

COSWORTH, John, of Cosworth, Cornwall, 2nd s. of Robert, 10 Dec. 1547, by Thos Hawley. Add. MSS. 16,940, fo. 202, and 7098, fo. 78 (fo. 59) ; Harl. MS. 5887, fo. 52, of London, mercer.

COSYN, Edward, of Charley Hall, co. Leic., s. and h. of Edward, clerk of the Carriages to K. Jas., 7 June 1664. Bysshe's Grants, fo. 21, Her. Coll., ?granted (13 March 1651 in Edmondson) and confirmed ; Harl. MS. 1105, fo. 21, 7 June 1664.

„   John, Alderm. and J.P. of Newcastle-upon-Tyne, grant 12 May 1647, by Ryley. Harl. MS. 1470, fo. 41 ; Guil. 408.

COTELL or COTEEL, Sir Thomas, descended from an ancient family of Cotels, Devon, confirmed by Segar. Add. MS. 12,225, fo. 34b. See also COTTELL. Harl. MSS. 6140, fo. 63, and 5887, fo. 112b, gu., semée de burrs argt.

COTES, Chr, of Hanslope, Bucks, 17 June 1575, by ? Cooke or G. Dethick. Harl. MS. 1422, fo. 123b.

„   John, alderm., coat and crest, by Barker. Harl. MS. 5846, fo. 21 ; Stowe MS. 692, fo. 30, as Cootes.

COTESFORD, John, of Launton, Oxfordshire, descended from Sir Roger and Catherine his wife, dau. and coh. of Sir Wm Shenshall or Shershall of Burton Shershall, Knt., who flourished temp. Ed. III., Quarterly, exemplified and confirmed and crest granted Feb. 1611-12, by Camden. Harl. MSS. 6095, fo. 18, and 1422, fo. 109 ; Guil. 71, as Cokesford.

COTTELL [COTTLE], Thos, of North Tawton, Devon, confirmed 8 Nov. 1580, by Cooke. Guil. 34 ; see Harl. MS. 5887, fo. 112b.

„   Sir Thomas, by Segar. See above, COTELL.

COTTINGTON, Sir Francis, ... Harl. MS. 1105, fo. 7b, by R. St. George, Clar.; Harl. MS. 1105, fo. 7b.

COULFE, Doctor, of Canterbury, confirmed or assigned 30 June 1615, by Camden. Harl. MSS. 1422, fo. 40, and 6095, fo. 38b ; Morgan's Sphere, p. 115 ; Guil. 147, and D. 14, fo. 128b, Her. Coll.

COURTHOPE, John, of Wyleigh, Sussex, 2nd s. of George, s. of John, certified 16 Feb. 1634-5, by Philpot, Somerset, etc. Harl. MS. 6179, fo. 67.

COVELL, Capt. Thos, of London, 10 Oct. 1629, by Segar. Add. MS. 12,225, fo. 32 ; C. 24 [Visit. Lond., 1634], fo. 117a, and Guil. 273,

COVENTRY, Richard, s. of Richard of Mollington, Cheshire, 24 Nov. 1603, 1 K. Jas., by Segar. Harl. MS. 1359, fo. 82ᵇ ; Add. MS. 12,225, fo. 32 ; William in Harl. MS. 1422, fo. 52.

„ Richard, of Grange . . . . 14 Nov. 1603, by Segar. Add. MS. 12,225, fo. 32 ; called Willm. in Harl. MS. 6179, fo. 15 ; Harl. MS. 6140, fo. 67ᵇ.

„ Thomas, of Crome D'Abitott, co. Worc., Esq., bencher of the Inner Temple, London, crest 10 Oct. 1602, by Camden. 10 Oct. in Harl. MS. 1422, fo. 37ᵇ: Add. MS. 14,295, fo. 120ᵇ : Harl. MSS. 1359, fo. 38ᵇ, and 6095, fo. 22ᵇ.

„ Sir Thomas, Baron Coventry, of Ailsborough, confirmed arms and crest and grant of supporters . . . ., by Segar. Add. MS. 12,225, fo. 28.

COWLEY, Robert, s. of Walter, s. of John, gent., of Salop, grant 18 Aug. 1597, by Dethick, Gart. Copy of grant, Q's Coll. Oxf. MS. 36, fo. 64.

„ Thomas, of Amsterdam, Feb. 1606, by Camden. Harl. MSS. 1422, fo. 19ᵇ, and 6095, fo. 6ᵇ.

„ Walter, London, Iremonger, } descendants of John, of Staffordsh., Esq.,
„ Edward, Apesley, co. Staff., { crest 8 Sept., 42 Eliz., 1600, by W. Dethick and Camden. Add. MS. 14,295, fo. 20 ; Harl. MSS. 6095, fo. 22ᵇ, and 1359, fo. 30.

COWPER, ..., Overleigh, Cheshire, 27 Sept. 1642. Berry and Burke's Armory ; Ormerod Hist. of Cheshire, i., 375.

„ George, of Runcton Holmes, Norfolk, by Harvey ? Clar. Le Neve MS. 352 ; Add. MS. 4966, fo. 28ᵇ.

„ John, of Stanton Drew, Somerset, s. of Richᵈ, of Winchcomb, Somerset, one of the Great pensioners attendant ordinary her most Royal person, granted 10 Dec. 1590, 33 Eliz., by W. Dethick (confirmed 23 April 1593). Stowe MS. 676, fo. 81, 90, 104 ; copy of grant, Q's Coll. Oxf. MSS. 36, fo. 26, and 27, fo. 120 ; Harl. MS. 6140, fo. 53ᵇ.

„ John, Moning, Essex, by Sir G. Dethick, Gart. Add. MS. 26,753, fo. 122ᵇ.

„ John, of London, by Cooke, Clar. Stowe MS. 670, fo. 52ᵇ.

„ John, of Ditcham, Sussex, s. of John, of D. (by Jane, dau. of . . . . Unwynne, younger son, of Horton als Morton, Wilts), s. of John by a dau. of Lewkenor, Kent, 9 Feb. 1614-15, by Camden. Harl. MSS. 1422, fo. 39ᵇ, and 6095, fo. 32. (Sotherton in margin.)

„ Mary, wife of Wᵐ Smith of London, ... by Cooke. Harl. MS. 1359, fo. 117ᵇ ; Stowe MS. 702, fo. 15.

„ Thomas, an ancient alderman of the city of Chester, 6 Nov. 1664, by Wm. Dugdale, Norr. Her. Coll.

„ Wm., als Thurgarton, of London and Notts, 1 Jan. 1549-50, by ? Hawley. Add. MS. 16,940, fo. 201ᵇ.

„ Wm., of Wye, Kent, ... 1633, by R. St. George, Clar. Harl. MS. 5887, fo. 114ᵇ.

Cox, Daniell, of Westminster, and Dr Daniell Coxe of Aldersgate St., London, 1648, by Squibb, Clar. Harl. MS. 6179, fo. 61ᵇ.

„ Edward (vel COKK), of London, gent., grant 21 or 26 Jan., 3 Q. Eliz., 1560-1, by G. Dethick. Harl. MS. 1359, fo. 35 ; 21 Jan., 1 Eliz., 1558-9, in Harl. MS. 1422, fo. 61 (Add. MS. 14,295, fo. 42, adds citizen and clothworker ; Inquis. post mortem 26 July 1620, 18 Jac., Wᵐ Cox, his son and heir) ; copy of grant, Q's Coll. Oxf. MS. 39, fo. 120 ; 25ᵗʰ January in Grants I., 246.

„ Thomas, see HAYWARD.

COXE, Thomas, of London, Dr in phys. and phys. in ord. to Chas. II., 20 Dec. 1665. Bysshe's Grants, fo. 23, Her. Coll. Harl. MS. 1105, fo. 21.

COYS, William (? of Bucks), s. of Roger, of London, testified by Ro. Cooke. Grants I., 389ᵇ.

CRACHERODE, Will., of Toppesfield, Essex, 15 July 1572, by Cooke, Clar. Harl. MS. 1137, fo. 42.

CRACROFT, ..., by Cooke, Clar. Stowe MS. 670, fo. 38ᵇ; Harl. MS. 6179, fo. 56.

CRAGGS, James, of city of Westminster (1 s. of Anthony, of Fawleyes and Wysel, als Wiserly, co. pal. Durham), one of the Secretaries, 18 Feb. 1690-1, by T. St. George, Gart., and H. [St. George], Clar. Stowe MSS. 714, fo. 132ᵇ, and 716, fo. 51ᵇ; Add. MS. 14,831, fo. 9; Grants IV., fo. 74.

CRANE, John, Clarke of the Kitchen to K. James, s. of John, s. of Wᵐ, of London, Esqʳ, confirmed 1606, by Camden. Harl. MS. 6095, fo. 21ᵇ; Guil. 289; Harl. MS. 5887, fo. 47ᵇ.

„ Sir Francis, of Mortlake, Surrey, 1 March 1624, by R. St. George, Clar. Harl. MS. 1105, fo. 6, 7, 11.

CRANFIELD, Edward, gent. usher, grandson of Lord Morley and Monteagle (s. of Edward), 25 March 1675, by Walker, Bysshe and Dugdale. Harl. MS. 6834, fo. 178; Grants III., fo. 11.

„ Lionel and } of London, confirmed 27 March 1613, by Camden. Add. MS. Thomas, } 14,295, fo. 64; Camden's Grants, 28, and certificate booke (not marked), 52, Her. Coll.

„ Randall, and to Sir Lionel, Knt., 2ⁿᵈ bro. to Randall, Aug. 1613, by Camden. Harl. MS. 6095, fo. 27ᵇ; alteration of arms granted 27 March 1613, change of crest 20 Oct., 19 Jac., 1621, by Segar; Add. MS. 12,225, fo. 34; Harl. MS. 6140, fo. 31; Lionel is Baron Cranfield and Lord High Treas. in Add. MS. 12,225, fo. 34.

CRANMER, Thos., Archbp. of Canterbury, ... Add. MS. 26,702, fo. 75ᵇ.

CRATFORD, ..., of Chelmarsh, co. Worc., 1613, by R. St. George, Clar. Stowe MS. 703, fo. 73.

CRAVEN, William, Alderm. and Sheriff of London, who came in Sheriff Smith's place, being lately put out of said office in Feb. 1600-1, gift 4 Feb. 1600-1, by W. Dethick and Camden. Add. MS. 14,295, fo. 116ᵇ; Harl. MS. 1359, fo. 37; 1601 in Stowe MS. 676, fo. 135; copy of grant, Q's Coll. Oxf. MS. 36, fo. 90.

„ Hon. William, Baron of Hampsted, grant of arms as an additional bearing to his other coat, which is granted in the 2ⁿᵈ place and supporters, by Segar. Add. MS. 12,225, fo. 32ᵇ.

CRAWLEY, ..., of Dorset, ..., Arg., a chev. gu. between 3 pears az., by Segar. Add. MS. 12,225, fo. 32ᵇ; Harl. MS. 6140, fo. 82.

„ . . . ., of Luton, Beds, or, on a fesse az. between 3 storks ppr., as many cross crosslets of the first, Quarterly, by Segar. Add. MS. 12,225, fo. 33; Harl. MS. 1531, fo. 166; different in Harl. MS. 6140, fo. 66ᵇ.

„ see SHRAWLEY, Kenelm, London, 1588, by Cooke. Stowe MS. 670, fo. 23; Harl. MS. 1359, fo. 113.

CREAGH, Sir Wᵐ, Knt., Newcastle-upon-Tyne, Northumberland, 3 March 1684-5, by Sir Wm. Dugdale and Norroy. Harl. MS. 6834, fo. 178; Grants III., fo. 257; Lansd. MS. 867, fo. 52.

CREED, William, D.D., prof. of Divʸ, Oxford, Canon of Ch. Ch., Archdeacon of Wilts, and Canon resid. of Sarum, 4 June 1663, by Walker. Add. MSS. 14,293, fo. 44, and 14,294, fo. 17ᵇ; Harl. MS. 1172, fo. 55; Guil. 259.

CREMOEER, ..., by Sir C. Barker, Gart. Add. MS. 26,702, fo. 56ᵇ.

CRESSEY, Henry, of Owlcotes, Notts, crest confirmed 21 June 1580, by Flower. MS. Ashm. 834, fo. 23ᵇ, copy of grant, Bodleian Lib.; Guil. 177; Stowe MS. 670, fo. 218ᵇ.

CRESWELL, Robert, of Purston (or Purslow), Northamptonsh. [? Preston, Northumbᵈ], gent., crest 20 Feb., 34 Q. Eliz., 1590, by W. Dethick. Stowe MS. 676, fo. 84 and 93; Harl. MS. 1359, fo. 19ᵇ; copy of grant, Q's Coll. Oxf. MS. 36, fo. 3; called Richard, s. of John, in Harl. MSS. 1441, fo. 103ᵇ, and 5847, fo. 54, and Add. MS. 12,454, fo. 54; Stowe MS. 703, fo. 58ᵇ.

CREWE, Thomas, of Kent, confirmed . . . . 1555-6 (Harvey's Grants). Add. MS. 16,940, fo. 25ᵇ.

CRICHE, ..., of Oxfordshire, and of London (ascribed to Edmond, of London, Add. MS. 4966, fo. 75), draper, master of Mercht. taylors 1624 ; 1619, by Segar, erm., on a pale sa., 3 crosses pattée fitchée or, a mullet for diff. Add. MS. 12,225, fo. 34 : Harl. MS. 1105, fo. 8.

CRIDLAND, John, Sergeant Major, of Spaxton, Somerset, and to nephews Francis, Henry, 1 June 1677, by Sir E. Walker, Gart. Her. Coll., fo. 64.

CRIKETOT, William, granted at Ilengast, in the feast of Corpus Xti 1410, 11 H. IV., by Thos. de Clervowe, Chevallier. Guillim Introduction, p. 8, and Camden's Remains, 222 : 9 Hen. V., 1421, in Harl. MS. 1178, fo. 45, 45ᵇ.

CRIMES, Thomas, citizen and haberdasher of London, 8 June 1575, by Cooke. Harl. MS. 1430, fo. 91ᵇ. *See also* GRYMES, with 4 quarterings named. Harl. MS. 1046, fo. 59ᵃᵇ ; Add. MS. 4966, fo. 96ᵇ.

CRIPPS, John, of Homestall, par. of East Grinstead, Surrey, 25 July 1662, 14 Chas. II. Bysshe's Grants and Her. Coll.: Guil. 349 ; Harl. MS. 1105, fo. 16ᵇ ; Add. MS. 14,293, fo. 13ᵇ.

CRISPE, Joan, dau. of Richard of Northampton, and wife to Richard (Robᵗ) Traps, Esq. and goldsmith of London, granted by Harvey 20 Nov. 1560, 3 Q. Eliz. Add. MS. 16,940, fo. 35ᵇ ; Harl. MSS. 1359, fo. 2ᵇ, and 1507, fo. 446, copy of grant, Brit. Mus., and Q's Coll. Oxf. MSS. 38, fo. 78 and 73, and 39, fo. 117 ; Le Neve's MS. 446 ; Family of Crispe, ii., 1.

   „ Ellis, of London, Sheriff, arms set outt by H. St. George, Richmond Her. Harl. MS. 1422, fo. 15ᵇ.

CROCKER, John, of Hooknorton, Oxon, Esq., confirmed 15 Nov. 1556, by Harvey. Add. MS. 16,940, fo. 10 ; Her. and Geneal., i., 80 ; Misc. Gen. et Her., i., 140, copy of grant, Brit. Mus. ; Grants I., 37ᵇ, 38.

CROFT, Sir Christopher, Knt., of York, Lord Mayor, confirmed 7 June 1649, by Ryley. Harl. MS. 1144, fo. 14 ; Surtees Soc., XLI., lii.; copy of grant, Brit. Mus.

CROFTS, William, Lord, supporters at Brussels 3 May 1658, by Sir E. Walker, Gart. Her. Coll., fo. 12.

CROKEY, Wᵐ, als JOHNSON, of Yorks, arms differenced 4 June 1496, by C. Carlile, Norr. Add. MS. 14,295, fo. 77ᵇ ; Stowe MS. 677, fo. 5 ; Harl. MSS. 1069, fo. 1, 1470, fo. 159, and 1507, fo. 3 ; copy of grant, Brit. Mus., and Harl. MS. 1172, fo. 2ᵇ, and Q's Coll. Oxf. MSS. 37, fo. 7, 38, fo. 19, and 146, fo. 18. *See* CROOKHEY below. Guil. 396.

CROME, Valentine, of Lincoln's Inn, 1 Nov. 1669, by Sir E. Walker, Gart. Her. Coll., fo. 63.

CROMER, Robert, of Yarmouth, 24 April 1494, by Richmond Clar. Harl. MS. 1116, fo. 38ᵇ.

CROMPTON, Thomas, of London, Dʳ of Law, s. and h. of Wᵐ (by Elizth., d. and h. of Thoˢ Boughton of Mardich, Essex), s. and h. of Thoˢ, of Stafford, arms quarterly, confirmed . . . . 1595, by Lee. Add. MS. 14,295, fo. 50; Harl. MSS. 1422, fo. 118, and 1359, fo. 23ᵇ.

   „ William, of Stone, co. Staff., crest 26 April 1562, by Flower. Add. MS. 14,293, fo. 126.

CROMWELL, Gregorie, Lord, coat and crest and supporters 1543, 33 H. VIII., by C. Barker, Gart. Add. MS. 14,294, fo. 55ᵇ : "geven hym by Mʳ Garter having the King's bill, signed for his discharge, or else he would not have given him any, for that his father was atteynted." Harl. MSS. 6179, fo. 15ᵇ, and 5846, fo. 21ᵇ ; Stowe MS. 692, fo. 31.

CROOKE, Sir John (Bucks), by R. St. George, Clar. Add. MS. 14,295, fo. 58 ; C. 26, fo. 97ᵇ, Her. Coll.

CROOKHEY als CROCKHAY als JOHNSON, William, grant 4 June 1496, by Carlisle. Harl. MSS. 1507, fo. 3, and 1470, fo. 159, copy of grant, Brit. Mus.; Gnil. 396 ; Harl. MSS. 1069, fo. 1, 1422, fo. 2. *See* CROKEY above.

CROOKS, ... of Winchester, Hants, gu., a saltire erm. betw. four fleurs-de-lis or, ... by Segar. Add. MS. 12,225, fo. 33ᵇ.

CROOME, ... paly bendy or and gu., quartering .... , by Segar. Add. MS. 12,225, fo. 33.

CROPLEY, Thomas, of co. Cambridge, ... , by Camden : arg., on a chief gu. three owls of the field. Harl. MSS. 1422, fo. 17, and 6095, fo. 1.

   „   Thomas, of Rockells hall in Shelland, Suff., s. of William, of Bury St. Edmunds, alteration of arms and crest 12 May 1635, by R. St. George. Harl. MS. 1470, fo. 98, 235 ; Guil. 222.

CROSMAN, Samuel, B.D., 1663, *see* TROTMAN.

CROSS, Robert, of Churlonge, Somersets., by Cooke's depy., 23 June 1584. Stowe MS. 670, fo. 8 ; copy of grant, MS. Rawl. B. 102, fo. 110, Bodleian Lib.

   „   Sir Robert, Knt. (s. of Wm., of Charlinch, Somerset), for services against the Spanish Armada 1588, at the burning of the Spanish fleet at Cadiz and for the winning of Cales 1596 ; crest April 1602, by Camden. Cott. MS., Faustina E. 1, fo. 58ᵇ ; Guil. 382 ; Harl. MS. 6140, fo. 42ᵇ.

CROUCH, John, of London, gent., s. of John, of Cornibury, nʳ Buntingford, Herts, 10 March 1608, by W. Camden, Clar. Harl. MSS. 1422, fo. 21, and 6095, fo. 12 ; Guillim 77 ; Harl. MS. 5887, fo. 63ᵇ.

CROUCHER, Henry, of Exton, co. Southants, High Sheriff, dated at the Office of Arms 14 Feb. 1658-9, by Bysshe. Harl. MS. 1172, fo. 34ᵇ, copy of grant.

CROW, Giles, of Brasted, Kent, allowed .... 1586, by Cooke. Add. MS. 4966, fo. 35 ; Harl. MSS. 1359, fo. 90, and 1422, fo. 93 ; Guil. 233.

   „   *See* Chʳ Crowe, arms gyronny of eight or and sa., on a chief of the 2ⁿᵈ two leopards' heads of the first, crest, Five arrows, one in pale and four in saltire or, barbed gu., feathered argᵗ. Caius Coll. Camb. MS. 551, fo. 30ᵇ ; Camden's Grants.

CROWE, Christopher, of East Bilney, Norfolk, 27 May 1614, by Camden. Harl. MS. 6095, fo. 41, and Le Neve's MS. 354.

CROWTHER, (1) John, of Middleton, (2) Richard, of Broadstone.

   „   (3) Thomas, of Sparchford,

   „   (4) Lewes, of Ludlow, and

   „   (5) Edward, of Millichapp, confirmed 20 Feb. 1562, by G. Dethick. Harl. MS. 1441, fo. 61 ; Stowe MS. 703, fo. 4ᵇ, and Q's Coll. Oxf. MS. 145, fo. 1ᵇ.

   „   John, of Exeter, coat and crest 27 March, 20 Hen. VIII., 1529, by T. Wriothesley, Gart. Le Neve MS. 463.

CRUGGE, ... crest .... Barker's Grants ; Harl. MS. 5846, fo. 28 ; Stowe MS. 692, fo. 30 ; Add. MS. 26,702, fo. 64ᵇ.

CRULE, John, of Cambray, under the dominion of the King of Spain, said to be descended from John (and Elizᵗʰ his wife, dau. to the Lord Penningʈon in Com. Lanc.), s. of Robᵗ, s. of Hugh, about 1288, quartering Pennington, 8 March 1631-2, by Segar. Add. MS. 12,225, fo. 33ᵇ ; Harl. MS. 6110, fo. 80.

CRUX, John, of Greenhouse in Milton, Kent, confirmed July, 7 Chas. I., 1631, by R. St. George. 10 July in Harl. MS. 1470, fo. 40, and 163 for copy of grant, British Mus. ; D. 18, fo. 58, Her. Coll. ; (Guil. 211, also borne by John Crux of Sheldwick in said co. of Kent).

CUDWORTH, John, of Werneth, co. Lanc., 23 Oct. 1613, by R. St. George. Add. MS. 14,295, fo. 61.

CUER, Thomas, of London, Chief sadler to the Queen, 20 Dec. 1561, by Harvey. Harl. MS. 1422, fo. 23 ; Add. MS. 16,940, fo. 40. *See* Anne Bennet his wife.

CUERTON, John, now dwelling at Bilbao in Spain, confirmed, no date, ... by Harvey. Ashm. MS. 834, fo. 49, copy of grant. Bodleian Lib.

CUFFE, John, of Ilchester, Somerset, granted .... , by Barker, 1526—49. Harl. MS. 5846, fo. 23 ; Stowe MS. 692, fo. 31ᵇ ; Guil. 367, as 1544.

CULCHETH, ...,   {crest in Harl. MS. 5846, fo. 26^b, a mooryan standing naked, sa., holding a target like a lion's face az., etc., and Stowe MS. 692, fo. 30^b, as CALCHETH. Stowe MS. 692, fo. 29, arg^t, a griffin az., membered or; coat only, Barker's Grants.

CULLEYMORE, James, of London, Jan. 1611-12, by Camden. Harl. MSS. 6095, fo. 14, and 1422, fo. 21^b; Guil. 293, as Robert.

CULLING, Thomas, of London, alderm., etc., esq., s. of W^m, of London, Devon, s. of Wm., s. of Wm., granted 9 Sept. 1657, and confirmed (3 Feb. 1661-2), by Bysshe. Harl. MS. 1105, fo. 19^b; copy of grant in Harl. MS. 1172, fo. 20 and 29; Bysshe's Grants, fo. 15, Her. Coll.

CULME, Hugh, Molland, Devon, quarterly, confirmed .... 1564 (Harvey's Grants). Add. MS. 16,940, fo. 38.

CUNYNGHAM, W^m, of Norwich, confirmed .... 155½ (Harvey's Grants). Add. MS. 16,940, fo. 17.

CUPPER, John, Oxon. (Harvey's Grants). Add. MS. 16,940, fo. 7^b.

CUNTRY, Thos., s. of Thomas, of Reculver, Kent, 14 Aug. 1612, by W. Camden, Clar. Harl. MS. 6140, fo. 25^b.

CURE, George, of London, 1588, by Cooke. Harl. MSS. 1359, fo. 113, and 1422, fo. 95; Add. MS, 4966, fo. 60^b.

CURLE (Anthony), of the Temple (Middle), by Cooke's deputy. Stowe MS. 670, fo. 8^b. See KYRLE. Harl. MS. 5887, fo. 4^b.

CURLL, W^m, of Hatfield, Herts, s. of Nicholas, out of Yorks, 17 Dec. 1586, by Flower. Guil. 42; MS. Ashm. 844, fo. 66, copy of grant, Bodleian Lib.

CURLEW, family of (CURLEY in Burke's Armory), testified ...., by G. Dethick, vert., on a chev. arg. 3 cinquefoils gu., same as Durlew in Stowe MS. 676, fo. 17. Harl. MSS. 1507, fo. 442, and 1359, fo. 3^b; Q's Coll. Oxf. MS. 37, fo. 20; as Durlew and Curlew in 39, fo. 13, for copies of "testamurs"; Le Neve's MS. 442.

CURLING, John, of St. Laurence, Isle of Thanet, s. of George, quartering Clarke, exemplified by Camden. ? Kent Vis. 1619; Stowe MS. 618, fo. 27^b.

CURRANCE, see URREN.

CURRIERS', Company of, of London, ..., by Cooke. Harl. MS. 1359, fo. 98.

CURTEYS, Griffin, of East Imborne, Berks, grant 2 June 1560, 2 Eliz., by G. Dethick. Stowe MS. 676, fo. 26^b; copy of grant, Grants I., 182, and Q's Coll. Oxf. MS. 37, fo. 37.

CURTIS, John, of London (s. of William, of Hatton, co. Warwick, etc.), confirmed 9 May 1632, by R. St. George. Harl. MS. 1470, fo. 228; Guil. 284; Harl. MS. 1085, fo. 16^b.

CURTICE [CURTEYS], Richard, Bp. of Chichester (Chester in MS. in error) 20 Feb. 1569-70, by G. Dethick, Cooke and Flower. Harl. MS. 1141, fo. 72; Q's Coll. Oxf. MS. 145, fo. 24.

CURTYS, Thomas, of the city of London, alderman, 20 Oct., 4 and 5 Phil. and Mary, 1557, by G. Dethick. Harl. MS. 1359, fo. 71; for copy of grant, Q's Coll. Oxf. MS. 39, fo. 88.

CURZON, Sir Robert, Knt., and Baron of the Exchequer, and was of Bylaugh, Norfolk, crest ...., Barker's Grants. Harl. MS. 5816, fo. 22^b; Stowe MS. 692, fo. 32.

CUST, Richard, of Stanford [Stamford?], co. Linc., 31 May 1663. Bysshe's Grants, fo. 19, Her. Coll.; Harl. MS. 1105, fo. 20; Add. MS. 14,293, fo. 5^b; Guil. 98.

„   Samuel, of Boston, co. Linc., ... 1649, by Bysshe. Harl. MS. 6832, fo. 413; Add. MS. 26,758, fo. 15^b, argent, on a chevron wavy sable, a death's head ppr.

CUTHBERT, Edward, and W^m, of Oundle, and brother Nathaniel, of Warnington, Northamptonsh., 12 June 1654, by Bysshe. Add. MSS. 26,758, fo. 16^b, and 14,293, fo. 2^b; Harl. MS. 1105, fo. 15^b; Stowe MS. 714, fo. 180.

CUTHBERT, Thomas, of Oundle, Northamptonsh., and to Richard and George, his brothers, entry damaged (by Bysshe), Clar. Harl. MS. 1105, fo. 40ᵇ and 15ᵇ.

CUTLER, ..., of the North . . . ., by Dalton, Norroy. Harl. MS. 1422, fo. 16ᵇ.

„ Sir John, Knt. and Bart., 27 March 1693, by T. St. George, Gart. and Clar. Harl. MS. 6834, fo. 178 ; Grants IV., fo. 132 ; Harl. MS. 1085, fo. 57.

„ John, of London, lately of Falthwaite, Yorks, 26 April 1585, by Cooke. Harl. MS. 1359, fo. 120ᵇ.

„ Nicholas, of Eye, Suffolk, coat and crest, Barker's Grants. Harl. MS. 5846, fo. 23ᵇ ; Stowe MS. 692, fo. 31ᵇ ; Harl. MS. 6179, fo. 15ᵇ.

„ Robert, of Ipswich, confirmed 21 July 1612, by Camden. Harl. MS. 1507, fo. 414 ; Misc. Gen. et Her., i., 228 ; Her. and Geneal., i., 83 ; Guil. 180 ; copy of confirmation, Q's Coll. Oxf. MS. 38, fo. 122 ; Le Neve's MS. 414 ; Grants II., 594ᵇ, 595ᵐ.

CUTTS, John, Lord Gowran, supporters 19 Dec. 1692. Grants IV., fo. 69.

D

DABBINS, ..., confirmed May 1616, by Camden. Harl. MSS. 1422, fo. 40ᵇ, and 6095, fo. 40ᵇ, Gu., five estoiles or betw. two flaunches chequy arg. and sa.

DACCOMBE, James, Stapleton, Dorset, ..., by Cooke. Stowe MS. 670, fo. 24.

DACRES, Henry, of London, born at Maifield, co. Stafford, coat and crest 24 Oct. 1524, by . . . . (Barker's Grants ; Harl. MS. 5846, fo. 31 ; Stowe MS. 692, fo. 33) ; Sir T. W[riothesley], Gart., and Tong, Norr., Le Neve's MS. 459 ; Harl. MS. 5887, fo. 81.

DACUS, Thomas, als DENNYS, of London, Quarterly coat and crest granted 4 Aug., 4 and 5 Phil. and Mary, 1557, by G. Dethick. Harl. MS. 1359, fo. 77ᵇ ; copy of grant in Latin, Q's Coll. Oxf. MS. 39, fo. 90 ; Grants I., 531.

DADE, ..., Norfolk, ... 1605, by Camden. Stowe MS. 706, fo. 18 ; Harl. MSS. 1085, fo. 25ᵇ, and 6140, fo. 74.

DAINES, Dr, of Suffolk, ... ratified by E. Bysshe, Gart.

DAKYNS, Arthur, of the city of York. At York 12 Oct. 1563, by Flower. Harl. MS. 6140, fo. 68ᵇ ; Stowe MS. 692, fo. 36ᵇ ; Harl. MS. 1453, fo. 74.

DAKEYN, Arthur, of Stubbing, co. Derby, confirmed 27 Aug. 1611, by R. St. George. Guil., p. 267 ; Harl. MS. 1093, fo. 33ᵇ.

DAKINS, George, of Yorkshire, gent., granted at London, by G. Dethick, Norr., 15 Dec., 2 Ed. VI., 1548. Harl. MSS. 1359, fo. 1ᶜ, and 1116, fo. 40 ; copy of grant, Q's Coll. Oxf. MS. 39, fo. 19 ; Grants I., 314.

DALBY, William, of London, ..., by Ro. Cooke, Clar. Harl. MSS. 1422, fo. 23ᵇ, 6179, fo. 6ᵇ, and 5887, fo. 12ᵇ.

DALE, Robert, of Hawkesley, co. pal. Chester, s. and h. of Robert, 9 Nov. 1602, by W. Dethick. Stowe MS. 714, fo. 149, copy of grant, Brit. Mus., and Add. MS. 5524, fo. 204ᵇ.

„ Roger (brother of the last), of Colyweston, Northhts., also Counsellor at law of Inner Temple and Lord of the Manor of Tixover, Rutland, 2nd s. of Robert, of Hawkesley, Cheshire, 9 Nov. 1602, by W. Dethick. Harl. MS. 1422, fo. 16 ; copy Add. MS. 5524, fo. 204ᵇ.

„ William, of London, Grocer, and of Brigstock, Northants, born in Cheshire, s. of Robert, of Wencle in par. of Prestbury, ... 1613 . . . ., by Camden. Harl. MSS. 1422, fo. 39, and 6095, fo. 30ᵇ.

„ William, Englishman, now in Flanders, born of an ancient family in Holland, s. of Cornelius, by Segar. Add. MS. 12,225, fo. 35.

DALLINGTON, Sir Robert, gent., of the Privy Chamber in ordinary to K. Charles, Master and one of the Governors of the King's hospitall founded in Charterhouse. Paynter's book, 237 ; Add. MS. 14,295, fo. 55ᵇ.

DALLISON, Martin, of Harringay als Hornsey, Middx., confirmed or granted 14 Dec. 1648, 24 Chas. I., by Squib, Clar. Guil. 95; called Marmaduke by Berry, perhaps Maximilian, argt., on a pile engrailed az. three crescents of the field.

„ William, of Leighton, co. Linc., esq., one of the Justices of the pleas holden before the King's and Queen's Majᵗⁱᵉˢ, crest 5 May, 3 and 4 Phil. and Mary, 1557, by G. Dethick. Misc. Gen. et Her., 2nd S., ii., p. 105; Harl. MS. 1359, fo. 44ᵇ, 69; copy of grant, Q's Coll. Oxf. MS. 39, fo. 83; Grants I., 252.

DALMARIUS, Julius Cæsar, grant 1 Jan. 1587-8, by W. Dethick, Gart. Stowe MS. 676, fo. 71, copy of grant, and Q's Coll. Oxf. MS. 37, fo. 102.

DALTON, Thomas, of Hull, Yorks, Alderman, gift . . . . 1563, by Flower. Add. MS. 14,295, fo. 39; Harl. MS. 1359, fo. 34ᵇ.

DALWIN, Mathew, of Polomie, Poland, 20 Dec., 4 Ed. VI., 1550, by G. Dethick. Harl. MS. 1359, fo. 60; copy of grant? in Latin, Q's Coll. Oxf. MS. 39, fo. 26; Grants I., 101.

DAM, John, of Much Hadham, Herts, 1 May 1582, by Cooke. (1591 in Harl. MSS. 1422, fo. 42ᵇ, and 1069, fo. 113ᵇ); Grants I., 199. *See also* DANE.

DAMPORT als DAMPITT [DAVENPORT], John, of Lovington, Som't, esq., s. of John, s. of John, 3rd s. of John of Bramhall, Chesh., 1 April 1582, by G. Dethick. Harl. MS. 1441, fo. 103, and Q's Coll. Oxf. MS. 145, fo. 54.

DANCASTLE or DANCASTER, John, of Wellhouse, Berks, granted in 1556 or 1561, by Harvey (Hawley), Clar., or G. Dethick; confirmed 25 Feb. 1586-7, by Cooke. MSS. Ashm. 840, fo. 409, and 858, fo. 211-12, copy of grant, Bodleian Lib.; Harl. MS. 1422, fo. 93; 1556 in Harl. MS. 1359, fo. 91ᵇ; Add. MS. 4966, fo. 65.

DANDY, *see* DAWNDY.

DANE (John? or Wᵐ, of Stortford), Herts, 1561, by Harvey, Clar. Berry's Supplt.; Add. MS. 16,940, fo. 28. *See also* DAM.

„ William, of London, confirmed . . . . 1561. (Harvey's Grants); Add. MS. 16,940, fo. 28.

DAPER, Richard, of Middx., confirmed . . . . 1558, 1 Q. Eliz. (Harvey's Grants); Add. MS. 16,940, fo. 15ᵇ.

DARBY, Charles, of St. Edmundsbury, Suffolk, 1588, by Cooke. Add. MS. 4966, fo. 84ᵇ; Harl. MSS. 1359, fo. 113, and 1422, fo. 95; Edmond in Stowe MS. 670, fo. 25.

DARE, Ananias, one of the assistant Governors of City of Raleigh, Va., by W. Dethick, Gart. Q's Coll. Oxf. MS. 36, fo. 120, copy of patent.

DARLEY, ... crest confirmed 10 April 1583, by W. Flower, Norr. Stowe MS. 706, fo. 4ᵇ; Harl. MS. 6179, fo. 11.

DARNALL, Adam, Thorneholme, co. Linc., esq., crest 20 Nov. 1566, by W. Harvey, Clar. Add. MS. 17,506, fo. 26ᵇ; Harl. MS. 5887, fo. 109.

DARNELL, Henry, Councellor, of Gray's Inn, ... 1603, by W. Dethick, Gart. Harl. MSS. 1441, fo. 104, and 5847, fo. 55; Add. MS. 12,454, fo. 54; Stowe MS. 703, fo. 62.

DART, *see* WALLIS.

DARTMOUTH, Lord (George Legge), supporters 10 March 1682-3, by W. Dugdale, Gart. Harl. MS. 6834, fo. 178; Grants III., fo. 188.

DASHWOOD, Francis (? Francis or George his brother), of London, esq., confirmed 24 Oct. 1662. Bysshe's Grants, fo. 14, Her. Coll.; Harl. MS. 1105, fo. 19; Guil., p. 269, late Alderman.

„ Francis, a silkman "at the Naked boy" in Cheapside, 1655, by E. Bysshe. Harl. MSS. 1441, fo. 152, and 1466, fo. 24.

DAVENANT, William, of Davenant in Essex, Quarterly . . . ., 1588, by Cooke. Harl. MSS. 1359, fo. 109, 1422, fo. 120ᵇ; called Davenport, Add. MS. 4966, fo. 57.

DAVENPORT, *see* DAMPORT.

DAVERS, James, co. Bucks, Danvers, Quarterly with Davers, by Cooke. Stowe MS.
    670, fo. 30 (John in Add. MS. 14,297, fo. 28ᵇ), Jeremy Davers of London
    in the margin.
DAVID, Robert (s. of John), s. of David Griffith of N. Wales, confirmed 20 April
    1581, by Flower. MS. Ashm. 844, fo. 6, copy of grant, Bodleian Lib.;
    Guil., p. 170; Harl. MS. 1422, fo. 78ᵇ, gules, on a bend argent a lyon
    passant sable.
DAVIDGE, ..., of Somerset, J.P., 2 April 1664, by Bysshe, Clar. Harl. MS.
    1105, fo. 40ᵇ; Bysshe's Grants, 36.
DAVIDSON, William, of London, s. of John, s. of Richard, crest 25 June 1575, by
    Cooke. Misc. Gen. et Her., i., 273, copy of grant, Brit. Mus. Le Neve's
    MS. 495.
    „   William (s. of John, s. of Richard), granted and confirmed 12 July 1586,
        by Flower. Guil., p. 156; MS. Ashm. 834, fo. 61, copy of grant,
        Bodleian Lib.
DAVIE, or DAVEY, John, Mayor of Exeter, grant 10 March, 33 Eliz., 1590-1, by
    W. Dethick, Gart. Stowe MS. 676, fo. 82; confirmation (? alteration)
    20 April 1594, then described as of Sandford and Kyrton, Devon, late
    Mayor of Exeter, also by W. Dethick, Gart. Stowe MS. 676, fo. 91ᵇ and
    107ᵇ; copy of grant, see Q's Coll. Oxf. MSS. 36, fo. 36, and 37,
    fo. 123.
DAVYS, John, of Ford, Devon, confirmed 39 Eliz. 1597, by W. Dethick, Gart.
    Stowe MS. 676, fo. 120; copy of grant and Q's Coll. Oxf. MS. 36,
    fo. 60.
DAVIES, John, the elder, of Middleton, Salop, s. of John, crest 24 Dec. 1623, by
    R. St. George. Harl. MSS. 1507, fo. 394, 1972, fo. 49, 1105, fo. 7, and
    1422, fo. 42; copy of grant, Q's Coll. Oxf. MS. 38, fo. 138; Le Neve's
    MS. 394.
    „   Thomas (from Wales), barber to K. Chas. I., and groom of the privy
        Chamber, 1 Dec. 1664, by Walker. Harl. MS. 1172, fo. 55; Add. MSS.
        14,293, fo. 47, and 14,294, fo. 16.
    „   Sir Thomas, of London, Knt. and Alderm. (s. of John, of London), and free
        of the Drapers and Merchᵗˢ Adventurers, ... 1677, by Sir E. Bysshe,
        Clar. Harl. MS. 1105, fo. 40; Bysshe's Grants, 34.
DAVIS, Richard, Bp. of St. Asaph, 20 Feb. 1559-60, by Harvey, Clar. Harl. MS.
    1386, fo. 110.
DAVISON, Sir Alexander, see DAVYSON.
DAVY, Henry, late Sheriff and Alderm. of Norwich, and elder brother
    „   Richard, late High Steward of Norwich, and his younger brother
    „   John, now living, and sisters Ellen and Isabel, the five children of Richard
        Davy of Easton, Norfolk, sometime Mayor of Norwich, by his wife
        Christian, dau. and heir of Ric. Bishop of Yarmouth, grant of arms and
        crest, undated and unsigned, to the posterity of said Richard, the father,
        among W. Dethick's Grants. Copy in Q's Coll. Oxf. MS. 36, fo. 108;
        Stowe MS. 676, fo. 35; 17 Nov. 1596, Harl. MS. 1085, fo. 50.
    „   Joan, als Trelake, wife to Sir Ralf. Warren, maior of London (1536 and
        1543), arms 10 May 1552; Add. MS. 16,940, fo. 206, by Hawley (?).
    „   Robert, of London, ye Queen's recʳ for S. Wales, s. of Jo., of Norwich,
        20 Jan. 1576-7, by Cooke. Harl. MS. 1422, fo. 78ᵇ; Stowe MS. 670,
        fo. 61ᵇ.
    „   William, John and Elizabeth, ... 1 Oct. 1552, ? by Hawley. Add. MS.
        16,940, fo. 206.
DAVYSON, Sir Alexander, of Newcastle-upon-Tyne, Northumb., 7 Chas., 1631, by
    Segar. Add. MS. 12,225, fo. 34ᵇ; 3 Jan. in Berry's supplᵗ, and Harl. MS.
    1105, fo. 8.
DAWBENEY, Oliver, confirmed 3 and 4 Phil. and Mary, 1556-7 (Harvey's Grants).
    Add. MS. 16,940, fo. 9.

DAWE, William (s. of Robert), of East Chelborough, Dorset, ... 1588, by Cooke, Clar. Harl. MS. 1166, fo. 89ᵇ.

DAWES, Abraham, s. of John, ..., co. Staff, 26 March 1613, by R. St. George. Paynter's Book II., 24ᵇ ; Add. MS. 14,295, fo. 60ᵇ.

„ William, of London, 2nd s. of Robert, of Longstrethin, Norfolk, 28 Feb. 1611-12, by Camden. Morgan's Sphere, 117 ; Harl. MS. 1441, fo. 149.

DAWNDY (DANDY). Arthur, of Cretingham, Suff., gent., grant 5 Jan., 2 Q. Eliz. Harl. MS. 1441, fo. 2ᵇ, 1559-60, by G. Dethick. Harl. MS. 1359, fo. 79 ; copy of grant, Q's Coll. Oxf. MSS. 39, fo. 107, and 145, fo. 3ᵇ ; Harl. MS. 5887, fo. 47 ; Grants I., 294.

DAWSON, Alexander, of the Manor of Spaldington, Yorks, 8 Feb. 1563-4, 6 Eliz., by Flower. Harl. MS. 1359, fo. 8ᵇ.

„ John, of Insterby (Sutterby), co. Linc., Barr. of the Inner Temple, now residing at Ballina-court, coˢ Tippʳ and Limerick, royalist, attested by Cooke, ..., his family of Sutterby, co. Linc., confirmed 12 Jan. 1663-4, by Walker, Gart. Copy of grant, Harl. MS. 1172, fo. 59 ; Add. MSS. 14,293, fo. 54, and 14,294, fo. 13ᵇ ; Guil., p. 342.

„ William, of Ayerley, Yorks, gent., 1 Feb. 1605-6, by R. St. George. Add. MS. 14,295, fo. 59 ; Harl. MS. 1422, fo. 14 ; C. 13 [Visit. Yorks, 1612], 200, Her. Coll.

DAY, Edward, of city of London, gent., s. of Edmond, s. of William, of Derbysh., 28 Feb. 1582-3, by G. Dethick. Harl. MS. 1441, fo. 71 ; 20 March in Q's Coll. Oxf. MS., Edmond, 115, fo. 16.

DEY (DAY), George, Bishop of Chichester, grant by C. Barker, Gart. Stowe MS. 692, fo. 36 ; Harl. MS. 1116, fo. 41ᵇ.

„ Henry, of Oxebonding, Norfolk, s. of Wᵐ, 2nd s. of Robᵗ, gent., confirmed 20 Nov. (? 45 Q. Eliz., 1602), by W. Dethick, Gart. (17 Nov. 1597 in Burke). Stowe MS. 676, fo. 141ᵇ ; copy of grant, Q's Coll. Oxf. MS. 36, fo. 105.

DAY, William, B.D., Provost of Eton and Dean of Windsor (s. of Richard, etc.), confirmed 28 Oct. 1582, by Flower. Harl. MS. 1422, fo. 19ᵇ ; Stowe MS. 706, fo. 21 ; Harl. MS. 6140, fo. 75 ; MSS. Ashm. 834, fo. 55, and 858, fo. 44, copy of grant, Bodleian Lib. ; Guil., p. 394.

„ William, of Eton, Bucks, June 1606, [? confirmed] by Camden. 5 July [? Camden's Grants], fo. 50 ; Harl. MSS. 1422, fo. 19ᵇ, and 6095, fo. 5ᵇ ; Guil., p. 394.

DAYNES, see DAINES.

DEACON, Henry, serjeant plumer to Q. Eliz., ..., by Cooke. Harl. MS. 1359, fo. 105.

DEALE, Anthony, of Feversham, Kent, s. of Anth., s. of Thos., grant 9 Sept. 1597, by W. Dethick and W. Camden, recorded by W. Segar. Add. MS. 12,225, fo. 35 ; Stowe MS. 676, fo. 121ᵇ ; Harl. MSS. 1422, fo. 38, and 6095, fo. 32ᵇ. Thomas, see Morgan's Sphere of Gentry, and for copy of grant, Q's Coll. Oxf. MS. 36, fo. 65.

DEAN, Sir Anthony, of Crutched Friars, s. of Anthony, of London, gent., decᵈ, s. of Anthony, of co. Glouc., 17 Dec. 1683, by Sir W. Dugdale, Gart. and Clar. Harl. MS. 6834, fo. 178 ; Grants III., fo. 221.

DENE, Henry, of Denefield (? Deneland), Hants, s. of John, of Deaneland, s. of Jas., 2nd s. of Mathew, s. of Wᵐ, s. of Robert, s. of Richᵈ, s. of Richard, "who lived in those dayes," 22 Nov. 1598, by Camden. Add. MS. 14,295, fo. 62ᵇ ; C. 17, 65ᵇ, Her. Coll. ; Harl. MSS. 1544, fo. 174, and 6086, fo. 62ᵇ.

DEANE, Mʳ John, of Mattingley, Hants, or I. of W., s. of John, of Wallingford, Berks, gent. (confirmed 1623, Burke's Armory), by Camden. Stowe MS. 677, fo. 8 ; Harl. MSS. 6179, fo. 66ᵇ, and 1544, fo. 151ᵇ.

„ William, of Gosfield, Essex (2nd s. of Wᵐ, s. of I., of co. Lanc.), confirmed 8 May 1577, by Flower. MS. Ashm. 834, p. 36, copy of grant, Bodleian Lib. ; Guil. 352.

DE GRANATA, Jacobus, Knt. of the Duchy of Brabant, arms and crest, 15 Aug. 1556, 3 and 4 Phil. and Mary, by Sir G. Dethick, Gart. Q's Coll. Oxf. MS. 39, fo. 79, for copy of testimonial ; Grants I., 81.

DEATH, William, of Dartford, Kent, ... 1589, by Cooke. Harl. MSS. 1359, fo. 100[b], and 1422, fo. 94[b]; Add. MS. 4966, fo. 88[b].

DECRYOLL or DEICROW, Benjamin, of Enfield, Middx., s. of Robert, s. of John, of Saul, Suff., descended from Decriol of Kent, Lieut. of Dover Castle, for wh. services the Key was borne in the Canton as an augmentation, confirmed . . . ., by Segar. Harl. MS. 1422, fo. 107 ; Add. MS. 12,225, fo. 35[b] ; Guil. 306 ; Harl. MS. 1105, fo. 11[b].

DEDYCOTT, Arthur, of Hackney, Middx., gift . . . . 1558. (Harvey's Grants) Add. MS. 16,940, fo. 21[b]; Derycote, Sheriff of London, Harl. MS. 1116, fo. 17[b] ; Add. MS. 4966, fo. 60.

DEE, John, of Moorelake, Surrey, Esq. Crest, Add. MS. 4966, fo. 60 ; 8 Q. Eliz., 1576 [sic ?], " D[r] John the astrologer," Quarterly of 6 (by Cooke ?), Harl. MSS. 1359, fo. 111, and 1422, fo. 122.

DEEDES, Julius, of Hythe, ... 1653, by E. Bysshe, Gart. Add. MS. 8932, fo. 225.

DEERING, Nicholas (s. of Nicholas, of Worgroot in Dorset), and to his brother Thomas, confirmed 13 Feb. 1664-5, by Walker. Add. MSS. 14,293, fo. 34, and 14,294, fo. 6 ; Guil. 159.

DEGGE, Simon, of Strongshull n[r] Uttoxeter, co. Staff., and of the Inner Temple, now one of H.M. Council and Justices for the Marches of Wales, 9 May, 13 Chas. II., 1661, by W. Dugdale, Norr. Harl. MS. 1105, fo. 60, and Her. Coll. (1662).

DEINCOURT, Baron, Sir Francis Leeke, Knt. and Bart., supporters 14 Nov. 1627, by Segar. Harl. MS. 1470, fo. 30, 42, copy of grant, Brit. Mus. ; Add. MS. 12,225, fo. 69[b], 1633.

DE LA DOWNE, John, of London, ... 1591, by Cooke. Harl. MS. 1359, fo. 112[b].

DE LA FOUNTAINE, Erasmus, of Belchamp St. Paul, Essex, 22 Feb. 1619-20, by Camden. Harl. MS. 6095, fo. 39 ; Guil. 136 ; Harl. MS. 6140, fo. 67.

DE LA HAY, George, of Weston, Surrey, s. and h. of Nevill De la Hay, crest Feb. 1600-1, by W. Dethick. Harl. MS. 1422, fo. 22[b].

DELALYND, { Alexander, Thomas and Cuthbert, sons of Sir Humphrey, Kt., of Twickenham. Grants I., 354, but query.
{ Thomas and Cuthbert, sons of Oliver, 20 Feb. 1577-8, by W. Dethick, York Herald. Harl. MS. 1171, fo. 60.

DE LA MOTT, ... de Normandie, arms 29 Nov. (3 Ed. VI. ?) 1549, by G. Dethick. Harl. MS. 1359, fo. 59[b]; copy in French, Q's Coll. Oxf. MS. 37, fo. 10, De la Mount, and 39, fo. 57 ; Grants I., 111.

DELAUNE, Gideon, of Blackfryars, London, exemplified 7 March 1612-13, by Segar. Add. MS. 12,225, fo. 35[b] ; C. 24, fo. 499 [Visit. Lond., 1634], Her. Coll., and Guil. 376.

DELILLERS, ... London, ... 1657 . . . . Burke's Armory.

DELL or DELVES, William, Sec[y] to W[m] Laude, Archb[p] of Cant[y], 16 Feb. 1637-8, by Borough. Harl. MS. 1105, fo. 55[b] ; 1631 in Harl. MS. 1441, fo. 57, and Add. MS. 26,702, fo. 90 ; Harl. MS. 5857, fo. 138, for copy of grant, Brit. Mus.

DELVES, see Parker's Glossary of Heraldry, Chron. Table, xiv.

DENE, see DEAN.

DENHAM, William, Citizen and Goldsmith of London, by G. Dethick. Harl. MS. 1441, fo. 78[b], and Q's Coll. Oxf. MS. 145, fo. 29[b].

DENNE, Thomas, Adisham, Kent, 1589, by Cooke's deputy. Stowe MS. 670, fo. 35[b]. (See BENNE.)

DENN, Vincent, D.C.L., s. of William, of Kingston, by Camden, Le Neve's MS. 357.

DENNIS, Philip, ... Arms 3 Edw. VI., 1548, Barker's Grants ; Add. MS. 14,294, fo. 56.

L

DENNIS, Thomas, *see* DACUS.

DENNY, Glover, of Raveningham, Norfolk, grant 9 March 1663-4, by Bysshe. Harl. MS. 1470, fo. 75, copy of grant, Brit. Mus., and Guil. 78. And to
" Phineas, of Toftmonks, ⎱ (his two uncles), sons of Thomas, of Langley,
" Edward, of Great Yarmouth, ⎰ Norfolk, decd., and to
" Sidrach (the issue of), of Toftmonks, decd., bro. to the said Thomas, of Langley aforesaid. Guil. 78.

DENSELL, Sir William, of Wye, Kent, Knt., augmentation and crest 15 July 1554, by Hawley. Harl. MS. 1507, fo. 9, 408 ; copy of grant, Q's Coll. Oxf. MS. 38, fo. 65 ; Le Neve's MS. 488.

DENTT, John, citizen and Salter of London, gift 20 Oct. (18 Q. Eliz.), 1576, by Cooke. Harl. MS. 1359, fo. 30 ; Add. MS. 14,295, fo. 18ᵇ.

DERWENTWATER, Earl of, Sir Francis Radcliffe, of Dilston, Northumbld., Knt., supporters 26 Jan. 1688-9, 4 Jac. 2 (*sir*) by T. St. George, Gart. Harl. MS. 6834, fo. 178 ; Stowe MS. 677, fo. 74, copy of grant, Brit. Mus. ; Grants IV., fo. 212.

" *see* DRAWATER and DRINKWATER.

DES BOUVERIE, *see* BOUVERIE.

DESSE, Sir Robert, Az., a chevron betw. three owls or, on a canton gules three lions passant guardant in pale of the second. Crest, On a chapeau gu., turned up ermine, an owl wings expanded or. Over the Crest " Vigilo." Berry's Armory.

DEVICKE, William, of Jarnessey (Guernsey ?), confirmed April 1612, by Camden. Harl. MSS. 1422, fo. 15, 6095, fo. 18 ; Guil. 343.

DEWE, Richard, of Abingdon, Berks, esq., 20 May 1661. Harl. MS. 1105, fo. 42ᵇ; ? by Bysshe, Clar.

D'EWES, Paul, of Stowlangtoft, Suff., altered 12 June 1617, by R. St. George. Harl. MSS. 1470, fo. 16, 231, and 5887, fo. 54ᵇ.

DEWEY, Thomas, of London, confirmed .... 1564 (Harvey's Grants), Add. MS. 16,940, fo. 27.

DEWHURST, William, of Dewhurst, co. Lanc., s. of John, s. of John, by R. St. George, Norroy, ... 1613. Harl. MSS. 6140, fo. 74ᵇ, and 6179, fo. 14 ; Stowe MS. 706, fo. 19ᵇ.

DIAMONT, *see* DIMAN, of London, Draper, arg., 5 fusils in fesse conjoined gu., each charged with a fleur de lis or, ... 1612, by Segar. Add. MS. 12,225, fo. 36 ; MS. Vincent, 154, fo. 5ᵇ, Her. Coll., and Guil. 371.

DICER, Sir Robert, of London, Bart., 27 June, 13 Chas. II., 1661. Bysshe's Grants, fo. 16, Her. Coll. ; Harl. MSS. 1105, fo. 19ᵇ, and 1172, fo. 27, copy of grant.

DICKENSON, Edmond, of Oxford, Dr in physic in Oxf., 31 March 1673, by Sir E. Bysshe, Clar. Harl. MS. 1105, fo. 40ᵇ ; Bysshe's Grants 35.

" Liming, s. of Robert, of Lydiard Tregoze, Wilts, 14 Nov. 1625, by Segar. Add. MS. 12,225, fo. 36 ; Guil. 162 ; Her. Coll. 140, fo. 26.

DICKONSON, William, of the city of Gedaneims [? Gedanum], 29 May 1557, letters of commendation from Sigismund Augustus, King of Poland. MS. Ashm. 844, fo. 13, copy, Bodleian Lib.

DICKINS, William, of Fleet St., London, descended out of Derbyshire from Hasel wood, Harl. MS. 6179, 26 June 1629, by Segar. Add. MS. 12,225, fo. 36ᵇ ; Dickens, 16 June 1625, in Guil. 257 ; Harl. MS. 6199, fo. 19ᵇ.

DIGHTON, Henry, of Hertford, Herts, " Owner of the Bell there," by Cooke. Stowe MS. 670, fo. 59ᵇ.

" John, of Woodsome, Yorks, gent., s. of John, crest 12 July 1590, by Cooke. Harl. MS. 1422, fo. 22 ; Add. MSS. 16,940, fo. 209, 26,753, fo. 124, and 17,506, fo. 27.

DYLKE, Richard, of Kirby Mallory, co. Leic., gent., crest 10 June 1574, by G. Dethick. Harl. MS. 1441, fo. 83 ; Misc. Gen. et Her., i., 9, copy of grant, Brit. Mus.; MS. Vinct. 162, fo. 178 (Her. Coll.); Q's Coll. Oxf. MS. 145, fo. 38.

DILLINGTON, Anthony, of Dillington, Norfolk, gent., ... 1575 ? Quarterly, by G. Dethick. Harl. MS. 1441, fo. 84, and Q's Coll. Oxf. MS. 145, fo. 39.

„ Robert, of Knighton Gorge in the Isle of Wight, crest 11 Jan. 1599-1600, by Camden. Add. MS. 14,295, fo. 91; Harl. MS. 1544, fo. 186ᵇ.

DIMAN, ..., of London, ..., Arg., on 5 fusils conjoined in fesse, gu. betw. 3 mullets sa., 4 fleurs de lis or, impaling Tuder, of Tuder, Northampts., by Segar. Add. MS. 12,225, fo. 36ᵇ; Harl. MS. 6140, fo. 28ᵇ.

DINNET, ..., of ...., Quartering, by Parlt., or by letters patent, Berry's Supplement [by patent, Burke's Armory].

DYSNEY, Lᵗ Col., ... 24 April 1651, by Bysshe. Add. MS. 26,758, fo. 15ᵇ; Harl. MS. 6832, fo. 413.

DISTILLERS' OF LONDON, the Master and Wardens, assistants and commonalty possessing the trade and mistere of, ... 9 Aug. 1630, by Borough. Harl. MS. 1441, fo. 105.

DIXE, John, of Herts, ..., by Harvey, Clar. Bannerman MS., No. 9, fo. 455.

DIX, John, formerly Ramsey (of Wickmer, Norfolk), exempl. Dix and Ramsey, quarterly, 19 May 1604, by Camden. Cotton MS. Faust., E. I., 46, copy of grant, Brit. Mus., Crest, by Segar, Gart., 1631. Harl. MS. 1085, fo. 44ᵇ.

„ John, D.D., ..., confirmed Dec. 1612, by Camden. Harl. MS. 6095, fo. 25ᵇ.

DYX, William, of Norfolk, 1 July 1548, by Hawley ? Add. MS. 16,940, fo. 202ᵇ.

DIXON, ..., of London (descᵈ from Dickson, of the Bpk. of Durham), by Cooke. Stowe MS. 670, fo. 81ᵇ.

DYXON, Gains, of Tonbridge, crest 20 April 1565, by Hervey. Misc. Gen. et Her., 2nd S., vol. i., p. 252, plate, copy of grant, Brit. Mus.

DIXON, George, of Ramsham, co. pal. of Durham, crest 14 Sept. 1615, by R. St. George. Stowe MS. 714, fo. 146; Add. MS. 14,295, fo. 107ᵇ; Guil. 365.

„ Robert, of Kings Langley, Herts, Esq., 14 July 1626, by R. St. George. Add. MS. 14,295, fo. 65; I. 9, 88ᵇ; Grants II., 662; Certificates 19 Nov. 1638, by W. Le Neve, fo. 663.

DOBBES, Richard, Plumstead, Kent, Sheriff of London (see his wife Glasse), grant 10 Aug., 35th H. VIII., 1543, by Hawley. Knighted and became Mayor of London 1551, and died 1556, leaving two daurs. only. Stowe MS. 677, fo. 66; Add. MSS. 16,940, fo. 200, and 7098, fo. 76ᵇ; Harl. MS. 1172, fo. 54ᵇ.

DOBELL, Walter, of Faumor (Falmere), Sussex, 7 Feb. 1605-6, by Camden. Harl. MSS. 1422, fo. 18ᵇ, and 6095, fo. 3ᵇ; Guil. 309, as 7 Feb. 1607; Harl. MS. 1562, fo. 122, 10 June, 2 K. Jac.

DOBSON, ..., cousin to Sir R. St. George, Norroy, who confirmed the coat and crest 1605. Add. MS. 14,295, fo. 80 (fo. 276ᵇ).

DOCHEN, Thomas, Doctor of Physick, borne at Campden in Gloucestershire, Student of Magdalen Coll., Oxford, ... 1594, by Lee. Harl. MS. 1359, fo. 10.

DODDING, Miles, of Kendal, Westmorld., one of the chief Clerks of the Crown Office, Court of K. Bench; crest 20 April 1587, by W. Dethick. Stowe MS. 676, fo. 72, copy of grant; Q's Coll. Oxf. MS. 37, fo. 103.

DODDS, William, of Hants, gift 1558. (Harvey's Grants) Add. MS. 16,940, fo. 7ᵇ.

DODE, ... Erm., a chief chequy or and az., by Cooke. Stowe MS. 670, fo. 58.

DODGE, John, of Wrotham, Kent, crest ? 16 Dec. 1546, by Hawley, Clar. Add. MS. 16,940, fo. 201ᵇ; (Her. and Geneal., i., 517); Harl. MS. 1548, fo. 177.

DODGE, Peter, Stopworth, Cheshire, etc., 8 April, 34 Ed. I., 1306, by Jaques, Hedingley. Harl. MS. 1116, fo. 37ᵇ ; copy of grant, Le Neve's MS. 506 ; *see* Her. and Geneal., i., 515, and Guil. 255 ; Grants II., 618. A forgery.

DODMER, Margaret, nxor. Sir Ralph, Mayor of London, grant 18 Feb. 1635-6, by C. Barker, Gart. MS. Ashm. 858, p. 23, "transcribed from an 8ᵛᵒ MS. of Sir Hy. Sᵗ George now in the custody of Silvanus Morgan, 25 Feb. 1661-2, fo. 212.

DODMORE, Rauf, of London, coat and crest. Barker's Grants : Harl. MS. 5846, fo. 31 ; Stowe MS. 692, fo. 35ᵇ.

DODSON, ..., 6 May 1617, by Sir Wᵐ Segar, Gart. Stowe MS. 697, fo. 48.

DODSWORTH, John, of Thornton Watlass, Yorks, crest 2 June 1610, by R. St. George. Add. MS. 14,295, fo. 81 ; B. 10, fo. 48. Her. Coll. ; Surtees Soc., Vol. XLI., p. xlvi. ; copy of grant, Brit. Mus., Harl. MS. 6140, fo. 51ᵇ.

DODWORTH, ..., of London . . . . by Cooke. Stowe MS. 670, fo. 27.

DOE, Charles, esq. (s. of Jonas, of Ludlow, Salop, a burgess of the town of Bridge-north), at Edgehill, and imprisoned for loyalty : Sheriff of London 1664 ; 15 Sept. 1664, by Walker. Add. MS. 14,294, fo. 9 ; Harl. MS. 1172, fo. 36.

DO, George, of Jesus Coll., Cambs, s. of John, citizen of London, 8 May 1662, by Walker. Harl. MSS. 1172, fo. 31, and copy of grant, 6179, fo. 30ᵇ.

DOLLING, John, of Worthe in the Isle of Purbeck, Dorset, gent., s. of Christʳ of the same, crest 17 May 1613, by Camden. Harl. MS. 6095, fo. 27 ; Add. MS. 14,295, fo. 84.

DOLMAN, Thomas, of Shawe, co. Berks, 1587, by Cooke. Harl. MSS. 1359, fo. 107ᵇ, and 1422, fo. 93ᵇ ; Add. MS. 4966, fo. 68ᵇ.

DONGAN, William, als THOGAN or GHOGAN, recʳ of H.M. first fruits, etc., in Ireland, descended from the Phogans of Munster, crest granted *temp.* Q. Eliz., by W. Dethick. Stowe MS. 676, fo. 34, copy of grant, *temp.* Q. Eliz. ; Q's Coll. Oxf. MS. 38, fo. 111.

DONHAULT, Gregory, of London, Sec. to Thomas, Lord Ellesmere, Lord Chancellor of England, s. of Roger, s. of Richard, of Hethencote, Northhants, out of Oxon., confirmed arms and impalement and grant of crest 26 May 1600, by Segar. Add. MS. 12,225, fo. 37 ; Harl. MS. 6140, fo. 29ᵇ, with impalement.

DONNYNG, John, of Chichester, confirmed . . . . 1565. (Harvey's Grants) Add. MS. 16,940, fo. 21 ; Harl. MS. 1562, fo. 49.

DOOR, ... of Cornwall and Devon, April 1605, by Camden. Harl. MSS. 1422, fo. 19, and 6095, fo. 4 ; Dore in Harl. MS. 1441, fo. 120.

DORCHESTER, Catherine Sidley, Bᵉˢ, supporters 8 Feb. 1685-6, by W. Dugdale, Gart. Stowe MS. 714, fo. 145ᵇ ; Grants III., 288 ; Lansd. MS. 867, fo. 52.

DOUBLEDAY, Thomas, of Middx. (and to his brethren), sons of Edward, of Westm., 5 March 1640-1, by Borough. Add. MS. 14,295, fo. 101, to the descendants of his father ; Harl. MS. 1105, fo. 57 ; Guil. 393.

DOUGHTY, William, of Hanworth, Norfolk, by Camden. Harl. MS. 1085, fo. 43.

DOVE, John, of Camberwell, Surrey, granted 23 Jan. 1572-3, by Cooke. Guil. 381 ; Harl. MSS. 1359, fo. 114, and 1422, fo. 95ᵇ ; Add. MS. 4966, fo. 97.

„ Thomas, Bp. of Peterboro', grant 5 May 1601, by W. Dethick and Camden, Clar. Stowe MS. 676, fo. 135, copy of grant, Q's Coll. Oxf. MS. 36, fo. 89.

DOWMAN, John, of Pocklington, Yorks, Doctor in both Laws, Archdⁿ of Suff., Canon Resid. of St. Paul's, London, Cardinal. 25 July 1526, 16 H. VIII., by Wriothesley, Gart., and Tonge, Norr. Harl. MS. 4900, fo. 20 ; Add. MS. 26,702, fo. 45ᵇ.

DOWNAM, ... Dʳ of Physic, *temp.* H. VIII. Add. MS. 26,702, fo. 45ᵇ.

„ William, Lord Bp. of Chester, granted 5 May 1561, by Dalton, Norr. Harl. MS. 1359, fo. 49ᵇ.

DOWNE, Henry, Visct. (DAWNAY), supporters 24 March 1697-8, by T. St. George. Grants IV., 250 ; copy of grant, Brit. Mus.
„ James or Thos., of Cobham, Surrey, 10 June 1572, crest, by Cooke. (John in Bannerman MS. 9) ; Harl. MS. 1433, fo. 133ᵇ.
DOWNES, ... by Cooke ; 1 and 4, arg., 3 palets wavy gu. (a mullet sa.) ; 2, arg., 6 mullets gu. ; 3, barry of 8 sa. and arg., in chief 3 plates ; crest, a wolfe's head argt. charged with a mullet sa. Harl. MS. 1359, fo. 87 ; Stowe MS. 670, fo. 62ᵇ ; Add. MS. 4966, fo. 66.
DOWNING, Edmond, of Pye, next par. of Waltham Holy Crosse, Essex, 1584, by Cooke. Add. MS. 4966, fo. 62 ; Harl. MS. 1359, fo. 98ᵇ ; Add. MS. 14,295, fo. 35ᵇ ; Guil., p. 172.
DOWNEING, Roger, H.M. serjeant skinner, 23 June 1665, by Sir E. Walker, Gart. Her. Coll., fo. 61.
DOYLY, John, Ewerden, Bucks, confirmed 1563. (Harvey's Grants) Add. MS. 16,940, fo. 48.
DRAGONER, Thomas, of Hoxton, Middx. .... (1587?), by Cooke. Harl. MSS. 1359, fo. 110 and 117, and 5887, fo. 84 ; Add. MS. 4966, fo. 28ᵇ.
DRAKE, Sir Francis, arms, crest and augmentation 20 June 1581, by Cooke. MS. Ashm. 834, i., fo. 38 and 44, copy of grant, Bodleian Lib. ; MS. Ashm. 844, fo. 39 ; Harl. MS. 1422, fo. 4 ; copy of grant, Harl. MS. 1172, fo. 5ᵇ ; Harl. MS. 1359, fo. 27, and Q's Coll. Oxf. MSS. 37, fo. 76, and 38, fo. 103 (146, fo. 29), and Brit. Mus., Harl. MS. 1052, fo. 5ᵇ ; Genealogist, vol. i., fo. 209 ; Add. MS. 4966, fo. 91 ; also for copies of grant, Her. and Geneal., viii., 310.
DRAPER als FARMER, ... Bucks .... by Cooke. Harl. MSS. 1422, fo. 90ᵇ, and 6179, fo. 19.
„ Christopher, of London, Alderm., confirmed .... 1560 (Harvey's Grants). Add. MS. 16,940, fo. 25.
„ Henry, of Colebrook, Middx., s. of John, of Bedfont, gent., Grant 14 Oct. 1571, by Cooke. Stowe MS. 670, fo. 60ᵇ, copy of patent, Q's Coll. Oxf. MS. 38, fo. 85 ; Guil. 311 (Grants II., 513) ; Harl. MS. 1105, fo. 2ᵇ.
„ Richard, of Middx., ... 1558, by Harvey, Clar. Add. MS. 16,940, fo. 15ᵇ.
„ Thomas, of Stroud Green, Middx., s. of John, 2 Aug. 1612, by Camden. Grants II., 592 ; Feb. 1613-14 in Harl. MS. 6095, fo. 26.
DRAPERS' COMPANY (patent in Latin), 10 March 1439-40, 17 H. VI., under the hand and seal of Brugges, Gart. (confirmed by Harvey, 1561, Add. MS. 16,940, fo. 40). Harl. MS. 4900, fo. 14ᵇ, 15 (Coat only, Add. MS. 26,702, fo. 62ᵇ) ; grant of a crest and supporters (1613), by Segar. Add. MS. 12,225, fo. 37 ; Her. and Geneal., i., 123.
DRAX, Thomas, of Woodhall, Yorks, confirmed 30 Nov. 1561, 4th Q. Eliz., by L. Dalton, Norr. Add. MS. 14,295, fo. 72 ; Harl. MSS. 1359, fo. 41ᵇ, and 6140, fo. 67ᵇ.
DRAYNER, als DRAGENER, Thomas, of Hoxton, Middx., ... (1587 ?), by Cooke. Harl. MSS. 1359, fo. 110, 117, and 5887, fo. 84.
DREW, Edmond, of Hayne, Devon, crest, a squirrel, etc., by Cooke. Stowe MS. 670, fo. 37.
DREWE, (Sir) Edward, Serjeant at Law, of Killerton, Devon, patent 1593, by Cooke. Harl. MS. 1164, fo. 90.
„ Martin, of Sharpeham, Devon, confirmed .... 1560 (Harvey's Grants). Add. MS. 16,940, fo. 43ᵇ, and also to Thomas, of Kent.
DRYWATER, als DERWENTWATER, ..., no other writing, ..., by Segar. Add. MS. 12,225, fo. 37ᵇ ; Harl. MS. 1422, fo. 15 ; Drawater, also Darwenwater.
DUCKE, Nicholas, of Lincoln's Inn (s. of Richard, of Heavitree, Devon, etc.), confirmed 23 June 1602, by Camden. Cott. MS. Faust. E. I., fo. 49ᵇ ; Guil. 374.

DUCKWORTH, Charles, rector of Dodleston, Cheshire, and Prebend. of Chester, 11 June 1672, by W. Dugdale, Norr. (Her. Coll.).

DUCY, Robert, esq., Alderm., of London, 28 Nov. 1622, by Camden.   Harl. MS. 6095, fo. 39, 28 Nov., 5 K. Ch. I., 1629 ; Bannerman MS. 9, fo. 459.

„   Sir William, Barronet, and Knight of the Bath, Baron Ducy and Visct. of Downe, Dep. E. M. Warrant 26 Dec. 1675, supporters 28 Feb. 1675-6, by Walker, Gart.   Harl. MS. 1172, fo. 48. copy of grant.   Add. MS. 14,293, fo. 25, 25ᵇ ; Grants III., fo. 19.

DUDLEY, John, esq., Sargᵗ of her Majesties pasterie, s. of Symon, of Elmley Lovitt, Norfolk, esq. [sic], 3 March 1588-9, by Cooke.   Add. MS. 14,295, fo. 47ᵇ ; 1582 in Harl. MS. 1359, fo. 96.

„   William, of London, Capt. of ye trayned bands, 18 June 1662.   Bysshe's Grants, fo. 9, Her. Coll. ; Harl. MS. 1105, fo. 18 ; Add. MS. 14,293, fo. 11ᵇ.

DUFFIELD, Anthony, of London, ... 1586, by Cooke.   Harl. MS. 1359, fo. 103.

DUGDALE, John, of Clithero, co. Lanc., crest 10 Aug. 1560, by G. Dethick.   Harl. MSS. 1441, fo. 86, and 5887, fo. 42 ; Stowe MS. 677, fo. 11ᵇ ; Add. MS. 14,295, fo. 52 ; I. 9, 98, and C. 24 [Visit. Lond., 1634], fo. 355, Her. Coll. ; Misc. Gen. et Her., N. S., iv., 103 ; Q's Coll. Oxf. MS. 145, fo. 42.

„   William, s. of Sir John, Norroy King of Arms, grandson to Sir Wᵐ Dugdale, Garter, augmentation 22 July 1698, Grants IV., 273, by Sir T. St. George, Gart. and Clar., and Berry IV., 271, and Cat. Her. Exhib. Soc. of Antiquaries, and Hamper's Life of Dugdale.

DUKE, George, of Wandsworth, Surrey, Capt. of a troop, and Major of a regᵗ of horse.   20 Oct. 1662, altered, augmentation 24 April 1663 or 1673, by Walker, Gart.   Add. MSS. 14,293, fo. 65, and 14,294, fo. 19 ; Harl. MS. 1172, fo. 64ᵇ ; Her. Coll., fo. 49, copy of grant.

„   Peter, of London, s. of Peter, of London, s. of Peter, of France, confirmed . . . . 1620, by Camden.   Harl. MS. 6095, fo. 37 ; Guil., p. 395.

„   Richard, of Powder Heys, Devon, arms and crest granted 10 Dec. 1554, by T. Hawley.   Add. MS. 16,940, fo. 39 and 207 ; Harl. MS. 1116, fo. 67 ; 1562, Quarterly coat confirmed, fo. 39 ; copy of grant, Q's Coll. Oxf. MS. 38, fo. 62.

DUKESON, Richard, S.T.P., and rector of St. Clements Danes, a chaplain to the King, 3 May 1666.   Bysshe's Grants, fo. 17, Her. Coll. ; Harl. MS. 1105, fo. 20.

DUKENFIELD, Robert, of D[nkenfield], Cheshire, confirmed . . . . 1613 or 1623, by R. St. George, Norr.   Guil. 57 ; Add. MS. 4966, fo. 32ᵇ (1613).

DUMMER, ..., az., 3 fleurs de lis or, on a chief of the 2ⁿᵈ a lion issuant gu., ..., by Segar.   Add. MS. 12,225, fo. 37ᵇ.

DUNCOMBE, John, of Stewkeley, Bucks, gift . . . . 1560, 3 Q. Eliz. (Harvey's Grants).   Add. MS. 16,940, fo. 18.

DUNHEVED, see LAUNCESTON.

DUN, Daniel, Doctor of the Lawe, now of Essex.   Add. MS. 4966, fo. 31, 8 Aug. 1588, by Cooke, copy of grant, Brit. Mus.
    Wᵐ, his brother, Dʳ of Physic, now of Bristol.   Harl. MSS. 1359, fo. 108ᵇ, 1422, fo. 107ᵇ, and 5887, fo. 91, Quarterly.

DUN (DUNN), Sir Daniel, Kt., Dean of the Arches, and his brother William, Doctor of Physic, incomplete grant of quarterly coat and crest, Dec. 1604, by Camden.   Cott. MS. Faustina E. I., 416, and Harl. MS. 6095, fo. 3ᵃ.

„   Sir Daniel, Doctor of the Civil Lawe, Quarterly Coat and Crest, 10 Feb. 1605-6, by Camden.   Harl. MSS. 6095, fo. 3ᵇ, and 1422, fo. 108, a new patent for alteration in Coat and Crest, 26 March 1607, by W. Camden. Harl. MSS. 6095, fo. 7, and 5887, fo. 91.

DUNCHE, William, of Little Wittenham, Berks, gift . . . . 1561 (Harvey's Grants). Add. MS. 16,940, fo. 39ᵇ.

DUNNING, Richard, of Denton, Norfolk, 14 Jan. 1664. Harl. MS. 1105, fo. 40 ; called Bunning in Bysshe's Grants 33, Her. Coll. *See* BUNNING.

DUNSTER, Giles, of Sevenington, Somersetsh., 7 June 1664. Bysshe's Grants, fo. 7, Her. Coll. ; Harl. MS. 1105, fo. 18 ; of Seavington, Kent, and 17th of June in Guil., p. 306 ; Harl. MS. 6179, fo. 48.

DUNTHORNE, William, of co. Camb., 2 March 1467-8, by T. Holme, first " Norroy." Stowe MS. 1047, fo. 206^b.

DUPPA, Thomas, gent., usher, daily waiter, crest 9 Feb. 167⅔, by Sir Wm Dugdale, Gart., and St. George, Norr. Harl. MS. 6831, fo. 78 ; Grants III., fo. 77.

„ Brian, D.D., Bishop of Winchester, Augmentation Aug. 1660, by Walker, Gart. Her. Coll., 33.

DURANT. . . . ., of Durant, co. Derby, July 1606, by Camden, Durant and St. Lyse quarterly. Harl. MSS. 1122, fo. 19^b, and 6095, fo. 5^b ; Guil., p. 55.

DURLEW, *see* CURLEW.

DURNING, Edward, of . . . ., Lancs. . . . . 1569, by Cooke. Harl. MS. 1422, fo. 42^b.

DYER, George, of Waterplace in Hertfordshire, ..., by Cooke. Harl. MS. 1359, fo. 99^b ; Add. MS. 4966, fo. 19.

„ Sir James, of Stoughton, Hunts, Knt., Lord Chief Justice of Com. Pleas, ye son of Richard, of Wynoalton, or Wymoalton, co. Somerset, crest, a falcon out of a coronet, grant 20 April 1575, by G. Dethick and Cooke. Stowe MS. 676, fo. 45^b, 47 ; Harl. MS. 1441, fo. 83, with remainder to nephew

„ James, as above (crest, a goat's head, etc.), with remaind^r to nephew Lawrence, same date. Copies of grants, *see* Q's Coll. Oxf. MS. 37, fo. 58, 61 (MS. 145, fo. 37^b) ; Grants I., 113, 269.

DYERS' COMPANY, 14 Oct. 1577, 19 Q. Eliz., crest and supporters added to their old arms, by Cooke. Harl. MS. 1359, fo. 75^b ; Add. MS. 14,295, fo. 44 (Nov.).

DYKE, DIKE, Thomas, of Horsham, Sussex, and to brethren

„ Robert, of London, merch^t, etc. Add. MS. 14,295, fo. 56 ; C. 24 [Visit. Lond., 1634]. 56, Her. Coll. ; Harl. MS. 1105, fo. 7^b.

DYMOCK, Francis, of Erdington, co. Warwick, quarterly, 17 June 1584 or 1589, 23 Eliz. [1580-81], by Cooke. Harl. MSS. 1359, fo. 100^b, and 1422, fo. 120^b ; Add. MS. 4966, fo. 89 ; Harl. MS. 5887, fo. 48 ; copy of grant, Harl. MS. 1116, fo. 34^b.

DYMMOCK, John, of London, coat and crest . . . ., Barker's Grants. Harl. MS. 5846, fo. 31^b ; Stowe MS. 692, fo. 36.

DIMOCKE, William, Master of the Assaye (? descended of Collier, *alias* Dymocke, of Stone, co. Staff.). Stowe MS. 706, fo. 67^b, by Camden, Clar.

DYNE, ..., of Greensted, Essex, ..., by Bysshe. Harl. MS. 1105, fo. 15.

DYNNE, Robert, of Heydon, Norfolk, gent., crest 28 June 1577, by Cooke. Add. MS. 14,295, fo. 81 ; Harl. MS. 1052, fo. 192, copy of grant, Brit. Mus. ; s. of Henry, 2nd s. of Robert, brother and heir of John, wh. Robert was s. of John by Jone, d. and coheir of John Aillwarte. Harl. MS. 5887, fo. 73^b.

DYOTT, John, of Stychbroke, co. Staff., crest granted 20 Feb. 1559-60, by G. Dethick. MS. Ashm. 858, pp. 113, 115, copy of grant, Bodleian Lib. ; Harl. MS. 1441, fo. 61^b ; (20 Feb., 2 Q. Eliz., 1559-60), in Stowe MS. 677, fo. 11, and Q's Coll. Oxf. MS. 145, fo. 2 ; Harl. MS. 5887, fo. 47.

DYSON, Henry, of Inkborough, co. Worc., 4 Feb. 1630-1, by R. St. George. Add. MS. 14,295, fo. 69^b ; C. 30, 72, Visit. of Worcestersh. 1634, Her. Coll. ; MS. Ashm. 858, pp. 123-4, copy of grant, Bodleian Lib. ; Harl. MS. 6179, fo. 39^b.

E

EADE, John, of co. Warwick, confirmed . . . . 15[6]$\frac{a}{6}$. (Harvey's Grants) Add.
MS. 16,940, fo. 29^b.

EALES, Luke, of Runcton Holme, Norfolk, one of her Majesty's physicians, and his
brother Thomas, 2 Nov. 1670, by Walker. Copy of grant, Harl. MS.
1172, fo. 61^b; Add. MSS. 14,293, fo. 73, and 14,294, fo. 21^b; Guil.,
p. 396.

EARLE, Erasmus, of Salle, Norfolk, esq., s. of Thos, s. of John, 12 April 1635, by
R. St. George. Add. MS. 14,295, fo. 105; Grants II., 496^b; Le Neve's
MS. 462.

„   Martin, of Tattersell, co. Linc., gent., 8 May 1558, by G. Dethick. Harl.
MS. 1141, fo. 85; Q's Coll. Oxf. MS. 145, fo. 40^b.

EARLES, John, D.D. (s. of Thos, Registrar of the Archbp's Court York), chaplain
to Chas. II. (after Dean of Westminster, Clerk of the Closet to Chas. II.
and Bp. of Salisbury), 1 Aug. 1660, by Walker. Harl. MS. 1172, fo. 70;
Add. MSS. 14,293, fo. 87. and 14,294, fo. 26; Guil., p. 282.

EARNING, Anthony, of London, Merchant, 6 Dec. 1662, 14 Chas. II. Harl. MS.
1105, fo. 16^b; Bysshe's Grants, fo. 2, Her. Coll.; Guil., p. 214; Harl. MS.
1086, fo. 14^b.

EAST INDIA MERCHANTS', Company of, grant of arms, crest and supporters 4 Feb.
1600-1, by W. Dethick, Camden and Segar. Add. MS. 12,225, fo. 79^b;
Stowe MS. 676, fo. 134; Morgan's Sphere, lib. iii., 107; Her. and General.,
i., 124; Add. MS. 5533, fo. 135; Q's Coll. Oxf. MS. 36, fo. 87, copy of
grant.

EAST INDIES, English Company trading to the, arms, crest and supporters 13 Oct.
1698, by T. St. George, Gart. and Clar. Grants IV., 282.

EASTDAYE, Henry, of Saltwood, Kent, ... by Cooke. Harl. MS. 1359, fo. 105^b;
called John in Stowe MS. 670, fo. 48^b, and Add. MSS. 14,297, fo. 48^b, and
4966, fo. 25 (Henry).

EASTMONT, John, of Sherborne, Dorset, 23 May 1670. Harl. MS. 1105, fo. 21^b;
Bysshe's Grants, fo. 24, Her. Coll.

EDDOWES, John, of Chalton, Cheshire, a benefactor to the College of Arms, 7 Nov.
1673. Harl. MS. 6179, fo. 46.

EDEN, Robert, of Durham, now of West Auckland . . . . 1573, by Flower. Add.
MS. 14,295, fo. 74^b (fo. 55), quarterly; Harl. MS. 6140, fo. 27^b.

EDGARE, Thomas, of Blewbery, Berks, coat and crest. Barker's Grants; Harl.
MSS. 5846, fo. 34, and 1422, fo. 17.

„   William, of Great Glemham, Suff., coat and crest. Barker's Grants; (10 Sept.
1545, Stowe MS. 677, fo. 21^b); 16 Sept., Harl. MSS. 1085, fo. 17^b, and
5846, fo. 33; Stowe MS. 692, fo. 38^b; Grants I., p. 7.

EDGE, Capt Thomas, of London, s. of Ellys, of Blackborne, co. Lanc., s. of John by
Alice, dau. of George Answorth of Answorth, co. Lanc., grant 5 Oct. 1621,
by Camden. Stowe MS. 677, fo. 39^b, 40, copy of grant, Brit. Mus.

EDGECOMBE, Peter, alias Piers, of Mt Edgcombe, Devon, crest 10 March 1573-4,
by R. Cooke, Clar. Grants I., 18.

EDISBURY, Kenwricke, Merthwell, co. Denbigh, servant to K. James, certified by
W. Camden (no date). Grants II., 596.

EDMONDES, ... of Cossington, Hants, descended from Edmondes of Baylies,
co. Sussex, Quarterly: 1 and 4, or, a fess vaire, in chief 3 martlets gu., a
crescent for diff. . . . . by Segar. Add. MS. 12,225, fo. 38.

„   . . . . of Sussex . . . . by Segar. gu., a fesse vaire, in chief 3 martlets or.
Add. MS. 12,225, fo. 38.

EDMONDS, Sir Clement, Clerk of the Counsel, Knt., July 1610, by Camden. Harl.
MSS. 1422, fo. 21, and 6095, fo. 12^b.

EDMUNDS, Henry, Worsborough Hall, Yorks, 1 Sept. 1665, by W. Dugdale, Norr.
Foster's Yorkshire Pedigrees; Visit. Yorks, 1665, Surtees Soc., p. 9.

EDMONDS, John, of Dodington, Oxon., coat and crest. Add. MS. 26,702, fo. 11 ; Barker's Grants ; Harl. MS. 5846, fo. 33 ; Stowe MS. 692, fo. 38ᵇ.

„   Symon, of London, mercht., 12 June 1640, by Sir J. Borough, Gart. Add. MS. 26,702, fo. 93 ; Guil., p. 381 ; Edwards in Harl. MS. 1105, fo. 57.

EDMONDES, Thomas, of Plymouth, Devon, 22 July 1599, by Camden. Harl. MSS. 1422, fo. 17, and 6095, fo. 1 ; Guil., p. 165.

EDMUNDS, Thomas, Worsborough Hall, Yorks, 1 Jan. 1647-8, by Bysshe or Ryley. *See* new grant to Henry Edmunds, 1665, and Foster's Yorkshire Pedigrees.

EDMONSON, Thomas, city of York .... 1612, by R. St. George, Norr. Stowe MS. 706, fo. 11 ; Harl. MSS. 6140, fo. 72, and 6179, fo. 13ᵇ.

EDULPH, EDOLFE or EDOULFE, Symon, of Brenset, Kent, gent., crest granted 3 July 1 Q. Eliz., 1559, by G. Dethick. Harl. MS. 1359, fo. 78 ; Q's Coll. Oxf. MS. 39, fo. 90 ; Add. MS. 16,940, fo. 6 (by Harvey and G. Dethick), ? new crest, 14 April 1562, 4 Eliz. ; MS. Ashm. 858, p. 22, copy of grant, Bodleian Lib.

EDWARD, William, of Salop, confirmed .... 1560. (Harvey's Grants), Add. MS. 16,940, fo. 14ᵇ.

EDWARDS, ..., of Southouse and London, granted .... by Cooke. Stowe MS. 670, fo. 3ᵇ ; Guil., p. 228, az., on a bend cottised argt. three martlets gules.

„   .... Quarterly, arg., 3 dragons' heads erased vert, each devouring a hand sinister couped ppr., vulned gu. ; quartering, 2 Morgan, 3 ...., 4 Cærleon ; 22 Sept., 2 Chas., 1626, by Segar. Add. MS. 12,225, fo. 38ᵇ ; Harl. MS. 1476, fo. 30.

„   Christopher, of London .... by Cooke. Stowe MS. 670, fo. 28.

„   Richard, of Henlowe, Beds, confirmed 27 Aug. 1632, by R. St. George, Clar. Add. MS. 14,295, fo. 56ᵇ ; C. 31, Visit. of Bedfordshire [1634], 63, Her. Coll.

„   Simon, of London, Merchant, 12 June 1640, by Borough. Harl. MS. 1105, fo. 57 ; Edmonds in Guil., p. 381 ; Add. MS. 26,702, fo. 93.

„   Thomas, of London, cheesemonger, descended out of Wales, arg., a fesse erm. cotised sa. between 3 martlets of the last .... by Segar. Add. MS. 12,225, fo. 38ᵇ.

EGERTON, Charles, augmentation for services in Ireland, crest and augmentation 20 Aug. 1574, by Narbon, Ulster King of Arms. Copy of grant, Brit. Mus. ; Add. MS. 14,295, fo. 49 ; *see* Harl. MS. 1359, fo. 23 ; Q's Coll. Oxf. MS. 146, fo. 30.

„   John, of Egerton and Oulton, Cheshire, confirmed crest ? 7 Aug. 1580, by Flower. MS. Ashm. 834, p. 24ᵇ, copy of grant, Bodleian Lib. ; Guil., p. 335.

„   Thomas, Knt., Keeper of the great seal, crest granted 20 May 1596, by W. Dethick. Stowe MS. 676, fo. 117, copy of grant, and in Latin in Q's Coll. Oxf. MS. 36, fo. 55.

EGLESTON, Thomas, Winchelsea, Sussex, ..., by Cooke. Stowe MS. 670, fo. 6ᵇ.

ELCOKE, Alexander, of Stopford, Cheshire, ... 1613, by R. St. George. Harl. MS. 1422, fo. 14.

ELD, Richard, Treasurer of the Companies in Ulster, confirmation 12 Sept. 1574, by Narbon, Ulster K. of A. MS. Ashm. 858, pp. 121-2, copy of grant, Bodleian Lib. ; Add. MS. 12,474, fo. 20.

ELDRED, Anne, *see* BLAIKWAY, 1652, copy of grant, by Bysshe. Harl. MS. 1172, fo. 18.

„   John, of London and Buckenham, Norfolk (4th s. of John, of Knetsall, Norfolk), difference granted 10 June 1592, by W. Dethick. Harl. MSS. 1422, fo. 42, and 1172, fo. 43 (Guil. 356) ; copy of grant, *see* Harl. MS. 6140, fo. 28ᵇ.

„   John, Colchester, Essex, 14 Feb. 1630-1, by R. St. George. Add. MS. 14,295, fo. 69 ; C. 21, [Visit.] Essex [1634], fo. 156, Her. Coll.

M

ELFRED, George, Hove, Sussex, 11 July 1682, by Sir Wm Dugdale, and Clar. Harl. MS. 6834, fo. 178 ; Grants III., fo. 156.

ELKYN [William], Alderman [and Mercer], of London, ..., coat and crest not given. Barker's Grants.   Harl. MS. 5846, fo. 34^b.

ELKIN, or ELKYN, the late W^m, citizen and Alderm., of London, late dec^d (and to his dau. Ursula), buried 20 Nov. 1595. By W. Dethick.   Stowe MS. 676, fo. 113, half a year after his death, who had for the same five pound. Never any king of armes could make a man a gentleman after his death but this Garter, ent^d by R. Brooke, York Herald.   Harl. MS. 1453, fo. 34 ; Certificate by W. Dethick, Gart. ; Q's Coll. Oxf. MS. 36, fo. 48 ; Grants I., 248.   See WYLKES, Alice.

ELKEN, Richard, of London, gent., grant 5 March, 4 Ed. VI., 1549-50, by G. Dethick, copy of grant, Brit. Mus.   Harl. MS. 1470, fo. 222, and Q's Coll. Oxf. MSS. 36, fo. 48, and 37, fo. 29, and 38, fo. 56 ; Harl. MS. 1359, fo. 7^b.

ELKINGTON, Thomas, of London, 22 Oct. 1608, by Camden, and to his uncles Henry, Tho., and Edward (see BURKE).   Harl. MSS. 1422, fo. 20^b, and 6095, fo. 10 ; Guil. 74.

ELLERKER, Edward, of Risby, Yorks, ... 1545, by C. Barker.   Harl. MS. 5807, fo. 33.

  „   Sir Rauf, of Risby, Yorks, gift of crest 20 March 1546, Barker's Grants. Harl. MS. 5846, fo. 33^b ; Stowe MS. 692, fo. 38^b ; Genealogist, i., 290.

ELYOTTE, ..., of London, crest, by Harvey, Clar.   Add. MS. 16,940, fo. 10^b.

ELLIOTT, of Suffolk (Richard), grant 8 April 1613 or Nov. 1614, by Camden, or, a fesse gu. between 2 bars gemelles wavy sa.   Crest, an elephant's head conped or, eared and tusked gu.   Harl. MS. 6095, fo. 31 ; Richard, Nov. 1613, in Harl. MS. 1422, fo. 39.

ELYOTT, Anne, dau. of John, gift . . . . 1563 (Harvey's Grants), sa., on a pile undée between 2 crastells [sic, Castells] or, a lion ramp^t az., langued and armed gu.   Add. MS. 16,940, fo. 14.

ELLYOTT, Edmond, citizen and Fishmonger of London, Scocheon deliv^d 12 June 1594, by Lee, arms and crest.   Harl. MS. 1359, fo. 31^b ; Add. MS. 14,295, fo. 26^b ; Stowe MS. 670, fo. 58^b ; William in Harl. MS. 6179, fo. 14^b.

ELIOTT, John, citizen and Mercer of London, crest given 8 March 1555-6, 2 and 3 Phil. and Mary, by Harvey.   Harl. MS. 1359, fo. 19 ; 7th of March in Add. MS. 14,295, fo. 12 ; Add. MS. 16,940, fo. 10^b ; Crest, a demi-pegasus gu., the mayne and wings gold ; Harl. MS. 6179, fo. 14^b.

ELYOTT, Thomas, of Greene place, Surrey, " per W. D[ugdale]."   Le Neve's MS. 255.

  „   Thomas and John, sons of Richard, " their consin William, master of the King's chancellerie," grant of arms and crest, 1492, on the day of the translation of St Thomas the Martyr of Canterbury (? 31 Dec.), by John Writhe, Gart.   Q's Coll. Oxf. MS. 38, fo. 13, copy of grant.

ELLIS, Humphrey, of Flints, Feb. 1587-8, 30 Q. Eliz., by Cooke.   Harl. MSS. 1359, fo. 108, and 1422, fo. 84^b ; Add. MS. 4966, fo. 57^b.

  „   John, St Paul's Churchy^d, London, Draper, Sheriff of Herts (1668), by Bysshe.   Harl. MS. 6179, fo. 32.

  „   John, of Yale, co. Denbigh, pensioner to Q. Eliz., Quarterly Coat.   Harl. MS. 1422, fo. 112^b.

ELLYS, Dame Joyce, dau. of John Elys of Devonshire, wife of Everard Feilding of Cold Newnam, co. Warw., coat only, Barker's Grants.   Harl. MS. 5846, fo. 37 ; Stowe MSS. 692, fo. 41, and 702, fo. 115.

ELLIS, Thomas, of Swynshed, co. Linc., coat and crest . . . ., Barker's Grants. Harl. MS. 5846, fo. 32^b ; Stowe MS. 692, fo. 38.

  „   Thomas, of Doncaster, Yorks, gent., Grant 1 Feb., 3 Ed. VI., 1548-9, by G. Dethick.   Harl. MS. 1359, fo. 59 ; copy of grant, Q's Coll. Oxf. MS. 39, fo. 21.

ELLISTON, Joseph, of Tillingham, 2nd s. of Matthew, of Heveningham Chestell, Essex, to them and their descendants, confirmed by R. St. George. Add. MS. 14,293, fo. 22.

ELLNOR, ..., Arg. on a cross sa. between 4 Cornish choughs ppr. 5 bezants, by Segar. Add. MS. 12,225, fo. 39.

ELTON, Nicholas, of London, Merch[t] Taylor, s. of Richard, of Kingston Lisle, co. Berks, confirmed by Camden and by Segar. Add. MS. 12,225, fo. 39 ; C. 24, fo. 457[a] [Visit. London, 1634], Her. Coll., and Guil. 404 ; Harl. MS. 1105, fo. 3.

ELWEYS, William, Broxton, Notts, Quarterly, exemplified by Cooke. Stowe MS. 670, fo. 31[b] ; Add. MS. 14,297, fo. 29[b].

EMERSON, Raffe, Foxton, co. Durham, by Thos. Wall, Gart., 1534-5, 26 H. VIII. (Burke's Armory) ; Harl. MS. 1397, fo. 257.

EMERY, Thomas, als AMERY, of Little Badow, Essex, 20 May 1628, by Segar. Add. MS. 12,225, fo. 39[b] ; Guil. 358, and C. 21, fo. 78 [Visit. Essex, 1634], Her. Coll.

EMMANUEL COLLEGE, Cambridge, 1 Jan. 1588-9, by Cooke, Clar. Cat. Her. Exhib. Soc. of Antiq., 69.

ENDERBY. . . . . arg., a fesse vert cotised (? betw. two barrnlets) gu., by Cooke ? . . . . Harl. MS. 1359, fo. 120 ; Add. MS. 4966, fo. 90[b].

ENGLAND. Sir George, of Great Yarmouth, Norfolk, 9 Nov. 1671, by Bysshe, Clar. Harl. MS. 1105, fo. 40 ; Add. MS. 29,785, fo. 3 ; Bysshe's Grants, 34.

ENGLEBERT, Hugh, of Lawrenny, co. Pembroke,
  ,, George, of London,
  ,, John, of Killington, Middlesex,
  ,, William, of London, sons of Nicholas, of Sherborne, Dorset, grandchildren of Roger, 27 May 1602, by Camden. Guil. 62.

ENGLISH, William, of Wadhurst, Sussex.
  ,, Henry, of Lincoln's Inn.
  ,, Thomas, of Buckland, nr. Maidstone, esq., 7 May 1662. Bysshe's Grants, fo. 13, Her. Coll.; Stowe MS. 703, fo. 70 ; Harl. MS. 1105, fo. 19.

EPES, Allen, of the Isle of Thanet, exemplified by Segar. MS. Rawl. B. 87, fo. 18, Bodleian Lib.

ERLSEMAN, John, of Westover, Isle of Wight, s. of John, of the same, grant 9 July 1592, by W. Dethick. Stowe MS. 676, fo. 88, 101, copy of grant ; Q's Coll. Oxf. MS. 36, fo. 20.

ESCAFFLES, Edward, rightly TRAFFLES.

ESKINTON, ... London, ... Oct. 1608. Burke's Armory. See ELKINTON.

ESSE or ASHE, ... Devon, confirmed Dec. 1613, by Camden. Harl. MSS. 1422, fo. 38[b], and 6095, fo. 28.

ESSEX, Edmond, of London, ... 1590, by Cooke. Harl. MS. 1359, fo. 96[b].
  ,, Sir William, of Wilts, ... H. VI. Add. MS. 26,702, fo. 31.

ESSINGTON, William and Thomas, sons of John, late of Cowley, nr. Essington, co. Glouc., descend[ts] of the elder house of two of the surname and family, confirmed 28 July 1610, by Segar. Harl. MS. 6140, fo. 77 ; Add. MS. 12,225, fo. 39[b] ; Guil. 371.

ESTCOURTE, Thomas, of Shipenmoyne, co. Glouc., Quarterly . . . . Nov. 1606, by Camden. Harl. MSS. 1422, fo. 108, and 6095, fo. 8.

ESTERCOMBE, see WARRE (Richard, an error, of Somerset, esq., 10 July 1576, by G. Dethick. Harl. MS. 1441, fo. 85).

ESTON, ... of Holme, co. Bedf., coat (neither date nor king). Add. MS. 14,295, fo. 107, certified by H. St. George, Norr.
  ,, John, of Southwark, Surrey, coat and crest . . . . Barker's Grants ; Harl. MS. 5846, fo. 33[b] ; Stowe MS. 692, fo. 38[b] ; Harl. MS. 1422, fo. 14[b].

ESTWICKE. Christopher, of Milton Grange, co. Bedf., gent., confirmed 15 Feb. 1579-80, by Sir G. Dethick, Gart. Copy of grant, Q's Coll. Oxf. MS. 38, fo. 101 ; Le Neve's MS. 419.

ETHERINGTON, Sir Richard, of Ebberstone, Yorks, Knt., confirmed 21 May 1613, by R. St. George. Harl. MS. 1359, fo. 43ᵇ.

„ Thomas, of Dryfeilde, Yorks, Esq., s. and h. of Wᵐ, grant . . . . 1567, by Cooke. Harl. MS. 1359, fo. 26 ; Add. MS. 14,295, fo. 15ᵇ.

ETON COLLEGE, ... 1 Jan., 27 H. VI., 1448-9. Copy of grant, Brit. Mus., Stowe MS. 840, fo. 60ᵇ ; Excerpta Hist., p. 47 ; Her. and Geneal. i., 119 ; Charta, 27 Hy. VI., No. 48 ; Cat. Her. Exhib. Soc. of Antiq., plate xxxvi.

EVANS, William, of London, gent., born in co. Merioneth, Wales, granted 20 Nov. 1581, by G. Dethick. Copy of grant, Q's Coll. Oxf. MS. 37, fo. 73 ; Stowe MS. 676, fo. 54.

EVELYN als AVELIN, George, of Lodington (Long Ditton), Surrey, gent., s. of John, s. of Roger, etc., crest 3 Aug. 1572, by Cooke. Harl. MS. 1507, fo. 115, copy of grant, Brit. Mus. ; Harl. MS. 1422, fo. 115 ; Misc. Gen. et Her., 2nd S., vol. i., p. 1, plate ; Cat. Her. Exhib. Soc. of Antiq. ; Q's Coll. Oxf. MS. 38, fo. 86 ; MS. 146, fo. 46.

EVENINGTON, see EVINGTON.

EVERARD, ... of Suffolk . . . . crest. Barker's Grants ; Harl. MS. 5846, fo. 34ᵇ ; Stowe MS. 692, fo. 38ᵇ.

„ Richard, of Hawkeden, Suff., 17 Sept. 1611, by Wᵐ Camden. Harl. MS. 1085, fo. 19.

EVERARD impaling WISEMAN. Quarterly coat. "I did see Robᵗ Cooke's hand at this impaled" (J. Withie). Harl. MS. 1359, fo. 113ᵇ ; Add. MS. 4966, fo. 62.

„ Robert, of Spaxton parish, Somerset, 1 Jan. 1660-61, by Walker, Gart. Her. Coll. 31.

EVERDS (rightly EVERAD, Harl. MS. 1116), Edward, ... at London 10 March (1 Q. Mary) 1553-4, by G. Dethick. Harl. MS. 1359, fo. 62ᵇ ; copy of certif. or grant, Q's Coll. Oxf. MS. 39, fo. 85 ; copy of grant, Harl. MS. 1116, fo. 45 ; Grants I., fo. 47.

EVERSHED, John, of Evershed, par. of Ockley, nr. Dorking, Surrey, 11 March 1696-7, by T. St. George, Gart. and Clar. Harl. MS. 6834, fo. 169 ; Misc. Gen. et Her., ii., 191 ; Grants IV., 222 ; Le Neve's MS. 463.

EVERY, John, of Somerset, Sergᵗ at arms to H. VIII., Ed. VI., Q. Mary and Q. Eliz. . . . . June 1604, by Camden. Harl. MSS. 1422, fo. 17ᵇ, 5839, fo. 2ᵇ, 2275, fo. 90ᵇ, and 1115, fo. 8ᵇ.

EVINGTON, Nicholas, s. of Richᵈ, s. of Richard, of Halsted, co. Linc., 1⅟2 Feb. 1612, by Camden. Harl. MS. 6140, fo. 61ᵇ ; Elsington in Caius Coll. Camb. MS. 551, fo. 31ᵇ.

EVINGDON als EVINGTON, Thomas, of Enfield, Middx., 2nd s. of Francis, of Casewick, co. Linc. (who bore arg., a fesse azure with a label of three points gules), arms and crest granted 10 Oct. 1614, by Segar. Add. MS. 12,225, fo. 40 ; Guil. 346, where he is called James, 2nd s. of Thomas, and Harl. MS. 6140, fo. 62 ; Evenington in Le Neve's MS. 351.

EWENS, John, of Wineanton, co. Somerset, arms and crest given 11 May 1578, by Cooke. Add. MS. 14,295, fo. 14 ; Harl. MSS. 1395, fo. 20ᵇ ? and 1422, fo. 51, alibi Baron of the Exchequer ; Harl. MS. 1166, fo. 88 ; Add. MS. 4966, fo. 84.

„ (Matthew) Baron of the Exchequer . . . . by Ro. Cooke, Clar. Harl. MS. 1359, fo. 104ᵇ and pedigree ; see Evans in Stowe MS. 606, fo. 46 ; Harl. MS. 5887, fo. 79.

EWER, Isaac, Col. of a regᵗ of foot under Genl. Sir Thoˢ Fairfax, 22 Feb. 1647-8, by Bysshe. Add. MS. 26,758, fo. 14, copy of grant ; Stowe MS. 677, fo. 36 ; Harl. MS. 6832, fo. 414.

„ William. See Stowe MS. 697, fo. 109ᵇ.

EXETER, City of, ... confirmed. (Harvey's Grants). Add. MS. 16,940, fo. 7.

„ The Merchants of, confirmed . . . . 1560. (Harvey's Grants), Add. MS. 16,940, fo. 12ᵇ.

EXETER, Merchant Taylors of, ... (Harvey's Grants), Add. MS. 16,940,
fo. 37ᵇ.

EXMEW, Sir Thomas, Mayor of London, 1517. . . . . Hen. VIII. Add. MS. 26,702,
fo. 36ᵇ.

EAY (EYE), Town of, Suffolk, grant 20 April 1592, by W. Dethick. Stowe MS.
676, fo. 95, copy of grant ; Q's Coll. Oxf. MS. 36, fo. 7.

EYNSHAM, Anneys, dau. of John, of London, Grocer, exemplified 28 Feb. 1453-4
(see also Randolf, John). MS. Ashm. 834, i., fo. 3ᵇ, copy of grant,
Bodleian Lib.

EYRE, Henry, of London, 1589, by Cooke. 1589 in Harl. MS. 1359, fo. 101, and
1583 in Harl. MS. 1422, fo. 94ᵇ.

„ Robert, of Eye, Suffolk, descended of the house of Hope of Darbishire and of
Eyre aforesaid by his mother ; coat and crest. Barker's Grants ; Stowe
MS. 692, fo. 90ᵇ ; Harl. MS. 5846. fo. 32ᵇ ; (? Add. MS. 16,940, fo. 19ᵇ,
Quarterly arms, confirmed 1558).

„ Thomas, of Buckingham, 8 April. 22 Ed. IV., 1482, by T. Holme, Clar. ;
entered 26 June 1566 at the Visitation, by Hervey. Stowe MS. 714,
fo. 169 ; Harl. MS. 3968, fo. 27ᵇ.

EYTON, William, of the house of Wickstie, co. Denbigh, and

„ Richard, his brother, esquire and sergeant of armes to Q. Eliz. : Quarterly
of 6 and crest confirmed 12 Aug. 1577, by G. Dethick. Harl. MS. 1441,
fo. 69, and Q's Coll. Oxf. MS. 145, fo. 13ᵇ ; Harl. MS. 1972, fo. 62.

F

FAGGE, Sir John, Bart. (among Cooke's Gifts). Stowe MS. 670, fo. 62ᵇ ; Add.
MS. 14,297, fo. 62ᵇ.

FAYREBEARD, Robert, of Northmore, co. Oxf., 19 Aug. 1640, by Borough. Harl.
MSS. 1105. fo. 57ᵇ, and 6179, fo. 23 ; Caius Coll. Camb. MS. 528, fo. 2,
for copy of grant ; Guil., p. 398.

FAIRBORNE, Sir Palmes, Knt., Commander-in-Chief of City of Tangier, s. of
Stafford Fairborne and grandson of Jervis, crest 25 Aug. 1677, by H. St.
George, Norr. Stowe MS. 714, fo. 120 ; Grants III., 64 ; Harl. MS. 6832,
fo. 355.

FAYRECHYLDE, Joan, wife unto John Lewys of Moorelake, Surrey, gift . . . . 1564.
Harvey's Grants, Add. MS. 16,940, fo. 6ᵇ and 56.

FAIRCLOUGH, Hugh, of London, Citizen and Clothworker, confirmed 2 Nov. 1583,
by G. Dethick. Harl. MS. 1441, fo. 68 ; Q's Coll. Oxf. MS. 145, fo. 12.

FAISH, ... by Cooke. Stowe MS. 670, fo. 63.

FALCONER, ... of London . . . . exemplified . . . . paly of 6, arg. and gu., on
a bend vert three trefoils slipped or . . . . by Segar. Add. MS. 12,225,
fo. 40.

FALDOE, Robert, of Maldon, Bedf., esq., crest 23 Aug. 1594, by Lee ; the arms of
Chamberlayne his wife, quarterly of 9, are also tricked. Add. MS. 14,295,
fo. 25 ; Stowe MS. 706, fo. 10 ; Harl. MSS. 1069, fo. 16ᵇ, and 670, fo. 57 ;
Add. MS. 14,297, fo. 57.

FANE, George, of Kent, crest, confirmed . . . . 1559. Harvey's Grants, Add. MS.
16,940, fo. 6.

FANSHAWE, Henry, of London, gift . . . . 15[6]⅔. Harvey's Grants, Add. MS.
16,940, fo. 16.

„ John, of Fanshawe Gate, co. Derby, Master of the Court of Remembrance to
Q. Eliz., assigned 14 Jan. 1571, by Cooke, G. Dethick and Flower. Stowe
MS. 676, fo. 41 ; Harl. MS. 1441, fo. 77 ; MS. Ashm. 834, fo. 28, copy of
grant, Bodleian Lib., and Q's Coll. Oxf. MSS. 37, fo. 125, 126, and 145,
fo. 14, 27 : Or, two chevrons erm. betw. three fleurs-de-lis sa. ; crest, a
dragon's head erased or charged with two chevrons (arms of Fanshawe of

Dronfield, co. Derby, according to Burke).   Add. MS. 7098, fo. 79 and 31[b], copy of grant, Brit. Mus.; Add. MS. 7098, fo. 79; Guil. 129; Reliquary, xxiii., 254.

FANSHAWE, Richard, Remembrancer of the Exchequer, augmentation by Royal Warrant, Castle of Elizabeth in Jersey, 8 Feb. 1649-50, by T. Lee, Chester Herald. See Walker's Grants, Her. Coll., fo. 3; L. ii., fo. 113, 114, Her. Coll.; Misc. Gen. et Her., ii., 121, copy of grant, Brit. Mus.

FARRINGTON, ... Abbott of Reding.   Add. MS. 26,702, fo. 55.

FARINGTON, William, of Worden, co. Lanc., gent., 4th s. to Sir Henry, of Farington in same co., Knt., crest altered 16 Dec. 1560, by Dalton. Arms Quarterly. Harl. MS. 1359, fo. 50; Her. and Geneal., i., fo. 81; Misc. Gen. et Her., i., 61, copy of grant, Brit. Mus.

FARMAREY, John, of London, Doctor of physick and first husband to Mary Snode (whom see), Dec. 1611, by Camden. Harl. MSS. 1422, fo. 36[b], 6095, fo. 17, and 5887, fo. 82[b]. (See LISTER.)

FARMER, Sir George, Knt., ... alteration . . . . 1591, by Cooke and Lee. Harl. MS. 1422, fo. 90[b], the anchors to be taken off the fesse.

„   George, one of the prothonotaries of the Court of Common Pleas (2nd s. of Bartholomew, of Ratcliff, co. Leic., gent., see Visit[n] 1619), alteration 20 Oct. 1663, by Walker. Harl. MS. 1172, fo. 63; copy of grant, Harl. MS. 1172, fo. 63; Add. MSS. 14,293, fo. 60, and 14,294, fo. 15[b]; Geneal., iii., 61; Guil., p. 310.

FARNABY, Henry, Alderm. of Truro, bore the ancient arms of Farnaby. Grants II., 646[b]; Le Neve's Notes, 257.

„   John, of City of Canterbury (s. of Thomas, of Keppington, Kent), served under Prince Rupert, Prince Maurice and others; imprisoned, plundered, sequestered and decimated; [grant] 3 May 1664, by Walker. Harl. MS. 1172, fo. 37; Add. MSS. 14,293, fo. 43, and 14,294, fo. 10[b]; Guil., p. 171.

„   Thomas, of London, gent., another coat, grandfather of Sir Chas., of Kippington, said to have had a grant in 1630. Grants II., 646 and 646[b].

FARNDON als FARENDON, Peter, of Sedlescombe, Sussex, gent., and to

„   Tobias, his brother, confirmed 28 Feb. 1634-5, by R. St. George. Harl. MS. 1470, fo. 5, copy of grant, Brit. Mus. (Guil., p. 260).

FARR, John, of Hepworth, Isle of Axholme, co. Linc., one of the Receivers for the Queen, s. of John, s. of John, etc., crest, grant 5 July 1582, by G. Dethick. Stowe MS. 676, fo. 57[b]; copy of grant, Q's Coll. Oxf. MS. 37, fo. 78; Grants I., 139.

FARARE, ... July 1609, by Camden. Harl. MSS. 1422, fo. 26[b], and 6095, fo. 11.

FARRER, Nicholas, of London . . . . 1588, by Cooke. Harl. MS. 1359, fo. 102[b].

FAUNCE, Robert, of Cliffe, Kent, a loyal person, 19 May 1663, by Sir E. Walker, Gart. Her. Coll., fo. 50.

FAUNTLEROY, Moor (s. of John, s. of W[m]), of Crondal, Hants, confirmed 8 Dec. 1633, by Borough. Harl. MS. 1470, fo. 102, copy of grant, Brit. Mus.; Guil., p. 251.

FAWETHER, John, of Briset, Suffolk, late of Henley upon Thames . . . . 1604, by Segar. Add. MS. 12,225, fo. 40[b]; Vincent MS. 154, fo. 1[b], Her. Coll., and Guil. 292.

FECKENHAM, Sir William, and Sir John Sitsylt, controversy 4 June 1332 decided in favour of Sir John Sitsylt of Duncombe, co. Hereford. Bossewell's Workes of Armorie, p. 81, and Collins' Peerage, ii., 584-5; Harl. MS. 980, fo. 51.

FEILD, see FIELD.

FEILDER, John, of Burrow Court, Hants, s. of John, Quarterly coat impaling Quarterly coat, circa Sept. 1638, au escocheon, confirmation or grant, by Borough. Add. MS. 14,295, fo. 90[b]; by R. St. George, Harl. MS. 1105, fo. 4.

FEKE, William, of London, given 2 May 1592, by Cooke. (W^m, of Wighton in Norfolk), Harl. MS. 1359, fo. 106^b ; Add. MS. 4966, fo. 85^b.

FENNOR, John, of the Manor of Beneweks, Sussex, grant 10 Nov. 1556, 3 and 4 Phil. and Mary, by Hawley. Harl. MSS. 1170, fo. 263, 1507, fo. 410, and 1116, fo. 42 ; copy of grant, Q's Coll. Oxf. MS. 38, fo. 69 ; Guil., p. 271 ; Grants II., 449 ; Le Neve's MS. 410.

FENTON, Thomas, Anthony and Christopher, sons of Christopher, of Crake, Yorks, 28 Feb. 1578, by Wm Flower, Norr. Stowe MS. 706, fo. 6 ; 1575 in Harl. MS. 6140, fo. 68^b.

FENWICK, Col. Roger, certified 29 June 1647, by Preston. Burke's Armory ; *see* Add. MS. 4966, fo. 44.

„ William, of Wallington, Northumberland . . . . crest, by G. Dethick, Gart. Add. MS. 32,659, fo. 12.

FERMOUR, John . . . . crest . . . . Barker's Grants, Harl. MS. 5846, fo. 35^b ; Stowe MS. 692, fo. 42 ; Harl. MS. 6179, fo. 13.

FERMOR, Alexander, of Welth or Walth, Sussex, gent., s. of W^m, s. of John, etc., crest 10 Nov. 1575, by Cooke. Harl. MSS. 1507, fo. 119, and 1422, fo. 119 ; copy of grant, Q's Coll. Oxf. MS. 38, fo. 91.

FERNE, John, of Crakemarsh, co. Staff., July 1583, by Flower. Harl. MS. 1453, fo. 75.

FEARNE, John, of Crake Marsh, co. Stafford, 2nd brother to W^m, s. of W^m, of Temple Belwood, co. Linc., 2 Feb. (? 1578-9), by G. Dethick. Harl. MS. 1441, fo. 67, and Q's Coll. Oxf. MS. 145, fo. 10^b.

FERNE, Robert, Bonsall, co. Derby . . . . 1644, by Sir H. St. George, Gart., and Le Neve, Norr. Stowe MS. 716, fo. 68.

„ William, in Temple Belwood, co. Linc., 2 Feb. 1578-9, by G. Dethick. Harl. MS. 1441, fo. 84^b, and Q's Coll. Oxf. MS. 145, fo. 40.

„ William, of Temple Belwood, co. Linc. (out of Derby), confirmed 27 April 1585, by Flower. MS. Ashm. 834, fo. 58, copy of grant, Bodleian Lib. ; Guil., p. 379 ; Reliquary, xxii., 50.

FERRAND, William, of Skipton within Craven, Yorks, gent., s. of Christofer, s. of W^m, etc., 20 March 1586-7, by Flower. Surtees Soc., XLI., p. xlii ; MS. Ashm. 844, fo. 68^b, copy of grant, Bodleian Lib. ; Harl. MS. 1422, fo. 13^b ; Guil., p. 74 ; *see also* Harl. MSS. 1422, fo. 13^b, and 1397, fo. 44^b, for Wm Farrant or Ferrand, D.C.L., of Mitcham, Surrey, by Glover, Somerset, Marshal to Norroy.

FERRERS, of Badesley and Tanworth, 1100, fo. 4^b, 36, 45, 59^b ; Warw. 1167, fo. 3 (a, b) ; 1563, fo. 25^b, 220^b.

„ Lord (Sir Robert Shirley), ... and supporters (Quarterings E. of P. Washington), 12 Dec. 1677, by Sir William Dugdale. Harl. MS. 6834, fo. 178 [?] ; Grants III., fo. 70.

FETHERSTON-HALGH, John, Stanhope Hall in the Bpk. [of Durham], crest confirmed to the ancestors of the above, by Flower. Add. MS. 14,295, fo. 78, ... (fo. 134).

FEVERSHAM (Sir George Sonds), Lord, supporters 28 March 1677, 11 Quarterings . . . . by Walker, Gart. Harl. MS. 6834, fo. 178 ; Grants III., fo. 53.

FIELD, Edmond, of Weston, Herts, s. and h. of Thomas, of same, grant 9 March 1653-4, confirmed 8 Dec. 1662, by Bysshe, and to his sister Susan. *See* Bysshe's Grants, fo. 8, Her. Coll. ; Harl. MS. 1105, fo. 16 ; Add. MS. 14,293, fo. 1.

FEILD, John, of Ardesloe, Yorks, gent., crest given 4 Sept. 1558, by Harvey. Harl. MSS. 1422, fo. 18^b, and 1359, fo. 33 ; Add. MSS. 14,295, fo. 33^b, 72, and 16,940, fo. 59.

FILKIN . . . . of Lincolnshire . . . . by R. St. George, Clar. Stowe MS. 703, fo. 72.

FILMER, Robert, of East Sutton, Kent, gent., gift of crest (?) 16 Sept. 1570, by

Cooke. Harl. MS. 1359, fo. 30, 120 ; Dec. in Add. MS. 14,295, fo. 20 ;
Add. MS. 4966, fo. 90^b.

FINCH, Sir Heneage, Lord Daventry, supporters 20 May 1674, by Walker, Gart.
Harl. MS. 6834, fo. 178 ; Grants III., fo. 36.

FYNCHE, Margaret, dau. and one of the heirs of James Finch (of Norwich ?), late
wife of John Dawes, Alderm. of London. Barker's Grants, Harl. MS.
5846, fo. 37^b ; Stowe MSS. 692, fo. 41, and 702, fo. 115.

FINET, Sir John, Kt., one of the assist. Masters of Ceremonies, temp. K. Jas. Harl.
MS. 6140, fo. 48 : Quarterly of 4 impaling quarterly of 19, and pedigree ;
certified by W. Camden. Grants II., 604^b, 606.

FINSEN, Anne, ux. Richard Nutbrowne of Barking, Essex, 1588, by R. Cooke :
gules, on a fess argent three trefoyles slipped vert. Harl. MS. 1359, fo. 95,
and Berry's Suppt. ; Harl. MS. 1441, fo. 136.

FIREBRACE, Henry (of Derbyshire), Chief clerk of the Kitchen to K. Chas. II. and
server to K. Chas. I., 1 Dec. 1677, by Sir Wm. Dugdale and H. St. George,
Norr. Harl. MS. 6834, fo. 178 ; Grants III., fo. 73.

FIRMAGE, Edward, of Ashfield, co. Suff., 1587, by Cooke. Harl. MSS. 1359,
fo. 107, and 1422, fo. 93^b ; Add. MS. 4966, fo. 68^b.

FYSHE (see FYSKE), confirmed 16 Nov. 1633. Burke's Armory.

„   Walter, of Stowemarket, Suff., ... by Cooke. Harl. MS. 1359, fo. 89^b ; Add.
MS. 4966, fo. 34^b : Sa., a chevron wavy betw. three fleurs-de-lis argt. ;
Crest, a tiger's head ermine maned and tusked or.

FYSHER, ... of Hatfield, Herts, ... by Barker, Gart.   Harl. MS. 5846,
fo. 35 ; Stowe MS. 692, fo. 42.

FISHER, ... of London, ... July 1614, by Camden : Or, three demi-lions
rampt., a fesse dancetté (indented) gu. ; [Crest] a demi-lion ramp^t gu.
holding a branch ppr. Harl. MSS. 6095, fo. 30, and 1422, fo. 39 ;
Morgan's Sphere, 114 ; Guil., p. 184.

„   Christopher, of London, gent., father of Henry, of Middle Temple . . . . by
Segar. Add. MS. 12,225, fo. 41 ; Guil. 208 ; Harl. MS. 6140, fo. 97.

„   Sir Edward, of . . . ., s. of Edward, of London, Alderm., s. of Rich^d, descended
out of Staffordshire, 4 Feb. 1607-8, by Camden. Harl. MSS. 1422, fo. 21,
and 6095, fo. 11^b ; Guil., pp. 208, 361.

„   Edward, of Mickleton, co. Glouc., 3rd s. of Richard, of Laeford (Latchford)
in Standen, Herts, Esq., descended from Hen., of Alrewas, co. Staff., Esq.,
temp. H. VI., confirmed arms and 12 quarters, by Segar. Entry very
indistinct. Add. MSS. 12,225, fo. 40^b, and 46,140, fo. 81^b ; Harl. MSS.
5857, fo. 140, and 6179, fo. 15 ; Guil., p. 184.

„   Henry, ... by Harvey (?) . . . . 1560. Harl. MS. 1116, fo. 56^b.

FYSHER, Henry, of Lydham Wycke, Wilts, 10 Oct. 1608, by Camden. Harl. MSS.
1422, fo. 20^b, and 6095, fo. 10 ; Guil., p. 361.

„   Jasper, of Corston, co. Warwick, crest, by Harvey, Clar. Add. MS. 16,940,
fo. 60^b, and Harl. MS. 1116, fo. 55^b.

FISHER, John, of Hunts, gent., 22 Ed. IV., 12 July 1482, by Thos. (Holme), Clar.
Add. MS. 6297, fo. 141 ; Harl. MS. 69, fo. 55^b ; MS. Ashm. 857, fo. 523-4,
copy of grant, Bodleian Lib.

„   John, Packington, co. Warwick, 1 Jan. 1551-2, by Thos. Hawley, Clar. Add.
MS. 16,940, fo. 205 ; Harl. MS. 1167, fo. 71^b.

„   John, Chilton Candover, Hants, after 1575, by Cooke. Harl. MS. 1544,
fo. 58.

FYSHER, John, of Corston, co. Warwick, confirmed 15[6]⅔ . . . . Harvey's Grants ;
Add. MS. 16,940, fo. 60^b.

„   Thomas, see HAWKINS, 1548.

FISHER, Thomas, of London (s. of John, of Woodstock, Oxon., out of Lanc.),
granted 26 April 1613, by Segar. Guil., p. 409.

„   William (of London, merch^t, s. of William), of Little Over, co. Derby, 10 Nov.
1660, by Walker. Add. MSS. 14,293, fo. 93, and 14,294, fo. 27^b ; Harl.

MS. 1172, fo. 70[b] ; Misc. Gen. et Her., 2nd S., ii., p. 228, and Genealogist,
N. S., vi., p. 180 ; Guil., p. 240 ; copy of grant, *see* Brit. Mus.

FISHMONGERS' COMPANY OF LONDON, arms, 19 Oct. 1512, by Wriothesley, Gart.,
and Benolte, Clar. MSS. Ashm. 858, fo. 17. and 844, fo. 14, copy of grant,
Bodleian Lib.; Add. MS. 26,702, fo. 34[b] ; Harl. MS. 1116, fo. 26[b] ;
Crest, Harl. MS. 5846, fo. 35[b], Barker's Grants.

FISKE, *see* FYSKE.

FITCHE, ... of Essex, descended from John Fitche of Fitche Castle in ye North,
25 Ed. I., 1297, Quarterly, 1 and 4 Fitche, 2 Allen, 3 Alges, by Segar and
Penson, Lanc. Her. Add. MS. 12,225, fo. 41.

„ Thomas, of Bradenham, Essex, s. of Robert in Harl. MS. 1422, fo. 14[b],
without the bordure as in the above, Stowe MS. 670, fo. 56.

FITZ ROY, Lady Anne ⎱ our dear and naturall daughters by our Right trusty and
„ Lady Charlotte ⎰ Right entirely beloved Cousin Barbara, Duchess of Cleveland, warrant, 28 Feb. 1672-3, at Whitehall. To bear our
royal arms in lozenge with a baston sinister ermine, as to Charles Fitzroy,
Earl of Southampton, their eldest brother, by Walker. Harl. MS. 1172,
fo. 47.

FITZ URYAN, John, Llangadock, co. Carmarthen (20 Feb. 1526 in Berry), *temp.*
Hy. VIII.: (argent), on a chev. gu. (sable) between three martlets sa. a
crescent arg., all within a border engrailed of the 2nd charged with eight
bezants. Crest, two swords ppr. in saltire, a martlet sa. charged with
a crescent. Add. MS. 26,702, fo. 46[b] ; Harl. MS. 1052, fo. 21, pedigree.
See Thos. JONES.

FITZWILLIAM, John, of London, Quarterly, confirmed . . . . 15[6]⅚ . . . . Harvey's
Grants, Add. MS. 16,940, fo. 32[b].

FLAMSTED, John, of Rushton, Northants, 28 June 1576, 13 Q. Eliz., by Cooke.
Harl. MS. 1359, fo. 121[b] ; Le Neve's MS. 252.

FLAYE, Thomas, of the city of Exeter, practitioner in phisicke, 27 Nov. 1628, by
R. St. George. Add. MS. 14,295, fo. 67 (I. 9, 91[b]).

FLEETE, Sir John, Knt., Alderm. of City of London, 30 May 1691, by T. St. George,
Gart. and Clar. Add. MS. 14,831, fo. 58 ; Grants IV., 77 ; Stowe MSS.
714, fo. 123, and 716, fo. 51 ; (13 May in Guil., p. 239).

FLEMING, Sir Francis, Lieut. of the Ordnance, 1549. Burke's Armory.

FLEMYNGE, John, of Sharlestone, Yorks, s. of John, s. of John, s. of William, and
of Alice his wife, d. and coh. of Henry Langfold, 25 Nov. 1571, 14 Q. Eliz.,
by Flower. Harl. MSS. 6140, fo. 70[b], 1422, fo. 23, and 1359, fo. 9 ; Misc.
Gen. et Her., vol. i., p. 1, copy of grant, Brit. Mus.

FLEMING, Thomas, of Southampton, Esq., after. a Knt., crest 3 June 1584, by
Cooke (gu., on a chev. betw. three owls arg. one erm. spot sa., Guil.).
Harl. MS. 1359, fo. 116[b] ; Add. MS. 14,295, fo. 30 ; Guil., p. 222 ; Add.
MS. 12,474, fo. 51[b] ; 29 May 1584 in Harl. MS. 5865, fo. 43, and 1588 in
Harl. MS. 1544, fo. 138 ; Add. MS. 4966, fo. 29[b] ; 29 May 1588 in Harl.
MS. 1544, fo. 138 ; Grants II., 480.

FLETCHER, Robert, of Stoke Bardolfe, Notts, by Cooke. Stowe MS. 670, fo. 28 ;
1552 . . . . Harl. MS. 1116, fo. 61[b].

„ Thomas, of London, gent., s. and h. of John, of Woodstock, Oxf. (descended
out of Lanc.), and to John Fletcher his son, 26 April 1613, by Segar.
Add. MS. 12,225, fo. 42 ; Harl. MS. 6140, fo. 63.

FLETCHERS' COMPANY [of London]. 12 Oct., 7 Ed. IV., 1467, by W. Hawkesloe,
Clar. Genealogist, iv., p. 127.

FLETEWOOD, John, of Lancashire, grant 6 Jan. 1538, by Barker. Copy of grant,
Q's Coll. Oxf. MSS. 38, fo. 26, and 39, fo. 18, and Brit. Mus., Harl. MSS.
1507, fo. 376, and 5846, fo. 38[b] ; in a later hand, Stowe MS. 692, fo. 41[b] ;
Le Neve's MS. 378.

FLEETWOOD, John, of Lancashire, gent., granted at London 1 July, 2 Ed. VI. . . . .
1548, by Dethick, Norr. Harl. MS. 1359, fo. 1[c] ; 4 July in Add. MS.

16,940, fo. 203, as Thos.; Argt. [and] or, undée per pale six martlets counterchanged, etc., Grants I., 316.

FLEETWOOD, John, of Penwortham, co. Lanc., confirmed 20 June 1564, by Harvey. Add. MS. 16,940, fo. 39^b; Cott. MS. Faustina E. 1, 29 ; Harl. MS. 1422, fo. 23 ; Guil., p. 398 ; Sir Willm. Fleetwood, Harl. MS. 5887, fo. 14^b.

FLETEWODE, Thomas, of London, Auditor of the co. Pal. of Cheshire and Flint, and one of the tellers of the Mint in the Tower of London, grant 1 June 1545, 37 Henry VIII., by Hawley. Sa., a chev. engr. checquy [lozengy] gu. and or betw. three silver roundels, each charged with a martlet sa. Crest, a demi-rabbit [squirrel ppr. collared and chained or, between his paws a branch of hazel fructed or] eating, stalked and leaved vert. Misc. Gen. et Her., 2nd S., vol. ii., p. 273, facsimile ; copy of grant, arms and crest, Q's Coll. Oxf. MS. 38, fo. 46.

„   Thomas, of London, 4 July 1548, by T. Hawley. Add. MSS. 7098, fo. 78^b, and 16,940, fo. 203, same arms as granted to John, by Dethick.

FLEXNEY, Rauff, of Oxford City, gent., gift . . . . 1592, by Cooke. Harl. MS. 1359, fo. 30 ; Add. MS. 14,295, fo. 19^b.

FLINT, FLYNTE, Robert, of city of Norwich, gent., grant 1 Jan., 3 Ed. VI., 1549-50, by Hawley. Harl. MS. 1507, fo. 402 ; Add. MS. 16,940, fo. 203^b, 205 ; Copy of grant, Q's Coll. Oxf. MS. 38, fo. 54 ; Grants II., 460 ; Harl. MS. 6140, fo. 42 ; Le Neve's MS. 463 [or 403].

FLOOD, see FLUDD.

FLOQUET, ... Harl. MS. 5846, fo. 38 ; Stowe MS. 692, fo. 40^b.

FLORIO, Celia (whose father came over with Philip, K. of Spain, into England), wife of James Molins of Shoe Lane, Middx., 23 Aug. 1614, arms (a crest ?) (? by Segar). Add. MS. 12,225, fo. 42 ; Harl. MS. 6140, fo. 79.

FLOWER, Richard, of Elye, co. Camb., gent., augmentation allowed 10 June, 1 and 2 Mary, 1554, by G. Dethick. Harl. MS. 1359, fo. 63 ; copy of grant, Q's Coll. Oxf. MS. 39, fo. 49 ; Grants I., 216.

FLOWERDEW, John, of Hethersett, Norfolk, 15 Oct. 1550, by Hawley (?). Add. MS. 16,940, fo. 204.

FLOYD, David, of Pengernoly, co. Carnarvon, s. and h. of Griffin, s. of David, descended from Theodore, the great prince of South Wales ; crest granted 17 Nov., 40 Eliz., 1598, by W. Dethick. Stowe MS. 676, fo. 124^b, copy of grant, Q's Coll. Oxf. MS. 36, fo. 69.

FLUDD, Thomas, of Milgate, Kent (s. and h. of David Fludd als Lloyd), confirmed 10 Nov. 1572, by Cooke. Harl. MS. 1422, fo. 119 ; Guil., p. 193 ; Harl. MS. 6170, fo. 21^b.

FLYER (FFLEERE), Ralph, Hints, Staff., 1614, 12 K. Jas., by St. George, Norr. Stowe MS. 706, fo. 15^b ; Harl. MS. 6140, fo. 73.

FOCHE, ... Wotton, Kent . . . . 1576, by Cooke. Burke's Armory.

FODEN, Thomas, Fulford, co. Staff., gent., 16 Feb. 1664-5, by W. Dugdale, Norr. Her. Coll. MS.

FOLIE, ... diff^t crest, by W. Ryley, Lanc. Her. Stowe MS. 703, fo. 64, a hand and arm embowed, etc.

FOLEY, Richard, of Stourbridge, co. Worc., 8 Feb. 1646-7, by Bysshe. Harl. MS. 6832, fo. 413^b; Add. MS. 26,758, fo. 16 ; (Thomas in Stowe MS. 703, fo. 70, see preceding diff. crest ; crest, a lion sejant arg. holding a shield of the armes).

„   Robert, of Stourbridge, co. Worc., High Sheriff (4th s. of Richard), arms confirmed with diff. : on a canton gu. a ducal coronet ar. Crest, the lyon holding a ducal coronet or in lieu of an escocheon. Augmentation 12 Dec. 1671, by Walker. Harl. MS. 1172, fo. 66 ; copy of grant, Add. MS. 14,293, fo. 69 ; Genealogist, ii., 37.

FOLJAMBE, Godfrey, of Walton, co. Derby, Esquire of the body to the King, crest 9 June 1513, by Wriothesley, Gart., and John Yonge, Norr. Harl. MS. 6592, fo. 36^b, copy of grant.

FOLJAMBE, Godfrey, of Walton, co. Derby, confirmed 28 May 1587, by Flower.
MS. Ashm. 844, fo. 68, copy of grant, Bodleian Lib.; Guil., p. 249;
Reliquary, xxii., 52.

FOLKES, Martin, of Grey's Inn, Middx., Counsellor at Law, 11 Mar. 1685-6, by
H. St. George, Clar. Stowe MS. 714, fo. 69ᵇ, copy of grant, Brit. Mus.;
Grants III., fo. 292; Lansd. MS. 867, fo. 52.

FOLLYOTT, John, of Perton, co. Worc., crest granted 16 May, 4 and 5 Phil. and
Mary, 1558, Quarterly of 6, by G. Dethick. Harl. MS. 1359, fo. 71ᵇ;
copy of patent, Q's Coll. Oxf. MS. 39, fo. 91; Harl. MS. 6140, fo. 53;
Grants I., 153.

FOLVILE, John, of Middlewich in Cheshire, confirmed 1599, by Camden. Harl.
MSS. 6095, fo. 23, and 1422, fo. 37ᵇ.

FONNEREAU, Zachary, marᵈ [? married] 1674; certificate of arms .... Add. MS.
14,831, fo. 13; Pedigree 3 D. 14, fo. 146ᵇ, Her. Coll.

FOOT, Thomas, of London, 1646, by W. Ryley, Lanc. Herald, and Ro. Browne,
Bluemantle. Stowe MS. 703, fo. 63; Harl. MS. 6832, fo. 413.

FOOTES, Thomas, gent. ("huisher daily waiter in ord. to the King"), s. of John, of
Michelham, Sussex, confirmed Dec. 1611, by Camden. Harl. MSS. 6095,
fo. 17, and 1422, fo. 56ᵇ.

FORDE, ... of Devonshire, Quarterly of 4, impaling [quarterly of] 6,
i.e., Forde of Hasting, atchievment, by Cooke (?). Harl. MS. 1359,
fo. 86ᵇ.

,, John, of Hastinge, Sussex, Quarterly of 4, as above, and crest, achievement
13 Nov. 1575, by Cooke (?). Harl. MSS. 1359, fo. 86ᵇ, and 1194, fo. 85ᵇ;
Add. MS. 4966, fo. 37, 67; Harl. MS. 1562, fo. 30ᵇ.

FORD, Lady Elizabeth, dau. of Wᵐ Forde of Hadley, Suff., wife of Bawdrye,
Barker's Grants. Stowe MS. 692, fo. 43; Harl. MS. 1116, fo. 28ᵇ.

,, John, of Ashburton, Devon, coat and crest .... Barker's Grants. Harl. MS.
5846, fo. 36 and 37; by Benolt, Clar., in Stowe MS. 692, fo. 41, 42; Add.
MS. 26,702, fo. 55ᵇ.

,, Richard, of Ford (see 1562 [? Harl. MS.]), s. of Charles, of Whithall, gent.,
2 s. of William, s. of William Atforde of Fordmore, Devon: Gules, a castle
triple towered argt., over the same a crown or.

,, (? FORTH), Robert, of Hadley, Suff., gent., grant 10 Dec. 1539 to him and
his posterity by Hawley, confirmed by Barker. Stowe MS. 692, fo. 43;
copy of grant, Q's Coll. Oxf. MS. 38, fo. 39; Harl. MS. 5887, fo. 92, as
Forth, and his dau. Lady Elizabeth Bawdry. [See FORTH.]

FOREST, ... co. Lanc. .... Feb. 1606, by Cooke (Camden): per pale gu. and sa.
a crescent, betw. the points an estoile of eight points or. Crest, an arm
(gu.) in armour, embowed or, holding a broken tilting spear. Harl. MSS.
1422, fo. 19ᵇ, 6095, fo. 6ᵇ, and 1441, fo. 123.

,, (Edward in 1513), prior of Lanthony .... Hy. VII. .... Add. MS.
26,702, fo. 40.

FORMAN, William, of Croxton, co. Linc., confirmed .... 1562. Harvey's Grants.
Add. MS. 16,940, fo. 20.

FORSETT, Edward, of Maribone, co. Middx., Nov. 1611, by Camden. Harl. MSS.
6095, fo. 16ᵇ, and 1422, fo. 36ᵇ; Guil. 411. (Or FAWCETT.)

FORSTER and FOSTER, for 24 coats see Stowe MS. 703, fo. 83—85.

FORSTER, ... of co. Cumb. .... by W. Dethick. Harl. MS. 1422, fo. 13ᵇ.

,, Mary, ux. .... White .... Forster quartering Bradley (not on a lozenge),
by Cooke. Stowe MS. 670, fo. 79; Harl. MS. 1359, fo. 98.

,, Mathew, of London, by W. Segar, Gart. Harl. MS. 6140, fo. 77ᵇ.

,, Thomas, of St. John Street, Middx., Esq., s. and h. of Thomas, s. of Roger,
2nd s. of Thomas, of Ederston, Northumberland, Esq., gift of crest
16 March 1596-7, 39 Q. Eliz., by Lee. Add. MS. 14,295, fo. 11ᵇ; Harl.
MSS. 1422, fo. 52, and 1359, fo. 18ᵇ; see Harl. MS. 5887, fo. 95, for the
quartered arms.

FORSTER, Sir Thomas, of St. John's Street, 27 Feb. 1604-5 or 1605-6, by Camden. Harl. MSS. 1422, fo. 18ᵇ, and 6095, fo. 3ᵇ; Guil., p. 315.

FORTH, Hugh, London . . . . 1646, by W. Ryley, Lanc. Her. Stowe MS. 703, fo. 64.

FOORTH, Robert, of Stretham, Surrey, coat altered in 1590, by Cooke. Harl. MSS. 1359, fo. 86ᵇ, and 1422, fo. 86ᵇ [sic].

FORTH, Robert, of Middx., see SCHETHER, his wife. Stowe MS. 702, fo. 115, coat and crest; Barker's Grants, Harl. MSS. 5846, fo. 39, and 5887, fo. 3.

FOSTER, Goddard, of Iden, Sussex, by Cooke, 1577, harts' heads; by Camden, 1602, talbots' heads. Harl. MSS. 6095, fo. 86ᵇ, and 1422, fo. 54; Add. MS. 4966, fo. 58ᵇ.

„   John, Badesley, Hampshire, confirmed 16 Nov. 1557. Harvey's Grants, Add. MS. 16,940, fo. 8ᵇ; Harl. MS. 5865, fo. 38.

„   Mary, see FORSTER.

„   Samuel, B.D., of Redgrave, Suff., 24 May 1678, by W. Dugdale and H. St. George, Norr. Stowe MS. 714, fo. 164; Grants III., 84.

FOTHERLEY, Thomas, of co. Linc., s. of Thos., of Rickmansworth, Herts, etc., gu., a fesse dancettée or, by Segar. Add. MS. 12,225, fo. 43; quartering Howse in Harl. MS. 1410, fo. 48.

„   Charles, of Burton, co. Linc., Archdeacon of Canterbury, 28 Feb. 1605-6, by Camden. Harl. MSS. 1422, fo. 19, 1359, fo. 10ᵇ, and 6095, fo. 5; Guil., p. 373.

„   Martin (Maurice in Guil.), Dean of Canterbury, 2ⁿᵈ bro., 28 Feb. 1605-6, by Camden, mullet or for diff. Harl. MSS. 1359, fo. 10ᵇ, 6095, fo. 5, and 1422, fo. 19; Guil., p. 373.

FOTHERSLEY, Thomas, of Rickmansworth, Herts, March 1623, by R. St. George. NOTE.—This coate and crest were tricked by my man John Giles by my order from a Trumpitt banner of . . . . Fothersly, lent me by . . . . Whitfield, esq., H. St. George, Clar. Add. MS. 14,295, fo. 65. Mountnessing, Essex.

FOULKE, ..., by Cooke. Harl. MS. 6179, fo. 19ᵇ.

FOULSHURST, ..., an esquire to Lord Andley at Poictiers 1356. Parker's Glossary of Heraldry, Chron. Table, p. xiv.

FOUNDERS' CO. OF LONDON, 13 Oct. 1590, by Cooke. Misc. Gen. et Her., i., 103, and History of the Company, by W. M. Williams.

FOUNTAINE, Thomas, of Huckett, Bucks, esq., s. of John, of Walton in the said co., Grant 20 June, 40 Eliz., 1597, by W. Dethick, arg., a fesse dancettée betw. 3 elephants' heads erased sa.; crest, an elephant's head erased sa. Stowe MS. 676, fo. 126ᵇ; copy of grant, Q's Coll. Oxf. MS. 36, fo. 74.

„   Thomas, of Hukott, Bucks, esq., confirmed. Or, a fesse between 3 elephants' heads erased sa., armed arg., gift [alteration] of crest, an elephant's head couped (erased in Le Neve) or, vulned gu., armed or, 1 Oct. or 12 Nov. 1604, by Camden. Harl. MSS. 1391, fo. 125, and 1533, fo. 15, for copy of grant, Brit. Mus.; Harl. MSS. 6095, fo. 2ᵇ, and 1422, fo. 18ᵇ, crest erased and dated 12 Nov.; Le Neve's MS. 276.

„   . . . ., of Belchamp St. Paul, Essex, 22 Feb. 1619-20, by Camden. See DE LA FOUNTAINE.

FOWELL, Arthur, Fowellscombe, Devon, May 1592, by Cooke, Clar., Berry's suppᵗ, argent, a chevron sable, on a chief gules three mullets pierced of the first.

FOWKE, Bartholomew, Chief Clerk of the Spicery in the Queen's House, ... 1580; copy of letters patent, Bodleian Lib., MS. Ashm. 834, fo. 36ᵇ; Guil., p. 173; Harl. MS. 5887, fo. 23.

„   Christopher, of London, confirmed . . . . 1562, Harvey's Grants. Add. MS. 16,940, fo. 11ᵇ.

FOWLE, John (s. of John), Sandhurst, Kent, exemplified 1602, by Camden. See Cat. Her. Exhib. Soc. of Antiq., 70.

FOWLER, ..., of Islington, Crest . . . ., Barker's Grants. Harl. MS. 5846, fo. 35 ; Stowe MS. 692, fo. 42.

„ . . . ., Salop, Quarterly . . . ., by Cooke. Stowe MS. 670, fo. 61.

„ Bryan, of Sowe ? co. Staff., coat and crest . . . ., Barker's Grants. Harl. MS. 5846, fo. 38ᵇ ; Stowe MS. 692, fo. 41ᵇ.

„ Daniel (s. of Wᵐ), of Stonhouse, co. Glouc., crest 13 March 1606-7. Harl. MS. 6095, fo. 20ᵇ ; Guil., p. 383 ; Harl. MS. 5887, fo. 23ᵇ and 74ᵇ, by Wᵐ Camden.

„ Edward, D.D., Bishop of Gloncester, confirmed 20 July 1693, by T. St. George, Gart. and Clar. Harl. MS. 6834, fo. 178 ; Grants IV., fo. 144 ; Harl. MS. 1172, fo. 54ᵇ ; Stowe MS. 677, fo. 70, and Harl. MS. 1185, fo. 57.

„ Francis, Leveson, now of Kinderton, s. and h. of Richard, of Harnage Grange, Salop, adopted heir to Sir Richd. Leveson, late of Trentham, co. Staff., K.B., assumed the Leveson arms by virtue of special warrant 1 Aug. 1664, by W. Dugdale, Norr., Her. Coll. and MS. Ashm. 857, pp. 287-8, copy of grant, Bodleian Lib.

„ Samuel, rector of Blunham, Beds ; brother Edward, Bp. of Gloucester ; exemplified 31 Jan. 1695-6, by T. St. George, Gart. and Clar. Grants IV., fo. 204.

„ Thomas, of Calais, ... 1534, by T. Benolte, Clar., Berry's Suppᵗ.

FOX, Henry, Yonlgreave, co. Derby, gent., 18 June 1664, by W. Dugdale, Norr. Her. Coll. : Or, a chevron gules between three foxes' heads erased azure (Berry).

„ John, of Ropley, co. Linc., gent., coat and crest. Barker's Grants, Harl. MS. 5846, fo. 37ᵇ ; Stowe MS. 692, fo. 41 ; Add. MS. 26,702, fo. 41.

„ John, of London, goldsmith . . . . 1586, by Cooke. Harl. MS. 1122, fo. 64ᵇ ; Add. MS. 4966, fo. 68.

„ John, of the Accatry Larder of H.M.'s House, by the King's Command, 20 Sept. 1661, by Sir E. Walker, Gart. Her. Coll., fo. 42.

FOXE, Michaell, of Chacham (Chacombe), Northants, 10 June 1551, ? by Hawley. Add. MS. 16,940, fo. 204ᵇ.

FOX, Nevinson, of Eastry Court, Kent, 21 June 1673, by Walker, Bysshe and Dugdale. Harl. MS. 1105, fo. 40ᵇ (Harl. MS. 6834, fo. 178) ; Grants III., fo. 3, an augmentation from the Earl Marshal.

„ Ralph, of High Holborne, Middx., confirmed 12 June 1632, by R. St. George. Harl. MS. 1470, fo. 52, copy of grant, Brit. Mus.; Guil., p. 197.

„ Simeon, Suffolk, ... by R. Browne, Bluemantle [?]. Harl. MS. 1411, fo. 153ᵇ, and Stowe MS. 703, fo. 72.

„ Stephen, Clerk of the Kitchen and of her Majesty's travelling expences, etc., granted at Brussels 30 Oct. 1658, by Walker. Guil., p. 197 : born of honest parents at Farley, Wilts, hath even from his youth been educated in the Royall family. Harl. MSS. 1105, fo. 40ᵇ, and 1172, fo. 72 ; Add. MSS. 14,293, fo. 97, and 14,294, fo. 33, patent dated 18 Nov. 1658 (copy in Brit. Mus.), Stowe MS. 677, fo. 78 ; Genealogist, i., 40 ; Her. Coll., fo. 4 and 30. See Eliz. WHITTLE, his wife.

FOXHALL, John, of London, gent., confirmation of arms, quarterings and crest, 29 Nov. 1579, by Cooke. Harl. MS. 1507, fo. 118 (copy of confirmation, Brit. Mus.), Harl. MSS. 1359, fo. 118ᵇ, and 1422, fo. 119, and Q's Coll. Oxf. MS. 38, fo. 102 ; Add. MS. 4966, fo. 100ᵇ ; Harl. MS. 5887, fo. 89.

FOXALL, John, of city of London, arg., two bars gu. . . . ., by Segar. Add. MS. 12,225, fo. 43ᵇ.

FOYLE, John, of Shaftesbury, Dorset, 1 Feb. 160⁵⁄₆, by Camden, by the Earl Marshal's consent. Harl. MSS. 1422, fo. 21, and 6095, fo. 11ᵇ ; Morgan's Sphere, 109 ; Harl. MS. 1541, fo. 181.

FRAMLINGHAM, ... ? 1586, by Cooke, ... Gu., on a chev. betw. three closed helmets arg. a mullet sa. charged with a crescent or. Crest, an elephant

statant or, tusked gu., wreathed round the neck vert. Harl. MSS. 1359,
fo. 111, and 1422, fo. 95ᵇ; Add. MS. 4966, fo. 60.

FRANCIS, Richard, of Tickenhall, ... Crest, by Camden, Clar. Harl. MS. 1093,
fo. 64ᵇ.

FRANCES, Andrew, of Wyndsor, Haberdasher, of London, coat and crest. Barker's
Grants, Harl. MSS. 5846, fo. 36ᵇ, and 5887, fo. 1.

FRAUNCES, Edward, of Derbyshire, confirmed 4 May 1577, by G. Dethick. Harl.
MS. 1441, fo. 87, and Q's Coll. Oxf. MS. 145, fo. 44.

FRANCEIS, Edward, Repton, co. Derby, Crest confirmed 20 Jan. 1606-7, by
R. St. George. Add. MS. 14,295, fo. 40, 54; of Barrow, Sargiant of the
Backehouse to K. James 1606, Harl. MS. 5887, fo. 20ᵇ.

FRANCKE, Captain of a troop of Horse in Ireland, 18 Jan. 1652-3, by Sir E. Bysshe,
Gart. Stowe MS. 703, fo. 71; Harl. MS. 1441, fo. 148ᵇ.

FRANKE, William, the New Works, Leicester, 6 Feb. 1689-90, by T. St. George,
Gart. and Clar. Harl. MS. 6834, fo. 178; Grants IV., fo. 57; Harl. MS.
1172, fo. 54ʰ.

FRANKLAND [als FRANCKLYN], Hugh, gent., of Nessinge, Yorks, gent., 8 Nov.
1566, by Flower. Surtees Soc., XLI., p. xli., copy of grant, Brit. Mus.

FRANCKLAND, William, of Rye, Herts, crest granted 3 March 1568-9, by G.
Dethick, Cooke and Flower. Harl. MS. 1359, fo. 54ᵇ; Q's Coll. Oxf. MS.
145, fo. 16ᵇ.

,, William, Rye, Herts, crest granted 3 March 1568-9, by G. Dethick. Guil.
239; Harl. MS. 1441, fo. 71; MS. Ashm. 844, fo. 26*, copy of grant,
Bodleian Lib., and Q's Coll. Oxf. MS. 39, fo. 142.

FRANKLIN, ..., of Willesden, Middx., ..., by Camden. Arg., on a fesse az. 3
dolphins embowed of the field. Crest, a dolphin embowed gu., transfixed
by two fish hooks saltirewise, etc. Harl. MSS. 1422, fo. 17, and 6095,
fo. 1.

FRANCKLIN, Henry (s. of Rowland), then upon his travels, grant 20 May (June)
1592, by W. Dethick. Stowe MS. 676, fo. 85ᵇ, 96; copy of grant, Q's
Coll. Oxf. MS. 36, fo. 9 and 13.

FRANKLIN, Richard, of York, gent., grant 25 Feb. 1580-1, by G. Dethick, Gart.
Copy of grant in Latin, Q's Coll. Oxf. MS. 37, fo. 77; Stowe MS. 676,
fo. 56ᵇ; Grants I., 83.

,, William, dean of Durham, ... 1530, by T. Tonge, Norr., Berry's Suppt.

FRAUNCIS, see FRANCIS.

FREAKE, Edmond, Bp. of Rochester, 1 April 1572, by G. Dethick, Cooke and
Flower. Harl. MS. 1441, fo. 77ᵇ, and Q's Coll. Oxf. MS. 145, fo. 27.

,, Robert, Iwerne Courtney, Dorset, 10 Aug. 1579, by Rob. Cooke. Grants I.,
122; Harl. MS. 1166, fo. 31.

FREBODY, John, s. of John, of Udimore, Sussex, April 1634, by R. St. George,
Clar. Harl. MS. 1562, fo. 178, Berry's Suppt.

FRECHEVILLE, John, Baron Staveley, 15 April 1665, supporters, by Walker.
Harl. MS. 1052, fo. 200, copy of grant, Brit. Mus.

FRECKILTON, Ferdinand, of Huntingdon, Quarterly, by Cooke. Harl. MS. 1359,
fo. 90ᵇ; Add. MS. 4966, fo. 65ᵇ.

FREDERICK, John, of London, merchᵗ, crest altered and coat confirmed 1647,
by Bysshe. Harl. MS. 6140, fo. 17ᵇ, 18; ? confirmed or regranted
to him as :—

,, Sir John, Kt., Alderm. and Lord Mayor of London, elect 22 Oct. 1661,
by Sir E. Walker, Gart. Harl. MS. 6179, fo. 29ᵇ; Her. Coll., fo. 42.

FREEAR, Thomas (John, Guil. 306), of London, D. Med., s. of John, also D. Med.,
and Ursula Castell, of East Hatley, co. Camb., Grant 12 Feb. 1602-3, by
Camden. (Thoˢ in Harl. MS. 1507, fo. 93, and Mary Shaw his wife);
John in Cott. MS. Faustina E. 1. fo. 65ᵇ. Harl. MSS. 1507, fo. 93 (copy
of grant, Brit. Mus.), 1359, fo. 26ᵇ, and 6095, fo. 18ᵇ, and Q's Coll. Oxf.
MS. 38, fo. 116; MS. 146, fo. 138.

FREEBODY, *see* FREBODY.

FREEMAN, John, of Moulton, s. and h. of Raphe, 28 May 1579, by R. Cooke, Clar. Bannerman MS. No. 9, p. 451.

„ Ralfe, of Aspden, Herts, s. and h. of W^m, of London, Esq., by St. George. Add. MS. 14,295, fo. 70.

„ Richard, of Bromfield, Essex, ..., by Segar. Add. MS. 12,225, fo. 43; Harl. MS. 6140, fo. 80^b.

FREMLIN, Gilbert, of Hartlip, Kent, s. of W^m, Crest granted 24 May 1567, by G. Dethick. Harl. MS. 1441, fo. 62; copy of grant, Q's Coll. Oxf. MSS. 38, fo. 88, and 145, fo. 2^b.

FRITH, ..., by Camden. Burke's Armory.

FRYTH or FRITH, Henry, of Wolverhampton, s. of Rowland, of Thornes, co. Staff. 4 July 1677, by Sir Wm. Dugdale, Gart. Harl. MS. 6834, fo. 178; Grants III., fo. 56; and H. St. George, Norr., Harl. MS. 6832, fo. 371.

FRYTH, ... Thornes, Shenstone, co. Staff., 1583. Burke's Armory.

FROBISHER, Francis, of Doncaster, Yorks, confirmed 1 April 1550, by (Harvey), Norr. Harl. MS. 1422, fo. 23; Add. MS. 16,940, fo. 10.

„ Sir Martin, by Cooke . . . . Stowe MS. 670, fo. 55^b.

FROMONDE, John [grant, by Walter Haywode, of Stratfeldsaye to, dat. the feast of St. Gregory the Pope, 5 Hen. IV., in French]. Add. Ch. 36,987.

FRUIN, ... of London, Erm., three bars az., out of the uppermost a lyon issuant . . . ., by Segar. Add. MS. 12,225, fo. 43^b.

„ Stephen, citizen and Skinner of London, brother to (Accepted Frewen) late Archbp. of York, 1 June 1665, by Sir E. Walker, Gart. Her. Coll., fo. 61; Stowe MS. 697, fo. 119.

FRYER, Francis, of London, gent., granted 10 April 1572, by G. Dethick, Cooke and Flower. Harl. MS. 1359, fo. 55^b; MS. Ashm. 844, fo. 42 (copy of grant, Bodleian Lib.); Harl. MSS. 1422, fo. 23, 1441, fo. 77^b, and 5887, fo. 44, and Q's Coll. Oxf. MS. 39, fo. 162, and MS. 145, fo. 28; Guil., p. 240; Harl. MS. 6140, fo. 70^b.

„ Thomas, *see* FREEAR.

„ . . . . five coats, *see* Stowe MS. 703, fo. 88, 89.

FULLER als FULWER, *see* FULWER.

FULLERS AND BRICKLAYERS (rather *see* TILERS AND BRICKLAYERS), Corporation of, 3 Jan. 1569-70, by G. Dethick, Cooke and Flower. Harl. MS. 1441, fo. 71^b.

FULMERSTON, Sir Richard, ... Barker's Grants, Stowe MS. 692, fo. 40^b.

FULMERSTONE, Richard, of Thetforth, Norfolk, esq., granted 15 June, 2 and 3 Phil. and Mary, 1556, by G. Dethick. Harl. MS. 1359, fo. 67^b; Grants I., 90; copy of grant, Q's Coll. Oxf. MS. 39, fo. 69.

FULWER, James, of London, Mercer, Merchant of the Staple and Mercht. Adventurer; descended of Thomas Fulwer, as is set downe below; crest granted 20 Dec., 3 Q. Eliz., 1560, by G. Dethick. Harl. MS. 1359, fo. 80^b; Grants I., 278; copy of grant, Q's Coll. Oxf. MS. 39, fo. 115.

„ John, lord of the manor of Temesford, Beds, esq., and Judge in the Guildhall of the Court of one of the Sheriffs of London; is descended of Thos Fulwer of Marks Hall, Essex, Esq., grandfather to the same John, and of Thos Fulwer, lord of Nettes in the Isle of Sheppey, Kent, esq., father to the same John, and of Marg^t, dau. and h. of Nicholas Clazell of Edgcott, Northts., esq., mother to the said John; Crest granted 20 Dec., 3 Q. Eliz., 1560, by G. Dethick. Harl. MS. 1359, fo. 80^b; copy of grant, Q's Coll. Oxf. MS. 39, fo. 116; Grants I., 103, 276.

FULLER als FULWER, Peter, of Shellers, Isle of Wight, quarterly . . . ., by Cooke, Clar. Stowe MS. 670, fo. 39^b.

FULWER, Ralphe, of London, gent., descended as above; crest granted 5 Feb., 3 Q. Eliz., 1560-61, by G. Dethick. Harl. MS. 1359, fo. 80^b; 20 Dec.

1560, *see* copy of grant, Q's Coll. Oxf. MS. 39, fo. 114 ; Grants I., 280.

FULLER alias FULLWAR, William, of Hollwell, Herts, gent., descended from Thomas Fulwar, arm., of Markeshall, Essex, "proavi sui," and Thomas Fulwar, arm., of Netts in the Isle of Sheppy, Kent, his father, etc. Certificate or testimonial in Latin, ... of July 1551, by Sir G. Dethick, Gart. *See* Q's Coll. Oxf. MS. 39, fo. 32.

FULWOOD, George, of Holborn, co. Middx., Esq., crest 10 July, 21 Q. Eliz., 1579, by Cooke, etc. ; seen and allowed by W. Dethick, Gart. Harl. MS. 1359, fo. 13 and 102 ; Add. MS. 14,295, fo. 7ᵇ ; Harl. MSS. 1093, fo. 115, and 6140, fo. 37.

„ William, an assist. Govʳ of the City of Raleigh, Va., by W. Dethick, Gart. Copy of grant, Q's Coll. Oxf. MS. 36, fo. 120.

FUNSTONE, Thomas, of Wymondham, Norfolk . . . . by Segar. Stowe MS. 677, fo. 8ᵇ ; Add. MS. 12,474, fo. 104ᵇ, as FONSTON.

FUTTER, John, of Thaxton, Norfolk, gift . . . . 1563 . . . . Harvey's Grants, Add. MS. 16,940, fo. 20.

FYSKE, Nicholas (Profr. in physics), of Studban, par. of Laxfield, Suff., 16 Nov. 1633, by Sir Wm. Segar, Gart. Grants I., 367 ; Add. MS. 12,225, fo. 44.

„ Nicholas, of Studham, par. of Laxford, Suff., prof. in physick, s. of Mathew, of the same, s. of William, of the same, who lived *temp.* Hen. VI., Ed. IV., Ric. III. and Hen. VII. ; crest 16 Nov. 1633, by Segar. Add. MS. 12,225, fo. 44 ; Grants I., 367.

G

GACE, ..., London, 15 Oct. 1649. Edmondson's Armory.

GAELL, Edward, of Hadleigh, Suff., ⎫ sons of John, of Hadleigh, 10 Jan. 1664-5.
„ George, of London, ⎬ Bysshe's Grants, fo. 17, Her. Coll. ; Harl.
„ Thomas, of Kelveden, Essex, ⎭ MS. 1105, fo. 16 and 18.

GAGE, Henry, s. and h. of John, of Haling, Surrey, and Margᵗ his wife, dau. to Sir Thomas Copley of said co., of ye above said arms and with a testimonial upon his going to travel that he is well extracted on both sides, 16 June 1626, by Segar. Add. MS. 12,225, fo. 44 ; Gage impaling Barnesley, Harl. MS. 5887, fo. 52ᵇ.

GALE, Francis, of Acombe, Yorks, gent., gift 26 March 1559, by Dalton. Harl. MS. 1359, fo. 33ᵇ ; Add. MS. 14,295, fo. 36ᵇ ; Harl. MS. 6140, fo. 70.

GALLARD, Joshua, esq., one of ye Receivers of ye King Chas. I., Exemplified, Quarterly, ..., by Segar. Add. MS. 12,225, fo. 44ᵇ.

GALLE, John, Dorset, confirmed . . . . 1558. Harvey's Grants, Add. MS. 16,940, fo. 6.

GALUERDET, GALIARDET, or GALLARD, Francois, a native of Rhodes, 17 Feb. 1536-7, 28 Hy. VIII., by Hawley, Receivᵣ General of the Hospital of St. John of Jerusalem, Quarterly of 4, grant. Misc. Gen. et Her., 2nd S., vol. i., p. 99, copy of grant, Brit. Mus.

GAMULL, ..., Cheshire, confirmation of arms and gift of a crest 1599, by Segar, Somerset Herald, then nominated Norroy, though not created nor the place assigned him, yet he added the seale of Norroy. Add. MS. 14,295, fo. 115 ; Harl. MS. 1359, fo. 36.

„ . . . ., of Buerton, Cheshire, new crest 1613, by R. St. George, Norroy, Berry's Supplᵗ.

„ . . . ., of Cheshire, ..., or, 3 mallets sa., by Segar, ... Add. MS. 12,225, fo. 44ᵇ.

GAMULL, Thomas, of Burton, Cheshire, 24 Feb. 1577, by Flower. Add. MS. 14,295, fo. 76 (92ª).

GAPE, John, Mayor of Sᵗ Alban's, Herts, 7 May 1684, by Sir Wm. Dugdale and Clar. Harl. MS. 6834, fo. 178 ; Grants III., fo. 239 ; Lansd. MS. 867, fo. 52.

GARDENER, ..., Ireland, by Cooke, ...   Stowe MS. 670, fo. 26ᵇ.

GARDNER, George, of Barwyk, Northumbld., gent., descended of Gardner, of Lancashire, crest 24 April, 19 Q. Eliz., 1577, by Sir G. Dethick, Gart. (father of Dʳ G., Dean of Norwich 1585). Harl. MS. 1359, fo. 18 ; Add. MS. 14,295, fo. 10ᵇ ; Harl. MS. 1441, fo. 87 ; Q's Coll. Oxf. MS. 145, fo. 43ᵇ ; Harl. MS. 5887, fo. 45.

GARDYNER, John, of Thundregepury, Herts, coat and crest. Barker's Grants, (1526—49), Harl. MS. 5846, fo. 42 ; Stowe MS. 692, fo. 47ᵇ.

GARDINER, Michael, of Greenford Magna, Middx., confirmed 16 June 1630, by R. St. George. Stowe MS. 677, fo. 43 ; Add. MS. 14,295, fo. 59 ; C. 24 [Visit. Lond., 1634], fo. 179, Her. Coll.

  „ William, of London, 1 March 1509-10, by T. Wriothesley, Gart., and Machado, Richmond Clar. Harl. MS. 1166, fo. 15ᵇ.

GARDENER, Richard, of Himbleton, co. Worc., 1 June 1592, by Cooke. Harl. MSS. 1359, fo. 106ᵇ, and 1442, fo. 54ᵇ ; Add. MS. 4966, fo. 93.

  „ Robert, of Lancashire. gent., yeoman of the Mouth to K. Edward VI., grant 20 July, 2 Ed. VI., 1548, by G. Dethick, Norr. Copy of grant, Q's Coll. Oxf. MS. 37, fo. 23, and Grants I., 338, Her. Coll. ; Harl. MS. 1116, fo. 40 ; a new coat 15 April, 3 Ed. VI., 1549, by G. Dethick, Norr. ; copy of grant, Q's Coll. Oxf. MS. 39, fo. 22, and Grants I., 326 ; Harl. MS. 1359, fo. 59 ; Crest confirmed 3 April 1560, then Sergeant of the Cellar, copy of confirmation, Q's Coll. Oxf. MS. 39, fo. 102, and Harl. MS. 2141, fo. 28 ; Misc. Gen. et Her., 3rd S., vol. iii., 141 ; Add. MS. 10,940, fo. 13.

  „ Thomas, of South Brent, Somerset, gent., grant 20 July, 3 and 5 Phil. and Mary, 1557, by G. Dethick. Harl. MS. 1359, fo. 70ᵇ ; copy of grant, Q's Coll. Oxf. MS. 39, fo. 82 ; Grants I., 214.

GARDINER, Thomas, of Holstead, Essex, s. of Thos., s. of Robert, alteration in crest 28 April 1600, by Camden, Clar. Le Neve's MS. 510 [or 500].

GARDYNER, Thomas, of Dedberbury, Oxon, crest . . . . 1578, by Cooke. Harl. MSS. 1359, fo. 119ᵇ, and 1442, fo. 54ᵇ ; Add. MS. 4966, fo. 96ᵇ.

GARDENER, Thomas, London, 1590, not "by Cooke." Stowe MS. 670, fo. 42ᵇ.

  „ William, of Bermondsey (Street) in Surrey, ..., by Cooke. Harl. MS. 1422, fo. 14 ; Stowe MS. 693, fo. 9.

GARDINER, William, of Norton Hall, near the Town of Bishop Norton, co. Linc., Esq., 9 or 8 March, 18 Hen. VIII., 1526-7, by T. Wriothesley, Gart., and T. Benolte, Clar. Le Neve's MS. 256 ; Add. MS. 17,506, fo. 27.

GARFOOTE, ..., by R. St. George, Clar., in Essex, ? 1634.

GARRAD, Jacob, of London, and his brother John, one of the grooms of the Privy Chamber to Chas. I. (sons of Thomas, late Sheriff of London), granted 18 Dec. 1632, by R. St. George. Guil., p. 184 ; Add. MS. 5533, fo. 15.

GARRARD, William, of Dorney, Bucks, coat and crest. Barker's Grants, Harl. MS. 5846, fo. 42ᵇ ; Stowe MS. 692, fo. 48.

  „ William, Felmingham, Norfolk, ... 1615, by W. Camden. Harl. MS. 1552, fo. 163, and Caius Coll. Camb. MS. 551, fo. 29.

GARRET, Sir George, Draper and Alderm. of City of London, ratified and confirmed . . . . 1634, by R. St. George. Guil., p. 170 ; Harl. MS. 1105, fo. 9.

GARSET, Robert, Esq., of the body to K. James, ... May 1614, 1 Feb. 1612, by Camden. Morgan's Sphere, 117 ; Harl. MS. 1441, fo. 149 ; as Garbet.

GARSTON (rightly GRAFTON), Richard, of London (3rd s. of Richard), confirmed . . . . 1584, by Cooke. Same coat as Grafton. Guil., p. 390. See GRAFTON.

O

GARTER, Bernard, of Brigstock, Northts., s. and h. of a 2nd son to Sir Wm Garter, Knt., grant of change in arms and crest 2 July, 10 Jac., 1612, by Segar. Add. MS. 12,225, fo. 45 ; C. 24 [Visit. Lond., 1634], fo. 569^b, Her. Coll., and Guil. 343 ; Harl. MS. 6140, fo. 66^b.

GARTH, Edward, of Penshurst, Kent, 5 Jan. 1548-9, ? by Hawley.   Add. MS. 16,940, fo. 205.

„   Richard, one of the six Clerks of the petty bag, of Morden, Surrey, gift 8 July 1564.   Harvey's Grants, Add. MS. 16,940, fo. 23 ; Harl. MS. 1561, fo. 216.

GASON, John, of Lee, par. of Ikham, Kent, given at London 10 June, 38 Hy. VIII., 1546, by ? Hawley.   Add. MS. 16,940, fo. 201 ; arms confirmed and crest given 28 Nov. 1589, 32 Q. Eliz., by Cooke. Harl. MS. 1359, fo. 28, 28^b, 100 ; Q's Coll. Oxf. MS. 146, fo. 461.

GASSON, Richard, s. of Rob., of Buntingford, Herts. now of London, 1608, by Camden.   Harl. MS. 1422, fo. 42^b.

GATES, Thomas, Colliton, Devon . . . . by Cooke.   Stowe MS. 670, fo. 35.

GATONBY, Anthony, of Gatonby, Yorks, July 1575, by Flower.   Harl. MS. 1453, fo. 74 ; Add. MS. 14,295, fo. 72^b.

GAUNTLETT, William, of Netherhampton, Wilts, gent., altered, coat confirmed, crest granted 19 July 1670, by Walker.   Harl. MS. 1172, fo. 69 ; Add. MSS. 14,293, fo. 79, and 14,294, fo. 23^b ; Guil., p. 347.

GAUS, William, by letters patent 2 Aug., 8 Jac., 1610.   Le Neve's MS. 421.

GAVELL, Robert, of Cobham, Surrey, esq., confirmed 12 Aug. 1572, by Cooke. Harl. MS. 1470, fo. 82 (copy of grant, Brit. Mus.) ; Guil., p. 333 ; Surrey Arch. Soc., iii., 349, and Misc. Gen. et Her., N. S., i., 320 ; Grants II., fo. 503 ; Stowe MS. 706, fo. 66.

GAWDY, Thomas, of Harleston, Norfolk, coat and crest.   Barker's Grants, Harl. MS. 5846, fo. 43 ; Stowe MS. 692, fo. 47.

„   Thomas, of Gawdy Hall, Norfolk, crest granted 20 or 25 Nov., 2 Q. Eliz., 1559, by G. Dethick.   Harl. MS. 1359, fo. 78^b ; Add. MS. 16,940, fo. 39^b ; copy of grant, Q's Coll. Oxf. MS. 39, fo. 103 ; Grants I., 298 ; Harl. MS. 5887, fo. 30.

GEDDING or JENYNS, William, Lancaster Herald [8 Hen. VIII., 10 Feb.] 1516[-17], [by Tho. Wriothesley, Gart., and Tho. Benolt, Clar].   Burke's Armory ; [Warw. Antiq. Mag., 104-5].

GEE, Samuel, of London . . . . 1592, by Cooke.   Harl. MS. 1359, fo. 106 ; Add. MS. 4966, fo. 92.

GEFFE, Nicholas, of Henborne, Berks, 4th s. of Andrew, of Nasing, Essex, s. of Thomas, of Broxbourne, Herts, 1 April 1579, by Cooke.   Harl. MSS. 1115, fo. 20, and 6179, fo. 19.

GEFFREY, Sir Robert, Knt., Sheriff of London . . . . 1676, by Bysshe ; Lord Mayor in 1686.   Burke's Armory.

GEFFREYS, Thomas, see JEFFREYS.

GELL, Anthony, of Hopton, co. Derby, 8 Feb. 1575-6, by Flower.   Harl. MS. 1453, fo. 74.

GENT, Thomas, of Bumstead at the Tower, Essex, 12 Nov. 1571, by Cooke.   Harl. MS. 1432, fo. 163, copy of grant.

GEOFFREYS, ... sa., a gryphon rampt. segreant within a bordure engrailed or . . . . by Segar.   Add. MS. 12,225, fo. 45.

GEORGE, John, of Bawdington . . . . with crest . . . . Hy. VIII.   Harl. MS. 5887, fo. 27 ; Add. MS. 26,702, fo. 41.

GERARD, Lord, of Brandon, supporters, at Oxford 1 May 1646, by Sir E. Walker. Her. Coll., fo. 11.

GERING, ... of the North, ... 1573, by G. Dethick.   Harl. MSS. 1422, fo. 16^b, and 1422, fo. 11^b, Or, two bars gu. each charged with three mascles (or lozenges) of the field, a canton . . . .

GERVIES, Arthur, of Essex, Master of the Pipe office, confirmed Gervies quartering

Serle .... 1610, by Camden (entered in the Office of Arms in book Essex, 6 Dec. 1610, S. Thompson, Wyndsor). Harl. MSS. 1422, fo. 110, and 6095, fo. 27.

GARVES (or GERVIS), William, of Great Pettley, co. Leic., ... May 1614, by Camden. Harl. MSS. 6095, fo. 30, and 1422, fo. 39 ; Gervis in Guil., p. 220.

GETHING, Richard, of London, Master of the Penn, by R. St. George, Clar. Harl. MS. 1105, fo. 10.

GIBBON, see PAYN, John, D.C.L.

GIBBON or GUYBON, ... of Westcliff, Kent, sa., a lyon rampt. guard. betw. three escallops argt., by Segar. Add. MS. 12,225, fo. 46. This coat is given to Thos Gibbon of Frith als Frid in Bethersden, Kent. Harl. MSS. 1422, fo. 82b, 6179, fo. 18, and 6140, fo. 28b.

GIBBON, Edmund, s. and h. of Francis (? Thomas in Guil.), of Rolvenden alias Rounden, Kent, gent. (viz., of Pumphouse there, Harl. MS. 1422, fo. 82b), confirmed 6 April 1629, by Segar. Add. MS. 12,225, fo. 45b, and Guil., p. 359 ; Harl. MSS. 6140, fo. 81b, and 6179, fo. 18b ; Grants I., 8.

GIBBON or GUYBON, John, of Dorset, esq., confirmation of arms and crest (? testified), by Segar : sa., a lion rampt. guard. crowned or betw. three escallops arg. Add. MS. 12,225, fo. 45b : Guil., p. 247 : Harl. MS. 1105, fo. 10b ; Grants I., 402.

GYBBS, ... Abbot of Catley Priory, co. Linc. Add. MS. 26,702, fo. 73.

„ .... of Warwickshire, by Cooke's deputy. Stowe MS. 670, fo. 7.

„ John, of Starford (Storford), Herts, ... by Cooke. Harl. MS. 1359, fo. 93b ; Add. MS. 4966, fo. 63.

GIBBES, John, of Stortford, Herts, arms and new crest, by W. Dethick ; coat of Gibbes of Devonshire, who denyeth this John to be of theire house ; entered by R. Brooke, York Her. Harl. MS. 1453, fo. 32b.

„ William, of South Perrott, Dorset, 13 Feb. 1600-1, by W. Dethick, Gart., and Camden, Clar. Harl. MSS. 1166, fo. 60b, and 6179, fo. 19b.

GYBSON, ..., Sergt at arms, ..., Hy. VIII., ..., with crest. Add. MS. 26,702, fo. 53.

„ Isaac, s. of William (see below), s. of Christopher, s. of John, of Staveley, Yorks, 4 March 1660-1, by Sir E. Walker, Gart. Her. Coll., 38.

GIBSON, John, of Welborne, Kt., Doctor of the lawe, 2 May 1574, by G. Dethick. Harl. MS. 1359, fo. 13 : Q's Coll. Oxf. MS. 145, fo. 28.

„ John, of Irby (? Ireleth), co. Lanc., esq., grant 15 Feb. 1582-3, by G. Dethick. Stowe MS. 676, fo. 59b : Harl. MS. 1441, fo. 78 ; 1580 in copy of grant, Q's Coll. Oxf. MS. 37, fo. 82 ; Grants II., 506.

„ Margaret, dau. and heir of Thomas, gent. (and wife of Ascew or Ascue), grant 5 Jan., 5 and 6 Phil. and Mary (? 1557-8), by G. Dethick. Harl. MS. 1359, fo. 80 ; copy of grant, Q's Coll. Oxf. MS. 39, fo. 84 ; Grants I., 274.

„ Robert, of Beckham Hall, Norfolk, gent., s. of Thos., s. of Robert, grant 6 May 1591 (by W. Dethick), and to one (' .... Gibson, that keepeth a taverne in London, ... arms and crest with a pedigree in wh. patent and pedigree great adoo is made about theyre ancienty. And they the first that ever used or bare any arms (entd by R. Brooke, York Her.). Harl. MS. 1453, fo. 34b ; Stowe MS. 676, fo. 93, 84 ; copy of grant in Q's Coll. Oxf. MS. 37, fo. 4 ; Guil., p. 403 ; Le Neve's MS. 355.

GYBSON, Thos, of London, gift .... 1560, ... Harvey's Grants, Add. MS. 16,940, fo. 14.

GIBSON, William, of Staveley, Yorks, confirmed 16 Jan. 1655-6, by Ryley. Harl. MSS. 1470, fo. 146, and 1105, fo. 11 (6 Jan.), declared void (Guil., p. 207) on the Restoration, regranted to his son Isaac.

GIDLEY, Bartholomew, of Gidley, Devon, and bro. John, of London, gent., 20 Nov.

1666, by Bysshe. Misc. Gen. et Her., N. S., iv., 19, copy of grant, Brit. Mus.

GIFFARD, ..., Chillington, Staff., crest 1523, another 1530. Berry.

GIFFARDSON, Roger, of Southwarke, ... Harvey's Grants, Add. MS. 16,940, fo. 10ᵇ.

GIFFORD, ..., crest . . . . Barker's Grants, Harl. MS. 5846, fo. 40ᵇ; Stowe MS. 692, fo. 46ᵇ, a hand argent holding a bunch of gillyflowers ppr.

„   John, D.D., of Hogsden als Hockston, Middx., 16 Oct. 1626, by R. St. George. Add. MS. 14,295, fo. 65ᵇ; C. 24 [Visit. of London, 1634], 572, Her. Coll.

GYGGES, Robert, Thomas and John, brethren, of Norfolk, 26 Feb. 1486-7, by T. Holme, Clar. Misc. Gen. et Her., 3 S., vol. i., p. 1, copy of grant, Brit. Mus. ; Grants II., 437 : Harl. MS. 6140, fo. 43.

GILBERT, Dorothie, dau. of Richard, ux. John Thompson, Audʳ to Q. Eliz., granted and allowed 22 May 1559, 1 Q. Eliz., by Harvey. Harl. MSS. 1359, fo. 11ᵃ, and 1115, fo. 16ᵇ; 1561 in Add. MS. 16,940, fo. 52 ; Stowe MS. 702, fo. 115.

„   Edward, of London, gift . . . . 15[6]⅝. Harvey's Grants, Add. MS. 16,940, fo. 45ᵇ.

„   George, of Clare, upon his pretended travailing into Italy and Germany aᵒ predicto (27 Nov. 1577, he aged 22), arms as William, same date with a second difference, ..., by R. Cooke. Copy of grant, Q's Coll. Oxf. MS. 37, fo. 65.

„   John, of Woodford, Essex, who was buried at Sᵗ Lawrence Jewry, nʳ Guild-hall, London, confirmed 1609, by Segar. Harl. MS. 1422, fo. 42ᵇ ; Add, MS. 12,225, fo. 46ᵇ ; Guil., p. 262.

„   Thomas, of Northberlingham, Norfolk, at Norwich, 7 Aug. 1576, by Cooke. Add. MS. 14,293, fo. 119, copy of grant, Brit. Mus.

GILBART, Thomas, of Sandwich, Kent, esq., ... Nov. 1595, by Lee. . . . . in Add. MS. 14,295, fo. 18 ; Harl. MS. 1359, fo. 16ᵇ.

GILBERT, Thomas, of Mayfield, Sussex, grant 8 Nov. 1616, by Segar. Add. MS. 12,225, fo. 46ᵇ ; Harl. MS. 6140, fo. 62ᵇ.

„   William, of Great Over, als Mickleover, co. Derby, gent., 4 Dec. 1576, by G. Dethick. Harl. MSS. 1441, fo. 85ᵇ, 6140, fo. 71ᵇ, and 5887, fo. 43 ; Q's Coll. Oxf. MS. 145, fo. 41ᵇ.

„   William, of London, D. Phys., confirmed 27 Nov. 1577, by Cooke. Stowe MS. 676, fo. 50ᵇ, copies of grant, Harl. MS. 1685, fo. 19.

GILBORNE, Sir Nichˢ, of Charing, Kent, ..., by Segar and Camden. No trick in Harl. MS. 1422, fo. 41 ; Harl. MS. 1441, fo. 139ᵇ.

„   William, citizen and Draper of London, ..., by Cooke. Stowe MS. 670, fo. 57ᵇ.

GILES, ..., Devon, ... by Cooke, ... Stowe MS. 670, fo. 63ᵇ.

„   . . . ., of co. Worc., and of the Custom House of London, 1630, by Segar. Add. MS. 12,225, fo. 47.

GYLES, Clement, of Melton Mowbray, co. Leic., gift . . . . 1562. (Harvey's Grants), Add. MS. 16,940, fo. 31ᵇ.

GILES, or GYLES, John, of Bowden, Devon, 10 June 1545, Visitation coat 1564 and 1620. Barker's Grants, Harl. MS. 5846, fo. 39ᵇ ; Stowe MS. 692, fo. 45ᵇ ; Add. MS. 16,940, fo. 200ᵇ, and Harl. MS. 6179, fo. 15, per fesse gu. and az., on a bend engrailed arg., etc.

GYLES, Thoˢ, citizen and Haberdasher of London, "assigned" 28 July 1579, by Cooke. MS. Ashm. 844, fo. 24, copy of grant, Bodleian Lib. ; Guil., p. 311.

GILL, Alexʳ, Chief Master or Teacher of Sᵗ Paul's School, London (1614), grant . . . ., by Segar. Add. MS. 12,225, fo. 46 ; Harl. MS. 5887, fo. 112, and 6140, fo. 77ᵇ.

„   Francis, s. of Wᵐ, of Ockendon, Essex, s. of Thoˢ, of Lincolnshire, crest

1 Sept. 1590, by Cooke. Add. MS. 14,295, fo. 119ᵇ ; Harl. MS. 6140, fo. 49ᵇ, 70ᵇ.

GILL, Raphe, Keeper of the Queen's Lyons to Q. E. and K. Jas. *circa* 1586, by Cooke. Harl. MS. 1422, fo. 76ᵇ, and 6140, fo. 53.

GILLEY, Samuel, s. of Mathew, s. of Wᵐ, who was fined for Sheriff of London. Confirmed 18 Dec. 1662, by Bysshe. Copy of grant, Harl. MSS. 1172, fo. 33, and 1105, fo. 19ᵇ ; Bysshe's Grants, fo. 16, Her. Coll.

„ William, fined for Sheriff of London. 1 June 1650, by Bysshe. Harl. MS. 1172, fo. 12, copy of grant ; Stowe MS. 697, fo. 106.

GILMAN, Henry, Twickenham, Middx. (*see* GUYLEMYN), by Cooke's deputies. Stowe MS. 670, fo. 47 ; Harl. MS. 1433, fo. 15.

GIMBER, *see* GYMBER.

GIOWSE, ..., by Cooke. Stowe MS. 670, fo. 14ᵇ.

GIPPS, Richard, of Horden, Middx., etc., 1 July 1624, by R. St. George, Clar. Harl. MSS. 1105, fo. 5, and 6179, fo. 69ᵇ.

GIRDLER, Joseph, utter barrister of the Inner Temple, 17 Dec. 1681, by Sir Wᵐ Dugdale and St. Geo., Clar. Harl. MS. 6834, fo. 178 ; Grants III., fo. 138.

GISLINGHAM, John, of Stuston, Suff., 7 Oct. 1576, by Cooke, Clar. Add. MS. 966, fo. 45.

GIUSTINIANI, George, Ambassʳ from Venice, and knighted, Augmentation by letter patent, R. Warrant, 1608. Harl. MS. 1507, fo. 397 ; Stowe MS. 840, fo. 64 ; copy, Q's Coll. Oxf. MS. 38, fo. 129 ; Rawl. MS. B. 102, fo. 52ᵇ, Bodleian Lib. ; for trick, *see* Le Neve's MS. 397.

GLADWIN, Thomas, Tapton in Chesterfield, co. Derby, Capt. of Foot, etc., Sheriff, 15 Jan. 168⅘, by T. St. George, Gart., and J. Dugdale, Norr. Harl. MS. 6834, fo. 178 ; Grants III., fo. 302 ; Lansd. MS. 867, fo. 52 ; Harl. MS. 1085, fo. 58.

GLASCOCK, William, of Much Dunmow, Essex, gent., and

„ John, of Rokeswell, Essex, gent., arms and crest confirmed 14 July 1571. 13 Q. Eliz., by Cooke. Harl. MS. 1359, fo. 14ᵇ ; MS. Ashm. 834, fo. 9 (copy of grant, Bodleian Lib.) ; Add. MS. 14,295, fo. 9 ; Guil., p. 233 ; Grants I., 266.

GLASSE, Alice, wife to Sir Richard Dobbes, Mayor of London, arms 5 April 1556, by ? Hawley. Add. MS. 16,940, fo. 208.

GLEDHILL, Thomas, Barkisland, Halifax, granted 23 Dec. 1612, by R. St. George. Harl. MS. 6179, fo. 15ᵇ ; Stowe MS. 706, fo. 14ᵇ ; Harl. MS. 6140, fo. 72ᵇ ; (confirmed 1632, by Segar, Burke's Armory).

GLOUCESTER, City of, grant 20 Oct. 1538, by C. Barker, Gart. MS. Ashm. 858, fo. 6-7, copy of grant, Bodleian Lib.

GLOVER, ... of Norfolk, Feb. 1611-12, by Camden. Harl. MSS. 6095, fo. 17ᵇ, and 1085, fo. 40ᵇ.

„ Alexander, of the Exchequer, confirmed circa 1605, by Camden. Harl. MS. 6095, fo. 19ᵇ ; ? called Humfrey, Harl. MS. 5887, fo. 13ᵇ.

„ Robert, Somerset Herald, crest granted 4 March 1577, by Cooke and Flower. (Stowe MS. 677, fo. 6ᵇ, adds : s. of Thomas, late of Este Clifford, s. of Thoˢ, of New Romney, Hants.) Exemplified, sa., betw. a chev. erm. three crescents arg. ; grant of crest, out of a cap or coronet sa. . . . . arg., a pair of wings sa. Harl. MS. 1359, fo. 86 ; Stowe MS. 677, fo. 6ᵇ ; MS. Ashm. 834, i., fo. 18, copy of grant, Bodleian Lib., and Stowe MS. 606, fo. 4 ; Add. MS. 4966, fo. 90ᵇ, copy of grant, Brit. Mus.

„ Thomas (Esquire of the body to K. Jas.), s. of Thomas, of Coventry, 11 April 1604, by Camden. (Kntᵈ 17 Aug. 1606. 3 April, Guil., p. 95.) 10 May, Harl. MS. 1359, fo. 38, and Add. MS. 14,295, fo. 118 ; Harl. MS. 6095, fo. 22 ; *see* Harl. MS. 5887, fo. 89.

„ Sir William, Sheriff of London, Dyer, Sheriff 1602-3, by Camden. Caius Coll. Camb. MS. 551, fo. 27 ; Harl. MS. 5887, fo. 88.

GLOVERS' COMPANY (now in the Leathersellers'), arms and crest 20 Oct. 1464, in
French, by Smert.   Harl. MS. 1359, fo. 74 ; Add. MSS. 14,295, fo. 42,
and 5533, fo. 135.

GOATLEY, Reynald, of Canterbury, Kent, ... by Segar, who has seen this coat
quartering Argoll.   Add. MS. 12,225, fo. 47 ; Harl. MS. 6179, fo. 88.

GODARD, Richard, Citizen and Alderm. of London, augmentation and crest 15 Aug.
1598, by W. Dethick, Gart., Camden and Segar.   Harl. MSS. 1422, fo. 52,
1470, fo. 241, and 1359, fo. 6ᵇ, copy of grant, Brit. Mus. ; Add. MS.
14,295, fo. 62ᵇ ; I. 9, fo. 30, Her. Coll. ; Guil., p. 211 ; Harl. MS. 5887,
fo. 25ᵇ.

GODDARD, William, of Middx. and East Woodhay, Hants, coat and crest (3 Dec.
1536, Harl. MS. 1544, fo. 145ᵇ).   Barker's Grants, Harl. MS. 5846, fo. 41ᵇ ;
Stowe MS. 692, fo. 47 ; Harl. MS. 1544, fo. 47ᵇ.

GODARD, William, of Westminster, gent. Usher for ye Hon. Court of Starchamber
and of her highness Chʸ the receipt of the Exchʳ, grant 6 April 1592, by
W. Dethick.   Stowe MS. 676, fo. 88 and 100 ; copy of grant, Harl. MS.
6140, fo. 54 ; Q's Coll. Oxf. MS. 36, fo. 18.

GODDYN [GODDEN], Agnes, dau. to John, of Kent, the wife of Wᵐ Clowes . . . .
by Cooke.   Harl. MS. 1359, fo. 117ᵇ ; Stowe MS. 702, fo. 115 ; Add. MS.
4966, fo. 196.

GODDEN, Anthony, of Addington, Kent, 1633, by W. Segar, Gart.   Harl. MS.
5887, fo. 114.

GODFREY, Oliver, of Willington, Kent, "found out and confirmed" 17 June,
21 Eliz., 1579, by G. Dethick.   Harl. MSS. 1441. fo. 103ᵇ, and 5847,
fo. 53ᵇ, and Add. MS. 12,454, fo. 53ᵇ ; Harl. MS. 1548, fo. 99, for
pedigree.

„   Oliver, of Wilmington, Kent. . . . . by Cooke.   Harl. MS. 1422, fo. 14ᵇ.

GODSALVE, Thomas, of the city of Norwich, coat and crest.   Barker's Grants,
Harl. MS. 5846, fo. 41ᵇ ; Stowe MS. 692, fo. 47.

GODWYN, Thomas, Bishop of Bath and Wells . . . . by Cooke.   Harl. MSS. 1359,
fo. 117, and 6179, fo. 12 ; Add. MS. 4966, fo. 28.

GOFFE, Stephen, D.D., and John, D.D., brothers, arms and augmentation 1 Ch. II.,
by Sir E. Walker, Gart.   Her. Coll., fo. 40.   See GOUGH.

GOFTON, Sir Humphrey, of Stokewell, Surrey, quarterly coat, 1 Aug. 1622, by
Camden.   Francis in Harl. MS. 1422, fo. 112 ; Harl. MS. 6095, fo. 40,
Francis ; Goston in Guil., p. 163.

GOLD, Christopher, of Stowmarket, Suffolk, " the King's Gunner," the canton, etc.,
augmented confirmation for beating down a piece of the steple at Bullen,
and so had a confirmation of those.   Stowe MS. 692, fo. 47 ; Barker's
Grants, Harl. MS. 5846, fo. 43.

GOLDSMYTH, ... his crest . . . .   Barker's Grants, Harl. MS. 5846, fo. 41 ;
Stowe MS. 692, fo. 46ᵇ : a hawk az., membered gn., guttée de sang.

GOLDSMITHS' COMPANY, ... crest and supporters . . . . 1571, by Cooke.   Her.
and Geneal., i., 122.

GOLIGHTLY, John, gift . . . . 1558 . . . .   Harvey's Grants, Add. MS. 16,940,
fo. 61.

GOLLOP, Thomas, Strode, Dorset, s. of Thos., of the same, 30 Oct. 1682, by Sʳ Wᵐ
Dugdale and Sᵗ George, Clar.   Harl. MS. 6834, fo. 78 ; Grants III.,
fo. 162.

GOMELDON, William, Esq., Jeweller unto the Queen, and his bro. Richard, sons of
Roger, late of London, Merchᵗ Adventurer and grandson of Wᵐ, of Porton,
Wilts, etc., 10 Nov. 1662, by Walker.   Harl. MS. 1172, fo. 32, copy of
grant.

GOMERSALL, ... of London . . . . by Sir G. Dethick, Gart.   Harl. MS. 6140,
fo. 54ᵇ.

GONVILLE AND CAIUS COLL., Cambridge, 15 Sept. 1575, by Cooke, Clar.   Original
at Caius Coll., Add. MS. 5822.

GOOCH, Pall, of Encle (Eccles), Norfolk, s. of Robert, of Dys, 8 Nov. 1580, by G. Dethick.   Harl. MSS. 1441, fo. 100, and 1422, fo. 22ᵇ, Paul, and Q's Coll. Oxf. MS. 145, fo. 50ᵇ.

GOOD, ... London . . . . by Cooke.   Stowe MS. 670, fo. 82.

GOODALL, Thomas, of Stoneham Earl, Suff., grant 1 March 1612-13, by Segar.   Harl. MS. 1470, fo. 23, 250 ; copy of grant, Brit. Mus., Add. MS. 12,225, fo. 47ᵇ ; Guil. 351 ; Harl. MS. 6140, fo. 66ᵇ.

GOODAY, Arthur, of Higham Ferrers, Northants, 11 Sept. 1600, by W. Dethick, Gart., and Camden, Clar.   Le Neve's MS. 356.

GOODCHILD, Elizabeth, dau. of Dunston, of London, gent., 2ⁿᵈ wife of Henry Brobredg of Sussex, Esq., 31 Aug. 1575, by G. Dethick.   Harl. MS. 1441, fo. 83ᵇ ; Q's Coll. Oxf. MS. 115, fo. 38ᵇ.

GOODERICH, Thomas, of Hardwick, Suff., Student at Law, s. of Thomas, of Bury St. Edmunds, grant 20 April 1594, by W. Dethick.   Stowe MS. 676, fo. 150, 112 ; copy of grant to Thomas the elder, Q's Coll. Oxf. MS. 36, fo. 41 and 106.

GOODRICH, Sir Henry, Knt. and Bart., alteration of crest 27 Aug. 1694, by T. St. George, Gart., and Clar., his brother John.   Misc. Gen. et Her., 2 S., vol. ii., p. 248 ; Grants IV., 175, copy of grant. Brit. Mus.

   „   John (½ bro. of Sir Hy.), alteration, Earl Marshal's Warrᵗ 21 Jan. 1697-8.   Grants IV., 244.

GOODRICKE, Richard, of London, confirmed . . . . 15[6]⅘.   Harvey's Grants, Add. MS. 16,940, fo. 34 ; Harl. MS. 5887, fo. 20.

   „   Richard, of Ribstone, Yorks, crest confirmed 1559, by L. Dalton, Norr.   Add. MS. 16,940, fo. 31.

GOODFELLOW, Christopher, of the Inner Temple, and Matthias, of London, sons of Matthias, of Cranford, Northhts., granted 16 April 1665, by Bysshe.   Guil., p. 261 ; Harl. MS. 6179, fo. 37ᵇ.

GOODINGE, Richard, of Boston, co. Linc., coat and crest.   Barker's Grants, Harl. MS. 5846, fo. 43ᵇ ; Stowe MS. 692, fo. 47ᵇ.

   „   George, of Debache, Suffolk, Crest by Cooke, 1576.   Harl. MS. 1085, fo. 26 and 16.

   „   . . . ., of Henley, Oxon, a patent.   Harl. MS. 6179, fo. 69ᵇ.

GOODLAW, Thomas, of Aspull, co. Lanc., 1581, by Flower, Norroy.   Harl. MS. 1437, fo. 47.

GOODMAN, Gawen, of Ruthin, co. Denbigh, 20 Nov. 1573, by Cooke.   Harl. MS. 1359, fo. 120ᵇ.

   „   Thomas, of Letherhead, Surrey, granted 12 May 1579, by Flower.   MS. Ashm. 834, fo. 21, copy of grant, Bodleian Lib. ; Guil., p. 386.

GOODRIDGE, Nicholas, of Totnes, Devon, July 1610, by Camden.   Harl. MSS. 1422, fo. 21ᵇ, and 6095, fo. 13 ; Guil., p. 76.

GOODWIN, John, of co. Bucks, confirmed . . . . 1550 or 1559.   (Harvey's Grants), Add. MS. 16,940, fo. 47ᵇ.

   „   John, of Surrey, ... 15[6]⅘.   (Harvey's Grants), Add. MS. 16,940, fo. 9 and 30ᵇ.

   „   John, of E. Grinsted, Surrey, Esq., confirmed 12 Nov. 1597.   Harl. MS. 1561, fo. 121ᵇ, by Camden ; Add. MS. 14,295, fo. 80ᵇ ; D. 11, 54, Her. Coll. ; 14 May 1605 in Morgan's Sphere, p. 117.

GOODWYN, Robert, of Portisberry, Somerset, crest 10 May 1553, by Hawley (?).   Add. MS. 16,940, fo. 206.

GODWIN, Thomas, of London, confirmed 15[6]⅘.   (Harvey's Grants), Add. MS. 16,940, fo. 51ᵇ.

GOODWIN, Thomas, London, out of Devon, ..., by G. Dethick.   Harl. MS. 1422, fo. 22ᵇ.

GOODWYN, William, of Bocking, Salop (Essex ?), coat and crest.   Barker's Grants, Harl. MS. 5846, fo. 44 ; Stowe MS. 692, fo. 47ᵇ ; Harl. MS. 1422, fo. 17.

GOODWYN, William, of Wells, Somerset, gent., grant 20 Feb., 1 and 2 Phil. and Mary, 1554-5, by G. Dethick. Harl. MS. 1359, fo. 63 ; copy of grant, Q's Coll. Oxf. MSS. 37, fo. 34, and 39, fo. 51 ; Grants I., 141-2, confirmed by W. Dethick ; Harl. MSS. 1116, fo. 42, and 1422, fo. 17.

GOODYER, Thomas, of New Windsor, Berks, 19 Oct. 1579, by Cooke. Harl. MSS. 1359, fo. 95, and 5887, fo. 29.

GOOKEINE, John, s. of Thomas, s. of Arnold Cockeine als Gookeine of Ickham, co. Camb., 7 Oct. 1609, by Segar. Add. MS. 12,225, fo. 47b ; Guil., p. 203 ; attested by Philipot, Somerset Her., Harl. MS. 6140, fo. 38 : impaling Denn quarterly, Harl. MS. 1432, fo. 212 ; copy of grant, Add. MS. 7098, fo. 80b.

GORE, Jerrard, of London, ... 1587, by Cooke. Harl. MSS. 1359, fo. 108b, and 1422, fo. 94 ; Add. MS. 4966, fo. 64.

GORING, Sir George, Knt., Master of the Horse to ye Queen, and Lieut. of the Hon. band of Pentioners, created by King Charles Baron Goring of Hurstpierpoint, Sussex, confirmation, quarterly of 9, and grant of supporters 10 May 1632, by Segar. Add. MS. 12,225, fo. 48.

GORNE, Sir Bartholomew de, a Dutchman, Quartermaster, seal and augmentation 1 April 1646, by Sir E. Walker, Gart. Her. Coll., fo. 27.

GORST, John, of London, citizen and mercht., and to John his father, 2 Dec. 1652, by E. Bysshe, Gart. Bysshe's Grants, 38. See also GOSSE.

GOSFRIGHT, George, of London, gent., s. of Andrew, late of Sandwich, Kent, s. of George, commonly called Gostred, 19 Feb. 1657-8, by Bysshe. Harl. MS. 1172, fo. 19, copy of grant.

GOSSE, ..., by Bysshe. Harl. MS. 6179, fo. 39.

GOSNOLD, Robert, of Suff., ... coat . . . . Barker's Grants, Harl. MS. 5846, fo. 43b ; Stowe MS. 692, fo. 48.

GOUGH, John, of Bishbury, co. Stafford, gent., 1 July 1664, by W. Dugdale, Norr. (Her. Coll.).

„ Dr John, and bro. Dr Stephen, arms and augmentation 1 July 1661, by Walker, Gart. Her. Coll., 40. See GOFFE.

„ William, gent., of the co. of Chester, grant 12 Dec., 21 Ed. IV., 1481, by T. Holme, Clar. Harl. MS. 1507, fo. 449 (copy of grant, Brit. Mus.), Harl. MS. 1359, fo. 3 ; Le Neve's MS. 449 ; Q's Coll. Oxf. MSS. 38, fo. 12, and 39, fo. 2 ; Grants II., 641.

GOULD (John), of Dorchester, Dorset, per saltire az. and or, a lyon rampt. counter changed, ..., by Segar. Add. MS. 12,225, fo. 48 ; C. 22 [Visit. Dorsetsh., 1623], fo. 157b, Her. Coll., and Guil., p. 399 ; Harl. MS. 105, fo. 8b.

„ Sir Henry, of Sharpham park, Somerset, a Justice of the Court of K. Bench, 7 July 1699, by T. St. George, Gart. and Clar. Add. MS. 14,831, fo. 87, and Grants IV., fo. 297.

GOULDING, ... Hill, Dorset, escocheon, by J. Borough. Harl. MS. 6179, fo. 23.

„ Robert, of Newherber, par. of Levington, Kent (s. of Henry), confirmed 13 May 1572, by Cooke. Guil., p. 174.

GOUNING, John, Mayor and Alderm. of Bristol, granted 22 Dec. 1662, by Bysshe. Harl. MSS. 1470, fo. 136, 1105, fo. 17, and 1441, fo. 131b, as Gunning, and Guil., p. 329 ; Bysshe's Grants, fo. 13, Her. Coll.

GOURNEY, Anne, wife of Richard, esq., citizen and Alderm. of London, dau. of Richard Johnson, of Hampstead, Essex, gift 12 March 1596, 39 Q. Eliz., by R. Lee, Clar., or his officer (?). Harl. MS. 1359, fo. 103. See JOHNSON.

GORNEY, Sir Thomas, of Stifford, Essex, Knt. and High Sheriff, 1622, arms allowed . . . . 1621, by Camden : Arg., a cross engrailed gu., in the dexter chief point a cinquefoil az. Harl. MS. 6095, fo. 40.

GOWRAN, Lord (Cutts), John, Baron of: supporters 19 Dec. 1692, by T. St. George, Gart. Harl. MS. 6834, fo. 178 ; Grants IV., fo. 69.

GRACE, Robert, Wilts, s. of John, of Somerset, ..., by Cooke. Stowe MS. 670, fo. 29[b].

GRAFTON, Richard (s. of Ralph, out of Cheshire), attested and ratified and confirmed (in a letter testimonial to Spain), by Flower, 16 Aug. 1577. MS. Ashm. 834, fo. 5[b] ; copy of grant, Bodleian Lib., 1512 [*sic*]. Guil., p. 390.

  ,, Richard, of London, confirmed . . . . 1560. (Harvey's Grants), Add. MS. 16,940, fo. 14 ; Harl. MS. 5887, fo. 21[b].

  ,, Richard, of London, 3rd s. of Richard, of London, Stationer and Printer, 3 March 1584-5, by Cooke. Add. MS. 14,295, fo. 30 ; Harl. MSS. 1359, fo. 116, and 1052, fo. 13[b] ; *see above* by Flower, Clar. Stowe MS. 670, fo. 1.

  ,, Richard, of London, Feb. 1605-6, by W. Camden. Harl. MSS. 1422, fo. 19, and 6095, fo. 4[b] ; Caius Coll. Camb. MS. 551, fo. 4[b] ; Morgan's Sphere, 109 ; Add. MS. 4966, fo. 62[b].

GRAHAM, *see* GRYME.

GRANDORGE, Humfrey, gent., 1st s. of John, 1st s. of Humfrey, of Flaskby, Yorks, gent., gift of crest 22 Nov. 1560, by L. Dalton, Norr. Harl. MS. 1359, fo. 46[b].

GRANGER, John, of London, ..., by Cooke, Clar. Stowe MS. 670, fo. 53.

GRASWINCLE, Sir Theodore, of Delfe in Holland, Augmentation at the Castle of St. German en laye, 10 Sept. 1649, by Sir E. Walker, Gart. Her. Coll., fo. 1.

GRATWICK, *see* GROTWICK.

GRAVATT, John, of London, free of the Comp[y] of Goldsmiths, Alderm. and deputy of Farringdon without, Fleet St. Ward, by Segar. Add. MS. 12,225, fo. 48[b] ; C. 21 [Visit. Lond., 1634], fo. 604[a], Her. Coll. ; Guil., p. 192.

GRAVE, James, of Heyton, Yorks, and to } sons of W[m], s. of Robert, s. of John, of
  ,, John, of London, gent.,   } Heyton aforesaid, Crest 12 June
                                 } 1591, by Cooke. Add. MS. 14,295,
fo. 23[b] ; Harl. MS. 1359, fo. 94[b] ; 12 Jan. 1591-2, by Cooke and Knight, Norr. (?), in Harl. MS. 1422, fo. 51 ; ? Grants II., 519.

GRAVENOR, azure, a garb or, *see* Le Neve's MS. 323 among Camden's Grants. *See* GROSVENOR.

GRAVESEND, Borough of, ... 1636, by W. Le Neve, Clar. Cat. Her. Exhib. Soc. of Antiq., 71.

GRAYE, Henry, of Gosfield Hall, Suff., 1576, by Cooke. Harl. MSS. 1422, fo. 85[b], and 1359, fo. 100[b] ; Add. MS. 4966, fo. 88[b].

GRAY, Sir Richard, Secretary of Ireland, July 1612, by Camden, arms also of Ann, dau. of Christopher Payton, his wife (*see* Anne Grey). Harl. MSS. 6095, fo. 23[b], and 1422, fo. 37[b].

  ,, Richard, of London, gent., s. of Walter, s. of Richard, descended of a younger brother of the Lord Gray of Rotherfield, copy of grant 23 June 1568, by Ro. Cooke. *See* copy in Records of the parish of Whitkerk exemplified.

  ,, Robert, Sheriff of London and Master of Merchant Taylors Co., 1635, and to Thomas Gray, his nephew, granted . . . . April 1635, by R. St. George, Clar. Harl. MS. 1470, fo. 14, 242 (copy of grant, Brit. Mus.) ; Grants II., fo. 658 ; Add. MS. 14,295, fo. 104 ; Guil., p. 405, and by Sir E. Bysshe to

  ,, William, of Hackney, Middx., 7 May 1652, and to his brethren, being of the kindred of Robert the Mercht. taylor. Harl. MS. 6140, fo. 75[b].

GREAVES, Sackville, of West Fairle, Sussex, esq., 28 Nov. 1671, by Sir E. Bysshe, Clar. Harl. MS. 1105, fo. 39, and Bysshe's Grants, 28.

P

GREDGEFIELD, William, ..., 1 April 1624, by R. St. George, Clar. Add. MS. 14,295, fo. 64ᵇ.

GREEKE (Thomas), Baron of Exchequer, crest Feb. 1611-12, by Camden. Harl. MSS. 1422, fo. 21ᵇ, and 6095, fo. 14ᵇ.

GREEN, ... 1725 [? 1625], by Le Neve? Burke's Armory.

GREENE, Edward, of Welby, Norfolk, gift 10 Aug. 1562. (Harvey's Grants), Add. MS. 16,940, fo. 61 : Grants II., 562.

,,   Edward, of Shenley, Herts, arms and crest 18 July 1571, by Cooke. Harl. MSS. 1359, fo. 24, and 1422, fo. 50ʰ ; Add. MS. 14,295, fo. 51ᵇ ; Q's Coll. Oxf. MS. 146, fo. 467 (coat as Thomas below).

,,   George, of Awkley, Yorks, 22 Oct. 1564, by Flower. Add. MS. 14,295, fo. 72ᵇ ; called Thoˢ by Guil., p. 367, and Harl. MS. 6140, fo. 69.

,,   Sir Richard, Knt., clerk of the check to the Hon. band of gent. pensioners, by R. St. George, Clar., not blazoned or tricked. Add. MS. 14,295, fo. 58.

,,   (or GREVE), Thomas, of Rotherham, Yorks, by letters patent in French 8 March, 13 H. VIII., 152[1-2], by Wriothesley, Gart., and Wall, Norr. Stowe MS. 706, fo. 10 ; see Edward above ; Harl. MS. 1433, fo. 18ᵇ.

GRENE, Thomas, of Knapton, Norfolk, gift .... (Harvey's Grants), Add. MS. 16,940, fo. 52.

GREENE, William, of Essex, gent., descended out of Yorks, confirmed 17 July 1494, 9 Hen. VII., by J. Richmond Clar. Stowe MS. 676, fo. 5 ; Misc. Gen. et Her., 2 S., vol. v., p. 360 (plate) ; Harl. MS. 1507, fo. 6ᵇ (copy of grant, Brit. Mus.) ; Harl. MS. 1422, fo. 113ʰ ; Add. MS. 14,295, fo. 77 ; Stowe MS. 692, fo. 47ᵇ ; copy of grant, Q's Coll. Oxf. MSS. 37, fo. 6, and 38, fo. 16, and 146, fo. 29.

,,   Sir William, of Oxfordshire, confirmed Feb. 1605-6, by Camden, Clar. Harl. MS. 6095, fo. 20 ; Guil., p. 157, adds father of Sir Michael ; Harl. MS. 5887, fo. 22ᵇ.

,,   William, of Mitcham, Surrey, fined for Alderm. and Sheriff of London. 6 Jan. 1663-4, by Bysshe, Clar. Harl. MS. 1470, fo. 66 ; (copy of grant, Brit. Mus.) Harl. MS. 1105, fo. 17 ; Bysshe's Grants, fo. 4, Her. Coll. ; Surrey Arch. Soc., iii., 350 ; Guil., p. 386.

GREENFIELD, John, son-in-law to Sir E. Walker, Gart., 3 Dec. 1661, by Garter. Her. Coll., fo. 43.

GREENHILL, Thomas, of the city of London, Chirugeon (7th s. of Wᵐ Greenhill of Greenhill, co. Middx., but 39th child by birth of the said Wᵐ, by Elizabeth his wife, dau. of John Jones of London), 1 Sept. 1698, by T. St. George, Gart. and Clar. Add. MS. 14,831, fo. 190 ; Grants IV., 276-7-8 ; Misc. Gen. et Her., 3rd S., v., 296.

GREENHOUGH, John, of Brandlesome, co. Lanc., 9 Nov. 1614, by R. St. George. Harl. MSS. 1422, fo. 109ᵇ, 6179, fo. 20ᵇ, and 6140, fo. 46, quarterly, fo. 73.

GREENSTREET (Peter in Guil., p. 405), of Ofspring, Kent, alteration 23 June 1642, by Borough. Harl. MS. 1105, fo. 58 ; alteration of crest and the martlet in the canton altered to an eagle, Caius Coll. Camb. MS. 551.

GREENWAYE, Ralph, ... Norfolk, gift .... 1558. (Harvey's Grants), Add. MS. 16,940, fo. 9.

GREENWELL, Wᵐ, of London, mercht. (descended from Greenwell of Greenwell Hill, co. Durham), crest given .... 1602, by Camden. (1601 in Add. MS. 14,295, fo. 120ᵇ) ; Harl. MSS. 1359, fo. 38ᵇ, 6095, fo. 1, and 1422, fo. 17.

GREETE, ... Staveley, Yorks, confirmed 1655. Burke's Armory.

GREGORY, George, of Nottingham, 4 July 1663, by W. Dugdale, Norr. (Her. Coll.)

,,   William, of Barnby upon Don [co. York] (s. of Roger, etc.), 23 Feb. 1600-1, 43 Eliz., by Segar. Surtees Soc., XLI., xlv., copy of grant, Brit. Mus. (?).

GRENEWAY, Capt. . . . . 1644, by W. Ryley, Lanc. Herald. Stowe MS. 703, fo. 63.

GRESHAM, John, Mercer, of London, s. of John, of Holtmarket, Norfolk, augmentation 20 Sept. 1537, by Hawley. Misc. Gen. et Her., ii., 311; F. 12, fo. 12, 128, Her. Coll.; (see wife Kath. Sampson) copy of grant, Brit. Mns., Sir Thomas, Harl. MS. 5887, fo. 20.

GRESHAM, Richard, Mayor and Alderm. of the Honble. city of London, 30 Nov. 1537, by Barker. Quarterings, Add. MS. 14,311, fo. 34, 36; Aubrey's Surrey, v., 371; Misc. Gen. et Her., ii., 311–312, copy of grant, Brit. Mus.; Le Neve's MS. 485.

GRETTON. . . . . family arms certified by Wm Ryley, Norr. Harl. MS. 6832, fo. 413ᵇ.

GREVE, Thomas, of Rotherham, see GREENE.

GREY, Anne, wife of Richard, of London, Alderm., arms. Barker's Grants, 1526—49, Harl. MS. 5846, fo. 40; Gray in Stowe MS. 692, fo. 46ᵇ; Grants I., 352ᵇ.

„ Henry, Lord Yelverton, supporters and quarterings 4 Nov. 1680, by Sir W. Dugdale. Harl. MS. 6834, fo. 178; Grants III., fo. 117.

GREY-TAWYERS', Crafte and Fraternyte of, the City of London, grant 27 Sept. 1476, 16 Edw. IV., by Holme; confirmed 11 Oct., 22 H. VIII., 1530, by Benolte. Harl. MS. 1470, fo. 54, copy of grant, Brit. Mus.

GRIFFITH, Thomas, of the city of Bristol, s. and h. of Edward, s. of John, of the same, exemplified 1 Nov. 1623, under hand and seale of the Office, by Segar (?). Add. MS. 12,225, fo. 48ᵇ.

GRILLS, John, Lanrethe, Cornwall, 19 Q. Eliz., 1577, by Cooke. Harl. MS. 1079, fo. 87.

GRIMES, ... wife of (?) Edward Anstin of Surrey . . . . 1611, by Camden. Harl. MSS. 1422, fo. 36, and 6095, fo. 15, No. 1.

„ Thomas, of London, citizen and Haberdasher, 8 June 1575, by Cooke. Harl. MS. 115, fo. 65; Add. MS. 4966, fo. 96ᵇ; Harl. MSS. 1359, fo. 114, and 1422, fo. 95ᵇ, as Crimes; Stowe MS. 670, fo. 68.

GRIMSBY, Town of, allowed or conferred . . . . 1592, by Rhee [Lee ?]. Add. MS. 17,506, fo. 35.

GRINDALL, Edmund, Bp. of London, 25 Dec. 1559, by G. Dethick. Harl. MSS. 1441, fo. 62ᵇ, and 1359, fo. 78ᵇ; grant in Latin, Q's Coll. Oxf. MSS. 39, fo. 109, and 145, fo. 3; Grants I., 49.

GROBHAM, Sir Richard, of Gt. Wishford, Wilts, 6 May 1599, by W. Camden, Clar. Harl. MS. 1443, fo. 50ᵇ; Stowe MS. 706, fo. 19; Harl. MS. 6140, fo. 31, 74.

GROCERS' COMPANY, arms and supporters granted by Benolte, crest granted 14 Oct., 4 Q. Eliz., 1562, by Harvey. Add. MSS. 14,295, fo. 28, and 16,940, fo. 52; Harl. MS. 1359, fo. 73.

GROSVENOR, Richard, of Eaton, Cheshire, esq., confirmation of the golden talbot, the ancient crest granted 20 Aug. 1597, 40 Eliz., by W. Dethick. Stowe MS. 676, fo. 125; Copy of grant, Brit. Mus., Harl. MS. 2022, fo. 90ᵇ, and Q's Coll. Oxf. MS. 36, fo. 70, in Latin; Grants I., 423.

GROSVENOR (GRAVENOR), azure, a garb or. Le Neve's MS., p. 323, among Camden's Grants.

GROTWICK, William, Ulverston, co. Lanc., crest 21 May 1607, by R. St. George. Harl. MS. 1562, fo. 120ᵇ; Add. MS. 14,295, fo. 79 (fo. 276); Harl. MS. 5887, fo. 49ᵇ; "doubtful whether he had a coat before," Stowe MS. 703, fo. 72; Harl. MS. 1105, fo. 10ᵇ.

GROVE, Robert, of Donhead St. Andrew, Wilts, and crest granted 20 June 1560, by Harvey. Add. MS. 16,940, fo. 25, and Hoare's Wilts, IV., i., 57; grant, Cat. Her. Exhib. Soc. of Antiq., 64.

GRYME, Henry, of Netherby, 1552, by Harvey, Norr. Harl. MS. 1116, fo. 61.

GUARES, Bernard de, by charter and Roy. Warrant 18 Sept., 24 H. VI., 1445. Harl. MS. 1178, fo. 43ᵇ.

GUDLAWE, Thomas, *see* GOODLAWE, 1581.

GUEVARA, Francis, of co. Linc., descended from Nicholas Uzlez (Velez) de Guevara of Segura, prov. of Guyposcoa in Spain, Knight of St. Iago, confirmed 1617, by Segar; also under the hand and seale of Gondemor, Ambass' Lieger in England for the King of Spain. Add. MS. 12,225, fo. 49; ped., Harl. MS. 807, fo. 119, quarterly : quarterly of 4, impaling Smyth. Harl. MS. 5805, fo. 104.

„ Johannes, of Stanigot, co. Linc., esq., 18 March 1604-5, by Segar and Camden, Clar. Harl. MS. 5805, fo. 104, copy of confirmation and pedigree, or rather a certificate of gentry. *See* preceding entry.

GUILDFORD (Nath. or Francis), Lord, supporters 12 Nov. 1683, by Sir Wm Dugdale. Harl. MS. 6834, fo. 178 ; Grants III., 208.

GUILDHALL, The fraternity of the Chapel of. Arms and crest originally granted by Walter Bellinger, Ireland King of Arms, and annulled by Thos. (Holme), Clar., who regranted the same coat and crest 16 July, 22 Ed. IV., 1482, which were confirmed 12 Oct. 1530 by Thos. Benolte, Clar. Q's Coll. Oxf. MS. 38, fo. 9, for copy and grant.

GUILLIM, John, Portsmouth Herald Extr^y, Earl Marshal's Warrant, 1603. Add. MS. 5756, fo. 276.

A GUILLIMS, John, of Westbury, in the forest of Dean, co. Glouc., by Harvey. Harl. MS. 1422, fo. 17.

GULL, William, of Sandwich, Kent, ... 1586, by Cooke. Harl. MSS. 1359, fo. 91, and 1422, fo. 93 ; Add. MS. 4966, fo. 30^b.

GULSTON, John, of Gray's Inn, Counsellor-at-Law, younger bro. and his elder bro. Theodore, Doctor of Physick, eldest son. Sons of Wm Gulston of Wymond-ham, co. Leic. Harl. MSS. 1422, fo. 20^b, and 6095, fo. 11 ; Guil., p. 358, by Camden.

GUNMAN, Christopher, "Commander of the Anne," 15 May 1676, ? by W. Dudgale. Harl. MS. 6834, fo. 178 ; Grants III., fo. 30.

GUNNING, Peter, S.T.D., Bp. of Chichester, s. of Peter, presbyter of Hove in Kent, 9 May 1670, by Walker. Add. MSS. 14,293, fo. 30, and 14,294, fo. 4 ; Harl. MS. 1172, fo. 51, copy of grant.

GUNNING, *see also* GOUNING.

GUNTER, ... his crest . . . . Barker's Grants, Harl. MS. 5846, fo. 42^b ; Stowe MS. 692, fo. 47 ; [Philip, of London, Harl. MS. 6140, fo. 37].

GURNEY, John, of Aylesbury, Bucks, 17 June 1669, by Bysshe, Clar.; *see also* GORNEY and GOURNAY. Harl. MS. 1105, fo. 22; Bysshe's Grants 27 ; Le Neve's MS. 505, and Proc. Soc. Antiq., 2nd S., xvi., 1897, p. 355.

„ Richard, als GURNARD, s. of Bryan G. als G., born at Kendal, co. Westmld., who for his integrity, gravity and prudence ye citizens of London had elected their Sheriff, exemplified 26 July 1633, by Segar. Add. MS. 12,225, fo. 49 ; C. 24 [Visit. Lond., 1634], fo. 307, Her. Coll., and Guil., p. 406 ; Harl. MSS. 5887, fo. 113^b, and 6140, fo. 71.

GUYAN, Marke, of Dines Hall, Essex, Knt^d by Chas. II., grant 3 Dec. 1671, ? by Sir E. Bysshe. Harl. MS. 1105, fo. 42.

GUYBON, *see* GIBBON.

GUYDOTT or GUIDOTTO, Anthonio, of Florence, 22 Dec. 1550, 4 Ed. VI. MS. Ashm. 858, fo. 15, 16, copy of grant, Bodleian Lib. ; Sir Anthony, augmentation by Barker, N. and Q., 2nd S., iv., 438, Bodleian Lib. ; MS. Rawl., B. cii, fo. 53 ; Le Neve's MS. 478.

GUYLEMYN als GUYLEMYN TROYTE, John, of Anglesey in Wales and then gentelman harbenger to the Q's Majestie, 16 Mary. Harl. MSS. 1433, fo. 15, and 1546, fo. 38, and Stowe MS. 670, fo. 47.

GYMBER, Fabyan, of London, gent., s. of W^m, s. of W^m, of Tempsford, s. of W^m, 5 Aug. 1590, by Cooke. Harl. MS. 1359, fo. 101^b ; Grants II., 499.

H

HABINGTON, ..., of Herts, by Hawley, Clar. Harl. MS. 1116, fo. 41ᵇ. *See* HANNINGTON.

HACKER, John, East Bridgford, Notts, Esq., a Justice of the peace, 28 Nov. 1611, by R. St. George, Norr. Add. MS. 14,295, fo. 59ᵇ; C. 34 [Visit. of Nottingham, 1662], fo. 3 ; Grants II., 611 ; Harl. MS. 6140, fo. 34ᵇ.

HACKETT, Roger, North Crawley, Bucks, s. of Thomas, of London, confirmed 1575, by Cooke, Clar. Stowe MS. 670, fo. 82.

HACKWELL, ... of co. Linc.. or, a bend betw. six trefoils slipped az. . . . . by Segar. Add. MS. 12,225, fo. 49ᵇ.

HACKWILL, John, s. of Wm., s. of Allan, s. of John, of Totnes, Devon, etc., grant of arms and crest . . . . 1601, by W. Dethick, Gart. Q's Coll. Oxf. MS. 36, fo. 123, copy of grant.

HACON, Sir Hubert, Kt., of Suffolk, 1536, by T. Wall, Gart. Bannerman's MS., No. 9, fo. 454.

HADDON, ..., crest . . . . Barker's Grants . . . . 1526—49. Harl. MS. 5846, fo. 50ᵇ ; Stowe MS. 692, fo. 54ᵇ.

HADLEIGH, town of, Suffolk, letters patent 22 Nov., 16 Jac. I. (18 Feb. 1618), by Camden. Cott. MS. Faustina E. 1, fo. 4 ; Suff. Arch. Instit., iii., 312.

HADLEY, George, East Barnet, Herts, only s. of George, citizen of London, 14 April 1685, by W. Dugdale, Gart. and Clar. Harl. MS. 6834, fo. 178 ; Grants III., fo. 271 ; Lansd. MS. 867, fo. 52.

HADNALL, ..., or, a maunch sa. ; crest, a buck's head erased or, ducally gorged az., attired sa., by Sir G. Dethick. Q's Coll. Oxf. MS. 145, fo. 26ᵇ.

HAGER, John, of Bourne, co. Camb., esq., crest and arms confirmed 2 Sept. 1605, by Camden. Harl. MS. 1359, fo. 25 ; Dec. in Add. MS. 14,295, fo. 111 ; Guil. 173, as Thomas.

HAKE (or HUKE), Thomas, Peterborough, Northants, by Cooke . . . . Stowe MS. 670, fo. 15.

HAKES, Joan, ux. . . . . Heneage. Stowe MS. 670, fo. 54ᵇ.

HALDENBY, Francis and Robert, of Haldenby, Yorks, brothers (quarterly of 6 given and granted), crest granted. Dated at York, 1 Dec. 1563, 5 Q. Eliz., by Flower. Add. MS. 14,295, fo. 72ᵇ ; Stowe MS. 692, fo. 56ᵇ ; Harl. MSS. 1422, fo. 111ᵇ, and 1359, fo. 41ᵇ.

HALE, Mathias, of Alderley, co. Glouc., Ld. Chief Baron of the Exchequer, 9 May, 13 Chas. II., 1661. Harl. MS. 1105, fo. 16ᵇ ; Bysshe's Grants, fo. 4, Her. Coll.

„ Thomas, of Clifford's Inn, gent., and to his brother Michael, 15 Sept. 1668, by Sir E. Walker, Gart. Her. Coll., fo. 65.

HALES, *see also* HALLES.

„ . . . . confirmed Feb. 1616, by Camden. Harl. MS. 6095, fo. 35ᵇ, and Caius Coll. Camb. MS. 551, fo. 24ᵇ.

„ James, of Dongeon, Kent, s. of Humphrey, s. of Sir James, a Justice C. P., s. of John, Baron of Exchequer, s. of John, s. of Henry, s. of John, s. of Thomas, of Haie Place, Haledon, Kent, and heir of Sir Robert Hales, Kt., lord of St John of Jerusalem in England and lord Treasurer of England, and also cousin to Sir Nicholas, 2 March 1570-71, by Cooke. Stowe MS. 670, fo. 60.

„ John, of Newington, Kent, 16 Nov. 1520, by Wriothesley and Benolte. Add. MS. 5506, fo. 109, copy of grant, Brit. Mus.

HALEY, Edward, of Edgware-bury, Middx., 27 Jan. 1679-80, by Wᵐ Dugdale, Gart., and Hy. St. George, Norr. Add. MS. 14,831, fo. 74 ; Grants III., fo. 99.

HALFEHIDE, Edward, of Aspdon, Herts, s. of James, of Yardley, Herts, crest confirmed 1564, by G. Dethick, Gart., Cooke and Norroy. Harl. MSS.

5823, fo. 25, and 1441, fo. 76, and Q's Coll. Oxf. MS. 145, fo. 25 ; Stowe MS. 703, fo. 28^b.

HALGAT, Robert [de Helmesworth, co. York], Bp. of Llandaff, 29 June 1539, by W. Fellow, Norr. Misc. Gen. et Her., N. S., i., 336, from Her. Coll., copy of grant, Brit. Mus.

HALIFAX, see WATERHOUSE.

HALL, Anthony, of Hampshire, gent., grant, by G. Dethick, Gart., 15 Feb., 6 Ed. VI., 1551-2. Harl. MS. 1359, fo. 61 : copy of grant, Q's Coll. Oxf. MS. 39, fo. 42 ; Grants I., 176.

„ Anthony, by Cooke, Clar. Stowe MS. 670, fo. 23.

„ Bartholomew, of Ipswich, Suff., s. of Thos, clerk of the Hanaper office in Chancery, s. of Thos., of Shirburn, Yorks, Crest 8 Feb. 1587-8, by Flower, Norr., and to the descendants of his grandfather. MS. Ashm. 844, fo. 74, pedigree and copy of patent, Bodleian Lib. ; Stowe MS. 677, fo. 32 ; Guil. 344.

„ Edward, of Bybrooke, par. of Kennington, Kent, 1588, by Cooke. Harl. MSS. 1359, fo. 113, and 1422, fo. 92 ; Her. and Geneal., ii., 431, of Wellesborough, Kent, 1583. See John, 1599, below, Add. MS. 4966, fo. 84^b.

„ John, s. of Amery, of Salford, co. Lanc., gent., gift at London 4 Nov. 1533, by Wriothesley and Tonge. Add. MS. 26,702, fo. 75^b ; Harl. MS. 1359, fo. 41 ; (Add. MS. 14,295, fo. 73, assigns this coat to Thomas Hall of Middle Walton, Yorks) ; Harl. MS. 6140, fo. 67^b.

„ John, of Everse, Salop . . . . coat and crest . . . . Barker's Grants, Harl. MS. 5846, fo. 48^b ; Stowe MS. 692, fo. 53^b.

„ John, the elder, of Wilsborough, Kent, and Edward, of Ashford, his kinsman, 27 June 1599, by W. Dethick, Gart., and Camden. Visit. Kent (43), by J. J. Howard, in Archæologia Cantiana, vol. vi., 252, copy of grant, Brit. Mus. See also Edward above.

„ Joseph, S.T.D., Bp. of Exeter, 12 May 1631, by R. St. George, Clar. Misc. Gen. et Her., 2nd S., vol. iii., p. 9, plate ; I. 23, fo. 67, Her. Coll. ; Add. MS. 14,295, fo. 67^b, as Joshua.

„ Nicholas, B.D., of Devonshire, treasurer of St. Peter's Cathedral, 20 March 1684-5, by Sir Wm Dugdale and Clar. Harl. MS. 6834, fo. 178 ; Grants III., fo. 260 ; Lansd. MS. 867, fo. 52.

„ Sarah, relict of Joseph, late of London, mercht., who died in the West Indies (sister of Sir Nathl and Sir Joseph Hearne, Kts., dec^d), etc. (mar^d to Sir Wm Hodges, bart.), and her two daus., Sarah, Lady Hodges, and Mrs Susanna Cottle, 20 Sept. 1699, by T. St. George, Gart. and Clar. Grants IV., 313 or 315 ; Stowe MS. 714, fo. 95.

„ William, see WALL.

HALLES, ... of London, Feb. 1605-6, by Camden : az., a chev. razuly or, etc. Harl. MSS. 1422, fo. 19, and 6095, fo. 5, and Cains Coll. Camb. MS. 551, fo. 4^b.

HALLETT, Sir James, London, goldsmith . . . . by Cooke. Stowe MS. 670, fo. 82^b.

HALLIDAY, William, ... 1623, see HOLLIDAY. See Le Neve's MS. 89, 280, 389.

HALLYDAYE, Sir Leonard, Knt., citizen and Alderm. of London, crest 21 Sept. 1605, by Camden. Harl. MS. 1470, fo. 11, for copy of grant, Brit. Mus., and Q's Coll. Oxf. MS. 38, fo. 119 ; Harl. MSS. 6095, fo. 4^b (23 Sept.), and 1422, fo. 19 ; Ld. Mayor, Harl. MS. 1359, fo. 37^b ; Guil. 345, as Halliday. This coat was granted by Mr Borough when he was Norroy to Wm Halliday of the city of London in 1623, the graunt in Latin, I have a copy of it, hee was questioned for this graunt before the Earl Marshal, it being in the province of Clarencieux. Add. MS. 14,295, fo. 117^b.

HALYLE (HALLILEY), John, of Dalston in Hackney, Middx., 15 May 1551, by Hawley. Add. MSS. 16,940, fo. 200^b, and 7098, fo. 77 (fo. 81), and if he died s.p. remainder to his brother Robert.

HALLOWAY, *see also* HOLLOWAY.

„ John, esq., Comptroller of the Custom house, London, quartering Thorey . . . . by Segar. Add. MS. 12,225, fo. 49ᵇ; Harl. MS. 6140, fo. 109ᵇ; Add. MS. 4966, fo. 26.

„ John, of the Univ. of Oxford, confirmed 10 Nov. 1631, by R. St. George, Clar. Add. MS. 14,295, fo. 56ᵇ: I. 9, 93, Her. Coll.; Harl. MS. 1405, fo. 4, in St. George's handwriting.

HALLOWOOD, Edward, of Chester, ⎫ attested by R. Holme, deputy to Garter. Harl.
„ Thomas, of London, salter, ⎭ MS. 6179, fo. 60ᵇ, different crests.

HALLOWS, ... of Derbyshire, ? 1647, by Sir E. Bysshe. Harl. MSS. 2275, fo. 40, and 6197, fo. 29ᵇ.

HALSEY, William, Gᵗ Gaddesden parsonage, and ⎫ 22 Jan. 1633-4, by R. St. George,
„ James, D.D., his brother, ⎬ Norr. Harl. MS. 5887, fo. 115;
⎭ Grants II., 655.

HALSTED, Laurence, Dep. to Dʳ Brady, Keeper of Records, Tower of London, 10 May 1688, by Sir T. St. George, Gart. and Clar. Harl. MS. 6834, fo. 178; Grants III., fo. 347.

„ Laurence, of Sunning, Berks, Esq., inhabiting yᵉ mansion house of yᵗ manuonr, and Lord of yᵉ same, also of London, out of Lancs, 20 Nov. 1628, by Segar. Add. MS. 12,225, fo. 50; C. 24 [Visit. Lond., 1634], fo. 42, Her. Coll.; Guil. 412; Harl. MS. 6140, fo. 79.

HALSWELL, Nicholas, of Gotehnrst, crest 1591, by Camden (? R. Cooke). Harl. MS. 1422, fo. 42ᵇ.

HAMBY, John, of Maltby, next Louth, co. Lincoln, esq., one of the auditors of the Prest, Crest 12 March 1568-9, by G. Dethick, Gart., Cooke and Flower. Crest blazoned, coloured; coat quartering Hansard, Greene and Slyght. Add. MS. 14,295, fo. 43ᵇ: MS. Ashm. 844, fo. 26, copy of grant, Bodleian Lib., and Q's Coll. Oxf. MS. 39, fo. 141 (MS. 145, fo. 18, and 146, fo. 40); Harl. MSS. 1422, fo. 113, and 1441, fo. 74; Guil. 315; Harl. MS. 1359, fo. 35ᵇ, to all either of his blood and name; Harl. MS. 1116, fo. 43ᵇ.

HAMERSLEY, Hugh, of London, s. of Hugh, s. of Richard, etc., exemplified, ratified and confirmed 22 Nov. 1614, by Camden. Stowe MS. 714, fo. 183; Harl. MSS. 6834, fo. 108, 6095, fo. 31ᵇ, and 1422, fo. 39ᵇ; Guil. 167; Grants II., 522.

HAMILTON, Collonel (under King William, 1693). Harl. MS. 6179, fo. 85ᵇ, *see* Lyon ordinary [ordinary of Arms, by Sir J. B. Paul, Lyon K. of A.].

HAMOND, Edward, of So. Wotton, ⎫ sons of Anthony, late of So. Wotton aforesaid,
Norfolk, M.A., ⎮ deeᵈ, 5 July 1698, by T. Sᵗ George, Gart.
„ Richard, ⎬ and Clar. Stowe MS. 714, fo. 128, Edmond
„ Nicholas, ⎭ fo. 119ᵇ; Grants IV., 269.

HAMMOND, James, of Salop, grant 30 April 1562, by Hervey. Stowe MS. 676, fo. 28ᵇ.

HAMOND, John, of Upton, Suffolk, ... by Cooke, Clar. Bannerman's MS. No. 9, fo. 453; Harl. MS. 1449, fo. 112.

„ John, of Camb., Dʳ of phys. to Henry, Prince of Wales, (Feb.) 1607-8, by R. St. George, Norr. Harl. MS. 1422, fo. 78; Feb. in Add. MS. 14,295, fo. 79ᵇ; Harl. MS. 6140, fo. 74.

HAMMOND, John, of Chertley Abbey, s. of Thos., s. of Giles, s. of Wᵐ, of Whaley, co. Lanc., s. of Thos., of Ferrybridge, Yorks, by R. St. George, Norr. Add. MS. 14,295, fo. 53ᵇ.

HAMOND, William, of Guildford, Surrey, crest 10 Aug. 1558, by Hervey. Copy of grant, Harl. MSS. 1116, fo. 52, and 1422, fo. 22; Add. MS. 16,940, fo. 26; Harl. MS. 5887, fo. 108.

HAMON, Thomas, of Nonyngton, Kent, coat and crest. Barker's Grants . . . . Harl. MS. 5846, fo. 56ᵇ; Stowe MS. 692, fo. 55ᵇ; Harl. MS. 5887, fo. 22ᵇ.

„ William, of Arreys, Kent, gift . . . . 1559. (Harvey's Grants) Add. MS. 16,940, fo. 45ᵇ.

HAMPSONE, Sir Robert, Alderm., 10 Oct. 1602, 44 Q. Eliz., by Camden. Harl.
MSS. 1422, fo. 18^b. and 6095, fo. 9^b ; Misc. Gen. et Her., 2nd S., vol. ii.,
p. 218 : Guil. 299.

HAMPTON, ... crest .... Barker's Grants, Harl. MS. 5846, fo. 51 ; Stowe MS.
692, fo. 54^b.

„   Robert, of London, descended from Hampton of co. Staff., confirmed
(? testified) .... by Segar. Add. MS. 12,225, fo. 50 ; C. 24 [Visit.
Lond., 1634], fo. 144, Her. Coll.; Guil. 137.

„   William, rector of Blechingley, Surrey, 13 Aug. 1662. Bysshe's Grants,
fo. 14, Her. Coll.; Harl. MS. 1470, fo. 105, copy of grant, Brit. Mus. ;
Harl. MS. 1105, fo. 19^b : Surrey Arch. Soc., iii., 351, and Guil. 70.

HANBURY, Francis, Wolverhampton, gent., 23 April 1664, by W. Dugdale. Burke's
Armory.

„   John, of Kelmarsh, Northts., 3rd s. of Walter, s. of Anthony, coat confirmed
and crest granted .... and to his brothers. See Visit., 1663, Staff., by
Camden ; Cott. MS. Faust. E. 1, fo. 64, copy of grant, Brit. Mus.

HANCOCK, Dancer, of London, escheator for Cambr. and Hunts, and also clerk
of the Records in the Tower of London, granted 10 April 1635, by Sir R.
St. George, Clar. Guil. 347 ; Harl. MS. 1105, fo. 6^b.

„   Edward, of Combe Martin, Devon, quarterly, 1588, by Cooke. Harl. MSS.
1359, fo. 114. and 1422, fo. 121 ; Grants II., 549.

„   John, of Blaxeley, Northants, gent., s. of Thomas, of Donnington, Salop,
confirmed 2 Nov. 1631, by St George (?). Add. MS. 14,295, fo. 56.

„   Richard, Cornhill, Lanc., s. of William, 11 Nov. 1614, by R. St. George,
Norr. Stowe MS. 706, fo. 15^b ; Harl. MSS. 6140, fo. 73, and 6197, fo. 12.

„   William, of Comb Martin, Devon, gént., 8 Dec. 1564, by Hervey. Harl. MS.
1359, fo. 53 ; Grants II., 549; copy of grant, see Q's Coll. Oxf. MS. 38,
fo. 80 ; Add. MS. 4966, fo. 97^b.

HANDCORNE, ... of London and co. Warw. .... 1627, by R. St. George, Clar.
Harl. MS. 1422, fo. 14^b.

HANDLEY, Henry (s. of William, of Wilford), of Nottinghamshire, and Gervase,
grant .... arms, arg., a fess between three goats passant, attired or,
21 June 1614, by Segar. Add. MS. 12,225, fo. 50^b ; 1612 in Harl. MS.
1422, fo. 16, Henry and Gervase, s. of W^m, of Wilford, Notts.

HANKE, John, Alderm. and Mayor of Chester, granted 6 Sept. 1580, by Flower.
MS. Ashm. 834, fo. 25, copy of grant, Bodleian Lib. ; Guil. 391.

HANMER, Sir Thomas, of Hanmer, Flints, Knt., crest 1 March, 1 and 2 Phil. and
Mary, 1554-5, by Sir G. Dethick, Gart. Copy of grant, Q's Coll. Oxf. MS.
39, fo. 55 ; Harl. MS. 1359, fo. 63^b ; Grants I., 220 ; Harl. MS. 1116,
fo. 44.

„   William, of the Fenns in Flints, s. of Wm., s. of Jenkin, etc., exemplified,
without date, by Cooke, Clar. Harl. MS. 1116, fo. 30.

HANNINGTON, William, of Hants, 2 May 1556, by Hawley (?). Add. MS. 16,940,
fo. 208 ; Harl. MS. 1116, fo. 41^b. Habyngton of Herts.

HANNS, Richard, of Oxford, 3 Dec. 1641, by J. Borough. Harl. MS. 1105, fo. 57^b;
Guil. 387.

HANS or HANSBY, Ralph, of Berverley, Yorks, allowed and assigned 10 Oct. 1582,
by Flower. MS. Ashm. 844, fo. 58, copy of grant, Bodleian Lib.; Guil.
207.

HANSHA, Alice, wife to Sir John Lyon, Maior of London, 10 July 1555, by
Hawley (?). Add. MS. 16,940, fo. 207^b.

HANSON, Robert, citizen and Alderm. of London, 20 June 1664, by Sir E. Bysshe,
Clar. Harl. MS. 1105, fo. 39 ; Bysshe's Grants 29.

HANSON, Edward, of Woodhouse, Yorks, gent., confirmed 17 July 1652, by W^m
Ryley, Norr. J. Watson's Halifax, p. 266.

HARBOURD or HARBORD, Charles, of Moor, Herts, esq., s. and h. of William, late
of Welton, Som^t, descended of the ancient family of Harbord in Wales, and

married the only dau. and heir of Rich⁴ Richmond of Babington ; yᵉ said Charles being at present principal officer of all the revenues belonging to Philip, Earl of Pembroke and Montgomery, and yᵉ sᵈ Charles being by yᵉ King made Auditor of the Duchy of Cornwall and surveyor genl. of all the King's houses, castles, lordships, manors, forests, chaces, etc., throughout England and Wales. N.B.—He was afterwards a Knt. and Andʳ Genl. to K. Chas. II. when Prince of Wales, and of his Privy Council, and on his accession to the Crown one of the Commissioners of the revenues assigned to the Q. Mother and Her Majesty Q. Catherine for their respective jointures and of their Council. 12 Nov. 1631, by Segar ; 2 June 1670, alteration in coat and augmentation, by Walker. Add. MSS. 12,225, fo. 50ᵇ, 14,293, fo. 71, and 14,294, fo. 20ᵇ ; Harl. MS. 1172, fo. 67, copy of grant.

HARBORNE, John, of Middx., s. of John, of Middx. (descended from Harborne of Norfolk, to whom Camden exemplified the arms), ratified or confirmed the same with grant of crest, 11 Jac., 1613, by Camden and Segar. Add. MS. 12,225, fo. 51 ; Harl. MSS. 6095, fo. 11, 1122, fo. 21, and 1359, fo. 13ᵇ ; Caius Coll. Camb. MS. 528, fo. 5 ; copy of confirmation, Harl. MS. 6140. fo. 29ᵇ.

„ Piers, now residing in city of Ayemonta in Spain, grant 25 July 1595, by W. Dethick, Gart. : arms, gu., a lion passant ar. betw. three bezants, an estoile for difference of a 3rd bro. ; crest, or, on a morion cap an eagle volant or, on the breast an estoile (or), beaked and membered. Stowe MS. 676, fo. 116 ; copy of grant, Q's Coll. Oxf. MS. 36, fo. 52.

„ William, of London, esq., 2nd s. of Wᵐ, of Yarmouth, Norf., esq., s. of George, of Salop, esq., confirmed 25 Sept. 1582, by Cooke, 24 Q. Eliz., to the posterity of Wᵐ his father. Copy of grant in Latin, Q's Coll. Oxf. MSS. 37. fo. 79, and 38, fo. 106, in Latin ; Harl. MSS. 1359, fo. 13ᵇ, and 1052, fo. 17ᵇ ; Add. MS. 14,295, fo. 8ᵇ ; Guil. 360 ; Add. MS. 4966, fo. 91.

HARBOTTLE, John, of Crowfeld, Sussex, confirmed . . . . 1559. (Harvey's Grants), Add. MS. 16,940, fo. 51ᵇ.

HARBY, Thomas, of Adysson, Northts., confirmed . . . . 1562. (Harvey's Grants), Add. MS. 16,940, fo. 15 ; Harl. MSS. 5887, fo. 56ᵇ, and 1116, fo. 54ᵇ.

HARBYN, Robert, of Newton (or Mavile), Somerset, gent., a patent May 1612, by Camden. Harl. MSS. 1422, fo. 37ᵇ, and 6095, fo. 23ᵇ ; Guil. 339.

HARDEN, see HORDEN.

„ . . . . crest . . . . Barker's Grants, Harl. MS. 5846, fo. 52 ; Add. MS. 26,702, fo. 1 ; Stowe MS. 692, fo. 54ᵇ, as HORDEN, which see.

HARDING, Hugh (Henry in Harl. MS. 1507, fo. 422), an Englishman in a duel at Perth with William de Sᵗ Lowe, a Scotchman ! for bearing the same arms. Sᵗ Lowe surrendered. Perth, 2 April 1312. Stowe MS. 840, fo. 63, pedigree copy in Brit. Mus., 1507, fo. 422 ; Harl. MS. 6592, fo. 43ᵇ ; Le Neve's MS. 422.

„ John, citizen and Mercht. Taylor of London (2nd bro. to Robert, Alderm. and Sheriff of London, s. of John, of Newport Pagnell, Bucks, grant of crest), arms and crest 30 Aug. 1568, by Sir G. Dethick and Cooke. Q's Coll. Oxf. MSS. 38, fo. 83, and 39, fo. 138, for copy of grant, and also Harl. MSS. 1470, fo. 415, 1441, fo. 74ᵇ, and 1359, fo. 53ᵇ ; Guil. 229 ; Grants I., 310, a crescent for difference ; Le Neve's MS. 415 ; Add. MS. 5887, fo. 45.

„ Robert, citizen and alderm. of London, now Sheriff of same city, s. of John, s. of John, of Newport Pagnell, Bucks, grant (? crest) 30 Aug. 1568, by Sir G. Dethick, Gart., Cooke and Flower. See brother John above. Q's Coll. Oxf. MSS. 38, fo. 83, and 39, fo. 137, for copy of patent, and also Harl. MSS. 1470, fo. 276, and 1359, fo. 53ᵇ ; Q's Coll. Oxf. MS. 145, fo. 21, and Guil. 229.

HARE, Hugh, of Totteridge (Herts), created Baron Coleraine in Ireland, confirmation

Q

of arms and crest and grant of supp^{rs} (1 May 1626), by Segar.   Add. MS. 12,225, fo. 51.

HARE, John, of London, confirmed . . . . 1563. (Harvey's Grants), Add. MS. 16,940, fo. 23.

„ Nicholas. Barker's Grants, Harl. MS. 5846, fo. 57 [in French], and Stowe MS. 692, fo. 52: Arg., a chevron sable between three griffins' heads az., on a chief gu. a mullet betw. two martlets or.

„ Nicholas, of Homersfield, Suff., crest 17 Dec., 37 H. VIII., 1545, by C. Barker, Gart. Grants I., 17.

„ Nicholas, of Homefield, Suff., gent., crest granted 17 Dec. 1545, 37 H. VIII., by Barker. Grants I., 17; 17 Sept. 1537 in Harl. MS. 1507, fo. 377, copy of grant, Brit. Mus., and Q's Coll. Oxf. MS. 38, fo. 23: Stowe MS. 692, fo. 54^b; Harl. MS. 5846, fo. 52^b; Le Neve's MS. 377, 325, etc.

„ Sir Nicholas, of Homersfield, 1 Dec. 1539. Add. MSS. 16,940, fo. 200, and 7098, fo. 75^b, then a Knight? fo. 6, by T. Hawley.

„ Nicholas, s. of John, of Stowe Bardolph, s. of John, of Humarsfield, Suffolk, gent., confirmed 24 Oct. 1574, by Cooke. Grants II., 498; Her. and Geneal., i., 82, copy of grant, Brit. Mus. ?

„ Sir Ralph, of Stowe Bardolph, s. of John, of London, alteration 12 Feb. 1613-14, by Camden. Grants II., 579; Her. and Geneal., i., 83; Harl. MSS. 6095, fo. 28^b, and 1422, fo. 38^b; Caius Coll. Camb. MS. 581, fo. 19^b; Le Neve's MS. 325.

HAREBREAD, ... of Yorks . . . . gu., a cross vair betw. four lions passant or, by Segar. Add. MS. 12,225, fo. 51^b.

HARES [HERIZ] alias SMYTH, William, of co. Leic., arms 8 Feb. 1499-1500, by Ch^r Carlyl, Norr. See fo. 374 in Modern Grants, Phillipps' Vol.: [Her. of Smith, p. 22]. (See SMYTH, Roger, crest 16 May 1565, by Sir G. Dethick. Topog. and Geneal., iii., 255, 259.)

HAREWELL, Edward, Wolverhampton, co. Staff., gent., 18 June 1663, by W. Dugdale, Norr. Her. Coll.; Harl. MS. 6179, fo. 30.

HARFFLETT als ATCHEQUER, Christ^r, of Kent, 9 May 1564, by Harvey. Harl. MS. 1115, fo. 3, and Q's Coll. Oxf. MS. 146, fo. 136. See CHEQUER and SEPTUANS also.

HARGILL, William, of Nun Monkton and of Clementhorp, Yorks, arms confirmed and crest given 1 Feb. 1580-81, 23 Eliz., by G. Dethick, Gart. Copy of grant, Q's Coll. Oxf. MSS. 37, fo. 74 (and 145, fo. 11); Harl. MSS. 1441, fo. 67^b, and 1359, fo. 33; Add. MS. 14,295, fo. 35, out of a mural crown gu. a lion's head or; 1585 in Harl. MS. 6140, fo. 69; Grants I., 167; Stowe MS. 676, fo. 55.

HARLAKENDEN, ... quarterly of 4: az., a fesse betw. three lyons' heads erased or; 4th quarter, Oxenbridge . . . . by Segar. Add. MS. 12,225, fo. 51^b.

HARLEY, John, Bp. of Hereford, granted at London 5 June 1553, 7 Ed. VI., by Sir G. Dethick, Gart. Copy of grant, Q's Coll. Oxf. MS. 39, fo. 45, in Latin; Harl. MS. 1359, fo. 61^b; Grants I., 37.

HARLOWE, Dame Elizabeth (wife of Sir Martin Bowes, Alderm. of London, Kt., and dau. of Wm Harlowe of London, gent.), ratified, confirmed and assigned, given and granted 16 March 1561-2, by Hervey. Add. MSS. 16,940, fo. 30, and 1359, fo. 57.

HARLOW, Pedach, of Gray's Inn, Esq., s. of Robert, of Preston, Northts. (dec^d in Stowe), patent 8 Sept. (28th in Stowe 703, fo. 60) 1629, by Segar. Add. MS. 12,225, fo. 52; Gnil. 292; Harl. MS. 6140, fo. 25.

HARMAN, John, of Moor Hall, co. Warwick, etc., arms and crest granted by Wriothesley, Gart., and Benolte, Clar.; confirmed 28 May 1582, by G. Dethick, Gart., and Cooke. Grant incomplete and alterations in pencil. Q's Coll. Oxf. MS. 37, fo. 81, copy of grant in Latin; of Yorks in Stowe MS. 676, fo. 59; Grants I., 67.

HARMAR, John, of co. Glouc., 1615, by Segar. Add. MS. 12,225, fo. 52 ; Harl. MS. 6140, fo. 80ᵇ.

HARPER, John or Richard, of Swarkeston, co. Derby, exemplified quarterly, Crest 3 Jan. 1565-6, by Sir G. Dethick. Harl. MS. 1441, fo. 104 ; Harpur in Q's Coll. Oxf. MS. 145, fo. 55 ; Stowe MS. 703, fo. 62 ; (Harl. MS. 1486, fo. 31ᵇ, 3 Jan. 1562-3 to Richd. Harpur) ; Richard in Le Neve's MS. 247 and 481.

„ John, treasurer of Christ's Hospital and Alderm. deputy of Bread Street Ward in London, s. of Thos., of Walton, co. Lanc., etc.; impaling Smith, by Segar. Add. MS. 12,225, fo. 52ᵇ ; C. 24 [Visit. Lond., 1634], fo. 374ᵇ, Her. Coll. ; Guil. 389.

HERPER als HARPER, Richard, of Cheshire, gift . . . . 1558. (Harvey's Grants), Add. MS. 16,940, fo. 32. See John above : Crest 3 Jan. 1565-6, by G. Dethick, Gart. Le Neve's MS. 481.

HARPER, William, of London, coat and crest . . . . Barker's Grants, Harl. MS. 5846, fo. 55 ; Stowe MS. 692, fo. 55ᵇ, now Lord Mayor, 4 Eliz., as Herper.

HARPHAM, Alice (dau. and h. of Walter, of March Chapple, co. Linc., originally out of Northumberland), wife of Thomas Philips of Lincolnshire, esq., 24 Mar. 1626-7, by Segar. Add. MS. 12,225, fo. 52ᵇ ; Grants I., 378.

„ Robert, of Marfleet, Yorks, confirmed 9 July 1657, by Ryley. Harl. MS. 1470, fo. 137 ; said to have been revoked, Guil. 295.

„ William, of the Inner Temple and of Yorkshire, 1 July 1656, by Ryley. Harl. MS. 1105, fo. 10ᵇ, 11.

HARRIE, Thomas, Rescrow in Cornwall, 10 March, 1 Ed. VI., 1546-7, by Hawley, Clar. Harl. MS. 1079, fo. 39.

HARRINGTON, Dʳ . . . . temp. Hen. VII. . . . . Add. MS. 26,702, fo. 51.

„ John, of Kelston, Somerset, s. of Allexander, descended of a younger bro. of Harrington of Briarley, Yorks, granted 12 Feb. 1568-9, by Sir G. Dethick, Gart., Cooke and Flower, and again 20 Sept. 1584 according to Stowe MS. 676, fo. 62. MS. Ashm. 844, fo. 43, copy of patent, Bodleian Lib., and Q's Coll. Oxf. MSS. 39, fo. 149, and 36, fo. 71 (MS. 145, fo. 18, 30 April 1569): Harl. MSS. 1359, fo. 54, 1441, fo. 74ᵇ, 5823 and 5847 ; Misc. Gen. et Her., N. S., iii., 17, and Guil. 413.

„ (John) of Kelston, Somerset, s. of John and Isabel his wife, dau. of Sir John Markham, Knt., sometime lieut. of the Tower, etc., with a label gu. of three points or quartering arg., a cross patonce az. ; crest differenced with the label as in the arms : confirmed and testified by Camden and Sir Wᵐ Dethick, Gart., 20 Nov. 1597, 40 Eliz. Harl. MS. 6095, fo. 37ᵇ ; copy of grant, Q's Coll. Oxf. MSS. 36, fo. 71, and 39, fo. 149.

HARRIS, see PRICKLEY.

HARRIS, Charles, Oxford and Middle Temple, s. of John, Alderm. and sometime Mayor of Oxford, a great sufferer for Chas. 1. ; 1 Aug. 1699, by T. St. Geo., Gart. and Clar. Grants IV., fo. 300. See John below.

„ Henry, the elder, of Great Missenden, Bucks, gent., 22 Aug. 1671, by Sir E. Bysshe, Clar. Harl. MS. 1105, fo. 22 ; Bysshe's Grants 27.

„ John, of the Inner Temple, gent. (Middle Temple according to Guil., p. 136), 10 April 1671, by Walker. Add. MSS. 14,293, fo. 83, and 14,294, fo. 24ᵇ ; Harl. MS. 1172, fo. 69ᵇ.

„ Nathaniel, S.T.P., J.C.D., confirmed by Camden, Clar. Harl. MS. 6179, fo. 133ᵇ.

„ Robert, of Leighton Stone, Essex, gent., two coats and crest given and granted 10 Nov., 3 and 4 Phil. and Mary, 1556, by Sir G. Dethick, Gart. Harl. MS. 1359, fo. 68 ; copy of grant, Q's Coll. Oxf. MS. 39, fo. 78 ; Grants II., 497, and I., 198.

„ Robert, of Chester, 31 Dec. 1558, quarterly, by Dalton. Harl. MS. 1359, fo. 44ᵇ.

HARRIS, Robert, formerly HERRIS, Justice of Peace, Middx., given, granted, ratified and confirmed 21 Dec. 1569, 12 Eliz., by Cooke : quarterly, with his mother's arms.   Harl. MSS. 1359, fo. 57, and 1422, fo. 114 : Q's Coll. Oxf. MS. 146, fo. 43 ; Grants I., 198, and II., 497 ; Harl. MS. 1115, fo. 2ᵇ.

HARRYS, Sir Thoˢ, Kt., Sergᵗ at law, since a baronet, July 1604, by Camden. Harl. MSS. 1422, fo. 18, 5839, fo. 3ᵇ, 2275, fo. 91ᵇ, and 1115, fo. 9ᵇ ; Guil. 403 ; Harl. MS. 6179, fo. 83ᵇ ; Add. MS. 18,582, fo. 63ᵇ.

HARRIS, William, of Hayne, Devon, 1592, quarterly, by Cooke.   Harl. MS. 1395, fo. 94ᵇ ; 1591 in Harl. MS. 1422, fo. 115ᵇ.

HARRISON, ... of Penrith, Cumberland, merchᵗ, of London, Nov. 1613, by R. St. George, Norr.   Harl. MS. 1422, fo. 83 ; Stowe MS. 706, fo. 22.

„ Gilbert, Alderm. and Sheriff of London, esq., descended of an ancient family surnamed Hardogson als Harrison, within the dutchy of Brunswic, whose arms in that country are here set out.   Grant of new arms 17 July 1633, by Segar.   Add. MS. 12,225, fo. 53 ; Guil. 389 ; Harl. MSS. 5887, fo. 113ᵇ, 6140, fo. 76ᵇ, and 1441, fo. 161ᵇ.

„ John, of London, s. of Wᵐ, s. of John, of Smythes, co. Derby, 5 May 1575, by Cooke.   Harl. MS. 1359, fo. 114ᵇ ; Surtees Soc., XLI., xli.

„ John, s. of Wᵐ, of Aldcliffe, co. Lanc., crest granted 10 Sept. 1616, by Segar. Harl. MSS. 1422, fo. 83, and 1507, fo. 116, copy of grant, and in Q's Coll. Oxf. MS. 38, fo. 128.

„ Robert, one of the Cursitors Court of Chancery, London, descended from Durham, by Segar . . . . Az., an eagle displayed regardant or, ducally gorged or, a chief erm.   Crest, on a cap of maintenance az., turned up erm., a bird sa.   Harl. MS. 1441, fo. 162ᵇ ; Add. MS. 12,225, fo. 53 ; C. 24 [Visit. Lond., 1634], fo. 593ᵇ, Her. Coll. : Guil. 210.

„ Thomas, of the North, of Finchampsted, descended out of Cumberland . . . . 1574, by Cooke.   Harl. MS. 1422, fo. 83 ; Caius Coll. Camb. MS. 528, fo. 8, copy of grant ; Add. MS. 4966, fo. 100 ; Stowe MS. 670, fo. 71.

HARRYSON, Thomas, sometime Mayor of the city of York, 2 Aug. 1592, by Knight, Norr.   Harl. MS. 1359, fo. 43.

HARRISON, William, of London, gent., s. of Michael, Penrith, Cumberland, 2nd s. of John, of Graystoke ; confirmed 24 Nov. 1607, by R. St. George, Norr. Harl. MS. 5887, fo. 59ᵇ ; Add. MS. 14,295, fo. 53ᵇ ; C. 24 [Visit. Lond., 1634], fo. 76ᵇ.

.. William, of Barlow Grange, Notts, s. of Wᵐ, of co. Bucks, Crest 1 Nov. 1609, by R. St. George, Norr.   Surtees Soc., XLI., xlvi., copy of grant, Brit. Mus.

„ William, of Aldcliffe, co. Lanc., father to farmer of the Customs, crest 10 Sept., 14 Jac., 1618 (1616), by Segar.   Int. MSS. P. Lewes, But int. MSS. J. Anstyes, Ar. Gart. the grant is to John, son of Wᵐ, of Aldcliffe. Add. MS. 12,225, fo. 33ᵇ ; Harl. MS. 1507, fo. 116, copy of grant, Brit. Mus. ; Guil. 336.

HARRY, Rowland, ... by Dalton, Norr. . . . . Harl. MS. 1422, fo. 112ᵇ ; Harris in Harl. MS. 6140, fo. 70.

HARSNETT, Samuel, Bp. of Chichester, patent . . . . Nov. 1613, by Camden.   Harl. MSS. 6095, fo. 28, and 1422, fo. 38ᵇ.

HART, Sir Percivall, Knt., ... coat . . . . Barker's Grants, Harl. MS. 5846, fo. 49 ; Stowe MS. 692, fo. 53ᵇ.

HARTE als HORTE, William, of Ensham, Oxon., 1 June 1581, by Sir G. Dethicke, Gart.   Harl. MS. 5887, fo. 88ᵇ.

HARTGRAVE, John, of Bullingbroke, co. Lincoln, coat and crest.   Barker's Grants, Harl. MS. 5846, fo. 47 ; Stowe MS. 692, fo. 53.

HARTLEY, John, of Manchester, co. Lanc., 2 Oct., 8 Chas., 1632, by Segar.   Add. MS. 12,225, fo. 53ᵇ ; [Visit.] Lanc. [1664], C. 37, fo. 12, Her. Coll., and Guil. 137.

HARTOPP, ... of Cambridgeshire . . . . a confirmation . . . . Oct. 1617, by Camden. Harl. MS. 6095, fo. 36.

HARTOP, Sir Edward, of Buckminster, co. Leic., bart., confirmed by Segar. Add. MS. 12,225, fo. 54 ; Guil. 256.

HARTOPP, Thomas, of co. Leic., s. of Wᵐ, s. of Thoˢ, s. of Richᵈ, s. of John, of Kent, given 18 May 1596, by Lee. Add. MS. 14,295, fo. 29ᵇ ; Harl. MS. 1359, fo. 32 ; among G. Dethick's grants, Add. MS. 26,753, fo. 124.

HARTROW, Richard, gent., "of a valiant courage, possessing arms and martial powers" (prowess ?), confirmed 19 Mar. 1579-80, by Flower. MS. Ashm. 834, fo. 23, copy of grant, Bodleian Lib.; Guil. 373.

HARTSTONGE, Ralph (2nd s. of James), of South Repps, Norfolk, 1576, by Cooke, Clar. Bannerman's MS., No. 9, p. 453.

HARVEY, Tobiah, of Womersley, Yorks, and brothers, 18 Sept. 1688, by T. St. George, Gart., and J. Dugdale, Norr. Harl. MS. 6834, fo. 178 ; Grants IV., fo. 18, 54, John and Samuel, Grants IV., fo. 71, 20 Nov. 1690, by St. George, Gart.

„ Sir Daniel, of Comb Nevile, Surrey, ... by Segar. Add. MS. 12,225, fo. 54.

„ Dionise (or Dennis), an assist. govʳ of Raleigh city, Virginia, arms . . . . by W. Dethick, Gart. Q's Coll. Oxf. MS. 36, fo. 120.

HERVEY, James, of Mardiche, Essex, confirmed . . . . 1559. (Harvey's Grants), Add. MS. 16,940, fo. 33ᵇ.

HARVEY, George, Capt. in the troops in Ireland, of Malden, Essex, youngest son of Roger, confirmed 3 Dec. 1603, by W. Dethick, Gart., and Camden. East Anglian, ii., 80, copy of grant, Brit. Mus.

„ John and Samuel, Womersley, Yorks, 20 Nov. 1690, by T. St. George, Gart. Harl. MS. 6834, fo. 178 ; Grants IV., 71. See Tobiah above.

HASELL, Edward, Dalemains Dacres ,Cumbˡᵈ, 4 May 1699, by T. St. George, Gart. and Norr. Grants IV., 258.

HASELLFOOT, ... London . . . . 1656. Edmondson's Armory.

HASLAM, ... Nottingham . . . . by Cooke. Harl. MS. 1422, fo. 13ᵇ.

HASLEDON alias CARTER, Wᵐ, of Manington, by Camden. Le Neve's MS. 357.

HASLEWOOD, Edmund, of Northampton, gent., coat and crest. Barker's Grants, Harl. MS. 5846, fo. 48 ; Stowe MS. 692, fo. 53ᵇ.

HASTINGS, William, of Hinton, Northants, 10 July 1685, by Sir Wm. Dugdale and Clar. Harl. MS. 6834, fo. 78 ; Grants III., fo. 273 ; Lansd. MS. 867, fo. 52.

„ Sir John, of Gloucestershire . . . . coat. Barker's Grants, Harl. MS. 5846, fo. 58.

HASTINGES, Sir Robert, of Darbie and Nottinghamshire: or, a maunch "mawtallée" [? maltaillée] gules . . . . Barker's Grants, Harl. MS. 5846, fo. 57.

„ Sir Robert, of Cambridgeshire : erm., [on] a chief az. two mullets pierced or. Barker's Grants, 1526—49, Harl. MS. 5846, fo. 57ᵇ.

HATTCHER (HATCHER), John, of Cambridge, gift 1561. (Harvey's Grants), Add. MS. 16,940, fo. 26 ; Harl. MS. 1116, fo. 56.

HATTON, George, Fulwell, nʳ Gloucʳ, ... by Cooke. Stowe MS. 670, fo. 18ᵇ.

HAUGHTON, John, of Gunthorpe, Norfolk, ... by Camden. Harl. MS. 6095, fo. 40ᵇ ; Le Neve's MS. 354.

HAWLE (? HAULE or DE AULA), Henry, of Wye [co. Kent], Esq., s. of George, s. of Thomas, 23 Nov. 1584, by Cooke. Harl. MS. 1422, fo. 92 ; (of Maidstone, Kent, in Burke) Harl. MS. 1359, fo. 99 ; Add. MS. 4966, fo. 19ᵇ.

HAVERSHAM, Baron (Sir John Thompson, Bt.), supporters 10 June 1696, by T. St. George, Gart. Grants IV., fo. 215.

HAVERCHAMP, Henry, of London, descended out of Germany, 1591, by Cooke ; confirmed by Segar. Harl. MSS. 1422, fo. 14ᵇ, and 6179, fo. 3.

HAVERS, John, of Wynfarthing, Norfolk, 10 March 1568-9, by Cooke, Clar Harl. MS. 1085, fo. 51ᵇ.

HAWARD (see Edmund HEYWOOD), confirmed Jan. 1616-17, by Camden : arg., two bendlets within a border gu. ; impaling, arg., a talbot statant sa., collared or. Harl. MS. 6095, fo. 34.

„   Samuel, s. of William, s. of Stephen, of the Isle of Hartye (? Thanet), Kent, patent 25 May 1612, by Segar. Add. MS. 12,225, fo. 54ᵇ ; Harl. MS. 6110, fo. 25ᵇ ; Arch. Cant., vol. vi., docquet.

HAWE, Henry, of Dudlington, Norf., gent., grant 15 Nov., 2 Q. Eliz., 1560, by Sir G. Dethick, Gart. Harl. MS. 1359, fo. 80 ; 20ᵗʰ Nov. in Harl. MS. 1441, fo. 63 ; copy of grant, Q's Coll. Oxf. MS. 39, fo. 112 (145, fo. 4), and according to Harl. MS. 1085, fo. 45, by W. Harvey, Clar., 1 Dec. 1563 ; Grants I., 270.

HAWES, James, citizen and clothworker, London, granted 1 Sept. 1559, by Harvey. Cott. MS. Faust. E. 1, 17 ; Add. MS. 16,940, fo. 41ᵇ ; Guil. 305.

„   James, citizen and Alderm. of London, grant of arms and crest (10 March 1566-7 in docquet [Q's Coll. Oxf.] MS. 145, fo. 11ᵇ), by G. Dethick, Gart. Q's Coll. Oxf. MS. 36, fo. 121, copy of grant ; Grants I., 143 ; Harl. MS. 1441, fo. 68.

HAWYS, Roger, of London, ... by Wriothesley, Gart. Add. MS. 26,702, fo. 57.

HAWKEBORNE, Dʳ John, Abbot of Chichester, Hen. VII. Add. MSS. 5848, fo. 88, in pencil, and 26,702, fo. 50.

HAWKESTONE, ..., an esqnire to Lord Audley at the battle of Poictiers 1356. Parker's Gloss. of Heraldry, Chron. Table xiv., note, etc.

HAWKEY, Thomas and John, brothers, of Llanrawren in Cornwall, and to Reginald, cousin, 28 June 1657 (by Sir E. Bysshe). Harl. MS. 1105, fo. 15ᵇ ; aº 1656 in Harl. MS. 1470, fo. 138, copy of grant, Brit. Mus.

HAWKINS, ..., sa., a lyon passant or on waves of the sea in base ppr., or barry undée arg. and az., in chief three bezants . . . . by Segar. Add. MS. 12,225, fo. 54ᵇ.

„   John, of Plymouth, Devon (? Admiral), confirmed. (Harvey's Grants), Add. MS. 16,940, fo. 23ᵇ ; Stowe MS. 703, fo. 89ᵇ. [Arms were granted to Sir John Hawkins, of Plymouth, the Naval Commander, by Harvey, Clar., 8 Q. Eliz., 1565 ; a canton was added by Cooke, Clar., in 1571. Burke's Armory.]

HAWKYNS als FYSHER, Thomas, of the Manor of Hawkeneste, co. Warw., coat and crest, 38 H. VIII., 1546, by Barker. Harl. MS. 5846, fo. 54ᵇ ; Stowe MS. 692, fo. 55ᵇ.

HAWKYNS als FISHER, Grant of arms and crest 10 May, 2 Ed. VI., 1548, by Hawley. Q's Coll. Oxf. MS. 38, fo. 49, for copy of grant; Add. MS. 16,940, fo. 202 ; see Stowe MS. 703, fo. 89ᵇ.

HAWLE, Henry, of Wye, Kent . . . . by Cooke. Harl. MS. 1359, fo. 99 ; Add. MS. 4966, fo. 19ᵇ.

HAWLES, William, of the Isle of Wight, co. Southampton, s. and h. of William, of City of Winchester, etc., 10 May 1574, by Sir G. Dethick, Gart. Harl. MS. 5823, fo. 34, and Q's Coll. Oxf. MS. 145, fo. 34 ; Stowe MS. 703, fo. 37ᵇ.

HAWLETT, Richard, of Stonham, Kent, s. of John, s. of Richard, of Yorks, 12 Aug. 1559, by Harvey. Harl. MS. 1115, fo. 4. See HOWLETT.

HAWSE, John, citizen and Alderm. of London, 10 March 1566-7, by Sir G. Dethick. Harl. MS. 1441, fo. 68. See HAWES.

HAWTHEN (? or HAWTAYNE), Edward, of ye Leye in Oxford, crest 20 Oct. 1566, by Harvey. Harl. MS. 1422, fo. 23.

HAWTHORNE, Robert, and . . . . Greenfield his wife, allowed 1 May 1661, by Walker, Gart. Her. Coll. 40.

HAWTON, ..., Arg., three bars and two mullets in chief sa., a crescent for diff. . . . . by Segar. Add. MS. 12,225, fo. 55.

HAWTREY, William, of the Chequers, Bucks, crest . . . . Barker's Grants, Harl. MS. 5846, fo. 53 ; Stowe MS. 692, fo. 56.

HAYDOCK, Thomas, of Greywell, Southants, ... coat and crest. Barker's Grants, Harl. MS. 5846, fo. 54 ; Stowe MS. 692, fo. 55.

HAYDON, John, of Cadhay, Devon, and to George, of St. Mary Overey, also Devon, with his difference ; coat and crest . . . . Barker's Grants, Harl. MS. 5846, fo. 55.

HAYE, ... of Yorkshire, now of London, erm., on a chief az. two mullets or ; patent . . . . 1628, by Segar. Add. MS. 12,225, fo. 55ᵇ ; Harl. MSS. 6179, fo. 53ᵇ, and 6140, fo. 78ᵇ, as LANE.

HAY, Master John, of the noble family of Erroll in Scotland, certificate 26 Aug. 1675, by Erskine, Lyon K. of A. Harl. MS. 1172, fo. 42, copy of.

HAYES, ... 1641, by W. Ryley, Lanc. Herald. Stowe MS. 703, fo. 63.

  „   Sir James, Great Badgbury, Kent, 8 May 1689, by Sir T. St. George, Gart. and Clar. Harl. MS. 6834, fo. 178 ; Grants IV., fo. 33.

  „   James, citizen and salter of London (leatherseller in 1605), s. of Alexʳ Hayes of Windsor, granted 13 May 1662, by Sir Edwᵈ Bysshe, Clar. Harl. MS. 1470, fo. 128, copy of grant, Brit. Mus. ; Bysshe's Grants, fo. 3, Her. Coll. ; Harl. MS. 1105, fo. 17 ; Guil. 190. And to

  „   Thomas, of Windsor, senʳ, his brother.

  „   Thomas, of Islington, Middx., Esq., Vice Chamberlain of London, 15 Feb. 1541-2, by T. Hawley, Clar. Add. MSS. 16,940, fo. 202, and 709, fo. 78 (fo. 56).

  „   Sir Thomas, Knt., of London, quarterly coat, confirmed by Camden, 1613. Harl. MSS. 1422, fo. 111, and 6095, fo. 30ᵇ ; Guil. 185.

  „   William, of the Warderobe (and Litley, Cheshire), patent Dec. 1615, by Camden. Harl. MSS. 6095, fo. 39ᵇ, and 1422, fo. 40 ; Le Neve's MS. 348.

HAYNE, Thomas, of Fryer Whaddon, Dorset, confirmed quarterly of 4 and grant of a new crest 4 Sept. 1607, by Segar. Add. MS. 12,225, fo. 55ᵇ; Harl. MS. 1470, fo. 56, 95, for copy of crest grant ; Guil. 360; Harl. MS. 6140, fo. 76ᵇ.

HAYNES, Nicholas, of Hackney, Middx., 4th s. of Richard, of Reading, confirmed . . . . 1578, by Cooke. MS. Ashm. 858, fo. 204-6, and 840, fo. 399, copy of grant, Bodleian Lib. ; Guil. 411.

  „   Thomas, sergeant of the Vestry in H.M.'s Chapel Royal, 2 Oct. 1661, by Sir E. Walker, Gart. Her. Coll., fo. 42.

  „   William, of London, eld. s. of Richard, of Reading, Berks, gent., and of Thomasine his wife, dau. and coh. of John Horley (Foxley in Add. MS.) of Berks, gent. ; quarterly of 4, the 1st coat and crest is confirmed, and the 2nd (Foxley) is allowed by R. Cooke, Clar., 10 June 1578, 20 Eliz. Harl. MSS. 1359, fo. 15, and 1422, fo. 116ᵇ ; Add. MS. 14,295, fo. 10ᵇ.

HEYWARD, Edward, of the Inner Temple, gent., s. of . . . . Heyward of Kerdiston, Norfolk, 21 June 1611, by Camden. Harl. MS. 6095, fo. 15ᵇ ; Guil., p. 94 ; Harl. MS. 1085, fo. 40.

HAYWARD, Henry, late of Tandridge Court, Surrey, gent., s. of Thoˢ, s. of Richard, descended of Michael Hayward of Hayward Castle, Wales ; ? an exemplification and grant of crest 10 April 1592, by W. Dethick, Gart. Copy of grant, Q's Coll. Oxf. MS. 36, fo. 10 ; Stowe MS. 676, fo. 85ᵇ, 96ᵇ ; Harl. MS. 1561, fo. 162.

  „   John, Hutton, Essex, and Joseph and Marie, 20 Feb. 167¾, by Sir Wᵐ Dugdale and St. George, Norr. Harl. MS. 6834, fo. 178 ; Grants III., fo. 80, brother and sister.

  „   Peter, of Brocton, Salop, 1559, by Harvey. Harl. MS. 1116, fo. 66.

  „   Rowland, of Acton Rounde, Salop, Esq., confirmed 25 Feb. 1560-61, by Sir G. Dethick. Harl. MS. 1441, fo. 64 ; Q's Coll. Oxf. MS. 145, fo. 5ᵇ.

HAYWARD, William, of Little Wenlock, Salop, 20 June 1637, by Sir J. Borough, Gart. Add. MS. 14,293, fo. 117.
„ Thomas, als Cox, of Forthampton, co. Glonc., 26 May 1666, by Sir E. Bysshe. Harl. MS. 1105, fo. 42.
HAYWODE, Walter, 5 Hen. IV., 1403-4, grants his arms with lands to Jno. Fromonde. *See* FROMONDE.
HEAD, Richard, of City of Rochester, Esq., } 4 Feb. 1664-5, 16 Chas. II., by Sir E.
„ John, of Malden, Essex, clerk, } Bysshe, Clar. Harl. MS. 1105, fo.
„ James, of Strood, Kent, } 21ᵇ; Bysshe's Grants, 25; Harl. MS. } 6179, fo. 44ᵇ, 72ᵇ.
HEALY, Richard, of Wells, D.C.L., 7 April 1698, by T. St. George, Gart. and Clar. Grants IV., fo. 262.
HEATH, Francis, of London Stone, 7 May 1662, by Sir E. Bysshe, Clar. Harl. MS. 1105, fo. 40ᵇ; Bysshe's Grants, 26.
HETHE, John, of London, confirmed . . . . 1558. (Harvey's Grants), Add. MS. 16,940, fo. 7ᵇ.
„ John, of London, Warden of the Fleet, crest 4 Aug. 1588, by Cooke. Harl. MS. 1422, fo. 22.
HEATH, Robert, of Brasted, Kent (Recorder of the City of London), s. of Robert of Eatonbridge, s. of Robert of Linfield, Surrey, Esq., exemplified, ratified and confirmed . . . . by Camden. Harl. MS. 6095, fo. 36ᵇ.
HETHE, William, of Alverchurche, co. Worc., gift 1560? (Harvey's Grants), Add. MS. 16,940, fo. 18ᵇ.
HEATHER, ..., of Heather in Derbyshire, [by] Bysshe, Gart. Harl. MS. 6832, fo. 413ᵇ.
HEBDON, John, s. of John, heretofore citizen of London, a merchᵗ in Russia, etc., born at Almostcliff, Yorks, etc., and Thomas, his brother, also a merchᵗ in Russia; dated at Brussels 28 March, 1658-9, by Walker. Harl. MS. 1172, fo. 72; Add. MSS. 14,293, fo. 100, and 14,294, fo. 33ᵇ; Her. Coll., fo. 31.
HEBER, Raynolde, of Marton-in-Craven, Yorks, s. of Thomas, Esquire, given by William Dethick, Gart., and Camden, 16 May 1599, 41 Q. Eliz. Harl. MS. 1359, fo. 9ᵇ.
HEBLETHWAYTE, James, of Malton, Yorks, gent., gift 1570, by Sir G. Dethick, Gart. Harl. MS. 1359, fo. 35; Add. MSS. 14,290, fo. 40, and 12,454, fo. 36ᵇ; Q's Coll. Oxf. MS. 145, fo. 36ᵇ.
HECHINS, William, Kentesbury, Cornwall, 8 Q. Eliz., 1565-6, by Harvey, Clar. Harl. MS. 1079, fo. 27ᵇ.
HEDGES als LACY, William and Charles, 25 Nov. 1687. Grants III., 336; Stowe MS. 714, fo. 94ᵇ—103; Lansd. MS., arms only, 867, fo. 52. *See* LACY.
HELLARD als HIGHLORD, John, and his brother Zachary, of London, merchant, sons of John, also of London, s. of Wᵐ, of Woodbury, Devon, gent., grant 26 May, 5 Chas., 1630, by Segar. Add. MS. 12,225, fo. 56; Gnil. 36; Harl. MSS. 1441, fo. 160, 6140, fo. 64ᵇ, and 1476, fo. 37; Grants I., 369; Misc. Gen. et Her., 3rd S., iv., 37.
„ Peter, prior of the minors of Bridlington, Yorks, patent 1 Oct., 9 Ed. IV., 1469, by Thomas Holme, Norr. Harl. MS. 1359, fo. 15ᵇ; Add. MS. 14,295, fo. 6; Surtees Soc., XII., xxxviii.; copy of grant, Brit. Mus.; Grants II., 628, and Proceedings Soc. of Antiq., 1897, April 1, p. 343, copy original; Vincent MS. 157, fo. 560; Le Neve's MS. 2, 9 and 511.
HELYAR, (? Justus) William, Devon, 7 April 1607, by Camden: az., a cross florettée arg. betw. four mullets pierced or; Crest, a cock gules or sable in front of a cross florettée or. Sloane MS. 3485, fo. 11; called Heler of Barnstaple in Harl. MS. 5839, fo. 9, and Belvin in Harl. MSS. 1422, fo. 19ᵇ, and 6095, fo. 7; Harl. MS. 1441, fo. 123ᵇ; Le Neve's MS. 283.
HEMYNG, Thomas, of Hitchin, Herts, coat and crest . . . . Barker's Grants, Harl. MS. 5846, fo. 54ᵇ; Stowe MS. 692, fo. 55ᵇ.
HEMINGS, John, *see* HENINGS.

HENDER, William, of Botreaulx Castle, Cornwall, 20 Nov. 1589, by Cooke. Harl. MSS. 1359, fo. 97, 1422, fo. 94ᵇ, and 1079, fo. 84 ; Add. MS. 4966, fo. 89ᵇ.

HENN als HEXE, Sir Henry, Knt. and Bart., of Wingfield, Berks, 28 Dec. 1642, by Borough. Harl. MSS. 1105, fo. 58, and 1470, fo. 27, 48, copy of grant, Brit. Mus. (s. of Willm., of Dorking, see below).

HENE, William, alias ESME, Dorking, Surrey, gent., confirmed 7 May, 39 Eliz., 1597, by Wᵐ Dethick, Gart. MS. Ashm. 1131, fo. 206ᵃ, copy of grant, Bodleian Lib.

HENLEY or HENDLEGH, Robert, of Somerset, Esq. (High Sheriff), a patent 26 Feb. 1613-14, by Camden. Harl. MSS. 6095, fo. 29, and 1422, fo. 38ᵇ ; Guil. 366 ; Stowe MS. 670, fo. 181ᵇ.

HENDLEY, Walter, of Kent, coat and crest. Barker's Grants, Harl. MS. 5846, fo. 53 ; Stowe MS. 692, fo. 55 ; Harl. MS. 5887, fo. 2.

HENNING, ... of Poxwell, Dorset : Barry undée of 6 arg. and az., on a chief az. three plates. 20 May, 9 Jac., 1611, by Segar. Add. MS. 12,225, fo. 56 ; Guil. 104.

HENINGS [HEMINGS ?], John, of London, gent., server a long time to Q. Eliz., K. James, K. Chas., s. and h. of George, of Droitwich, co. Worc., confirmed 2 March 1629-30, by Segar. Grants I., 392 ; Add. MS. 12,225, fo. 56ᵇ, as Henings.

HENSHAW, Thomas, of London, s. of Robert, of Prestbury, Cheshire, s. of Edward, of same co. ; crest 26 June 1611, by Sir R. St. George, Norr. Grants II., 657 ; Harl. MSS. 1156, fo. 47ᵇ, and 1359, fo. 1ᵇ, as HINCKSHAWE, which see ; a silkman, Harl. MS. 6140, fo. 39ᵇ.

HENSLEY, Richard, Capt. of the Pioners at the siege of Kinsale in Munster against the invading Spaniards and rebellious Irish. Dublin, 25 April 1602, by Danˡ Molyneux, Ulster K. of A. Harl. MS. 1441, fo. 9 ; Nichols' Leic., 4th pt., 272, copy of grant in Brit. Mus.

HENSLOWE, Thomas, of West Burhurst, Hants, s. of Raphe, etc., confirmed Feb. 1591-2 at the Office of Arms, by W. Dethick, Gart. Stowe MS. 676, fo. 87, 98 ; copy of patent, Q's Coll. Oxf. MS. 36, fo. 14 ; Misc. Gen. et Her., 2nd S., vol. iv., p. 350.

HENXMAN, Edward, als LE HENCHMAN, gent., patent dated at Windsor 24 April 1549, 3 Ed. VI., by Barker. Harl. MS. 1359, fo. 82 ; Le Neve's MS. 42.

HEPBURN als RICHARDSON, ... one of the grooms of the Privy Chamber to K. James, confirmed . . . . 1608, by Camden. Harl. MS. 6095, fo. 36ᵇ.

HEPDEN, ... of Essex, erm., five fusils conjoined in fesse gu., by Segar. Add. MS. 12,229, fo. 56ᵇ.

HERBERT, of Caerbury (? Henry), Baron ; Suppʳˢ 25 May 1694, by T. St. George, Gart. Grants IV., 167, V., 5 ; copy of grant, Brit. Mus., Add. MS. 31,896, fo. 85ᵇ.

  „ Edward, Baron Herbert, of Castle island, Ireland, arms and crest confirmed and grant of supporters 10 Jan. 1624, by Segar. Add. MS. 12,225, fo. 58 ; Misc. Gen. et Her., 2nd S., ii., p. 169, gives 1624 ; Powysland Club, v. 165 ; Le Neve's MS. 502.

  „ Sir George, of Swansea, co. Glamorgan, Knt. (s. of Richard, a natural son of Wᵐ, Earl of Pembroke), coat and crest . . . . Barker's Grants, Harl. MS. 5846, fo. 53ᵇ ; Stowe MS. 692, fo. 55.

  „ John, of Cardiff, co. Glamorgan, gent., 13 Nov. 1574, by W. Dethick, York Her. Le Neve's MS. 213.

  „ John, of Overton, Yorks, J.P. and quorum . . . . 1563, by Flower ; died s.p. Harl. MS. 1453, fo. 74 ; Stowe MS. 706, fo. 8ᵇ, by Dalton (who died in 1561).

  „ als ROBERTS, John, of Cardiff, co. Glamorgan, gent., grant 13 Nov. 1574, by Wᵐ Dethick, York Herald. Copy of grant, Q's Coll. Oxf. MS. 37, fo. 56. See ROBERTS.

R

HERBERT, Thomas, city of York, s. of Christopher, s. of Richard, of York, 29 April 1614, by R. St. George, Norr. Stowe MS. 706, fo. 16ᵇ ; Harl. MSS. 6179, fo. 11, and 6140, fo. 73.

  „   Sir William, Knt., Master of the King's horse (server to the King's Majesty, 2ⁿᵈ son to Richᵈ, natural son of William, Earl of Pembroke, Stowe MS.), coat and crest. Barker's Grants, Harl. MS. 5846, fo. 53ᵇ ; Stowe MS. 692, fo. 55 (in a later hand).

HERD, Richard, of London, ... by G. Dethick, Gart. Harl. MS. 1441, fo. 79 : argt., a chev. gu. betw. three water bougets sa. ; crest, a demi-goat saliant ppr., etc. Stowe MS. 703, fo. 35ᵇ.

HERD, Richard, and ⎫ sons of Thomas Herde, s. of Wᵐ, of London, etc. (granted
  „   Thomas,   ⎭ by Sir G. Dethick and) exemplified 23 April 1589, with the motto " moderata durant," by W. Dethick, Gart. Stowe MS. 676, fo. 77 ; copy of exemplification in Q's Coll. Oxf. MS. 37, fo. 112, and MS. 145, fo. 30, a new coat (the other being also borne by the name of Busshell) : argt., on a chev. gu. three crescents or between three lozenges sa. ; crest, as above, etc.

HEREFORD, City of, augmentation of arms, crest, suppʳˢ and motto for valiant defence against the Scots ; given at Oxford, 16 Sept. 1645, by Walker. Add. MSS. 14,293, fo. 108, and 14,294, fo. 36 ; Harl. MS. 1172, fo. 73 ; Dingley's Hist. from Marble, pt. I., p. ccxii., Camden Soc.

HERMAN, Edmond, one of the grooms of the Privy Chamber ; of the parish of Langley Marish, Bucks, coat and crest . . . . Barker's Grants, Harl. MS. 5846, fo. 54 ; Stowe MS. 692, fo. 55ᵇ.

  „   Nicholas, of Middleton Storry, Oxford, confirmed 10 Dec. 1630, by Segar. Add. MS. 12,225, fo. 57 ; Guil. 289 ; Harl. MS. 6140, fo. 64ᵇ.

HERON, Giles, Chipchase, Northumbld., crest confirmed . . . . 15 . . . . by (L. Dalton, Norr.). Add. MS. 16,940, fo. 26ᵇ.

  „   James, of Eyling Green, par. of Hamsted Norris, Berks, 1 June 1652, by E. Bysshe, Gart. Harl. MS. 1441, fo. 162ᵇ, copy of grant, Brit. Mus.

HERRICK, Robert, and ⎫ sons of John, of Haughton, co. Leic., confirmation of crest
  „   William,   ⎭ 8 May 1598, by W. Dethick, Gart. and Camden. Harl. MS. 5887, fo. 105 ; Misc. Gen. et Her., 2nd S., i., p. 34. copy of grant, Brit. Mus.

  „   Sir William, Knighted by K. James, and his goldsmith, patent . . . . 1605, by Segar and Camden. Add. MS. 12,225, fo. 57 ; Harl. MS. 6095, fo. 22 ; Guil. 40 ; Harl. MSS. 5887, fo. 90ᵇ, and 6140, fo. 81.

HERRYS, Arthur, of Crixsey, co. Essex, esq., 3rd s. of Wᵐ of Southminster, esq., s. of John, of Prytwell, Essex, crest granted 19 or 29 Nov. 1578 to the posterity of John for ever, by Flower. MS. Ashm. 834, fo. 20, and 844, fo. 9, copy of grant, Bodleian Lib., and Q's Coll. Oxf. MS. 38, fo. 97 ; Harl. MS. 1359, fo. 59 ; Guil. 136 ; Grants II., 623, and in Brit. Mus., Harl. MS. 1116, fo. 38.

HERRIS, Arthur, of Hartfordshire, quarterly Arms . . . . by Cooke. Add. MS. 4966, fo. 58ᵇ ; Harl. MS. 1359, fo. 92.

HERTER, Col. Philip, a German who served in the King's army, augmentation at the Hagne 4 June 1649, by Walker. Her. Coll., fo. 27.

HESKETH, Sir Thomas, of Rufford, co. Lanc., Knt., s. and h. of Robt., alteration of crest confirmed 30 Nov. 1561, by Dalton, Norr.: quarterly of 8. Harl. MS. 1359, fo. 52.

HESSE, John Van, lord of Piershill and Werna in Holland, patent 1 Jas. I., ... Feb. 1621. Add. MS. 6297, fo. 309 ; MS. Ashm. 858, fo. 88. See VAN HESSE.

HESTERCOMBE, see WARRE of Hestercombe.

HEWITT, ... 1586, by Cooke (see HUETT). Harl. MS. 1359, fo. 119 : or, on a pile gu. three escallops of the field. Add. MS. 4966, fo. 90.

HEWETT, Charles, of Dublin, gent., late deputy there of the Queen's Majesties wars, and comptroller-genl. for H.M.'s imports, etc. (? coat confirmed) and crest granted 10 Dec. 1597, by W. Dethick, Gart.   Q's Coll. Oxf. MS. 36, fo. 75, for copy of patent.

HEWETT (George), Visct. of Gowran and Baron of Jamestown, supporters 4 May 1689, by T. St. George, Gart.   Harl. MS. 6831, fo. 178; Grants IV., fo. 35; Stowe MS. 590, fo. 3, 4.

„   Sir Thomas, Shircoaks, Notts, old arms restored 12 June 1618, by R. St. George, Norr.   Harl. MS. 1422, fo. 16; copy, Brit. Mus., Add. MS. 5524, fo. 206, gules, a chevron, etc.

HEWET, Sir William, Maior of London; 4 Nov. 1553, by ? Hawley.   Add. MS. 16,940, fo. 206ᵇ.

HUETT, William, of Milbroke, Beds, esq., grant 1 May 1579, and to issue of Robert his father, by Cooke.   Harl. MS. 1441, fo. 10, entered in Bedf. Vis., 1634, copy of grant in Brit. Mus.

HEWETT, William, of London, crest 20 May 1598, by W. Dethick, Gart.   Harl. MS. 1422, fo. 23.   (See Charles HEWETT.)

HEWSE, HEWESE, see HUGHES.

HEYDON, Martha, late wife of John, late Sheriff and Alderm. of London, and dau. of Nicholas Rose of London, grant 10 Jan. 1582-3, by Cooke.   Stowe MS. 676, fo. 60; Q's Coll. Oxf. MS. 37, fo. 83, for copy of grant.   (See also ROSE.)

HEYES, George, of Ratingden, Essex, gent., grant 2 Aug. 1563, by Sir G. Dethick.   Harl. MS. 1441, fo. 65; Q's Coll. Oxf. MS. 145, fo. 7ᵇ; called Leys in Grants II., 652.   See LEYS.

HEYGATE, see HIGHGATE.

HEYMAN, Peter, of Sellinge, Kent, gent., 1 May 1547, by T. Hawley, Clar.   Add. MSS. 16,940, fo. 202, and 7098, fo. 78.

HEYNES, Simon, of Mildenhall, Suff., s. of John, gent., confirmed 20 Sept. 1575, by Cooke.   Original in Public R. O., Lond., copied 24 March 1638-9.   See Stowe MS. 677, fo. 13; Misc. Gen. et Her., i., 250; copy of grant, Q's Coll. Oxf. MS. 38, fo. 93; Guil. 332; Grants II., 525.

HEYNSHAM or HEYNSHAW, see HINSHAM, EYNSHAM and KEINSHAM, John.   See Stowe MS. 703, fo. 13.

HEYWARD, Edward, see HAYWARD.

HEYWOOD, Edmund, of London, descended from Heywood of Mottram, Cheshire, confirmed June 1616, by Camden; exemplified impaling the arms of Magdalen Wiburbury, his wife.   Stowe MS. 677, fo. 7; Haward in Harl. MS. 6095, fo. 34.

HICHAM, Sir Robert, Attorney to Q. Anne, a confirmation, crest given 1604, by Camden.   Harl. MSS. 6095, fo. 21ᵇ, and 5887, fo. 55ᵇ.

HICKES, Baptist, grant of supporters . . . . probably by Segar.   Add. MS. 12,225, fo. 57ᵇ.

HICKES, Sir Michael, and   } Knts., sons of Robert Hickes of London, Esq., by
„   Sir Baptist, of London,   } Julia, the dau. of William Arthur of Clapham, Somerset, Esq., 1 Feb. 1604-5, by Camden.   Cott. MS. Faust. E. 1, 60ᵇ; Harl. MSS. 6095, fo. 4, 1422, fo. 18ᵇ, and 5887, fo. 90ᵇ.

„   Thomas, an apothecary of London in Fleet St., sett out by Vincent . . . .   Harl. MS. 1422, fo. 14ᵇ.

„   William, esq., s. and h. of Sir Michael, Knt., dec⁴, testified 1619, by Segar, R. St. George, Norr., H. St. George, Richmond, and Brooke, York Herald.   Add. MS. 12,225, fo. 57ᵇ; Grants I., 428, Her. Coll., and Guil. 128.

HICKIE, Michael, gent., sec. to Henry, Earl of Thomond, 18 April 1688, by R. Carney, Ulster K. of A.   Grants II., 463.

HICKMAN, Henry, D.C.L. and Chancellor to the Ld. Bp. of Peterborough, s. of Anthony, of London, citizen, s. of Walter, of Woodford Hall, Essex, etc., arms confirmed and crest granted 1 Dec. 1590 to William, Walter, Henry, D.C.L., Anthony, Eleazar and Matthew, gent., sons of Anthony, by W. Dethick, Gart. Q's Coll. Oxf. MS. 36, fo. 2, copy of grant ; Stowe MS. 676, fo. 83ᵇ and 92ᵇ. (Harl. MSS. 1453, fo. 32ᵇ, and 3526, fo. 141ᵇ : arms with a crest, by W. Dethick, Gart., for which he had 10ˡ ; this coate is the auncient arms of Byrmingham ; entered by R. Brooke, York Herald.)

HICKMOTT, John, of Kent, ... by Barker. Add. MS. 26,702, fo. 1.

HIGFORD, Henry, of Boxley, Kent, 10 Feb. 1663-4. Bysshe's Grants, fo. 7, Her. Coll. ; Harl. MS. 1105, fo. 18.

HIGHGATE, Reignold, of Fearing, Essex, coat and crest, confirmed 9 Nov. 1549. Add. MS. 14,295, fo. 100 ; Barker's Grants, Harl. MS. 5846, fo. 56ᵇ ; Stowe MS. 692, fo. 56 ; allowed at the Visitation of London, 1634 and 1687, to the Heygate Family, a tortean for distinction.

HIGHLORD, *see* HELLARD.

HIGHMORE, Abraham, sometime Major and Lient.-Col. in the service of Chas. I., s. and h. of Edward, rector of Stickland, Dorset, s. and h. of Richard, rector of Hinton Martell, Dorset, 28 July 1683, with remrʳ to the heirs of his grandfather, by Sir Wᵐ Dugdale, Gart., and Sir H. St. George, Clar. Harl. MS. 6179, fo. 75 ; Add. MS. 14,830, fo. 104 ; Grants III., fo. 200, and ped. 2, D. 14, fo. 167, Her. Coll. ; Harl. MS. 6832, fo. 212.

HILL, ... of London, gn., two bars erm. on a chief . . . . a lion passant or ; Crest, a lion statant or between a pair of wings gn. charged with two bars erm. . . . . by Camden. Harl. MS. 6095, fo. 25ᵇ ; and Customer of Yarmouth Harl. MS. 1422, fo. 42.

„ Daniel, M.A., Prebend. of Rochester, 5 July 1699, by T. St. George, Gart. and Clar. Grants IV., fo. 295 ; Stowe MS. 693, fo. 5ᵇ.

„ Coat quartered by Ro. Bynge, which *see*, by Cooke. Harl. MS. 1359, fo. 89ᵇ ; Add. MS. 4966, fo. 35ᵇ.

„ Elizabeth, dau. to John Hill and wife to Davy Woodruff of London, gift . . . 1561, 3 Q. Eliz. (Harvey's Grants), Add. MS. 16,940, fo. 19ᵇ.

„ { Alice, ux. Reginald Corbett, Justice C.B., daughter of
„ { Jane, elder sister of Sir Rowland, and wife of John Gratewood ;
„ { Elizabeth, younger sister of Sir Rowland, and wife of John Barker ; 3 Nov. 1562, to the descendants of Jane and Elizabeth. By Harvey. MS. Ashm. 834, fo. 47, copy of grant, Bodleian Lib., and Q's Coll. Oxf. MS. 37, fo. 40 ; Grants II., 559 ; Proc. Soc. Antiq., 1897, 2nd S., xvii., p. 350.

„ Humphrey, Sillvington als Silton, Salop, by Cooke's depʸ. Stowe MS. 670, fo. 9.

„ John, als DE LA HULL, of Little Pype, co. Staff., grant 12 May 1560, by Sir G. Dethick, Gart. MS. Ashm. 858, fo. 116, 117, copy of grant, Bodleian Lib.

HILLS, John, of London, auditor . . . . by Cooke. Harl. MSS. 1422, fo. 42, and 1359, fo. 109, auditor, sa., a chevron betw. three leopards' faces sable ; Add. MS. 4966, fo. 57.

HILL or HILLS, John, of London, gent., 15 March 1586, by Cooke. Harl. MS. 1422, fo. 42 ; Stowe MS. 714, fo. 100, copy of grant, Brit. Mus. ; Harl. MSS. 1422, fo. 42, and 1359, fo. 109 ; Guil. 197, sable, a chevron betw. three cats argt., etc. ; Add. MS. 4966, fo. 30ᵇ.

„ Nicholas, of Bromesgrove, Worc., 10 Aug. 1560, by Sir G. Dethick, Gart. Harl. MSS. 1441, fo. 100, and 5847, fo. 48ᵇ, and Q's Coll. Oxf. MS. 145, fo. 49ᵇ ; Harl. MS. 5887, fo. 25.

„ Richard, of Dorney, Bucks, sa., on a fess arg. betw. three cats of Montaigne (cats-a-mountain) passant or a cross sarcellic betw. two coquilles (cocks) gu., crest ; coat and crest. Barker's Grants, Harl. MS. 5846, fo. 46 and 47ᵇ.

„ Richard, of Paxton, Somt. . . . . by Cooke. Stowe MS. 670, fo. 26.

HILL or HILLS, Richard, of Sutton, Surrey, s. of William, by Cooke, 1588.   Stowe
　　MS. 670, fo. 24[b], 25, impaling Morley fo. 24[b], and Onslow fo. 25.
　„　Robert, D.D., s. of Ralph, of Ashbourne, co. Derby, patent Nov. 1615, by
　　Camden.   Harl. MSS. 6095, fo. 40, and 1422, fo. 40 ; Guil. 394 ; Le
　　Neve's MS. 349.
　„　Sir Rowland, of London, maior . . . . coat . . . .   Barker's Grants, Harl. MS.
　　5846, fo. 46[b], see a grant by Harvey, Clar., 3 Nov. 1562, to the descendants
　　of his sisters Jane, wife of John Gratewood, and Eliz[th], wife of John
　　Barker, copy of grant, Bodleian Lib. ; Grants II., 559.   See Jane and
　　Eliz[th] HILL above.
HILLERSDEN, Thomas, of Hocklife, Beds, gift of crest . . . . 1596, by Lee.   Add.
　　MS. 14,295, fo. 121[b] ; Harl. MSS. 1422, fo. 95[b], and 1359, fo. 39.
HINCKSHAWE, Thomas, of London, silkman, by Rich[d] St. George, Norr., crest
　　26 June 1611.   Harl. MSS. 1359, fo. 1[a], and 1156, fo. 47[b], as Henshaw.
HINDMARSH (?) . . . . by Sir G. Dethick.   Q's Coll. Oxf. MS. 145, fo. 52.
HINSHAM, HINSHAW or HEYNSHAW, John, of Chichester, " being one of the
　　Queenes yeomen of the seller," 20 Dec. 1565, by Sir G. Dethick.   Harl.
　　MS. 1441, fo. 67 ; Heynsham in Q's Coll. Oxf. MS. 145, fo. 10 (or
　　HENYSHAW, which see).
HINXMAN, Edward, see HENXMAN, 1549.   Burke's Armory.
HIPPESLEY, John, of Cameligh, Somerset, confirmed . . . . 1564, 6 Q. E.   (Harvey's
　　Grants), Add. MS. 16,940, fo. 33[b] ; Harl. MS. 5887, fo. 34[b], with quartering
　　and impalement.
HITCHCOCK als ARRAS, George, s. of Robert, of Bucks, 30 Nov. 1560, by Dalton,
　　Norr.   Add. MS. 16,940, fo. 22 ; Harl. MSS. 1359, fo. 14[b], and 1422,
　　fo. 107[b].
HITE, William, of Gotehurst, Somerset,　　｜1 June 1663.   Bysshe's Grants,
　„　Thomas, ｝of Staplegrove, Somersetsh.,　｝fo. 11, Her. Coll. ; Harl. MS.
　„　John,　　　　　　　　　　　　　　 ｜1105, fo. 19.
HIXON, Thomas, of Greenwich, gent., Keeper of His Majesties Standing Wardrobe
　　theire, confirmed . . . . 1617, by Camden ; exemplified, ratified and con-
　　firmed arms of Hixon of co. Camb.   Harl. MS. 6095, fo. 36[b] ; Guil. 217 ;
　　impaling Cave, 4 quarters, Harl. MS. 5887, fo. 100[b].
HOBBS, Thomas, of Gray's Inn, 12 Nov. 1603, by Camden.   Morgan's Sphere, 117.
　„　Thomas, of St. Clement Danes, Middx., Chirurgeon to the King, crest 9 June
　　1687, by Sir T. St. George and H. St. George, Clar.   Harl. MS. 6834,
　　fo. 178 ; Grants III., fo. 314 ; Stowe MS. 677, fo. 69 ; Harl. MSS. 1172,
　　fo. 54[b], 6179, fo. 63, and 1085, fo. 58 ; Lansd. MS. 867, fo. 52.
HOBSON, Thomas, s. of Thomas, of Merington, Bpk. of Durham, gent., granted
　　16 Jan. 1657-8, by Ryley.   Harl. MS. 1470, fo. 145, copy of grant, Brit.
　　Mus. ; (1648, probably an error for 1657-8, in Harl. MS. 1105, fo. 11) ;
　　Guil. 357.
HOBY, Edward, s. of [Sir] Thomas, of Bisham, co. Berks, exemplified 10 June 1570,
　　by Sir G. Dethick, Gart.   MS. Ashm. 858, pp. 230-2, copy of grant,
　　Bodleian Lib., and in Q's Coll. Oxf. MS. 37, fo. 70.
HOBBY, [Sir] Edward, s. of Sir Edward, Kt. (of Thomas, as above) (also in his
　　lifetime was sent embassador to ye French King), quarterly of 6 ; 6 June
　　1580 [? 1570, as above], by Sir G. Dethick, Gart.   Harl. MSS. 1441,
　　fo. 100, and 5847, fo. 48[b] ; Grants I., 69, patent in Latin as Hoby ; 1581
　　in Q's Coll. Oxf. MS. 145, fo. 49[b] ; crest, Stowe MS. 676, fo. 52[b].
HOBY, Peregrine, of Bysham, Berks, natural son of Sir Edward, of Bisham, Berks,
　　17 Nov. 1664.   Harl. MS. 1105, fo. 20[b] ; Bysshe's Grants, fo. 20, Her.
　　Coll. ; MS. Ashm. 840, fo. 433-5, copy of grant, Bodleian Lib. ; Harl. MS.
　　1115, fo. 69, copy of grant, Brit. Mus.
HODDESDON, otherwise BARNET, Robert, of Herts, confirmed and granted 1 May,
　　30 Hy. VI., 1452, by (? Leigh), Clar.   Stowe MS. 714, fo. 172, copy of
　　grant, Brit. Mus. ; Grants II., 463.

HODGES, ... of London, ... Oct. 1610, by Camden : or, three crescents sa., on a canton of the 2ᵈ a crown of the 1ˢᵗ ; patent. Harl. MS. 1422, fo. 21ᵇ ; Her. and Geneal., iv., p. 96 ; Harl. MS. 6095, fo. 13, copy of grant, Brit. Mus.

HODGIS, Richard, of Highgatt, Middx., gift .... 1561. (Harvey's Grants), Add. MS. 16,940, fo. 20ᵇ.

HODGES, William, s. and h. app. to Owen Hodges, steward of the Household to Prince Ludovic, Duke of Richmond and Lenox, and afterwards steward of ye household to his brother Edmund (gallice Esmé), Duke of Lenox and Earl of March ; which Owen was s. and h. of Roger, of Ilminster, Somerset, esq. ; confirmed 31 Dec. 1628, by Segar. Add. MS. 12,225, fo. 58.

  „ Sir William, of Middx., Bart., now of Cadiz, 23 Nov. 1698, by T. St. George, Gart. and Clar. Add. MS. 14,830, fo. 112, and Grants IV., fo. 287, maried Sarah HALL, see.

HODGKINSON, Richard, of London, ... by Segar. Add. MS. 12,225, fo. 58ᵇ ; Guil. 138 ; Harl. MSS. 6140, fo. 58ᵇ, 1105, fo. 13, and 1441, fo. 162.

HODGSON, ... (Sussex), erm., on a chief gu. three cutlasses erect arg., hilted or ; quartering Goldsmith .... 1628, by Segar. Add. MS. 12,225, fo. 58ᵇ ; Harl. MSS. 1076, fo. 201, and 5887, fo. 115.

  „ (Essex) .... 1631 .... Burke's Armory.

HODSHON, Richard, Alderm. of Newc.-on-Tyne, 15 Aug. 1575, by Flower. Harl. MSS. 1453, fo. 74, and 5887, fo. 97ᵇ.

HODSON, Christopher, of Cambridge, gent., s. of Henry, of ye same, crest 28 July 1592, by Cooke. Harl. MS. 1359, fo. 101ᵇ ; Stowe MS. 714, fo. 148, fo. 91 says 18ᵗʰ July.

HOET, Peter, of London, mercht.. 22 March 1663-4. Harl. MSS. 1105, fo. 17ᵇ, and 1470, fo. 122, copy of grant, Brit. Mus. ; Bysshe's Grants, fo. 6, Her. Coll. ; Guil. 130.

HOGHTON, Richard, of Park Hall, co. Lanc., crest 2 Nov. 1606, by R. St. George, Norr. 20ᵗʰ Novr. in Add. MS. 14,295, fo. 60ᵇ ; Misc. Gen. et Her., 3rd S., vol. i., p. 193 ; Harl. MS. 5887, fo. 49.

HOLBECH, Edward, Satcliffe, co. Linc., ... by Cooke. Stowe MS. 670, fo. 17.

HOBECHE, Thomas, of Stowe, co. Linc., same coat as the last, 14 Jan. 1586-7, by Cooke. Add. MS. 4966, fo. 65 ; Harl. MSS. 1359, fo. 91ᵇ, and 1422, fo. 93 : Surtees Soc., XLI., xlii., copy of grant, and Harl. MS. 1172, fo. 7, 22. See RANDES, Thomas.

HOLBECK, Roger, of Wichingham, Norfolk, s. of Thomas, of Westhall, Suff., confirmed .... June 1613, by Camden. Harl. MS. 6095, fo. 27 ; Guil. 248.

HOLDEN, Ralph, of Holden, Lanc., by Dalton, Norr. Add. MS. 14,295, fo. 76ᵇ (94ᵇ).

HOLDEN, Robert, of Hockridge in Cranborne, Kent, 20 May 1663. Harl. MS. 1105, fo. 17ᵇ ; Add. MS. 14,293, fo. 3 ; Bysshe's Grants, fo. 6, Her. Coll. ; Guil. 117 ; Harl. MS. 6179, fo. 62.

HOLDERNESSE, John Ramsy, Lord R., Visct. Haddington and Earl of, dated at ye great scale 22 Jan., 18 Jac. I., 1620-1. Harl. MS. 1507, fo. 424, and Q's Coll. Oxf. MS. 38, fo. 132, copy of Roy. Warrant, etc.

HOLES, Thomas de, arms from Domvile by deed 16 Rich. II., 1392-3. Harl. MS. 1988, fo. 12ᵇ ; Norfolk Arch. Soc., vii., 319 ; Misc. Gen. et Her., N. S., i., 188.

HOLFORD, William, of Welham, co. Leic., esq., High Sheriff 1616, alteration, etc.,

  „ Richard, of Edith Weston, co. Rutland, and

  „ Richard, of Wistow, co. Leic., High Sheriff co. Leic.,

1 Jan. 1621-2, by Camden. Harl. MS. 1507, fo. 386, and Q's Coll. Oxf. MS. 38, fo. 134, copy of grant ; Morgan's Sphere of Gentry, 118 ; Harl. MS. 5887, fo. 110 ; Le Neve's MS. 386.

HOLGILL, ... Master of the Savoy, ... Add. MS. 26,702, fo. 55.

HOLL, Thomas, of Aylsham, Norfolk, 26 Aug. 1576, by Cooke, Clar.   Bannerman's
   MS., No. 9, fo. 452.
HOLLAND, George, West Angmering, Sussex, 14 June 1581, by G. Dethick, Gart.
   Harl. MS. 1562, fo. 144ᵇ.
   „   John, ... az., semée-de-lis a lion rampant guardant arg. . . . . 1583, by
      R. Glover, Somerset;   18 May 1601, by Camden ;   19 May 1601, by Segar.
      Add. MS. 12,225, fo. 59.
   „   Joseph, ... 28 Dec. 1588, by Cooke or W. Dethick.   Harl. MS. 1122,
      fo. 121ᵇ, azure, a lyon rampant guardant argent.
   „   Thomas, maior of Dartmouth, Devon, gent., s. of Robᵗ, s. of Wᵐ, grant
      20 June 1599, by W. Dethick, Gart. (and ? Camden).   Stowe MS. 676,
      fo. 130ᵇ ; Q's Coll. Oxf. MS. 36, fo. 81, copy of grant.
HOLLES, see HOLES and HOLLIS.
HOLLOND, Sir Thomas, of Berow in Anglesey (confirmed 25 Nov. 1635, Egerton
   MS. 2586, fo. 125), by J. Borough, Gart.   Harl. MS. 1105, fo. 56 ; Add.
   MS. 26,702, fo. 91.
HOLLIDAY, Sir Leonard, see HALLIDAY.
   „   William, of London, grant 13 Feb. 1623-4, 21 Jac. I., in Latin, by Borough,
      Norr.   MS. Ashm. 857, fo. 502-3, copy of grant, Bodleian Lib. ; Add. MS.
      14,295, fo. 117ᵇ (granted by J. Borough when Norroy, for this he was
      questioned before the Earl Marshal, it being in the province of Clarenceux) ;
      Harl. MS. 1507, fo. 389, copy of grant, Brit. Mus., and Q's Coll. Oxf. MS.
      38, fo. 137 ; Le Neve's MS. 89, 280, 389.
HOLLYNSHED, Hugh, als HOLLYNSIDE, of Bosley, Cheshire, lord of the Manor of
   Heyton, Staff., arm., crest, "a Bonocus head," etc. (see also CANDETOR ?) ;
   granted crest 1 July, 2 Q. Eliz., 1560, by Sir G. Dethick, Gart.   Harl. MS.
   1359, fo. 79ᵇ ;   MS. Ashm. 858, fo. 148, copy of grant, Bodleian Lib., and
   Q's Coll. Oxf. MS. 39, fo. 108 ;   Grants I., 254, "original grant in Brit.
   Mus.," "argent, a cross sable, a canton ermines."
HOLLYS, ... crest . . . . (? 24 May 1550, Burke).   Barker's Grants . . . . Harl.
   MS. 5846, fo. 51ᵇ ; Stowe MS. 692, fo. 54ᵇ.
HOLLES, Gervase, augmentation 4 Dec. 1649 by letters patent of that date from
   Chas. II. ; alteration Jan. 1649-50 at Jersey.   MS. Ashm. 858, fo. 57—59,
   copy, Bodleian Lib. ; by Sir E. Walker, Gart., Jan. 1649-50, Her. Coll. 2.
HOLLIS, William, of co. Notts, Knt., 24 May 1563, 5 Eliz., by Sir G. Dethick.
   Harl. MS. 1441, fo. 66ᵇ ; 1550 in Q's Coll. Oxf. MS. 145, fo. 10.
HOLLYS, Sir William, of Haughton, Notts, crest, 13 June 1587, by Flower.   MS.
   Ashm. 834, fo. 70, copy of grant, Bodleian Lib. ; Harl. MS. 5887, fo. 35.
HOLLOWAY, John, esq., Controller of the Customs House, London, arms signed by
   Segar, Gart.   Add. MS. 4966, fo. 26.
   „   Henry, by St. George.   Harl. MS. 1105, fo. 9ᵇ.   See also HALLOWAY.
HOLLMAN, George, of Devonshire, a councillor of Lincoln's Inn ;   July 1607, by
   Camden.   Harl. MSS. 1422, fo. 20ᵇ, and 6095, fo. 10ᵇ ; Caius Coll. Camb.
   MS. 551, fo. 31.
HOLMAN, George, of London, esq., 1606, by Camden, Clar.   Harl. MS. 1441,
   fo. 149.
HOLMDEN, Anthony, of Tenches, par. of Lingfield, Surrey, by Segar.   Add. MS.
   12,225, fo. 59ᵇ.
HOLMEDEN, John, of Surrey, now of London, 20 June 1577, 19 Q. Eliz., by Cooke.
   Harl. MSS. 1359, fo. 101, and 6140, fo. 53ᵇ ; Add. MS. 14,295, fo. 28ᵇ.
HOLME, ... of East Holme, co. Lanc., June 1613, by R. St. George, Norr.   Add.
   MS. 14,295, fo. 80 (see Harl. MS. 1422, fo. 80ᵇ) same coat, but crest
   (Harl. MS. 6140, fo. 74ᵇ) out of a ducal coronet or.   See HULME, William.
HOLMES, John, of North Mymms, Herts, crest 1 Nov. 1551, by Hawley.   Harl.
   MS. 1359, fo. 8 ; Add. MSS. 16,940, fo. 205, and 14,295, fo. 72ᵇ.
   „   Thomas, of co. Camb., confirmed . . . . 1558.   (Harvey's Grants), Add. MS.
      16,940, fo. 9ᵇ.

HOLMES, Sir Robert, Knt., 3rd s. of Henry, of Mallow, co. Cork, etc., Rear Adml.,
Capt, and Govr of the Isle of Wight. Harl. MS. 6179, fo. 24. Augmentation
19 Jan. 166⅝, by Walker. Add. MS. 14,294, fo. 29 ; Her. Coll., 65.

HOLSTOKE, William, of London, gift . . . . 1562. (Harvey's Grants), Add. MS.
16,940, fo. 31{b} ; Harl. MS. 5887, fo. 78.

HOLSTON, William, Suff., 24 March, 16 H. VIII., 1524-5, by Wriothesley and
Benolte, Clar. Add. MS. 26,702, fo. 56 ; Harl. MS. 1422, fo. 30{b} ; crest
granted by Barker, Harl. MS. 5846, fo. 51{b} ; Stowe MS. 692, fo. 54{b} ;
Harl. MS. 1116, fo. 41.

HOLTON or ERNLES ? (coat, but ? the crest), az., on a bend or three eagles displayed
gu. ; crest, a woman's head couped at the shoulders, crined, wreathed about
the temples . . . . (bust ppr., habited gu.), by Camden. Harl. MSS. 5839,
fo. 2, 2275, fo. 90, 1115, fo. 8, and 1422, fo. 17{b} (? Ernle, Stowe MS. 706,
fo. 25) ; Le Neve's MS. 270.

HOLYMAN, John, Bp. of Bristol, arms 20 Nov. 1554, by ? Hawley. Add. MS.
16,940, fo. 207.

HOMBRESTON, of co. Hereford, crest 6th June 1554, by Hervey, Clar. Le Neve's
MS. 493-4.

HONYWOOD, Sir William (?) [the whole entry scratched through except the name].

„ John, of Gray's Inn, coat and crest . . . . Barker's Grants, Harl. MS. 5846,
fo. 48.

„ Thomas, of Send Newington, Kent, and

„ Robert, of Petts, and to all descendants of John, of Casebourne, grandfather
of Thomas ; ? an alteration from a more confused bearing, 10 Nov. 1576,
by Cooke. MS. Ashm. 834, fo. 4{b}, copy of grant, Bodleian Lib. ; Guil. 221.

HOOKE, John, of Bramshot, Hants, confirmed, crest 20 Oct. 1600, by Wm Dethick,
Gart., and Camden. Add. MS. 14,295, fo. 87 ; Guil. 398 ; Harl. MSS.
6179, fo. 61, 1544, fo. 74, and 5887, fo. 6.

HOOPER or HOWPER, John, Bp. of Worcester and Gloucester, granted 5 Sept. 1552,
6 Ed. VI., by G. Dethick, Gart. Harl. MS. 1359, fo. 61{b} ; copy of patent,
Q's Coll. Oxf. MS. 39, fo. 44, burned 9 Feb. 1555-6 ; Grants L., 29 ; Harl.
MS. 1116, fo. 40{b}.

„ John, of city of New Sarum, Wilts, etc., confirmed quarterly coat, crest
granted 15 Nov. 1562, by Hervey. Add. MS. 14,295, fo. 86 ; Harl. MS.
1422, fo. 113 ; Add. MS. 16,940, fo. 45 ; Harl. MS. 1116, fo. 47{b}.

HOPE, Ralph, Yeoman of Her M.'s Robes, confirmed . . . . by Harvey. Harl. MS.
1422, fo. 82 ; Stowe MS. 706, fo. 20{b}, says mar. ye da. of Pigion.

HOPER, see HOOPER.

HOPERTON, Adam, of Gilshope, Yorks, crest 28 Aug. 1612, by R. St, George.
Surtees, XLI., xlvii. ; copy of grant, Brit. Mus., Harl. MS. 6179, fo. 13{b} ;
Harl. MS. 6440, fo. 72.

HORDE, George, London, ... 10 March 1558-9, by Harvey. Harl. MS. 1422,
fo. 22 ; Add. MS. 16,940, fo. 35.

HORDEN, see HARDEN.

„ Edward, s. of Alexander, of Horden, Kent, confirmed 1 Jan. 1586-7, by
W. Dethick, Gart. Harl. MS. 1422, fo. 108{b} ; Stowe MS. 676, fo. 67{b}, and
Q's Coll. Oxf. MS. 37, fo. 95, for copy of grant in Latin ; Add. MS.
26,702, fo. 1.

„ Thomas, of Kent, 24 May (14 H. VIII.) 1522, grant in French by
T. Wriothesley, Gart., and T. Benolte, Clar. Stowe MS. 706, fo. 11{b} ;
Add. MS. 26,702, fo. 1. Crest, by Barker, Gart. See also HARDEN.

HORNBROOKE, Richard, or HORNIBROOK (s. of Richard, of Exeter), of the lifeguards
of the horse, given 16 Dec. 1663, by Walker. Add. MSS. 14,293, fo. 49,
and 14,294, fo. 17 ; Harl. MS. 1172, fo. 56, grant of arms ; and [afterwards]
Bluemantle pursuivant at arms [1665, d. 1667], Guil. 403.

HORNE, ... crest . . . . Barker's Grants, Harl. MS. 5846, fo. 52{b} ; Stowe MS.
692, fo. 54{b}.

HORNE, Robert, Bp. of Winchester, arms only, 10 Feb., 3 Eliz., 1560-1, by G. Dethick, Gart. Grants I., 65; see Memo. in Le Neve's MS., fo. 428.

HORNEBY, Henry, of Linc. . . . . Add. MS. 26,702, fo. 67^b.

HORNER, Sir John, of Coleford, Som^t, Knt., coz. and heir of Sir Thos. Horner, Knt. . . . . 1584, by Cooke. Harl. MS. 1359, fo. 117; Add. MSS. 14,295, fo. 40^b, and 4966, fo. 28.

HORNYOLD, John, of Hanley Castle, co. Worc., crest confirmed . . . . 1560. (Harvey's Grants), Add. MS. 16,940, fo. 51.

HORSEMAN, ... arms, or, three galtraps gu.; crest, a cup or enflamed gu. . . . . 1590, by Cooke. Harl. MS. 1359, fo. 101.

  „ Robert, of Rypon in Yorkshire, now of London, 26 May 1590, by Cooke, Clar. Harl. MS. 1359, fo. 105; Stowe MS. 670, fo. 46^b; Add. MS. 14,297, fo. 16^b; Harl. MS. 6140, fo. 55. (Different coats.)

HORSEFALL, John, Ld. Bp. of Ossory in Ireland, granted . . . . Feb. 1591-2, by W. Dethick, Gart. Stowe MS. 676, fo. 85, 95^b; copy of grant, Q's Coll. Oxf. MS. 36, fo. 8.

HORSFALL, Richard, of Storrs Hall, York, 1612, by R. St. George, Norr. Harl. MS. 1422, fo. 14.

HORTE, see HARTE.

HORTON, ... crest . . . . Barker's Grants, Harl. MS. 5846, fo. 50; Stowe MS. 692, fo. 54.

HOSKINS, ... of co. Mon., barry of 6 or and vert, a bordure erm. . . . . by Segar. Add. MS. 12,225, fo. 59.

  „ Charles, of London, confirmed . . . . 1563. (Harvey's Grants), Add. MS. 16,940, fo. 29.

HOUGH, Ralph, of London, par. of St. Margaret, Lothbury, 30 March 1650, by Sir E. Bysshe, Gart. Harl. MS. 1441, fo. 13, copy of grant, Brit. Mus.; Misc. Gen. et Her., 2nd S., vol. i., p. 288; Harl. MS. 6179, fo. 93^b.

HOUGHTON, John, see HAUGHTON.

  „ Ralph, of London, gent., s. of John, of Honghton, co. Lanc., s. of Ralph, s. of Nicholas, s. of John, originally descended from a younger honse of Houghton of Houghton Tower in ye County. 1 July 1626 in Add. MS. 14,295, fo. 98; by Segar, Add. MS. 12,225, fo. 55.

  „ Toby, of King's Cliffe, Northants, 1 November, 26 Eliz., 1584. Bannerman's MS., No. 9, fo. 510, 1584, by Cooke; Harl. MS. 1359, fo. 117^b; Add. MS. 4966, fo. 20.

HOULTE, William, city of London, gent., crest 18 June 1582, by Sir G. Dethick. Harl. MSS. 1441, fo. 74^b, and 1422, fo. 22^b; Q's Coll. Oxf. MS. 145, fo. 21, as Holt.

HOUSE, ... late Alderm. of London, Quarterly . . . . by Cooke. Stowe MS. 670, fo. 48. Same coat as Ric. Howse, but a difft. crest.

HOVEDEN, John, of Felban, Ireland, see HOVENDEN.

HOVELL, ... Suff. . . . . confirmed . . . . 1587, by Flower. Harl. MSS. 1422, fo. 46, 6140, fo. 69^b, and 1085, fo. 24.

  „ Allen, s. of Joshua, of Plymonth, merch^t, 5 Aug. 1652, by Sir E. Bysshe. Harl. MSS. 1441, fo. 146^b, and 1172, fo. 79, vide 44, ye armes in ye greate book of funerals; Stowe MS. 703, fo. 70; Harl. MS. 1466, fo. 24^b, as Howell, 1654.

HOVENDEN, John, of Kelleban, Ireland, arms confirmed and granted 1585, by Cooke, Clar. Harl. MS. 1359, fo. 88^b; Misc. Gen. et Her., N. S., i., 233; Her. Coll., F. 12, fo. 217, incomplete at College; Add. MS. 4966, fo. 52^b; Harl. MS. 5887, fo. 37.

HOWARD, ... originally of Kent . . . . by J. Borough. Harl. MS. 1105, fo. 55^b; Add. MS. 26,702, fo. 90.

HOW, Annabella, see SCROOPE.

HOWE, George . . . . an assistant Govr of Raleigh city, Virginia, arms . . . . by W. Dethick, Gart. Q's Coll. Oxf. MS. 36, fo. 120.

s

HOWE, John, of Emble, par. of Stowgumber, Somt., gent., pat. 10 Dec. 1625, by Segar. Add. MS. 12,225, fo. 60 ; Guil. 193.

HOW, Richard, of the city of London (s. of Sir Richard How, Knt., dec⁴, late Sheriff and Alderm. of London), and his two sisters, viz. :—
„ Elizabeth, and ⎱ 30 Oct. 1691, by T. S⁴ George, Gart. and Clar. Add. MS.
„ Susanna,   ⎰ 14,830, fo. 123, and Grants IV., fo. 97 ; Harl. MS. 1085, fo. 56.

HOWE, Roger, of London, merclt. . . . . by Segar. Add. MS. 12,225, fo. 59ᵇ ; Vincent MS. 154, fo. 10, Her. Coll., and Guil. 192.

HOWELL, John, of St. Albans, Herts, confirmed . . . . by Segar. Add. MS. 12,225, fo. 60.

HOWLAND, Rich⁴, D.D., Cambridge, s. and h. of John, of London, gent., arms confirmed and crest given by patent 20 Jan. 1584-5, and to descendants of his father, by Cooke. Harl. MS. 1359, fo. 120 ; 10ᵗʰ Jan. in Add. MS. 14,295, fo. 45. See Harl. MS. 5887, fo. 2ᵇ, for Howland, Counsellor, of Gray's Inn, ? Sir Giles ; the three brothers Knighted by K. James.

HOWLETT, Richard, of Sidnam, Kent, esq., s. of John, s. of Richard, of Newton, Yorks, given by Wᵐ Harvey, Clar., at London 12 Aug. 1559, 1 Q. Eliz. Add. MSS. 14,295, fo. 6ᵇ, and 16,940, fo. 53ᵇ ; Harl. MSS. 1359, fo. 12ᵇ, and 1115, fo. 4. See HAWLETT.

HOWMAN, Roger, of city of Norwich, Dʳ in Physic, 5 May 1684, by Sir W. Dugdale, Gart., and H. St. George, Clar. Misc. Gen. et Her., N. S., i., 397 ; Grants III., 236 ; copy of grant, Brit. Mus., Lansd. MS. 867, fo. 52.

HOWSE, Richard, of Edmonton, Middx., confirmed . . . . 1563. (Harvey's Grants), Add. MS. 16,940, fo. 51 ; Harl. MS. 1422, fo. 22.

HOWSSON, John, D.D. and chaplain to K. James, confirmed Feb. 1605-6, by Camden. Harl. MS. 6095, fo. 20 ; Guil. 399 ; (Bp. of Oxon. and Durham), Harl. MS. 5887, fo. 22ᵇ.

HOWSON, William, Wigtoft, co. Linc., gent., descended from Thomas, s. of William, 10 Feb. 1602-3, by W. Dethick, Gart., and Camden, Clar. Grants I., fo. 342, 351.

HUBBARD, ... one of the Clerks of the Chancery, by Cooke. Harl. MSS. 1359, fo. 104, and 5887, fo. 11.

HUBBERD or HUBERD, Edward, of Birchanger, Essex, gent., one of the six clerks in Chancery, s. of Richard, s. of John, sometime citizen and mercer of London (who mar. Elizabeth, d. and h. of the valiant Capt. Gongh) : Quarterly arms confirmed and crest granted 19 May 1578, by Sir G. Dethick, Gart. ; confirmed with three stars added to the crest (of the lion's head) 2 June 1590, by W. Dethick, Gart. Harl. MS. 1441, fo. 82ᵇ ; Q's Coll. Oxf. MSS. 36, fo. 117, and 37, fo. 119 (and 145, fo. 37) ; Stowe MS. 676, fo. 36, 80ᵇ ; Add. MS. 4966, fo. 92.

HUBARD, Thomas, of Callie (Calais) . . . . coat . . . . Barker's Grants, Harl. MS. 5846, fo. 49 ; Stowe MS. 692, fo. 53ᵇ.

HUBBY alias HUBY, John, Norwich, s. of Matthew, gent. of the horse to Hy., late Earl of Cumberland, 15 May 1676, by W. Dugdale. Harl. MS. 6834, fo. 178 ; Grants III., fo. 27.

HUCKELL, ... (s. of Nicholas), of Hitchin . . . . 1581, by Cooke, Clar. Bannerman's MS., No. 9, 459.

HUDDASDON, William, of Guy's Cliffe, co. Warwick, by Cooke. Harl. MS. 1359, fo. 114ᵇ ; Add. MS. 4966, fo. 100.

HUDSON, John, of London, s. of Robert, s. of Thomas, of Apletreeweck, Yorks, crest 10 Feb. 1577-8, by Cooke, Clar. Stowe MS. 670, fo. 39ᵇ. See HULSON.

HUDDY, Richard, of Nethway, Devon, 13 Feb. 1570-1, by Cooke or G. Dethick. Harl. MS. 1422, fo. 123.

HUGGEN, Robert, of Bradenham, Norfolk, 8 or 28 H. VIII., by T. Wall, Gart. Bannerman's MS., No. 9, 452.

HUGGESSEN, ... confirmed .... 1624, by Segar. Harl. MSS. 6140, fo. 25, and 6179, fo. 40.

HUGHES, ... Mr Dudley's serv^t. Arms, gu., a fret argt. on a canton or, a pheon gu. Stowe MS. 670, fo. 4^b.

„ Reignold, of London, gen., s. of, etc., exemplified 1 Aug. 1590, by R. Cooke. Harl. MS. 5805, fo. 160^b.

HUYS, Thomas, of co. Glouc., a gift .... 1558. (Harvey's Grants), Add. MS. 16,940, fo. 9^b ; Harl. MS. 6140, fo. 32, with difft. crest, phys. to Q. Eliz.

HEWSE or HEWESE, William, Bp. of St. Asaph 1573—1601 ; 10 Dec. 1573, by Sir G. Dethick, Gart. Harl. MS. 1441, fo. 81 ; Q's Coll. Oxf. MS. 145, fo. 33 ; Harl. MS. 5847, fo. 32, as Hewese, and 5823, fo. 33, as Hewse.

HUGHES, William, of Llewerllyd, Flints (s. of Hugh), crest confirmed 28 .... 1620, by Sir Richard St. George (Norr.). Harl. MS. 2006, fo. 96 ; by T. Wall, Gart., 38 H. VIII., Harl. MS. 1977, fo. 207.

HUGON, Robert, of East Bradenham (Bucks), 20 May 1546, by ? Hawley. Add. MS. 16,940, fo. 201 ; Bannermau's MS., No. 9, 452.

HULBERT, George, ... Justice .... granted .... March 1639, by Borough, Gart. Harl. MSS. 1105, fo. 56, and 1441, fo. 57^b ; Add. MSS. 26,702, fo. 91^b, and 4966, fo. 33^b ; Guil. 390.

HULL, John, of Hameldon, Surrey, 1527, by Wriothesley, Gart., and Benolte, Clar. Harl. MS. 1433, fo. 32, and 5846, fo. 49^b ; Stowe MS. 692, fo. 54.

„ John, of London and Northamptonshire, 20 July 1616, by W. Camden, Clar. Harl. MS. 6095, fo. 34 ; to his kindred and nephews, Harl. MS. 1422, fo. 42^b ; Cains Coll. Camb. MS. 551, fo. 24 ; Guil. 196 ; Harl. MS. 1433, fo. 175^b.

„ John, of Battersea, Surrey, esq., s. and h. of John, of Newport Pagnell, Bucks, s. of William, of Essam, Northants, confirmed 25 Jan. 1624-5, by Segar. Add. MS. 12,225, fo. 60^b ; Guil. 196 ; Harl. MS. 6140, fo. 76^b.

„ Joseph, of Stoke-by-Nayland, Suff., J.P. and barr.-at-law, of Linc. Inn, 7 Feb. 1680-81, by W. Dugdale, Gart., and H. St. George, Clar. Stowe MS. 714, fo. 98^b ; Grants III., fo. 126.

HULLS, Thomas, of Norbury and Astley, Cheshire, esq., Quarterly coat confirmed, a gift of crest, by Flower, 3rd day .... 8 Eliz., 1566. Harl. MSS. 1422, fo. 118^b, 1359, fo. 10, and 1507, fo. 95, copy of grant, Brit. Mus., and Q's Coll. Oxf. MS. 38, fo. 81.

HULME, William, of Over Hulme, par. of Leeke, co. Staff., s. of Thos., s. of W^m, s. of Nicholas, s. of W^m, etc., crest granted 1 July 1613, by R. St. George, Norr. Q's Coll. Oxf. MS. 36, fo. 97 ; copy of grant, Harl. MS. 1422, fo. 80^b, as HOLME, which see, and also Add. MS. 14,295, fo. 80 ; Harl. MS. 6140, fo. 74^b ; Le Neve's MS. 423.

HULSON, John, of London, ... gift .... 1560 .... (Harvey's Grants), Add. MS. 16,940, fo. 22^b.

„ John, of London, gent., crest given 10 Feb., 20 Eliz., 1577-8, by Sir Gilbert Dethick, Gart. Q's Coll. Oxf. MS. 145, fo. 46 ; Harl. MSS. 1441, fo. 88^b, and 1359, fo. 29 (and 105^b, crest drawn differently) ; Stowe MS. 670, fo. 39^b ; Add. MS. 4966, fo. 25.

HULTON, Adam, of the Parke, co. Lanc., gent., crest given 10 Dec. 1561, by Dalton. Her. and Geneal., ii., 536 ; Harl. MS. 1359, fo. 52 bis.

HUMBLE, Peter, see UMBLE, and Le Neve's MS. 357.

HUMPHREY, Charles, of Rishangles, Suff., confirmed and ratified by Camden, Clar., and after in possession of

„ Thomas, of Dublin, his brother, 26 Jan. 1638-9, by Thos. Preston, Ulster. Harl. MS. 1470, fo. 96, 262 ; Guil. 177 ; attestation of a certificate for Thomas, by Camden, Harl. MS. 1105, fo. 1.

HUMFREY, Richard, of Rettendon, Essex, Quartering Warner, by Segar. Add. MS. 12,225, fo. 60^b ; Guil. 364 adds s. of Richard, s. of Richard, etc.

HUMPHREY, William, gent., Save Maister to the Queen's mints within the Tower of

London, grant 30 (? 8) June 1562, by Harvey. Harl. MS. 1507, fo. 375, copy of grant, Brit. Mus., and Q's Coll. Oxf. MS. 38, fo. 79; Harl. MSS. 1359, fo. 19, and 1422, fo. 22 ; Add. MS. 16,940, fo. 40ᵇ ; Her. and Geneal., i., 82 ; Grants II., 566 ; Le Neve's MS. 375, 274.

HUN, Thomas, of Dedham, Essex, 8 Sept. 1572, by Sir G. Dethick. Harl. MS. 1441, fo. 73 ; Q's Coll. Oxf. MS. 145, fo. 19ᵇ ; Harl. MSS. 5847, fo. 18ᵇ, and 5823, fo. 19ᵇ.

HUNCKES, Sir Thomas, of Clapton, co. Glouc., about 1605, by D. Molyneux, Ulster K. of A. Harl. MS. 5887, fo. 38ᵇ.

HUNLOKE, Henry, of London, 14 Dec. 1587, by Cooke. Harl. MSS. 1359, fo. 108, and 1093, fo. 17ᵇ ; Add. MS. 4966, fo. 64.

„ { Sir Henry, Bt., of Wingerworth, 19 Dec. 1674, "mullets removed," W. Dugdale. Harl. MS. 6834, fo. 178 ; Grants III., fo. 9 ; J. J. Howard's R. Cath. Fam., ii., 102, 105.

„ { Sir Henry, of Wingerworth, co, Derby. 14 June 1688, by Sir T. St. George, Gart. Grants IV., fo. 9.

HUNNYNGES, William, esquire, one of the Six Clerks of the Council, crest and arms confirmed 10 Nov. 1549 (3 E. VI.), by C. Barker, Gart. Harl. MS. 1116, fo. 40.

HUNNIS, William, of Middx. gent., of the Queen Majesties Chapel, and "Master of her highness children in the same," granted 14 Feb. 1568-9, by Sir G. Dethick, Gart., Cooke and Flower. Harl. MSS. 1441, fo. 70, and 1359, fo. 54 ; MS. Ashm. 844, fo. 6, copy of grant, Bodleian Lib., and Q's Coll. Oxf. MS. 39, fo. 136 (and 145, fo. 15ᵇ).

HUNSTON, William, of Walepoll, Norfolk, gent., crest 6 Feb., 3 and 4 Phil. and Mary, 1556-7, Quarterly of 4 . . . . by Sir G. Dethick, Gart. MS. Ashm. 840, fo. 383-4, copy of grant, Bodleian Lib., and Q's Coll. Oxf. MS. 39, fo. 75 ; Harl. MS. 1359, fo. 68ᵇ ; Grants I., 202.

HUNTE, Alice, dau. of H. of Sevenoaks in Kent . . . . by Cooke. Harl. MS. 1359, fo. 92 ; Add. MS. 4966, fo. 37ᵇ.

HUNT, James, of Dantzic, s. of Robert, of Stokegreve (Stokegreen), Devon, ... 1592, by Cooke. Harl. MSS. 1359, fo. 63ᵇ, and 1422, fo. 63ᵇ ; Add. MS. 4966, fo. 25.

„ John, of Paddon, Devon, 2 June 1510, by T. Wriothesley, Gart. Grants I., 404ᵃ.

„ John, of Lyndon, Rutland, granted 20 July 1585, by Cooke. Harl. MSS. 1359, fo. 88, and 1422, fo. 63ᵇ ; Guil. 263 ; Add. MS. 4966, fo. 19, 45.

HUNTINGDON (Col. Robt., Stanton Harcourt, co. Oxford), or, fretty sa., on a chief of the 2nd three mullets or [a chief per fesse of the 2nd and gules, on the upper part three mullets or]. Harl. MS. 1105, fo. 20ᵇ and 42ᵇ ; Bysshe's Grants, fo. 21, Her. Coll. ; one of yᵉ commissioners for the Excise, Harl. MS. 6179, fo. 44ᵇ.

HUNTON, William, of East Knoyle, Wilts, ... 1578, by Cooke. Harl. MS. 1359, fo. 105ᵇ ; Add. MS. 4966, fo. 24ᵇ.

HURDIS, { Thomas, Atherstone-upon-Stower, co. Warwick, and of London, mercht., grant 30 July 1695, by T. St. George, Gart. and Clar. Grants IV., fo. 204. And

„ { William, of Stoke Newington, Middx., sons of James, of Atherstone, deceased.

HURT, Thomas, of Ashbourne, co. Derby, crest 4 Sept. 1565, by Flower. MS. Ashm. 858, fo. 161, copy of grant, Bodleian Lib. ; Reliquary, xxii., 51 ; Le Neve's MS. 491.

HUTCHINSON, { Edward, of Wickham, Yorks, by Flower, by letters patent 4 July 1581. Harl. MS. 1359, fo. 8ᵇ ; MS. Ashm. 834, fo. 46, copy of grant, Bodleian Lib. ; June in Guil. 387.

HOCHINSON or HUCHINSON, { Edward (s. of Richard), of Wykeham, Yorks, confirmed 4 June 1581, and to his brethren, by Flower. MS. Ashm. 834, fo. 46, copy of grant, Bodleian Lib. ; Guil. 387 ; Harl. MS. 6140, fo. 68ᵇ.

HUTTOFT, Henry, of Hants, ... Add. MS. 26,702, fo. 76ᵇ.
HUTTON, ... crest, a camel's head per pale sa. and arg. betw. two wings counter-
      changed, etc., holding a broad arrow-head in his mouth or, etc.   Barker's
      Grants . . . . Harl. MS. 5846, fo. 50 ; Stowe MS. 692, fo. 51 ; Harl. MS.
      6179, fo. 12.
   „   Matthew, D.D., Dean of York, grant 20 July 1584, by G. Dethick, Gart.
      Stowe MS. 676, fo. 63 ; Exemplified 1 May in MS. Ashm. 858, fo. 237-8,
      copy of grant, Bodleian Lib., and Q's Coll. Oxf. MS. 37, fo. 87 ; Grants I.,
      fo. 71.
   „   Richard, of Goldsborough, Yorks, gent., 2nd s. of Anthony, s. of John, s. of
      William, of Penrith, Cumb., 27 June 1599, by W. Segar, Somerset Herald
      and Norroy nominate. Add. MSS. 12,225, fo. 61, and 14,295, fo. 115 ;
      Harl. MS. 1359, fo. 36 ; Q's Coll. Oxf. MS. 146, fo. 136 ; Guil. 161,
      5ᵗʰ June.
   „   Thomas, of Dry Drayton, co. Camb., 16 Nov. 1528, by Wriothesley, Gart.,
      and Benolte, Clar.   Harl. MS. 1172, fo. 8, copy of grant.
   „   Sir Timothy, of Marske in Richmondshire, Yorks, Knt., and
   „   Sir Thomas, of Popleton, sons of Mathew, late Archbp., by W. Dugdale, Norr.
      Add. MS. 14,295, fo. 54ᵇ ; C. 40, 132 [Visit. Yorks, 1665, Her. Coll.] ;
      see also by R. St. George, 1608, Harl. MS. 6140, fo. 50.
HUYSH, Sylvester, of Donyford,   ⎫
   „   William, of Dunster,   ⎬ co. Somerset, kinsmen, confirmed 1589,
   „   Rowland, of South Brent, and ⎪ by Cooke. Burke's Armory.
   „   Richard, of New Inn, Middx., ⎭
HYDE, ... crest . . . . Barker's Grants, Harl. MS. 5846, fo. 51 ; Stowe MS.
      692, fo. 53, 54.
   „   Bernard, descended out of Notts and Herefordshire, 6 Sept. 1609, by Segar.
      Add. MS. 12,225, fo. 61 ; C. 24 [Visit. of Lond., 1634], fo. 18ᵇ, Her.
      Coll. ; Guil. 364 ; Harl. MSS. 1441, fo. 162, 5887, fo. 106, and 1476,
      fo. 36.
   „   George, of South Denchworth, Berks, crest confirmed 22 Nov. 1600, by
      Camden. Cott. MS. Faust. E. 1, fo. 50ᵇ ; 20ᵗʰ of Nov. in Stowe MS. 714,
      fo. 99 ; MSS. Ashm. 858, fo. 208, and 840, fo. 411, copy of grant, Bodleian
      Lib. ; Misc. Gen. et Her., N. S., iii., 53 ; Gough MS., Bodleian Lib., Berks,
      16, fo. 72ᵇ. See also CATER. Le Neve's MS. 473.
HIDE, John, of London, ⎫ sons of Edward, s. of Edward, s. of Jenkin, 2nd s. of
      and   ⎬ Robert, of Norbury, Cheshire, 2 April 1571, by Cooke.
   „   Edward,   ⎭ Harl. MSS. 1359, fo. 90ᵇ, and 1442, fo. 60ᵇ ; Gents.
                         Mag., 1864, ii., 221 ; Harl. MS. 5887, fo. 67 ;
      Add. MS. 4966, fo. 65ᵇ.
   „   Capt. John, of St. Katherine, Middx. (out of Cheshire), confirmed 5 Aug.
      1637, by the Kings of Arms and Heralds. Guil. 371.
HYDE, Laurence, Viscount, supporters 25 Nov. 1681, by Sir William Dugdale.
      Harl. MS. 6834. fo. 78 ; Grants III., fo. 142.
HIDE, Robert, of Albury, Herts, ... 1586, by Cooke. Add. MS. 4966, fo. 81ᵇ ;
      Harl. MSS. 1359, fo. 115ᵇ, 1422, fo. 60ᵇ, and 5887, fo. 21 ; Thomas in
      Stowe MS. 670, fo. 17.
HYDE, William, of South Denchworth, Berks, crest 31 July 1562, by Harvey.
      Harl. MS. 1422, fo. 113 ; Add. MS. 16,940, fo. 29 ; Grants II., 481ᵇ, 548 ;
      Harl. MS. 1116, fo. 48.
HIDE, William, of Whetstone, Middx., 9 June 1691, by St. George, Gart. and Clar.
      Stowe MS. 714, fo. 170 ; Add. MS. 14,830, fo. 105 ; Grants IV., fo. 85 ;
      Harl. MS. 1085, fo. 56.
HYNDE, ... crest . . . . Barker's Grants, Harl. MS. 5846, fo. 50ᵇ ; Stowe MS.
      692, fo. 54.
   „   Austyne, of city of London, sheriff, gift, by Hawley, 1 Oct., 4 Ed. VI., 1550,
      copy of grant, Q's Coll. Oxf. MSS. 37, fo. 25, and 39, fo. 29 ; Harl. MS.

1359, fo. 5 ; Add. MS. 16,940, fo. 204 ; Grants II., 478 ; Harl. MS. 1116, fo. 44ᵇ.

HYNDE, Elizabeth, dau. to Thomas Hynde, confirmed . . . . 1559. (Harvey's Grants), Add. MS. 16,940, fo. 13ᵇ.

HYND, Rowland, of Hedsor, Bucks (s. and h. of Austin, of London, Alderm.), allowed . . . . 1583, by Cooke. Harl. MS. 1359, fo. 98ᵇ ; Add. MS. 14,295, fo. 32 ; Guil. 159 ; Add. MS. 4966, fo. 62ᵇ.

HYRNE, Clement, of Inglosse at Heveringham, Norfolk, esq., late maior city of Norwich 1593, s. of Nicholas, of Draiton in said co., and father to

HEARNE or HIRNE, Thomas, now one of the Alderm. of Norwich, grant of arms and crest 22 Nov. 1596, by Wᵐ Dethick, Gart. Stowe MS. 703, fo. 59ᵇ ; Q's Coll. Oxf. MS. 37, fo. 94, copy of grant, and Stowe MS. 676, fo. 67 ; Harl. MS. 1453, fo. 33, " the arms given being those of Englosse, saving the differencing of the Canton, entᵈ by R. Brooke, York Herald."

HIRNE, Thomas, s. of Clement ; marr. Ann, dau. of . . . . Thurston, of Hopney, Suff. ; coat and impalement . . . . by Wᵐ Dethick. Harl. MSS. 1441, fo. 104, and 5847, fo. 54ᵇ ; Add. MS. 12,454, fo. 54 ; Stowe MS. 703, fo. 59ᵇ.

I

IBSGRAVE, William, of Langley, co. Herts . . . . coat and crest . . . . Barker's Grants, Harl. MS. 5846, fo. 59ᵇ ; Stowe MS. 692, fo. 58 ; Harl. MS. 5887, fo. 82, three quarterings.

ILBERT, William, Buckfastleigh, Devon, 28 Nov. 1692, by T. St. George, Gart. and Clar. Harl. MS. 6834, fo. 178 ; Grants IV., fo. 122 ; Harl. MS. 1085, fo. 56.

ILES, Thomas, of Fulham, Middx., alteration . . . . by Sir R. St. George, Clar. Add. MS. 14,295, fo. 56 ; (I. 23, fo. 32 [Her. Coll.]) ; Harl. MS. 1105, fo. 7ᵇ.

INDIA, THE MERCHANTS OF, incorporated as "the Company of Merchants of London trading with the East Indies"; grant of arms and crest 4 Feb. 1600-1, by W. Dethick, Gart., and Camden. Q's Coll. Oxf. MS. 36, fo. 87, copy of grant. See EAST INDIES.

INGE (William in Guil. 259), of Leicester, 22 Feb. 1641-2, by J. Borough, Gart. Harl. MS. 1105, fo. 58.

INKERSALL, ... gu., a fesse dancettée erm. betw. six trefoils slipped or, by Segar. Add. MS. 12,225, fo. 63 ; C. 28 [Visit. of Herefordsh., 1634], fo. 45, 2nd Index, Her. Coll., and Guil. 135.

INNES, Robert, of Edinburgh, W. S., s. of Robert, of Readhall, s. of Adam, of same, 12 June 1693, by A. Areskine, Lyon K. of A. Misc. Gen. et Her., N. S., ii., 395, copy of grant, Brit. Mus.

IPSWICH TOWN, confirmation of arms, crest and supporters granted 20 Aug. 1561, by Hervey. Add. MS. 16,940, fo. 59 ; 24 of Aug. in copy of grant, Q's Coll. Oxf. MS. 38, fo. 77 ; Misc. Gen. et Her., 2nd S., vol. ii., p. 343 ; Cat. Her. Exhib. Soc. Antiq., 65.

IRELAND, James, s. of John, s. of John, of co. Hereford, s. of Hugh, of co. Salop, descendants of Ireland of co. Lanc., Esq., gift 1602, by Wᵐ Segar, Somerset Her. als Norroy nominate. Harl. MS. 1359, fo. 37 ; 1601 in Add. MS. 14,295, fo. 117, and Add. MS. 12,225, fo. 65 ; Guil. 127.

„ Sir John, Knt., of Langley, co. Hereford, coat and crest . . . . Barker's Grants, Harl. MS. 5846, fo. 59 ; Stowe MS. 692, fo. 58.

IREMONGER, William, of Chattcutt, co. Lanc. [Chatcnll, co. Staff. ?], ... by Camden. Harl. MSS. 1422, fo. 12, 6179, fo. 2, and 1441, fo. 46.

IRMONGERS' COMPANY, 1 Sept. 1455, 34 Hen. VI., by Lancaster Herald ; confirmed 16 . . . ., 22 H. VIII., 1530, by Benolt ; reconfirmed 27 May 1560, by Hervey. Add. MS. 16,940, fo. 44 ; Her. and Geneal., i., 37 ; *see* Burke's Armory.

ISAAKE, Samuel, town clerk of Exeter, sequestered, but restored by writ of mandamus *temp.* Chas. II., etc. ; augmentation 6 June 1670, by Walker. Add. MSS. 14,293, fo. 85, and 14,294, fo. 25 ; Harl. MS. 1172, fo. 76 ; Guil. 258. *See* IZAAK.

ISAACKSON, Henry and [William ?], L.D.D. (of Fifield, Essex), by W. Segar. Grant, Harl. MS. 1105, fo. 30.

ISONS, John, of Trontesdale, Yorks, gent., 11 May 1613, by R. St. George, Norr. Add. MS. 14,295, fo. 61 ; Harl. MS. 6179, fo. 22[b].

ITHELL, Thomas, Doctor of the Civil Lawe and Master of Jesus Coll., Camb. ; s. of Piers Ithell of Billesden, co. Leic., Esq. ; a patent 10 July 1575, 17 Q. Eliz., by Cooke. Harl. MS. 1359, fo. 114[b] ; Add. MS. 4966, fo. 91[b].

IVAT, Thomas, Esq., Searcher of the port of the City of London ; s. of William, who marr. Margaret, dau. of W[m] Littleton als Lodge, sometime of Cresset, Salop, esq., and niece to Sir Thomas Littleton, Knt., lord mayor of London 1583 ; coat confirmed and crest granted 27 June 1626, Quarterly of 8, by Segar. Stowe MS. 677, fo. 9[b] ; Add. MS. 12,225, fo. 65 ; Guil. 131 ; Grants I., 372 ; Harl. MS. 6140, fo. 76[b].

IVE or IVES, John, Northants, confirmed . . . . 1562. (Harvey's Grants), Add. MS. 16,940, fo. 34[b] ; Harl. MS. 5887, fo. 50 ; IVES, Harl. MS. 1116, fo. 47.

IZAAK, Samuel, town clerk of the city of Exeter, etc., 6 June 1670, by Walker ; royalist, imprisoned by sea and land, etc. Harl. MS. 1172, fo. 76 ; Add. MS. 14,293, fo. 85 ; Isaacke in Add. MS. 14,294, fo. 25 ; sequestered, but restored by writ of mandamus *temp.* Chas. II., etc. ; Guil. 258. *See* ISAAKE.

IZOD, John, chief gentleman Ussher to Q. Anne 1606, of Tuddington, Glouc., 1592, by Cooke. Harl. MSS. 1359, fo. 104, and 1422, fo. 95 ; Add. MS. 4966, fo. 85[b] ; Harl. MS. 5887, fo. 47.

J

JAKMAN [JACKMAN], Edward, of Harton, Essex, gift . . . . 1561. (Harvey's Grants), Add. MS. 16,940, fo. 52[b] ; Harl. MS. 5887, fo. 51.

JACSON, ... crest . . . . Barker's Grants, Harl. MS. 5846, fo. 59[b] ; Stowe MS. 692, fo. 58.

JACKSON, ... of Kilwonldegrove, Yorks, ... by Segar : gu., three suns ppr., a chief indented erm. (? gn., two bars dancettée erm., on a chief az. three suns or). Add. MS. 12,225, fo. 61[b] ; Harl. MS. 6140, fo. 66[b].

    ,, John, of Gatonbye, Yorks, gent., ... 1563, by Flower. Add. MS. 14,295, fo. 36 ; Harl. MSS. 1359, fo. 33[b], and 6140, fo. 69[b].

    ,, John, one of the trompeters to Q. Eliz., s. of John, of Westchester, confirmed 1 June 1584, 26 Q. Eliz., by Sir Gilb[t] Dethick, Gart. (of Stockport in Harl. MS. 5860, fo. 48, and ? if arms granted by Chas., K. of Sweden). Harl. MSS. 1422, fo. 48, and 1359, fo. 23 ; Add. MS. 14,295, fo. 48 ; Q's Coll. Oxf. MS. 145, fo. 9 ; Harl. MS. 6140, fo. 35.

    ,, Richard, of Killingwold Grange, s. of Anthony, s. of Richard, ... 1613, by R. St. George, Norr. Harl. MS. 1422, fo. 48, and ? by Segar, Add. MS. 12,225, fo. 61[b].

    ,, Robert (s. of John, of Kendal, Westmorland), chiefest Master Warden for the Society and Co. of the Girdlers in London, now of Englefield, Middx., gent., etc., arms and crest granted 24 Aug. 1596, by W. Dethick, Gart. Copy of grant, Q's Coll. Oxf. MS. 36, fo. 57.

JACKSON, Robert, of Keswick, Cumberland, ... by Cooke. Harl. MSS. 1359, fo. 97ᵇ, and 1422, fo. 48 ; Keswick, Yorks, Add. MS. 4966, fo. 87ᵇ.

„ Thomas, of Duddingstone, Northampt., 10 Aug. 1689, by T. St. George, Gart. and Clar. Harl. MS. 6834, fo. 178 ; Grants IV., fo. 53.

JACOB, Catherine, d. and h. to John Jacob of Myddle, Salop, and wife to Hugh or John Whitebroke of Bridgenorth in the said co. ; confirmed . . . . 1563. (Harvey's Grants). Add. MS. 16,940, fo. 44ᵇ ; Harl. MS. 1116, fo. 55.

„ . . . . of Stratford, Bow, and one of the Custom House, gent., by Wᵐ Segar, Gart. Harl. MS. 5887, fo. 111.

„ Thomas, of Wotton Bassett, Wilts, confirmed 24 June 1633, by Sir R. St. George, Clar. Harl. MS. 1470, fo. 155, copy of grant, Brit. Mus. ; Gnil. 189 ; Harl. MS. 1105, fo. 13.

JACOMB, Thomas, D.D., s. of John, of Burton Lazers, co. Leic., 20 April 1672, by Walker. Harl. MS. 1172, fo. 66, copy of grant ; Add. MS. 14,293, fo. 68 ; Guil. 381 ; Harl. MS. 6179, fo, 59.

JADWINE or JADEWINE (or JADSWINE), Robert, gent. (mar. Cecilia, dau. of Sir Francis Clark, K.B.), s. and h. of Thomas, of London, gent. (by Lucy, dau. of John Skillicorne of Preshall, co. Lanc., arm.), s. of Wᵐ, of Barwick, Esq., etc. ; gift, by Dethick (? Wᵐ) . . . . confirmed 21 Sept. 1629, by Segar. Add. MS. 12,225, fo. 61ᵇ ; Guil. 365 ; Grants I., 358 ; Harl. MS. 6140, fo. 64ᵇ.

JAKES, John, of London, ... by Cooke. Harl. MSS. 5887, fo. 24, and 1359, fo. 88 ; Add. MS. 4966, fo. 52.

JAMAICA, ... Seal, 3 Feb. 1661-2, by Sir E. Walker, Gart. Her. Coll., fo. 5.

JAMES, [Bartholomew], Mayor of London (1479—1480) . . . . Ed. IV. . . . . Add. MS. 26,702, fo. 36ᵇ.

„ of Cornewall, 26 July 1641, by Borough. Harl. MS. 1105, fo. 57ᵇ.

„ Francis, of Barrow Court, Somerset, Doctor of lawe and a Master in Chancery, s. of John, of One [Onn] parva, co. Staff., and bro. of William, S.T.D. and dean of Durham, confirmed by Camden. Harl. MSS. 1422, fo. 41, and 6095, fo. 18.

„ (John), M.D., a physitian, ... by Cooke, Clar. Stowe MS. 670, fo. 11.

„ Martin, of London, esq., and registrar of the High Court of Chancery, crest granted 10 Sept. 1574, by Sir G. Dethick, Gart. Harl. MS. 1441, fo. 81 ; copy of grant, Q's Coll. Oxf. MS. 36, fo. 104 (and MS. 145, fo. 32ᵇ).

„ Roger, of Upminster Hall, Essex, and ⎱ (sons of Roger, of London, a native
„ John, his brother ⎰ of Cheshire), James and Moreskins quarterly and two crests, 18 Nov. 1611, by Camden. Harl. MSS. 1422, fo. 109, and 6095, fo. 16ᵇ ; Arch. Cant., iv., 242 ; Her. and Geneal., ii., 428, and vi., 680 ; Roger, brewer, Guil. 323.

„ Thomas, D.D., warden of All Souls', Oxford, formerly an officer in the army ; 29 April 1668. Harl. MS. 1105, fo. 20ᵇ ; Add. MS. 14,293, fo. 6ᵇ ; Bysshe's Grants, fo. 20, Her. Coll. ; Gnil. 274.

JANSON, Brian, of London, free of the Drapers . . . . May 1605, by Camden : impaling Lee. Harl. MSS. 1422, fo. 19, and 6095, fo. 4.

„ William, of Tunbridge, Kent, 11 Feb. 1646-7, ? by Bysshe, Clar. Harl. MS. 4198, fo. 53ᵇ.

JARRETT, James (s. of Wᵐ), London, merchant, 19 May 1696, by T. St. George, Gart. and Clar. Grants IV., 236, and Burke.

JASON, Robert, of Enfield, Middx., confirmed 10 March 1588-9, by Wᵐ Dethick, Gart. Harl. MS. 1470, fo. 57, copy of grant, Brit. Mus. ; Misc. Gen. et Her., 2nd S., vol. iii., p. 49 ; Guil. 166 ; 12 July 1588 in Harl. MS. 6140, fo. 31ᵇ, and 4 quarterings.

JASSON, Simon, s. of Sebastian, of Burton on Trent, co. Staff., crest 6 Nov. 1610, by R. St. George, Norr. MS. Ashm. 858, fo. 118, copy of grant, Bodleian Lib. ; Add. MS. 14,295, fo. 79 ; see Harl. MSS. 5887, fo. 40ᵇ, and 6140, fo. 41.

JAWDRELL, Robert, of Wytcham, Isle of Ely, co. Camb., Esq., gift of crest 2 July 1597, by Lee, Clar.   Harl. MS. 1359, fo. 39ᵇ ; Add. MS. 14,295, fo. 121ᵇ, " coat awaiting proof."

JAY, Henry, of London, Alderm., 4 May 1601, by Camden.   Harl. MSS. 1422, fo. 17ᵇ, and 6095, fo. 1ᵇ ; Guil. 120.

JEFFREY, John, of Mexham, co. Denbigh, s. of Jeffrey, s. of Hugh, s. of Robert Vehan, lineally descended from Kenrick Rywallon, 12 October 1614, by R. St. George, Norr.   Grants II., 463ᵇ.

JEFFEREY, Thomas, of London, gent., ... 1542, by C. Barker.   Stowe MS. 692, fo. 58 ; Add. MS. 19,816, fo. 114.

JEFFREYS, Sir George, Baron Jeffreys of Wem, supporters 21 Nov. 1685, by W. Dugdale, Gart.   Stowe MS. 714, fo. 126ᵇ ; Grants III., 277 ; Lansd. MS. 867, fo. 52.

JEFFERYES, James, s. of Richard, of Little Bursted, Essex, exemplified 20 Feb. 8 Jac., 1610-11, by Segar.   Add. MS. 12,225, fo. 62 ; C. 21 [Visit. of Essex, 1634], fo. 148, Her. Coll.; called John in Add. MS. 14,293, fo. 20 ; Guil. 318 ; Harl. MS. 6140, fo. 80.

JEFFERSON, Simon, of London, gent., 2nd s. of Anthony, of Ripon, Yorks, confirmed, a patent . . . . by Segar.   Add. MS. 12,225, fo. 62.

JEGON, John, Corpus Xᵗⁱ Coll., Camb., D.D., ... by Cooke, Clar.   Stowe MS. 670, fo. 49.

JEKYLL, Thomas, of Bocking, Essex, and of Clifford's Inn, Attorney, Chief clerk of the paper office of the King's Bench, and lover of arms, antiquities, and of Mathematical sciences ; s. and h. of John Stocker Jekyll, late of Newington, Middx., gent., etc. ; alteration of old coat and crest 6 Feb. 1627-8, by Segar : quartering Stocker, Barnehouse, and Brihyton ?   Add. MS. 12,225, fo. 62ᵇ ; Guil. 158.

JEMMET, Philip, of London, brewer, who was fined for Alderman ; 17 Nov. 1670, 22 Ch. II.   Bysshe's Grants, fo. 25, Her. Coll. ; Harl. MSS. 1105, fo. 21ᵇ, and 6179, fo. 40ᵇ ; Proc. Soc. of Antiq., 1897, fo. 355 ; Le Neve's MS. 504.

JENKES, George, of the county of Salop, crest given 1 May 1582, 25 Q. Eliz., by Cooke.   Harl. MS. 1359, fo. 121ᵇ.

JENKYNS, Roger, of London, confirmed 3 June 1611 (9 Jac. I.), by Segar, with six quarterings.   Add. MS. 12,225, fo. 63 ; Jones in Guil. 388.   See JONES, Harl. MS. 6140, fo. 39.

JENKINSON, ... Tunstal, Norfolk, and Oulton, Suff., confirmed 8 Nov. 1563, by Harvey.   Burke's Armory.

„   . . . . Norwich . . . . 1687 . . . .   Burke's Armory.

„   Anthony, citizen of London, a great traveller, granted 14 Feb. 1568-9, by Sir G. Dethick, Gart., Cooke and Flower.   MS. Ashm. 844, fo. 3, copy of grant, Bodleian Lib., and Q's Coll. Oxf. MS. 39, fo. 147; Harl. MSS. 1359, fo. 54ᵇ, and 1441, fo. 70 ; Guil. 87 ; Grants II., 629ᵇ.

„   Sir Paul, of Walton, Bart., Sheriffe, Derby, 14 April 1687, by Sir T. St. George, Gart., and J. Dugdale, Norr.   Harl. MS. 6834, fo. 178 ; Grants III., fo. 310 ; Lansd. MS. 867, fo. 52 ; Harl. MS. 6179, fo. 60.

„   Sir Robert, of London, confirmed 2 Nov., 16 K. Jas., 1618, by Camden.   Cott. MS. Faustina, E. 1, fo. 62ᵇ ; Guil. 87 ; Grants II., 577 ; Crisp's Visit. England and Wales, notes, ii., 47.

JENER, ... Prothonotary of Com. Pleas . . . . II. VIII.   Add. MS. 26,702, fo. 39ᵇ.

JENNER, Sir Thomas, Kt., ... Recorder of London, augmentation and alteration 5 June 1684, by Sir Wᵐ Dugdale and H. St. George, Clar.   Harl. MS. 6834, fo. 178 ; Grants III., fo. 241 ; Lansd. MS. 867, fo. 52.

JENNERY, Thomas, citizen of London, and his brothers William, Henry and George, s. of Henry, of Wetherden, Suff., 10 Dec. 1661, by Sir E. Walker, Gart.   Her. Coll., fo. 44.

T

JENNEY, ... erm., a bend gu. betw. two cottices sa.; confirmed .... by Segar. Add. MS. 12,225, fo. 62ᵇ ; Harl. MS. 6140, fo. 30.

JENNENS, ... Lord Mayor ([Sir] Stephen in 1508), H. VII. Add. MS. 26,702, fo. 38ᵇ ; Harl. MS. 6179, fo. 15.

JENINGS (Peter in Guil., p. 304), of Silsden, Yorks, grant 26 May 1641, by Borough. Harl. MS. 1105, fo. 57ᵇ ; Caius Coll. Camb. MS. 551, copy of grant.

JENNYNS, Ralph, of Churchill, Somerset, crest confirmed .... 1563. (Harvey's Grants), Add. MS. 16,940, fo. 53.

JENINS [JENNINGS], William, Lancaster Herald, 10 Feb. 1516-17, by Wriothesley [Gart.] and Benolt [Char.]. Harl. MS. 1167, fo. 82ᵇ.

JENOYRE, ... of Essex .... by Cooke. Harl. MS. 1359, fo. 86ᵇ ; Add. MS. 4966, fo. 66ᵇ. Alverstone alias Jenoure of Bygotts in Dunham Magna, Harl. MS. 6140, fo. 46.

JENYSON, Thomas, Yokefleet, Yorks, confirmed .... 1559, by Dalton, Norr. Add. MS. 16,940, fo. 35ᵇ.

JEPSON, Robert, of London, gift .... 1562. (Harvey's Grants), Harl. MS. 1116, fo. 47 ; Add. MS. 16,940, fo. 44.

JERMYN, Henry, of Wickham Bishop, Essex, assigned 9 Aug. 1664, by Sir Edw. Bysshe, Clar. Guil. 161.

  ,,   Sir Thomas, of Suffolk, crest 1 Sept. 1552, by ? Hawley. Add. MS. 16,940, fo. 205.

JERVEIS or JERVEYS [JERVOISE], Thomas, of Weoley, co. Worc., confirmed (155- or 156-), (Harvey's Grants) : sa., a chevron betw. three Eagletts [displayed ?] arg. ; crest, a tyger head erased arg. [sa. ?], mayned and tufted arg. Add. MS. 16,940, fo. 22 ; Harl. MS. 1422, fo. 22ᵇ.

JESSOPPE, Richard, of Broomhall, Yorks, granted 13 July 1575, by Flower. MS. Ashm. 834, fo. 11, copy of grant, Bodleian Lib. ; Harl. MS. 1453, fo. 74 ; Guil. 402.

JESSOPP, Thomas, of Gillingham, Dorset, ... by Cooke. Harl. MSS. 1359, fo. 90, and 1422, fo. 51ᵇ ; Add. MS. 4966, fo. 35.

JESUS COLLEGE, Cambridge, grant of crest 6 July 1575, by Cooke. Her. and Geneal., i., 120, copy of grant, Brit. Mus. ; Add. MS. 5822, fo. 1.

JEVON, Daniel, and brother } of Sedgley, co. Staff., confirmed 10 Jan. 1651-2, by
  ,,   Thomas,   }   Ryley. MS. Ashm. 858, fo. 135ᵇ, copy of grant, Bodleian Lib. ; Misc. Gen. et Her., N. S., iv., 384.

JEWKES, Edward, sergeant of the Bathe (? Bake) House within the Queen's princely palace ; in time of wars he to be standard bearer for the band, and Tynall of the Household, and for services in connection with the late dangerous attempt of the Spanish called the "invincible navie"; arms quarterly and crest granted .... 1593, by W. Dethick, Gart. Copy of grant, Q's Coll. Oxf. MS. 36, fo. 28 ; Stowe MS. 676, fo. 105 [has "Serjeant of the Bath to her Magesty"].

JEYNER, John, of London, son of Christopher Jeyner of Sussex, ... 1591, by Cooke. Harl. MSS. 1359, fo. 102, and 1422, fo. 23 ; Add. MS. 16,940, fo. 209 (and Stowe MS. 670, fo. 46, as JOYNER), which see.

JOBSON, Sir Francis, of Essex, letters patent April 1553, 7th Ed. VI., for new coat for services to Hen. VIII., signed by the King at Westminster. MS. Ashm. 834, fo. 43, copy of letters patent, Bodleian Lib. ; Guil. 404.

  ,,   Walter, of Snayth, Yorks .... by Cooke. Harl. MS. 1359, fo. 75ᵇ ; Add. MSS. 14,295, fo. 75ᵇ, and 4966, fo. 36.

JODRELL, see JAWDRELL.

JOHNSON, ... crest .... Barker's Grants, Harl. MS. 5846, fo. 60 ; Stowe MS. 692, fo. 58.

  ,, ... deputy of St Buttolph's, Aldersgate Ward, London : arg., a pheon az. betw. three mascles gu., by Segar. Add. MS. 12,225, fo. 63ᵇ ; C. 24 [Visit. of Lond., 1634], fo. 84ᵇ, Her. Coll. ; Guil. 374.

JOHNSON, ... of the Tower, ... June 1609, by Camden. Harl. MSS. 1422, fo. 18. 5839, fo. 3ᵇ, 2275, fo. 90ᵇ, and 1115, fo. 9ᵇ ; Guil. 339.

„ . . . . co. Linc. Quarterly : 1 and 4, or, a water bouget sable, on a chief of the last three bezants ; 2 and 3, gu., three fleurs-de-lis in bend arg. betw. two cottises vair. Crest, out of a ducal coronet per pale arg. and azure two wings expanded counterchanged. ["Subscribed by Robert Cooke als Clarenceux roy de Armes To Johnson.] Add. MS. 17,506, fo. 36ᵇ ; see Le Neve's MS. 258.

„ Ann, dau. of Richard, of Hempstead, Essex, ux. Richard Gourney, citizen and Alderm. of London, grant 12 March 1596-7, by Lee. Q's Coll. Oxf. MS. 146, fo. 185 ; Add. MS. 14,295, fo. 11 ; Stowe MS. 702, fo. 115.

„ Edward, Tunbridge, Kent, s. of James, of Lewisham, Kent, and of Joan his wife, d. and h. of Rob. Cheesman, who mar. the daur. and heir of . . . . Woodhall and Yaxley ; 10 May 1570, by R. Cooke, Clar. Stowe MS. 670, fo. 60ᵇ ; Add. MS. 14,297, fo. 60ᵇ.

„ Jane and Elizabeth, see MORDAUNT.

„ John, of Norfolk, now Linc. . . . . by Cooke, Clar. Stowe MS. 670, fo. 39.

„ Nicholas, of Milton Bryan, Bedf., and to his brothers

„ Francis, and } argent, on a pile azure three ounces' heads erased of the first ;
„ William, } 8 May 1632, by R. St. George, Clar. Misc. Gen. et Her., N. S., ii., 121, copy of grant, Brit. Mus.

„ Richard, of Gainsborough, co. Linc., confirmed 7 May 1579, by Flower. MS. Ashm. 834, fo. 21, copy of grant, Bodleian Lib. ; Guil. 34 ; Harl. MSS. 6179, fo. 40ᵇ, and 1115, fo. 65.

„ Robert, of London, s. of John, of Goldinton, Bedf., by Camden. Morgan's Sphere, 118 ; see Harl. MS. 6110, fo. 61ᵇ.

„ Robert, preacher, of North Luffenham, Rutland, B.D., founder of grammar schools and hospitals at Oakham and Uppingham ; confirmed 23 March 1592-3, by Cooke. Misc. Gen. et Her., N. S., i., 452 ; Harl. MS. 1359, fo. 122 ; Add. MS. 4966, fo. 41ᵇ ; John in Stowe MS. 670, fo. 53ᵇ ; Le Neve's MS. 252.

„ Rowland, surveyor of the Queen's works at Berwick, new crest granted 20 or 25 May 1569, by Sir Gilbᵗ Dethick, Cooke and Flower. MS. Ashm. 844, fo. 22, copy of grant, Bodleian Lib., and Q's Coll. Oxf. MS. 39, fo. 154, and (MS. 145, fo. 22ᵇ) ; Harl. MSS. 1441, fo. 75ᵇ, and 1422, fo. 74ᵇ ; Guil. 388 ; Harl. MS. 5887, fo. 44, for grant of Coat of Arms from Geo. Bullock, see Brit. Mus., Add. Charter 19,882.

„ Thomas, of Yorks . . . . 1563-4, by Flower. Harl. MS. 1453, fo. 74.

„ Capt. Thomas, of Great Yarmouth, Norfolk (s. of Thomas, 4ᵗʰ time bailiff of Great Yarmouth, and his grandfather James, several times also), 10 Sept. 1660, by Walker. Sequestered and decimated, Harl. MS. 1172, fo. 71 (81) ; Add. MSS. 14,293, fo. 92, and 14,294, fo. 27 ; Guil. 186 ; see Harl. MS. 1085, fo. 42 ; Harl. MS. 6179, fo. 55.

„ William, of Ingham, Norfolk, 23ᵗʰ July 1633, in the 9ᵗʰ yeare of oᶠ soveraign lord King Charles, by R. St. George, Clar. [Gu., on a saltire ar. five crosses moline of the field ; Crest, a wolf's head erased per pale crenellée ar. and gu.] Harl. MS. 5887, fo. 114.

„ William [by Sir C. Barker . . . . Azure, a fesse embattled or between three cocks' heads erased ar., beaked gu., combed or. Barker's Grants]. Add. MS. 26,702, fo. 76ᵇ ; [see Visit. of Lond., 1634, Harl. Soc., under Jesson].

„ William, als CROKEY, see CROKEY.

„ William, and } sons of William, of Willingdaledoe, Essex, crest 20 May 1577,
„ Charles, } by Cooke. Harl. MS. 1422, fo. 16 ; copy of grant, Add. MS. 5524, fo. 208.

„ William (JONSON), of Tunbridge, Kent, confirmed 11 Feb. 1646-7. Harl. MS. 4198, fo. 53ᵇ.

JOHNSON, William, of Bowden Park, Wilts, 26 Dec. 1663. Harl. MS. 1105, fo. 17; Bysshe's Grants, fo. 4, Her. Coll.

JOLLES, John, als JOYLES, of London, after Lord Mayor (deputy gov^r of the merchant Advent', Caius Coll. Camb. MS.), grant 14 July 1604, by Camden. Harl. MSS. 1422, fo. 18, 5839, fo. 3^b, 2275, fo. 90^b, and 1115, fo. 9^b; MS. Ashm. 858, p. 18, copy of grant, Bodleian Lib.

JOLLY, Robert, of Hatton Garden, par. of St. Andrew, Holborn, in the suburbs of London, 7 Oct. 1692, by T. St. George, Gart. and Clar. Harl. MS. 1172, fo. 64^b; Add. MS. 14,831, fo. 110, and Grants IV., 119; Harl. MS. 1085, fo. 56.

JOLLYE, William, of Leeke, co. Staff., and to all the descendants of John, his grandfather; crest 27 Aug. 1614, by R. St. George, Norr. Harl. MS. 1470, fo. 266; Guil. 255; Harl. MS. 1105, fo. 9^b.

JONES, ... crest .... hiatus in the blazon (? not given by Barker). Barker's Grants, Harl. MS. 5846, fo. 60^b; Stowe MS. 692, fo. 57^b.

„ (or JHONES) .... of London, dyer : gu., a cross betw. four pheons or, by Segar. Add. MS. 12,225, fo. 63^b; Harl. MS. 6140, fo. 79.

„ .... of London .... parti per pale az. and gu. three lyons rampt. argt., a mullet for diff. ; Quarterly of 8 (3 Milo, E. of Hereford, 4 Newmarch); by Segar. Add. MS. 12,225, fo. 64.

„ Edward, of Walpole, Norfolk .... 1587, by Cooke. Harl. MS. 1422, fo. 65; Stowe MS. 670, fo. 19^b, as Johns; Add. MS. 4966, fo. 30.

„ Edward, of Lansayre, Dyffryn Clwyd, co. Denbigh, confirmed by R. St. George, Norr. Add. MS. 14,295, fo. 58^b; (descended from the family of Trevor of C. in said co., Harl. MS. 6067, fo. 38). Quarterly : 1 and 4, parted per bend sinister ermine and ermines and a lyon rampant within a bordure engrailed or ; 2 and 3, gu., a cross crosslet set upon three gryces [grieces] or. Crest, a lyon couchant guardant gu., tail betwixt his hinder legs and reflexed over his back.

JHONES, Francis, Alderm. of London, s. of John, s. of John, of Loostone, par. of Claverley, co. Salop, 12 Nov. 1610, by Camden. Harl. MSS. 1422, fo. 21^b, and 6095, fo. 13^b; Morgan's Sphere of Gentry, ii., p. 110; Her. and Geneal., vol. vi., p. 323, as Jones; Guil. 171.

JONNES, Griffin, of Merionethshire (? Monmouthshire), confirmed 18 Nov., 12 Q. Eliz., 1569, by Sir G. Dethick. Harl. MS. 1441, fo. 69; Q's Coll. Oxf. MS. 145, fo. 13; Harl. MS. 5887, fo. 46.

„ Sir Henry (used at funerall) .... by Cooke, Clar. Stowe MS. 670, fo. 13^b.

JONES, John, of Monmouthshire, s. of Nicholas, 21 May (March) 1573, by Sir G. Dethick. Harl. MS. 1441, fo. 79; "March" in Q's Coll. Oxf. MS. 145, fo. 30.

„ Robert, of Scarborough, Yorks, 23 Feb. 1612-13, by R. St. George, Norr. Add. MS. 14,295, fo. 60^b; Grants II., 636; Le Neve's MS. 496.

JONES (or JONNES), Sir Roger, citizen and Sheriff of London, and his brother

„ Thomas, Bishop of Meath, 14 Sept. 1604, by Camden. Sir Roger died in the year of his shrievalty, 24 July. Copy of grant, Brit. Mus., Stowe MS. 703, fo. 59^b; Harl. MSS. 6095, fo. 2, and 1422, fo. 18, where Roger is put as James; Harl. MS. 4600, fo. 55^b; copy of grant in Bannerman's MS., No. 9, 489.

JONES, Roger, als JENKENS, of London, descended from the house of Trevor in Wales : parti per bend sinister ermine and erminois, a lyon rampt. or, a crescent for diff., with 4 quarterings, 3 June, 9 Jac., 1611, by Segar. Add. MS. 12,225, fo. 63; Guil. 388.

JOHN or JONES, Thomas ap John, fitz Urian of Llangaddock, co. Carmarthen, gentⁿ, mace bearer or sergeant-at-arms to Hen. VIII., granted 20 Feb. 1526-7, by Wriothesley. Harl. MS. 1052, fo. 21, pedigree; Add. MS. 26,702, fo. 46^b; Guil. 223. *See* FITZ URYAN.

JONES, Walter, of Dingestow, co. Mon., s. of John and Agnes, dau. of John

Thomas, etc. ; crest granted 16 July 1593, by W. Dethick, Gart. Stowe MS. 676, fo. 89, 102 ; Copy of grant, Q's Coll. Oxf. MS. 36, fo. 22 and 32.

JONES, Walter, city of Worcester, born at Witney, Oxon., s. of Henry, of the same, s. of John, 2nd s. of John, of Greysmond, co. Mon., 45 Eliz., 1603, by consent of Gilbert, Earl of Shrewsbury, by W. Dethick, Gart. Harl. MS. 1422, fo. 107 ; copy of grant, Add. MS. 5524, fo. 206.

,, William, of Lanwarne, co. Hereford, s. of William, confirmed 8 Jan. 1566-7, by Sir G. Dethick, Gart. Harl. MS. 1441, fo. 68ᵇ ; Q's Coll. Oxf. MS. 145, fo. 12ᵇ ; June in Harl. MS. 5887, fo. 46.

JOANES. William, of Keevil, Wilts . . . . by Cooke. Harl. MSS. 1359, fo. 102ᵇ, and 1422, fo. 65 ; Stowe MS. 670, fo. 33ᵇ.

JONES, William, s. of Thomas, s. of William, s. of Richard, of Holt, co. Denbigh : arg., a lyon rampant vert vulned on the shoulder az. ; coat confirmed and crest granted 16 June 1607 (by R. St. George in Add. MS. 14,293). Add. MS. 12,225, fo. 64 ; 21 of June in Add. MS. 14,293, fo. 121 ; copy of grant, Brit. Mus. ; 16th of June in Add. MS. 14,295, fo. 78ᵇ ; Guil. 175, approved by Segar, Gart.

JORDAN, ... Dec. 1604, by Camden ; same coat as Sir William, with crescent sa. Harl. MSS. 5887, fo. 31ᵇ, and 6095, fo. 3.

JORDEN, ... of Callyce . . . . sa., an eagle displayed in bend between ii cottises ar., on a chief or, iii oak leaves vert. Barker's Grants, Stowe MS. 692, fo. 58.

JORDAN, Edmund, of Gatwick, Surrey, s. of William, s. of John, etc., confirmed (as used on seals 13 or 30 Ed. I:, 1284) and grant of crest. Quarterly of 8 : 1 Jordan, [2 Jordan], 3 Codrington, 4 Saltman, 5 Barwick, 6 Hussey, 7 Hussey, and 8 Nesseile. 18 Feb. 1628-9, 4 Chas., 1629, 5 Charles I., by Segar, Gart. Add. MS. 12,225, fo. 64ᵇ ; Harl. MSS. 6140, fo. 81ᵇ, and 1105, fo. 8 bis.

,, Edmond, of Gatwick, Surrey, High Sheriff 1628, s. of William, etc., alteration 2 June 1631, by R. St. George, Clar. C. 2 [Visit. Surrey, 1623], 72, Her. Coll. ; Add. MS. 14,295, fo. 67ᵇ ; Guil. 211 ; see copy of grant, Brit. Mus., Add. MS. 7098, fo. 79ᵇ and 79·ᵇ, 1 May 1632 ; Harl. MS. 1105, fo. 8.

,, Sir William, of Wiltshire . . . . Nov. 1604, by Camden. Harl. MSS. 6095, fo. 2ᵇ, 1422, fo. 18ᵇ, and 5887, fo. 10ᵇ.

JOURS, Luke, of Ipswich, Suff., 15 Sept. 1664, ? by Sir E. Bysshe, Clar. Harl. MSS. 1105, fo. 40ᵇ, and 1085, fo. 16ᵇ.

JOWELES als JOWLES, John, of Surrey, s. of John, of Alkham, Kent, 1620, by Segar. Add. MS. 12,225, fo. 64ᵇ ; Guil. 335.

JOYLES, see JOLLES.

JOYLIFF, Richard (s. and h. of John, of Estover, Dorset), formerly Capt. of one of the trayned bands ; 28 March 1664, by Walker. Harl. MS. 1172, fo. 37 ; Add. MSS. 14,293, fo. 41, and 14,294, fo. 11ᵇ ; Guil. 334.

JOYNER, John, of London, s. of Christopher, of Sussex, granted . . . . 1591, by Cooke, Clar. Stowe MS. 670, fo. 46 ; see JEYNER, Harl. MSS. 1359, fo. 102, and 1422, fo. 23 (Jeyner) ; Add. MS. 16,940, fo. 209.

JUBBS, William, of Wymondham, Norfolk, and ⎫ 3 Nov. 1664, by Sir E. Bysshe,
   ,, John, of the same place, his kinsman, ⎭ Clar. Harl. MS. 1105, fo. 39ᵇ ; Bysshe's Grants, 32.

JUDDE, Andrew, Maior of London, 3 March 1551-2, by ? Hawley. Add. MS. 16,940, fo. 205. See Mary MATHEW, his wife, 1558, by Harvey.

JUMPER, William, of London, merchᵗ, 24 Feb. 1651-2, by Ed. Bysshe. Harl. MS. 1105, fo. 15 ; Stowe MS. 703, fo. 70.

JUSTICE, ... Coventry . . . . by Camden. Burke's Armory.

,, Mary, wife to John Yates, of Lyvord [Lyford], Berks, 20 Feb. 1551-2, by ? Hawley. Add. MS. 16,940, fo. 204ᵇ.

K

KAY, Arthur, of Woodsome, Yorks, crest, a gift, 22 Oct. 1564, by Flower. Harl. MS. 1359, fo. 42ᵇ; Robert in Add. MS. 14,295, fo. 72ᵇ; Harl. MS. 6140, fo. 68.

„ John, of Dalton, Yorks, gent., crest granted at Wakefield 7 Oct. 1564, by Flower. Add. MS. 14,295, fo. 72ᵇ; Harl. MSS. 1359, fo. 42ᵇ, and 6140, fo. 68.

KEARSLEY, Henry, of London, gent., s. of Oliver, of Deane, co. Lanc., granted 2 Jan. 1655-6, by Sir Ed. Bysshe, Gart. Harl. MS. 2275, fo. 40, 44, copy of patent, Brit. Mus.; confirmed 20 Oct. 1662, by Bysshe [Clar.], Harl. MS. 1441, fo. 51ᵇ; copy of grant, Harl. MS. 1105, fo. 18ᵇ, and Guil. 187; registrar of all goods, ships, wares and merchandise that should be seized, etc., 6 Sept., 6 Chas. I., 1631—1648 (Harl. MS. 1441), removed by parliament and restored 12 Chas. II., Guil. 187; Bysshe's Grants, fo. 12, Her. Coll.; Harl. MS. 1441, fo. 150.

KEBELL, ... crest .... Barker's Grants, Harl. MS. 5846, fo. 62ᵇ; Stowe MS. 692, fo. 61.

KEBLE (Henry), Lord Mayor of London (1510) .... Hy. VII., with crest. Add. MS. 26,702, fo. 38ᵇ, diff. coat on fo. 45.

KECK, Nicholas, 4th s. of John, s. and h. of Geoffrey, of Long Marston, co. Glouc., descended of an ancient and worthy family; confirmed .... by Segar. Add. MS. 12,225, fo. 65ᵇ; Harl. MS. 1397, fo. 190ᵇ; Grants I., 16ᵃ.

KEELING, John, of Hackney and the Inner Temple, Esq., s. of Thomas, of Newcastle-under-Line, co. Staff.; Quarterly, 30 April 1632, by Segar. Stowe MS. 677, fo. 53; Add. MSS. 12,225, fo. 65ᵇ, and 14,262, fo. 47; Guil. 179; Reliquary, xv., 259.

KEELING, Sir John, Kt., Lord Chief Justice, King's Bench, by Sir E. Bysshe. Harl. MS. 1457, fo. 327ᵇ.

KELK, ... by Cooke, Clar. Stowe MS. 670, fo. 51; Harl. MS. 6140, fo. 53.

KELLETT, Matthew, of Ripley, Surrey, 1 or 15 Oct. 1550, by Hawley. Add. MS. 16,940, fo. 204; Guil. 164; Harl. MS. 1115, fo. 66ᵇ.

KELLY, William, s. of .... Kelly of Torrington, Devon, ... 1589, by Cooke, Clar. Stowe MS. 670, fo. 35; Add. MS. 14,297, fo. 33.

KELSEY, John, of Chelmsford, Essex, and his brother Henry and all the issue of their father George, of Thorpe, Essex, granted 24 June 1634, by R. St. George, Clar. Harl. MS. 1470, fo. 12, copy of grant, Brit. Mus.; Guil. 344.

KEMBER, of the North, ... 14 Hen. VII. .... 1498-9, by John Writhe, Gart. Harl. MS. 1422, fo. 15ᵇ.

KEMBLE, George, of Wydell, Wilts, new crest granted 21 Nov. 1602, by Camden. MSS. Ashm. 858, fo. 202-3, and 840, fo. 407, copy of grant, Bodleian Lib.

KEMPE, ... crest .... Barker's Grants, 1526—49, Harl. MS. 5846, fo. 64; Stowe MS. 692, fo. 61.

KEMP, Edward, of Dover, Esquire of the body to the King, 1614, by Segar. Add. MS. 12,225, fo. 66; Harl. MS. 6140, fo. 25ᵇ.

KEMPE, William, of South Malling, Sussex, 1 Dec. 1662, by Sir E. Bysshe, Clar. Harl. MS. 1105, fo. 16ᵇ; Add. MS. 14,293, fo. 12ᵇ; Misc. Gen. et Her., 2nd S., vol. iii., p. 372, plate; Bysshe's Grants, fo. 2, Her. Coll.; 6ᵗʰ Decʳ in Guil., p. 125.

KEMPTON, ... the younger .... Az., a fesse betw. three fleurs-de-lis or (Kympton), by R. Cooke, Clar. Stowe MS. 670, fo. 23.

„ Edw., of London, ... 1587 .... by Cooke. Harl. MS. 1422, fo. 94; Add. MS. 4966, fo. 56ᵇ, same crest and coat as William Kimpton, tho' only two fleurs-de-lis in chief.

„ Robert, of Gray's Inn, gent., granted 15 Sept. 1579, by Cooke. (1577 in

Stowe MS. 676, fo. 49); copy of grant, Q's Coll. Oxf. MSS. 37, fo. 66, and 38, fo. 98, sable, a pelican betw. three fleurs-de-lis or.

KIMPTON, William, of Monken Hadley, Middx., Alderm. of London, 3 April 1574, by Cooke. Harl. MS. 1359, fo. 109ᵇ; Misc. Gen. et Her., i., 46, and Monken Hadley, by F. C. Cass, p. 54; original grant, Add. Charters, No. 6218, Brit. Mus.

KENDALL, John, of co. Leic., exemplified 22 Aug. 1443, 21 Hen. VI., by "Clarnsew" King of Arms (? Leigh). MSS. Ashm. 844, fo. 16, and 858, fo. 109, copy of grant, Bodleian Lib., and (Staff. Visit., 1614, C. 10, fo. 133, Her. Coll.); Guil. 412; in Egerton MS. 996, fo. 86ᵇ, with seal of Clar.

KENE, John, North Cove, Suff., gift 3 May 1562. (Harvey's Grants), Add. MS. 16,940, fo. 59ᵇ; Harl. MS. 1085, fo. 15.

KENNE, Christopher, of Kenne, Somers., Esq., crest given 8 April 1561, 3 Q. Eliz., by Harvey. Harl. MS. 1359, fo. 19ᵇ; Add. MS. 16,940, fo. 27ᵇ.

KENESTON, *see* KYNASTON.

KENNETT, Sir Thomas, Alderm. of Coventry . . . . by Dethick, Gart. Burke's Armory.

KENSEY, John, Esq., J.P., co. Hertford, and Capt. of a troop of horse in Shropshire, 1651, by Ryley, Norr. Harl. MS. 1441, fo. 153ᵇ.

KENT, John, of Devizes, Wilts, s. of Roger, of Coppenhall, Cheshire, 24 June 1615, by St. George, Norr. Harl. MSS. 1422, fo. 14, and 6140, fo. 73ᵇ.

KENWRICKE, Richard, s. of Robert, of King Sutton, Northants, Esq., Quarterly of 6 and crest 1613, marshalled by W. Camden, Clar. Grants II., 584; Harl. MS. 5887, fo. 104ᵇ, and Stowe MS. 677, fo. 17ᵇ.

KENYAN, Thomas, of London, ... 1590, by Cooke, Harl. MS. 1359, fo. 103ᵇ.

KEPPES, Thomas, of Hothfield, Kent, out of co. Worc. (seal bearer to Edwᵈ, Lord Littleton, Keeper of the great seal, etc.), Augmentation 8 April 1646 at Oxford, by Walker. Add. MS. 14,293, fo. 106; Harl. MS. 1172, fo. 73; MS. Ashm. 858, fo. 48, copy of grant, Bodleian Lib.; Grants I., fo. 401; Her. Coll., fo. 26 [? Walker's Grants].

KERCHER (Robert), D.D., of Norfolk, confirmed April 1606, by Camden. Harl. MS. 6095, fo. 21; Guil. 359; Harl. MS. 5887, fo. 32ᵇ.

KERRIDGE, Thomas (Capt., a distinguished diplomatist *temp.* Chas. I.), granted 17 June 1629, by Sir R. St. George, Clar. Guil. 343; Grants II., 643ᵇ; Le Neve's MS. 479.

KERY, Thomas, Clerk of the Privy Seal . . . . by Cooke. Harl. MSS. 1422, fo. 23, and 6140, fo. 37ᵇ and 70ᵇ.

KETELBYE, ... crest . . . . Barker's Grants, Harl. MS. 5846, fo. 63; Stowe MS. 692, fo. 61.

KETLING, Arthur, now residing in Germany, descended of an ancient family in Ireland, s. of John, s. of Robert, of Nicholstowne Castle, co. Tipperary; patent 16 or 18 July 1612, by Segar. Add. MS. 12,225, fo. 66.

KETRIDGE, Richard, of London, ... 1593, by Cooke. Harl. MS. 1359, fo. 112; Add. MS. 4966, fo. 25; Harl. MS. 5887, fo. 73ᵇ.

KETTILL, William, and his son John, and to the posterity of either of them, by Cooke, Clar., 10 June 1573. Stowe MS. 670, fo. 80; Add. MS. 4966, fo. 53.

KEVALL, George, of London, gent., 15 July 1577, by Cooke, Clar. Proc. Soc. Antiq., 1897, p. 352.

KEVETT, Thomas, of Coventry, Alderm., granted . . . . 1558, by Sir G. Dethick, Gart. Harl. MSS. 5823 and 5847; Q's Coll. Oxf. MS. 145, fo. 19ᵇ; Guil. 184; (? confirmed by Cooke 1583, Harl. MS. 1470, or 1573-4, Q's Coll. Oxf. MS. 145); called Knevet, Harl. MS. 1441, fo. 73ᵇ; Harl. MS. 1470, fo. 6, 184 and 185ᵇ.

KEY, Anne, wife to Alderm. Allot (Lord Mayor of London 1590): sa., a chevron ar., a flower de lice in chief ar., by W. Dethick, Gart. Add. MS. 26,753, fo. 122ᵇ; (Stowe MS. 590, fo. 8, for Allott pedigree) dau. of Edmund, wife

1st of Henry Malishe of London ; Harl. MSS. 1453, fo. 35[b], and 3526, fo. 14[b]. *See* ALLETT.

KEYLE, ... crest .... Barker's Grants, Harl. MS. 5846, fo. 62[b] ; Stowe MS. 692, fo. 61.

KEYLLE, Thomas, of London, coat and crest. Barker's Grants, Harl. MS. 5846, fo. 61[b] ; Stowe MS. 692, fo. 61.

KEINSHAM [KEYNSHAM], George, Tempsford, Bedf., confirmed 14 Nov. 1570, by Sir G. Dethicke, Cooke and Flower. Harl. MS. 1441, fo. 76[b] ; Q's Coll. Oxf. MS. 145, fo. 26.

KEYS, Roger, and ⎱ letters patent 19 May 1449, 27 H. VI. Excerpta
„ Thomas, and his desc[ts], ⎰ Historica, 49 ; Her. and Geneal., i., 137. *See* ETON COLLEGE.

KEYT, Roger, of Dorset, ... 1586, by Cooke. Harl. MS. 1359, fo. 112[b].

„ William, of Dorset, Quarterly .... 1586, by Cooke. Harl. MSS. 1359, fo. 103, and 1422, fo. 116 ; Roger in Stowe MS. 670.

„ William, of Chesselborne, Dorset, ... 1588, by Cooke. Harl. MSS. 1359, fo. 108[b], and 1422, fo. 94 ; Add. MS. 4966, fo. 87.

Kidermister, Edmund, of Langley Marish, Bucks, one of the six clerks in the Court of Chancery, s. of John, of Langley, confirmed 17 Nov. 1594 (or 1593), by W. Dethick, Gart. Stowe MS. 676, fo. 112 ; copy of grant, Q's Coll. Oxf. MS. 36, fo. 46.

KIDERMASTER, Thomas, of Colshall, co. Warwick, and of Lincoln's Inn, by Segar. Add. MS. 12,225, fo. 66[b] ; Harl. MS. 6140, fo. 78[b].

KYDWELLYE, ... crest .... Barker's Grants, Harl. MS. 5846, fo. 63[b] ; Stowe MS. 692, fo. 61.

KILBY, Humphrey, esq., major to the Orange reg[t] of trayned bands (or serg[t]-major to reg[t] of foot, London), 13 November 1660, by Walker. Harl. MS. 1441, fo. 130[b] ; Her. Coll. 35 ; a glasseman on Ludgate Hill, Harl. MS. 6179, fo. 38[b].

KILLINGWORTH, John, of Balsham, co. Camb., after of Bradley, Suff., gent., s. of Richard, of same counties, gent., etc., arms confirmed and crest granted by Sir G. Dethick. Q's Coll. Oxf. MS. 36, fo. 66, for copy of grant, confirmed by W. Dethick, Gart., 25 Nov. 1586 ; Stowe MS. 676, fo. 122 ; (Harl. MS. 6179, fo. 55[b], of Northumberland, by St. George).

KIMPTON, *see* KEMPTON.

KINDER, William, of Notts, 10 Feb. 1614-15, by R. St. George, Norr. Add. MS. 14,295, fo. 55[b].

KINGE, ... of London, sa., on a chevron betw. three cross crosslets or as many escallops of the field ; Crest, a hand [cubit arm erect] grasping a [broken] spear, by Camden. Harl. MSS. 6095, fo. 7, and 1422, fo. 36[b].

KING, ... London, 1590 : sa., a chev. erm. charged with three escallops gu. ; crest, a talbot's head erased sa., eared and collared or (Berry).

„ Alexander, of London, ... 1592, by Cooke. Harl. MSS. 1359, fo. 103, and 1422, fo. 36[b].

„ Edward, of Bromley, Kent, 20 Feb. 1660-61, by Sir E. Walker, Gart. Her. Coll. 37. ? Ancestor of Duckworth King, Bart.

„ (Peter) of London, goldsmith .... by Cooke. Add. MS. 4966, fo. 100[b] ; Stowe MS. 670 ; Harl. MSS. 1359, fo. 118[b], and 1422, fo. 36[b].

KYNGE, Richard, of Staynefield, Suff., ... 1589, by Cooke. Harl. MS. 1359, fo. 94[b].

KING, Richard, of Sherborne, Dorset, J.P., and of the Inner Temple, Counsellor-at-law, granted [6th or] 10 April 1641, by Borough, Gart. (1 April in Harl. MS. 1105, fo. 57) ; Guil. 245 ; Q's Coll. Oxf. MS. 146, fo. 471 ; Misc. Grants IV., 24.

„ Richard, Exeter, 14 Jan. 1691-2, by T. St. George, Gart. and Clar. Harl. MS. 6834, fo. 178 ; Grants IV., fo. 110 ; Harl. MS. 1085, fo. 56.

KYNG, Robert, of Much Baddow, Essex [2nd s. of John], gift 15⅝ [28 July 1562], (Harvey's Grants), Add. MS. 16,940, fo. 60.

KING, Robert, of Somersetshire, and at this tyme one of the Gent. Ushers to the King and Queen's most excellent Majesties, granted 15 April, 2 and 3 Phil. and Mary. 1556, by Sir G. Dethick. Copy of grant, Q's Coll. Oxf. MS. 39, fo. 64 ; Harl. MS. 1359, fo. 67 ; Grants I., 238.

„ Thomas, of Stanyford, Suff., ... by Cooke. Stowe MS. 670, fo. 43.

„ Thomas, Alderman of Coventry, co. Warwick, 26 Dec. 1683, by Sir Wm. Dugdale, Gart. and Clar. Harl. MS. 6834, fo. 178 ; Grants III., fo. 229.

KINGDOME, Capt. . . . . . London, by W. Dugdale, Norr. Harl. MS. 6179, fo. 39.

KINGFORD, Robert, of Youlkstone, par. of Morwinstow, Cornwall, 23 Oct. 1691, by T. St. George, Gart. and Clar. Grants IV., 94 ; Stowe MSS. 714, fo. 71ᵇ, 128ᵇ, 161 (23ʳᵈ Oct.), and 716, fo. 51ᵇ ; Harl. MSS. 6179, fo. 74, and 1085, fo. 56.

KING'S COLLEGE, Cambridge, Letters Patent of Hen. VI., 1 Jan. 1450-1, Record Office. 1448-9 in Cat. Her. Exhib. Soc. of Antiq., p. 60 ; copy of grant, Excerpta Historica, 362 ; Her. and Geneal., i., 119.

KINGSTON or KYNGESTON, John de, prior to combat with a French knight, letters patent at Westm. 1 July (Aug.), 13 R. II., 1389. Stowe MSS. 840, fo. 55ᵇ, and 679, fo. 116 ; Harl. MS. 1507, fo. 426 ; N. and Q., 1st S., iii., 88, and pat. rolls. 13 R. II., pars. i., m. 37 ; Prynne's 4th Institute, p. 68 ; see Stowe MS. 697, fo. 116, for trick ; Le Neve's MS. 426.

KIPPES, Thomas, see KEPPES.

KYPPING, Robert, of Kent, 16 Jan. 1545-6, by Hawley. Add. MS. 16,940, fo. 201.

KYRBYE, ... arg., two bars gu., on a canton of the last a lion's head erased or ; crest, out of a ducal coronet per pale or and argent an elephant's head gules, ears arg., tusks or, ... ? 1586, by Cooke. Harl. MSS. 1359, fo. 111, and 1422, fo. 92ᵇ ; crest, Add. MS. 4966, fo. 60ᵇ.

KIRBY, ... Crosby, co. Lanc., Quarterly . . . . by R. St. George. Stowe MS. 716, fo. 55. 1 and 4, arg., two bars gu., on a canton of the last a cross moline or ; 2 and 3, arg., on a bend sa. three lozenges arg. charged with a cross [saltire] sa. Crest, a lion statant arg., collared and holding in its dexter forepaw a cross crosslet or.

KYRKEBY, Jone, wife to Sir William Laxton, Mayor of London. 20 July 1556, by Hawley. Add. MS. 16,940, fo. 208 ; Harl. MS. 1116, fo. 46, copy of grant.

KIRKE, see Michael LOWE. Stowe MS. 670, fo. 52, probably a quartering.

„ Capt. David, s. of Jervice, of London, merchant, late of Dieppe in France, s. of Thurston, of Greenhill, par. Norton, co. Derby, etc., after Knt. and Govʳ of Newfoundland ; 1 Dec. 1631, by R. St. George, Clar. Stowe MS. 677, fo. 62 : and his brothers both by sea and land, augmentation ; no date (? same). For the capture of De Raymond, the French Admiral, in Harl. MS. 1196, fo. 48.

„ George, Master of the Robes and one of H.M.'s bedchamber, 20 June, 33 Jac. [VI. of Scotland], 1600, by J. Balfour, Lyon K. of A. Grants II., 670, and I., 9, 115 ; Stowe MS. 677, fo. 59.

„ Lewis, capt. and governor of a fort in Canada captured ⎫
from the French, ⎪
„ Thomas, capt. and Vice Admiral of the family fleet (or ⎬ bros. of Capt.
merchantmen), ⎪ David aforesaid.
„ John, and ⎱ land lubbers, "both by sea and land," ⎭
„ James, ⎰

KIRTON, Edward, of Almesford, Somerset, certified by R. Cooke. Visit. Middx., 1568 ; Grants II., 523.

KYRTON, Stephen, Alderm. of London ; 1573, by Cooke or G. Dethick. Quarterly of 4. Harl. MS. 1422, fo. 113.

KYRWIN, William, of London, freemason, s. of John, of Yorkshire, descended from

U

Curwen ; confirmed 1 Jan. 1586-7, by W. Dethick, Gart. Stowe MS. 676, fo. 69ᵇ ; Q's Coll. Oxf. MS. 37, fo. 99, copy of grant.

KITCHEN, John, of Pelyn, co. Lanc., coat and crest. ? This a 2nd grant or [there was] a subsequent grant to this. Barker's Grants, Harl. MS. 5846, fo. 64ᵇ ; Stowe MS. 692, fo. 61ᵇ bis.

KYTCHYN, John, of Islington, Middx., from Belper, co. Derby, granted 12 Feb. 1578-9, by Flower. MS. Ashm. 34, fo. 13, copy of grant, Bodleian Lib. ; Guil. 234 ; Harl. MS. 5887, fo. 88ᵇ ; Reliquary xxii., 244.

„ John, of Gray's Inn, impaling Gaywood or Mayfield ?, by Cooke. Stowe MS. 670, fo. 20.

KITCHEN, Robert, s. of Richard, of co. Lanc., grant (?45 Q. Eliz.) by W. Dethick, Gart. Stowe MS. 676, fo. 141 ; copy of grant, Q's Coll. Oxf. MS. 36, fo. 103.

KITCHINMAN, ... (Helmsley, Yorkshire), patent . . . . April 1616, by Camden. Harl. MSS. 6095, fo. 35ᵇ, and 1422, fo. 40ᵇ : argt., on a pile sable betw. two cross crosslets fitchée gu. three lozenges of the field.

KYTSON, ... crest . . . . Barker's Grants, Harl. MS. 5846, fo. 63ᵇ ; Stowe MS. 692, fo. 61.

„ Thomas, of Hengrave, Suff., grant 14 April 1527, by Wriothesley and Benolte. Visit. of Suffolk [1561], by J. J. Howard, ii., 97. 99 ; Add. MS. 26,702, fo. 53ᵇ ; Harl. MSS. 1395, fo. 54, and 1441, fo. 72ᵇ ; Guil. 241.

„ Thomas, of Hengrave, Suff., alteration of arms and crest 13 Feb. 1568-9, by Sir G. Dethick, Gart., Cooke and Flower. Copy of grant, Q's Coll. Oxf. MSS. 39, fo. 148 (MS. 145, fo. 18ᵇ) ; Harl. MSS. 1359, fo. 54, and 1441, fo. 72ᵇ.

KNAPLOCK, Robert, of Winchester, Hants, confirmed . . . . 1601, by Camden, Clar. Harl. MS. 1441, fo. 143.

KNAPP, Henry, of Hintlesham, Suff., ... 1576, 18 Q. Eliz., by Cooke. Harl. MSS. 1359, fo. 123, and 1085, fo. 15ᵇ.

„ Henry, of Woodcot, Oxon., confirmed or granted 2 Sept. 1669, by Sir Ed. Bysshe, Clar. Harl. MS. 1105, fo. 40 ; Guil. 346 ; Bysshe's Grants, 4, 33.

KNATCHBULL, Richard, Mersham, Kent, ... 1574, by Cooke. Harl. MSS. 1359, fo. 107, and 1422, fo. 93ᵇ ; Add. MS. 4966, fo. 30.

KNESWORTH, ..., Lord Mayor (Thomas, 1505) ; 12 Hen. VII., 1496-7 [Sheriff 1495-6] ; E. IV. [?], Add. MS. 26,702, fo. 37.

KNIGHT, ... crest . . . . Barker's Grants, Harl. MS. 5846, fo. 62 ; Stowe MS. 692, fo. 61.

„ Arthur, and ⎱ . . . . of London, sons of John, out of Kent, by Segar. Add.
„ Stephen, ⎰ MS. 12,225, fo. 66ᵇ ; C. 24 [Visit. Lond., 1634], fo. 508ᵇ, Her. Coll. ; Guil. 371.

„ Bezaliel, of Banbury, Oxf., ... by J. Borough, Gart. Add. MS. 26,702, fo. 89ᵇ ; Harl. MS. 1105, fo. 55ᵇ.

„ Francis, of Mitcham, Surrey, Sir John, of Bristol, and Fitzherbert and Isaack, 10 Feb. 1668-9. Bysshe's Grants, Her. Coll. Harl. MS. 1105, fo. 20ᵇ and 21* : argt., three pales gu., on a (fo. 21) canton of the 2ⁿᵈ a spur and leather or ; crest, out of a mural coronet arg. an eagle volant or.

„ George, Mayor of Bristol. 18 Oct. 1652, by Bysshe, Gart. Harl. MS. 6832, fo. 413ᵇ ; Add. MS. 26,758, fo. 16.

„ Henry, als BROTHERS, of Clerkenwell, citizen of London and free of the company of Brewers (s. of Richard Knight alias Brothers of Lowton, Bedf.). 25 July 1664, by Walker. Add. MSS. 14,293, fo. 38, and 14,294, fo. 10 ; Harl. MS. 1172, fo. 53 : (Guil. 320) copy of grant.

„ Humphrey, of the cittie of London, coat and crest. Barker's Grants . . . . Harl. MS. 5846, fo. 64 ; Stowe MS. 692, fo. 61ᵇ.

„ John, of Charwelton, Northants, gent., s. of Thomas, etc. ; collaterally descended from Knight of Salop ; arms confirmed with diff. and crest given

8 May 1613, 11 K. Jac., by Camden. Copy of grant, Q's Coll. Oxf. MS. 38, fo. 125 ; Harl. MSS. 6095, fo. 27, and 1359, fo. 19ᵇ.

KNIGHT, John, Surgeon-Chirurgeon, 1 June 1661, by Sir E. Walker, Gart. Her. Coll., 40.

„   Michael, of Westerham, Kent, s. of Christopher, of Cudham, Kent, and Mary his wife, dau. and sole h. of John Platt of Wigan, co. Lanc. ; Knight and Platt quarterly, 20 Feb. 1662, by Sir Ed. Bysshe, Clar. Bysshe's Grants, fo. 5, Her. Coll. ; 18th Feb. in Harl. MS. 1105, fo. 17ᵇ ; Add. MS. 14,293, fo. 4ᵇ ; Guil. 394.

„   Nathan, of Ruscombe, Berks, a barrister of Lincoln's Inn ; 30 Nov. 1670. Bysshe's Grants, fo. 26, Her. Coll. ; Harl. MS. 1105, fo. 21ᵇ.

„   Richard, of Sᵗ Dennes in Hants, quarterly arms confirmed and crest given .... 1583, by Cooke. Harl. MSS. 1359, fo. 120, 1394, fo. 120, and 1422, fo. 117ᵇ ; Add. MS. 14,295, fo. 33.

„   Richard, of Cowden, Kent, } 24 Aug. 1671, by Sir E. Bysshe, Clar.
„   Richard, of the same, his uncle, } Harl. MS. 1105, fo. 22 ; Bysshe's Grants, 28.

„   Robert, of Bromley, Kent, gent., grant 14 July 1548, by T. Hawley. Copy of grant, Q's Coll. Oxf. MS. 38, fo. 48 ; Add. MS. 16,940, fo. 203 ; Stowe MS. 677, fo. 6 ; (Grants II., 485).

„   Thomas, of Hoo, co. Southants (a clerk of the signet to H. VIII. and under treasurer of his mint, Guil. 318), coat and crest granted 8 April 1546, by Barker. Harl. MS. 5846, fo. 64ᵇ ; Stowe MS. 692, fo. 61ᵇ ; Harl. MS. 1470, fo. 90, 183, copy of grant, Brit. Mus. ; Grants I., fo. 5.

„   William (Fellow of New Coll., Oxf.), letters patent, 20 July 1514, by gift from Maximilian the Emperor ; Prothonotary of the apostolical seat and Ambassʳ from H. VIII. to Emperor Maximilian ; Bishop of Bath and Wells 1541—47 ; d. 29 Sept. 1547. Q's Coll. Oxf. MS. 38, fo. 24, and Harl. MS. 1507, fo. 417, for copy of letters patent ; Berry's Appdx. ; Le Neve's MS. 417.

„   William, of Southampton, Hants, Collector of the subsidies ; 4 Feb. 1549-50, by Hawley. Add. MS. 16,940, fo. 203ᵇ ; Harl. MS. 1544, fo. 190ᵇ.

„   William, of Abthorpe, Northants, brother of Thomas, of Hoo, named above, coat confirmed and crest granted 24 March 1565, by Hervey. Harl. MS. 1470, fo. 89, 183, copy of grant, Brit. Mus. ; Guil. 319 ; Grants I., fo. 6.

KNIGHTBRIDGE, Anthony, of Chelmsford, Essex, and to
„   Richard, } his brothers, May 1663. Harl. MSS. 1105, fo. 17, and 1470,
„   John,   } fo. 129, copy of grant, Brit. Mus. ; Bysshe's Grants, fo. 3, Her.
„   George, } Coll. ; Guil. 126.

KNIGHTLEY, William, of Kingston-upon-Thames (1623), by Camden. Morgan's Sphere, 118.

KNIPE, Christopher, of London, s. of James, of Wharton, co. Lanc., gent., arms confirmed and crest granted 10 Nov. 1616, by Segar. Add. MS. 12,225, fo. 67 ; Guil. 193 ; Grants I., 411, 415 ; Harl. MSS. 5887, fo. 115, and 6140, fo. 77.

KNOLLER, Robert, of Herne, Kent, ... 1626, by Segar : arg., on a bend cotticed sa. a lyon passant guardant erm., crowned or. Add. MS. 12,225, fo. 69.

KNOWLER, Robert, of Stroode, par. of Herne, Kent, grant 10 April 1626, by Segar : arg., on a bend betw. two cottices sa. a lyon passant guardant of the field, crowned or. Add. MS. 12,225, fo. 69ᵇ ; Stowe MS. 618, fo. 231ᵇ.

KNOT, Anthony, rector of Whitchurch, and to his brethren, sons of Anthony ; granted 15 April 1632, by Sir R. St. George, Norr. Harl. MS. 1470, fo. 212, copy of grant, Brit. Mus. ; Guil. 307 ; Harl. MS. 6179, fo. 26.

KNOWLES, Richard, of Cold Ashby, Northants, s. of Roger, 8 Nov. 1580, by Sir G. Dethick, Gart. Harl. MS. 1441, fo. 100ᵇ ; Q's Coll. Oxf. MS. 145, fo. 50 ; Harl. MS. 1085, fo. 16ᵇ.

KNOLLES, Sir Robert, coat .... Barker's Grants, Harl. MS. 5846, fo. 61^b ; Stowe MS. 692, fo. 60 *bis.*

KNOWSLEY, Robert, of North Burton als Fleming, Yorks (mar. Anne, dau. and coh. of the parson of Rudston) ; 13 Sept. 1612, by R. St. George, Norr. Stowe MS. 706, fo. 15 ; Harl. MS. 6140, fo. 72^b.

KYNASTON, Bryan, of Thornington, Essex, ... by Cooke. Harl. MS. 1359, fo. 117^b ; Add. MS. 4966, fo. 29.

„ John (KENESTONE), of the Woodhouse, co. Salop, s. of Thomas, s. of Jasper, s. of Jenkins, 2nd s. of Philip Kynaston in the Stockes, Salop, esq. ; 19 (or 29) April 1569, by Sir G. Dethick, Gart., Cooke and Flower. Harl. MS. 1441, fo. 72^b ; copy of grant, Q's Coll. Oxf. MS. 39, fo. 153 (and MS. 145, fo. 18) ; Harl. MS. 1359, fo. 56.

KYNNE, Robert, Send, co. Glouc., ... by Cooke. Stowe MS. 670, fo. 63.

KYRLE, Anthony, of the Middle Temple, crest 10 Jan. 1584-5, by Cooke. Q's Coll. Oxf. MS. 38, fo. 108, copy of grant ; Grants I., fo. 14 ; Harl. MS. 5887, fo. 4^b ; Stowe MS. 670, fo. 8^b ; Add. MS. 14,297, fo. 8^b ; quarterly in Harl. MS. 6140, fo. 44^b.

L

LACY, John, of London, mercer in Cheapside, bd. [bur.] 14 Sept. 1606 ; .... by Cooke. Harl. MS. 1359, fo. 118 ; Add. MS. 4966, fo. 96 ; Harl. MS. 5887, fo. 37^b, and wife.

„ Thomas, } of Spilman Hall, Suff., gent., ... ?1575, by Sir G. Dethick.
„ John, } Harl. MS. 1441, fo. 84 ; Q's Coll. Oxf. MS. 145, fo. 39.
„ William, }

„ William, als HEDGES, of city of London, mercht., } and to the desc^{ts} of his
„ Charles, D.C.L., } great-grandfather John
Lacy. E. Marshal's Warrant 25 Nov. 1687, by H. St. George, Norr. Stowe MS. 714, fo. 94^b, 103 ; Grants III., 336 ; Lansd. MS. 867, fo. 52.

LADE, Robert, of Gray's Inn, Esq., s. and h. of Vincent, of Bareham, Kent, etc., "approbat." of ye aforesaid arms quartering Mumbray .... by Segar. Add. MS. 12,225, fo. 67 ; Harl. MSS. 6140, fo. 79^b, and 1441, fo. 154^b.

LAKE, Edward, Chancellor dioc. of Lincoln, 30 Dec., 19 Chas. [1643] ; Augmentation by Chas. I. for services at Edge Hill. *See* Baronetages. Berry ; Harl. MS. 6832, fo. 247 ; 12 June 1661 in Le Neve's MS. 508.

„ John, of Normanton, Yorks, gent., arms confirmed and crest a gift at Wakefield (7 Oct. Harl. MS. 1394, fo. 37^b) 1564, 6 Q. Eliz., by Flower. Harl. MSS. 1359, fo. 42^b, and 1422, fo. 111^b ; Add. MS. 14,295, fo. 73.

LAKINGTON, Edward, of Washbourne, Devon, confirmation of arms and grant of crest ; quarterly of 8 and 5 others named .... by Segar. Add. MS. 12,225, fo. 67^b.

LAMBARD, John, of Ledbury, co. Heref., gent., and at this time shryve to the King's Majestie of the city of London, grant 15 July 1551, by Hawley. Add. MS. 16,940, fo. 201^b, as Lambert ; Her. and Geneal. i., 80 ; 1552 in Arch. Cant., vol. v., 247.

LAMBE, Thomas, of Trimley in Thurlestone, Suff., confirmed arms and crest 3 July 1559, 2 Q. Eliz., by Harvey. Harl. MS. 1359, fo. 22^b ; Add. MSS. 14,295, fo. 47^b, and 16,940, fo. 36.

LAMBERT, Richard, of London, gift 1564. (Harvey's Grants), Add. MS. 16,940, fo. 46^b ; Harl. MS. 5887, fo. 10.

LAMLEY, Francis, of Clipston, Northants, gules, on a fess argent three mullets sable between three fowles argent ; a pedigree of the family extracted by the Industry of Robert Cooke, Clarenceux, and Edmond Knight, Norrey, both Kings of Armes, etc. Bannerman's MS., No. 9, fo. 511.

LANDOR (als LAUNDER ?), Walter, Rugeley, co. Staff., 11 June 1687, by Sir T. St. George, Gart., and J. Dugdale, Norr. Harl. MS. 6834, fo. 178 ; Grants III., fo. 320 ; Berry ; Lansd. MS. 867. fo. 52.

LANE, ... crest .... Barker's Grants, Harl. MS. 5846, fo. 70 ; Stowe MS. 692, fo. 64ᵇ.

„ . . . ., or, a chev. erminois ? betw. three mullets pierced az. ; patent .... by Segar. Add. MS. 12,225, fo. 67ᵇ.

„ Sir George, Knt., a clerk of the P.C. (s. of Sir Richard, of Tulske, co. Roscommon, Bart.). 18 years Sec. to James, Duke of Ormond, etc.; augmentation 9 April 1661, by Walker. Add. MSS. 14,293, fo. 26, 14,294, fo. 2 ; Harl. MS. 1172, fo. 49, copy of grant ; Genealogist i., 376.

„ Sir Richard, Knt., Keeper of the Great Seal Chas. II., Roy. Warrant at Castle of Elizabeth, Isle of Jersey, 8 Feb. 1649-50. Harl. MS. 1470, fo. 73, 79 ; MS. Ashm. 858, fo. 55—57, copy of grant, Bodleian Lib. ; Augmentation and alteration at Jersey 17 Dec. 1649, by Sir E. Walker, Gart., Her. Coll., 1.

„ Sir Richard, of Tulske, co. Roscommon, Knt. and Bart., s. of George, and 2nd s. of Henry, of Cowarth, Berks, by Anne Norris, his wife, consin german unto Sir John Norris ; crest 6 April 1661, by Walker. Harl. MS. 1052, fo. 210, copy of grant, Brit. Mus.

„ (Thomas), Bentley, Staff., s. of John, crest and augmentation : a canton of the arms of England for services by Col. John Lane after the battle of Worcester ; 5 Feb. 1678, by Sir Wᵐ Dugdale, Gart., and Sᵗ George, Norr. Harl. MS. 6834, fo. 178 ; Grants III., fo. 150ᵇ ; Harl. MS. 6179, fo. 98 ; Gent. Mag., i., 279 ; Boscobel Tracts, ed. by J. Hughes, 2nd ed., 293-4.

„ William, of Lewes, Sussex, 16 Dec. 1668, by Bysshe, Clar. Add. MSS. 26,758, fo. 16ᵇ, and 14,295, fo. 81ᵇ ; Harl. MSS. 6179, fo. 25ᵇ, and 6832, fo. 113ᵇ.

LANGDALE, Marmaduke, Baron of, Holme, Yorks ; supporters 9 Oct. 1660, by Walker. Stowe MS. 677, fo. 67.

LANGFORD, John, of Salford (? Shelford), Bedf., March 1607, by Camden. Query Langford quartering Rogeres. Harl. MSS. 6095, fo. 8ᵇ, and 1422, fo. 108 ; Guil. 104.

„ John, of Gray's Inn, patent, quarterly of 4 .... by Segar. Add. MS. 12,225, fo. 68 ; C. 24 [Visit. Lond., 1634], fo. 408, Her. Coll. ; Guil. 206, he of Alington ; Harl. MS. 6140, fo. 75ᵇ.

LANGHORN, William, of Barnard's Inn, s. of William, of Bedford, gent., 20 Jan. 1610-11, 8 K. E. ?, [8 Jas. l.] by Camden. Harl. MSS. 6095, fo. 15, and 1422, fo. 35ᵇ ; Guil. 316 ; Harl. MS. 6140, fo. 40ᵇ.

LANGLAND, see LONGLAND.

LANGLEY, John, citizen and fishmonger of London (out of Lanc.), confirmed 4 June 1632, by Sir Richᵈ Sᵗ George, Clar. Q's Coll. Oxf. MS. 36, fo. 128, copy of grant ; Harl. MS. 1470, fo. 33 and 247, copy of grant, Brit. Mus. ; Guil. 385.

„ Richard (town clerk of London, Harl. MS. 6095, fo. 23, same arms), of Lincoln's Inn, gent., s. of Roger, of Shrewsbury, Salop, gent., youngest s. of Roger, of Madeley, Salop ; arms confirmed and crest given 20 Jan., 40 Eliz., 1597-8, by Camden. Add. MS. 14,295, fo. 120 ; Harl. MSS. 1359, fo. 38, and 1422, fo. 37ᵇ ; Guil. 357.

„ Thomas, North Grimston, Yorks, gent., 10 Sept. 1666, by W. Dugdale, Norr. Her. Coll.

LANGSTON, Robert, prothonotary of the common pleas (prothonotaries Apostolicalis Metropolitane), doctor of both laws (? D. Can. L. and D.C.L.), coat. Barker's Grants, Harl. MSS. 5846, fo. 69, and 1422, fo. 68 ; Stowe MS. 692, fo. 64.

LANGTON, James, of Kingston, Surrey, gent., 4th in descent from Christopher, said to be brother of the Baron of Walton, a little from Preston in Andrez

(Amounderness), co. Lanc., etc.: confirmed 29 Aug. 1592, by W. Dethick, Gart., on the testimony of several Cumbrians. Q's Coll. Oxf. MS. 37, fo. 122, copy of confirmation.

LANGTON, John, of Langton, co. Linc., crest confirmed . . . . 1562. (Harvey's Grants), Add. MS. 16,940, fo. 24b.

„ John, of Stantonmore, Middx., 7 Dec. 1577, by Sir G. Dethick, Gart. Harl. MS. 1441, fo. 88; Q's Coll. Oxf. MS. 145, fo. 45; Grants I., 19.

„ William, of Broughton, co. Lanc., Esq., confirmed 25 Jan. 1657-8, by Ryley. Harl. MSS. 1105, fo. 11, and 1470, fo. 139; "Made void," Guil. 384 and Berry.

LANT, Thomas, Portcullis Pursuivant, s. of Thomas, s. of Henry, of Staffs, 16 March 158⅞, by Cooke. Stowe MS. 670, fo. 24; Le Neve's MS. 477.

LANWORTH (LANGWORTH), Edward, of Backsted, Sussex: arg., three dragons' heads couped sa., langued gu.: crest, a dragon's head rased erm., collared and langued gu., by Sir G. Dethick, Gart. Add. MS. 26,753, fo. 122b.

LANY, John, Cratfold, Suff., confirmed 12 July 1561, by Harvey. Add. MS. 16,940, fo. 13b: Proc. Soc. Antiq., 1897, p. 350.

LARDER, Thomas, of Somerset, 12 Feb. 1467-8, 7 Ed. IV., by Thos. [Holme], Clar. (Clar. at this time was W. Hawkeslow.) Add. MS. 6297, fo. 143; 7 Ed. III., MS. Ashm. 857, fo. 524-5; 7 Ed. IV., copy of grant, Bodleian Lib.; Harl. MS. 69, fo. 56, 7 Ed. IV. [The correct date is probably the 17th of Edw. IV., 1477-8, see Misc. Gen. et Her., 4th S., v., 268.]

LARKYN, Thomas, of the city of Westminster, Middx., esq., unsigned grant and confirmation 28 Nov. 1611, by Camden. Harl. MS. 1410, fo. 44: chequy argt. and gu., on a cross az. five keys paleways or; crest, a lark az., beaked and legged or, standing on a key of the last.

LARKING, Thomas (or LARKHAM), by Cooke. Stowe MS. 670, fo. 74; Dr of physic, Add. MS. 4966, fo. 67b.

LASCELLS, George, of Estkyrk, co. Yorks, crest 1557. Barker's Grants, Harl. MS. 5846, fo. 71; Stowe MS. 692, fo. 64b; MS. Ashm. 858, fo. 23b, transcribed from an 8vo MS. of Sir Hy. St. George now in the Custody of Sylvanus Morgan, 25 Feb. 1661-2, fo. 211.

LASCOE, William, of Halam, Notts,

„ Henry, } citizen and grocer of London,

„ Francis, }

„ George, citizen and mercer of London,

} sons of William, of Haleham, decd; 20 Feb. 1663-4, by Sir Ed. Bysshe, Clar., and Wm Dugdale, Norr. Stowe MS. 716, fo. 52b; Harl. MS. 1105, fo. 18; Bysshe's Grants, fo. 9, Her. Coll.

LASSETTA, Stanislaus, d'Lopinic "e familia Ravitarum," addition and augmentation by letters patent temp. H. VIII. MS. Ashm. 858, fo. 1-2, copy of letters, Bodleian Lib.

LATCH (John in Stowe MS. 677, fo. 8b): Arg., on a fesse undée az. betw. three escocheons gu. as many lozenges or; "testified" . . . . by Segar. Add. MS. 12,225, fo. 68; "procured by me, R. Mundy," see Stowe MS.; Add. MS. 12,474, fo. 104b.

LATIMER (Thomas Osborne), Visct., supporters 23 May 1674, by Walker. Harl. MS. 6831, fo. 178; Grants III., fo. 40.

LAUNCE, John, of Halesworth, Suff., s. of John; 8 Nov. 1580, by Sir G. Dethick, Gart. Harl. MS. 1441, fo. 100b; Misc. Gen. et Her., N. S., iv., 209; Grants I., 123.

LAUNCESTON als DUNHEVED, Borough of, Cornwall, 24 July 1573, by Cooke, Clar. Misc. Gen. et Her., 2nd S., vol. iii., p. 120, facsimile; copy of grant, Brit. Mus.; Cat. Her. Exhib. Soc. of Antiq., p. 67.

LAUNDER, John, Newhall, co. Lanc., 10 June 1687, by Sir T. St. George and John Dugdale, Norr.: Sa., three mullets of six points in bend argt. betw. two cottises indented or, for Launder of Stafford. Harl. MSS. 1085, fo. 58, and 6834, fo. 178; Grants III., fo. 317; Berry; Lansd. MS. 867, fo. 52.

LAVENDER, Nathl, of London, s. of Elyas, s. of William, of Standen, Herts; coat confirmed and crest granted 7 May 1628, by Segar. Add. MS. 12,225, fo. 68^b; Guil. 397 calls him Nicholas; (see Harl. MS. 1531, fo. 152).

LAW or LAWE, . . . of the North . . . . as entered in the books of the office of arms by Segar. Add. MS. 12,225, fo. 69.

LAWERELL, William, alias WOMBWELL, out of Lanc., 9 July 1565, by Flower, who assigned the crest of Wombwell to the above contrary to the laws of arms. Harl. MS. 1052, fo. 45^b and 51; copy of grant, Harl. MS. 1754, fo. 55^b.

LAURENCE, ..., Sheriff, Rugby . . . . 1559, by Harvey. Harl. MS. 6140, fo. 36^b; Berry.

LAWRENCE (M^r), Quarterly: 1 and 4, sa., three pigeons volant or; 2 and 3, gu., a chev. arg. betw. three griffins' heads erased or. Crest, two hands ppr. lying flat on the wreath holding a garland of bayes vert. Add. MS. 26,753, fo. 123.

LAURENCE. [A trick only, with "Maiore larances" over, and "brown" below the shield.] Arg., a cross raguly [? embattled] gu., on a chief of the last a lion passant guardant silver. Crest, a stag's head erased sa. [? ar. guttée sa.] gorged with a coronet arg., attired or. Stowe MS. 703, fo. 71. [Compare the arms and crest granted to William Laurence of St. Ives, 30 October 1562.]

LAWRENCE, ..., Quarterly: 1 and 4, arg., a cross raguly gu.; 2 and 3, arg., two bars, and in chief three mullets gu. [Washington], [over all on the fesse point] a crescent sable for difference. Crest, a demi-turbot erect arg., the tail upwards, a crescent also for difference; a vellum escocheon with his (Cooke's) name to it. [Miscel. Grants, iv., 129]; Stowe MS. 670, fo. 62; Add. MSS. 14,297, fo. 62, and 4966, fo. 90^b.

LAURENCE, John, Alderm. of London, and to his brothers

„ Abraham, and } sons of Abraham, granted 19 Nov. 1652, by E. Bysshe, Gart.,
„ Richard, } confirmed 18 Sept. 1664: arg., a cross raguly gu., a canton ermines; crest, two trunks of a tree raguly in saltire environed with a chaplet vert. Harl. MS. 1105, fo. 15; Stowe MS. 703, fo. 70 and 71; Harl. MS. 1441, fo. 149^b; Bysshe's Grants, fo. 10, Her. Coll.; Harl. MS. 6179, fo. 31.

LAWRENCE, Richard, of Foxcote, co. Glouc., s. [and h.] of Richard, of the same, granted 1597, 41 Eliz., by W. Dethick, Gart. Stowe MS. 676, fo. 128^b; Q's Coll. Oxf. MS. 36, fo. 77, copy of grant; Misc. Gen. et Her., i., 204, "Argent, a cross ragulé, in the first canton a Lyon passant Gu., And for his Creast . . . . The hed of A Foxe proper having one bezant vppon his necke."

LAURENCE, Thomas, of London, goaldsmyth, by Wm Dethick, Gart., for which he had five pounds, 1594. Harl. MS. 1453, fo. 32, entered by the then York Herald, Ralph Brooke; Guil. 261, arg., a cross raguly, on a chief az. three leopards' heads or.

LAWRENCE, William, St Ives, Hunts, Esq., crest 30 Oct. 1562, by Hervey. Add. MSS. 14,295, fo. 101^b, and 16,940, fo. 53^b.

LAWSE, Thomas, of Kent, D^r of the Civil Law . . . . 1584, by Cooke. Add. MS. 4966, fo. 59; Harl. MS. 1359, fo. 87^b; Add. MS. 14,295, fo. 36; Guil. 87; Harl. MS. 1085, fo. 38.

LAWSON, George, ... with crest . . . . Hen. VIII. Add. MS. 26,702, fo. 47.

„ George, of Barfield, Essex, gent., coat and crest. Barker's Grants, Harl. MS. 5846, fo. 69; Stowe MS. 692, fo. 64.

„ Ralph, of Burgh, Yorks, crest 2 Jan. 1592-3, by Knight, Norr. Surtees Soc., XLI., xliii.; Misc. Gen. et Her., N. S., iii., 29, copy of grant, Brit. Mus.

„ Thomas, of Little Usworth, in the Bishopric of Durham, and to Robert Lawson of Rocke, Northumberland, and to William, John, George and Rowland, all six being the sonnes of William Lawson of the same place, gent., 28 Feb. 1558-9, by Dalton. Harl. MS. 1359, fo. 45^b; MS. Ashm. 834, fo. 13, copy of grant, Bodleian Lib.; Guil. 392.

LAWTON, William, of Church Lawton, Cheshire, crest, by Cooke.   Harl. MS. 1442, fo. 16ᵇ.

LAYCOCK, George, Southwell, Notts. coat confirmed and crest granted 20 Nov. 1613, by R. St. George, Norr.   Harl. MS. 1470, fo. 22, 258, copy of grant, Brit. Mus. ; Lacock in Guil. 346.

LAYFIELD, D.D. (Edward), Archdeacon of Essex and rector of All Hallows, Barking, ... 1639, by Borough.   Harl. MSS. 1105, fo. 55ᵇ, and 1441, fo. 57ᵇ ; Add. MS. 26,702, fo. 90ᵇ ; Guil. 185.

LAYWORTH, ... of Oxfordshire, D.D., ... by Segar.   Vaire, on a saltire gu. five fleurs-de-lis or.   Crest, a lapwing ppr. laying his talons on a liz. (sic, i.e., a fleur-de-lis).   Add. MS. 12,225, fo. 68ᵇ.

LEADER, Oliver, of Much Stoughton, Hunts, coat and crest.   Barker's Grants, Harl. MS. 5846, fo. 80 ; Stowe MS. 692, fo. 73.

LEAKE or LEEKE, Rt. Hon. Sir Francis, Knt. and Bart., created by Jas. I. Baron Deincourt, of Sutton, co. Derby ; confirmation of coat impaling Cary, confirmation of crest, grant of supporters 14 Nov., 1 Chas., 1627, by Segar. (1633 in Add. MS. 12,225, fo. 69ᵇ) ; Harl. MS. 1470, fo. 30, 42, copy of grant, Brit. Mus.

LEAR, Sir Peter, Bart., of Ipplepen, Devon, and late of London, mercht., 12 Nov. 1660, by Walker.   Misc. Gen. et Her., 3rd S., vol. i., p. 233, copy of grant, Brit. Mus.

LEATT, Nicholas, of London, s. of Nicholas, of Horsley, co. Derby ; a patent 13 Dec. 1616, by Camden.   Harl. MSS. 6095, fo. 35, and 1422, fo. 40ᵇ ; Guil. 330.

LEE, ... by Browne, Bluemantle [?].   Stowe MS. 703, fo. 71.

„   Elizabeth, dau. of John, of Stamford, co. Linc., and wife to Sir John Lyon, late of London, Knt. and Alderm.; 6 Oct. 1564, by Sir G. Dethick. Harl. MS. 1441, fo. 65 ; Q's Coll. Oxf. MS. 145, fo. 7ᵇ ; Grants II., 652.

„   John, D.D., Archdeacon of Rochester, s. of Thomas, late of London, gent., decᵈ, by Ann, dau. of T. Warner and sister and h. of Thomas Warner, Bp. of Rochester ; 20 Nov. 1665.   Harl. MS. 1105, fo. 20ᵇ ; Bysshe's Grants, fo. 19, Her. Coll., and Visit. of Kent [1663—68], D. 18, fo. 179ᵇ.

„   Sir Richard, of Sopwell, Herts, Knighted for services done at Bulleyne ; 26 Oct., 36 H. VIII., 1544, alteration or augmentation, two coats and crests.   Barker's Grants, Harl. MS. 5846, fo. 67ᵇ ; Stowe MS. 692, fo. 64ᵇ, 65 ; Grants I., 20.

„   Richard, of Hickham, Middx., ... 1592, Quarterly, by Cooke.   Harl. MS. 1359, fo. 105ᵇ and 119 ; Q's Coll. Oxf. MS. 146, fo. 472 ; Harl. MS. 4966, fo. 24ᵇ, 95.

„   Robert, ... Quarrendon, 18 August 1530, by Wr[iothesley], Gart., and Benolte, Clar.   Add. MS. 26,702, fo. 47 ; Cat. Her. Ex., 62.

„   Robert, Alderm. and Sheriff of city of London (s. of Humphrey, descended from Reginald Lee, chief patron and founder of the Parish Church of Lee, co. Staff.) ; grant 20 Dec. 1593, by W. Dethick, Gart.   Harl. MS. 1422, fo. 51 and 75ᵇ ; Add. MS. 14,295, fo. 15ᵇ ; Harl. MS. 1395, fo. 26 ; Stowe MSS. 676, fo. 89ᵇ, 103, and 716, fo. 68ᵇ ; Q's Coll. Oxf. MS. 36, fo. 24, 29, for copy of grant of arms, also MSS. 38, fo. 112, and 146, fo. 31.   Harl. MS. 1453, fo. 33ᵇ, for entry by R. Brooke, York Herald, as follows : "patent 1593, per W. Dethick, Garter, who doth derive him to descend of Reginald Lee, chief patron and founder of the parish church of Lee in Staffordshire, wherein he greatly fayleth, for the said Reginald Lee died without issue, leaving his 2 sisters his heyres, for this arms and derivacion Garter had 10 pounds."

„   Thomas, of Clatercott, Oxon., ar. confirmed . . . . 1561.   Harvey's Grants, Add. MS. 16,940, fo. 16.

„   Thomas, of London, out of Chesh., confirmed 25 Oct. 1583, by Flower : arg., on a chev. engrailed betw. three leopards' faces sa. a crescent or. MS. Ashm. 844, fo. 56, copy of grant, Bodleian Lib.; Guil. 260.

LEECHFORD, Sir Richard, of Shelwood, Surrey, attested 22 Nov. 1606, by Segar. Misc. Gen. et Her., i., 54, copy of grant, Brit. Mus.

LEEKE or LEETE, Thomas, of Gray's Inn, descended out of Shropshire; by Segar. Add. MS. 12,225, fo. 70; C. 24 [Visit. Lond., 1634], Her. Coll.; Guil. 68.

LEESON, Robert, Whitefield North [?co. Northampton], by Harvey, Clar., ... 1566. Harl. MS. 6179, fo. 62ᵇ.

LEETE, see LETE.

LEFREYS, Anthony, Dorset, ... crest . . . . 1564. (Harvey's Grants), Add. MS. 16,940, fo. 6ᵇ.

LEGAT, Thomas, of Dagwhams (Dagenams), Essex, 2 May 1554, by ? Hawley. Add. MS. 16,940, fo. 207.

LEGATT, William, of Sutton, Hornechurche, Essex, gift . . . . 1559. (Harvey's Grants), Add. MS. 16,940, fo. 24ᵇ.

LEGGE, Robert, of London, treasurer of the ships . . . .   Barker's Grants, Stowe MS. 692, fo. 65.

„   Col. William, one of the grooms of H.M.'s bedchamber; Crest (? April) 1662, by Sir E. Walker. Her. Coll., fo. 46; Harl. MS. 6179, fo. 49.

LEIGHE, ... crest . . . .   Barker's Grants, Harl. MS. 5846, fo. 69ᵇ; Stowe MS. 692, fo. 64ᵇ.

LEIGH, ... clerk . . . . by R. St. George, Norr. Harl. MS. 1422, fo. 15ᵇ.

LEYGHE, John, esq., lord of the manor of Holton, Dorset, crest . . . .   Barker's Grants, Harl. MS. 5846, fo. 67ᵇ; Stowe MS. 692, fo. 65.

LEIGH, Piers a, 1495, see ASHTON.

LEGH, Sir Piers, of Bradley and Lyme, co. Lanc., and Hanley, Cheshire, in token of his descent from Piers Legh, a hero of Cressy; grant of augmentation 11 June 1575, by Flower. MSS. Ashm. 858, fo. 175-7, and 840, fo. 397-8, copy of grant, Bodleian Lib.; "for services rendered to the Black Prince at Cressy by his father-in-law Sir Thomas Danyers," in Genealogist, v., p. 142, and Earwaker's East Cheshire, ii., 303; Le Neve's MS. 482, for confirmation to Richard Legh of Bradley by W. Dugdale, Norroy, 8 April 1665.

LEIGHE, Richard, of High Leigh, Cheshire, Esq., Coat confirmed and crest granted 20 July, 3 and 4 Phil. and Mary, 1567, by Sir G. Dethick, Gart. Harl. MSS. 1116, fo. 41, and 1359, fo. 69ᵇ; Q's Coll. Oxf. MS. 39, fo. 71, for copy of grant; Grants I., 208.

LEIGH (LIGH), Richard, of High Leigh, esq., Cheshire, now living, father to Richard; 3 Dec. 1580, by Sir G. Dethick, Gart. Harl. MS. 1441, fo. 101; Q's Coll. Oxf. MS. 145, fo. 51.

„   Robert, of Bekingham, Cheshire, 20 Nov. 1552, by ? Harvey, Norr. Add. MS. 16,940, fo. 206.

„   Sir Thomas, Alderm. of London, with crest . . . . Add. MS. 26,702, fo. 70.

LEYGH, Sir Thomas, Maior of London; 3 Sept. 1555, by ? Hawley. Add. MS. 16,940, fo. 207ᵇ.

LEIGHE, William, of Sutton, Surrey, 7 July 1609, by Camden. Harl. MSS. 1422, fo. 21, and 6095, fo. 12; Guil. 289; Harl. MS. 1561, fo. 164.

LELLO, ... of co. Hereford: erm., on a canton gu. a cross moline or . . . . by Segar. Add. MS. 12,225, fo. 70.

LE MAIRE . . . . 1 March 1624-5, by R. St. George, Clar. Harl. MS. 1105, fo. 7.

LEMAN, John, of London, Alderm., patent 25 Jan. 1615, 12 K. Jas., by Camden. Harl. MSS. 6095, fo. 31ᵇ, and 1422, fo. 39ᵇ; Guil. 240.

LE MARCHANT, William, s. of James, ⎫ of the Isle of Guernsey; 27 May 1689, by
„   Eleazar, s. of Thomas,   ⎬   T. St. George, Gart., and Hen. St. George,
                                  ⎭   Clar. Stowe MS. 714, fo. 128ᵇ; (1683
in Stowe MS. 716, fo. 51ᵇ); Grants IV., 39.

x

LEMITAIRE, George, of city of Westminster, esq., s. of Thomas, s. of Nicholas, who came forth of Normandy; coat confirmed and grant of crest 14 June, 4 Jac., 1606, by Segar. Add. MS. 12,225, fo. 70ᵇ; Guil. 395 says 14 June, 14th Jas. I. (1616) (? confirmed by Le Neve 1634-5); in Grants I., 381, 14 Jac., 1616.

LEMPSTER, Lord (Sir William Farmer, Bart.), supporters 3 June 1692, by T. St. George, Gart. Harl. MS. 6834, fo. 178; Grants IV., fo. 115.

LENDON, Capt. Robert or John, born of honest parents at Allington, Devon, an officer in the Navy Royal 1648; dated at Brussels 10 May 1658, by Walker. Add. MSS. 14,293, fo. 96, and 14,294, fo. 32ᵇ; Harl. MS. 1172, fo. 76ᵇ; Guil. 314; Her. Coll., fo. 30.

LE NEVE, William, York Herald (after Knt. and Clar. K. of Arms), etc.; arms confirmed and crest granted 5 May 1627, by Segar. Add. MS. 12,225, fo. 70ᵇ; Guil. 130; Le Neve's MS. 456.

LEONARD, ... of Knowle (Kent), arms allowed at his funeral by Cooke's deputy. Stowe MS. 670, fo. 5ᵇ; Grants I., fo. 26.

„ John, ... Kent, ... 1558? confirmed. (Harvey's Grants), Add. MS. 16,940, fo. 8.

LENNARD or LEONARD, Samson, s. of William, 2nd s. of John, of Shepsted, Kent, and younger bro. to John, who was father to Samson Leonard, Knt., Lord Darcy, father of Rich., now Lord Darcy, 1628, ? Dacre . . . . 1626, by Segar (6 quarterings). Add. MS. 12,225, fo. 71; Harl. MS. 6140, fo. 81; Guil. 128.

„ William, Watford, Herts, ... or, three chevronels sa.; crest, a greyhound passant or, collar and " terrett " sa., studded or; by Sir G. Dethick, Gart. Add. MS. 26,753, fo. 122ᵇ.

LENTON, John, of Adwincle, Northants, Quarterly of 6 and crest confirmed 21 May 1584, by Cooke. Q's Coll. Oxf. MS. 146, fo. 41; Add. MS. 14,295, fo. 47; Harl. MS. 1359, fo. 87ᵇ; March in Harl. MS. 1422, fo. 114; Guil. 239; Add. MS. 12,474, fo. 52ᵇ; Harl. MS. 5887, fo. 9ᵇ; Add. MS. 4966, fo. 59ᵇ.

LE TALOR, John, of London, Esq., arms confirmed and crest granted 20 July 1572, by Cooke. Misc. Gen. et Her., 2nd S., vol. iv., p. 273; Muskett's Suffolk Manorial Families, i., 241.

LETE, see also LEEKE and LEETE.

LETE, ... of Bury Sᵗ Edmunds, Suff.: Arg., on a fesse gu. betw. two matches roled and fired ppr. a martlet or . . . . by Segar. Add. MS. 12,225, fo. 71; Harl. MS. 6140, fo. 61ᵇ.

LETHBRIDGE, Thomas, Clifford's Inn, s. of . . . . L. of Hatherley, Devon, ... 1652, by Sir E. Bysshe. Harl. MS. 1441, fo. 147; Stowe MS. 703, fo. 71.

LETHERSELLERS' Co., London, arms and crest at London 20 May, 19 Ed. IV., 1479, by John Moore, Norr.; supporters and impalements (Quarterly 1 and 4 (2 and 3, Glovers' arms, 1464, by John Smart, Gart.) 7 Nov. 1505, 21 H. VII., by Richmont, Clar.; confirmation 11 Oct., 22 H. VIII., 1530, by Thoˢ Benolt, Clar. Q's Coll. Oxf. MS. 38, fo. 11, copy of grants, etc.; MS. Ashm. 858, fo. 26-7, copy of grant, Bodleian Lib.; Harl. MSS. 1453, fo. 127, and 1359, fo. 74ᵇ; Add. MSS. 14,295, fo. 42ᵇ, 43, and 5533, fo. 135.

LEVERSAGE, William, of Whelock, Cheshire, confirmed 24 Sept. 1580, by Flower. MSS. Ashm. 834, fo. 25ᵇ, and 858, fo. 39, copy of grant, Bodleian Lib.; Guil. 298.

LEVESON, John, s. of Sir Walter, of Wolverhampton, co. Staff.; crest, a demi-arm couped arg., gauntletted sa., thereon two gemelles, a fesse oundy arg. [?]. Barker's Grants, Stowe MS. 692, fo. 65ᵇ; Harl. MS. 5846, fo. 68ᵇ.

LEVESON or LEWSON, John, of Wolverhampton, co. Staff., 2nd s. of Walter, of same, confirmed 26 Nov. 1561, ? by Dalton. Harl. MS. 1359, fo. 52; Grants II., 686; Quarterly arms, Harl. MS. 5887, fo. 61ᵇ.

LEVETT, John, and of Salehurst, Sussex, sons of John, of same, s. of William, of
„   Thomas,   Warbleton, Sussex, coat confirmed and crest granted 16 Dec.
1607, by Segar. Add. MS. 12,225, fo. 71ᵇ.

LEVING, Thomas, s. of Thomas, s. of Walter, co. Derby, granted or confirmed
10 Sept. 1611, by Sir R. St. George, Norr., as I am informed by the family.
Guil. 245; Stowe MS. 706, fo. 13ᵇ; Harl. MSS. 6179, fo. 13ᵇ, and 6140,
fo. 72.

LEVINZ, Sir Cresswell, Serg᷑ at law, and the descendants of his great-grandfather,
19 Aug. 1699, by St. George, Gart. and Clar. Harl. MS. 14,831, fo. 76,
and Grants IV., 303.

LEWYN, William, *see* LOWEN.

LEWIN, Thomas, the King's Coachman, descended out of the Bishoprick of
Durham; 28 May 1640, by Sir John Borough, Gart. Harl. MSS. 1105,
fo. 57, and 1441, fo. 57ᵇ; Add. MS. 26,702, fo. 93; (Guil. 133, born at
Siston, co. Leic., now Servant to his Majesty).

LEWES, Lady, wife to Sir John Cookes or Cootes, Mayor of London; 2 June 1545,
by ? Hawley. Add. MS. 16,940, fo. 200ᵇ.

„   Barnaby, of Stock, Dorset, gent., out of Montgomery, confirmed 16 Feb.
1594-5, by W. Dethick, Gart. Q's Coll. Oxf. MS. 36, fo. 43, for copy of
confirmation; Stowe MS. 676, fo. 11.

LEWYS, David, D.C.L., Judge of the Admiralty. [1558 ?]. Quarterly : 1, chequey
or and sa., on a fess gu. three leopards' faces jessant-de-lis or ; 2, arg.,
a chev. gu. betw. three oak leaves vert. Crest, on a wreath or and sable
a dragon's head erased vert, langued gules, gorged with a crown argent.
By Sir G. Dethick, Gart. Add. MS. 26,753, fo. 123.

LEWES, John, of Mortlake, Surrey, gift . . . . 1564. (Harvey's Grants) *see* wife
Joan Fayrechild, Add. MS. 16,940, fo. 6ᵇ and 56.

LEWIS, John, recorder of Doncaster, etc., assigned, allowed and confirmed 22 Oct.
1586, by Flower. MS. Ashm. 844, fo. 65, copy of grant, Bodleian Lib. ;
Guil. 133.

LEWES, Robert, and of Rossenden in Bleane, Kent, gent., exemplified by
„   Bevill,   Camden . . . . arg., a chev. gu. betw. three beavers' tails
ppr. ; crest, a demi-beaver ppr. Harl. MSS. 1422, fo. 20,
and 6095, fo. 9 and 19 ; Guil. 256 ; Harl. MS. 5887, fo. 9ᵇ.

LEWIS, Ros (? Rees), of Kery . . . . II. VII. Add. MS. 26,702, fo. 47ᵇ.

„   Thomas, of London, esq., 14 Dec. 1661. Bysshe's Grants, fo. 10, Her. Coll.;
Harl. MS. 1105, fo. 18ᵇ.

LEWKAR, *see* LOCAR.

LEYCESTER, Sir Ralph, of the manor of the Toftes, Cheshire, Knt., granted by
Gilb. Dethick, Norr., 15 May, 2 Ed. VI., 1548. Q's Coll. Oxf. MSS. 37,
fo. 19, 38, fo. 52, and 39, fo. 15, for copy of grant, ex. Mag. Reg. ;
G. Dethick, Gart., Harl. MSS. 1507, fo. 445, and 1359, fo. 2ᵇ ; Grants I.,
312 ; Le Neve's MS. 445.

LEYS, George, Rathington, Essex, 2 Aug., 4 Eliz. . . . . 1562, by Sir G. Dethick,
Gart. Grants II., 652 ; Heyes in Harl. MS. 1441, fo. 65, and Q's Coll.
Oxf. MS. 145, fo. 7ᵇ.

LYDDELL [LIDDELL], Thomas, of Ravensworth Castle, co. Durham, 21 Aug. 1615,
by R. St. George. Add. MS. 14,295, fo. 70ᵇ ; C. 32, fo. 58 [Visit. of]
Durham [1615].

LIGHTBOURNE, John, of Manchester, and of Gray's Inn, J.P. co. Lanc., and to his
brother
„   James, also of Manchester, 3 June 1662, by W. Dugdale, Norr. Add. MS.
14,830, fo. 88 ; Grants I. ; 28ᵗʰ June in Harl. MS. 1105, fo. 60 ; Guil.
366 ; 30ᵗʰ June in Harl. MS. 1470, fo. 120.

LIGO, Thomas, of Stoke Mandeville, Bucks, 4 June 1632, by R. St. George, Clar.
Harl. MS. 1105, fo. 12ᵇ.

LYLY, ... gu., three lillies arg. stalked and leaved vert, a bordure of the 2ⁿᵈ and a crescent for diff. ; quartering Gabott .... by Segar.   Add. MS. 12,225, fo. 73[b].

LILLY, Thomas, of South Lynn, Norfolk, 12 June 1662.   Bysshe's Grants, fo. 22, Her. Coll. ; Harl. MSS. 1105, fo. 21, and 6179, fo. 54.

„   William, of London, gent., coat confirmed and crest granted 25 April 1593, by W. Dethick, Gart.   Stowe MS. 676, fo. 90, 104[b] ; Q's Coll. Oxf. MS. 36, fo. 27, for copy of grant.

LYNDSEY, Edward, of London, gent., and of Bucksted, Sussex, Esq., s. of Miles, of Dent, Yorks, Esq., etc., confirmation of arms quartering Ingledew ; crest granted 20 June 1608, by Segar.   Add. MS. 12,225, fo. 73[b] ; Harl. MS. 6140, fo. 81[b] ; Guil. 211, 20 Jan. 1608, by Segar and R. St. George, Clar.; 20 July in Harl. MS. 1562, fo. 188[b].

LYNSEY, William, s. of Simon, of London. Browne Baker, servant to the Earl of Dorset .... by Segar.   Add. MS. 12,225, fo. 74 ; Vinc[t] MS., No. 154, fo. 3[b] ; C. 27, fo. 38 [Visit. Sussex, 1633], Her. Coll., and Guil. 211.

LINGE, John, s. of Laurence, of Warcop, Westmorld., crest granted 13 June 1589, by W. Dethick, Gart., and his brother

„   Peter, called LE LINGE, now of Bassingborne, co. Camb.   Q's Coll. Oxf. MS. 37, fo. 111, copy of grant ; Stowe MS. 676, fo. 76[b].

LE LINGNE, Danyell, of Harlaxton, co. Linc., s. of Anthy., s. of John, of Velenzeive, prov. of Hainault ; confirmation of arms and gift of crest (or patent in Harl. MS. 6095) 20 Jan. 1619-20, by Camden.   Cott. MS. Faustina E. 1, fo. 5, copy of grant, Brit. Mus.; Harl. MSS. 1359, fo. 43[b], and 6095, fo. 42 ; Guil. 68 ; according to Add. MS. 14,259, fo. 63, these arms were confirmed " by the office of arms " ; see L. 20, fo. 1, Her. Coll., afterwards Sir Daniel De Ligne ; Harl. MS. 6140, fo. 67.

LINLEY, Sir Henry, Middleham, crest .... April 1607, by R. St. George, Norr. Add. MS. 14,295, fo. 79 .... (fo. 276).

LINSTEAD, William, of South Burlingham, } 7 May 1672, by Sir E. Bysshe, Clar. Norfolk, and   } Harl. MS. 1105, fo. 89[b] ; and
„   Thomas, his brother,   } Bysshe's Grants, 31.

LISBURNE, Visct. (John Vaughan), 25 July 1695, supporters by T. St George, Gart. Grants IV., 201.

LISLE, ... of St Martins-in-the-Fields, Middx. : erminois, on a chief az. three lions ramp. or ; by Segar.   Add. MS. 12,225, fo. 71[b] ; Harl. MS. 6140, fo. 78.

„   Sir Arcold de (a Frenchman), Lieut.-Col. of a regt of Horse ; augmentation at Oxford 3 March 1645-6, by Sir E. Walker, Gart.   Her. Coll., 1.

„   Arthur Plantagenet, Visct., filius bastard of Ed. IV.; coat and crest, by Barker.   Harl. MS. 5846, fo. 2 ; Stowe MS. 692, fo. 9.

LYSTER, ... of Yorke .... coat and crest ....   Barker's Grants, Harl. MS. 5846, fo. 70[b] ; Stowe MS. 692, fo. 64[b].

LISTER, Edward, of London, D. phys., patent 20 April 1602, by Camden.   (William in Add. MS. 14,295, fo. 73) ; Harl. MS. 6095, fo. 25 ; Guil. 104 ; Harl. MS. 5887, fo. 82[b].

„   Gylbert, of Yorkshire, Crest .... by Harvey (Norr.).   Add. MS. 16,940, fo. 6[b].

„   John, of Kingston-upon-Hull, Crest 12 Nov. 1613, by R. St. George, Norr. Surtees Soc., XLI., xlviii. ; Add. MS. 14,295, fo. 61[b], and Her. Coll., B. 21, fo. 208.

„   Laurence, of Midhope, Yorks, Crest .... 1564, by Flower.   Add. MS. 14,295, fo. 73 (fo. 29).

„   William, of Midhope, crest 1557.   Harl. MS. 1116, fo. 63, ? by Harvey.

LITTELL, see LYTTELL, Thomas, of Bray, Berks, ... 1563.

LLOYD, Col. Sir Charles, Quarter-Master-Gen., and his brother } Augmentation at
„   Sir Godfrey,   } the Hague April

1649, by Walker. Add. MSS. 14,293, fo. 109, and 14,294, fo. 36ᵇ; Harl. MS. 1172, fo. 73; Her. Coll., fo. 28.

LLOYD, Giles, of London, descended out of Wales, crest 10 Q. Eliz. (? 1587), by Cooke. Harl. MS. 1359, fo. 111; Add. MS. 4966, fo. 97ᵇ.

„ John, of London, 1 April 1627, by Segar, Gart. Harl. MS. 1085, fo. 2.

LOADES, Henry, Chamberlain of London, crest 30 July 1687, by Sir T. St. George, Gart. and Clar. Harl. MS. 6834, fo. 178; Grants III., 327; Lansd. MS. 867, fo. 52; Harl. MS. 1085, fo. 59.

LOCAR, Emannell, of Bridgewater, ... Barker's Grants, Add. MS. 26,702, fo. 15; Harl. MS. 5887, fo. 58.

LOCK, Michael (? Ashton Giffard, Wilts, and Stoweeliffe, Hants), crest 5 July, 1 and 2 Phil. and Mary, 1555, by Sir G. Dethick, Gart. Q's Coll. Oxf. MS. 39, fo. 53, for copy of grant; see a testimonial for arms in MS. Ashm. 844, fo. 1; Harl. MS. 1359, fo. 63ᵇ; Locke in Grants I., 77; Harl. MS. 1116, fo. 45ᵇ, copy of grant.

LOCKSMITH, see MARSHALL.

LODGE, Sir Thomas, Maior of London 1562; 15 Aug. 1556, by Hawley? Add. MS. 16,940, fo. 208.

LOGYNS [LOGGINS], Symond, ... gift . . . . 1560 . . . . (Harvey's Grants), Add. MS. 16,940, fo. 46ᵇ; Harl. MS. 5887, fo. 46ᵇ.

LONDON. Robert, of Albye, Norfolk, J.P., served in the late war against the rebels under Col. Sir Ed. Walker, Knt. and Bart.; 10 Feb. 1664-5, by Walker. Add. MSS. 14,293, fo. 35, and 14,294, fo. 6ᵇ; Harl. MS. 1172, fo. 51ᵇ; East Anglian, iii., 8; Guil. 76.

„ William, of Leighton Buzzard, Beds, gent., grant 1 March 1537-8 or 1538-9, by Hawley. Harl. MS. 1507, fo. 400, and Q's Coll. Oxf. MS. 38, fo. 22, copy of grant; Le Neve's MS. 400.

LONE, John, ⎫ of Cambridge, [and ?] Linton, co. Cambr., brothers, 10 April 1695,
„ William, ⎭ by T. St. George, Gart. and Clar. Grants IV., 190.

LONG, ... of Norfolk, 16 Feb. 1651-2, by E. Bysshe, Gart. Harl. MS. 1105, fo. 15.

LONGE, Edward, of Monckton juxta Broughton Gifford, Wilts, 1588, by Cooke. Harl. MSS. 1359, fo. 95, and 1422, fo. 80ᵇ; Stowe MS. 670, fo. 33ᵇ.

LONG, Gifford, of Rood Ashton, ... 1589 . . . . Berry.

„ Mary, dau. of Symond, of the Isle of Wight, wife unto George Owen (Burke says Sir William Allen, Lord Mayor 1572), gift 1558. (Harvey's Grants), Add. MS. 16,940, fo. 9ᵇ and 61ᵇ.

„ Miles, of New Sleaford, Linc., and Staple Inn, 14 Feb. 1666-7. Bysshe's Grants, fo. 19, Her. Coll.; Harl. MS. 1105, fo. 20.

„ Robert, of Souldon, Herts (Norf. in Harl. MS. 1105, fo. 8ᵇ), 26 Oct. 1632, by Segar. Add. MS. 12,225, fo. 72; Harl. MS. 1105, fo. 8ᵇ.

LONGE, Thomas, of Trowbridge, Wilts, gift . . . . 1561. (Harvey's Grants), Add. MS. 16,940, fo. 17ᵇ.

LONG, William, of Beckington, Wilts, s. of Thomas, s. of William, s. of Henry, 1561, by Harvey. Harl. MS. 1422, fo. 80ᵇ, ascribed also to . . . . Long, Capt. of a troop of Horse, 1642; Add. MS. 4966, fo. 86ᵇ; Harl. MS. 6140, fo. 74ᵇ.

LONGFORD, ..., ux. John Mills of Cashiobury . . . . paly of 6 gu. and or, a bend argᵗ; ? confirmed by Camden. Stowe MS. 706, fo. 54ᵇ; Harl. MSS. 1422, fo. 38ᵇ, and 6095, fo. 28.

LONGLAND, Edward, of Tingwick, s. of John, of ye same place, Bucks; a difference in the arms and a different crest, by R. Cooke. Stowe MS. 670, fo. 51ᵇ.

„ John, Bp. of Lincoln (from 1520 to 1547), H. 8 [Her. Coll.?]; Add. MS. 26,702, fo. 60; Harl. MS. 6179, fo. 12ᵇ.

„ John, Archdeacon of Buckingham (1544—50, 1559—89), by R. Cooke, Clar. Stowe MS. 670, fo. 18.

LONGLEY, John, of London, gift 1560-61. (Harvey's Grants), Add. MS. 16,940, fo. 18.

LONSDALE, John Lowther, Visct., supporters 28 Feb. 1697-8. Grants IV., fo. 254.

LONYSON, John, esq., citizen and goldsmith and Mr of the Mint in England; 20 June 1575, by Cooke or G. Dethick. Harl. MS. 1422, fo. 122b.

LORAINE (LORREYN), William, s. of Richard, of Kirkharle, Northumberland, 17 Feb. 1639-40, by Borough. Harl. MSS. 1105, fo. 56b, and 1069, fo. 109b; Thomas in Harl. MS. 1441, fo. 58, and Add. MS. 26,702, fo. 92h; Guil. 372; Harl. MS. 5857, fo. 139.

LORT (als LORD), ... of co. Pembroke, confirmed .... 163-, by Sir J. Borough, Gart., and Sir R. St. George. Harl. MS. 6179, fo. 48.

LOSSE, Hugh, of Stanmore-the-Lesse, Middx., coat and crest. Barker's Grants, Harl. MS. 5846, fo. 71; Stowe MS. 692, fo. 65.

    "   Sir Hugh, of Coddock, Suff.: Quarterly, arg. and sa., a saltire party per saltire betw. four fleurs-de-lis, all counterchanged .... 1633, by Segar. Harl. MS. 6140, fo. 35; Add. MS. 12,225, fo. 72b.

LOTYSHAM, ... of Somerset, ... 1609, by Camden. Morgan's Sphere, 109; Harl. MSS. 1422, fo. 21, and 6095, fo. 12.

LOUTLEY, Thomas, of Middx., ... 1560. Harvey's Grants, Add. MS. 16,940, fo. 11h.

LOVE, Nicholas (Richard), of Basing in Froxfield, Southants, gent., 5 Feb. 1612-13 or 7 Dec. 1613, by Camden. C. 19, fo. 32, 107, Visit. of Hampsh., 1622, erroneously called Richard, and 7 Sept. in Morgan's Sphere, 111; Add. MS. 14,295, fo. 63b and 88; see Harl. MSS. 5865, fo. 41b, and 1544, fo. 151; Le Neve's MS. 500.

    "   Robert, of Kerstead, Norfolk, 10 Dec. 1663. Bysshe's Grants, fo. 6, Her. Coll.; Harl. MS. 1105, fo. 17b; Add. MS. 14,293, fo. 8; called Lowe in Guil. 189.

LOVEDEN, ... Loveden, Berks, ... (1589, Berry), by Cooke, Clar. Stowe MS. 670, fo. 32h; Harl. MS. 1441, fo. 138b.

LOVELASSE (LOVELACE), William, of Canterbury, Sergeant-at-law, being one of the heirs of Richard Lovelace, Knt., late Marshal of Caillys, decd s.p.; according to the custom of gavelkinde in .... it descended to John Lovelace of King's Downe, Esq., s. of William, bro. of Sir Richd, which John had issue Thomas, and the said William had issue the foresaid William, Sergt.-at-law. Quarterly: arms confirmed and crest given to William and to the posterity of his grandfather William, etc., 2 Dec. 1573, 16 Q. Eliz., by Cooke. Add. MS. 4966, fo. 66b; Harl. MS. 1359, fo. 13b; Q's Coll. Oxf. MS. 146, fo. 35; Harl. MS. 1422, fo. 113h; Add. MS. 14,295, fo. 8; MS. Ashm. 834, fo. 3, copy of patent, Bodleian Lib.

LOVELL, Thomas, of Laxfield, Suff., 25 June 1579, by Sir G. Dethick, Gart. Harl. MS. 1441, fo. 140b; Q's Coll. Oxf. MS. 145, fo. 35; Harl. MS. 5887, fo. 43.

LOWE, Humfry, of Southmills, par. of Blouham, Beds, esq., coat confirmed and crest granted 28 July 1628, by Segar. Add. MS. 12,225, fo. 72b; ? MS. Ashm. 834, fo. 16; Guil. 193.

    "   Humphrey, of Bromsgrove, co. Worc., Esq., High Sheriff, exemplified 8 Feb. 1657-8, by Sir E. Bysshe; diff. coat from Michael Lowe, who died s.p.; granted by Cooke. Add. MS. 26,758, fo. 13b; Stowe MS. 677, fo. 61, copy of grant; Harl. MS. 6832, fo. 414.

    "   John, "juris peritus," gen., grant .... Oct. 1602, by W. Dethick, Gart. Stowe MS. 676, fo. 136; Q's Coll. Oxf. MS. 36, fo. 91, copy of grant.

    "   John, City of Westminster, one of the under chamberlains in the court of the receipt of H.M.'s Exchequer; 25 May 1694, by T. St. George, Gart. and Clar. Add. MS. 14,831, fo. 166; Grants IV., 170; Stowe MS. 714, fo. 153; Harl. MS. 1085, fo. 58.

Lowe, Michell, of Stafford, ... 1592, by Cooke. (*See* Bysshe). Harl. MSS. 1359, fo. 113ᵇ, and 1422, fo. 51ᵇ; (and of Finmore, co. Staff., 1578) Add. MSS. 4966, fo. 84, and 26,758, fo. 13ᵇ. [Robert, *see* Love.]

„ William, of Shropshire, ... 1586, by Cooke. Harl. MSS. 1359, fo. 89ᵇ, and 1422, fo. 51ᵇ; Add. MS. 4966, fo. 34ᵇ.

Lowen, John, of the manor of Gerpyns, Essex, gift .... 1559. Harvey's Grants, Add. MS. 16,940, fo. 16ᵇ; Harl. MS. 5887, fo. 54, for John, of London, draft.

„ William (Lewyn), of London, D.C.L., s. of Edm., s. of John, of Herts, etc., confirmed (more probably granted) .... 1575, by Cooke. Stowe MS. 676, fo. 46; Q's Coll. Oxf. MS. 37, fo. 59, copy of grant.

Lownde, Sir Alexander, Knt., a captain, served in the wars of Gascoyne and Guienne, France, etc. [No references. *See* below, Thomas.]

„ Jerard, of Pocklington, Yorks, confirmed by ? Harvey or Dalton. [No references.]

„ John, of Overton, par. of Astbury, Cheshire, s. of William, s. of Richard; coat confirmed and crest granted 18 June 1612, by Sir R. St. George, Norr. Harl. MS. 1069, fo. 37ᵇ; copy of grant, Brit. Mus., Harl. MS. 2146, fo. 77; (Launndes, Harl. MS. 6179, fo. 14); Grants II., 583; Harl. MS. 6140, fo. 74.

„ Thomas, late of Orpington, Kent, gent., s. of Leonard, s. of John, of co. Lincoln, gent., descended collaterally of the ancestors of that house, name and family. [Az., fretty Arg. within a bordure or, over all a canton bendy of six gu. and vair. Longvale, quartered by Bray : vair, three bendlets gu. Harl. MS. 5887, fo. 24ᵇ, shews the mantling Az., lined Argent, and makes the arms a fret within the bordure.] Confirmed or exemplified at the Office of Arms, London, 20 June, 38 Q. Eliz., 1596, by Wᵐ Dethick, Gart. Q's Coll. Oxf. MS. 36, fo. 58, copy of grant, and MS. 146, fo. 137; Add. MS. 14,295, fo. 116ᵇ; Stowe MS. 676, fo. 18. Sometime a taylour .... 1596, by W. Dethick, Gart., for which he had 5ᴴ. The canton is the Lord Braye's arms ; the armes is the armes of Sir Alexander Lownd, Knt., that lived in Ed. III. tyme, etc., entered by R. Brooke, York Herald. Harl. MSS. 1453, fo. 35, and 5887, fo. 24ᵇ. [Add. MS. 14,295, fo. 116ᵇ, says : This arms without the canton is acknowledged to be the ancient arms of Sir Alexʳ Lownde, Knt.]

Lucar, *see* Locar.

Lucas, ... of Cornwall, ... erm., two lions combatant gu. .... by Segar. Add. MS. 12,225, fo. 73; Harl. MSS. 6140, fo. 81, and 5887, fo. 85ᵇ *bis*.

„ Margaret, dau. of John, of Halden, Kent, ux. Robert Browne, gent., granted 10 Dec., 4 Ed. VI., 1550, by G. Dethick, Gart. Harl. MS. 1359, fo. 60ᵇ; Q's Coll. Oxf. MS. 39, fo. 31, for copy of grant (eosen and heir of Thomas Lucas of London, gent.). John Lucas married Margaret, d. and h. of Jo. Penne and of Joan his wife, d. and h. of Sir Robert Brackenbury, Knt., Lieut. of the Tower, *temp.* R. III. Achievement 8 Nov. 1571, by Cooke, viz.—Quarterly : 1 Lucas, 2 Hills, 3 Penne, 4 Brackenbury, 5 Balliewle, 6 Paynell. Harl. MSS. 1422, fo. 111ᵇ, and 1359, fo. 11; Q's Coll. Oxf. MS. 146, fo. 19; Grants I., 306.

„ Richard, ... coat and crest .... Barker's Grants, Harl. MS. 5846, fo. 69ᵇ; Stowe MS. 692, fo. 64ᵇ.

Lucke, John, of Rotherfield, Sussex, confirmed quartered arms (and crest), by Segar. Add. MS. 12,225, fo. 73.

Luckyn, William, 2nd s. of William, of Lado in Essex, 24 June 1611, by Camden. Harl. MS. 1422, fo. 16ᵇ; Morgan's Sphere, 117; Harl. MS. 1085, fo. 9; Thomas in Le Neve's MS. 357.

Ludford, Symond, of London, gift .... 1560. (Harvey's Grants), Add. MS. 16,940, fo. 32ᵇ; Harl. MS. 5887, fo. 65.

LUGGAR, Nathaniel, of Bodmin, etc. (a Royalist), granted at the Hague 20 Dec. 1650, by Walker. Add. MSS. 14,293, fo. 95, and 14,294, fo. 32 ; Harl. MS. 1172, fo. 70ᵇ ; Guil. 263 ; Her. Coll., fo. 29.

LUKE, Sir Walter, of Corupull (Cople), Beds, Kt., crest 1 Oct. 1544, by T. Hawley. Add. MSS. 16,940, fo. 200ᵇ, and 7098, fo. 77 (fo. 32) ; six quarterings, Harl. MS. 6140, fo. 41.

LUPTON, Roger, ... H. VII..... Add. MS. 26,702, fo. 52ᵇ, and Berry.

LUPUS, Ambrose, s. of Baptist, of "Castello maiori" of Busto in Normandy, in the republic of Malan ; augmentation and crest granted ? 45 Eliz. .... by W. Dethick, Gart. Q's Coll. Oxf. MS. 36, fo. 96, copy of grant in Latin ; Stowe MS. 676, fo. 138ᵇ, names his sons Peter and Joseph.

LUSHER or LASHER, James, of London : gu., a lyon passant betw. three dexter gauntlets erect, their backs affrontée or, by Segar. Harl. MS. 6140, fo. 26 ; Add. MS. 12,225, fo. 78ᵇ ; Harl. MS. 6140, fo. 27.

„   James, of London, and   } Quarterly : 1 and 6 Lusher, 2 Combarford,
„   Nicholas, of Sharlands, Surrey, }   3 Erneford, 4 Pembridge and 5 Coding-
                                               ton. Crest, a matlet [martlet ?] or, by
    Cooke, Clar. Stowe MS. 670, fo. 39.

LUTHER, of Essex, confirmed July 1614, and
„   Anthony, of Kelvedon, Essex, patent Nov. 1614, by Camden. Harl. MSS. 1422, fo. 39, and 6095, fo. 30ᵇ.

LUTLEY, see LOUTLEY.

LUTMAN, ..., confirmed by Sir Will. Dethick, Gart. Harl. MS. 6179, fo. 58.

LYDDIAT, John, of Walsall, co. Staff., s. of Hugh, s. of John, all of the same ; 19 Oct. 1614, by R. St. George, Clar. Caius Coll. Camb. MS. 528, fo. 7 ; Harl. MS. 1052, fo. 182 ; (copy of grant, Brit. Mus., Harl. MS. 1380, fo. 27) ; Add. MS. 14,295, fo. 61ᵇ ; MS. Ashm. 858, fo. 119, copy of grant, Bodleian Lib. ; C. 36, fo. 200ᵇ [Visit. Staffordsh., 1663], Her. Coll.

LYFELD, Thomas, of Stoke Dauburne (d'Abernon), Surrey, gent., grant 10 May, 2 Q. Eliz., 1560, by Sir G. Dethick, Gart. Q's Coll. Oxf. MS. 39, fo. 101, copy of grant ; Harl. MS. 1359, fo. 79 ; Grants L., 292, compare with Harl. MS. 6140, fo. 46ᵇ.

LYNACRE, ... crest .... Barker's Grants, 1526—49, Harl. MS. 5846, fo. 70 ; Stowe MS. 692, fo. 64ᵇ.

LYNCH, ... Dʳ Phisicke and Archdeacon of Wilts .... H. 8 [Her. Coll. ?] ; Add. MS. 26,702, fo. 51.

LYNCHE, Simon, of Staple, Kent, s. of William, s. of Symon, of Cranbrooke, gent., confirmed 10 Dec. 1572, by Cooke. Misc. Gen. et Her., N. S., iv., 351, copy of grant, Brit. Mus.

LYNE, Richart, of Hants, 25 Nov. 1555, by T. Hawley. Add. MS. 16,940, fo. 207ᵇ ; Harl. MS. 1562, fo. 113 ; Add. MS. 7098, fo. 78ᵇ (fo. 122) ; Harl. MS. 5865, fo. 49.

LYON, Sʳ John, Maior of London ; 1 Oct. 1550, by Hawley, Clar. (his 1ˢᵗ wife Alice Hansha, 1555, by Hawley ; his 2ⁿᵈ wife Elizth. Lee, 1564-5, by G. Dethick). Add. MS. 16,940, fo. 204 ; Harl. MS. 1359, fo. 5ᵇ ; Q's Coll. Oxf. MSS. 37, fo. 26, and 39, fo. 28, copy of grant, ex. Mag. Reg., Gilb. Dethick ; Grants II., 652, 462 ; Harl. MS. 1115, fo. 66ᵇ.

LYTTELL, Thomas, of Bray, Berks, confirmed .... 1563. (Harvey's Grants), Add. MS. 16,940, fo. 53 ; (Harl. MS. 1105, fo. 4, for an Essex family).

M

MABB, John, ... Chamberlayn of London ; 10 Nov. 1571, by Cooke. Harl. MS. 1359, fo. 119ᵇ ; Grants II., 521 ; Add. MS. 4966, fo. 60ᵇ.

MacCARTHY, Charles, Visct. Carthey of Muskery ; 21 Sept. 1639, by T. Preston, Ulster. Le Neve's MS. 463.

MACK DERMOD, Edmund, and ⎱ descended from Thomas Mack of Crosnah, co.
„ Cormuck, his son, ⎰ Roscommon, etc. ; crest granted 16 April 1599, by Wᵐ Dethick, Gart. Q's Coll. Oxf. MS. 36, fo. 82, for copy of grant ; Stowe MS. 676, fo. 131.

MACHEN, Richard, of Witcomb, Gloucestershire, s. of Thomas, s. of Henry, gent. ; patent, Quarterly, 1 June 1615, by Segar. Add. MS. 12,225, fo. 74 ; Harl. MS. 6140, fo. 63ᵇ ; Guil. 225 ; Harl. MS. 1441, fo. 50, copy of grant.

MACHET, ⎧ John, rector of Lambeth, 1570—74, and chaplain to Math. Parker
⎪ (Archbp. of Canterbury, 1559 to 1575), descended out of Leicester-
⎪ shire, and to
„ ⎪ Samuel, ⎱ brethren, sons of John Machet of Gynningham, Norf.,
„ ⎨ Mathew, and ⎬ 27 Jan. 1626-7, by Segar. Add. MS. 12,225, fo. 78 ;
„ ⎩ Nathaniel, ⎭ 5 July 1626, Harl. MSS. 1085, fo. 43 ; and 5887, fo. 114.

MACKAY, Patrick, of London, mercht., Certif. of arms 22 March 1706. Le Neve's MS. 484.

MACKWORTH, John, and his brother ⎱ to use "a parcel" of the arms of John
„ Thomas, ⎰ Touchet, Lord Audley of Haley, by con-
sent ; 1 Aug. 1404 . . . . Q's Coll. Oxf. MS. 38, fo. 3, copy of deed in French ; Harl. MS. 1410, fo. 23ᵇ ; Add. MS. 6670, fo. 208 ; Parker's Glossary of Heraldry, Chron. Table, p. xiv., note k ; Grants II., fo. 677.

MADYSON, Edmond, of Hunaby, co. Linc. . . . . 1587, by Cooke. Harl. MSS. 1359, fo. 107, and 1422, fo. 93ᵇ ; Add. MS. 4966, fo. 69.

MADDISON, Sir Lionel, of Newcastle-upon-Tyne, etc., reassumed their paternal coat 5 June 1635 and to his bros., by W. Le Neve, Norr. Harl. MS. 1441, fo. 10ᵇ, copy at large, Brit. Mus. ; Visit. Durham, 1575, Philipson's Ed., Notes, p. 61, and Surtees Soc., XLI., l. ; Stowe MS. 677, fo. 57 ; Grants II., 608.

MADDOX, ... of Masterley, Salop, and of London, ... party per pale gu. and az., two lyons passant or, by Segar. Add. MS. 12,225, fo. 78.

MADOCKS, John, of co. Middx., gent., s. of Thomas, late of Salop, gent., of the bedchamber to Ed. VI., Q. Mary and Q. Eliz. ; crest granted 26 March 1592, by W. Dethick, Gart. Stowe MS. 676, fo. 88 and 100ᵇ ; Q's Coll. Oxf. MS. 36, fo. 19, copy of grant ; Guil. 306 ; Grants I., fo. 28.

MAIDSTON, Robert, of Boxted, Essex, ... 1614, by Camden. Morgan's Sphere, 118.

MAJOR, John, of the Borough of Leicester, and to his father
„ Anthony, of Kempston, Notts ; crest 15 May 1646, by Sir E. Bysshe, Gart. Harl. MS. 1441, fo. 149ᵇ ; Stowe MS. 703, fo. 70, and Berry's Armory. [See also MAYOR.]

MAKARETH or MAKERETH, ... of co. Lanc. . . . . by Cooke. Harl. MSS. 1359, fo. 119, and 6140, fo. 39 ; Add. MS. 4966, fo. 90.

MALBON, George, of Bradeley, Cheshire, 20 Aug. 1683, by Sir Wᵐ Dugdale and Norroy. Harl. MS. 6834, fo. 178 ; Grants III., fo. 205.

MALBY, Arthur, of London, born in Norfolk (akin to Sir Nicholas Malby, Knt.), father of Thos., who mar. Lettice, dau. of Hy. Clifford and of his wife, sister of Walter, 1ˢᵗ Earl of Essex, etc. ; arms and crest granted 24 Nov. 1589, by W. Dethick, Gart. Stowe MS. 676, fo. 79ᵇ ; Q's Coll. Oxf. MS. 37, fo. 117, for copy of grant.

Y

MALDEN, Town of, Essex, 30 April 1562, by Sir G. Dethick, Gart. Harl. MS. 1441, fo. 65ᵇ; Q's Coll. Oxf. MS. 145, fo. 8; Grants II., 652; Harl. MS. 1116, fo. 48ᵇ.

MAL(D)ENBECK, John, of Danzic in Prussia, a gift of arms by letters patent Westmʳ 16 Jan. 1533-4; alteration 16 July 1534, by Wriothesley. Harl. MS. 4900, fo. 2ᵇ, 7ᵇ; Grants II., 692.

MALLOM, John, of Walter-Acton, Norfolk, 4 May 1685, by Sir Wᵐ Dugdale and Clar. Harl. MS. 6834, fo. 178; Grants III., 266; Lansd. MS. 867, fo. 52; Harl. MS. 1085, fo. 59.

MALLORY, Richard, Alderm. of London, confirmed 155 .... or 156 .... Harvey's Grants, Add. MS. 16,940, fo. 58.

MALTBY..... of Maltby in Cleveland, Yorks, ... arg., on a bend gu. three garbs of malt or, by Segar. Add. MS. 12,225, fo. 74ᵇ.

MALTE, John, of London (tayler, by K. H. VIII. in Stowe MS.), coat and crest .... Barker's Grants, Harl. MS. 5846, fo. 30ᵇ and 78ᵇ; Stowe MS. 692, fo. 69ᵇ.

MALTYWARD, Robert, of Rougham, Suffolk, esq., Barr.-at-law; 26 May 1663, by Sir E. Walker, Gart. Her. Coll., fo. 50; Harl. MS. 1085, fo. 31.

MALYART, Thomas, of Somerset .... Add. MS. 26,702, fo. 77.

MALYN, John, of Calleys .... coat and crest. Barker's Grants, Harl. MS. 5846, fo. 7ᵇ; Stowe MS. 692, fo. 69.

„   William, M.A., s. of Henry, of Staplehurst, Kent, granted after 1564, by Cooke, Clar. Harl. MS. 1116, fo. 69ᵇ, copy of grant, Brit. Mus.

DE MANDAVILE, Sir Otho, s. of Peter, arms granted to Peter by Ed. III.; exemplified and confirmed to son (17 R. II., pt. i., m. 5) 1377-8: gu., three leopards or, collared with crowns az. Harl. MS. 1507, fo. 426; MS. Ashm. 835, fo. 365, copy of grant, Bodleian Lib.

MANDERE, Thomas, of Leigh, Devon, augmentation 16 Dec. 1660, by Walker, Gart. Her. Coll., fo. 30. See Thos. MAUNDY.

MANFELD, Lancelot, of Skirpenbeck, Yorks, confirmed 20 Sept. 1563, by Flower. MS. Ashm. 844, fo. 72*, copy of grant, Bodleian Lib.; Guil. 77.

MANINGHAM, J., ..., by Ro. Cooke .... Add. MS. 5855, fo. 130.

MANINGTON or MONINGTON, of Cornwall, ... Quarterly, by R. Cooke. Stowe MS. 670, fo. 29ᵇ.

MANLOVE, Rowland, of co. Staff., ... by R. St. George, Clar. Stowe MS. 703, fo. 73.

MANLY, William, of London, 4 quarterings. Visit. of Lond., 1633; see Add. MS. 4966, fo. 44.

MANN, Edward, of Ipswich, Suff., sometime comptroller of that part; granted 2 March 1662, by Sir Ed. Bysshe, Clar. Bysshe's Grants, fo. 5, Her. Coll.; Harl. MSS. 1105, fo. 17ᵇ, and 1470, fo. 121, copy of grant, Brit. Mus.; Guil. 360.

MAN, Henry, Bp. of the Isle of Man; 27 Jan., a. 37 [Hen. VIII.], 1545-6, Frydaye, "az., a masculyn wᵗʰ iiij flower de Luces, one at each end, or, within and without the masculyn set v yong men's heads argent, eared or." Harl. MS. 5846, fo. 74ᵇ, coat .... by Barker; Stowe MS. 692, fo. 68ᵇ, Henry, Richard in the margin ["Azure, a masculyn wᵗʰ iiij flower de Luces, one at each end, or, within and without the masculyn then sett v yong men's heads sylver, heered golde, couppey, over all a pontifycall myter garnysshed or and ar., wᵗʰ pendaunte or, lined and taselyd or"].

„   John, of Lynzeh (Lyndsell), Essex, confirmed .... 155– or 156–. (Harvey's Grants), Harl. MS. 1359, fo. 50ᵇ; Add. MS. 16,940, fo. 57.

„   John, of Bolingbroke, co. Linc., J.P. and feodary of the Duchye of Lancaster within the said county; given 5 April 1561, 3 Eliz., by Dalton. Harl. MS. 1359, fo. 50ᵇ.

MANN, John, of city of Norwich, 4 Jan. 1664-5, by Sir E. Bysshe, Clar. Harl. MS. 1105, fo. 38*, 39; Bysshe's Grants, 29.

MANNE, William, s. of John, of Holy Cross, city of Canterbury, Knt., 10 June 1601, by Camden. Add. MS. 14,295, fo. 62 ; C. 16, fo. 218 [Visit. of] Kent [1619].

MANNAKER, Adrian, a Dutch gen., Mayor of the city of Middleburge in Zeeland (Knighted by K. James at Greenwich 20 June 1609), grant 28 June 1609, by Segar. Add. MS. 12,225, fo. 75.

MANNING, ... of Kent, descended of ancient and noble family, so called from Manning, a town in Saxony, whence they came into England before ye Conquest and have settled also in Frisia or Friesland ; confirmed with 11 quarterings and crest . . . . by Segar. This, with a pedigree, Add. MS. 12,225, fo. 74b ; C. 16, fo. 133 [Visit. of Kent, 1619], Her. Coll. ; Guil. 137 : Harl. MS. 1432, fo. 158.

  ,, George, } of Downe, Knt., crest 20 April 1577, by Sir G. Dethick, Gart.
  ,, Henry, } Kent Visit., 1619, edited by J. J. Howard, p. 271 (Arch. Cant.); Harl. MS. 1441, fo. 86b, and Q's Coll. Oxf. MS. 145, fo. 43, copy of grant, Brit. Mus.

MANSBRIDGE, John, of London, gent., citizen and Mercht. taylor, allowed at Visit. of London, 1568, by Ro. Cooke, Clar. Stowe MS. 670, fo. 60.

MANSELL, Francis, now of Guildford, Surrey, who provided the ship and with great loyalty and fidelity assisted his Majesty's transportation after the unfortunate battle of Worcester (or, three manacles sa., on a chief gu. a lion passant guardant or) ; 14 Feb. 1664½, by Walker, Gart. Her. Coll., fo. 60 ; Berry's Armory.

MANSUR, Richard, of London, see MORYSON.

MANWARINGE, Sir John, coat and crest . . . . Barker's Grants, 1526—49, Harl. MS. 5846, fo. 72 ; Stowe MS. 692, fo. 68.

MAPES, (Leonard), of Feltham and Rollesby, Norfolk, ... Francis, of . . . ., Mapes quartering Blount, confirmed . . . . 1587 (by W. Dethick, Gart., and Cooke, Clar.). Caius Coll. Camb. MS. 551, fo. 31 (among Camden's Guifts [1587?]) ; Harl. MSS. 1552, fo. 228, and 1441, fo. 152 ; Le Neve's MS. 354.

MAPLES, Sir Thomas, of Long Stow, Hunts, Bart., testified 10 Feb. 1632, by Wm Segar, Kt, Gart. Harl. MS. 1105, fo. 2b.

MAR, Edmund, of Colchester, 7 May 1611, by Camden. Harl. MS. 6179, fo. 35.

MARBURY, Sir Anthony, of Lambeth, Surrey, testification of Knighthood, descent and arms, with quarterings, 10 May 1616, by Wm Segar and Camden. Add. MS. 12,225, fo. 76b ; Guil. 336.

MARCHE, ... Clarke of the Star Chamber, London, ... 1587, by Cooke, Clar. : gu., a horse's head couped betw. three cross crosslets fitchée argent ; crest, a griffin's head erased az. holding in his beak a rose gu., stalked and leaved vert. Stowe MS. 670, fo. 20b.

MARCH, John, of co. Linc., granted 11 Aug. 1576, by G. Dethick, Gart. Q's Coll. Oxf. MS. 37, fo. 63, for copy of grant, and MS. 145, fo. 44b ; Stowe MS. 676, fo. 48b ; Add. MS. 26,753, fo. 120b : arms, arg., a cross flory az. betw. four talbots' heads erased sa. ; crest, a talbot's head erased (lion's head couped ?) arg. charged with a cross flory az. Stowe MS. 703, fo. 48 ; Add. MS. 26,753, fo. 120b.

  ,, Stephen, of Newport, I. of W., attested by Wm Penson, Lanc. Herald, 16 Nov. 1633. Harl. MS. 1422, fo. 57b.

MARCHAND or MARCHAM, John (s. of William), of Bucks, confirmed or granted . . . . 1582, by Cooke. Marcham in Add. MS. 14,295, fo. 31b ; (Guil. 267, Marchand).

MARDEN, ... of city of London, ... or, a bend gu., in the sinister chief point a chough, by Segar. Add. MS. 12,225, fo. 78b.

MARFFYN, see MERVIN.

MARIANUS, Sir Angelus, from Cremona, Italy, 8 Nov. 1557, by G. Dethick, Gart. Grants I., 21 : on a bend or a lion rampant gu. ; crest, a talbot's head and neck.

MARIGNY-CARPENTER, Jacob de, a French gent., Augmentation and alteration of arms, Crest and supporters at Hockstraet in Brabant, 23 Aug. 1653, by Sir E. Walker, Gart. Her. Coll., fo. 1.

MARKAUNT or MERKAUNT, John, of Colchester, crest 7 May 1612, 10 K. Jas., by Camden. Harl. MS. 1172, fo. 9, copy of grant, Brit. Mus.; (Harl. MSS. 1541, fo. 183ᵇ, and 6065, fo. 101, as Markaunt); Harl. MS. 1085, fo. 19; Edmond in Le Neve's MS. 355.

MARKS, ... of Suffolk, ... gu., semée-de-lis or, a lyon rampant and a canton erm. .... by Segar. Add. MS. 12,225, fo. 77ᵇ.

MARKES, Richard, of Beverley, Yorks, gen., 10 May 1560, by G. Dethick, Gart. Surtees Soc., XLI., xl., copy of grant, Brit. Mus.

MARLER, Richard, of co. Northants, gent., crest granted 2 July 1566, by Sir G. Dethick, Gart. Stowe MS. 676, fo. 30; Q's Coll. Oxf. MS. 37, fo. 44, copy of grant; Grants I., fo. 256.

„ Walter, of London, s. of Walter, of London, gent., 10 Oct., 27 Eliz., 1585, by Cooke. Add. MS. 14,295, fo. 33; Harl. MSS. 1359, fo. 98ᵇ, 1453, fo. 5, and 1069, fo. 28ᵇ; Add. MS. 4966, fo. 62.

MARLOW, Abbot, ... arg., on a fesse per fesse indented az. and purpure, betw. three pinks or, stalked and leaved vert, as many trefoils slipped argt. Add. MS. 26,702, fo. 40.

MARPLE, Richard, senʳ, of Edenstow (or Edwinstow), co. Derby, confirmed 20 Sept. 1574, by Flower. MS. Ashm. 844. fo. 71. copy of grant, Bodleian Lib.; Guil. 276: This patent was procured by Thos. Drury and by him written with his own hand and delivered by me Somerset for my father (in law) Norroy on Tuesday, 7 Nov. 1587, 29 Eliz., Reliquary, xxii., 244.

MARRIETT [MARYETT], Thomas, of Remenham, Berks, Esq., arms confirmed and crest given 16 June 1586, 28 Q. Eliz., by Cooke. Harl. MS. 1359, fo. 14, 89; copy of grant in Harl. MS. 1172, fo. 4; Add. MS. 14,295, fo. 8ᵇ; Grants II., 491; Add. MS. 4966, fo. 35ᵇ.

MARRONE, (DE ROAN) .... arms 15 Sept., 4 Ed. VI., 1550, by Sir G. Dethick, Gart. Certificate in French, Q's Coll. Oxf. MSS. 37, fo. 24, and 39, fo. 25; Harl. MS. 1359, fo. 60; Grants I., 117; Q's Coll. Oxf. MS. 140, fo. 25, copy of grant; Stowe MS. 676, fo. 18ᵇ.

MARSHE, ... of London, grocer, ... on a piece of vellum, by Cooke, made certayne Scotchn. for his buryall Monday, 25 Oct. 1602. Add. MS. 14,295, fo. 27ᵇ; Harl. MSS. 1359, fo. 118ᵇ, and 1422, fo. 57ᵇ; Stowe MS. 670, fo. 70; Add. MS. 4966, fo. 101.

„ Gabriel, Servant to the Duke of Buckingham, ... 1627. Harl. MSS. 1422, fo. 57ᵇ, and 5887, fo. 111.

MARSH, John, s. of John, of Marton, par. of Langdon, Kent, confirmation and grant of crest 10 June 1616, by Segar. Add. MS. 12,225, fo. 75ᵇ; Harl. MS. 1470, fo. 208 and 74, copy of grant, Brit. Mus.; Guil. 383 says 16ᵗʰ June; Grants I., 391; Harl. MS. 6140, fo. 76.

MARSHE, Richard, of Worcestershire, coat and crest .... Barker's Grants, Harl. MS. 5846, fo. 71ᵇ; Stowe MS. 692, fo. 66.

MARSH. Richard, and ⎫ of Longdon, Kent, confirmed .... by Segar. Add.
„ Thomas, his eldest son, ⎭ MS. 12,225, fo. 75.

MARSHE, Thomas, Clerk of the Council of the Star Chamber, 21 May 1571, by Cooke. Misc. Gen. et Her., 2nd S., vol. iv., p. 56, facsimile: Stowe MS. 670, fo. 20ᵇ; Add. MS. 14,297, fo. 38ᵇ; a new coat 8 March 1578-9, by Sir G. Dethick, Gart., Harl. MS. 1441, fo. 82ᵇ; Q's Coll. Oxf. MS. 145, fo. 37, and Add. MS. 12,442, fo. 27, copy of grant, Brit. Mus.; died 1624 in Harl. MS. 1422, fo. 57ᵇ; Harl. MS. 6179, fo. 15ᵇ; see Harl. MS. 1116, fo. 92ᵇ; Stowe MS. 703, fo. 40ᵇ; Cat. Her. Exhib. Soc. of Antiq., No. 220.

MARSHALL, ... of London, crest .... Barker's Grants between 1526—49, Harl. MS. 5846, fo. 77; Stowe MS. 692, fo. 69ᵇ.

LOCKSMITH alias MARSHALL, ... servant to Sir Francis Bacon : arg., a chev. between three horseshoes sa., a chief gu. . . . . by Segar.   Add. MS. 12,225, fo. 72 ; Harl. MS. 6140, fo. 49.

MARSHALL, Henry, of Carlton, Notts, confirmed 1 June 1562.   (Harvey's Grants), Add. MS. 16,940, fo. 57ᵇ ; Grants II., 564 ; Misc. Marescall, ii., pt. 2, p. 90.

„   John, Alderm. of London ; 15 Sept. 1556, by Hawley ?   Add. MS. 16,940, fo. 208ᵇ.

„   John and Henry, of Southwark, s. of Richard, of Cockwood, Yorks, s. of Thos., s. of Richard ; 21 Dec. 1611, by Camden, and pedigree.   Harl. MS. 6095, fo. 16 ; Morgan's Sphere of the Gentry, p. 111 ; Harl. MS. 1561, fo. 134.

„   John, of London, vintner, 14 Dec. 1647, by E. Bysshe, Gart.   Harl. MS. 6140, fo. 18.

„   Nicholas, s. of Ralph, s. of William, all of Barking, crest 10 Dec. 1578, by Cooke, Clar.   Le Neve's MS. 493.

„   Richard, of Ivy House in the par. of Strood or Street, co. Somerset, 1 June 1573, by Sir G. Dethick.   Harl. MS. 1441, fo. 79ᵇ ; Q's Coll. Oxf. MS. 145, fo. 31.

„   Robert, of the Castle of Carrigonan, co. Cork, one of H.M.'s Council in the province of Munster, and George, his brother, one of H.M.'s esquires : out of Yorks.   Harl. MSS. 5887, fo. 104, and 6140, fo. 42.

MARSHAL, Thomas, of Mitchelham, Sussex, s. of Edward, of Hitchin, 2 Dec. 1612, by Camden.   Morgan's Sphere, 117 ; Caius Coll. Camb. MS. 551, fo. 28ᵇ.

MARSHAM, Robert, of Little Melton, Norfolk, 12 May 1517, 9 H. VIII., by T. Wriothesley, Gart.   Le Neve's MS. 352.

„   ⎧ Thomas, of Grafton Park, Northants, arm. ;
„   ⎨ John, of Whornes Place, Kent, one of the six Clerks in Chancery ;
„   ⎩ Ferdinando, Esqʳᵉ of the body to the King ; alteration of arms at Oxford 11 March, 20 Chas., 1644-5, by Walker, Gart.   Add. MS. 14,294, fo. 30ᵇ ; Her. Coll., 25.

MARSTON, John, Esq., late of the Middle Temple, councillor at the lawes, now of the city and county of Coventry, s. of John, s. of Ralph, of Salop ; exemplified (29) Nov. 1587, by Wᵐ Dethick, Gart.   Q's Coll. Oxf. MS. 37, fo. 98, for copy of exemplification ; Stowe MS. 676, fo. 69, s. of Ralph, s. of John.

MARTEN, ... of Bildeston, Suff., ... 1600.   Berry.

MARTON or MARTYN, Annie, mother to . . . . Askewe . . . . 1589, by Cooke.   Harl. MS. 1359, fo. 100 ; Stowe MS. 702, fo. 115 ; Harl. MS. 1441, fo. 144ᵇ.

MARTYN, Sir Christopher, of Barton (or Bourton), co. Camb., Knt., granted June 1601, and to his brethren, by Camden.   Cott. MS. Faustina E. 1, 44 ; Harl. MSS. 1422, fo. 17ᵇ, 5839, fo. 2ᵇ, 2275, fo. 90ᵇ, and 1115, fo. 8ᵇ ; Guil. 212, 214.

MARTIN, Cuthbert, of London, esq., and sometime Alderm., descended out of Lanc., s. of William ; afterwards Knighted ; 31 Aug. 1615, by Segar.   Add. MS. 12,225, fo. 75ᵇ ; C. 21 [Visit. of Essex, 1634], Her. Coll. ; Harl. MS. 6140, fo. 62ᵇ.

MARTON, John, of London, ...   Add. MS. 26,702, fo. 77.

MARTYN, John, of co. Devon, 24 Q. Eliz. . . . . 1581, "who went round about the world with Sir Francis Drake, 1577 " : gu., on a chev. or three talbots passant sa. ; crest, on a sphere an eagle arg., ducally gorged, by Sir G. Dethick.   Harl. MSS. 1441, fo. 102ᵇ, and 5847, fo. 52 ; Q's Coll. Oxf. MS. 145, fo. 53.

MARTYNE, Richard, of London, esq., now as well Warden of the Exchange and money within the Tower of London, as also of coynage of golde and silver within the same place, or elsewhere within the realme of England, as also one of the assistants of the society of the minerall and batrye workes within the said Realme of England. Allowed and crest granted to him 10 Jan. 1572-3. Harl. MSS. 1359, fo. 21ᵇ, and 1422, fo. 51 ; Add. MS. 14,295, fo. 15 ; Harl. MS. 1116, fo. 43ᵇ.

MARTYN, Roger, of Long Melford, Suff., Alderm. of London, gift between 155 . . . . and 156 . . . . (Harvey's Grants), Add. MS. 16,940, fo. 58ᵇ.

MARTINUS, Samuel, practical Master in theology, History and philosophy ; by Nation a Bohemian, s. of Peter, a man well deserving the ecclesiastical function ; by Segar. Add. MS. 12,225, fo. 76.

MARTYN, Thomas, of Martins, Dorset, gent., augmentation to arms and crest 20 Nov., 2 and 3 Phil. and Mary, 1556, by Sir G. Dethick. Q's Coll. Oxf. MSS. 37, fo. 35, and 39, fo. 58, for copy of grant in French ; Harl. MS. 1359, fo. 64 ; Stowe MS. 676 ; Grants I., 115.

MARWOOD, William, of Plymouth and Plimstock, Devon, esq., crest given . . . . 1596, by R. Lee. Add. MS. 14,295, fo. 122 ; Harl. MS. 1359, fo. 39ᵇ.

MASCALL, ... of Essex and of London, mercht., Sept. 1671, by Sir E. Bysshe, Clar. Stowe MS. 697, fo. 121.

MASHAM, William, of Shakerland Hall, Suff., and now citizen and Alderm. of London ; 12 Jan. 1583-4, by Sir G. Dethick. Harl. MS. 1441, fo. 69ᵇ ; June in Q's Coll. Oxf. MS. 145, fo. 14.

MASON, Richard, esq., 5 Feb. 1668-9, by Sir E. Walker, Gart. Her. Coll., fo. 65 ; Stowe MS. 697, fo. 118ᵇ.

„   Stephen, of London, ... gift . . . . 1560 . . . . (Harvey's Grants), Add. MS. 16,940, fo. 57.

„   John, s. of William, of Yorks, Coat confirmed and crest granted by Cooke. Harl. MS. 1410, fo. 59 and 59ᵇ.

MASSEY, John de, of Tatton, appellant,   ⎫ claimed same arms ; both disallowed at
„   John de, of Pottington, defendant,   ⎭ Gloucester 14 Nov., R. II. (? 1378). Harl. MS. 1507, fo. 423, and Q's Coll. Oxf. MS. 38, fo. 143, for copy of proceedings ; Le Neve's MS. 423.

„   Toby, one of yᵉ captains of yᵉ Militia of yᵉ city of London, and painter-stainer, by Segar. Add. MS. 12,225, fo. 76 ; Harl. MS. 6140, fo. 79.

MASSIE, Sir Geffrey, of Tatton, coat and crest . . . . Barker's Grants, Harl. MS. 5846, fo. 72 ; Stowe MS. 692, fo. 68.

MASSINGBERD, Thomas, of Gunby, co. Leic., gift arms 27 May, 6 H. VIII., 1514, by T. Wriothesley, Gart., and T. Benolte, Clar. Crest by same to same, 10 May, 5 H. VIII. Add. MS. 17,506, fo. 38ᵇ.

MASTER, James, of East Landen, Kent, and ⎫ 2 May 1608, by Camden. Visit. of
„   John, of Sandwich, Kent,   ⎭ Kent, 1619—44, edited by Howard; Arch. Cant., vol. v., 238 ; Her. and Geneal., ii., 434, copy of grant, Brit. Mus. ; Le Neve's MS. 356.

„   Michael, of Wilsborough, Kent. Marshal of the Hall to K. James ; exemplified 20 May 1620, by Segar. Misc. Gen. et Her., 2nd S., vol. iv., p. 72, copy of grant, Brit. Mus.

„   Richard, of Northants (or Oxfordshire), crest 2 July 1566, by G. Dethick, Gart. Stowe MS. 676, fo. 30.

„   Richard, Doc. Phys. and phys. to Q. Eliz., s. of Robert, of Wilsborough, Kent ; arms and crest 1 Dec. 1568, by G. Dethick, Gart., Cooke, and Flower. (Exemplified to Michael Master of Wilsborough, Kent, Marshal of the Hall to King Jas., by Segar, 20 May 1620.) Harl. MS. 1441, fo. 70ᵇ, as Masteres ; Q's Coll. Oxf. MS. 39, fo. 133, copy of grant in Latin (MS. 145, fo. 16) ; Misc. Gen. et Her., 2nd S., vol. iv., p. 72 ; Her. and Geneal., ii., 433 ; 1 Nov. in Harl. MS. 1422, fo. 78 ; Arch. Cant. (Visit. Kent), vol. iv., p. 259 ; MS. Ashm. 844, fo. 46, copy of grant, Bodleian Lib. ; Gnil. 180 ; Grants I., 91.

„   William, of Heytesbury, Wilts, arms and crest. Barker's Grants ; (Maister in Harl. MS. 5846, fo. 75ᵇ) ; Stowe MS. 692, fo. 69 ; Harl. MS. 5887, fo. 5.

MASTER, William le, LL.D. and D.D., of Camb., grant 17 Nov. 1587, by W. Dethick, Gart. Stowe MS. 676, fo. 73 ; Harl. MS. 1422, fo. 78 ; Q's Coll. Oxf. MS. 37, fo. 105, copy of grant in Latin.

MATCHET, John, 1627, see MACHET.

MATHER, Christopher, of Seacroft, Yorks, 11 Feb. 1575-6, by Flower. MS. Ashm. 834, fo. 15, copy of grant, Bodleian Lib.; Her. and Geneal., iii., 260 ; Guil. 41.

MATHEW, Dame Mary, wife of Sir Andrew Jude, late Lord Mayor of London ; 5 or 10 Oct. 1558, by Hervey. Misc. Gen. et Her., 2nd S., vol. ii., p. 1, facsimile ; dau. and h. of Thomas Mathew of Colchester, Essex, see Add. MS. 16,940, fo. 52b ; Cat. Her. Exhib. Soc. of Antiq., No. 212.

„ (William), of Tresengar in Cornwall.

MATTOCK, Nicholas, of Hitchin, Herts, grant 23 July, 9 H. VII., 1494, by Richmont Clar. Laurence's Nobility of the Brit. Gentry, 9 ; Misc. Gen. et Her., 2nd S., vol. v., p. 329, facsimile ; Harl. MS. 1507, fo. 7, copy of grant, Brit. Mus. ; Q's Coll. Oxf. MS. 38, fo. 17, copy of grant.

MAUDELEY, John, of Somerset, arms and crest . . . . Barker's Grants, Harl. MS. 5846, fo. 78 ; Stowe MS. 692, fo. 69b.

MAUDLEY, Roger (s. of John, s. of Richard, of Nonney, co. Somerset, gent.), confirmed 18 June 1532, by Benolte. Stowe MS. 676, fo. 14 ; copy of grant, Q's Coll. Oxf. MS. 37, fo. 9, ex. Mag. Reg., G. Dethick ; (1537 in Berry) ; Grants II., 531.

MAUNDY, Thomas, confirmed . . . . 1657, by Bysshe, Gart. Add. MS. 26,758, fo. 16b ; Richard in Harl. MS. 6832, fo. 414 ; see Harl. MS. 6179, fo. 89, for Maunder in Cumberland, out of Cornwall. See Thos. MANDERE.

MAUTEBEY, ..., erm., on a bend betw. two cottises engrailed gu. three garbs or ; May 1612, a patent by Camden. Harl. MS. 6095, fo. 18.

MAWSON, Charles, Chester Herald, s. of Thomas, of Great Wigston, co. Leic., Captain of Horse under Ld. Loughborough; 24 Dec. 1692, by T. St. George, Gart. and Clar. Harl. MS. 6834, fo. 178 ; Grants IV., 125 ; Harl. MS. 1085, fo. 56 ; Le Neve's MS. 492.

„ Peter, s. of Nicholas, of Mill Beck, Kendal, a person of eminent loyalty, 10 Feb. 1661-2, by Sir E. Walker, Gart. Her. Coll., fo. 44.

MAXEY, Anthony, of Bradwell, Essex, ... 1587, by Cooke. Harl. MSS. 1359, fo. 110, and 1422, fo. 93b ; Add. MS. 4966, fo. 30b.

MAY, ... of Charterhouse, Somerset, and Rawmore, Sussex, 1573 : sa., a chev. or betw. three roses arg., a chief of the 2nd ; crest. Berry.

„ . . . . of London, draper : gu., a fesse betw. eight billets or . . . . by Segar. Add. MS. 12,225, fo. 76b.

„ Elizabeth, wife to John Tedcastell . . . . 1590, by Cooke. Harl. MS. 1359, fo. 94 ; Stowe MS. 702, fo. 115.

„ Thomas, of Kent, 1 May 1440, by Roger Leigh, Clar. Grants II., 629, and Le Neve's MS. 510.

„ Thomas, Master of the Marshalsea ; 24 March 1574, by ?Cooke or G. Dethick. Harl. MS. 1422, fo. 121 ; (called Way in Harl. MS. 1359, fo. 118) ; Harl. MS. 5887, fo. 68, 68b.

„ Thomas, s. of Richard, of Wadhurst, Sussex : arms, gu., a fesse betw. eight billets or ; crest, a lion's head and neck couped. Harl. MS. 1422, fo. 12 ; Add. MS. 12,225, fo. 71b ; Harl. MS. 1441, fo. 46.

„ Thomas, of Stoke by Nayland, Suff., 4 Jan. 1687-8, by Sir T. St. George, Gart. and Clar.: gu., two barulets erm. bew. six billets or. Harl. MS. 6834, fo. 178 ; Grants III., fo. 339 ; Lansd. MS. 867, fo. 52.

MAYCOCKE, ... printer, Little Britain, London, confirmed. Harl. MS. 6179, fo. 51b.

MAYCOTE als MACKWITH, Cavagliero, of Reculver, Kent, 2 Nov. 1604, by Camden. Harl. MSS. 1422, fo. 18b, and 6095, fo. 2b ; Guil. 157.

MAYDELEY, ... crest .... Barker's Grants, Harl. MS. 5846, fo. 75 ; Stowe MS. 692, fo. 69ᵇ.

MAYDWELL, Thomas, of Geddington, Northants, gent.
„ Thoby, and   } his bros., sons of Lawrence, of Gretton, s. of Thos., s.
„ Richard, of Gretton, } of William, etc., confirmed 3 Dec. 1621, by Camden. Q's Coll. Oxf. MS. 38, fo. 135 ; Harl. MS. 1507, fo. 387, copy of grant, Brit. Mus. ; Harl. MS. 1172, fo. 53ᵇ ; (entered in the large book of patents, p. 388) ; (1634 in Berry) ; Le Neve's MS. fo. 387, 388 and 358.

MAYFIELD, Owen, Alderm. and Mayor of Cambridge ; 9 Oct. 1684, by Sir W. Dugdale and Clar. Harl. MS. 6834, fo. 178 ; Grants III., 248 ; Lansd. MS. 867, fo. 52.

MAYHEWE, Robert, of Clippesby, Norfolk, confirmed 9 Nov. 1563, by Hervey. Guil. 284 ; Grants I., 314.
„ .... of Hemingston, Suff., by Camden. Harl. MS. 1085, fo. 16.

MAYNARD, Henry, of Esten, Herts, ... 1590, by Cooke. Harl. MS. 1359, fo. 101ᵇ.
„ Sir William, Knt. and Bart., created Baron Maynard of Wicklow in Ireland by K. Jas. ; confirmation of arms (quarterly of 4) and crest and grant of supporters 26 Nov. 1621, by Segar. Add. MS. 12,225, fo. 77.

MAYNE, Alexʳ, of London, ... 1626, by Segar. Add. MS. 12,225, fo. 77.

MAINE, Bennett, of Creslowe, Bucks, crest June 1604, by Camden. Harl. MS. 6095, fo. 18ᵇ ; Stowe MS. 677, fo. 5 ; Mayne in Guil. 254 ; Harl. MS. 5887, fo. 4ᵇ.

MAYOR, John, of Southampton [Gu., an anchor erect in pale arg., on a chief or two roses of ye first ; crest, out of a wreath a Greyhound's head couped gu., collared or], descended out of the parish of Hanway in the isle of Jersey from Sʳ Marins Mayor or Mager, who flourished in the time H. VII. and VIII. and served in the wars of H. VII., by Segar .... Add. MS. 12,225, fo. 77ᵇ.

MAYOR, MAIOR,   } Captain of Lubecke. Add. MS. 26,702, fo. 76.
MEYGER, Sir Marke,   } Augm. per letters patent at Greenwich 10 Dec.
(Mark MAJOR, a German,)   } 1533, H. VIII., natᵈ temp. H. VIII. [Knighted at
MEYER, Sir Mark,   } Greenwich by Hen. VIII., Stowe MS. 676]. MS. Ashm. 858, fo. 4-5 [has Major], copy of grant, Bodleian Lib. ; Harl. MS. 4900, fo. 1ᵇ [has Meyger] ; [Harl. MS. 1408, fo. 41, has Marcus Mayger] ; Stowe MS. 676, fo. 15 [has Maior]; Grants II., 691.

MEIR (MEYER), MAYER or MAYOR, Matthew, of the North, granted 9 Nov. 1547, 1 Ed. VI. [Gu., an oak tree in pale betw. two swans arg., thereon an anchor sable pendant, on a chief or a pellet charged with a portcullis chained and ringed of ye 4th betw. two roses dimidiated of the field. Crest, a greyhound's head couped and pted p pale arg. and vert within a plume of [4] feathers arg. and vert (Stowe MS. 676)], by Gilb. Dethick, Norr. Q's Coll. Oxf. MSS. 37. fo. 13, and 39, fo. 8 ; Harl. MS. 1507, fo. 434, copy of grant in Latin, Brit. Mus. ; Harl. MS. 1359, fo. 4ᵇ ; Sir Matthias, of the isle of Jerseys, gu., an anchor erect in pale or, on a chief of the second three roses of the field, in Berry ; Grants I., 107 ; Le Neve's MS. 434.

MEADOWS or MEDOWS, James, D.D., Quartering Brock, by Segar and Camden, crest, etc., ... 1600. Add. MSS. 14,295, fo. 77, and 12,225, fo. 79 ; Harl. MSS. 6140, fo. 35ᵇ, and 1441, fo. 161ᵇ.

MEADOWS, Sir Philip, his lady was dau. and h. of .... Lucy ; 20 Feb. 1662-3, by Walker. Her. Coll., fo. 49 ; Harl. MS. 1172, fo. 72ᵇ.

MEAUTIS, John, of Calais, 12 Aug. 1494, by Richmont aℓs Clar. Misc. Gen. et Her., 3rd S., vol. i., p. 65, copy of grant, Brit. Mus.

MEDLEY, Robert, of London, s. of John, of Newsted, Yorks, 25 June 1580, by Cooke. Harl. MS. 1359, fo. 122ᵇ.

MEEREST or MEEREHURST, Henry, serjant of ye Bakehouse to H. VIII., by T. Benolt, Clar. I. 9 ; H. 8 [Visit. Herefordsh. and Wales, 1530, Her. Coll.] ; Harl. MSS. 6179, fo. 20, and 1397, fo. 118ᵇ.

MEGGS, William, of London, 24 June 1579, by Cooke. Harl. MS. 1359, fo. 104ᵇ ; 4th of June in Add. MS. 14,295, fo. 16ᵇ ; Add. MS. 4966, fo. 86.

MELDRED, John, Alderm. of London 1425. *See* MELRETH.

MELLOR, John, of Came, Dorset, confirmed 24 June 1586 ; s. of John, by . . . . dau. of John Wolley ; by W. Dethick, Gart. 20ᵗʰ of June in Stowe MS. 676, fo. 65ᵇ ; Q's Coll. Oxf. MS. 37, fo. 92, copy of grant.

[MELRETH, William, Mercer, Alderm. of London 1430, Sheriff 1425-6, M.P. for London 1427, 1429, 1432 (*see* Beaven's Aldermen of the City of London). A slip is inserted on which Joseph Foster has written :
"Ar. 109, last page but 4.
John Meldred, Alder. of London 1425."

Arundel MS. 109 is a missal of the 15th century bequeathed by William Melreth, Alderman of London, to the Church of St. Laurence, Old Jewry, in January 1446. The last page but 4 in this MS. has nothing about arms on it ; it is part of the text of the missal and runs straight on. On fo. 263ᵇ, or two pages from the end, is an illumination of The Trinity, with a donor kneeling (? Melreth) and two coats of arms.

At the top of the slip Joseph Foster has written : "important & valuable. With additions from 'the Labored pedigrees,' by Mundy, Withie & others." The MS. here referred to I have been unable to trace.]

MELTON, John, of Tottenham High Cross, Middx., 31 Aug. 1626, by R. St. George, Gart. Add. MS. 14,295, fo. 65 ; J.P. and 1 Sept. in Guil. 363.

  ,,   William s. of William, late of city of Chester, ratified and confirmed 2 Jan. 1560-1, by Dalton. Harl. MS. 1359, fo. 48ᵇ.

MENNES, Mathew, of the Inner Temple, esquire, s. of Andrew, gent., s. of Matthew, of Kent, gent., a patent 10 July 1616, by Camden. Harl. MSS. 6095, fo. 34ᵇ, and 1422, fo. 40ᵇ ; Guil. 260 ; copy of grant Harl. MS. 1432, fo. 160.

MEORYE, ... crest . . . . Barker's Grants, Harl. MS. 5846, fo. 76ᵇ ; Stowe MS. 692, fo. 69ᵇ, slightly different crest, though probably intended for the same, as

  ,,   George, of North Hall, Essex, coat and crest . . . . Barker's Grants, Harl. MS. 5846, fo. 72ᵇ ; Stowe MS. 692, fo. 68ᵇ, as John.

MERCHANT ADVENTURERS OF LONDON, The Company of, grant of arms, crest and supporters 13 Nov. 1616, by Segar and Camden. Add. MS. 12,225, fo. 79. *See also* EAST INDIA.

MERCHANTS' (FELLOWSHIP OF), trading with Braband, Flanders, Holland and Selland (John Wyllshe, their master), by Roger Machado, Richmont Clar. (No date—betw. 1493 and 1516.) MS. Ashm. 858, fo. 27, 28, copy of grant. Bodleian Lib.

MERCHANTS TRADING TO FRANCE, To the Governor and Company of, French Merchants, grant of arms, crest and supporters, by Segar. Add. MS. 12,225, fo. 79ᵇ.

  ,,   TRADING TO CANARIES, 1 June, 17 Chas. II., 1665, by E. Walker, Gart. Add. MS. 5533, fo. 12.

MERCHANT TAYLORS, of the fraternity of S. John Baptist in London, arms and crest 23 Oct. 1480, by Thomas (Holme), Clar ; confirmed 22 Hen. VIII., 1530, by (Benolte), Clar. ; coat altered, new crest and supporters 23 Dec. 1586, by Cooke. Mercht. Taylors' Guild, by C. M. Clode, 1875 ; Add. MS. 14,295, fo. 21 ; Harl. MS. 1359, fo. 72ᵇ. In both MSS. 1556 an error for 1586.

MEREDITH, Edward ap, s. of Griffith, s. of Thomas, of Milenoth, co. Radnor . . . .

Z

1574, by Cooke. Harl. MSS. 1359, fo. 113[b], and 1422, fo. 95[b] ; Add. MS. 4966, fo. 61[b].

MEREDETH, Sir William, of Stanstye, co. Denbigh, Knt., paymaster of the King's Majesties forces in the Low Countries (lineally descended from Eouvdd, one of the principal and auntient Nobility of Wales), to the which William Meredith, his brethren and their posterity W. Camden, Clar., assigned, ratified and confirmed his crest, Quarterly (? 1607). Q's Coll. Oxf. MS. 146, fo. 43 ; Add. MS. 14,295, fo. 111 ; Harl. MSS. 1359, fo. 25, and 1422, fo. 114[b].

MERFYNLAND, ... crest . . . . Barker's Grants, Harl. MS. 5846, fo. 77[b] ; Stowe MS. 692, fo. 69[b].

MERRETT, Christopher, D[r] in physic and fellow Coll. of Phys., London, and

,, Francis, his brother, 13 July 1666. Byshe's Grants, Her. Coll., fo. 18 ; Harl. MSS. 1105, fo. 20, and 1470, fo. 112, copy of grant, Brit. Mus. ; Guil. 401.

MERRICK, ..., a gent. to the comp of Russia ; he mar. . . . ., dau. of Sir Francis Cherry ; az., a fess undée arg., in chief two mullets pierced or, impaling Cherry ; 24 Oct. 1601, by Segar. Harl. MS. 6140, fo. 36 ; Add. MS. 12,225, fo. 80.

MERICK, Andrew, of West Camell in Somerset, ... 1589, by Cooke. Harl. MSS. 1359, fo. 96, and 1441, fo. 132[b].

,, Gelly, of Hascard, co. Pembroke, gent., crest 1 Dec. 1583, by G. Dethick, Gart. Stowe MS. 677, fo. 9 ; Q's Coll. Oxf. MS. 38, fo. 107, copy of patent ; Grants I., 200 ; Stowe MS. 606, fo. 60[b]. copy of patent.

MERRICK, Jan, Ambassador from England to Russia 1614, ? certified ; perhaps not a grant. Caius Coll. Camb. MS. 528, fo. 5.

MERRIFIELD, Ralph, of Thornhill and Denisham, Dorset, s. of John, of the house of Merrifield, Somerset, coat confirmed and crest granted 10 Sept. 1616 or 1623 (14 Jac.), by Segar. Add. MS. 12,225, fo. 80 ; Guil. 124 ; Harl. MSS. 6179, fo. 32[b], and 6140, fo. 77.

MARFFYN (MERVIN), Thomas, of Dover Court, Kent, gent., crest. Barker's Grants, Harl. MS. 5846, fo. 73 ; Stowe MS. 692, fo. 68[b].

MERYWEATHER, Edward, of Barfreston, Kent ; Nov. 1607, by Camden. Harl. MS. 1422, fo. 20[b] ; of Eythorn [co. Kent] in Harl. MS. 6095, fo. 9[b].

MERREWETHER, John, of Sheperswould or Sibbertswold, Kent, s. of Richard, s. of Edward ; served in the expedition to Calais, and also in Flanders ; crest 26 July 1609, by Segar ? and Camden. Add. MS. 14,295, fo. 99 ; Harl. MS. 6140, fo. 25[b] bis.

METCALFE, Mathew, s. of Lucas, of Bedal [Bedale, co. York], 29 Sept. 1581, by Cooke. Surtees XLI., xli., copy of grant, Brit. Mus. ; Grants I., 16.

,, Thomas, gent., citizen and goldsmith of London, granted 25 March, 1 and 2 Philip and Mary, 1554-5, by Harvey. Q's Coll. Oxf. MS. 39, fo. 54, copy of grant ; Harl. MS. 1359, fo. 62 ; Grants II., 543 ; Merchant taylor in Harl. MS. 5887, fo. 58.

METHAM, Dorcas (SMITH), dau. of John, of High Holborn, Middx., and

,, Isaac, of One house, all in ye Co. of Suff., by Sir R. St. George, Clar. Harl. MS. 1441, fo. 153.

MEWSSE, Arthur (alias Mowss), 2nd s. of Richd., s. of Richd., of Wooburn, Bedf., quartering Scott, 13 Dec. 1623, by Segar. Add. MS. 12,225, fo. 80[b] ; Guil. 210.

MEYGER, see MAYOR.

MEYSEY, John, of Shakenhurst, co. Worc., 10 Nov., 25 H. VIII., 1518, (?) by Benolte. Harl. MS. 1422, fo. 16 ; Add. MS. 19,816, fo. 115 ; Harl. MSS. 5887, fo. 50, and 1116, fo. 39[b].

MICAULT, family of, of L'Isle de France, certificate at length by Pierre d'Hozier, Toloze Herald, 18 June 1621 [1634 ?]. Harl. MSS. 1441, fo. 8[b], and 1442, fo. 21.

MICAULT, Claude de, Certificate by Pierre d'Hozier, Toulouse Herald, 18 [?28] June 1634. Harl. MS. 1470, fo. 154 [? the same document].

MICHELL, Humphrey, of Old Windsor, Berks, out of Yorkshire ; confirmed 7 Apr. 1581, by Flower. MS. Ashm. 844, fo. 39, copy of grant, Bodleian Lib. ; Guil. 259.

MITCHELL, William, of Mortham, Yorks, ... by Bysshe. Stowe MS. 703, fo. 70.

MICKLETHWAYT, Elias, ... 6 Nov. 1626, by Borough. Surtees, xxxvi., p. 280, copy of grant, Brit. Mus., Harl. MS. 1105, fo. 1ᵇ.

MIDDLECOT, ..., of co. Linc., ... az., an eagle displayed erm., on a chief gu. three escallops or, by Segar. Add. MS. 12,225, fo. 81.

MIDDLETON, David, of Westerham, Kent, descended from Middleton of Belsay Castle, Northumberland ; confirmation of arms, quarterly of 4, and crest 17 Dec., 8 Jac , 1610, by Segar. Add. MS. 12,225, fo. 80ᵇ ; Guil. 382 ; Harl. MS. 1562, fo. 128ᵇ.

„ Hugh, of London, Goldsmith, created a baronet 22 Aug. 1622, and of Ruthin, co. Denbigh, made " a new ent or river of fresh water " ; 6th s. Richard, s. of David, receiver of North Wales, etc. ; grant of new coat and crest 1 Nov. 1622, by Camden. Q's Coll. Oxf. MS. 38, fo. 136, and Harl. MS. 1507, fo. 382, copy of grant ; Le Neve's MS. 382.

MIDELTON, William, of co. . . . ., gent., 23 Apr., 10 Eliz., 1568 (or 1560), by Sir G. Dethick, Gart. Harl. MS. 1441, fo. 88 ; Q's Coll. Oxf. MS. 145, fo. 45.

MIHILL, ... Norfolk, confirmed . . . . by R. Cooke, Clar. Harl. MS. 1422, fo. 82, sable, a fesse betw. three lozenges ermine, a crescent for diff. ; crest, a mailed arm embowed argt. holding a scimitar arg., handle or ; and Stowe MS. 706, fo. 20.

„ Robert, of Northampton, ... 1587, by Cooke, Clar. Harl. MS. 1442, fo. 82 ; Stowe MS. 706, fo. 20.

MYLBORNE [MILBOURNE], Sir John, Alderm. of London, coat and crest . . . . Barker's Grants 1526—49 ; Harl. MS. 5846, fo. 75 ; Stowe MS. 692, fo. 69 ; Harl. MS. 5887, fo. 92 ; Lord Mayor 1521, with crest, Hen. VII., in Add. MS. 26,702, fo. 39.

„ Richard, D.D., Bp. of (St. David's 1615 and of Carlisle 1621), confirmed June 1615, by W. Camden, Clar. Harl. MSS. 1422, fo. 40, and 6095, fo. 32ᵇ.

MILDEMAY, Thomas, of Mursey, Essex, gent., patent of arms and crest by Hawley, at London 15 May 1542, 34 H. VIII. Harl. MSS. 1359, fo. 5ᵇ, and 1507, fo. 433, copy of grant, Brit. Mus. ; and Q's Coll. Oxf. MSS. 38, fo. 42, and 39, fo. 3, copy of grant ; Add. MSS. 16,940, fo. 200, and 7098, fo. 76, 25ᵗʰ of May ; Le Neve's MS. 433.

MILDMAY, Sir Walter, of Chelmsford, Essex, Knt., coat and crest 38 Hy. VIII., 1546, changed in 1566. Stowe MS. 692, fo. 68 ; Barker's Grants, Harl. MS. 5846, fo. 71ᵇ ; Stowe MS. 692, fo. 65ᵇ.

„ Sir Walter, Knt., of Essex, after Chancellor of the Exchequer ; grant or gift 20 May 1552, 6 Ed. VI., by Sir Gilb. Dethick, Gart. Original grant, Cott. MS. Faustina E. 1, 15 ; Q's Coll. Oxf. MS. 39, fo. 43 (and also 100 for another coat), copy of grants ; Harl. MS. 1359, fo. 29ᵇ ; Guil. 147, restitution of the ancient arms 20 Aug. 1583, by Cooke, declaring Sir W. Mildmay's descent from the time of K. Stephen ; Misc. Gen. et Her., ii., 261 ; Harl. MS. 245, fo. 142, 145 ; MS. Ashm. 858, fo. 234-6, copy of grant, Bodleian Lib.

MILDEMAY, Sir Walter, Knt., of Apethorne, Northants, descended of Thos. Mildmay of Chelmsford, Essex, arms confirmed and crest granted 10 Nov., 1 Q. Eliz., 1559, by Sir Gilb. Dethick, Gart. Q's Coll. Oxf. MS. 39, fo. 100 ; Harl. MS. 1359, fo, 78.

MYLEHAM, Gregory, of Barningham, Norfolk, certificate 4 Feb. 1614-15, by Segar. Add. MS. 12,225, fo. 83ᵇ.

MILESON, Edward, of Bury St. Edmunds, Suff., (arms) crest 1612, by R. St. George, Norr.   Add. MS. 14,295, fo. 81 ; C. 15 [Visit. of Suff., 1612], col. 2, fo. 250 ; Harl. MSS. 1085, fo. 25, 6179, fo. 12, and 6140, fo. 69.

MILITARY COMPANY, the arms of the, and others exercising military discipline of arms in the artillery Garden of London, by Segar and Camden (fo. 10) ; confirmed March 1639, by Borough (fo. 10ᵇ).   Add. MS. 26,758, fo. 10 and 10ᵇ, trick.

MILL, Edmond (of Pulbergh, Sussex, 1359), 12 Aug., 29 H. VI., 1450. by John Smert, Gart.   Cott. MS. Faustina E. 1, 12, copy of grant in French ; Q's Coll. Oxf. MS. 146, fo. 462 ; Harl. MS. 1359, fo. 17 ; Add. MS. 14,295, fo. 19ᵇ ; Harl. MS. 1116, fo. 48ᵇ.

„   Hugh, of Putford, Devon, clerk, 17 July 1661, by Sir E. Walker, Gart.   Her. Coll., fo. 41.

„   John, of Southampton (? Banneret), s. of Richd., s. of Thomas, who was full cozen to Edmond Mill of Pulbergh, Sussex ; augmentation, three hinds' heads erased ppr., and the crest guttée d'eau, confirmed by Benolt, 25 H. VIII., 1533-4.   Add. MS. 14,295, fo. 19ᵇ ; Harl. MS. 1359, fo. 17 ; Q's Coll. Oxf. MS. 146, fo. 462 ; Harl. MSS. 5887, fo. 51, and 1116, fo. 48ᵇ.

„   John, B.D., fellow of Queen's Coll., Oxf., and Preb. of Exeter ; 1 July 1678, by W. Dugdale, Gart., and H. St. George, Norr.   Stowe MS. 714, fo. 167, copy of grant, and Grants III., fo. 90.   Sable, a millstone or with a fer de moulin thereon (in fesse) of the first, and on a chief arg. three eaglets displayed gu.   Crest : A dexter arm habited with a bachelor of divinity's sleeve sa., the hand ppr. holding an open book arg., covered gules.   Harl. MS. 6179, fo. 46.

„   John, Chaplain in Ordinary, a new coat 3 July 1684, by Sir Wᵐ Dugdale, Gart. and Clar.   Harl. MS. 6834, fo. 178 ; Grants III., fo. 243 (and Burke) ; alteration and addition, Lansd. MS. 867, fo. 52.

MILLER, ..., 4 coats [Millor . . . ., Millor of co. Linc. or London, Miller of Came, co. Dorset, Richard Myller of Plumpton in Cumberland].   Stowe MS. 703, fo. 88.

„   Sir John, of Islington, Middx., Knt., s. of Henry, of Barnstaple, Devon, by Segar.   Add. MS. 12,225, fo. 81ᵇ ; C. 28, fo. 36 [Visit. Middx., 1634], 2ᵈ Index, Her. Coll. ; Guil. 375.

„   Major John, born at Ballienston, co. Armagh (s. of Robert, of Huntingdon), a captain in the "Colestreamers" under Monke, Adjutant-Genl., etc. ; 27 May 1672, by Sir E. Bysshe, Gart.   Add. MS. 14,293, fo. 67 ; Harl. MS. 1172, fo. 65ᵇ ; (Guil. 69) ; copy of grant, Harl. MS. 6179, fo. 123.

MYLLER, Rychard, of Plompton in Cumberland, ... by Cooke.   Harl. MSS. 1359, fo. 97, and 1422, fo. 85 ; Add. MS. 4966, fo. 87.

MILLER, Thomas, Mayor of Chichester and J.P. ; 16 Feb. 168½, by Sir W. Dugdale and Clar.   Harl. MS. 6834, fo. 178 ; Grants III., fo. 255 ; Lansd. MS. 867, fo. 52.

MILLETT, John, of Hayes Court, Middx., Esq., s. of Richard, s. of John, of the same ; a patent . . . . Dec. 1616, by Camden.   Harl. MSS. 6095, fo. 35, and 1422, fo. 40ᵇ.

MILLS, Francis, servant to Sir Francis Walsingham, Knt., by Cooke . . . . Harl. MSS. 1359, fo. 94ᵇ, and 1422, fo. 89.

„   John, of Cashiobery in Thundridge by Warr (Ware), Herts, and his brother

„   Thomas ; a patent Nov. 1613, by Camden. Mills impaling Longford.   Harl. MSS. 6095, fo. 28, and 1422, fo. 38ᵇ.

MILLES, Richard, of Knightington, Berks, ... 1588, by Cooke.   Harl. MS. 1359, fo. 115ᵇ ; (by Rouge Crosse, Harl. MS. 1441, fo. 136) ; Harl. MS. 5887, fo. 24 ; Add. MS. 4966, fo. 84ᵇ ; Harl. MS. 6179, fo. 19.

MILLS, Richard, of London, Esq., 18 Feb. 1662.   Bysshe's Grants, fo. 12, Her. Coll. ; Harl. MS. 1105, fo. 19.

MILLES, Thomas, of Norton Court, near Faversham, esquire for the body of
K. James the first, and chief Customer of Kent ; given 12 Oct. 1586, by
Cooke. Harl. MSS. 1359, fo. 114ᵇ, and 1422, fo. 89, and of Anne, his
wife, dau. of John Polley als Polhill, gent., of Otford in Kent, ... Jan.
1609, by Camden. Milles impaling Polley, quartering Buckland and
Sandbach, Harl. MS. 6095, fo. 10ᵇ ; (Add. MS. 4966, fo. 100).

MILLS, William, of London, descended from Mills of Cornwall : az., a mill clock in
fess or, 3 April 1628, by Segar. Add. MS. 12,225, fo. 81 ; Harl. MS.
1092, fo. 113, as Mill.

MILNER, ..., Cornwall and Yorks : erm., three wolves' heads ppr. couped gu.
. . . . patent, by Camden. Harl. MS. 6095, fo. 24ᵇ.

MILTON, John [Captain ?], of London (mayor added), [testified] by W. Ryley,
Lancaster Herald. Stowe MS. 703, fo. 64.

MILWARD, John, D.D., Attendant Chaplain of divinity to the Queen's most
excellent Majesty ; 10 May (42 Eliz.) 1600, by W. Dethick, Gart.
Grants I., 344—7.

MINERALL AND BATTREY WORKES AND CORPORATION (or MINERS), arms, crest and
supporters 20 Feb. 1569-70, by Sir G. Dethick, Cooke and Flower. Q's
Coll. Oxf. MS. 145, fo. 24ᵇ ; Harl. MS. 1441, fo. 72 ; and MS. Ashm. 844,
fo. 19, 20, 27, copy of grant, Bodleian Lib.

MINES, ROYALL, Corporation of : arms, crest and supporters 28 May 1568, by Sir G.
Dethick, Cooke and Flower. Harl. MS. 1441, fo. 72ᵇ ; Q's Coll. Oxf. MS.
145, fo. 17.

MINGAY, John, of Armingall, Norfolk, ... 1590, by Cooke. Harl. MS. 1422,
fo. 23ᵇ.

MINSHULL, Sir Richard, alteration in, or a new crest. Hy., Lᵈ Mowbray and
Matravers, Dep. E. Marshal's Warrᵗ, 4 July 1642, to Sir William le Neve,
[Clarencieux] King of Arms. Harl. MS. 2119, fo. 220, copy of grant, and
Berry's Armory ; Le Neve's MS. 473.

MINTERNE, John, of Newland in Batcombe, Dorset, ... 1581, by Cooke, Clar.
Harl. MS. 1166, fo. 50.

MITCHELL, William, of Mortham, co. York, ... by Bysshe. Stowe MS. 703,
fo. 70.

MITTON, see MYTTON.

MOIGNE, Sir William, Knt., grant 2 Nov. 1391, 15 R. II., by Thoˢ Grendale of
Fenton. Topographer, ii., 192 ; Guil., Introd., p. 8 ; Camden's Remains,
218, 1st edn.

MOLE, John, of Molton, Devon, ... 1592 (Berry), by Cooke. Harl. MSS. 1422,
fo. 15ᵇ, and 1359, fo. 96ᵇ.

MOLESWORTH, ... a stockingseller in London, who hath stood on the Pillory and
byn condemned in the Star Chamber ; by Wᵐ Dethick, Gart. ; entered by
R. Brooke, York Herald. Harl. MS. 1453, fo. 32ᵇ. [Small trick of Arms :
Vair, an inescutcheon Azure, all within a bordure Gules, charged with eight
crosses crosslet Argent.]

„ John, of Helpeston, Northampt., gent., descended out of Cornwall : an
escocheon on vellum, by Camden. Stowe MS. 706, fo. 68.

MOLIN, Nicholas de, Ambassador from Venice, Knighted, augmentation by Royal
Warrant 24 Jan., 3 Jac., 1605-6. Q's Coll. Oxf. MS. 38, fo. 118 ; Harl.
MS. 1507, fo. 397 ; Stowe MS. 840, fo. 58, copy of warrant ; for trick see
Le Neve's MS. 397 ; MS. Rawl., B. 102, fo. 11, Bodleian Lib.

MOLINS, James, in Shoe Lane, London, chirurgeon, and his wife Florie, 23 Aug.
1614, by Segar. Add. MS. 12,225, fo. 82 ; Guil. 322 ; Harl. MS. 6140,
fo. 79.

MOLLITOR, Joachim, senator of Hamburg, augmentation by letters patent 1 Oct.
1538. MS. Ashm. 858, fo. 8, 9, copy of grant, Bodleian Lib.

MOLLYNER or MULLYNER, Laurence, of Bramford, Suff., 21 May 1664, by Sir E.
Bysshe, Clar. Harl. MS. 1105, fo. 39ᵇ ; Bysshe's Grants, 31.

MONINGS, Edward, of Waldershare, Kent, confirmed 20 Nov. 1570, by Cooke. Guil. 93.

MONINGTON, *see* MANINGTON.

MONKE. John, of Hurston, 5th s. of Richd., of Ashington, Sussex ; 10 Nov. 1615, by Segar. Misc. Gen. et Her., 2nd S., vol. i., p. 84, facsimile copy of grant, Brit. Mus.

MONMOUTH, Humphrey, of London, Alderm. . . . . coat and crest. Barker's Grants, Harl. MS. 5846, fo. 73 ; Stowe MS. 692, fo. 68ᵇ.

MONOUX, ..., crest . . . . Barker's Grants, Harl. MS. 5846, fo. 77 ; Stowe MS. 692, fo. 69ᵇ.

MONOX, George, Mayor of London, gent., patent 4 Oct. 1514, by T. Wriothesley, Gart., and Benolte. Guil. 362 ; Grants II., 555, as recited in exemplification to nephew George, next mentioned.

„ George, of Walthamstow, Essex, nephew and heir to George ; 1514, exemplified 10 June 1561, by Hervey. Guil. 362 ; Grants II., 555 ; Harl. MS. 1531, fo. 148.

MONNOX, Henry, of Hemmingford Grey, Hunts, Esq., arms and crest granted 10 May 1557, 3 and 4 Philip and Mary, by G. Dethick, Gart. Q's Coll. Oxf. MS. 39, fo. 72, copy of grant ; Harl. MS. 1359, fo. 69ᵇ ; Grants I., 206.

MONTE-ACUTO, William de, Earl of Salisbury, by letters patent from E. III., 16 Sept., 13 Edw. III., 1339. Lansd. MS. 872, fo. 14, copy of Roy. Warrant, Brit. Mus. ?

MOONE, *see* NONNE.

MOUNTGOMERY, George, Dean of Norwich, Bp. of Derry in Ireland ; confirmed . . . . 1605, by Camden. Harl. MSS. 6095, fo. 20, and 5887, fo. 19ᵇ.

MORE and MOORE, for 34 coats *see* Stowe MS. 703, fo. 79—82.

MORE, ... of Oxford, crest, a demi-lyon rampant or charged with a fesse lozengy of iiij per pale gu. and sa., langued gn., a crescent sa. for diff. . . . . by Sir G. Dethick, Gart. Add. MS. 26,753, fo. 123 ; Guil. 225.

MORE, Alexander, of Grantham, co. Linc. . . . . Feb. 1635, by Borough. Harl. MSS. 1105, fo. 56ᵇ, and 1441, fo. 58 ; Add. MS. 26,702, fo. 92 ; Guil. 102.

„ Edward, of Crabet, Sussex, s. of John More of the same, out of Salop, grant *temp.* Q. Eliz., by Sir G. Dethick, Gart. Q's Coll. Oxf. MS. 36, fo. 113, for incomplete copy of grant, Stowe MS. 676, fo. 34ᵇ.

MOORE, Edward, of Alvechurch, co. Worcʳ, and to William Moore, merchᵗ ; 12 May 1666, by Sir E. Walker, Gart. Her. Coll., fo. 62.

„ John, of Kirkedale, co. Lanc., gent., crest 10 Nov., 3 Eliz., 1561, by Dalton. Harl. MS. 1359, fo. 51.

MORE, John, a Cheshire man, a noble in Spain (Bilbao), s. of Stephen (by a dau. of John Ridley, esq.), s. of Roger by a dau. of Pigott of Salop ; Certified 24 Jan. 1581-2, by Flower and his deputy R. Glover, Somerset Her. MS. Ashm. 834, fo. 50, 51, 52, copy of grant, Bodleian Lib., in Latin ; Q's Coll. Oxf. MS. 38, fo. 104, copy of grant in Latin, and MS. 146, fo. 136 ; Le Neve's MS. 372.

MOORE, John, of Ipswich, Suff., ... 1586, by Cooke. Harl. MSS. 1422, fo. 13, and 1359, fo. 89ᵇ ; Add. MS. 4966, fo. 35ᵇ.

MORE, John, Sec. to Q. Anne Boleine, wife to Hen. VIII., and

„ Edmond, of Shoreditch, sons of Thomas, s. and h. Robert, of co. Linc., gent. ; 14 July 1593, by Cooke. Misc. Gen. et Her., i., 309 ; Her. and Geneal., i., 83 ; Add. MS. 14,293, fo. 20ᵇ ; Harl. MS. 1137, fo. 125, quartering Gent ; Grants II., 488.

MOORE, John, the elder, of New Sarum, gent., ? coat and crest 1597, by R. Lee, Clar. Q's Coll. Oxf. MS. 146, fo. 32 ; Add. MS. 14,295, fo. 122ᵇ ; Harl. MS. 1359, fo. 40.

MORE or MOORE, John, of London, Dʳ in Physic, new arms and crest 22 Jan. 1626-7, by Sir R. St. George, Clar. Harl. MSS. 1422, fo. 13, and 1092,

fo. 183 ; alteration Add. MS. 5524, fo. 207ᵇ ; MS. Ashm. 858, fo. 159,
copy of grant, Bodleian Lib. ; Q's Coll. Oxf. MS. 36, fo. 126, *see*, and MS.
146, fo. 45 : five coats, perhaps belonging to two Doctors of the name ;
alteration 2 May 1627, by R. St. George, Clar. Harl. MS. 1422, fo. 13,
No. 4, altered from argent, three morecocks ppr., and crest, a morecock
ppr. to argent, a cross pattée, in chief two escallops of the 2ⁿᵈ ; Crest,
a more's head ppr., thereon a chapeau gu. turned up ermine and in his ear
a pearl. Add. MS. 5524, fo. 207ᵇ, copy of grant.

Moor or More, Sir John, Knt., Alderm. and late Lord Mayor of London, s. of
Charles, 25 Aug. 1683, and to descendants of his father, by Sir W. Dugdale,
Gart., and Sir H. St. George, Clar. 28 Sept. in Stowe MS. 714, fo. 102ᵇ ;
Harl. Soc., VIII., 278 ; Grants III., 231 ; copy of grant, Brit. Mus.

More, Nicholas, of the Inner Temple, s. and h. of John, s. of Edward, s. of Gawyn,
s. of Richd., late of Binfield, Bedf., by Elizabeth Brocas ; crest 28 April
1569, by Sir G. Dethick, Cooke and Flower (two crests in Berry). Harl.
MS. 1441, fo. 75ᵇ ; MS. Ashm. 834, fo. 27 ; Q's Coll. Oxf. MS. 38, fo. 84,
and 39, fo. 152, for copy of grant (MS. 145, fo. 22ᵇ) ; Guil. 225 ; Grants I.,
236.

Moore, Thomas, of Larden, Salop, s. of Edmund, 27 Nov. 1561, by Harvey.
Harl. MSS. 1422, fo. 13, and 1430, fo. 78ᵇ ; Add. MS. 16,940, fo, 23ᵇ,
confirmed (?) by Lee, Porteullis, Marshal to Clar., 1584 ; Harl. MS. 5887,
fo. 57ᵇ.

  „ Thomas, of Newington, Middx., gent., 14 May 1576, by Cooke. Harl. MSS.
1422, fo. 13, and 1359, fo. 27 (1172, fo. 3ᵇ) ; Add. MS. 4966, fo. 94ᵇ,
copy of grant, Harl. MS. 1172, fo. 3ᵇ.

Moore, Thomas, of Angram Grange, Yorks, bar.-at-law, Inner Temple, and
  „ William, his brother ; 26 May 1670, by W. Dugdale, Norr. (Her. Coll.)
  „ Thomas, of Wigenhall, Norfolk, 11 June 1654, by Sir Edw. Bysshe, Gart.
Harl. MS. 6179, fo. 61 ; Proc. Soc. Antiq., 1897, p. 355 ; N. and Q.,
2nd S., vol. ii., 171.

  „ William, lord prior of Worcester (1518—36). Add. MS. 26,702, fo. 58ᵇ.

Moor, William, Mayor of Colchester ; 1664, 14 Chas. II., by Sir E. Bysshe, Clar.
.... Harl. MS. 1105, fo. 39 ; Bysshe's Grants, 28.

Morar, Robert, of London (s. of Robert, to whom these arms were confirmed),
attestation Morar impaling West, by Segar .... Add. MS. 12,225,
fo. 82ᵇ.

Mordaunt, John, of Turvey, Bedf., Crest 29 Feb. 1512-13, by T. Wriothesley
and Benolte. Le Neve's MS. 507.

  „ Dame Elizabeth, wife to Sir Charles, of Little Massingham, Norfolk, Bart.,
and Mʳˢ Jane, daus. and coheirs of Nicholas Johnson of London, draper ;
14 Jan. 1664-5. Bysshe's Grants, fo. 26, Her. Coll. ; Harl. MS. 1105,
fo. 22.

Morden, *see also* Murden and Norden.

Morden, John, of Esthall, Kent, given .... 3 Q. Mary ; altered 1586, by Cooke.
Harl. MS. 1359, fo. 90.

Morewood, John, of Alpeton, co. Derby, late high sheriff (s. of Rowland, late of
Oakes, par. of Bradfield, Yorks, decᵈ, s. of John), 28 June 1678, with
remainder to the posterity of his uncles Andrew, Joseph and Francis, by
W. Dugdale, Gart., and H. St. George, Norr. Stowe MS. 714, fo. 165 ;
Harl. MS. 6140, fo. 96, copy of grant, Brit. Mus. ; Guil. 113 ; Grants III.,
87 ; altered to vert, an oak tree arg., fructed or, Harl. MS. 6179, fo. 43ᵇ.

Morgan, Francis, a Judge of King's Bench, confirmed 1 May 1558, by Harvey.
Her. and Geneal., i., 81 ; Add. MS. 16,940, fo. 57ᵇ, of Heyford, Northts.
(quite a diff. coat and crest to Harl. MS. 1422, fo. 45ᵇ) ; ? Harl. MS. 5887,
fo. 25.

  „ Henry, Bp. of Bangor, arms 5 Dec. 1553, by ? Hawley. Add. MS. 16,940,
fo. 201.

MORGAN, Henry, Bp. of St. David's, arms 2 April 1554, by ? Hawley. Add. MS. 16,940, fo. 206^b.

   ,,   Hugh, Apothecary to the Queen, and now of London, and of her most honorable household, s. of John, of Bardfield, Essex, etc.; grant 2 March 1587-8, by W. Dethick, Gart. Stowe MS. 676, fo. 72^b; Q's Coll. Oxf. MS. 37, fo. 104, copy of grant. He died s.p. 1612, aged 103, Guil. 212. After confirmed to Robert Morgan, 1613, by Camden, Harl. MS. 3526, fo. 98^b.

   ,,   John, of Chester (4 Dec. 1608, by Sir R. St. George, in Stowe MS. 716, fo. 55), but the certificate had neither date nor King's name: arg., on a bend engrailed sa. three cinquefoils ermine, on a chief az. a cross patonce betw. two fleurs-de-lis or, a martlett for diff.; crest, a dragon's head crased gu., about his neck two collars dancettée or. Add. MS. 14,295, fo. 54^b; 4 Dec., Harl. MS. 6140, fo. 37^b; Le Neve's MS. 412.

   ,,   Lewis, of Gray's Inn, Edward Somerset, Marquis of Worc.; granted to him the liberty of bringing the portecullis (his crest) under the coronet of a marquis in an escocheon, 3 July 1656. Harl. MS. 1470, fo. 72.

   ,,   Robert, of Little Hallingbury, Essex, confirmed . . . . 1613, (Visⁿ) by Camden. (See Hugh MORGAN.) Guil. 212; Harl. MS. 3526, fo. 98^b.

   ,,   Thomas, of Eston, Somerset, ... 1591, by Cooke. Harl. MS. 1422, fo. 23^b.

   ,,   William, D.D., Bishop of Llandaff (1594—1601), by W. Dethick, Gart. Q's Coll. Oxf. MS. 36, fo. 110, copy of incomplete grant.

   ,,   William, of Blackmore, co. Hereford, ratified and confirmed 27 May 1602, by Camden: arg., a lion ramp. sa., ducally crowned or. Guil. 177; Stowe MS. 670, fo. 59^b.

MORLAND, Samuel, gent., 14 Feb. 1656-7, by E. Bysshe, Gart. Add. MS. 14,293, fo. 9; 24th Feb. in Harl. MS. 1105, fo. 15^b.

   ,,   Sir Samuel, Knt. and Bart., augmentation 16 Aug. 1661, by Walker (as Sir S. Morland, Knt. and Bart., gent. in ordinary of the privy Chamber to K. C. II.). Harl. MS. 1105, fo. 13; Her. Coll., fo. 41.

MORLEY, ... of Glynde, Sussex, ... by Cooke. Harl. MS. 1422, fo. 15^b.

   ,, ... of Yorks, ... by Segar. Add. MS. 12,225, fo. 82; ? see Harl. MS. 6140, fo. 51^b, Quarterly of 6.

   ,,   Isabella, dau. of Christopher, of co. Durham, wife of Hy. Anderson of Newcastle-upon-Tyne; confirmed 10 Feb. 1574-5, 17 Eliz., by Sir Gilb. Dethick. Misc. Gen. et Her., 2nd S., vol. iv., p. 161; and Q's Coll. Oxf. MS. 145, fo. 36^b; Harl. MS. 1441, fo. 82, 10 Feb. 1573-4.

   ,,   John, of Barnes, Hants, ... 1575, by Cooke. Harl. MSS. 1544, fo. 93, and 6140, fo. 53^b.

   ,,   John, of Estington, ... (? 1575), by Cooke. Harl. MS. 1359, fo. 98; of East Havant, Sussex, in Harl. MS. 1422, fo. 117, and Add. MS. 14,295, fo. 30^b; see Sir Edward Morley impaling Devenish, Harl. MS. 5887, fo. 101; Add. MS. 4966, fo. 63^b.

   ,,   Robert (DE MORLE), 6 Jan. 1349. Camden's Remains, 222.

   ,,   Robert, of Erdington, co. Warw., coat confirmed and crest granted 20 Nov. 1560, by Hervey. Harl. MS. 1116, fo. 54; (Add. MS. 16,940, fo. 58), copy of grant, Brit. Mus.

MORPETH TOWN, co. Northumb., 20 May 1552, [a parcell of] the arms of Sir Roger De Marlay, the founder thereof being assigned by Hervey, Norr. Her. and Geneal., i., 119, and Misc. Gen. et Her., ii., 216; Add. MS. 16,940, fo. 8; Cat. Her. Exhib. Soc. Antiq., 63.

MORRANT, Edward, of the Exchequer, crest . . . . 1575, by Cooke. Harl. MSS. 1359, fo. 119^b, and 1422, fo. 95^b, as Morant.

MORRYCE, Sir Christopher, Knt., master of the ordnance, coat and crest . . . . Barker's Grants, Harl. MS. 5846, fo. 74^b; Stowe MS. 692, fo. 69; Harl. MS. 5887, fo. 9.

   ,,   Francis (MORRILL), esquire of the Ordnance, Jas. I., by R. St. George, Clar. Bannerman's MS., No. 9, 451.

MORRYS, Rees, of London, gent., patent granted 30 Dec. 1587. 30 Q. Eliz. (by Cooke). Harl. MS. 1359, fo. 86 ; 20th Dec. in Harl. MS. 1422, fo. 62 ; Roger in Add. MS. 4966, fo. 91.

MORRISE, Thomas, of Coxwell, Berks, gent., confirmed 8 Aug. 1562, by Sir G. Dethick. Harl. MS. 1441, fo. 66, and Q's Coll. Oxf. MS. 145, fo. 9 ; Grants I., 170, II., 652.

MORRIS, Thomas, of Wansted, Essex, Clerk of the Ordnance, confirmed or granted . . . . by R. St. George, Clar. Guil. 365.

MORISON, (? Sir) Charles, of Caysho, Herts, Esq., s. of Sir Richard, dec⁴ ; 20 May 1586, by Cooke. Harl. MS. 1052, fo. 19ᵇ, copy of grant, Brit. Mus. ; Harl. MSS. 1422, fo. 62, and 1359, fo. 107ᵇ ; MS. Ashm. 834, fo. 68, 69, copy of grant, Bodleian Lib., 21 May 1587 ; Guil. 351 ; Add. MS. 4966, fo. 30 ; Harl. MS. 6140, fo. 52.

MORYSONE, Richard, of London, grant, coat and crest . . . . Barker's Grants, Harl. MS. 5846, fo. 78 ; Stowe MS. 692, fo. 69ᵇ, written Morysond.

MORRYSON, Thomas, of the pipe office . . . . by Cooke. Harl. MSS. 1359, fo. 119ᵇ, and 1422, fo. 62 ; Add. MS. 4966, fo. 97.

MORRILL, Francis, esquire of the ordnance to K. James, by R. Sᵗ George, Clar. Bannerman's MS., No. 9, fo. 451. [See also MORRYSE.]

MORTAGH, William, of . . . . co. Down, " for his particular services and loyalty to Hy. IV." : gu., a chevron arg. between three men's heads ppr. ; crest, a demi-sea-horse arg., crined, finned and tayled or ; by Ulster. Harl. MS. 1172, fo. 53ᵇ.

MORTIMER, John, of Cheshunt, Hunts, s. of Mark, of London, merchᵗ, dec⁴ ; 14 June 1688, by St. George, Gart. and Clar. Stowe MS. 714, fo. 124 ; Harl. MS. 6834, fo. 49 ; Grants IV., 8 ; Guil. 132 ; Harl. MS. 6179, fo. 71.

MORTOFTE, Valentine, s. of William, s. of John, of Itringham, Norfolk, exemplified and confirmed . . . . Feb. 1606-7, by Camden. Harl. MSS. 1422, fo. 20, and 6095, fo. 7ᵇ ; Guil. 225 ; Add. MS. 4966, fo. 33.

MORTON, Thomas, of Lechlade, co. Glouc., 15 May 1515, by Wriothesley. Harl. MS. 1561, fo. 113 ; (Berry's Armory) Harl. MS. 1433, fo. 60.

MOSDELL, Stephen, of Southwark, Surrey, esq., s. of Thomas, of Kings Cleere, Hants, s. of Thomas, borne in Germany ; 13 May 1665. Bysshe's Grants, fo. 24, Her. Coll. ; Harl. MS. 1105, fo. 21ᵇ.

MOSE, ... of Petworth, Sussex, 24 Feb. 1670-1, ? by Sir E. Bysshe, Clar. : erminois, a cross pattée arg. Harl. MS. 1105, fo. 42.

MOSELEY, Maurice, of London, mercht., confirmation crest, by Segar. Add. MS. 12,225, fo. 82ᵇ ; Harl. MSS. 5887, fo. 113, and 6140, fo. 81.

MOSLEY, Nicholas, of London, Alderm., s. of Edward, of Hough, co. Lanc., gent., etc., coat confirmed and crest granted 17 Feb. 1592-3, by Cooke. Misc. Gen. et Her., N. S., iii., 98 ; Family Memoirs, by Sir O. Mosley ; Harl. MS. 1470, fo. 22, copy of grant, Brit. Mus. ; Harl. MSS. 1359, fo. 104, and 1422, fo. 120 ; Grants II., 489 ; Add. MS. 4966, fo. 85ᵇ.

MOSSETT, William, of Chipping Barnet, Herts, M.A., and to his brothers and all descendants of Thomas Mossett of Whitby, Yorks; confirmed 10 May 1585, by Flower. MS. Ashm. 844, fo. 60, copy of grant, Bodleian Lib. ; Guil. 248.

MOTT, Mark, of Braintree, Essex, s. of Thos., of Bocking, Essex, crest 10 Nov. 1615, by Segar. Eastern Counties Collectanea, i., 16 ; C. 21 [Visit. Essex, 1634], Her. Coll., and Guil. 93 ; Add. MSS. 12,225, fo. 83, and 12,474, fo. 116ᵇ.

MOULSON, { John, of Hargrave, Stubs, Chesh., and
„ { Thomas, his brother, of London, being truly descended from the coheirs of Rosengrave, Oreby and Hargrave; exemplified . . . . by Camden. Grants II., fo. 590 ; Harl. MSS. 1422, fo. 112, and 6095, fo. 40.

MOULT, Francis, of Tollerton, Notts, 10 Feb. 1586-7, by Sir T. St. George,

Gart. and Norr. Harl. MS. 6834, fo. 178 ; Grants III., fo. 305 ; Lansd. MS. 867, fo. 52 ; Harl. MS. 1085, fo. 58.

MOULTON, William, and } of Yorkshire and of London .... 1571, by Cooke. Harl.
,, Robert, } MS. 1359, fo. 102.

MOUNTAGU, George, D.D. and Dean of Westminster, a patent .... June 1613, by Camden. Harl. MS. 6095, fo. 27ᵇ.

MOUNTFORDE, Thomas, S.T.D., of the same name and family of Hackforth, Yorks, confirmed 18 Feb. 1602-3, by Camden. Stowe MS. 676, fo. 137ᵇ ; Harl. MSS. 6095, fo. 18ᵇ, and 1422, fo. 2ᵇ ; Q's Coll. Oxf. MSS. 36, fo. 94, 38, fo. 117, and 146, fo. 20 ; Harl. MSS. 1470, fo. 189ᵇ, and 1507, fo. 100, copies of grant, Brit. Mus., in Latin, and in Harl. MS. 1172, fo. 7ᵇ.

MOWAT, Sir Roger, of Inglestoane, Kt., Bart. ; 26 March 1674. Scots Grants, Le Neve's MS. 485.

MOWBRAY, Thomas de, Earl Marshal, and of Nottingham, letters patent or writ of privy seal at Westminster for crest 12 Jan. 1393-4. Stowe MS. 840, fo. 54, 55 ; P. R., 17 Ric. II., pt. i., m. 2 ; " to bear the crest of the King's eldest son with a diff." in Lansd. MS. 872, fo. 17 ; Gent. Mag., ii., 398.

MOWDY, Edmund, of St. Edmundsbury, Suff., grant 6 Oct. 1540, by T. Hawley, Clar. Add. MSS. 7098, fo. 76 (fo. 21), and 16,940, fo. 200 ; Harl. MS. 1422, fo. 17.

MOWSE, als MEWESS, Arthur, 2nd s. of Richard, s. of Richard, of Woodburne, co. Bedf., assigned 13 Dec. 1623, by W. Segar, by Patent. Guil. 210.

,, See TYDUR.

MOYLE, Robert, of the prothonotary office (and Inner Temple), by Borough. Harl. MS. 1105, fo. 55 ; Add. MS. 26,702, fo. 89.

MOYLYN, ... crest .... Barker's Grants, Harl. MS. 5846, fo. 77ᵇ ; Stowe MS. 692, fo. 69ᵇ.

MOYSER, James, of Firlington, Yorks } sons of Adam, of the same place, patent
,, Thomas, his brother, } 31 Dec. 1566, by Dalton. Harl. MS. 1359, fo. 45.

MUCKELOWE, ... crest .... Barker's Grants, Harl. MS. 5846, fo. 76 ; Stowe MS. 692, fo. 69ᵇ.

MULSHOE, Robert, of Gothurst, Bucks, or of Thingdon, Northants, 10 Dec. or Nov. 1587, by W. Dethick, Gart. : erm., on a bend sa. three goats' heads erased arg. Harl. MS. 1359, fo. 21 ; Le Neve's MS. 368. See Joane VINCENT.

MUN, John, of Hackney, Middx., etc., confirmed 2° Aug. 1562, by Harvey. Add. MS. 16,940, fo. 15 ; Harl. MS. 1476, fo. 34 ; see 6140, fo. 62.

MUNDAY, ... Ld. Mayor of London (Sir John, 1522), Hen. VII. Add. MS. 26,702, fo. 37ᵇ.

MUNDEN, Dame Susanna, relict of Sir Richard, Knt., who died in H.M.'s service at sea, etc., 9 Oct. 1680, unto the children and to her husband's brother Sir John, Rear Adml of the King's fleet, by H. St. George, Clar. Stowe MS. 714, fo. 168 ; Grants III., 111.

MUNDYE, ... crest .... Barker's Grants, Harl. MS. 5846, fo. 75ᵇ ; Stowe MS. 692, fo. 69ᵇ, as Monday ; see Harl. MS. 1045, fo. 111ᵇ, for Stephen Mundy of the Inner Temple.

MURDEN, Richard, of Morton Morrell, co. Warwick, exemplified, ratified and confirmed Dec. 1618, by Camden (arms of Morden als Murden of Branston, Northants). Harl. MS. 6095, fo. 3ᵇ ; Guil. 195.

MURGATROD, Michael (Sec. to Archbp. Whitgift), s. of William and wife Frances, d. of Edward Hippon, of Fetherston, Yorks, and of Cambridge University, grant 2 Jan. 1598-9, by W. Dethick, Gart., and Camden. Q's Coll. Oxf. MS. 36, fo. 72 and 84, copy of grant in Latin ; Stowe MS. 676, fo. 125ᵇ and 132.

MURIEL, ... crest .... Barker's Grants. Harl. MS. 5846, fo. 76ᵇ ; crest in Stowe MS. 692, fo. 69ᵇ.

MURYELL, Edward, of London, [arms] with crest, Hen. VII. Add. MS. 26,702, fo. 52.

MURPHY, Col. John, 16 May 1663, by a certificate of Athlone herald, in Ireland. Guil. 399.

MOSCOVIANS, The, of London, i.e., "Muscovy or Russian merchts.," arms, crest and supporters 2 April 1555, by ? Hawley. Add. MS. 16,940, fo. 207ᵇ.

MUSGRAVE, George, of Nettlecomb, co. Somerset, and his brothers; exemplified 6 April 1690, by the E. Marshal's Warrant. Harl. MS. 6834, fo. 178 ; Grants IV., fo. 67.

„ Richard and William and the descendants of John, their great-grandfather.

MUSITIONES, Company of, of London, ... Oct. 1604, by Camden. Harl. MSS. 1422, fo. 18, and 6095, fo. 2.

MUSKETT, Henry, of Halstead, Suff., gent., 13 Sept. 1576 (Harl. MS. 1105, fo. 1), by Ro. Cooke, Clar. Harl. MS. 2146, fo. 161, copy of grant, Brit. Mus.

MUSSENDEN, Francis, of Healing, co. Linc., Quarterly, by Cooke, Clar. Stowe MS. 670, fo. 46ᵇ.

MUSTERS, John, of Tuthill Street, Westminster, 12 Aug. 1611, by W. Ryley, Norr. Harl. MS. 6832, fo. 413, confirmed by E. Bysshe, Gart. Harl. MSS. 1441, fo. 150ᵇ, and 6832, fo. 413.

„ Sir John, of Hornsey, Middx., Kt., 13 March 1682 ; 25 November 1682, grant, alteration of colours of bend, by Sir Wm. Dugdale, Gart., and Sir Hy. St. George, Clar. Harl. MS. 14,830, fo. 146 ; Grants III., 167 (194, alteration of bend from az. to gu.) ; Harl. MS. 6179, fo. 43ᵇ.

MYLSENT, John, of Barham, par. of Great Linton, co. Cambr., letters patent 1 June 1557, 3 and 4 Phil. and Mary, by (? Harvey or Dalton) Norr. Cott. MS. Faustina E. 1, 23, incomplete, copy of grant, Brit. Mus., ? no blason.

MYNNE, Henry, als MEENE, of St. Margaret's, Ilketshall, Suff., 27 Aug. 1662. Bysshe's Grants, fo. 8, Her. Coll. ; Harl. MS. 1105, fo. 18 ; Add. MS. 14,293, fo. 11ᵇ.

MYLTON als MYTTON, ... of Oxon., ... by Segar. Add. MS. 12,225, fo. 83.

MITTON, Edward, of co. Staff., confirmation of arms, quarterly of 6, by Segar . . . . Add. MS. 12,225, fo. 81ᵇ ; Harl. MS. 6140, fo. 78.

„ William, see MELTON.

N

NABBS, William, of Stafford, 20 Dec. 1675, by W. Dugdale, Gart. Harl. MS. 6834, fo. 178 ; Grants III., fo. 17.

NANDICK, William, of Elston, Yorks, by R. St. George, Clar. Stowe MS. 703, fo. 74.

NAPER, Alexander als Sandye, of Devon, gent., 1 Aug. 1577, 20 Eliz., by Cooke. Crest, 1 Aug. 1575, Harl. MSS. 1144, fo. 2, and 1359, fo. 86 ; Add. MS. 4966, fo. 94.

„ Robert, of London, descended of the ancient house of Mercaston (Merchistoun) in Scotland, Quarterly, allowed by Ro. Cooke, Clar., 6 Nov. 1576, 18 Q. Eliz. Harl. MS. 1359, fo. 85ᵇ. Quarterly : or, a bend chequy arg. and az., etc.

NAPIER, Sir Robert, of Lnton Hoo, co. Bedf., descended from the ancient Earls of Lenox, confirmed quarterly of 9 and two crests and supporters, by Segar. Add. MS. 12,225, fo. 83ᵇ.

NAPPER, Richard, of Grange, Dorset, Ld. Chief Baron of Ireland, by Cooke . . . . Harl. MS. 1422, fo. 16ᵇ ; different bird for crest in Stowe MS. 670, fo. 56ᵇ. Argt., a saltire sa., etc. Crest, on a mount vert a stork ppr.

NATCOMBE or NUTCOMBE, John, of Devonshire, s. of Nicholas, s. of John, s. of Richard, ... March 1657, by Sir E. Bysshe, Gart. Harl. MS. 1172, fo. 24, copy of grant.

NAUNTON, William, coat and crest *temp.* Ed. III., 1326—77. (In the tyme of K. Ed. III. the armes) his crest given by Garter, but fyrste he gave him a lyon's head erased, thereon three trefoils slipped or, and after this other. Stowe MS. 692, fo. 71 ; Barker's Grants, Harl. MS. 5846, fo. 79.

NAVIE, ROYALL, the Corporation of the, arms and crest . . . . 1573, by Sir G. Dethick, Gart.   Harl. MS. 1441, fo. 81ᵇ ; Q's Coll. Oxf. MS. 145, fo. 33ᵇ.

NALER or NAYLER, William, London, one of the six clerks of the Chancery, gift 10 Feb. 1564-5, by Harvey. Q's Coll. Oxf. MS. 145, fo. 17ᵇ ; Add. MS. 16,940, fo. 29ᵇ ; Harl. MS. 1441, fo. 74, confirmed 30 June, 9 Eliz., 1567, by Ro. Cooke, Clar. ; Harl. MS. 2146, fo. 174, then registrar of the Court of Chancery ; Stowe MS. 703, fo. 23 ; Harl. MS. 1116, fo. 79ᵇ.

NEALE, ... of Warnford, Hants, ... 1579.   Berry's Armory.

„   Richard, D.D., Bp. of Lichfield 1610—14, of Lincoln 1614—17, etc., Archbp. of York ; ob. 31 Oct. 1640 ; a patent Jan. 1613-14, by Camden.   Harl. MS. 6095, fo. 24, 26 ; Guil. 255.

NEALL, Dʳ Richard, Deane of Westminster 1605, a patent . . . . Nov. 1612, by Camden.   Entry erased in Harl. MS. 6095, fo. 28 ; Guil. 255.

NEDHAM, John, of Wymondsley, Herts, s. of James, s. of Christopher, s. of John, called Black John Nedham of Nedham Grange, co. Derby ; coat confirmed and crest granted 18 Feb. 1586-7, by Cooke.   Stowe MS. 714, fo. 92, 136 ; MS. Ashm. 834, fo. 65 and 66, copy of grant, Bodleian Lib. ; Harl. MSS. 1359, fo. 110ᵇ, and 1422, fo. 65 ; Guil. 243 ; Grants I., 289 ; Add. MS. 4966, fo. 65 ; Harl. MS. 5887, fo. 22, 27ᵇ, 34, 91 ; Reliquary, xxii., 68.

NEGUS, Francis, of Bow St., Covent Garden, London, 11 Dec. 1683, by Sir Wᵐ Dugdale and Clar.   Harl. MS. 6834, fo. 178 ; Grants III., fo. 219 ; Add. MS. 31,896, fo. 38ᵇ, has "Mʳ Negus, Secretary to yᵉ Duke of Norfolk, p Sʳ Hen. St. George, 1684 " ; Harl. MS. 6179, fo. 74.

NELSON, ... of Mawdesley, co. Lanc., ? confirmed 26 June 1587, by Cooke. Guil. 94.

„   . . . . of the Poultry (? Pantry), crest confirmed . . . . by R. St. George, Norr. Add. MS. 14,295, fo. 79ᵇ . . . . (fo. 276).

„   Thomas, of Elsath Hall, York, now of the pantry ; 29 Jan. 1607-8, by R. St. George.   Add. MS. 14,295, fo. 75 (fo. 56ᵃ) ; Harl. MS. 5887, fo. 59ᵇ.

NEME, John, of Woodnesborough, Kent, 16 July 1574, by Cooke.   Harl. MS. 1359, fo. 122ᵇ.

NERBONNE, Pierre de, grant by Hen. VII. for good service ; in French, 23 June 1502.   Pat. Roll, 17 Hen. VII., p. 1, m. 1 ; MS. Ashm. 858, fo. 60, copy of grant, Bodleian Lib.

NETHERSOLE, John, of Nethersole (Wingham Wold), Kent, gent., 10 May 1578, by Cooke : per pale gu. and az., three griffins segreant or.   Harl. MS. 1105, fo. 20ᵇ.

NETTES, Richard, ? Capt., one of the Gentlemen Ushers to Q. Anne, ... by Segar. Add. MS. 12,225, fo. 85.

NEVILL, Sir John, Chevet, Yorks, ... 1513, 5 H. VIII., by T. Wriothesley, Gart. Harl. MS. 1422, fo. 122.

„   John, citizen and grocer of London, 26 March 1633-4, by Sir R. St. George, Clar.   Add. MS. 14,295, fo. 104 ; Grants II., fo. 656.

NEVELL, Mary, relict of John, Vice Adml., West Indies, 15 Dec. 1697, to the descendants of the Adml., by St. George, Gart. and Clar.   Grants IV., 239.

NEVINSON, Thomas, Eastry, Kent, ... 1570, by Cooke, Clar. : or, a chevron betw. three eagles displayed az., beaked and legged gu. ; crest, a lynx statant ppr., etc.   (Berry) ; Stowe MS. 670, fo. 40ᵇ.

NEWARK-UPON-TRENT, Town and Corporation of, 8 Dec. 1561, by Sir G. Dethick, Gart.   Harl. MS. 1441, fo. 65ᵇ ; Her. and Geneal. 119 ; 1561 in Q's Coll.

Oxf. MS. 145, fo. 8[b] ; C. Brown's Annals of Newark, 78 ; Cat. Her. Exhib. Soc. of Antiq., 66 ; Grants II., 652.

NEWBOLD, Abbot of Evesham, ... arg., on a fess sa. betw. three gillyflowers gu., slipped vert, a mitre or betw. two roses or. (? Arms 1505, by Wriothesley, MS. Ashm. 858, fo. 28, copy of grant, Bodleian Lib.) ; Add. MS. 26,702, fo. 34 ; Stowe MS. 692, fo. 70.

NEWCASTLE-UPON-TYNE, Town of, 16 Aug. 1575, by Flower, crest and supporters. MSS. Ashm. 834, fo. 12[b], and 858, fo. 39, copy of grant, Bodleian Lib.

NEWCE, ... Much Haddam, Herts, and Ditchingham, Norfolk, by Cooke, Clar., ... 1575 : sa., two pales arg., a canton erm. ; Crest, on a mount vert a garb or. Berry ; see Harl. MS. 5887, fo. 76[b], for John, of the Court of Wardes, impaling Garnett ; Harl. MS. 1234, fo. 126.

  „ Clement, of Much Hadham, Herts, arms 1 June 1549, by Hawley. Add. MS. 16,940, fo. 201[b] ; Harl. MS. 1433, fo. 4.

NEWCOMBE, William, of Exeter, Devon, arg., a fesse embattled betw. two escallops sa. ; Crest, out of a mural coronet or a falcon sa. (? tail arg.), July 1611, by Camden (patent). Harl. MS. 6095, fo. 15[b] ; (1163, fo. 15) ; Le Neve's MS. 300.

NEWCOMEN, Charles, of London, and ⎱ . . . ., by Ro. Cooke, Clar. Stowe MS. 670,
  „ John, of co. Linc. ⎰ fo. 9[b].

NEWDIGATE, Walter, of Newdigate, Surrey, Quarterly . . . . by Cooke. Stowe MS. 670, fo. 7.

NEWDYKE, Robert, gent., of Worcester, s. of Robert, s. of Richard, s. of Henry, of Worc., gent., etc. ; mar. Margaret, 2nd dau. and coh. of Rich. Osney, of Worcester, gent. Newdyke coat by Cooke, confirmed and the crest (and ? Osney quartering) given 1 Dec. 1580, by Sir Gilb. Dethick, Gart. Harl. MSS. 1422, fo. 118, and 1359, fo. 23[b], set down in vellum under the hand of Ro. Cooke ; Add. MSS. 14,295, fo. 49[b], and 26,753, fo. 122[b] ; Q's Coll. Oxf. MS. 37, fo. 75, copy of 1580 grant ; Grants I., 258.

NEWFOUNDLAND, Company of, arms, crest, supporters and motto, by Borough. Caius Coll. Camb. MS. 551.

NEWLAND, William, of Newsillsbnry, Barkway, Herts, 29 April 1693, by T. St. George, Gart. and Clar. Harl. MS. 6834, fo. 178 ; Grants IV., fo. 135 ; Harl. MS. 1085, fo. 57.

NEWMAN, Gayus (s. of Gabriel, s. of Thomas, of Norfolk), confirmed 12 Nov. 1610, by Camden. Harl. MSS. 1422, fo. 21[b], and 6095, fo. 13[b] ; Guil. 267, the 12th Nov. ; Le Neve's MS. 294 ; Grants II., 582.

  „ George, ... June 1611, by Camden : or, a fess dancettée betw. three eagles displayed sa. Harl. MSS. 6095, fo. 15[b], and 1422, fo. 35[b].

  „ John, of London, grocer, ... by Cooke. Harl. MS. 1359, fo. 96.

  „ John, citizen and chirurgeon of London (s. of John, of Stamford, co. Linc.), grant 15 Feb. 1663-4, by Walker. Add. MSS. 14,293, fo. 52, and 14,294, fo. 13 ; Harl. MS. 1172, fo. 57 ; (Guil. 253) copy of grant.

  „ Thomas, citizen and mercht. of London, ... by Ryley, Lanc. Her. Harl. MS. 6832, fo. 413.

  „ Richard, of Fifehead Magdalen, Dorset, and Evercreech, Somerset (see recital of pedigree) ; augmentation 2 April 1664, by Walker. Add. MSS. 14,293, fo. 40, and 14,294, fo. 11 ; Harl. MS. 1470, fo. 71 ; Harl. MS. 1172, fo. 54, copy of grant.

NEWTON, Sir John, of Hather, co. Linc., Bart., 20 May 1662, by Sir E. Walker, Gart. Her. Coll., fo. 47.

  „ . . . . by E. Norgate, Windsor Herald, ... Stowe MS. 703, fo. 71.

  „ Sir John, of Richmond Castle, Somt., Knt., twelve coats confirmed and crest granted 12 Dec., 10 Q. Eliz., 1567, by Sir G. Dethick, Cooke and Flower. Q's Coll. Oxf. MS. 39, fo. 130 ; MS. Ashm. 834, fo. 34, copy of grant, Bodleian Lib. ; N. and Q., 1st S., ii., 428 ; Arch. Institute, 1851, p. 239 ; Guil. 125 ; Harl. MS. 1754, fo. 116.

NEWTON, Sir Robert, of London, Bart.,⎫ sons of Thomas, of Easton, Northts.,
    and his two brothers,   ⎪ 14 Feb., 13 Chas. II., 1660-1. Bysshe's
„ Richard, and   ⎬ Grants, fo. 9, Her. Coll. ; Harl. MS.
„ Thomas,   ⎪ 1470, fo. 118, copy of grant, Brit.
                     ⎭ Mus., and Harl. MS. 1105, fo. 18.
„ William, and⎱ sons of John, of Axmouth, Devon, who mar. Mary, dau. of
„ Humfrey,   ⎰ William Boteler of Biddock, co. Bedf., Esq., etc. ; by Segar
         . . . . Add. MS. 12,225, fo. 85.
„ William, next Trent, co. Linc., granted or confirmed 14 June 1660, by
        Walker. Guil. 263.

NICH, see NYE.

NICHOLAS, Eighteen coats, see Stowe MS. 703, fo. 86.
„ . . . . az., a fesse betw. three lyons' heads erased or . . . . by Segar. Add. MS.
      12,225, fo. 84ᵇ: borne also by John Nycolas of London, controller of the
      work of the bridge. John Nicholas, girdler, of London, clarke of the
      bridge-house, Harl. MS. 5887, fo. 73.
„ Sir Edward, Knt., principal Sec. of State *temp.* Chas. II., augmentation and
      crest at Jersey 17 Dec. 1649, by Walker, Gart. Her. Coll., 2 : (Berry's
      Armory); Harl. MS. 6179, fo. 46ᵇ ; (grant 1st L. 2, 104ᵇ, Her. Coll.).
„ John, of Winterborne Earl, Wilts, ... 1612, by Segar. Add. MS. 12,225,
      fo. 84 ; Guil. 223, and Berry.
„ John, s. of Edward, of Winterborne Earle, Wilts, 10 Feb. 1623-4, by Sir R.
      St. George, Clar. Add. MS. 14,295, fo. 64 ; C. 22, 27, Wilts [Visit.,
      1623].
„ Thomas, of co. Glouc., patent Dec. 1620, by Segar. Add. MS. 12,225,
      fo. 84 ; Harl. MS. 6140, fo. 63ᵇ ; Guil. 223.

NYCHELLE, John, of London, coat and crest. Barker's Grants, Harl. MS. 5846,
      fo. 79 ; in Stowe MS. 692, fo. 70ᵇ, styled Master John Nychells of London,
      gent. ; his wyfe was Sir Steven Jenyns' daughter, the mayre.

NICHOLLS, ... of Islep Willen, Bucks : az., three eagles displayed in bend betw.
      two cottises engrailed or, either side whereof three cross crosslets fitchée
      or . . . . by Segar. Add. MS. 12,225, fo. 86.

NYCOLLS, Francis, of Hardwick (Hardwyck), Northants, ... 1588, by Cooke.
      Harl. MSS. 1359, fo. 108ᵇ, and 1422, fo. 84ᵇ ; Add. MS. 4966, fo. 56.

NYCOLL, John, of London, gift . . . . 155 . . . . or 156 . . . . (Harvey's Grants),
      Add. MS. 16,940, fo. 24.

NICHOLL, John, one of the assistant governors. Raleigh, Vᵃ, arms granted : per
      bend arg. and gu., five fusils counterchanged . . . . by W. Dethick, Gart.
      Q's Coll. Oxf. MS. 36, fo. 120.

NICHOLLS, John, of Garth, co. Montgomery, gent. (? John Dugdale or T. St. George,
      Gart.), by Norroy : arg., a fesse az. betw. six laurel leaves vert. "A grant,"
      Harl. MS. 1172, fo. 54ᵇ.
„ John, of Trewane . . . . by Camden. Harl. MS. 1079, fo. 92.

NICOLL, Paul, of Hendon Place, Middx., ... 1650, by Ed. Bysshe. Harl. MS.
      6179, fo. 46ᵇ ; Stowe MS. 677, fo. 70ʰ ; Harl. MS. 1172, fo. 54ᵇ ; Add. MS.
      26,758, fo. 16ᵇ.

NICOLLS, Richard, Tilney, Norfolk, 1 Jan. 1550-51, by ? Hawley. Add. MS.
      16,940, fo. 204ᵇ.

NICHOLSON, ... of Seale, Kent, ... by Sir G. Dethicke. Harl. MSS. 5847,
      fo. 54, and 1441, fo. 103ᵇ : Stowe MS. 703, fo. 58ᵇ, a trick, not a grant.
„ Francis, Governor of Maryland ; 9 March 1693, by T. St. George, Gart. and
      Clar. Grants IV., 153 ; Harl. MS. 1085, fo. 57.

NICOLSON, Otes, of London, Examʳ in the Court of Chancery, s. of Thomas, s. of
      William, s. of Nicolas, of Cumberland ; grant 7 Sept. 1596, by W. Dethick,
      Gart. Stowe MS. 676, fo. 115ᵇ ; Harl. MS. 1422, fo. 22 ; Q's Coll. Oxf.
      MS. 36, fo. 51, copy of grant; Add. MS. 14,293, fo. 19ᵇ, as Thomas; Guil.
      90 ; Harl. MS. 5887, fo. 63ᵇ ; Le Neve's MS. 488.

NYCOLSON, Robert, of London, Quarterly .... 1588, by Cooke. Harl. MSS. 1359, fo. 109, and 1422, fo. 120 ; Add. MS. 4966, fo. 31.

NICOLSON, William, of co. Lincoln, gent., grant 26 Feb. 1535-6, 27 Hy. VIII. Stowe MS., by T. Tong, Clar. ; Harl. MS. 1422, fo. 84ᵇ ; Stowe MS. 677, fo. 5ᵇ ; Q's Coll. Oxf. MSS. 145, fo. 54ᵇ, and 146, fo. 20, copy of grant, Brit. Mus.

NYGHTINGALE, Richard, of London, s. of Robert, of Lytchfeld, Quarterly .... 1593, by Cooke. Harl. MSS. 1359, fo. 111ᵇ, and 1422, fo. 120 ; Add. MS. 4966, fo. 24.

NOADS, George. of Shepallbury. Herts, etc., confirmed or granted 10 Feb. 1634-5, by Sir R. St. George, Clar. Guil. 133 ; Stowe MS. 703, fo. 73.

NOELL, see NOWELL.

NONE or NOONE, Robert, of Walton-upon-the-Wold, co. Leic., Nov. 1611, by .... , Camden. Harl. MSS. 6095, fo. 16, and 1422, fo. 35ᵇ.

„ George, see NOUNE.

NORBORNE, Walter, of Hill Marten. Wilts, sometime reader of the Inner Temple ; s. of John, s. of Humphrey, both of Studley, Wilts ; 22 June 1651, by Sir E. Bysshe, Gart. Harl. MS. 1172, fo. 13, copy of grant.

„ Walter, and ⎱ of Calne, Wilts, s. of Walter, of the same, reader of Inner
„ John, ⎰ Temple, etc. ; 14 July 1660, by Walker. Add. MSS. 14,293, fo. 103, and 14,294, fo. 34 ; Harl. MS. 1172, fo. 71 ; Guil. 284 ; Cat. Her. Exhib. Soc. of Antiq., 72.

NORCLYFFE, Thomas, of Great Gomeronll, Yorks, patent 11 July, 4 (K. Jas.), 1606, by R. St. George, Norr. Add. MS. 14,295, fo. 78ᵇ ; Harl. MSS. 1359, fo. 43ᵇ, and 6140, fo. 53 ; Genealogist, vol. vi., p. 35.

NORCOTT, see NORTHCOTE.

NORDEN, John, of the Manor of Easthill, Kent, gent., grant 1 Nov. 1556, 3 and 4 Philip and Mary. by G. Dethick, Gart. Q's Coll. Oxf. MS. 39, fo. 76, copy of grant ; Harl. MS. 1359, fo. 6 ; altered in 1586, by R. Cooke, Clar., see Harl. MS. 1422, fo. 51ᵇ ; Grants I., 196 ; Add. MS. 4966, fo. 69ᵇ. See MORDEN.

NORFOLK, Thomas, Duke of, augmentation, letters patent 1 Feb. 1513-14, 5 H. VIII., for service at the battle (Flodden) near Browxton, Northumbld., against the Scots ; orig. 5 H. VIII., Ro. 37 and 38. Stowe MS. 840, fo. 62, copy of letters patent, Brit. Mus. ; Cotton MS. Julius C., vii., fo. 237 ; Harl. MS. 1178, fo. 45 ; Lansd. MS. 872, fo. 13—16.

NORHOPE, ... of Nottingham, alias CLEARKE, now of Kent : Quarterly, arg. and vert, a cross counter componée of the same, by Segar. Add. MS. 12,225, fo. 87.

NORREYS, Lord, ... arms of Venables, by T. St. George, Clar. and Norr. Harl. MS. 6834, fo. 178 ; Grants III., fo. 333 ; Lansd. MS. 867, fo. 52.

NORRIS, ... a patent .... 1622, by Camden : arg.. a cross pattée flory sa. between twelve billets az. Harl. MS. 6095, fo. 39.

„ Francis, citizen and Alderm. of Norwich ; 3 May 1665. Bysshe's Grants, fo. 27, Her. Coll. ; Harl. MS. 1105, fo. 22.

NORREYS, Thomas, of Orford, co. Lanc., confirmed 9 Nov. 1581, by Flower. MS. Ashm. 844, fo. 54, copy of grant, Bodleian Lib. ; Guil. 383.

NORTH, ... of Walkeringham, Notts, ... 42 Eliz., 1600, by Segar. Add. MS. 12,225, fo. 85ᵇ ; C. 29 [?C. 9, Visit. co. Nottingham, 1614], Her. Coll. ; and Guil. 104.

„ (Edward, of Felsham, in Stowe MS.) .... crest .... Barker's Grants, Harl. MS. 5846, fo. 79ᵇ ; Stowe MS. 692, fo. 71.

„ Sir Edward, of Kirtling, co. Camb., Knt., coat altered and crests : this in confirmation from Mʳ Garter for that afore he had p pale, etc. Barker's Grants, Harl. MS. 5846, fo. 79ᵇ ; Stowe MS. 692, fo. 71.

„ Edward, of Tewin, Herts, servt. to K. Chas. ; s. of Edward, of Tewin, s. of Edward, Master of Harriers to Ed. VI., s. of John, s. of Robert, of the same parish and co., lords of the manor of Merden ; grant 25 Feb. 1633-4, by R. St. George. Stowe MS. 677, fo. 42 ; copy of grant, Brit. Mus., Harl. MS. 6179, fo. 74.

NORTH, John, of Cubley. co. Derby, grant, arms and crest, 21 June 1676, by W. Dugdale, Norr. Harl. MS. 6834, fo. 178 ; Misc. Gen. et Her., N. S., i., 301 ; Grants III., p. 33 ; Cat. Heraldic Exhib. Soc. of Antiq., No. 242.

NORTHCOTE, Walter, of Crediton, Devon, 1 Jan. 1570-71, by Cooke, Clar. Grants II., 517 ; Harl. MS. 1359, fo. 105, as Norcott; 1590 in Harl. MS. 1422, fo. 23ᵇ; per Rouge Crosse in Harl. MS. 1441, fo. 133.

NORTHEN, see Paul BAYNING.

NORTHEY, Henry, of Bocking, Essex, gent., given and granted at London 10 July, 2 and 3 [? 2 and 4] Philip and Mary [1556 ?], by Sir G. Dethicke. Q's Coll. Oxf. MS. 39, fo. 65, copy of grant 1556 ; and Harl. MS. 1359, fo. (68) and 81ᵇ; Genealogist, iii., p. 72 ; Grants I., 194 ; Harl. MS. 6179, fo. 72ᵇ; Stowe MS. 606, fo. 78, copy of grant.

NORTHFOLKE, James, of Westminster, ... by W. Ryley, Lancaster Herald. Stowe MS. 703, fo. 64.

NORTHINE, John, of London, ... by Cooke. Harl. MS. 1359, fo. 93ᵇ; Add. MS. 4966, fo. 63ᵇ.

NORTHLAND, Thomas, of Sussex, gent., grant London 10 Nov. 1482,, by Thos. (Holme), Clar. Misc. Gen. et Her., 2nd S., iv., pl., 136, copy of grant, Brit. Mus. ; Cat. Her. Exhib. Soc. of Antiq., 61.

NORTHOVER, ... of Alercourt, Somerset, a patent . . . . May 1614, by Camden. Harl. MSS. 6095, fo. 29ᵇ, and 1422, fo. 39 ; Guil. 372.

NORTON, ... stationer of London . . . . by Segar. Add. MS. 12,225, fo. 85ᵇ. This is the entire entry.

,, Bonham, (the King's printer), assigned Feb. 1611-12, by Camden. Harl. MS. 6095, fo. 17ᵇ; Guil. 73 ; of Stratton in Shropshire, Harl. MS. 6140, fo. 41.

,, Robert, of Halesworth, Suff., 1 May 1548, by ? Hawley. Add. MS. 16,940, fo. 202ᵇ.

,, Sampson, (Master of the Ordnance temp. H. VIII.). Add. MS. 26,702, fo. 62 ; Harl. MS. 5846, fo. 93ᵇ; Stowe MS. 692, fo. 83.

,, William, of Berlington, co. Worc., ... by Cooke. Harl. MS. 1359, fo. 116 ; Add. MS. 4966, fo. 28ᵇ.

,, William, a stacioner and bookbynder, of London, 36 Eliz., 1594, by Wᵐ Dethick, Gart. ; after death of Norton " he and his issue relinquished it "; entered by R. Brooke, York Herald. Harl. MS. 1453, fo. 35.

NORWICH, City of, confirmed . . . . by Harvey. Berry's Armory.

NORWOOD, Thomas, of (Astwood) co. Bucks, Esq., arms confirmed and crest given 1 Nov. 1585, 27 Q. Eliz., by Cooke. Harl. MS. 1359, fo. 21ᵇ, and 1422, fo. 51 ; 5ᵗʰ Nov. in Add. MS. 14,295, fo. 15 ; Guil. 53.

NOSWORTHY, Edward, of Truro, Cornwall, s. of Francis, s. of John ; 27 June 1661, by Sir E. Bysshe, Clar. Harl. MSS. 1172, fo. 28, copy of grant ; 1105, fo. 19ᵇ; Bysshe's Grants, fo. 15, Her. Coll.

NOTT, John, s. of John, s. of John, of Ansford, Kent, ... 1587, by Cooke's Depy. [?]. Stowe MS. 670, fo. 20 ; Harl. MS. 5887, fo. 86.

,, William, of . . . . crest 3 June, 1554, by ? Hawley. Add. MS. 16,940, fo. 207.

NOUNE or NOONE, George, of Fostocke, Norfolk, ... by Cooke. Harl. MS. 1359, fo. 99 ; Add. MS. 12,474, fo. 55 ; Stowe MS. 670, fo. 6ᵇ; Add. MS. 4966, fo. 20.

NOURSE, John, of Chillingplace and Wood Eaton, Oxon., Esq., s. of John, of Melton, Bucks : Nourse impaling Engham and two crests, 28 May 1629, by W. Segar, Gart. (? 27 May 1630). Add. MS. 12,225, fo, 86 ; 27ᵗʰ May 1629 in Guil. 71 ; Harl. MSS. 6140, fo. 64ᵇ, and 1441, fo. 160,

NOWELL (NOEL), Andrew, of Dalby, co. Leic., confirmed 10 Feb. 1582-3, by Cooke.
Harl. MS. 1359, fo. 93; MSS. Ashm. 834, fo. 39, and 858, fo. 40, copy of
grant, Bodleian Lib.; Guil. 319; Add. MS. 4964, fo. 36ᵇ; Harl. MS.
5887, fo. 28, 89ᵇ.

NOWER, John, of Ashford, Kent, 10 Oct. 1663, by Sir E. Bysshe, Clar. Bysshe's
Grants, 36; Harl. MS. 1105, fo. 40ᵇ.

NOYES, William, of Burian, co. Cornwall .... (1591), by Cooke. Harl. MS.
1359, fo. 112ᵇ; 1591 in Harl. MS. 1422, fo. 23ᵇ; Stowe MS. 670, fo. 45.

NURSE, Thomas, Doctor in physic, s. of John, Alderm. of Leicester; 15 April 1662,
by Walker. Harl. MS. 1172, fo. 30; copy of grant, Harl. MS. 6179,
fo. 30ᵇ. [See also NOURSE.]

NUTBROWNE, Nicholas, of Barking, Essex, ... 1588, by Cooke: erm., on a chief
sa. three lions' heads erased arg.; and his wife, Anne FINSEN, whom see.
Harl. MSS. 1359, fo. 95, and 1441, fo. 137ᵇ.

NUTCOMBE, John, of Devonshire, s. of Nicholas, s. of John, s. of Richard, ...
March 1657-8, by Sir E. Bysshe, Gart. Harl. MS. 1172, fo. 24. See
NATCOMBE.

NUTHALL, John, of Catenhall, Cheshire, confirmed 13 June 1582, by Flower. MS.
Ashm. 844, fo. 52, copy of grant, Bodleian Lib.; 3 June 1581 in Harl.
MS. 1359, fo. 83ᵇ, and quarterly of 4; Guil. 352, and Berry.

NYE alias NICH, ... of Sussex: paly of 6 arg. and sa., per fesse counterchanged
.... by Segar. Add. MS. 12,225, fo. 84ᵇ.

•

O

OFFLEY, Francis, descended from Sir Thomas [Mayor of London 1556-57].
Le Neve's MS. 509. [See below.]

„ Hugh, of London, Alderm., 5 Sept. 1588, 30 Q. Eliz., by Cooke. "The
armes was otherwise; but now these confirmed." Harl. MS. 1359,
fo. 14ᵇ and 109; "altered," Add. MS. 14,295, fo. 9; Harl. MS. 6179,
fo. 14ᵇ; Add. MS. 4966, fo. 57.

„ Sir John, of London, ..., by Borough. Harl. MSS. 1105, fo. 55, and 1441,
fo. 57; Add. MS. 26,702, fo. 89.

„ Sir Thomas, Mayor of London, 5 May 1547, by ? Hawley. Add. MS. 16,940,
fo. 202ᵇ; Le Neve's MS. 509.

OGDEN, John, ..., for his faithful services to the King, temp. Chas. II., ...,
Berry's Armory.

OGLE, Sir John, Col. of a regt of foot under the command of the United Provinces
of Holland, and prefect and Govr of the city of Utrecht, descended of the
Barons of Bothal of the North, testified 10 Jan., 12 Jac., 1614-15, by
Segar. Add. MS. 12,225, fo. 86ᵇ; Grants I., 356.

„ Mark, of Eglingham, Northumbld., gent., out of the house of Musgrave in
that co., grant 18 Aug., 26 H. VIII., 1534, for services in Scotland, by
T. Hawley, Norroy. Copy in full, Harl. MS. 1507, fo. 401; Q's Coll. Oxf.
MS. 38, fo. 35, copy of grant; see Le Neve's MS., fo. 401.

„ Richard, of Pinchbeck in the partes of Holland, co. Linc., Esq., coat and
crest. Barker's Grants, Harl. MS. 5846, fo. 80; Stowe MS. 692, fo. 73.

OGLETHORPE, ..., Yorks, ... 1596, by Lee. Add. MS. 14,295, fo. 73ᵇ
(fo. 33ᵇ).

OKEOVER, Philip, of Okeover, co. Staff., confirmed 6 March 1585, by Flower.
MS. Ashm. 844, p. 61, copy of grant, Bodleian Lib.; Guil. 355.

OKES, John, of Westminster, doctor, out of Peover, Cheshire, certified 4 June
(May) 1608, by R. St. George, Norr. Add. MS. 14,295, fo. 78ᵇ,
(fo. 138); Harl. MSS. 6179, fo. 13ᵇ, and 6140, fo. 74.

OKEY, Col. John, a patent 1653 (? by Bysshe), he was executed at Tyburn 1662 as
a Regicide. Harl. MS. 6179, fo. 29ᵇ.

OLDFIELD, Anthony, of Spalding, co. Linc., a patent, Nov. 1616, by Camden. Harl. MSS. 6095, fo. 35, and 1422, fo. 40ᵇ ; Anthony in Add. MS. 12,474, fo. 80.

„ Philip, of Bradwell, Cheshire, confirmed 7 Feb. 1578, by Flower. MS. Ashm. 834, fo. 17ᵇ, and 858, fo. 39, 145, copy of grant, Bodleian Lib. ; Guil. 74.

„ Roger, of London, ..., 1608, by Camden, Arms, or, on a pile engrailed az. three garbs or ; Crest, a griffin's head and neck erased, per fesse indented az. and or, thereon three guttes de sang. Cains Coll. Camb. MS. 551, fo. 27ᵇ ; Morgan's Sphere (ii.), 117 ; Harl. MS. 5887, fo. 64ᵇ.

„ Samuel, of London, attested by Jo. Philipot. Harl. MS. 1422, fo. 124ᵇ.

OLDISWORTH, Edward, of Poultons Court, co. Glouc., Esq., 1st s. of Nicholas, 31 Jan. 1569-70, by Cooke. Harl. MS. 1359, fo. 115.

OLDESWORTHE, Edward, and his brethren, sons of Nicholas, of Paltons Court, co. Glouc., Esq., crest confirmed 15 June 1569, by Sir G. Dethick, Gart., Cooke and Flower. MS. Ashm. 844, fo. 29, copy of grant, Bodleian Lib. ; Harl. MS. 1441, fo. 71ᵇ ; Q's Coll. Oxf. MS. 39, fo. 158, copy of grant ; Harl. MS. 1359, fo. 55 ; Guil. 292 ; Add. MS. 4966, fo. 95ᵇ.

OLYFFE, John, of Foxgrove, co. Kent, gift 1560 (Harvey's Grants). Add. MS. 16,940, fo. 26ᵇ.

OLIVER, Sir Benjamin, of Exeter, Devon, Erm., on a chief sa. 3 lions rampt. arg., grant 30 Nov. 1671, by Sir Edw. Bysshe. Visit. Oxford and Bucks, Her. Coll. and Ms. *penes* me. Copy of grant, Brit. Mus.

OLIVER or OLYVAR, Robert, of Blandford, Dorset, 1 July 1547, by T. Hawley, Clar. Add. MSS. 16,940, fo. 202, and 7098, fo. 78 (fo. 55) ; Harl. MS. 6179, fo. 56ᵇ.

ONEBY als ONDEBY, Dame Mercy, relict of Sir John (to his descendts.), s. of John, s. of John, of Ondeby, co. Leic., 7 Aug. 1680, by Sir H. St. George, Clar. Harl. MS. 6834, fo. 178 : Grants III., fo. 108, and same date and reference to John, of Barwell, co. Leic., s. of Thomas, of Sheppay, co. Leic., 3rd s. of John, of Ondeby aforesaid.

ONLEY, Edward, one of the gent. pensioners for the Q's body guard, s. of Thomas, 2nd s. of John, of Cotesby, Northts., crest granted 7 Sept. 1597, by W. Dethick, Gart. Q's Coll. Oxf. MS. 36, fo. 63, copy of grant ; Stowe MS. 676, fo. 121 ; Harl. MS. 1422, fo. 13ᵇ ; Le Neve's MS. 253.

ONSLOW or ANSLOW or ANNESLEY, 1588, ux., *see* Hill, Richard, and Stowe MS. 670, fo. 25 ; Harl. MS. 5887, fo. 30.

OPIE, Thomas, of Bodmin, 6 Aug. 1573, by Cooke. Harl. MS. 1079, fo. 178ᵇ.

ORANGE, John, of the Middle Temple, ..., 35 Q. Eliz., 1593, by Cooke. Berry's Armory.

ORFORD, Edward, Earl of, supporters 10 June 1697. Grants IV., fo. 225.

ORGAN, Richard, of Lamborne, Bucks [Berks], a Justice of peace, by Camden. Harl. MSS. 1422, fo. 17ᵇ, 5839, fo. 2ᵇ, 2275, fo. 90ᵇ, and 1115, fo. 8ᵇ ; Morgan's Sphere, 107.

ORLIBAR, Robert, of Harrold, } brothers, 1 April 1652, by Ed. Bysshe,
„ George, of Pudington, Beds, } Gart. Harl. MS. 1105, fo. 15ᵇ ; Add.
„ John, of London, } MS. 14,293, fo. 4 ; Bysshe's Grants, fo. 7, Her. Coll.

ORME, William, Hanse Hall, co. Staff., 18 Feb. 1662-3, by W. Dugdale, Norr. Her. Coll.

ORPWOOD, Thomas, of Abingdon, Berks, 1st s. and h. to Paul, sometime Mayor of Abingdon, &c., 1st s. of Thomas, sometime Mayor also, 31 Oct. 1600, by Camden, to Thomas and his brothers William, Robert, Richard, Lionel and Francis. Cott. MS. Faustina E. I., 43 ; Guil. 166.

OSBALDESTON, John, of Osbaldeston, Esq., s. and h. of Sir Alexʳ, of co. Lanc., Knt., gift of crest 24 Nov. 1560, 3 Eliz., by Dalton. Harl. MSS. 1359, fo. 47, and 1441, fo. 46.

OSBORNE, John, of Hartlip, Kent, crest 3 May 1573, by Cooke. Visit. Kent, 1619, p. 33 ; Dr. Howard, Arch. Cant., v., 227 ; Her. and Geneal., ii., p. 434, copy of grant, Brit. Mus.

OSBOURNE, John, of Debenham, Suff., 2 Aug. 1578, by Cooke. Harl. MSS. 1359, fo. 86ᵇ, 1422, fo. 76ᵇ, and 1085, fo. 26ᵇ ; Add. MS. 4966, fo. 67.

OSBORN, Sir Jan, chevalier, of Brussels, 3rd s. of Ulric, etc. ; dated at Brussels 1 Sept. 1658, by Walker. Add. MSS. 14,293, fo. 98, and 14,294, fo. 33 ; Harl. MS. 1172, fo. 72, as Sir John, descended out of Norfolk ; Her. Coll., fo. 30 ; Harl. MS. 6179, fo. 79ᵇ.

OSBOURNE, Peter, of London, ... by Cooke. Harl. MS. 1359, fo. 93ᵇ ; Add. MS. 4966, fo. 63.

OSSULSTON, Lord (Charles [John] Benet, Knt. [K.B.]), supporters, ? arms also (crest 24 Nov. 1682) ; 18 March 1694-5, by T. St. George, Gart. Grants IV., 182.

OUDART, Nicholas, s. of Christopher ; born in Mechlin in Brabant ; Sec. to Sir William Boswell, Knt., resident with the States General, and to Sir Ed. Nicholas, principal Sec. of State ; made a free denizen of England by Chas. I. ; confirmed at Oxford 1 May 1645, by Walker. Add. MS. 14,294, fo. 28.

OUTLAWE, Thomas (s. of Rafe) .... of Wichingham, Norfolk, a patent .... June 1613, by Camden. Harl. MS. 6095, fo. 27ᵇ ; Guil. 193.

OVER, ... or, on a bend az. a fret of the field .... by W. Segar. Add. MS. 12,225, fo. 86ᵇ.

OVERBURY, Thomas, of Aston sub Edge, co. Glouc. .... by Cooke. Harl. MS. 1359, fo. 105.

OVERMAN, ... of Southwark, Surrey : az., a chev. betw. three fleurs-de-lis or, on a chief of the last a lyon passant guardant gu. .... 1628, by Segar. Add. MS. 12,225, fo. 87.

OWEN, Edward, of Shrewsbury, gent., grant of a canton and crest 8 Dec. 1582, by Cooke. Harl. MS. 1359, fo. 92ᵇ ; MS. Ashm. 858, fo. 138, copy of grant, Bodleian Lib. ; Harl. MS. 1422, fo. 62 ; Misc. Gen. et Her., 2nd S., vol. ii., p. 249 ; Add. MS. 4966, fo. 59 ; Sheriffs of Montgomeryshire, by W. V. Lloyd, 39.

  ,,   George, of the co. of Oxford, (had William and ....) Stowe MS., coat and crest .... Barker's Grants, Harl. MS. 5846, fo. 80ᵇ ; Stowe MS. 692, fo. 73.

  ,,   Lewis, of Crewthyn, co. Carnarvon, 14 March 1616, by Segar. Egerton MS. 2586, fo. 226, copy of grant, Brit. Mus.

  ,,   Thomas, of Lincoln's Inn : quarterly of 4 (Ireland, O'Heley and Cole) .... by Cooke. Harl. MS. 1359, fo. 92ᵇ ; Add. MS. 4966, fo. 59 ; for differences see Harl. MS. 5887, fo. 72.

OWEN, see LONG.

OXBURGH, Thomas, of Linn, Norfolk, ... 1613, by Camden. Quarterly of 4 : 1 Oxburgh, 2 Hever, 3 ...., 4 .... Harl. MSS. 6095, fo. 40ᵇ, and 1441, fo. 152ᵇ.

OXENDEN, John, ... 6 Feb. 1445-6, 24 H. VI., by John Wryxworth, (Guyon) King of Arms. Visit. Kent [1619], 88 ; Arch. Cant., vi., p. 277 ; 1428 in MS. Ashm. 858, fo. 64 (but wrongly), copy of grant, Bodleian Lib.

OXENHAM, William, of South Tawton, Devon, 7 March 1694-5, by T. St. George, Gart. and Clar. Stowe MS. 714, fo. 132 ; Grants IV., 181 ; Harl. MS. 6179, fo. 93ᵇ.

OXWICKE, ... Norfolk and London, mercht. ; pedigree subscribed by W. Ryley, Lancⁱ, see arms. Harl. MS. 6179, fo. 97.

P

PACE, ... of London : coat, or, on a cross quarterly az. and gu. a bird, etc. ; crest, a boar's head caboshed, standing in pale sa. a cross crosslet fitchée and an ankker in saltire on the neck, armed, snowted and eared or, ? vulned. Coat and crest in later hand. Barker's Grants, Harl. MS. 5846, fo. 84ᵇ ; Stowe MS. 692, fo. 78 ; Add. MS. 26,702, fo. 47. Pacey. ? A crest for the next named.

„ Mʳ Richard, "the King's high and principall secretarye," granted 12 Feb. 1517-18, 9 H. VIII., by T. Wriothesley and Benolt. Q's Coll. Oxf. MS. 38, fo. 30, copy of grant ; Harl. MS. 1359, fo. 7ᵇ ; Grant in Reg. Off.

PACKE, Christopher, (Lord Mayor of London), 26 July 1683, by Sir William Dugdale, Gart., and St. George, Clar. Harl. MS. 6834, fo. 178; Grants III., fo. 202 ; Harl. MS. 6179, fo. 52.

„ John, of London, High Sheriff of Suff. ; 20 Jan. 1696-7, by T. St. George, Gart. and Clar. Add. MS. 14,831, fo. 41 ; Grants IV., 218.

PACKER, William, ... 1645, by W. Ryley, Lanc. Herald. Stowe MS. 703, fo. 63.

PACKINGTON, Thomas, of Edgworth, Middx. ; testified by Segar. Add. MS. 12,225, fo. 87ᵇ ; Vincent's Surrey, C. 129, fo. 541 ; Harl. MS. 6140, fo. 80ᵇ.

PADDON, Robert, of Hinton Dawbeny, Hants, 16 May 1590, by Cooke. Harl. MSS. 1359, fo. 100, 1422, fo. 94ᵇ, and 1544, fo. 1ᵇ.

PADDY, Nicholas, Lancaster Herald, and ⎱ 24 June 1590, by Cooke. Harl. MSS.
„ William, Dʳ Phys., his brother,   ⎰ 1422, fo. 22ᵇ, and 1359, fo. 103ᵇ ; Stowe MS. 692, fo. 77.

PAGE, Rt. Hon. Sir Richd., Knt., a gift of crest and arms quarterly, confirmed 1 Feb. 1530-31, 22 H. VIII., by Benolt. Add. MS. 14,295, fo. 12 ; Harl. MSS. 1359, fo. 19, and 1422, fo. 116ᵇ.

„ Col. Sir Richard, at Oxford, 6 May 1645, by Walker. Add. MSS. 14,293, fo. 110, and 14,294, fo. 36ᵇ ; Harl. MS. 1172, fo. 72ᵇ ; Her. Coll., fo. 25.

„ William, of Hegesett, Suff., gent., grant 16 Sept. 1552, by Sir G. Dethick, Gart. Ex. Mag. Reg. ; Stowe MS. 676, fo. 21ᵇ ; Q's Coll. Oxf. MS. 37, fo. 30, copy of grant ; Grants I., 192 ; Harl. MS. 5887, fo. 50, as Edward, and Harl. MS. 1116, fo. 47.

PAGET, Robert, Sheriff of London ; 1536. Berry's Armory.

PAGETT, William, born in London, Clarke of the Privy Counsel and one of the four clarkes of his highness signet, grant 1 June 1541, by Hawley. Q's Coll. Oxf. MS. 38, fo. 40 ; Harl. MS. 1507, fo. 406, copy of grant, Brit. Mus. ; Grants II., 541 ; Le Neve's MS. 406.

PAGET, Sir William, of Bromley, co. Staff., Knt., alteration of coat and crest (after 1540) ; " he had other afore of Clarenceux which he mislıked," etc. Barker's Grants, Harl. MS. 5846, fo. 85ᵇ ; Stowe MS. 692, fo. 78ᵇ.

„ Sir William, Lord of Beaudesert, confirmation, by letters patent dated at Westminster, of his arms, crest and suprs., by Ed. VI. (1547—53). Her. Coll., M. 14, fo. 48 ; MS. Ashm. 834, fo. 45ᵇ, and 844, fo. 23, 24, 25, copies of letters patent, Bodleian Lib.

PAGITT, Thomas, of the Middle Temple, London, s. and h. of Richard, of Cranford, co. Northampt., 24 Feb. 1575-6, by Cooke. Harl. MS. 1470, fo. 148 ; 1584 in Add. MS. 14,295, fo. 38ᵇ, and Harl. MS. 1359, fo. 116 ; Guil. 243 ; Add. MS. 4966, fo. 62ᵇ.

PAGRAVE, John, of Colsford, Somerset, ... by Cooke. Harl. MS. 1359, fo. 116ᵇ ; Add. MS. 4966, fo. 29.

PALMER, ... Crest, a demi-panther, etc. Barker's Grants, Harl. MS. 5846, fo. 81 ; Stowe MS. 692, fo. 78. Arms and crest, a demi-dragon, etc. Harl. MS. 5846, fo. 81 ; Stowe MS. 692, fo. 78.

„ Anthony, of Stockdale, co. Northampt., ... 1580, by Cooke. Harl. MSS. 1422, fo. 91, and 1359, fo. 112ᵇ.

PALMER, Henry, Beakesbourne, Kent, ... 1586, by Cooke. Stowe MS. 670, fo. 13.

„ John, of Hartlipp, Kent, Quarterly .... 1576, by Cooke. Harl. MS. 1359, fo. 105 ; Q's Coll. Oxf. MS. 146, fo. 472.

„ John, s. of John, ..., by R. St. George, Norroy. Harl. MS. 5887, fo. 72ᵇ.

„ John, M.A., Archdeacon of Northampton, ⎫ all sons of Joseph, late of
„ Elias, of Stepney, Middx., ⎬ Cropredy, Northants, gent.,
„ Nathaniel, of Kingston-upon-Hull, ⎭ decᵈ, 3 May 1670, by Walker. Add. MSS. 14,293, fo. 74, and 14,294, fo. 22 ; Harl. MS. 1172, fo. 61ᵇ ; Guil. 118, copy of grant.

„ Richard, of Wokingham, Berks, s. and h. of Richard, of the same, 20 Feb. 1665-6 (16 Chas. II., 1663-4), by Sir Edw. Bysshe. Harl. MS. 1172, fo. 34ᵇ ; MSS. Ashm. 840, fo. 429, and 858, fo. 212, 213, copy of grant, Bodleian Lib. ; Harl. MS. 6179, fo. 30.

„ Thomas, with Welsh-Bardic verse, Quarterly, not a grant. [Grants] II., 682, Her. Coll.

„ William, of Lemington, co. Glonc., 5 Oct. 1553, by ? Hawley, Clar. Add. MS. 16,940, fo. 206.

„ William, of Hill, Bedf., a Justice of the Peace, s. of Robert, of the same, grant, Feb. 1634-5, by Sir R. St. George, Clar. Q's Coll. Oxf. MS. 36, fo. 127, copy of grant, and also Harl. MSS. 4600, fo. 59, and 1531, fo. 175ᵇ ; compare Harl. MS. 5887, fo. 72ᵇ.

PALSHEYDE, ..., crest ...., Barker's Grants. Harl. MS. 5846, fo. 83 ; Stowe MS. 692, fo. 78.

PALTOCK, Edward, of Kingston-upon-Thames, Surrey, gent., s. of Robert, of the same, gent., arms confirmed and crest granted to him and descendants of his father, 14 Feb., 9 Jac., 1611-12, by Segar. Harl. MSS. 1470, fo. 170, and 1420, fo. 41, as George ; Surrey Arch. Soc., iii., 351 ; Harl. MS. 1359, fo. 65, copy of grant ; Guil. 138, as Edmund.

„ John, of Kingston-upon-Thames, Surrey, s. of Robert, gent., coat confirmed and crest granted 14 Feb., 9 Jac., 1611-12, by Segar. Add. MS. 12,225, fo. 88ᵇ.

PAMPHLIN, Robert, yeoman of the Robes to Q. Eliz. See Add. MS. 5822, fo. 43ᵇ ; Harl. MS. 6140, fo. 51.

PANTON, Henry, of Lewes, Sussex, Doctor of physic, patent 4 July 1615, by Camden. Harl. MSS. 6095, fo. 38ᵇ, and 1422, fo. 40.

PARAMORE, ..., of Shropshire, given ...., 1574, by Cooke. Harl. MS. 1359, fo. 115ᵇ, arg., on a fesse az. three crescents of the field ; Add. MS. 4966, fo. 91ᵇ.

„ Thomas, of Sar, Isle of Thanet, Kent, allowed and assigned 1585, by Cooke. Harl. MS. 1359, fo. 99 ; Guil. 88 ; Add. MS. 4966, fo. 20ᵇ.

„ Thomas, of Canterbury, sometime late maior of that city, s. of John, of Preston, s. of Henry, s. of Thomas, of Paramore Street in Ashe, juxta Sandwich, patent ...., May 1616, by Camden. Harl. MSS. 6095, fo. 34, and 1422, fo. 40ᵇ.

PARBO or PERBO, Edward, of Lincoln's Inn, Esq., s. of Capt. Parbo, who was in the wars at St. Quintin's and at Newhaven, s. and h. of Thomas, s. and h. of James, of Pevor, Cheshire ; patent 14 Nov. 1620, by Segar. Add. MS. 12,225, fo. 92 ; Harl. MS. 6140, fo. 63ᵇ.

PARKE, ..., crest ...., Barker's Grants. Harl. MS. 5846, fo. 85 ; Stowe MS. 692, fo. 78.

„ Thomas, of Wisbech, Isle of Ely, confirmed 1628, by Segar. Add. MS. 12,225, fo. 88ᵇ ; 1618 in Harl. MS. 1422, fo. 13ᵇ ; Guil. 161.

PARKER, Thomas, of the Willows (Walsham), Suff., Austin Parker of Stanton, and to George and Richard their brethren, erm., on a chief vert 3 bucks' heads cabossed or, 18 Feb. 1609-10, by Segar, Gart. Add. MS. 12,225, fo. 89 ; H. 24, Heralds' College ; Guil. 161 ; Harl. MSS. 1085, fo. 25ᵇ, and 6140, fo. 39ᵇ.

„ ...., of Margate, Isle of Thanet, ..., by Borough. Harl. MSS. 1105, fo. 55, and 1441, fo. 59 ; Add. MS. 26,702, fo. 88ᵇ ; Guil. 307.

PARKER, Henry, Fryth Hall, Essex, gent., grant 4 or 21 Feb. 1537-8, by Barker. Q's Coll. Oxf. MS. 38, fo. 37 ; Harl. MS. 1470, fo. 113, copy of grant, Brit. Mus. ; Harl. MS. 5846, fo. 86ᵇ ; Misc. Gen. et Her., 3 S., vol. i., p. 97 ; Guil. 344 ; Grants I., 9 ; Harl. MS. 5887, fo. 2.

,,   John, of Ratton, Sussex, Esq., arms confirmed and crest granted 20 June, 2 and 3 Philip and Mary, 1556, by Sir G. Dethick, Gart. Q's Coll. Oxf. MS. 39, fo. 68, copy of grant ; Harl. MS. 1359, fo. 67ᵇ ; Add. MS. 32,659, fo. 141.

,,   John, of Lambeth (1 s. of Matthew, Archbp. of Canterbury), crest and different coat assigned (from 1559, coat, the archbishop's) 28 May 1572, and by another patent to his brother Mathew, by Cooke, Clar. (MS. Ashm. 844, fo. 7, copy of grant, Bodleian Lib., alteration of arms and gift of new crest to John and Mathew). Her. and Geneal., i., p. 82 ; Misc. Gen. et Her., N. S., i., 408 ; Guil. 307.

,,   John, of London, s. of Roger, ..., by Cooke, Clar. Stowe MS. 670, fo. 47.

,,   John, Sibertswold, Kent, grant 6 May 1588, by Cooke. Harl. MSS. 1359, fo. 104ᵇ, 1422, fo. 89ᵇ, and 1470, fo. 106 ; Guil. 248 ; Stowe MS. 670, fo. 24, 38, different crests, and Add. MSS. 14,297, fo. 22, 36, and 4966, fo. 85.

,,   Matthew, Archbp. of Canterbury, arms 28 Nov. 1559, by Sir G. Dethick, Gart. MS. Ashm. 834, fo. 8, copy of grant, Bodleian Lib. Harl. MSS. 1359, fo. 78ᵇ, and 1441, fo. 62 ; Q's Coll. Oxf. MS. 145, fo. 3 ; Her. and Geneal., i., 81 ; Guil. 307 ; Grants I., 55.

,,   Nicholas, of Finglesham, Kent, s. of William, of the same, out of Norfolk, Patent 10 Sept. or Dec. 1608, by Segar. Add. MS. 12,225, fo. 89 ; Harl. MS. 6140, fo. 36ᵇ.

,,   Thomas, of Gloucester, ... temp. H. VIII., ... Add. MS. 26,702, fo. 51ᵇ.

,,   Thomas,   ⎤ sons of Thomas, s. of Thomas, of Yorksh., brothers ; con-
,,   William and   ⎬ firmed 20 April 1563, by Flower. MS. Ashm. 834, fo. 5,
,,   Martyn,   ⎦ copy of grant, Bodleian Lib. ; Guil. 396.

,,   William alias Malverne, Lord Abbot of Gloucester, 1515, with crest, ... Add. MS. 26,702, fo. 59ᵇ.

,,   William, of London, ..., 1591, by Cooke. Harl. MSS. 1359, fo. 103ᵇ, and 1422, fo. 89ᵇ.

,,   William, of London, draper, s. of Philip, of St. Wem, Cornwall, 10 April 1661, by Walker, Gart. Her. Coll. 39.

PARKES, Margaret, dau. of Thomas, of Bassingbourne, co. Linc., wife or widow of Robert Wythens, Sheriff of London, grant 10 Jan. 1593-4, by W. Dethick, Gart. Q's Coll. Oxf. MS. 36, fo. 45, copy of grant ; Harl. MSS. 1453, fo. 34, and 3526, fo. 143.

,,   Richard, of Willingworth, co. Staff., 4 Feb. 1614-15, by Ric. St. George. Add. MS. 14,295, fo. 62 ; Grants II., fo. 666 ; C. 10 [Visit. Staff., 1614], 95ᵇ ; C. 36 [Visit. Staff., 1663], fo. 52ᵇ ; Harl. MS. 1052, fo. 206ᵇ ; Add. MS. 31,896, fo. 39, copy of grant, Brit. Mus. ; Add. MS. 7025, fo. 202 ; orig. grant, Grants II., 666 ; Le Neve's MS. 502.

PARKHURST, John, Bp. of Norwich, 4 Sept. 1560, by G. Dethick, Gart. (allowed to Alderm. Robert Parkhurst without the crescent, by R. St. George, Clar., and Segar, Gart., ..., 1631). Harl. MS. 5823, fo. 4, see ; Harl. MSS. 1441, fo. 63, and 1359, fo. 79ᵇ ; Q's Col. Oxf. MS. 39, fo. 109, copy of grant, and MS. 145, fo. 3, which see ; Grants I., 51.

,,   Sir William, of London, Kt., and ⎤ 10 Sept. 1624, by R. St. George. Harl.
,,   Robert (mentioned above), some ⎮ MS. 1441, fo. 46 ; Add. MS. 14,295,
       time Alderman of the City of   ⎬ fo. 64ᵇ ; I. 22, 103, and Certif. (not
       London,   ⎦ marked) 48 [Her. Coll.] ; Q's Coll. Oxf.
                                                             MS. 145, fo. 4 ; see Harl. MS. 1422, fo. 12.

PARKHURST, Sir William, Knt., grant. arg., a cross ermines betw. 4 roebucks trippant ppr., Feb. 1631-2, by Segar. Add. MS. 12,225, fo. 89ᵇ; Q's Coll. Oxf. MS. 145, fo. 4; ermine in Harl. MS. 5887, fo. 111ᵇ, an Alderm. of London [? Sir Robert Parkhurst, Kt., Alderm.].

PARKENS, John, of London, ..., 1589, by Cooke. Harl. MS. 1359, fo. 100.

PARKIN, Philip, of Coleman Street, London, 1 May 1570, by G. Dethick, Gart. Harl. MS. 1422, fo. 16; Paskin in Harl. MS. 5887, fo. 33; Add. MS. 5524, fo. 207ᵇ.

PARKINS, Richard, of Mattisfield, Berks [co. Worcester], confirmed 18 Aug. 1559, by Hervey. MS. Ashm. 858, fo. 159, copy of grant, Bodleian Lib.

    ,,   William, of Merston Jabet, co. Warw., 11 July 1682, by Sir Wᵐ Dugdale and Clar. Harl. MS. 6831, fo. 178; Grants III., fo. 153.

PARKINSON, James, als Fetherston, gent., co. Westmorland in the barony [? Deanery] of Kendal, crest 17 May 1566, by Sir G. Dethick, Gart. Cott. MS. Faustina E. 1, 18ᵇ, copy of grant, Brit. Mus.

PARR, Q. Katharine, angmentation . . . ., temp. Hy. VIII., ... ? letters patent; Berry's Armory.

    ,,   John, of London, principal embroder to the Queen, s. of Robert, of Stilley, co. Warw., who was descended from Thurston Parr, of Parwith, co. Lane., Quarterly of 6, grant of coat and crest 20 Sept. 1590, by W. Dethick, Gart. Stowe MS. 676, fo. 80; Q's Coll. Oxf. MS. 37, fo. 118, copy of grant. These three crests or badges, with the armes of Parre, and four other forged coats, by Wm. Dethick, Gart., for which and a forged pedigree he had ten pounds as the said Parre confessed. Entered by R. Brooke, York Herald. Harl. MS. 1453, fo. 32.

PARRINCHEFE or PERRINCHEFE, Richard, D.D., Prebendary of Westminster, ... 1665 ? (Basset on E.P.).

PARRIS, Robert, of Hitchin, Herts, 15 June 1573, by Cooke. Harl. MSS. 1359, fo. 101, and 1422, fo. 94ᵇ; s. of Thomas, of Hitchin, gent., in Stowe MS. 677, fo. 33.

PARRY, Edith, ux. Nicholas Wheeler, "only for her tyme," etc., by Cooke, Clar. Stowe MS. 670, fo. 12ᵇ.

    ,,   Henry, S.T.D., Chaplain to the Queen, s. of Henry, s. of William, of Worme-bridge, co. Hereford (no date), marshalled by W. Camden. Grants II., 588.

    ,,   John, of Morehampton, co. Hereford (1569), s. of Stephen, s. of John, 2 s. of Myles, s. of Henry ap Griffith ap Henry ap Jones, Arg., a fess between three lozenges within a bordure az.

    ,,   William, attaynted for high treason 1578-9, ? crest, by Sir G. Dethick. Harl. MSS. 5847, fo. 46ᵇ, and 1441, fo. 89ᵇ; Add. MS. 26,753, fo. 121,121ᵇ; Q's Coll. Oxf. MS. 145, fo. 47ᵇ; Harl. MS. 5887, fo. 39; the traytor, Harl. MS. 1116, fo. 74ᵇ; see also fo. 74 for another coat.

PARSONS, John, s. of John, late of Steyning, Sussex, 23 April 1661, 13 Ch. II. Bysshe's Grants, fo. 1, Her. Coll.; Harl. MS. 1105, fo. 16ᵇ; Add. MS. 14,293, fo. 13; Guil. 380.

    ,,   Sir John, of Boveny and Langly, Bucks, (s. of John); marr. Elizabeth, d. and h. of Sir John Kederminster of Langley, Master of the Rolls; alteration of old coat and crest, quartering Kederminster and Hampden, by Segar . . . . Add. MS. 12,225, fo. 89ᵇ; Harl. MS. 6140, fo. 79.

PARTRIGE, Ashabell, of London, Esq., one of the chief and principall gouldsmiths to Q. Eliz.; 30 April 1559, by Harvey. Harl. MS. 1172, fo. 45, copy of grant; Add. MS. 14,295, fo. 90; Guil. 235; Grants I., 333; Harl. MS. 5887, fo. 60.

    ,,   Hugh, borne in the North parts, gent., granted at London 5 Feb., 2 Ed. VI., 1548-9, by Gilb. Dethick, Norr. Copy of grant, Q's Coll. Oxf. MSS. 37, fo. 17, and 39, fo. 12, and Harl. MS. 1507, fo. 439, in Brit. Mus. (ex. Mag. Reg., G. Dethick); Harl. MS. 1359, fo. 4; Grants I., 334; Le Neve's MS. 439.

PARTRIDGE, James, s. and h. of Henry, 2nd s. of Robert, younger bro. of Henry, of
Allestree, Kent ; confirmed 4 March 1630-31, by Segar.   Add. MS. 12,225,
fo. 90 ; Guil. 119 ; Harl. MS. 1441, fo. 162.

PARTRYCHE, Miles, of London, grant . . . .   Barker's Grants, Stowe MS. 692,
fo. 78b.

PERTRICHE or PARTRICHE, Nicholas, of London, coat and crest . . . .   Barker's
Grants, Harl. MS. 5846, fo. 82 ; Stowe MS. 692, fo. 77, as Partriche.

PARTRICHE, William, of Syseter, co. Glouc., gent., s. of John, s. of William, s. of
Roger, of Kendal, in co. York, gent. ; confirmed 20 April 1561, by Dalton.
Q's Coll. Oxf. MS. 38, fo. 76, copy of grant ; Harl. MS. 1359, fo. 50b ;
confirmed 1566, by Harvey, in Harl. MS. 1422, fo. 15.

PARVIS, Edward, of Surrey, gent., and to the posterity of his bro. Henry ; arms
confirmed and ratified 3 Dec. 1597, by Wm Dethick, Gart., Camden and
Segar.   Harl. MSS. 1422, fo. 52, 1470, fo. 253, and 1359, fo. 1b ; Guil.
226 ; copy of grant.

   „   Henry, of Surrey, gent., 12 Jan. 1581-2, by Sir Gilbert Dethick, Gart.
Harl. MS. 1441, fo. 80b, and Q's Coll. Oxf. MS. 145, fo. 32.   And again,
3 Dec. 1597, (to him) and his brother Edward, by W. Dethick, Gart.,
Camden and Segar.   Add. MS. 12,225, fo. 90 ;   (copy of grant, Harl. MS.
1359, fo. 1b) ;   Harl. MSS. 1422, fo. 52, and 1470, fo. 253 ; Surrey Arch.
Soc., iii., 352 ; Guil. 226 ; Harl. MSS. 5887, fo. 45b, and 6140, fo. 76b.

PASCHALL, John, of Much Baddowe, Essex, Esq., arms and crest given 1558,
4 and 5 Philip and Mary, by Harvey.   Q's Coll. Oxf. MS. 146, fo. 467 ;
(2 Q. Eliz., 1560, in Add. MS. 16,940, fo. 31b) ; Harl. MS. 1359, fo. 24 ;
Add. MS. 14,295, fo. 51b.

PASKE or PASHE, ..., D.D. : Quarterly, az. and sa., in the 2nd and 3rd a fleur-de-lis
silver . . . . by Segar.   Add. MS. 12,225, fo. 90b.

PASKIN or PARKIN, Philip, of Colman St., London, 1 May 1570, by G. Dethick,
Gart.   Harl. MS. 1422, fo. 16 ; Paskin in Harl. MS. 5887, fo. 33 ; Add.
MS. 5524, fo. 207b.

PASSEMER or PATTISMORE, John, of Passemer Heys and of Sweton, Devon ; crest
. . . .   Barker's Grants, Harl. MS. 5846, fo. 83b ; Stowe MS. 692, fo. 78 ;
Add. MS. 26,702, fo. 74b.

PATENSON, John, of London, confirmed . . . . 1560, 3 Q. Eliz.   (Harvey's Grants),
Add. MS. 16,940, fo. 30 ; Vintner . . . . Harl. MS. 5887, fo. 76.

PATENTEES FOR ALAMODES, RENFORCES AND LUTESTRINGES, 14 March 169½, by
T. St. George, Gart. and Clar.   Harl. MS. 6834, fo. 178 ; Grants IV.,
fo. 112.

PATMER, see BRIGGS.

PATRICKSON, Anthony, of Stokehowe, Cumbld., ... 1592, by Cooke.   Harl. MS.
1359, fo. 106b ; Add. MS. 4966, fo. 93.

PATTISMORE, see PASSEMER.

PAULE, William, D.D., Chaplain in ordy and dean of Lichfield ; 18 Feb. 1660-1, by
Sir E. Walker (died Bp. Oxford).   Her. Coll. 37.

PAULE, Richard, of Norfolk, ... by Cooke.   Harl. MS. 1359, fo. 105 ; called
Henry in Stowe MS. 670, fo. 65.

PAULET, see WINCHESTER.   Grants III., 119b.

PAWLETT, ..., nat. s. of Sir William Morgan of Winchester, by Sir W. Segar,
Gart.   Harl. MS. 1544, fo. 194.

PAYLER, William, of York, J.P. East Riding, confirmed 20 Oct. 1585, by Flower.
MS. Ashm. 834, fo. 59, copy of grant, Bodleian Lib. ; Guil. 274.

PAYNE, Edward, ... 3 Feb. 1646-7, by E. Bysshe, Gart.   Harl. MS. 6140, fo. 18.
Confirmed 1662. see next entry.

   „   Edward, Richard, Robert, Charles and Henry, sons of Edward, late of East
Grinsted, Sussex, 25 Feb. 1661-2, 13 Chas. II.   Bysshe's Grants (? fo. 1),
Her. Coll. ; Harl. MS. 1105, fo. 16b ; Add. MS. 14,293, fo. 14b ; Guil.
393.

PAYNE, Elizabeth, dau. of John, of Denbigh, gent., wid. of Henry Reignolds, "being now of great age," and (REIGNOLDS [als PAYNE], Henry, son of the above); grant June 1588, by W. Dethick, Gart. Stowe MS. 676, fo. 75; Q's Coll. Oxf. MS. 37, fo. 109, copy of grant. *See also* John PAYNE and REIGNOLDS. Grants I., 145.

PAINE, Isaac, Adrian, Nicholas and William, of the city of Norwich, 10 Feb. 1670-71. Harl. MS. 1105, fo. 22. By Bysshe, Clar.

PAYNE, John, of London, par. of St. Clement's without Temple Bar, gent., grant 10 April 1556, by T. Hawley. Add. MS. 16,940, fo. 207ᵇ; Q's Coll. Oxf. MS. 38, fo. 61, copy of grant; Add. MS. 7098, fo. 77ᵇ (fo. 35).

PAYN als GYBON, John, D.C.L., Advocate of the Court of Arches and a master in Chancery; crest 24 Nov. 1570, by Cook. MS. Ashm. 844, fo. 48, copy of grant, Bodleian Lib.; Guil. 273.

PAYNE, John, s. of John, of co. Denbigh, and PAINE, Henry; REIGNOLD, Henry, als PAINE, s. of Elizabeth, full sister to the aforesaid John; crest 19 May 1575, by Sir G. Dethick. Harl. MSS. 1441, fo. 83ᵇ, and 5847, fo. 37; Q's Coll. Oxf. MS. 37, fo. 60, copy of grant, and MS. 145, fo. 38; Stowe MS. 676, fo. 46ᵇ; Grants I., 145, Her. Coll., transcript imperfect.

„ John, of London, ... 1586, by Cooke. Harl. MSS. 1359, fo. 90, and 1422, fo. 64, ? coat same as William, 1586; Add. MS. 4966, fo. 35.

„ John, s. of Richard, of John, of Nantwich, Cheshire, gent., 1 Oct. 1601, by Segar. Harl. MS. 1172, fo. 25, copy of grant.

„ John, of Stoke by Neyland, Suff., s. of John, 23 July, 13 Jac., 1615, by Segar. Add. MS. 12,225, fo. 88; Harl. MS. 1172, fo. 10ᵇ, copy of grant.

„ John, of Hough, co. Line., ... 1661. Bysshe's Grants, Her. Coll., fo. 26?; Harl. MSS. 1105, fo. 18ᵇ, and 6179, fo. 31, one of ye secondaries of ye Exchequer and of ye Inner Temple.

PAINE, Sir Joseph, Knt., Mayor of Norwich; 1 Sept. 1660, by Walker. Add. MSS. 14,293, fo. 88, and 14,294, fo. 26; Harl. MS. 1172, fo. 70, as Payne; Guil. 189, as Payne.

PAYNE, Nicholas, of Wallingford, Berks, Clerk and comptroller of the Queen's Household (2nd s. of John, of Houghton, co. Staff.); confirmed 12 Jan. 1586-7, by Flower. *See* MS. Ashm. 834, fo. 64, 65, copy of grant, Bodleian Lib.; Guil. 121; ? William.

PAINE, Robert, s. and h. of Robert, of Midlow, Hunts, 14 Nov., 2 Jac., 1604, by Segar and Camden. Add. MS. 12,225, fo. 87ᵇ (88 Sir Robt.); Harl. MSS. 6140, fo. 77ᵇ, and 5839, fo. 42ᵇ; Guil. 89.

PAYNE, Thomas, of Dunham, Norfolk, by Cooke, ... Harl. MSS. 1359, fo. 64, and 1422, fo. 64; Add. MS. 4966, fo. 34.

„ William, of London (s. of Philip, of Chepstow, Suff., s. of Philip, s. of John, of Chepstow, s. of Thomas, of Wales); confirmed or granted .... 1586, by Cooke. Guil. 259, same arms as John, 1586.

PAYNELL, Jeffrey, ... gu., two chevrons and a bordure arg., by Camden .... Morgan's Sphere, 118.

PAYNTER, *see* CAMBORNE.

„ Humphrey, one of H.M.'s sergeant chirurgeons in ordinary (royalist) at Oxford, 21 Feb. 1645-6, by Walker. Add. MS. 11,294, fo. 31; Her. Coll., fo. 26. Coat afterwards altered.

„ John, of Sprowle, Norfolk, gent., s. of Robert, gen., 4 July 1609, by Segar. Add. MS. 12,225, fo. 90ᵇ; Jan. in Guil. 291.

PAYNTER STAYNERS, Company of, grant 3 Feb. 1484-5, 2 R. III., by Sir T. Holme, Clar., confirmed 11 Oct. 1530, 22 H. VIII., by Benolt. Harl. MS. 1470, fo. 190; MS. Ashm. 858, fo. 40, copy of grant, Bodleian Lib., and 834, p. 63; Her. and Geneal., i., 121.

PAYNTON, John, town clerk of city of Oxford, 8 July 1679, by W. Dugdale, Gart., and H. St. George, Norr. Stowe MS. 714, fo. 118ᵇ; Grants III., 93; Guil. 372.

c c

PAYTON, Anne, dau. of Christopher Payton and wife of Sir Rich. Gray, Sec. of Ireland, a patent, July 1612, by Camden. Stowe MS. 706, fo. 50 ; Harl. MSS. 1422, fo. 37ᵇ, and 6095, fo. 23ᵇ.

PEACHEY, William, of London, mercht., s. of Edward, of Petworth, Sussex, 20 Feb. 1663-4, by Sir E. Bysshe, Clar. Bysshe's Grants, 40.

PEYCOCK, ..., of Waterford in Ireland, crest . . . ., Barker's Grants. Harl. MS. 5846, fo. 84ᵇ ; Stowe MS. 692, fo. 78.

PEACOCK, ..., Redburne, co. Hereford, 2 May 1598, by W. Dethick, Gart., Camden and Segar. Harl. MS. 1422, fo. 15.

„ John, of Cowley, Berks, 27 June 1640, by Borough. Harl. MSS. 1105, fo. 57, and 1441, fo. 58ᵇ ; Add. MS. 26,702, fo. 93 ; Guil. 367.

„ Simon, of Burne Hall, co. Durham, 10 Nov. 1688, by T. St. George, Gart., and J. Dugald [Dugdale], Norr. Stowe MS. 714, fo. 158 ; Grants IV., 27 ; Guil. 233.

PEAK, Richard, of Garboldisham, Norfolk, 1624, by R. St. George, Norroy. Harl. MS. 1085, fo. 51ᵇ.

PEKE, Edward, Sandwich, Kent, arms as next (? crest differs), by Cooke. Stowe MSS. 670, fo. 8ᵇ, and 618, fo. 65ᵇ.

„ Edward, of Holdchurch Gate in Kent, 2 March 1584-5, by Cooke. Harl. MS. 1359, fo. 101.

PEAKE, Richard, of London, 2nd s. of Francis, 3rd s. of William, late of Lutterworth, s. and h. of John, etc., at London, 13 Sept. 1598, by W. Dethick, Gart., and Camden (wings in crest ermine). Harl. MS. 1359, fo. 36ᵃ.

„ Robert, of Walton, co. Linc., crest confirmed . . . . 1562 (Harvey's Grants). Add. MS. 16,940, fo. 38.

„ ⎧ Thomas, of Grays Inn, gent., 1st s. of Francis, 3rd s. of William, of Lutterworth, s. and h. of John, of Tyrlington, commonly called Turlington, and

„ ⎩ Richard, of co. Leic., of London, gent., 13 Dec. 1598, by W. Dethick, Gart., and Camden (different crests), wings in crest arg. (13 Dec. in) Add. MS. 14,295, fo. 115ᵇ, 116. Harl. MS. 1359, fo. 36ᵃ.

„ Thomas, of London, merchant tayler, ..., by Segar. Add. MS. 12,225, fo. 91.

PEAK, Sir William, Knt., Alderm. of the city of London (s. of Boniface Peak of Achurch, Northants), 20 July 1664, by consent of Sir Robert Peake of the city of London, governor of Basing, and Col. in the service of the King, by Walker. Add. MSS. 14,293, fo. 39, and 14,294, fo. 10 ; Harl. MS. 1172, fo. 54 (see Guil. 187), copy of grant.

PEARD, ..., of Devonshire, ..., May 1606, by Camden. Harl. MS. 6095, fo. 5ᵇ ; of Barnstaple, Harl. MS. 1422, fo. 19.

PEARSE, Thomas, of Court, par. of Bigby, or Bigbury, Devon, granted 12 Aug. 1641, arg., two bars sa. and 6 estoiles gu., 3, 2, 1, by Borough. Peirse, 1644, in Harl. MS. 1105, fo. 57ᵇ ; Cains Coll. Camb. MS. 551, copy of grant ; Guil. 89.

PECK, John, of Winchelsea, Sussex, ..., by Cooke. Add. MS. 4964, fo. 85 ; Harl. MS. 1359, fo. 106ᵇ.

„ Thomas, late mayor and head Alderm. of Norwich, and one of the Justices of the peace, grant, by (by Gart.) Sir G. Dethick. Stowe MS. 676, fo. 35ᵇ ; Q's Coll. Oxf. MS. 36, fo. 109, copy of grant.

„ William, of Wood Pelling, Norfolk, gent., attestation of arms and crest by Segar, ... Add. MS. 12,225, fo. 92ᵇ ; Stowe MS. 677, fo. 9 "pcured p me R. Mundy."

PECKHAM, Peirs, of the city of London, confirmed by Rogier Richmont als Clarencieux, 30 June 1494, 9 H. VII. Q's Coll. Oxf. MS. 38, fo. 15, copy of grant ; Harl. MS. 1359, fo. 7 ; Grants II., 535.

PEDLEY, James, of Abbotsley, Hunts, esq., High Sheriff, by Segar, ... Add. MS. 12,225, fo. 91ᵇ ; Harl. MS. 6140, fo. 65ᵇ ; his dau. married Bigg, "procured by me, R. Mundy"; Stowe MS. 677, fo. 7ᵇ; Add. MS. 12,474, fo. 107ᵇ.

PEIRCE, Sir Edmond, Knt., Doctor of Law, Royalist, taken prisoner 1640, served in H.M. life guards, etc., alteration of coat and augmentation 20 May 1661, by Sir E. Walker, Gart.   Harl. MS. 1441, fo. 54, copy of grant, Brit. Mus., and *see* Edward Percy.

Harl. MS. 1441, fo. 54 [slip inserted with abstract of Patent to ? Sir Edward Percie 20 March 1642, ? to Sir Edmund Pierce in 1661].

Whereas Sir Edward Percie, Knt., Doctor of Law, hath from the beginning of the unnatural divisions and rebellion in his Majesties Kingdoms and dominions with great zeale and affections applied himself to his Majesties just cause and interest, and in the year one thousand six hundred forty two was by his Majestie from Yorke upon speciall trust and confidence imployed into the County of Kent, where, falling into the hands of rebells upon the account of his loyalty, he was for divers weeks detained prisoner by them from which after he had with much difficulty obtained his liberty, the war being then begun and his Majestye settled in the Citty of Oxford, he sometime served in his Majesty's Life Guards and shortly after he was made Colonell of a Regiment of Horse, wherewith he faithfully and actively served his Majestie at severall Battles fought with Rebells at Newbery, Cheriton, Copredy Bridge, Lostwithiel, and taking of the Cittys, Townes and fortes of Winchester, Bristol, Gloucester, Leicester, Wardour Castle, Arundel Castle, Lipiat Castle and Woodhouse and divers other places, and in those services received several wounds, and whereas also for much of the said time hee the said Sir Edward Percie was by his Majesties especiall Commission constituted *judge Marshal and Advocate General* of his Majesties Royall arms whereby and in Consideration of his service performed therein and of his Constancy, Courage and fidelity, his Majesty hath not only dignified him with the Order and degree of Knighthood, but hath esteemed him worthy of some peculiar marks and addition of armes to be borne by him and conveyed to posterity as a testimony of his loyalty and service.

Arms : Or, upon a pile az. an unicorn rampant of the first; altered to or, an unicorn rampant az.; and for augmentation, upon a canton az. a fleur-de-lis or.

Grant of crest : A unicorn's head erased az., attired and gorged with a ducal crown or.   Granted by Edward Walker, Gart., 20 Aug. 1661. A Master in Chancery; Knighted at Greenwich 10 July 1645. (Knights, 1558—1752, Add. 32,102 [fo. 133 has 10 July 1645, to Sir Edmund Peerce of Greenwich, LL.D., Mʳ of Chancery].)

PEERSE, Edmund, of Alveston, co. Warwick, 10 June or July 1605, by Camden. Harl. MSS. 1422, fo. 19, and 6095, fo. 4ᵇ; Guil. 360; Le Neve's MSS. 384 and 280.

PEYRSE, John, of Norwold, Norfolk, confirmed 20 Aug. 1560, 2 Q. E. (Harvey's Grants).   Add. MS. 16,940, fo. 17ᵇ; Harl. MS. 2198, fo. 6.

PEIRSE, John, of East Greenwich, } both servers in ordinary of H.M.'s Chamber,
Kent, and brother   } sons of Henry, of Bedale, s. of Marmaduke,
„   Richard,   } s. of Thos., s. of Thos. [? Petter Peirce of Bedall], confirmed 19 Dec. 1634, by R. St. George, Clar.   Surtees Soc., XLI., xlix., copy of grant, Brit. Mus.

PEERS, John, Essex (*see* John Piers), ..., by Cooke.   Stowe MS. 670, fo. 74; Add. MS. 4966, fo. 67.

„   Robert, of Westdowne, Kent, crest . . . ., 1588, by Cooke.   Harl. MSS. 1359, fo. 86, 1422, fo. 91ᵇ, and 1141, fo. 2; Add. MS. 4966, fo. 91ᵇ; Stowe MS. 703, fo. 89.

PEIRS, Sir Thomas, of Westfield, Kent, a Knight of Nova Scotia, Vert, two sceptres in saltire or; crest, a jamb holding 2 sceptres as in the arms, by

Borough.   Harl. MS. 1105, fo. 55[b], and Caius Coll. Camb. MS. 551 ; Add. MS. 26,702, fo. 90.

PEERSON (see also PIERSON), ... patent, ..., April 1616, by Camden, per fesse embattled az. and gu., 3 suns in splendour gold, and another, or confirmation June 1616, with quarterly coat, 3 and 4, arg. a talbot statant sa., collared or.   Harl. MS. 6095, fo. 33[b], 34 (June in Harl. MS. 1422, fo. 40[b], 111).

PEIRSON, D[r] John, of Cambridge (after Bp. of Chester), ..., 1666.   Bysshe's Grants, fo. 17, Her. Coll. ; Harl. MS. 1105, fo. 20.

PEISLEY, Capt. William, of Knocknemeas, Kings Co., testified 24 Nov. 1638, by Albon Leverett, Athlone Officer of Arms of Ireland.   Stowe MS. 677, fo. 14[b].

PELEGRINI, John Dominicke, born in Nice tr'er visitour and president of the messengers of the Duke of Savoy, Letters patent at Westminster, augmentation 30 June 1629.   MS. Ashm. 858, fo. 83-4, copy of grant, Bodleian Lib.

PELL, ..., of Dymbleby, co. Linc., a scotion delivered on paper by R. Lee, Clar., 19 Oct. 1594.   Harl. MS. 1069, fo. 9[b] ; Add. MS. 14,295, fo. 22.

PELLE, Geoffrey, of Kyng's Lynn, Norfolk, by Camden, Clar.   Le Neve's MS. 354.

PENDLETON, Francis, of Norwich, ...   1612, by Camden, Clar.   Le Neve's MS. 353.

PENDRETH, Miles, of Northbourne, Kent, ... 1586, by Cooke.   Harl. MSS. 1359, fo. 89[b], and 1422, fo. 51[b] ; Add. MS. 4966, fo. 34[b].

PENNANT, Peires, one of the four Gent[n] Ushers to Q. Eliz., s. of Hugh ; arms confirmed and crest given, 2 May 1580, to him and the issue of Hugh, his father : Quarterly of 4, by Cooke.   Harl. MSS. 1359, fo. 120, and 1422, fo. 118[b] ; Add. MS. 14,295, fo. 44[b] ; Harl. MS. 1972, fo. 30, copy of grant in Brit. Mus., Quarterly : 1 Pennant, (2) Yswitan Wyddell (which he bears as his paternal coat, 1667), 3 Philip Phithean and (4) Griffith Lloyd.

PENINGE, Antony, of Keterberye and Ipswich, Suff., gent., s. of Arthur, late of Keterberye, dec[d], etc. ; grant 1 June 1594, by W. Dethick, Gart.   Stowe MS. 676, fo. 108[b] ; Harl. MS. 1359, fo. 20[b] ; Q's Coll. Oxf. MS. 36, fo. 38, copy of grant ; Harl. MSS. 1560, fo. 263, and 1422, fo. 51 ; Add. MS. 14,295, fo. 14[b].

PENYFATHER, William, of London, by Segar . . . . (and ? Camden).   Same coat assigned as by Camden in Burke's Armory ? (which or both ?) ; Add. MS. 12,225, fo. 91.

PENEYFATHER, William, younger son of John, of Barton under Needwood, co. Staff., ... 1603, confirmed by ? Segar : parti per fess or and gu., a bend erm., a mullet for diff. ; crest, a lion sejant ar. sustaining an oval shield charged per fess or and gu., a bend erm., a mullet on his shoulder for diff. gu.   Berry's Armory.

PENNE or PENNY, Thomas, of London, Doctor of physic, 1 July 1574, 16 Q. Eliz., by Cooke.   Harl. MSS. 1359, fo. 121[b], and 5887, fo. 64 ;   Le Neve's MS. 253.

PENNE, see LUCAS, Margaret.

PENNYMAN, James, of Ormesby in Cleveland, Yorks, s. and h. of William, of Mourton in the said co., dec[d], s. of Robert ; arms confirmed and crest granted 10 May 1599, by Segar.   Add. MS. 12,225, fo. 91[b] ; Surtees Soc., XLI., p. xliv. ; Guil. 339 ; Grants I., 360.

PENPONT, Richard, of Trewodo, Cornwall, ...   Add. MS. 14,315, fo. 45.

PENRUDDOCK, George, of Penruddock, Cumberland, by C. Barker, Gart., 20 May 1548.   Visit. Eng. and Wales, ii., p. 46, facsimile of grant in colours.

PENSAY, Edward, 1st s. of John, s. of Percival, sometime of Preston in Amunderness, ... by Segar.   Add. MS. 12,225, fo. 92[b].

PENSON, William, Lanc. Herald, E. M.'s Warrant, 14 Feb. 1614.   Harl. MS. 1107, art. 27, fo. 31.

PENTECOST als ROWLAND, Thomas, Abbot of Abingdon, Berks. Add. MS. 26,702, fo. 69.

PENTON, Henry, Counsellor-at-law and a bencher of Lincoln's Inn, and his brothers
  ,, Godson, late Mayor of Winchester, } 4 Aug. 1698, by T. St. George, Gart.
  ,, Stephen, rector of Wathe, Yorks.   }   Add. MS. 14,831, fo. 26 ; Grants IV., 275.

PENYSTON, Thomas, lord of Hawrugge, Bucks., esq., crest granted 8 July or Aug. 1564, by Harvey : a pedigree by T. Holme, Clar. ; an achievement of 25 coats and 3 crests confirmed 8 Feb. 1573-4, by Cooke, and 13 other coats painted. Q's Coll. Oxf. MS. 146, fo. 37, copy of confirmation ; Q's Coll. Oxf. MS. 38, fo. 90 ; Harl. MSS. 1470, fo. 156, and 1507, fo. 106, copy of grant, Brit. Mus. ; Harl. MS. 1422, fo. 4 ; Genealogist, vol. i., p. 1 ; Harl. MSS. 5887, fo. 49, and 6140, fo. 55, for 36 Quarterings ; Harl. MS. 1116, fo. 36.

PEPYS, Thomas, of South Creyke, Norfolk, gift . . . . 1563. (Harvey's Grants), Add. MS. 16,940, fo. 20ᵇ.

PERBO, see PARBO.

PERCIE, Sir Edward, Knt., D.C.L., rightly Edmond Peirce. See PEIRCE.

PERCY, Thomas, of Islington, Middx., 10 Aug. 1546, by ? Hawley. Add. MS. 16,940, fo. 201 ; Harl. MS. 5887, fo. 28ᵇ.

PERNE, Andrew, Dean of Ely and Master of Sᵗ Peter's Coll., Camb. ; 15 June 1574, by Sir G. Dethick, Gart. Harl. MSS. 5823, fo. 35, and 1441, fo. 140 ; Stowe MS. 676, fo. 43ᵇ ; Q's Coll. Oxf. MS. 37, fo. 55, copy of grant (MS. 145, fo. 35) ; Grants I., 31 ; Stowe MSS. 670, fo. 71ᵇ, and 703, fo. 38 ; Add. MS. 4966, fo. 94.

  ,, Andrew, D.D., Dean of Ely ; crest . . . . 1572, by Cooke, Clar. Stowe MS. 670, fo. 71ᵇ.

PERRENCHEPE, Richard, D.D., preb. of Westminster, ... 1665, by Bysshe. Harl. MS. 1105, fo. 12ᵇ.

PERROTT, Abraham, out of North Wales, 10 Sept. 1646, by Ryley, Norr. : an escutcheon. Harl. MS. 6179, fo. 57.

PARRAT (or PERROTT), George, lawfully descended of Owen, etc., out of Pembroke-shire, 16 May 1549, by Sir G. Dethick. Harl. MS. 1441, fo. 79ᵇ ; Q's Coll. Oxf. MS. 145, fo. 30ᵇ, see ; copy Brit. Mus., Harl. MS. 6832, fo. 341 ; Misc. Gen. et Her., 3rd S., iii., p. 1.

PERROTT, James, of Amersham, Bucks, sometime of Norleigh Fowler, Oxon . . . . . . Dec. 1664, by Sir E. Bysshe, Clar. Bysshe's Grants, fo. . . . . Her. Coll. ; Add. MS. 14,293, fo. 9ᵇ ; Harl. MS. 1105, fo. 17ᵇ.

PERSSE, Thomas, of Islington, grant of a canton of his own arms by Thomas Percy, s. and h. of Sir Thomas Percy, 12 April 1549, 3 Ed. VI. MS. Ashm. 862, fo. 181, copy of grant, Bodleian Lib.

PERT, ..., descended out of ye North : Arg., on a bend gu. three lozenges or, by Segar, Somerset Herald. Add. MS. 12,225, fo. 92.

  ,, Thomas, Dʳ . . . . Add. MS. 26,702, fo. 66ᵇ. Quarterly : arg. and gu., in each quarter a lion rampant reguardant or, on a chief dancettée arg. three pellets.

PESHALE, Richard, s. of Humfrey, confirmed die mercurii prox. post festum Paschae, 14 H. VI., 1436, by Joan, late wife of William Lee of Knightley. Camden's Remains, 220 (1st Edit.) ; Guil. Introd., p. 8.

PETCHILL, Thomas, of Normanton, nʳ Grantham, co. Linc., and
  ,, John, of the Mid. Temple . . . . 1661. Bysshe's Grants, fo. 11, Her. Coll. ; Harl. MS. 1105, fo. 18ᵇ.

PETER, Lord, of Germany [Dominus Petrus ex partibus Germaniæ oriundus, Queen's Coll. Oxf. MS.], 5 Dec. 1553, by Sir G. Dethick, Gart. Stowe MS. 676, fo. 23ᵇ, and as Dʳ Petrus, Harl. MS. 1359, fo. 62, and copies of grant in Latin in Q's Coll. Oxf. MSS. 37, fo. 33, and 39, fo. 56 ; Grants I., 41.

PETER, Robert, of Devonshire, Auditor to H.M. Exchequer, 3rd s. of John, of the same shire and brother to Rt. Hon. Sir William Peter, Knt. and Chancellor of the Order of the Garter; confirmed 1 Jan. 1573-4, by Sir G. Dethick. Harl. MS. 1441, fo. 80 ; Q's Coll. Oxf. MS. 145, fo. 31, has June ; 1 June 1573 in R. C. Families, by J. J. Howard, i., 57.

PETRE, Sir William, of Ingarston, Essex, Knt., Secretary [of State] . . . . coat and crest. Barker's Grants, 1526—49, Harl. MS. 5846, fo. 85ᵇ ; Stowe MS. 692, fo. 78ᵇ.

PETERMAN, Rose, one of the servers or sewers of H.M. Chamber ; 27 June 1681, by Sir W. Dugdale, Gart., and H. St. George, Clar. Stowe MS. 714, fo. 156 ; Grants III., 135.

PETERSON, William, of Lewes, Sussex, gift . . . . 1565. (Harvey's Grants), Add. MS. 16,940, fo. 55ᵇ, of London, haberdasher ; Harl. MSS. 5887, fo. 61, and 6140, fo. 42ᵇ.

PETIT, ..., of Hexstall, Staff., ... 1583 : arg., a chev. gu. betw. three bugle horns sa. stringed of the second ; crest, a demi-wolf salient. Berry.

PETRE, see PETER.

PETRUS, see PETER above.

PETRUS, ... 5 Dec., 1 Q. Mary, 1553, by G. Dethick. Harl. MS. 1359, fo. 62 ; confirmed, Q's Coll. Oxf. MSS. 37, fo. 33, and 39, fo. 56, in Latin ; Grants I., 41 ; Stowe MS. 676, fo. 23ᵇ, as Lord Peter.

PETT, John, London, gent., 9 Sept. 1519, by Wriothesley, Gart., and Benolte, Clar. Harl. MS. 1430, fo. 94ᵇ.

PETTIE, ... crest . . . . Barker's Grants, Harl. MS. 5846, fo. 83 ; Stowe MS. 692, fo. 78.

PETTUS, Thomas, of Norwich, Alderman and Maior, ... 1614, by Camden, Clar. Le Neve's MS. 352.

PETTY, Robert, of Otford, Kent, s. of George and nephew of Robert Petty of Otford ; 12 April 1644, by Sir H. St. George, Gart. Stowe MS. 714, fo. 185.

PETTYWARD, John, of London, Alderm., mercht. (s. of Roger, s. of John, of St. Edmundsbury, Suff.) ; 16 July 1660, by Sir E. Walker, Gart. Add. MSS. 14,293, fo. 90, and 14,294, fo. 26ᵇ ; Harl. MS. 1172, fo. 71 ; Stowe MS. 677, fo. 65 ; Guil. 292 ; Harl. MSS. 1466, fo. 24ᵇ, and 1441, fo. 151ᵇ.

PETULA, Marcus Antonius, a Venetian, augmentation 1 May 1551, by Sir G. Dethick, Gart. Q's Coll. Oxf. MS. 39, fo. 35, copy of grant ; Grants I., 105.

PETYT, William, of the Inner Temple, and his brother } 29 May 1690, by T. St.
  „   Sylvester, of Barnard's Inn, gent.,   } George, Gart. and Clar.
                                                        Add. MS. 14,830, fo. 73 ;
                                                        Grants IV., 59.

PEWTERERS', Company of, London, 13 Aug. 1451, 29 Hen. VI., by (R. Leigh), Clar. Cott. MS. Faustina E. 1, 26, copy of grant, Brit. Mus. A new grant 26 May, 1533, by T. Benolte, Clar. History of the Pewterers' Company, by C. Welch.

PEYTON, Henry, of the Examiners' Office (Court of Chancery) ; 24 July 1641, by Borough. Harl. MS. 1105, fo. 57ᵇ ; Caius Coll. Camb. MSS. 551 and 542, copy of grant ; Guil. 101. Edward Peyton, knt. and bart., testified to his kinship with this Henry, he to bear coat with some meet distinction to avoid the multiplicity of difference, 20 Nov. 1633 : a bordure erm. added to the paternal coat, and a collar erm. added to the crest p certif. of Arthur Cresheld, 30 Nov. 1638.

PHILLIPS, ... of London, apothecary, by Segar. No arms given. Add. MS. 12,225, fo. 93. See PHILLIPS, John, below.

  „   Edmund, of London, descended out of Dorsetsh. ; 10 Dec. 1633. Guil. 215, by Segar ; Add. MS. 12,225, fo. 93 ; C. 24 [Visit. of London, 1634], fo. 454, Her. Coll.

PHILLIPS, Fabian, late of Yarpole and Leominster, co. Hereford, one of the Council
of Wales, s. of Robert Phillipps, s. of Thomas, s. of John, of Yorks, " that
valiant gentleman " ; confirmed 14 June 1579, by Sir G. Dethick, Gart.
Q's Coll. Oxf. MS. 37, fo. 69, copy of confirmation (MS. 115, fo. 48) ;
Stowe MS. 676, fo. 51ᵇ ; Harl. MS. 1441, fo. 90 ; Le Neve's MS. 453.

PHILLIPPE, James, of Brignell, Yorks, a patent of crest 26 May 1560 (2 Eliz.), by
Dalton. Harl. MS. 1359, fo. 46.

PHILIPPES, James, of Brignal, Yorks, ... 1561, by Flower. Harl. MS. 1422,
fo. 46 ; Add. MS. 14,295, fo. 73.

PHILLIPPS, John, of London, gent., ... by ? Sir G. Dethick, Gart. Harl. MS.
5823, fo. 55ᵇ ; (? Add. MS. 12,225, fo. 93).

PHILIP, Morgan, als WOLF, of London, from Wales, 1 March 1551-2, by ? Hawley.
Add. MS. 16,940, fo. 205.

PHILIPS, Robert, of Wispington, co. Linc., confirmed 28 June 1665, by Sir E.
Walker, Gart. Her. Coll., fo. 62.

PHILLIPPS, Thomas, Esq., Capt. of 100 foot, served in France 10 years, and also in
Ireland, 15 Oct. 1600, by D. Molineux, [Ulster] King of Arms. Stowe
MS. 703, fo. 60ᵇ ; (see Harl. MS. 1441, fo. 104ᵇ), copy of grant.

PHILLIPS, Thomas, of Netley, Salop, ... by Borough, Gart. Harl. MS. 1105,
fo. 55 ; Add. MS. 26,702, fo. 89.

PHILIPPES, William, of London, esq., s. of John, of London, s. of Robert, of
Bridgnorth, Salop, s. of Hugh, of co. Denbigh, 15 Dec. 1574, by Ro. Cooke,
Clar. Grants I., 199 ; Harl. MS. 1422, fo. 46.

PHILLIPPS, William, of Tamworth, co. Warwick, and of Beeley, co. Worc., ... by
Cooke. Harl. MSS. 1359, fo. 115, and 1422, fo. 46 ; Add. MS. 4966, fo. 84ᵇ.

PHILLIPSON, Rowland, als THERWALL, of Calgarth, Westmld., and
  „   Miles, als THERWALL, of Thwaterden Hall, sons of Christʳ, s. of Robert, s. of
Rowland, etc. ; coat confirmed and crest granted 18 May 1581, by Cooke.
Misc. Gen. et Her., 2nd S., vol. iv., p. 193, facsimile ; copy of grant,
Brit. Mus.

PHILPOT, Nicholas, of Hereford, s. of Nicholas, s. of Nicholas, of Poston and
Vowchurch, co. Hereford, assignment of colours 31 Dec. 1683, by Sir Hy.
St. George, Clar. Harl. MS. 6834, fo. 178 ; Grants III., 227.

  „   John, of London, Alderm., temp. R. II. Berry.

PHIPPES, ..., London, 22 July 1656 : arg., on a pile rising from the dexter chief
to the sinister base sa. a lion rampant of the first ; crest. Berry.

FFYSYCIONS OF LONDON, The Company and Science of, grant. Barker's Grants,
Stowe MS. 692, fo. 42.

PICKAS, James, of Sussex, groom of the Chamber to Ed. VI., Queens Mary and
Eliz. ; arms and crest under the hand of R. Cooke, Clar., but without seale,
date or name. Q's Coll. Oxf. MS. 146, fo. 42 ; Harl. MS. 1359, fo. 40 ;
Add. MS. 14,295, fo. 48ᵇ.

PICKERING, Hester, sole h. of William, of Oswaldkirk, Knt., wife of Edward
Wotton of Kent, 18 March 1580-81, on an escocheon of pretence, by Cooke.
MS. Ashm. 844, fo. 41, copy of grant, Bodleian Lib.

  „   Robert, of Walford, Cheshire, testified . . . . by Segar. Add. MS. 12,225,
fo. 93ᵇ ; Harl. MS. 1562, fo. 90 ; altered at the Visitation of Sussex, 1634,
Harl. MS. 6140, fo. 78ᵇ.

  „   William, of London, gent., s. of William, of Malpas, Cheshire, crest 28 Jan.,
35 Q. Eliz., 1592-3, by Edward Knight, Norr. Add. MS. 14,293, fo. 18 ;
Misc. Gen. et Her., 3rd S., vol. ii., p. 177.

PICTON, John, of Cheshire, gent., confirmed . . . . 1486, by Thos. (Holme), Clar.
Harl. MSS. 1359, fo. 51ᵇ, and 1470, fo. 236, copy of grant, Brit. Mus.

PIDGEON, Elizabeth (d. and eventual sole h. of Thomas Pidgeon, mayor and aldermi.
of Coventry), 2nd wife Sir John Dugdale, Norroy, 1 Jan. 1684, by Sir Wᵐ
Dugdale and Clar. Harl. MS. 6834, fo. 178 ; Grants III., fo. 233 ;
(Hamper's Life of Dugdale, 519).

PIERPONT, Robert, Visct. Newark and Baron Pierpont of Holme Pierpont in Notts, confirmation of arms and crest, grant of supporters, ... 1623, by Segar. Add. MS. 12,225, fo. 94.

PIERS, John, of Essex, ... sa., a chevron ermine betw. three lions' heads erased arg., a chief or ; crest, a griffin's head and neck engrailed sa., bezantée and ducally gorged or. Peers in Stowe MS. 670, fo. 74, the chevron arg., but no crest ; Harl. MS. 1105, fo. 42ᵇ, ? by Bysshe.

PIERCE, Michael, and } sons of Thomas, of Great Missenden, Bucks, 3 June 1632,
  „ Edmond, } by Sir R. St. George. Add. MS. 14,295, fo. 69ᵇ.

PIERSON (Richard), of London, draper, and } arg., two chevronels az. betw. three
  „ Thomas, of Olney, Bucks, } leaves erect vert, by Segar. Add.
MS. 12,225, fo. 94, and Burke.

  „ Thomas, of Westminster, ... 1577, by Cooke : arg., two chevronels sa., on a canton of the last an eagle displayed of the field ; crest, out of a ducal coronet or an ostrich's head betw. two ostrich feathers arg. Harl. MSS. 1359, fo. 106, and 1422, fo. 91ᵇ ; Add. MS. 4966, fo. 92ᵇ.

  „ Thomas (of the receipts a teller of H.M.'s Exchequer and Usher of the Star Chamber), s. of Nicholas, s. of Robt. and born on the borders of co. Lanc. and Cumberld., confirmed 21 Oct. 1577, by Flower: arg., two chevronels sa., betw. three oak leaves erect ppr. Guil. 116 ; MS. Ashm. 844, fo. 70*, copy of grant, Bodleian Lib.

  „ Thomas, of the city of York, ... 1612, by R. St. George, Norr. : az., three suns in pale or betw. two palets wavy erminois ; crest, a sun ppr. rising out of a cloud. Stowe MS. 706, fo. 14 ; Harl. MS. 6179, fo. 13ᵇ.

PIGOT, Gervase, of Thrumpton, Notts, 1 July 1664, by W. Dugdale, Norr. (Her. Coll.) ; Harl. MS. 1105, fo. 60, 6 Dec. 1662.

PIKE, Henry, see PEKE [? PEKE (PEAK), Edward].

PYLBOROUGHE, ... crest . . . . Barker's Grants, Harl. MS. 5846, fo. 83ᵇ ; Stowe MS. 692, fo. 78.

PILKINGTON, James, Bp. of Durham, confirmation of arms 10 Feb. 1560-61, 3 Q. Eliz., by Sir Gilb. Dethick, Gart. Q's Coll. Oxf. MS. 145, fo. 5 ; Add. MS. 14,295, fo. 24 ; Harl. MS. 1359, fo. 20 ; confirmed 1 Aug. 1575, by Flower, MS. Ashm. 834, fo. 12, copy of grant, Bodleian Lib. ; Guil. 54 ; Pilkington Family, p. 57.

PINDAR, Reginald, see PYNDAR.

PINDER, Richard, of the Isle of Axholme, co. Linc., gent., s. of William, s. of Robert, s. of John, of the same, 12 April 1558, by Sir G. Dethick. Harl. MSS. 1441, fo. 85ᵇ, and 5847, fo. 40 ; Q's Coll. Oxf. MS. 145, fo. 41 ; Stowe MS. 670, fo. 74ᵇ ; (Harl. MS. 1476, fo. 127) ; [Harl. MS. 1476, fo. 127.—This Coat, azure, a chevron between three lions' heads erased ermin, crowned or. Creast, a lyons head erased ermin, crowned or. This Coat is confirmed by Clarencieux to one Pinder in Cheapside. See under Thomas PYNNER.]

PINFOULD, Richard, of Dunstable, Beds, gent., arms and crest devised, ordained and assigned by mee, Richmont als Clar., at London, 8 Oct. 1501, 7 H. VII. Harl. MS. 1359, fo. 22 ; 18ᵗʰ Oct. in Add. MS. 14,295, fo. 46 ; copy of grant, Harl. MS. 1172, fo. 3.

PINMAKERS, Company of, London, incorporated 28 April, 3 Jac. ; arms and crest 19 Aug. 1606, by Camden. Stowe MS. 677, fo. 23.

PINNER, Francis, of Bury St. Edmund's, Suff., 2 May 1612, by Camden. Harl. MSS. 1422, fo. 41, and 1172, fo. 8ᵇ, copy of grant ; Caius Coll. Camb. MS. 551, fo. 27ᵇ ; Morgan's Sphere, 117.

PYNNER (Thomas), the Queen's Master Cook, whose father was a pinmaker in Northampton, 8 June 1574, by Cooke. Harl. MS. 1422, fo. 95ᵇ ; Stowe MS. 678, fo. 71ᵇ ; confirmation of altered crest 12 Aug. 1577, Thomas Pynner, esq., clerk of the kitchen to the Queen, by G. Dethick, Harl. MS. 1441, fo. 87ᵇ ; Q's Coll. Oxf. MS. 145, fo. 44ᵇ ; ? to whom Cooke confirmed

the arms of Ric. Pyndar, as above, Harl. MS. 1476, fo. 127 [see Richard
PINDER] ; Add. MS. 4966, fo. 67ᵇ bis.

PISING, Hugh, with John and Richard, his brethren . . . . 1591, by Cook. Harl.
MS. 1422, fo. 23ᵇ.

PITCHER, Francis, a Piedmontese, arms confirmed . . . . March, 2 and 3 Philip and
Mary, ... 1555-6, by Sir G. Dethick, Gart. Q's Coll. Oxf. MS. 39,
fo. 62, copy of grant ; Harl. MS. 1359, fo. 61 ; Grants I., 79.

PITFELD (Charles, of Hoxton, Middx.), by Norgate, Windsor Herald. Stowe MS.
703, fo. 71.

PITT, William, of Stapleton, Dorset, 13 Aug. 1604, by Camden. Harl. MSS. 1422,
fo. 18, 5839, fo. 3ᵇ, 2275, fo. 91ᵇ, and 1115, fo. 9ᵇ ; Morgan's Sphere, 107.

PITTMAN, Geoffrey, of Woodbridge, Suff., at the time High Sheriff, coat confirmed
and crest granted by Segar . . . . Add. MS. 12,225, fo. 93ᵇ.

PLAISTED, ... Sussex, by Cooke, Clar. Harl. MS. 1562, fo. 201, 46ᵇ.

PLAISTERERS' COMPY., of London, 15 Jan. 154⅜, 37 H. VIII., by T. Hawley, Clar.
Grants I., 417 ; Misc. Gen. et Her., i., 138-9 ; Her. and Geneal. I., 122, copy
of grant, Brit. Mus.

PLANTNEY [Henry ?], of Wolverhampton [by Cooke, Clar.] : sa., a lion rampant
betw. eight trefoils slipped arg. ; Crest, a tiger's head erased or, tufted and
maned gu. [Granted 1583, Burke.]

PLATT, James, of Plaisted, Essex, 6 Feb. 1578, by Cooke, Clar. Harl. MS. 1359,
fo. 17ᵇ.

„ John, of Playstow, Essex, gent., s. and h. of John and Philippa his wife, dau.
of Thos. Shukburgh of Shukburgh, co. Warwick, Esq., 3rd s. of John,
of Wigan, co. Lanc., gent., and of Alice his wife, dau. of Thos. Standish of
Standish, co. Lanc. ; Quarterly coat (Platt and Standish), confirmed
6 Feb., 21 Eliz., 1578, by Cooke. Harl. MS. 1359, fo. 17ᵇ, has James ;
Harl. MS. 1422, fo. 117, has John ; Add. MS. 14,295, fo. 21ᵇ, has James.

„ John, s. of John, of Wigan, co. Lanc., first given 22 Nov. 1559, 2 Q. Eliz.,
by Dalton ; confirmed 6 or 11 March 1564-5, 8 Q. Eliz., by Harvey. Harl.
MS. 1359, fo. 17ᵇ, 48 ; Add. MSS. 16,940, fo. 55, and 14,295, fo. 21ᵇ.

„ Richard, of London, brewer, Arg., fretty sa., on each fret a plate, by Camden.
Morgan's Sphere, 117, and Harl. MS. 1422, fo. 95ᵇ ; Father to Sir Hugh,
Knt., Harl. MS. 1359, fo. 114, and 68, by Cooke ; Harl. MS. 5887, fo. 5ᵇ,
and Stowe MS. 670, fo. 68ᵇ ; Add. MS. 4966, fo. 97ᵇ.

PLEASAUNCE, William, of Brandon Ferry, Suff., 6 Sept. 1576, by Cooke. Harl. MS.
1085, fo. 22.

PLEAYLL als PLEAHILL, William, of St. Andrew's, Holborn, London (s. of William,
of same, s. of Richard or Philip, of Little Dunmowe, Essex, s. of William,
of Barniston or Barmiston, also in Essex), 27 Jan. 1679-80, by Sir W.
Dugdale, Gart., and H. St. George, Norr. Add. MS. 14,831, fo. 90, and
Grants III., fo. 96.

PLEDYERD, Thomas, of Bottesham, co. Camb., gift . . . . 1565. (Hervey's Grants),
Add. MS. 16,940, fo. 24ᵇ.

PLEY, George, of Weymouth, Dorset, 9 Oct. 1667, by Sir E. Walker, Gart. Her.
Coll., fo. 64.

PLOTT, Anthony, of Plymouth, ... 1587, by Cooke. Harl. MSS. 1359, fo. 109ᵇ,
and 1422, fo. 94 ; Add. MS. 4966, fo. 64.

„ William, of the city of Hereford, descended of the Kentish family, arms
and crest exemplified by Segar. Add. MS. 12,225, fo. 94ᵇ ; Grants I., 14ᵃ.

PLUMBE, William, of Merworthe, Knt., confirmed 10 June 1563. (Harvey's
Grants), Add. MS. 16,940, fo. 6, and Burke.

PLUMME, Edward, of Hawkedon, Suff., by R. St. George, Clar. Harl. MS. 1085,
fo. 21ᵇ.

PLUMER, June, dau. to John, of London, draper, wife to John Lowen of Essex, gift
. . . . 1559. (Harvey's Grants), Add. MS. 16,940, fo. 44ᵇ ; Harl. MS.
1116, fo. 56.

D D

PLUMMER, ... parti per chev. counterflory arg. and gu., three martlets counter-
changed .... by Segar.   Add. MS. 12,225, fo. 95ᵇ.
PLUMSTED, Bartholomew, of Calthorp, Norfolk, 30 Aug., 18 Q. Eliz., 1576, by
Cooke.   Harl. MSS. 1359, fo. 123, and 1085, fo. 42ᵇ.
POE, Leonard, of London, esq., s. of James, s. of Richard, of Poes field, co. Derby,
6 July 1599, by Camden, Clar.   Le Neve's MS. 358.
POLASON, see PULASON.
POLLEY als POLHILL, (impalement) see under Thomas MILLES, p. 173.
POLSON, Randolph, of Northfleet, Kent, 7 June 1665, by Sir E. Walker, Gart.
Her. Coll., fo. 60.
POLWHILE or POLWYLLE, John, of Polwhile, Cornwall, s. of John, s. of Stephen,
s. of Giles (? Oates), arms differenced and crest granted 16 Feb. 1568-9,
by Sir G. Dethick, Gart., Cooke, and Flower.   Q's Coll. Oxf. MS. 39,
fo. 135, copy of grant (MS. 145, fo. 15ᵇ); MS. Ashm. 844, fo. 2, copy of
grant, Bodleian Lib. ; Harl. MSS. 1359, fo. 55, and 1441, fo. 70ᵇ ; Guil.
69 ; Harl. MS. 1079, fo. 74ᵇ.
PONET, see POYNET.
POOLE, [Captain Richard, 2nd s. of Thomas Poole, s. and h. of Captain Richard
Poole of] New Shoreham, Sussex, [descended from co. Chester, confirmed
by W. Roberts, Ulster K. of A., 31 May] 1648 : az., semée-de-lis or,
a lion rampant guardant of the second, on a canton az. [arg.] a ship in
full sail ppr. ; crest, a mermaid in profile ppr. holding in her hands a naval
crown or. [Geneal., v., 116] ; Berry.
POOLE or POLE, ... Quarterly, by .... Cooke, Clar.   Stowe MS. 670, fo. 62,
["a vellam Escutcheon in Collours subscribed Pole." Quarterly : 1 and 4,
Arg., a chevron between three crescents Gules ; 2 and 3, ... a chevron
ermine between three fleurs-de-lis .... Crest, a falcon, wings endorsed
Argent] ; Add. MS. 14,297, fo. 62.
   „   David, Bp. of Peterborough, arms granted 15 June, 3 and 4 Philip and Mary,
1557, by Hawley.   Q's Coll. Oxf. MS. 38, fo. 68, copy of grant ; grant in
P.R.O., see Misc. Gen. et Her., i., 231 ; Harl. MS. 1359, fo. 58, grant ;
Grants II., 464.
   „   Godfrey, of High Hedge, co. Derby, confirmed arms (quarterly) and crest
.... 1578, 20 Eliz., by Flower.   Harl. MSS. 1359, fo. 44, and 1422,
fo. 109ᵇ.
   „   William, of Poole in Wherall (Wyrral), Cheshire, grant in French of crest
13 April, 4 Hen. VIII., 1513, by T. Wriothesley, Gart., and John Yonge,
Norr.   Harl. MSS. 2022, fo. 91, and 6140, fo. 49ᵇ.
POPE, ..., of London, ... by Cooke, Clar.   Stowe MS. 670, fo. 27.
   „   Francis, of London, draper, gift .... 155- or 156-. (Harvey's Grants).
Add. MS. 16,940, fo. 55ᵇ ; Harl. MS. 5887, fo. 57.
   „   Robert, of Salop, gent., crest confirmed 21 Feb. 1572-3, by Sir G. Dethick,
Gart.   Harl. MS. 1441, fo. 73ᵇ ; Q's Coll. Oxf. MS. 145, fo. 20.
   „   Thomas, of Dodyngton, Oxf., coat and crest. Barker's Grants, Harl. MS.
5846, fo. 85 ; Stowe MS. 692, fo. 78ᵇ.
POPLEY, Sir Derrick, of Bristol, Kt., confirmed .... 1672, 24 Chas. II., by
Walker.   Guil. 214.
PORDAGE, William, of Rodmersham, Kent, s. of John, 20 March 1570-71, by Cooke.
Harl. MS. 1359, fo. 122ᵇ.
PORT, Henry, of Cheshire, 27 June, 1506, by Chr. Carlyle als Norroy.   Harl. MS.
1116, fo. 39.
PORTER, ... crest ....   Barker's Grants, Harl. MS. 5846, fo. 82ᵇ ; Stowe MS.
692, fo. 78.
   „   .... of the Isle of Wight, ... by Cooke, Clar.   Stowe MS. 670, fo. 48.
   „   Richard, of St. Margaret's in South Elmham, Suff., s. of Nicholas, s. of John,
gen., of co. Linc., confirmed 1 June 1606, by Segar, Gart.   Add. MS.
12,225, fo. 95ᵇ ; Harl. MS. 1085, fo. 27 ; Le Neve's MS. 480.

PORTLAND, Earl of (William Bentinck), supporters (created 9 April 1689) 3 July 1689, by T. St. George, Gart. Grants IV., 49 ; Harl. MS. 6834, fo. 178.

PORTSMOUTH, Louise Renée, Duchess of, supporters 18 June 1674, in French, by E. Walker, Gart. Harl. MS. 6834, fo. 44 ; Grants III., 44.

POTENGER, Richard, of Burfield, Berks, 19 Nov. 1664, 16 Chas. II. Bysshe's Grants, fo. 18, Her. Coll. ; Harl. MS. 1105, fo. 20 ; MS. Ashm. 851, fo. 198.

POTENSON, see PATENSON.

POTKYN, ... crest .... Barker's Grants, Harl. MS. 5846, fo. 84 ; Stowe MS. 692, fo. 78, as Pootkyn.

POTKIN, William, of Sevenoaks, Kent, gent., grant 25 May 1517, by T. Wriothesley, Gart., and Benolte, Clar. Stowe MS. 676, fo. 11 ; copy of patent in French, Q's Coll. Oxf. MS. 37, fo. 8 ; ex. Mag. Reg., by G. Dethick ; Proc. Soc. Antiq., 2nd S., xvi., 1897, fo. 348 ; Harl. MS. 6140, fo. 45[b] ; see also Harl. MS. 1116, fo. 47, for John Potkin [of Reculver], something illicit.

POTT, John, of Lincoln's Inn, s. of Roger, confirmed or granted 1583, by Cooke. Harl. MS. 1359, fo. 98[b] ; Add. MS. 14,295, fo. 31 ; Guil. 68 ; Add. MSS. 12,474, fo. 51[b], and 4966, fo. 63.

POTTER, Christopher, "M[r]," i.e., "Provost" of Queen's Coll., Oxf., ... by Borough. Harl. MSS. 1105, fo. 55, and 1441, fo. 57; Add. MS. 26,702, fo. 88[b] ; Guil. 216.

POTTS, John, Stancliff, co. Derby, 19 Nov. 1611, by R. St. George, Norr. Harl. MS. 1093, fo. 19.

POULLEY, see PULLEY.

POULTON, William, of Berwyke St. Leonard's, Wilts, gent., coat confirmed and crest granted 27 Aug. 1565, by G. Dethick, Gart. Harl. MS. 1441, fo. 9[b], copy of grant, Brit. Mus.

POUNT, ... by Dethick, Gart., ... Harl. MS. 1483, fo. 72[b] ; Stowe MS. 677, fo. 7.

POVEY, John, one of the Clerks in the Courts of the Queen (s. of Davie, s. of John, of Cheshire), confirmed 12 May 1588, by Flower. MS. Ashm. 844, fo. 76, copy of grant, Bodleian Lib. ; Guil. 138.

„ Justinian, of London, Esq. (Auditor-General to Q. Anne and Auditor in reversion to the King James), s. of John, Citizen of London and free of the company of the Imbroiderers, patent Nov. 1614, by Camden. Harl. MSS. 6095, fo. 31[b], and 1422, fo. 39[b] ; Guil. 138.

POWELL, Edmond, of Sampford, Oxon., coat and crest granted . . . . Barker's Grants, Harl. MS. 5846, fo. 86 ; Stowe MS. 692, fo. 78[b] ; or, two cheveronells, etc., Harl. MSS. 6179, fo. 15 [fo. 38[b]], and 5887, fo. 10. [Harl. MS. 5846, fo. 86 : Gold, 2 cheveronells betweene two lyons pawes rased g., armed b., betweene the cheveronells 3 wells b. ; his crest, 2 lyons pawes indosant erased thorow an annulet or, armyd b. ; w[reath] or and s. ; m[antlet] g., Lined Argent. Stowe MS. 692, fo. 78[b], has the same, but iij lions pawes rased gouls, armed asure .... and in eche pawe an annelett golde. Harl. MS. 5887, fo. 10, has 3 paws.]

„ Edmond ap, of Sandford in com. Oxford, confirmed .... 1565, 7 of Q. Eliz. (Harvey's Grants), Add. MS. 16,940, fo. 30[b], Quarterly for Ap ppowell, Or, a lion rampant [sables, a fece engrailed gules, on a wrethe argent and sables an armyd arme from the elbowe upwarde, garnyshed golde, holding therein a courtelace hilted and pomelyd golde, attached to the pomel a lace gules, tacelid golde].

„ John, Surveyor-General of [all her Majesties] Ordnance (3rd s. of Andrew, of Bruton in Somerset), assigned .... 1584, by Cooke. Harl. MSS. 1359, fo. 117, and 1422, fo. 63 ; Guil. 387 ; Add. MS. 4966, fo. 28.

POWLE, Stephen, of London, gent., out of Essex, Quarterly coat confirmed .... March 1587-8, by W. Dethick, Gart. Q's Coll. Oxf. MS. 37, fo. 100, copy

of confirmation in Latin ; 1586 in Stowe MS. 676, fo. 70 ; Proc. Soc. of
Antiq., 2nd S., xvi., 1897, fo. 353.

Powle, Thomas, of London, esq., clerk of the Crowne to the Queen's Majesties
Court of Chancery, one of the six clerks, and comptroller of the Hanaper
in the same Court, and Steward of Her Majesty's Forest of Waltham,
co. Essex ; arms and crest (in lieu of old arms and crest granted 10 May
1559) granted 7 May 1569, by Sir G. Dethick, Gart., Cooke and Flower.
Q's Coll. Oxf. MS. 39, fo. 155, copy of grant, MS. 145, fo. 79 ; MS. Ashm.
858, fo. 215, copy of grant, Bodleian Lib. ; Harl. MSS. 1359, fo. 56, and
1441, fo. 73, as Poole ; Proc. Soc. Antiq., 2nd S., xvi., 1897, fo. 351 ; Le
Neve's MS. 373.

„   Thomas, of Cranbrook, Essex, grant 5 April, 2 and 3 Philip and Mary, 1556,
by Hawley, Clar. Proc. Soc. of Antiq., 2nd S., xvi., 1897, p. 349 ; 10 May
1559, by Hervey, Q's Coll. Oxf. MS. 38, fo. 71 ; Harl. MS. 1507, fo. 373,
copy of grant, Brit. Mus. ; Add. MS. 16,940, fo. 37 ; Grants II., 562 ; Le
Neve's MS. 373.

Powell, Thomas, of Whittington, Salop, crest 5 July 1574, by Cooke. Add. MS.
14,293, fo. 118.

Power, Francis, of Blechington, Oxon., 8 June 1601, by Camden. (Morgan's
Sphere, 117) ; Harl. MSS. 1422, fo. 111ᵇ, and 6179, fo. 20ᵇ.

„   John, of Whitchurch, Bucks, gent., ... 1478, 18 E. IV., by Thos. (?Holme),
Clar. Harl. MS. 5524, fo. 219, copy of grant ; Stowe MS. 676, fo. 4 ;
Q's Coll. Oxf. MSS. 37, fo. 5, and 38, fo. 10, copy of grant, ex. Mag. Reg.,
Gilb. Dethick ; Grants II., 435 ; grandfather of Henry, Visct. Valentia.

Powney, John, of Old Windsor, Berks, gent., grant 3 May 1662, by Sir E. Bysshe,
Clar. Bysshe's Grants, fo. 3, Her. Coll. ; Harl. MS. 1470, fo. 257, copy of
grant, Brit. Mus. ; Harl. MS. 1105, fo. 16ᵇ ; Guil. 373.

Powys, Thomas, of Henley, Salop, sergt.-at-law, ... by Sir E. Bysshe, Clar.
Harl. MS. 1105, fo. 21ᵇ ; Bysshe's Grants, fo. 24, Her. Coll.

Poynant, Michell, of London, clerk of the Chancery, etc., 14 March 1508-9, by
Chr. Carlyle, Norr. MSS. Ashm. 840, fo. 377-8, and 858, fo. 251-2, copy
of grant, Bodleian Lib. ; Stowe MS. 676, fo. 7.

Poynet or Ponet, John, Bp. of Winchester, 1 April, 5 Ed. VI., 1551, by
G. Dethick, Gart. (Her. Coll.), Grants I., 25.

Poynter, John, of Lincoln's Inn, co. Middx., registrar of the affidavit office in
Chancery (s. of Samuel, registrar of same), 28 May 1694, by T. St. George,
Gart. and Clar. Add. MS. 14,830, fo. 112 ; Grants IV., fo. 161 ; Stowe
MS. 714, fo. 154 ; Harl. MSS. 1172, fo. 54ᵇ, and 1085, fo. 57.

„   Richard, of London, a patent 4 June 1612, by Camden. Harl. MS. 6095,
fo. 23ᵇ ; Poyntell in Harl. MS. 1422, fo. 37ᵇ, and 1441, fo. 99ᵇ, June
1620.

Pragell (? Pringle), John, captain of foote men in Berwick, coat and crest by
Flower, dated at York 10 June, 4 E(liz., 1562). Stowe MSS. 692, fo. 77ᵇ,
677, fo. 18, and 706, fo. 8ᵇ, as Preagle.

Prannell, Henry, of London, Alderm. and Vintner, s. of William, of Martyr
Worthy, Hants, patent . . . . 1584, by Cooke. Harl. MS. 1359, fo. 116 ;
Add. MSS. 14,295, fo. 30ᵇ, and 4966, fo. 29.

Pratte, ... of Reston . . . . crest . . . . Barker's Grants, Harl. MS. 5846,
fo. 84 ; Stowe MS. 692, fo. 78.

Pratt, ..., d. of Charles, of Southwark, esq., ux. Sir Edward Osborne, of London,
. . . . by Cooke, Clar. Stowe MS. 670, fo. 48ᵇ.

„   . . . . of Reyston Hall, Norfolk, or, on a chevron sable betw. three pellets, each
charged with a martlet or, as many mascles of the last. Bysshe's Grants,
fo. 22, Her. Coll. ; Harl. MS. 1105, fo. 21.

„   Ralph, of Statherne, co. Leic., " R.P. by God's blessing & virtue wh. only
enobleth men " ; grant 23 Aug. 1601, by Camden. (Ralph Pratt of
Southwark, Surrey, gent., 1600, in Add. MS. 14,295, fo. 117ᵇ) ; Harl. MS.

6140, fo. 26ᵇ ; Cott. MS. Faustina E. 1, 59ᵇ ; Harl. MS. 1359, fo. 37ᵇ, as of Southwark, Surrey ; Guil. 367 ; Crispe's Frag. Gen., i., 56 ; Cat. Her. Exhib. Soc. of Antiq., 70.

PRATT, Roger, one of the eleven assistant Govᵗˢ of Raleigh, Virginia, arms granted, erm., on a chief gu. three fusils arg. . . . . by W. Dethick, Gart. Q's Coll. Oxf. MS. 36, fo. 120.

PREAGLE, see PRAGELL.

PRENTISE, Simon, of Burstow and Marshland, Norfolk, ... by Harvey, Clar. Bannerman's MS. 9, 45.

PRESCOTT, Alexander, of London, s. of William, of Cople, co. Lanc., descended of Prescott of Prescott, crest . . . . March 1611, by Camden. (Father of Sir John Prescott, High Sheriff 1627.) Harl. MSS. 6095, fo. 14ᵇ, and 1122, fo. 35ᵇ.

PRESTLEY, William, of the cittie of London, descended from Prestley of Beting in Yorks, patent . . . . Feb. 1619-20, by Camden. Harl. MS. 6095, fo. 37.

PRESTON, John, of Preston, Westmorld., by R. St. George. Crest altered . . . . June 1605 in Add. MS. 14,295, fo. 79ᵇ and 110 ; Harl. MS. 1359, fo. 24ᵇ, coat as Harl. MS. 1422, fo. 78, but crest differs ; Add. MS. 26,702, fo. 25ᵇ ; Harl. MSS. 6179, fo. 18, and 6140, fo. 24.

PRESTWICH, ... of Holme, co. Lanc. : Arms, gu., a mermaid arg., comb and glass or ; crest, a mermaid ppr. . . . . by Barker. Berry's Armory.

PRESWOOD, Thomas, of the county of Devon, gift . . . . 1564. (Harvey's Grants), Add. MS. 16,940, fo. 45.

PRETTYMAN, ..., ... on a fesse cottised . . . ., betw. three fleurs-de-lis . . . ., a lyon passant . . . . . by Segar. Add. MS. 12,225, fo. 95.

„ John, of Boughton, Suff., Kt., s. and h. of William, 28 July 1599, by Segar ; patent . . . . 1607, by Camden. Add. MS. 12,225, fo. 94ᵇ ; Harl. MS. 6095, fo. 25.

PREWETT, William, of Bristol, 1 Oct. 1672, 24 Chas. II., by Sir E. Bysshe, Clar. Harl. MS. 1105, fo. 40 ; Bysshe's Grants, 33.

PRICE, Sir John, of Portcham, co. Hereford, Knt., coat and crest. Barker's Grants, Harl. MS. 5846, fo. 86 ; Stowe MS. 692, fo. 78ᵇ.

PRYCE, John, of Barton Regis, nr. Bristol, co. Glouc., s. of Gregorie, of the same, esq., 8 April 1573, by Cooke. Add. MSS. 14,295, fo. 26, and 6179, fo. 15 ; Harl. MS. 1422, fo. 57.

PRICE, John, of Kingston-upon-Thames, etc., exemplified 1602, by Camden. Guil. 272 ; (? see Harl. MS. 5887, fo. 6ᵇ, sa., a cock arg., combed and wattled gules, three red feathers in his tayle and three at the end of his winge) ; see Le Neve's MS. 427.

„ Thomas, of Brecon, 1632, see PRISE.

PRICKLY als HARRIS, ..., or, a chevron erm. betw. two [three] passion nails az. . . . ., by Segar. Add. MS. 12,225, fo. 95 ; C. 24, [Visit. of London, 1634], fo. 75, Her. Coll. ; Guil. 304, as of London.

PRICKLEY, Hugh, of Prickley, s. of Richard, for services in discovering the great Mortimer, Earl of March and Ulster, had [for his crest] a chapean with a crownet [thereon] inbattayle, an armed arm, with a fiste-hammer or pole-axe [ppr.], to his posteritie for ever, by letters patent 6 Ed. III., 1332 ; lineally descended from Adam, of Pricley, temp. Etheldred the Saxon. Harl. MS. 2146, fo. 201.

PRIDYAUX or PREDYAUX, John, of Nutwell, Devon, confirmed 16 May 1558. (By Harvey, see Harl. MS. 1359, fo. 15) ; Add. MS. 16,940, fo. 7ᵇ, and Burke.

„ Thomas, of Nutwell, Devon, esq., coat first given by Harvey, now altered thus by Lee, Clar., 1594 ; crest as it was. Q's Coll. Oxf. MS. 146, fo. 463 ; Harl. MSS. 1359, fo. 15, and 1069, fo. 10 ; Add. MS. 14,295, fo. 9ᵇ ; Stowe MS. 670, fo. 58ᵇ.

PRINCE, Richard, of Abbey foregate, nr. Shrewsbury, 2 Nov. 1584, by Cooke. Harl. MS. 1359, fo. 117ᵇ ; Add. MS. 14,295, fo. 40ᵇ ; MS. Ashm. 858, fo. 134, copy of grant, Bodleian Lib. : Add. MS. 12,474, fo. 54ᵇ, by Ley, Portcullis ; Add. MS. 4966, fo. 29.

PRINGLE ?, see PRAGELL.

PRINNE, Edward, born in Portugal, s. of Richard, of the same, 2nd s. of Richard, of Bristol, etc., crest granted 10 Aug. 1582, by Cooke. Q's Coll. Oxf. MSS. 36, fo. 101, and 37, fo. 80, copy of grant in Latin ; Stowe MS. 676, fo. 58ᵇ ; see also W. Dethicke. [Possibly this refers to the grant by Dethick to Edward Prynne of Shropshire 21 May 1588 (Harl. MS. 1069, fo. 31) ; see The Her. of Worcestershire, ii., 452, and the next entry.]

PRINNE, Edward, capt. and Knt. of the order of Christ in Portugal, arms and crest was made in pedigree 21 May 1588, subscribed by W. Dethick, Gart., etc. See Q's Coll. Oxf. MS. 146, fo. 42 ; Add. MS. 14,295, fo. 48 ; Harl. MS. 1359, fo. 23.

PRISE, Thomas, of Brecknock, co. Brecknock, Esq., grandchild and heir male to Sir John, of the same, Kt., etc., new coat and crest 20 June 1632, by Sir R. St. George, Clar. Add. MS. 14,295, fo. 103 ; styled a knight in Harl. MS. 1301, fo. 25.

PROBY, Ralph (Peter in pencil), of Bramton, Hunts, ... 1586, by Cooke. Harl. MSS. 1359, fo. 110ᵇ, and 1422, fo. 93ᵇ ; Add. MS. 4966, fo. 68.

PROCKTER, Richard, of London, ... by Cooke. Harl. MS. 1359, fo. 114ᵇ ; Add. MS. 4966, fo. 94.

PROUD, ... of Shropshire, steward of the College of Westminster, a confirmation April 1606, by Camden. Harl. MS. 6095, fo. 20ᵇ ; Guil. 411 ; Harl. MS. 5887, fo. 29ᵇ.

PROUZE, Richard, of Exeter, ... 1589, by Cooke. Harl. MSS. 1359, fo. 100, and 1422, fo. 94ᵇ.

PROWSE, William, of Clyſte, Somt., gent., crest 7 Sept. 1573, by Cooke. Misc. Gen. et Her., N. S., iv., 400, and 2nd S., i., 110, copy of grant, Brit. Mus.

PRUJEAN, Francis, of London, Dʳ in physic, 20 March 1651-2, by E. Bysshe, Gart. Harl. MS. 1105, fo. 15 ; ? confirmed by Sir Edward Walker, Gart., 10 April 1661, then a Knight, Her. Coll., fo. 39 ; Cat. Her. Exhib. Soc. of Antiq., 72.

PRUST, Hugh, of Gorfon [Gorven], Devon, ... (Visit. of Devon [1620], by H. St. George, Richmond Her., and Sampson Lennard, Bluemantle), deputies for [Camden], Clar. Harl. MS. 1422, fo. 15.

PRYOTTE, John, born in the North. 1 Oct., 1 Ed. VI., 1547, by G. Dethick, Norr. Harl. MS. 1507, fo. 430, copy of grant in Latin, Brit. Mus., and Q's Coll. Oxf. MS. 37, fo. 11 ; Harl. MS. 1359, fo. 5 ; Grants I., 109.

PRYOTT, John (a Northern gent., Stowe MS. 696), 5 Oct., 2 Q. Eliz., 1560, by Sir G. Dethick, Gart. Q's Coll. Oxf. MS. 39, fo. 110, copy of grant ; Harl. MSS. 1359, fo. 79ᵇ, and 1410, fo. 16 ; Le Neve's MS. 430.

PUCKERING, John, Sergt.-at-law (s. of Robert, late of Flamborough, gent.), confirmed 26 June 1579, by Flower. MS. Ashm. 834, fo. 22, copy of grant, Bodleian Lib. ; Guil. 372 ; Stowe MS. 670, fo. 55, quarterly of 6, among Cooke's gifts.

PUCKLE, John, of Elynborne, Sussex, s. of John, of London, by William Camden, Clar. Harl. MS. 6067, fo. 14, 29, copy of grant, Brit. Mus. ; Harl. MS. 1562, fo. 4.

PUDSEY, ... confirmed . . . . 1566, by W. Harvey, Clar. Harl. MS. 1167, fo. 85ᵇ.

PULASON or POLASON, Thomas, of London, gift . . . . 1564, 6 Q. Eliz. (Harvey's Grants), p. pale arg. and sa., three lions rampt. counterchanged of the field ; [crest] a crown, thereout a demi-peacock displayed or. Add. MS. 16,940, fo. 30.

PULESTON, Roger, of Emral, Flints, crest . . . . 1582, by Cooke. Harl. MS. 1422, fo. 95 ; Add. MS. 14,295, fo. 31ᵇ.

PULFORD, John, of London, gent., s. of Thomas, of Farendon, Cheshire, etc., grant

. . . . 1589-90, 32 Eliz., by W. Dethick, Gart. Stowe MS. 676, fo. 78^b; Q's Coll. Oxf. MS. 37, fo. 115, copy of grant.

PULLEY (or POULLEY), ... Essex, ... Feb. 1639, by Borough. Harl. MS. 1105, fo. 56 ; Add. MS. 26,702, fo. 91^b ; Harl. MS. 4966, fo. 33.

PULLEYN, John, of Kelleng Hall, Yorks, ... Add. MS. 26,702, fo. 75^b.

PULLEYNE, Walter, of Scotton, Yorks, confirmed . . . . 1551 (by Harvey, Norr.). Add. MS. 16,940, fo. 13.

PURCELL, Thomas, of Shrewsbury, esq., quarterly of 4, and gift of crest . . . . April 1597, by Lee. Q's Coll. Oxf. MS. 146, fo. 42 ; Add. MS. 14,295, fo. 121 ; Harl. MSS. 1422, fo. 114, and 1359, fo. 39.

PUREFOY, Thomas, of co. Leic., arms by patent from John de Wellesborough, as in remainder to the manor of Fen Drayton, and Wellesborough, co. Leic., 21 R. II., in the feast of St John the Apostle. Harl. MS. 980, fo. 302, 209 ; Add. MS. 6297, fo. 137.

PURPETT, John, of Levington, Suff., gift . . . . 1560 (Harvey's Grants) : per fesse or and sa., a pale engrailed counterchanged. Add. MS. 16,940, fo. 38^b.

PYE, Edmund, of London, granted 2 March 1634-5, by Ric. St. George, Clar. Guil. 245 ; copy of grant in Lot 618 sold P[uttick] and S[impson] 18 May 1899.

  ,, Sir Walter, Knt., Attorney of the Court of Wards and Liveries, and his brother

  ,, Sir Robert, of St Stephen's, Westminster, Auditor of the Receipt of the Exchequer, confirmed 11 (or 12) Feb. 1632-3, by Sir R. St. George. Add. MS. 14,295, fo. 70^b ; C. 25, fo. 45 [Visit. of] Herefordshire [1634] ; Harl. MS. 1105, fo. 1^b and 10.

PYEED, ... crest . . . . Barker's Grants, Harl. MS. 5846, fo. 82^b ; Stowe MS. 692, fo. 78.

PYLE, Edward, of Pottery Court, par. of Wallop, Hants, 20 June 1663, by Walker. Add. MSS. 14,293, fo. 58, and 14,294, fo. 14 ; Harl. MS. 1172, fo. 58.

  ,, Gabriel, of Wilts, Knt., ... by Camden. Harl. MS. 1422, fo. 16.

  ,, Richard, gent. (now sergeant chirurgeon to His Majesty, Her. Coll., fo. 30), his Majesty's servant at the Hague ; 1 June 1650 (by Walker, Gart.). Add. MSS. 14,293, fo. 105, and 14,294, fo. 35 ; Harl. MS. 1172, fo. 71^b ; Guil. 258.

PYNCOMBE, John, of South Molton, Devon, esq., s. and h. of John, by Ann, his wife, d. of Richard Doderidge and sister of Judge Doderidge, now living, s. of John, of ye same place ; coat confirmed and crest granted 18 July 1616, by Segar. Add. MS. 12,225, fo. 96 ; Guil. 386 ; Grants I., 383.

PYNDAR, Reginald, of Kemplay, co. Glouc., 30 Sept. 1682, by Sir W. Dugdale and St. George, Clar. Harl. MS. 6834, fo. 178 ; Grants III., 159.

PYOT, Richard, of London (Sheriff), grant 1 Dec. 1610, by Camden ; exhibited at Lichfield 1663. MS. Ashm. 858, fo. 112-13, copy of grant, Bodleian Lib. ; Harl. MSS. 1422, fo. 16, 21^b, and 6095, fo. 14 ; Guil. 360.

Q

QUADRING, ... of Linc., ... by Ro. Cooke. Stowe MS. 670, fo. 39.

QUARLES, John, s. of John, late citizen and draper of London, dec^d, and to his brethren, confirmed 15 Feb. 1577-8, by Cooke. MSS. Ashm. 834, fo. 16^b, and 858, fo. 218-19, copy of grant, Bodleian Lib. ; Guil. 214.

QUASH, Andrew, of Exeter, confirmed 9 March 1626-7, by Segar. Harl. MSS. 1422, fo. 13^b, and 6179, fo. 2.

QUASH or QUACH, John, of Norwich, grant . . . . 1588, by Cooke. Harl. MS. 1422, fo. 13^b.

QUEENS' COLLEGE, Cambridge, arms 26 H. VI. (1447-8), by Margaret, his Queen, her own six quarters in a border vert ; crest 10 May 1575, by Cooke, Clar. Add. MS. 5822.

QUICKERELL or QUYKERELL, John, ... Add. MS. 26,702, fo. 58ᵇ.

QUILTER, William, of Staple, Kent, 12 June 1552, by Sir G. Dethick, Gart. Harl. MS. 1441, fo. 65ᵇ ; 1551 in Q's Coll. Oxf. MS. 145, fo. 8.

QWYRE, Bartholomew, of London, ... by Cooke, Clar. Stowe MS. 670, fo. 18.

R

RADCLIFF, Jasper, of Courthall in Hockworthy, Devon, 20 June 1693, by T. St. George, Gart. and Clar. Grants IV., 142 ; Harl. MS. 1085, fo. 57.

RAGAZON, Jacobus, of Venice (Veneto), or a Venetian, addition to arms, letters patent *temp.* Philip and Mary. Harl. MS. 6179, fo. 13 ; MS. Ashm. 858, fo. 2. copy of grant, Bodleian Lib.

RAINEY, William, 1620. *See* John REYNY.

RALEIGH, the Governor and Assistants in the City of Raleigh in Virginia, with the appurtenances, arms granted . . . . by W. Dethick, Gart. Undated. Q's Coll. Oxf. MS. 36, fo. 120, copy of grant.

RALLINES, Thomas, Dʳ (of physic ?), crest by Camden. Harl. MS. 5887, fo. 54.

RAMME, Francis, of Hornchurch, Essex, ... 1590, by Cooke. Harl. MS. 1359, fo. 103 ; Q's Coll. Oxf. MS. 146, fo. 471.

RAMRYGGE, Thomas, Abbot of St Alban's (1484—92), Hen. VII. Add. MS. 26,702, fo. 64ᵇ.

RAMSAY, Sir John, Earl of Holderness, supporters, etc., dated at the Great Seal, 22 Jan. 1620-1, 8 Jac. Q's Coll. Oxf. MS. 38, fo. 132, copy of R. Warrant, etc. ; Harl. MS. 1507, fo. 201ᵇ ; Le Neve's MS. 424, 472.

RAMSDEN, John, of Longley, Yorks, April 1575, by Flower. Harl. MSS. 1453, fo. 74, and 1422, fo. 23ᵇ ; Guil. 167.

RANDALL, Anthony, of Kentisbury, Devon. Randall and Woolfe, quarterly, confirmed 1 July 1588, 30 Q. Eliz., by Cooke. Harl. MSS. 1359, fo. 13, and 1422, fo. 116 ; Add. MS. 14,295, fo. 8.

RANDYLL, Edward, of London, gent. (grandson Thomas), s. and h. of Vincent (and his wife Elizabeth Hardinge), s. and h. of Thos. (and Alice, d. and h. of Thomas Shelley), 2nd s. of Gilbert, of Hunsdon, Herts, gent., arms quarterly confirmed and crest given 22 May 1573, 15 Q. Eliz., by Cooke. Q's Coll. Oxf. MS. 146, fo. 41 ; Harl. MS. 1359, fo. 22ᵇ ; March in Harl. MS. 1422, fo. 114 ; Add. MS. 14,295, fo. 46ᵇ, quartering Shelley and Harding. *See* Thomas RANDYLL, 12 Dec., H. VII., by S. Thos. Holme, Clar.

„   Edward, of Surrey, gent., s. of Edward, of London, s. of Vincent, also of London, s. of Thomas, etc., confirmed . . . . by Camden ; exemplified by T. Holme, Clar., 1485-6. Cott. MS. Faustina, E. 1, 56.

RANDOLL, Justis, of London, ... by Cooke. Harl. MSS. 1359, fo. 119ᵇ, and 1422, fo. 92ᵇ ; Add. MS. 4966, fo. 61.

RANDALL, Richard, of Wolston Northts., and   } allowed before 1597, by Cooke: gu.,
„   Thomas, of Bonnington, co. War.   }   on a cross arg. five horse-shoes
                                                    sa. Guil. 349 ; Richard, of Wilford, co. Warwick, in Harl. MS. 1422, fo. 92ᵇ.

RANDYLL, Thomas, of Northants, gent., ? exemplified, arms and crest given 12 Dec. 1 Hy. VII., 1485, by Thos. Holme, Clar. (after Knt.) ; grandfather of Edward. Q's Coll. Oxf. MS. 146, fo. 41 ; Cott. MS. Faustina, E. 1, 56, in a note ; Harl. MS. 1359, fo. 22ᵇ.

RANDE, William, of Northants, and } arms and crest of, 3 July 1579, by Cooke,
„   Nicholas, his grandfather,   }   Harl. MS. 1359, fo. 122.

RANDES, Henry, D.D., of Holbech and Bp. of Rochester, and after of Lincoln, and of the High Court of Parlt. to H. VIII., and a confirmation to,

„ Thomas, of Lincoln (s. of Henry, Bp. of Rochester and after of Lincoln, which Henry took the name of Holbeach from his native place, according to the custom of Ecclesiastics), alteration in blazon and grant of crest 10 July 1599, by Camden. Harl. MS. 1507, fo. 94b, and Q's Coll. Oxf. MS. 36, fo. 77, and 38, fo. 115, copy of grant (MS. 146, fo. 21) ; Cott. MS. Faustina, E. 1, fo. 66b ; Harl. MSS. 1422, fo. 3, 1470, fo. 164, and 1172, fo. 7 and 22, copy of grant ; Harl. MSS. 1359, fo. 26b, and 6095, fo. 18b ; Stowe MS. 696, fo. 130 ; 29th July in Guil. 121.

RANDOLF, John, of London, mercer, grant of another coat with difference 28 Feb. 1453-4. See EYNSHAM. MS. Ashm. 834, i., fo. 3b, copy of grant, Bodleian Lib.

RANDOLPH, Thomas, of Badilsmere, co. Camb., confirmed 15 March 1570-71, 13 Q. Eliz., by Cooke. MS. Ashm. 834, fo. 29, copy of grant, Bodleian Lib. ; Guil. 105.

RANT, Roger, of North Walsham, Norfolk, gent., s. of Robert of the same, gent., confirmation of arms and gift of crest 26 Jan. 1580, 22 Q. Eliz., by Cooke. Harl. MS. 1359, fo. 14b, 94 ; Add. MS. 14,295, fo. 96.

„ William, of Yelverton, Norfolk, ... 1574, by Cooke. Harl. MS. 1085, fo. 38b ; (Berry).

RATCLIFF, Charles, of Todmorden, co. Lanc., gent., confirmation of arms and gift of crest 5 Nov., 3 Eliz., 1561, by Dalton. Harl. MSS. 1422, fo. 122b, and 1359, fo. 51.

RAVEN, of Creeting, Suff. ? certified by W. Camden, no date. Grants II., 601.

„ John, Dr in physic and medicine, fellow of Coll. of Phys., London, and sworn phys. to ye late Q. Anne and K. Chas. I. (s. of John, late Richmond Herald), confirmed (Grants I., 389, Her. Coll.) by Segar. Add. MS. 12,225, fo. 96 ; Guil. 223 ; see also different arms under Camden ; Harl. MS. 6179, fo. 54.

„ William, of Long Melford, Suff., confirmed 15 Oct. 1561. (Harvey's Grants), Add. MS. 16,940, fo. 42.

RAVENSCROFT, George, of Bretton, Flints, ... Harl. MS. 1422, fo. 123b.

RAW, George, of Skipton, Yorksh., merchant adventurer and haberdasher of London, confirmed 20 Jan. 1563, by Flower. MS. Ashm. 834, fo. 6, copy of grant, Bodleian Lib. ; Guil. 243 ; Harl. MS. 6179, fo. 41 ; Proc. Soc. of Antiq., 1897, 2nd S., xvi., p. 351.

RAWE, George, of Sandwich, Kent, esq., 20 Jan. 1573, by Cooke. Harl. MS. 1359, fo. 122b ; Le Neve's MS. 497.

RAWDON, Marmaduke, of London, Capt. and Commander of one select band of 300 men of armes of the said city of London, coat exemplified and crest granted 24 Sept. 1618, by Camden. Add. MS. 14,295, fo. 73b ; Harl. MSS. 6095, fo. 38, and 1359, fo. 10b ; Guil. 335. See also THOROGOOD.

„ Marmaduke, of London, (19 Feb. in Guil. 336) 1639, by Borough. Harl. MS. 1105, fo. 56 ; Add. MS. 26,702, fo. 91b ; Guil. 336.

RAWLETT, Sir Ranffe, Kt., borne in the county of Leicester and now dwelling nighe St. Alban's in the Manor of Gorhams in the county of Herts, coat and crest 1 Ed. VI., 1547. Barker's Grants, Harl. MS. 5846, fo. 87 ; Stowe MS. 692, fo. 82 and 90b.

RAWLINS or RAWLYNS, John, of Aldermanbury, London, descended from David ap William Jenkyn, crest confirmed 12 Nov. 1562 (Harvey's Grants), by Harvey and G. Dethick. Harl. MS. 1422, fo. 107b ; Add. MS. 16,940, fo. 60 ; Harl. MS. 6179, fo. 20b.

„ John, of Woking, Surrey, 2 Feb. 1623-4, by R. St. George, Clar. Harl. MS. 1561, fo. 192.

RAWLINS, Margaret, d. of William, of London, grocer and merchant adventurer, and wife of James Bacon, Alderm. of city of London ; 13 Nov. 1570, by

E E

Sir G. Dethick, Cooke and Flower.   Harl. MS. 1441, fo. 76ᵇ ;   Q's Col. Oxf. MS. 145, fo. 25ᵇ.

RAWLINS, Richard, Archdeacon of Huntingdon, ... Hen. VIII.   Add. MS. 26,702, fo. 60ᵇ.

„   Thomas, of Wakering, Essex, crest 2 Jan. 1559-60, by Sir G. Dethick, Gart. Harl. MSS. 1441, fo. 101, and 5847, fo. 50ᵇ ; Stowe MS. 676, fo. 25 ; Q's Coll. Oxf. MS. 37, fo. 38, copy of grant (1566 in MS. 145, fo. 51ᵇ) ; Misc. Gen. et Her., 2nd S., vol. iv., p. 225 ; Harl. MS. 5887, fo. 26ᵇ ; Grants I., 184.

RAWLIN, Thomas, D. Med., exemplified and confirmed . . . . 1601, by Camden. Harl. MSS. 1422, fo. 107ᵇ, and 6095, fo. 12ᵇ and 22 ; Guil. 338 says 1610, and of Hereford ; 1605 in Le Neve's MS. 292.

RAWLINSON, Robert, of Carke in Cartmel, co. Lanc., and of Gray's Inn, and Vice-Chancʳ Co. Pal. of Lanc., 20 May 1662, by W. Dugdale, Norr.   Harl. MS. 1105, fo. 60, and Her. Coll. [? Dugdale's Grants].

RAWORTH, Robert, of Gray's Inn, a person of known integrity and ability, 10 May 1665, by Sir E. Walker, Gart.   Her. Coll., fo. 60.

„   Robert, citizen and merchant of London (s. of Henry, of Wollaton, Notts), 4 Jan. 1680-81, by Sir Hy. Sᵗ George, Clar., Sir Wᵐ Dugdale, Gart.   Add. MS. 14,830, fo. 199 ; Grants III., fo. 123 ; Stowe MS. 714, fo. 99ᵇ.

RAWSON, John, of Pickbarne, Yorks, Capt. of Horse to Chas. II., 28 Aug. 1665, by W. Dugdale, Norr.   Her. Coll. [Dugdale's Grants ?].

RAYMONDE, ..., of London, crest . . . . 1547.   Barker's Grants, Harl. MS. 5846, fo. 88ᵇ ; Stowe MS. 692, fo. 82.

„   Thomas, of Danmow.   Add. MS. 31,896, fo. 30.

RAYMOND (see John, 1588), 20 Sept. 1581, by Cooke : sa., a chev. betw. three eagles displayed arg., on a chief or a rose betw. two fleurs-de-lis gu.   Harl. MS. 1442, fo. 17.

„   John, of Little Dunmow, Essex, gent., grant 15 Nov., 2 and 3 Philip and Mary, 1555, by Sir G. Dethick, Gart.   Harl. MS. 1116, fo. 44 ; Q's Coll. Oxf. MS. 39, fo. 60, copy of grant ; Harl. MS. 1359, fo. 1ᶜ ; Grants I., 224.

„   John, of London, gent., purveyor H.M. Pottery [Poltry, i.e., Poultry]. Crest 20 Sept. 1588, by Ro. Cooke, Clar.   Grants I., 225, Her. Coll.

„   Sir Jonathan, Knt. and Alderm. of London, 11 April 1687, by T. St. George, Gart. and Clar.   Harl. MS. 1172, fo. 67ᵇ ; Misc. Gen. et Her., 2nd S., vol. ii., fo. 59 ; Grants III., 312 ; Lansd. MS. 867, fo. 52.   Az., an eagle displayed erm., on a chief embattled arg. three plates (silver).   Crest: out of a mural crown a demi-eagle displayed erm., charged on the breast with three plates as in the arms, beaked sa.   Harl. MSS. 1085, fo. 58, and 6179, fo. 59ᵇ.

RAYNES, Robert, of Nottingham, confirmed . . . . 1558.   (Harvey's Grants), Add. MS. 16,940, fo. 8ᵇ.

RAYNOLDS, see REANALDS, REYNOLDS and PAYNE.

„   John, of Attleburgh, Norfolk, gent., and ⎱ and their posterity, confirmed
„   Henry, his brother,   ⎰ 14 Oct. 1576, 18 Q. Eliz., by Cooke.   Harl. MSS. 1470, fo. 97, 213, and 1359, fo. 122 ; Guil. 182 ; Grants II., 507.

READ, see also REDE.

„   . . . ., of Faccombe, Hants, colours, etc., assigned by Earl Marshal's Warrant 26 March 1640.   Grants II., 674.

„   Allan, draper, of Sᵗ Dunstan's-in-the-West, by Bysshe, Gart.   Harl. MS. 1441, fo. 149ᵇ.

READE, John, of London : gu., a chevron or betw. three fleurs-de-lis, two in chief or and one in base arg., ... 1599, by Camden.   Morgan's Sphere, 117 ; (see Guil. 225, az., three cock pheasants or).   (John, s. of George, s. of Leonard.)

READ, Peter, of Gymmyngham, Norfolk, augmentation, etc., 1535, by the Emp. Chas. V. Harl. MS. 1552, fo. 136.

READE, Thomas, of Barton, Berks, ... by Cooke. Harl. MS. 1359, fo. 115 ; Add. MS. 4966, fo. 95ᵇ.

READ, William, and ⎱ sons of James (or William), of Wichford, Essex, confirmed
  „ Thomas, ⎰ 20 Jan. 1653-4, by Bysshe, Gart. Add. MS. 26,758, fo. 16.

READHEAD, Robert, gent., Servant and one of the grooms in her Majestie's Chamber, now Castellan or Keeper of the Castle at York, s. of Bartholomew; of Sheriff Hutton Castle, Yorks, sometime servant to Ed. VI., etc., augmentation and crest granted 10 May 1598, by W. Dethick, Gart. Q's Coll. Oxf. MS. 36, fo. 73, copy of grant ; Provost marshal at Ostend, Stowe MS. 676, fo. 126, and one of the shewers in Ordinary, etc. ; Surtees Soc., XLI., xliii.

READING [Borough of], in Berks [confirmed 6 Oct.] 1566 [by Harvey, Clar.]. (Berry).

REANALDES, see REYNOLDS, RAYNOLDS and PAYNE.

REANALDES, ..., one of the clerks of the privy seale, April 1607, by Camden. Harl. MSS. 1422, fo. 20, and 6095, fo. 7.

REBOW, John, of Colchester, Essex, granted 10 April 1685, by Sir Wᵐ Dugdale, Gart., and Sir Hy. Sᵗ George, Clar. Grants III., 263 ; Guil. 364 ; Lansd. MS. 867, fo. 52 ; Harl. MS. 1085, fo. 59.

REDDALL, George, of Lincolnshire, coat and crest . . . . Barker's Grants, 1526—49 ; Harl. MS. 5846, fo. 88.

REDDICHE, Alexander, of Redditch, co. Lanc., confirmed 15 May 1587, by Flower. MS. Ashm. 844, fo. 68, copy of grant, Bodleian Lib. ; Guil. 177 ; Grants I., 10.

REDE, see also READE.

  „ Sir Edward, of Norwich and Beccles, Suff., 15 May 1521, 13 Hen. VIII., by T. Wriothesley and Benolte, Clar. : Az., on a bend wavy or three Cornish choughs ppr., a border engrailed arg. charged with torteaux and pellets alternately. Stowe MS. 693, fo. 76ᵇ.

  „ Sir Richard, of Acton, Middx., Knt., coat and crest (a bugle's head, etc.). Barker's Grants, 1526—49 ; Harl. MS. 5846, fo. 89ᵇ ; Stowe MS. 692, fo. 82ᵇ.

  „ Robert, of Chedingston, Kent, Chief Justice of the K.'s Bench, crest granted 6 Aug. 1518, by T. Wriothesley, Gart., and Benolte : A shoveller bendy of six arg. and sa., beaked and membered or. Stowe MS. 676, fo. 12 ; MS. Ashm. 834, fo. 1, copy of grant, Bodleian Lib. ; Stowe MS. 692, fo. 82 ; Harl. MS. 5846, fo. 89ᵇ, has Reske ; and Add. MS. 26,702, fo. 44ᵇ [has Rede].

  „ William, of the city of Bristol. . . . . 1565, 8 Q. Eliz. (Harvey's Grants), Add. MS. 16,940, fo. 41ᵇ.

REDING, George (of London), descended from Reding of Reding Hall, co. Hereford, exemplified, ratified and confirmed Nov. 1609, by Camden. Harl. MSS. 1422, fo. 20ᵇ, and 6095, fo. 11 ; Guil. 333.

REDMAN, ..., procter in the Arches Court, by Segar. Add. MS. 14,295, fo. 73ᵇ (fo. 35ᵇ) ; Harl. MS. 5887, fo. 83.

  „ Richard, and his brother ⎱ s. of John, Mayor of Wilton, Wilts,
  „ Thomas, proctor in the Court of ⎬ grant 9 July 1599, by W. Dethick,
  Arches, registrar principal, etc., ⎰ Gart., and Camden. Q's Coll. Oxf. MS. 36, fo. 83, copy of grant ; Stowe MS. 676, fo. 131 ; Cott. MS. Faustina, E. I, fo. 63.

  „ William, Bp. of Norwich, D.D., arms confirmed and crest given at London 1 May 1595, by Lee. (1594 in Harl. MS. 1422, fo. 51 ; Add. MS. 14,295, fo. 22ᵇ) ; Harl. MS. 1359, fo. 30ᵇ ; 27ᵗʰ May in Stowe MS. 670, fo. 59 ; 17ᵗʰ May in Add. MS. 14,297, fo. 70.

REE, Richard, of Kidderminster, ... 1589, by Cooke. Entered again 1634, see Sir H. St. George ? at Visit. [of Worcestersh., 1682-3 ?] ; Harl. MS. 1422, fo. 124ᵇ.

REED als SMITH, Thomas, of Norfolk, 15 Jan. 1481-2. See SMITH.

REEPES, Henry, s. and h. of John, 2nd s. of Henry, crest 30 Nov. 1560, by Dalton. Harl. MS. 1359, fo. 47.

REEVE, see REVE.

„ Agnes (ux. Sir Edw. Walker, Gart.), d. of Dr John Reeve, of Bookham, Surrey, J.P.), 1 July 1660, by Walker, Gart. Her. Coll., 32.

REICHEL, Servatius, Wenceslaus, Lazarus and Israel, s. of Nicholas, and to their cousins Nicholaus, Stanislaus, Johannes and Paul, s. of Stanislaus, granted 9 Sept. 1554, by Emperor Ferdinand. Berry.

REIGNOLDS, see PAYNE, PAINE, and REYNOLDS.

RELFE, John, one of the Clerks assistants in the House of Lords, 28 Jan. 1692-3, by T. St. George, Gart. and Clar. Harl. MS. 14,830, fo. 179 ; Grants IV., 127 ; Harl. MS. 1085, fo. 57.

RELF, William, of London, ... gift . . . . 1561 . . . . sa., two chevrons erm. betw. three greyhounds' heads, etc. (Harvey's Grants), Add. MS. 16,940, fo. 59.

RENFORCES, Patentees of, see PATENTEES.

REPPES, Henry, see REEPES.

RESCROWE (DERESCROWNE), Thomas, of Derescrowe, Cornwall, 10 March 1547-8, by ? Hawley. Add. MS. 16,940, fo. 202.

REST, ... with crest, Hen. VIII. Add. MS. 26,702, fo. 35 ; Harl. MS. 1049, fo. 67ᵇ, 68ᵇ, grocer. Memo.—John Rest, Lord Mayor of London 1516. Stowe MS. 692, fo. 82.

REAVE, Anthony, of Breade, Sussex, coat confirmed and crest granted 13 July 1633. Guil. 247 ; by Segar, Add. MS. 12,225, fo. 96ᵇ ; Harl. MS. 1096, fo. 161.

REVE, Francis, of Maldon, Suff., ... 1590, by Cooke. Harl. MSS. 1359, fo. 103. 1422, fo. 90ᵇ.

REVELL, George, 1577, see KEVALL.

„ John, of London, gift . . . . 1561 : per chev. engrailed sa. and or or argent, two chaplets ? (Harvey's Grants), Add. MS. 16,940, fo. 38 [has "p cheveron engr sables and ar., two chastells in chif argent, in poinct on a pellett afleurdelys gold, on a wrethe argent & sables an antelupes head razid azur, mayned, horned & tusked golde, holding in his mouthe a braunche of acorns in their pper couller "].

„ Robert, of Shortloud Legg, co. Derby, crest granted 10 July 1545, 37 Hen. VIII., by William Fellows, Norr. MS. Ashm. 858, fo. 154 and 162, copy of grant, Bodleian Lib. ; Stowe MS. 706, fo. 12ᵇ, and to John Revell of co. Derby confused ; see also Harl. MSS. 1093, fo. 83, and 6140, fo. 71ᵇ ; Reliquary, xxii., 51.

REWSE, Symon, esq., of Hedgeston (? Hoxton), 1 April 1632, by Segar. Add. MS. 12,225, fo. 96ᵇ, inserted about 15 May 1730 from grant brought to Mr Shier's office.

REYNARDSON, Thomas, of Plymouth, Devon, 10 Dec. 1632, by Segar. Add. MS. 12,225, fo. 96ᵇ ; Guil. 373 ; Harl. MS. 6140, fo. 80ᵇ.

REYNER, William, of Overton, Hunts, ... 1588, by Cooke. Harl. MSS. 1359, fo. 108ᵇ, and 1422, fo. 94 ; same arms and crest as John Reyner in Stowe MS. 670, fo. 26, etc., see Raynor in the Armories ; Add. MS. 4966, fo. 57ᵇ ; Quarterly coat, Harl. MS. 6140, fo. 45.

REYNES, Thomas, of Hampstead, Middx., gent., granted . . . . 2 and 3 Philip and Mary, 1555-6, by Sir G. Dethick, Gart. Q's Coll. Oxf. MS. 39, fo. 59 ; Harl. MS. 1359, fo. 64 ; Grants I., 222 ; Harl. MS. 1116, fo. 44.

REIGNOLTE, ... crest . . . . Barker's Grants, Harl. MS. 5846, fo. 90ᵇ ; Stowe MS. 692, fo. 82ᵇ.

REYNOLDS, see RAYNOLDS, REANALDES and PAYNE.

REYNOLDS, ... (? 1664), by Sir E. Bysshe.   Harl. MS. 1105, fo. 39 ;   Bysshe's Grants 29.
 „ Henry, of Belstead, Suff., s. of Robert, of the same, arms altered, crest granted .... 1584, by Cooke. Add. MS. 14,295, fo. 41 ; Harl. MSS. 1359, fo. 116ᵇ, and 1422, fo. 60ᵇ ; Guil. 102 as Reginale ; Add. MS. 4966, fo. 29ᵇ.
REIGNOLDS, Thomas, and } gent., sons of Henry, of Denbigh, crest granted to
 „ John,   } Henry, of Denbigh, gent., and to William and Thos. and John here named, temp. Q. Eliz., by W. Dethick, Gart. (See PAYNE, p. 193.) Stowe MS. 676, fo. 37ᵇ ; Q's Coll. Oxf. MS. 36, fo. 116, copy of grant ; Grants I., 145.
REYNY, John, of city of London, s. of Roger, etc., 16 March 1619-20, by Camden. Misc. Gen. et Her., i., 191 ; (called Wᵐ Rainey in Harl. MS. 6095, fo. 37); Guil. 216.
RICCARD alias RICHARDS, Charles, of Hecke, Yorks, ... 1595, by Lee. Harl. MS. 1422, fo. 124 ; Add. MS. 14,295, fo. 75.
RICCARD, Charles, of Heck, Yorks, a confirmation in a scutcheon 11 Aug. 1612, by R. St. George, Norr. Stowe MS. 706, fo. 15.
RYCARD, Thomas, of Heittesfeld, Yorks, 24 Jan. 1519, by T. Wriothesley, Gart. Le Neve's MS. 513 ; temp. H. VIII., by Norroy, Harl. MS. 1422, fo. 17.
RICE, rightly PRICE, John, of Barton Regis, co. Glouc., s. of Gregory, confirmed 8 April 1573, by Cooke. Harl. MS. 1422, fo. 57, and Add. MS. 14,295, fo. 26, as PRYCE, which see.
RICE, Richard, of Preston, Suff., Quarterly .... 1586, by Cooke's deputy.   Stowe MS. 670, fo. 17ᵇ ; Robert in Harl. MS. 5887, fo. 17.
 „ William, of Boemer (Medmenham), Bucks, grant 2 May, 2 and 3 Philip and Mary, 1556, by Hawley. Q's Coll. Oxf. MS. 38, fo. 67, copy of grant ; Harl. MS. 1470, fo. 248 ; Bodmar in Harl. MS. 1507, fo. 409 ; Grants II., 455 ; Add. MS. 16,940, fo. 208 ; Guil. 160 ; Le Neve's MS. 409.
RICH, ..., of Otford, Kent, 1 April 1656. Harl. MS. 1105, fo. 16. ? By Bysshe, Clar.
 „ Edward, of Horndon on the Hill, Essex, ? crest, a patent 30 May 1579, by Cooke : Rich quartering Shaa. Harl. MSS. 1359, fo. 120, and 1422, fo. 121ᵇ ; Add. MS. 4966, fo. 90.
 „ Thomas, of Leyton (or Lexden), Essex, ... 1590, by Ro. Cooke, Clar. : per pale sa. and gu., a cross bottonnée betw. four fleurs-de-lis or ; Crest, on the stump of a tree couped and erased or, a hawk, wings endorsed arg., preying on a pheasant ppr. Stowe MS. 670, fo. 38ᵇ ; Berry.
 „ Sir Richard, of Brendiche, Essex, coat exemplified and crest. Barker's Grants, Harl. MS. 5846, fo. 87 ; Stowe MS. 692, fo. 82ᵇ, " Rich. and his wife in the other book " ; see also Harl. MS. 6834.
RICHARDS, Edward, of Yaverland, Hants. Harl. MSS. 1544, fo. 43ᵇ, and 5865, fo. 43ᵇ.
RICHARDSON, Capt. Edward, served in Ireland, certified 22 May 1647, by Wᵐ Roberts, D.C.L., Ulster K. of Arms. Genealogist, i., 201, copy of grant, Brit. Mus.
 „ Edward, of Ripon, Yorks, gent., grant 20 March 1649-50, by Ryley. Surtees Soc., XLI., lii, copy of grant, Brit. Mus. ; Genealogist, i., 201.
 „ Ferdinando, of Gloucester, of the privy chamber, 1588, by Cooke. Harl. MSS. 1359, fo. 95ᵇ, 1422, fo. 88ᵇ, and 6140, fo. 47.
 „ John, of city of Durham, crest 18 Sept. 1615, by R. St. George, Norr. Surtees Soc., XLI., xlviii, copy of grant, Brit. Mus.
 „ Sir Thomas, of Horringham, Norfolk, Knt., Lord C. J. of Com. Pleas, 3 Feb. 1627-8, by R. St. George, Clar. Harl. MS. 1422, fo. 88ᵇ ; alteration, Harl. MS. 1116, fo. 29.
RICHARS, Edmond, of Fringe, Norfolk, ... 1613, by Camden. Harl. MS. 6095, fo. 40ᵇ ; Le Neve's MS. 353.

RICHERS, John, of Stalham, Norfolk, 24 July 1664. Bysshe's Grants, fo. 16, Her. Coll.; Harl. MS. 1105, fo. 19[b].

RICHMAN or RICHMOND, Richard, of Hedenham, Norfolk, crest 1576, by Cooke, Clar. Bannerman's MS., No. 9, 453. ["The Coat conf. to this famylie is: Er., on a cheif sa. a Grip. pa. or; Crest, a falcon rousant er., beaked & l. or, p Robertum Cook, Clar., 1576, A° 18 Eliz."]

RIDDELL (RYDELL) alias BONNER, John, of Swarford, Oxon., Esq., and his cousin
  „ Anthony, of Campden, co. Glouc., gent., 16 May 1574, by Cooke. Add. MS. 14,295, fo. 25; alias Benne in Harl. MS. 1422, fo. 52.

RYDGWAYE als PECOK, John, of Karsebill Abbot [Abbot's Careswell], Devon, 20 Feb. 1540-41, by T. Hawley. Add. MSS. 16,940, fo. 200[b], and 7098, fo. 77 (? fo. 31).

RIDGEWAYE, Sir Thomas, of Torre, Devon, Kt., s. of Thos. and Maria, d. and coh. of Grace, d. and sole heir of John Borenhouse of Marsh, Devon, Esq., and grandchild of John Ridgeway of Torre, Devon, Esq.; grant 4 May 1602, by Camden. Cott. MS. Faustina, E. 1, 55[b]; Guil. 216; 10 quarterings, Harl. MS. 6140, fo. 46[b].

RIDGES, William, fined for Sheriff and Alderm. of London; 22 March 1664-5, by Bysshe, Clar. Harl. MS. 1105, fo. 40; Bysshe's Grants, fo. 35; Harl. MS. 1410, fo. 15.

RYDLEY, Thomas, M.A., confirmed 11 July, 23 Q. Eliz., 1581, by Flower. MS. Ashm. 844, fo. 53, copy of grant, Bodleian Lib.; Guil. 149.

RIDSDALL, George, of co. Linc., 20 Aug. 1547, by ? Hawley. Add. MS. 16,940, fo. 202.

RIGBY, Alexander, of Burgh, co. Lanc., ... 1573, by Flower. Harl. MS. 1422, fo. 42[b].
  „ Alexander, of Wigan, co. Lanc., ... by St. George, Norr. Harl. MS. 1422, fo. 15[b].

RIGDON, Robert, of Dowesby, Lincoln, ... 1601, by Camden. Harl. MSS. 1422, fo. 71, and 6140, fo. 40[b].

RIGGES, Ralph, of Farnham or Fareham, Surrey, s. of Thomas, who died seised of the manor of Farnham, s. of Thomas, of Southampton, confirmed by Segar, testified by W[m] Le Neve, 23 Oct. 1640. (See also Mary BLAKE, his wife.) Add. MS. 12,225, fo. 97; C. 19 [? Visit. Hampshire, 1622], fo. 124, Her. Coll.; and Guil. 195; Grants I., 419.

RIGGS, William, of the par. of Clerkenwell, Middx., one of the King's Auditors, coat and crest . . . . Barker's Grants, Harl. MS. 5846, fo. 91; Stowe MS. 692, fo. 82[b].

RIPPON (RYPON), Walter, of London, gent., coachmaker to Q. Eliz., s. of Jeoffrey, s. of Thos., s. of Thos., s. of Rich., s. of John, s. of Arnold, of Yorks, gent., crest 19 June 1590, by Cooke. Add. MS. 14,295, fo. 42[b]; Harl. MS. 1359, fo. 96[b].

RISLEY, William, of Chetwell, Bucks, ... by Cooke, Clar. Stowe MS. 670, fo. 41.

RIVERS, ..., Chafford, Kent, ... 1583: arms, az., two bars dancettée or, in chief three bezants. Berry.
  „ Elizabeth, Countess, arms and supporters 9 Nov. 1680. Grants III., 119. See also SCROOPE, by W. Dugdale, Gart., and St. George, Clar.

RYVERS, Sir John, Knt., Alderm., confirmed and crest granted 2 May 1581, by Cooke. Harl. MS. 1359, fo. 87[b]; MS. Ashm. 834, fo. 37; (1583 in Harl. MS. 1422, fo. 117[b], and Add. MS. 14,295, fo. 34[b]); Guil. 358; Add. MS. 4966, fo. 58, ? copy of grant, Bodleian Lib.

ROBARTES, Richard, esq., s. and h. of John, late of Truro, Cornwall, s. and h. of Richard, of the same, patent 2 Jan. 1614-15, 12 K. Jas., by Camden. (Grafton in margin.) Harl. MSS. 1422, fo. 39[b], and 6095, fo. 31[b]; Guil. 103.

ROBBINS, see also ROBINS.

ROBBINS, John, of Dover, a captain, 19 Dec., 1 Q. Eliz., 1558, by Dalton. Harl. MS. 1359, fo. 45 ; copy of grant, Harl. MS. 1116, fo. 69.

ROBERTS, ... Salop and Somerset, ... 1578. Berry's Armory.

„ John : Harberts, surnamed Roberts [Robart in Stowe MS.], of Cardiff, N. Wales ; confirmed 13 Nov. 1574, by W. Dethick, Garter. [In Harl. MS. 1453, fo. 35, there is a trick of the Arms.—Quarterly : 1, Per pale Az. and Gules, three lions rampant Argent ; 2. Argent, on a bend cottised Sa. three mullets of the field ; 3, Ar., a lion rampant Sable, crowned Or ; 4, Gules, a lion rampant within a bordure engrailed Or.] " These 4 Coates Garter hath past by patent to one Robertes of Caerdiff in Wales, wch Robertes father was a Pedler and Bastard to one Sr Robert, a Preist, for the mayntenance of wch Armes the said Garter hath forged a most false pedigree : The first Coate is Herbertes, borne by the Earle of Worcester, who is Lo. Herbert of the same. The second is the anntient Armes of Andrewes of Northamptonshire ; the 3 is the Armes of the Lo. Morley. The 4 is the Cheif Coate of the Earle of Shrewsbury." Entered by R. Brooke, York Herald. Harl. MS. 1453, fo. 35 ; Stowe MS. 676, fo. 44 ; copy of grant, Q's Coll. Oxf. MS. 37, fo. 56.

„ Thomas, of Little Braxted, Essex, gent., exemplified quarterly coat (Hobson of Shipley, Sussex), and crest 1626, by Segar. Add. MSS. 12,225, fo. 97b, and 14,293, fo. 22b ; (s. of Thos., s. of Clement, see Guil. 335) ; Harl. MS. 6140, fo. 80.

„ William, of Sutton Chenell, co. Leic., a patent May 1614, by Camden. Harl. MSS. 6095, fo. 30, and 1422, fo. 39 ; Guil. 384 ; Grants I., 22.

ROBINS, see also ROBBINS.

„ George, of Hackney, Middx., 10 May 1672, by Sir E. Bysshe, Clar. Bysshe's Grants, fo. 31 ; Harl. MS. 1105, fo. 39b ; alteration in crest 19 March 1672-3, by Bysshe, Bysshe's Grants, fo. 34, and Harl. MS. 1105, fo. 40.

„ John, of Netherhall in the par. of Stoketon, co. Worc., coat and crest. Barker's Grants, Harl. MS. 5846, fo. 88 ; Stowe MS. 692, fo. 82.

BOBYNSON, Francis, of London, gift . . . . 1561. (Harvey's Grants), Add. MS. 16,940, fo. 42.

ROBINSON, Henry, Bp. of Carlisle, arms granted 25 July 1598, by W. Dethick, Gart. Stowe MS. 676, fo. 127 ; Q's Coll. Oxf. MS. 36, fo. 76, copy of grant in Latin.

„ Henry, of Cransley, Northants, descended out of Yorkshire, ... Nov. 1611, by Camden, patent. Harl. MSS. 1422, fo. 35, and 6095, fo. 16b ; Grants II., 570.

„ Henry, of Langford, Essex, clerck, 26 Sept. 1671, by Sir E. Bysshe, Clar. Harl. MS. 1105, fo. 22 ; and Bysshe's Grants, 28.

„ Sir John, Knt. and Bart. (nephew to Dr William Land, Archbp. of Canterbury), Lord Mayor of London and Lieut. of the Tower of London ; augmentation 20 Oct. 1663, by Walker. Add. MSS. 14,293, fo. 59, and 14,294, fo. 15, letters patent at Whitehall 13 Oct., Harl. MS. 1172, fo. 62 ; copy of grant, Stowe MS. 677, fo. 68 ; Genealogist, i., 153.

„ William, Alderm. of the city of York, 1 Aug. 1626, 14 K. [James I., 1616], by R. St. George, Norr. Stowe MS. 706, fo. 17 ; Add. MS. 14,295, fo. 72 ; 1616 in Harl. MS. 6140, fo. 73b.

„ Sir William, of Newby, Yorks, Knt., granted and confirmed 20 Feb. 1634-5, 10 Chas., by Sir W. Le Neve, Norr. Surtees Soc., XLI., xlix, copy of grant, Brit. Mus.

ROBOTHAM, Robert, of Raskill, Yorks, granted 8 Dec. 1560, 3 Eliz., by Dalton. Harl. MS. 1359, fo. 47b ; Her. and Geneal., i., 81 ; Misc. Gen. et Her., 2nd S., vol. i., p. 269.

ROBSON, Thomas, Gyles and Robert, sons of James, late of Cambridge, gent., confirmed 3 May 1635, by R. St. George, Clar. Add. MS. 5822, fo. 28.

ROCH, Sir Bartholomew le, a Frenchman, Captain of the fireworkers, 6 May 1645 at Oxford, by Sir E. Walker, Gart. Her. Coll., fo. 27.

ROCHE, ... crest, a roebuck's head . . . . Barker's Grants, Harl. MS. 5846, fo. 89 ; Stowe MS. 692, fo. 82.

ROCHDALE, Richard, of London, in the par. of St. Michael the King, 9 Dec. 1656, ? by Bysshe, Clar. Harl. MS. 1105, fo. 15b.

ROCKE, Richard, of Shrewsbury, confirmed 6 March 1603, 1 Jac., by Camden. MS. Ashm. 858, fo. 133, copy of grant, Bodleian Lib. ; Harl. MSS. 5839, fo. 2, 2275, fo. 90, and 1115, fo. 8.

RODES, William, of Skyrket, Yorks, confirmed 21 Aug. 1585, by Cooke. Harl. MS. 1359, fo. 88b ; Add. MS. 14,295, fo. 75 ; Misc. Gen. et Her., 2nd S., vol. iii., p. 293 ; Guil. 364 ; Add. MS. 4966, fo. 52.

RODWAY, ..., of London and Tottenham, ... arg., on a fesse az. betw. three bugle horns stringed sa. as many roses or, by ? Segar. Add. MS. 12,225, fo. 97b.

ROE, Sir Thomas, of Bulwick, Northants, lately of Beckenham, Kent, etc., exemplified 30 April 1632, by R. St. George, Clar. Harl. MS. 1441, fo. 60b, copy in Brit. Mus. *See also* ROWE and RAWE.

ROGER, Christopher, of Sutton, Kent, ... 1593, by Cooke. Harl. MS. 1359, fo. 111b, and 1422, fo. 60 ; Add. MS. 4966, fo. 24.

ROGERS, Mary, ux. John Harrington, of Kelston, Somerset, esq., d. of Jane (widow of Sir George Rogers of Cammington, Somerset, decd), dau. and sole h. of Edmond Winter of Cliffe, Devon, by his wife Elnor, dau. and heir of Silvester Sydenham, Arms quarterly of 6 given and granted to Mary Harrington by her mother Jane Harrington 20 Sept. 1594, to be exemplified by Mr Garter (*i.e.*, W. Dethick). Q's Coll. Oxf. MS. 37, fo. 85, copy of exemplification, etc.

   „   Ralfe, of London, ... 1586, by Cooke. Harl. MSS. 1359, fo. 90b, and 1422, fo. 60 ; Add. MS. 4966, fo. 69.

   „   Richard, of Little Ness, Salop, ... 1578, by Cooke. Harl. MSS. 1359, fo. 119, and 1422, fo. 60 ; Add. MS. 14,295, fo. 51 ; in Stowe MS. 670, fo. 72, the crest is without the mount vert, and also in Add. MS. 4966, fo. 94b.

   „   Robert, of Coulton, Norfolk, grant, 26 Jan. 1576-7, by W. Dethick, York Herald. Stowe MS. 676, fo. 54b ; Q's Coll. Oxf. MS. 37, fo. 64, copy of grant ; Proc. Soc. of Antiq., 1897, 2nd S., xvi., p. 352.

ROLLE, ... crest . . . . Barker's Grants, Add. MS. 26,702, fo. 56 ; Harl. MS. 5846, fo. 90 ; Stowe MS. 692, fo. 82b.

   „   (William ?), of Hele, Devon, clerk, with crest. Add. MS. 26,702, fo. 56.

ROLPH, Edmond, goldsmith, of London, arg., three crows sa., a trefoil in chief vert, by Camden. Morgan's Sphere, 117.

ROMMEY, William, of London, gent., arms and crest by patent 26 Sept. 1593, by Wm Dethick and Cooke. Harl. MS. 1359, fo. 10b ; 16 Dec. in Harl. MS. 1422, fo. 95 ; Harl. MS. 5887, fo. 12b ; Add. MS. 4966, fo. 84b.

ROMNEY, John, of Middleton in Kent, gent., grant 7th or 11th April 1615, by Segar. Add. MS. 12,225, fo. 98 ; Guil. 262 ; Harl. MS. 6140, fo. 62b ; 9th in Bannerman's MS., No. 9, 450.

RONE, Edward, of Middx., 6 Nov. 1598, by Camden and W. Dethick, Gart. Add. MSS. 14,295, fo. 63, and 31,896, fo. 30 ; Antony in Harl. MS. 1116, fo. 80b.

ROOE, *see also* ROWE and RAWE.

   „   Roger, of Alport, co. Derby, ? by R. St. George, Norr.; elder brother of Sir Friend (Francis) Rooe, and to the heirs of his body, 9 June 1608 (*alibi* 1605) (another coat and crest 9 July 1612). Harl. MS. 1422, fo. 79b ; Add. MS. 14,295, fo. 71, as Roe and 1605 ; Stowe MS. 716, fo. 55, per pale or and gu., a lion, etc. [per pale or and gu., semée of trefoils slipped, a lion rampant, all counterchanged ; crest, an arm embowed, habited Gules, holding in the hand ppr. a garb Or] ; Harl. MS. 5887, fo. 56b.

Roof, Sir William, Iremonger, Lord Maior of London, ... 1595, by Cooke. Harl.
MS. 1422, fo. 79^b.

Rook, ..., arg., a fess betw. three chess rooks gu., confirmed , . . . 1631, by
Segar. Add. MS. 12,225, fo. 98 ; Harl. MS. 6140, fo. 65.

Rooke, ..., of Tipton, Essex, ... alteration . . . . by Cooke. Harl. MS. 1442,
fo. 16^b.

Rookes, George, of London, 1 May 1640, by Borough. Harl. MSS. 1105, fo. 57,
and 1441, fo. 58 ; Add. MS. 26,702, fo. 93^b ; Guil. 322.

,, George, of Stony Stratford, Bucks, former arms approved and allowed 29 Oct.
1640, by W. Le Neve. Grants II., 616.

Roper, Thomas, of Eltham, Kent, ... 1587 or 1578 ?, by Sir G. Dethick, Gart.
Harl. MS. 1441, fo. 89 ; Q's Coll. Oxf. MS. 145, fo. 46^b ; Harl. MSS. 5887,
fo. 39, and 6140, fo. 27^b.

Roscarrock, Richard, of Cornwall, Crest 1 Nov. 1553, by ? Hawley. Add. MS.
16,940, fo. 206^b.

Rose, Judith, widow of Sir Maurice Diggs, Bart., ⎫ daus. and coheirs of George
now wife of Daniel Sheldon of Ham ⎪ Rose of Easter Gate, Sussex,
Court, Surrey, and ⎪ 16 Feb. 1681-2, by Sir W^m

,, Margaret, relict of Sir Joseph Sheldon, Kt., ⎬ Dugdale, Gart. and Clar.
late alderm. and sometime Lord Mayor of ⎪ Harl. MS. 6834, fo. 178 ;
the City of London, ⎭ Grants III., 149 ; and Berry.

,, John, of Lyme Regis, Dorset, granted 2 Nov. 1639, by Borough, Gart.
Harl. MSS. 1105, fo. 56^b. and 1441, fo. 58^b ; Add. MS. 26,702, fo. 92^b ;
Guil. 120 ; Harl. MS. 6140, fo. 17 ; Richard in Harl. MS. 6140, fo. 17.

,, Martha (d. of Nicholas, of London), ux. John Heydon, late Sheriff and
Alderm. city of London, grant 10 Jan., 24 Eliz., 1582-3, by Cooke. Q's
Coll. Oxf. MS. 37, fo. 83, copy of grant : Stowe MS. 676, fo. 60.

Rosenbrick, Michael, a Prussian born, augmentation (a chief) granted at London
29 May 1568, by G. Dethick, Gart. Q's Coll. Oxf. MSS. 36, fo. 119, copy
of grant in Latin, and 39, fo. 132 ; (born at Pedam or Sedain in Prussia,
Stowe MS. 676) ; Harl. MS. 1359, fo. 61^b ; Grants I., 35.

Rosse, John, a student in the Inner Temple, s. of Thomas, of Wadesden, Bucks,
grant (? 45 Q. Eliz.), by W. Dethick, Gart. Stowe MS. 676, fo. 139 ; Q's
Coll. Oxf. MS. 36, fo. 98, copy of grant.

Rossetur, Richard, of Somerby, co. Linc., ... 1592, by Cooke. Harl. MS. 1359,
fo. 112 ; Add. MSS. 17,506, fo. 27^b, and 4966, fo. 25^b.

Rotheram, George, Quarterly . . . . by Wm Dethick, Gart. "This second coat
being the chiefe armes of Gray, now Earle of Kent, Garter hath given
away without any difference to one George Rotheram, and made a false
pedegree to mayntayne the same, which abuse of it bee not redressed. The
said Earles heyres are in danger thereby to be disinherited." Entered by
R. Brooke, York Her. Harl. MS. 1453, fo. 34 ; see Edward in Harl. MS.
5887, fo. 10.

Rothwell, James, of Coldrey, Hants, Assistant Surveyor of the Ordnance, 1 March
168⅞, by Sir T. St. George, Gart. and Clar. Harl. MS. 6834, fo. 178 ;
Grants III., fo. 345 ; Lansd. MS. 867, fo. 52.

,, Stephen, of Ewarby, co. Linc., descended out of the family of Rothewell, co.
Lanc., 1 April 1585, 27 Q. Eliz., by Flower. MS. Ashm. 834, fo. 60, copy
of grant, Bodleian Lib.; Harl. MS. 1359, fo. 82^b ; Guil. 365 ; Harl. MS.
5887, fo. 4^b.

Roundell, William, of Hutton Wansley, Yorks, 20 April 1676, by W. Dugdale,
Norr. Harl. MS. 6834, fo. 178 ; Grants III., 25 ; and Edmondson's
Armory.

Rowbatch, Giles, of Lytton, co. Hereford, s. of Thomas, s. of Pierce Rowbatch of
Letton, co. Hereford, confirmed March 1614, by Camden. (John in Harl.
MS. 1422, fo. 38^b) ; Harl. MS. 6095, fo. 29^b ; Guil. 62.

Rowe (see also Rooe and Rawe), William, of Pontefract, Yorks, 20 Oct. 1651, by

F F

Ed. Bysshe. Harl. MSS. 1466, fo. 24, and 1441, fo. 152 ; copy of grant, *see* Proc. Soc. Antiq., 1897, p. 354 ; N. and Q., 2nd S., vol. xi., p. 171.

ROWE, John, of Lewes, Sussex (s. of William), confirmation of arms, quartering Drew of East Grinsted, Sussex, and crest 24 May 1614, by Segar. Add. MS. 12,225, fo. 98[b] ; Misc. Gen. et Her., i., 161 ; Guil. 186.

„ Robert, of Windle Hill, co. Derby, ⎫ sons of Henry, of Windle Hill afore-
  and his brother   ⎬ said, s. of William, crest 9 July
„ Roger, of London,   ⎭ 1612, by R. St. George, Norr. Add.
MS. 14,295, fo. 109 ; Harl. MS. 1422, fo. 78 ; Stowe MS. 706, fo. 19 ; Grants I., 245.

„ Samuel, of Macclesfield, Cheshire, gent., one of the fellows of the Soc. of Gray's Inn, confirmed 10 March 1653-4, by Ryly. Harl. MS. 1470, fo. 64 ; 20th of March, and declared void on the Restoration according to Guil. 236 ; Local Gleanings Mag., by J. P. Earwaker, 1880, 429.

„ Thomas, of Clapham, Bedf., now Alderm. of London, s. of Robert, 2nd s. to Reynold, of Kent ; Crest granted 23 April 1567, by Sir G. Dethick, Gart., and Flower. Q's Coll. Oxf. MS. 39, fo. 127, copy of grant ; Harl. MS. 1359, fo. 56[b].

ROE, *see also* ROOE and ROWE.

ROE, Sir Thomas, Knt., of Bulwick, Northants, out of Kent, Chancellor (of the Garter), s. of Robert, esq., etc., attested 30 April 1632, by R. St. George, Clar. Harl. MS. 1441, fo. 59[b] ; copy of grant, Add. MS. 4966, fo. 44[b].

ROWLAND, Thomas, *see* PENTECOST.

ROWLEY, John, of Barkway, Herts, granted 11 Dec. 1639, by Borough. Harl. MSS. 1105, fo. 56[b], and 1441, fo. 57[b] ; Add. MS. 26,702, fo. 92 ; 20th Dec. in Guil. 106.

ROWSE, Thomas, of London, merchant, 13 April 1647, by E. Bysshe, Gart. Harl. MSS. 1105, fo. 15 *bis*, and 6140, fo. 18.

ROWSEWELL, William, of Ford, Devon, ... by Ro. Cooke. Stowe MS. 670, fo. 27[b].

ROYAL FISHING OF GREAT BRITAIN, the Gov[rs] and Compy. of all the, 13 Dec. 1664, by Walker. Add. MSS. 14,293, fo. 36, and 14,294, fo. 7 ; Harl. MS. 1172, fo. 44 ; copy of grant, Cat. Her. Exhib. Soc. of Antiq., 72.

ROYAL COMPANY, 20 Jan. 1662-3, by Sir E. Walker, Gart. Her. Coll., fo. 4.

ROYAL SOCIETY, arms and supporters, 30 June 1663, by Walker. MSS. Ashm. 836, fo. 123, and 845, fo. 150, copy of grant, Bodleian Lib. ; Her. Coll., fo. 5.

ROYDEN, Robert, of Exeter, 31 July, 9 H. VII., 1494, by Richmond and Clar. Harl. MSS. 5887, fo. 50, and 1116, fo. 38[b].

ROYLE, John, of Leftwich, Cheshire, gent., confirmed 17 Nov. 1654, by Ryley. Harl. MSS. 1470, fo. 176, 273, and 1105, fo. 11 ; Guil. 76.

ROYS, Job, ... gu., a gryphon segreant arg., on a chief of the 2nd three roses of the first . . . . by Segar. Add. MS. 12,225, fo. 98[b] ; Harl. MS. 1105, fo. 5.

ROISE, John, of London, gent., granted 2 July, 5 Q. Eliz., 1563, by Sir G. Dethick, Gart. 1562 in Q's Coll. Oxf. MS. 39, fo. 124, copy of grant ; Harl. MS. 1359, fo. 70 ; Grants I., 212.

RUBENIUS, Sir Petrus Paulus, Sec. to the King of Spain, letters patent augmentation 25 Dec. 1631 at Westminster. MS. Ashm. 858, fo. 86, 87, copy of grant, Bodleian Lib.

RUCHE, ... crest, a lion's head erased vert, dropped arg., ? guttée de l'armes. Barker's Grants, Harl. MS. 5846, fo. 90[b] ; Stowe MS. 692, fo. 82[b].

RUDD, Anthony, D.D., Bp. of St. David's, 12 Aug. 1597, by R. Lee, Clar. Stowe MS. 714, fo. 101, copy of grant, Brit. Mus.

„ John, of Wynterton, co. Lincoln, "Ar., a canton b., thereon vii martlets arg., iij, i & iij g., 3 cupps covered or, a crescent [?] or ; this canton was the olde armes of Lewes le Shatt [le Chat ?] of France, who at Muterell was taken prisoner by the sayd John, & therefor had thes Armes sett forthe but no pattent of them.' Barker's Grants, Stowe MS. 692, fo. 80ᵇ, in a later hand.

Rudd, Matthew, the younger, of Woodham Walter, Essex, s. of Matthew, the elder, sometime of Chelmsford, Essex, and now of Furnival's Inn, exemplified 12 Nov. 1634, 10 Chas., by Sir R. St. George, Clar. Add. MS. 14,293, fo. 18ᵇ; Harl. MS. 1105, fo. 36.

Rudehall, ... crest . . . . Barker's Grants, Harl. MSS. 5846, fo. 90, and 6179, fo. 22ᵇ; Stowe MS. 692, fo. 82ᵇ; see Coat, Harl. MS. 1116, fo. 24ᵇ.

Rudge, Edward, of London, salter, s. of Thomas, of Evesham, co. Worc., out of Cheshire, 1 June 1634, by R. St. George, Clar. Grants II., 665.

Rudiarde, Thomas, of Rudiarde, co. Staff., coat confirmed and crest granted 3 Oct. 1579, by Wᵐ Dakins, Norr. MS. Ashm. 845, fo. 163, copy of grant, Bodleian Lib. Probably a forgery [certainly spurious] as there was no such Norroy. See also Smethwick.

Rugg, William, of Norwich, gent., crest 2 March, 2 Q. Eliz., 1559-60, by Sir G. Dethick, Gart. Q's Coll. Oxf. MS. 39, fo. 106, copy of grant; Harl. MS. 1359, fo. 79.

Rugge, William, of Fellingham, Norfolk, esq., 26 July 1568, by Cooke. Add. MS. 14,295, fo. 64; C. 15, fo. 4ᵇ [Visit. of] Norfolk [1613]; Harl. MS. 1359, fo. 94ᵇ.

Rusburgh, John, of Baldoke (Herts), confirmed 155- or 156-, arg., a chev. sa. between three bears conchant ppr.; crest, a stork sa., purfled arg., membered and beaked gu. (Harvey's Grants), Add. MS. 16,940, fo. 32ᵇ; see also fo. 42, and Harl. MS. 1422, fo. 22; Grants II., 546.

„ Richard, of Aylsham, Norfolk, 16 Nov. 1558, by Hervey. Harl. MS. 1422, fo. 22; Add. MS. 16,940, fo. 32ᵇ and 42; Grants II., 546; Le Neve's MS. 514.

Rushe, Sir Francis, of Essex, ... Jan. 1605, by Camden. Crest, The head dead, the hair and beard sandy colour. Harl. MSS. 1422, fo. 18ᵇ, and 6095, fo. 3.

Russell, ... of Worcestershire, crest . . . . Barker's Grants, Harl. MS. 5846, fo. 91; Stowe MS. 692, fo. 82ᵇ.

„ John, of London, master carpenter of the King's Majesty, granted 15 Oct., 6 Ed. VI., 1552, by Sir Gilb. Dethick, Gart. Q's Coll. Oxf. MS. 39, fo. 40, copy of grant; Harl. MS. 1359, fo. 60; Grants I., 308; Misc. Gen. et Her., 3rd S., vol. v., p. 121.

„ Thomas, of Charlton, Kent, 25 March 1650, by Sir E. Bysshe. With consent of Sir William Russell, Bart., of Streynsham, Thomas to bear the difference of a fifth brother. Add. MS. 14,262, fo. 46ᵇ.

„ William, of Pensey (Pevensey), Sussex, gent., crest 20 Feb., 3 and 4 Philip and Mary, 1556-7, by Sir Gilbert Dethick, Gart. Q's Coll. Oxf. MS. 39, fo. 74, copy of grant; Harl. MSS. 1422, fo. 122, and 1359, fo. 69; Grants I., 204; Harl. MS. 5887, fo. 98ᵇ.

„ Sir William, of (Deblow?), of Chippenham, co. Cambr., Knt., Treasurer of the Navee Royal, confirmed . . . . Dec. 1618, by Camden. Cott. MS. Faust., E. 1, fo. 62ᵇ; Harl. MS. 6095, fo. 36.

Rustat, Tobias, Yeoman of the Robes to his Majesty, crest 30 Dec. 1676, by W. Dugdale, Norr. Add. MS. 14,830, fo. 77; Grants III., 31; Harl. MSS. 1441, fo. 130ᵇ, and 6832, fo. 371ᵇ; Crispe's Visit. Eng. and Wales, notes, i., 87.

Ruthall, (Richard, of Mowshome, co. Bucks), coat and crest. Barker's Grants, Harl. MS. 5846, fo. 88ᵇ; Stowe MS. 692, fo. 82.

„ Dr Thomas (Bishop of Durham), with crest. Add. MS. 26,702, fo. 66ᵇ; Harl. MS. 6179, fo. 22ᵇ.

Rutter, Abraham, of the city of Exeter, Devon, ... by Segar. Add. MS. 12,225, fo. 99.

RYDER, ⌈ Anthony (s. of John, of Newbury, Berks), Physician to the late K. Charles
⎩ during the late Rebellion, and to Chas. II. in foreign parts ; and
  ,, ⌊ John, of Newbury, physician, eldest bro. of Anthony, 10 July 1662, by
Walker. Add. MS. 14,293, fo. 33 ; Rider in Add. MS. 14,294, fo. 5ᵇ ;
Harl. MS. 1172, fo. 51ᵇ ; Guil. 394.

,, John, of Leigh, par. of Churchstow, Devon, 6 May 1662, by Sir E. Walker.
Her. Coll., fo. 46.

RYE, William, of Whitwell, co. Derby, 1575, by W. Flower, Norr. Harl. MS.
1093, fo. 81.

RILEY, ..., of co. Lanc., ... or, a fess betw. three crosses formée vert .... by
Segar. Add. MS. 12,225, fo. 97.

RYLEY, William, Bluemantle pursuivant of arms, by Borough. Harl. MS. 1105,
fo. 56 ; Add. MS. 26,702, fo. 91 ; Harl. MS. 6179, fo. 30.

RYMPYNDEN, John, of Letherhed, Surrey, gent., grant 17 Feb. 1516-17. by
Wriothesley and Benolt. Add. MS. 26,702, fo. 60 ; Q's Coll. Oxf. MS.
38, fo. 29, copy of grant in French.

RYVES, John, of Damory, Dorset, gift .... 1564. (Harvey's Grants), Add. MS.
16,940, fo. 58ᵇ.

RYVETT, James, of Briset in Suffolk, Crest, by Harvey, Clar. Add. MS. 16,940,
fo. 41ᵇ ; Harl. MS. 1116, fo. 66.

S

SABB, John, of Gray's Inn and Norfolk, ... by Ro. Cooke. Stowe MS. 670,
fo. 36ᵇ ; Add. MS. 4966, fo. 90 ; Harl. MS. 6179, fo. 19.

SABIN, John. Beakesbourne, Kent, M.D., grant 29 May 1663, by Sir Ed. Bysshe,
Clar. Bysshe's Grants, fo. 3, Her. Coll. ; Harl. MS. 1470, fo. 132, copy
of grant, Brit. Mus. ; Harl. MS. 1105, fo. 17 ; Guil. 242.

SABLE, of Norfolk, ... 1589, by Cooke : arg., on a pale betw. two anchors sa.
three estoiles or. Harl. MS. 1359, fo. 119.

SABYSCH, Capt. Charles Frederick, a native of Silesia in Germany, who had faithfully
served his late Majesty in the Condition of Engineer, at the Hague 4 June
1649, by Sir E. Walker, Gart. Her. Coll., fo. 29.

SACHEVERELL, George, of Nottingham, s. and h. of Valence, decᵈ, nat. s. to Herry,
late of Morley, co. Derby, grant 11 May 1665, by W. Dugdale, Norr.
(Her. Coll.)

SACRE, ... Kent, ... 1614 .... gu., two bars erm., in chief three martlets or ;
Crest, au elephant or in a wood ppr. Not the Christopher Sacker coat.
Berry.

SAKER, Christopher, of Feversham Abbey, Kent, a confirmation 1615, by Camden.
Harl. MSS. 6095, fo. 39ᵇ, and 1422, fo. 40 ; Le Neve's MS. 346.

SACKVILLE or SACHEVILLE, John, of city of Bristol, s. of John, of the same, gent.,
grant temp. Q. Eliz., by Sir G. Dethick. Stowe MS. 676, fo. 37 ; Q's Coll.
Oxf. MS. 36, fo. 115, copy of grant.

,, Thomas, one of the gent. Ushers in Ordinary to James I., testified 9 June
1622, by consent of Richard, Earl of Dorset, by Segar, Camden and
Sir R. St. George. Add. MS. 12,225, fo. 99 ; Guil. 411 ; Harl. MS. 6140,
fo. 66ᵇ.

SADLER, John, of Edmonton, Middx., gift .... 1558. (Harvey's Grants), Add.
MS. 16,940, fo. 19.

SADLEIR, Sir Ralph (or Paul), of Standon, Herts, Knt., made banneret at the battle
of Musselborough in Scotland, Chancellor of the duchy of Lancaster and of
the Queen's privy Council, granted 14 May 1542, 34 H. VIII., by Barker ;
altered (to Sir Paul Sadler) 4 Feb. 1575-6, by Cooke and Flower ; died s.p.
MS. Ashm. 834, fo. 14ᵇ, copy of grant, Bodleian Lib. ; Guil. 410.

SADLER, Thomas, esquire of the body to oure Soverayne Lord the King [James], Register to the B[ishop] of Sarum, Justice of Peace in the County of Herts [Knighted 8 Aug. 1623], s. of William, s. of John, s. of Robert, exemplified [testified by Camden]. Cotton MS. Julius, B. xi., 111ᵇ.

SADLERS' COMPANY, of London, az., a chevron betw. three saddles furnished or; grant of supporters and crest 20 Oct. 1585, 27 Q. Eliz., by Cooke. Harl. MS. 1359, fo. 73ᵇ.

SAFFIN, John, ... 17 Sept. .... Add. MS. 14,295, fo. 41ᵇ; by Segar, Add. MS. 4966, fo. 21ᵇ; Harl. MS. 6140, fo. 36ᵇ. See CHAFFIN.

ST. ALBANS, Earl of, Supporters at Breda May 1660, by Sir E. Walker. Her. Coll., fo. 13.

ST. AMAND (SENTAMONDE), Anthony, coat and crest .... Barker's Grants, Harl. MS. 5846, fo. 97; Stowe MS. 692, fo. 83, 86.

ST. AUBYN (SEYNT AUBYN), Thomas, of Clowance, Cornwall, 18 March 1545, crest by Gart. Barker's Grants, Harl. MS. 5846, fo. 92ᵇ; Stowe MS. 692, fo. 87; Visit. Engl. and Wales, iv., 1.

ST. GEORGE, Sir Henry, Richmond Herald, Knt., augmentation by letters patent 26 Sept. 1627 (grant of Gustavus Adolphus, King of Sweden). Guil. 433; Grants II., 693, 695.

„ Nicholas, grants of arms and crest .... by Sir R. St. George. Imperfect. Harl. MS. 1172, fo. 63ᵇ, 64, 53ᵇ.

SEYNTHILL, Peter, of Devonshire, grant of coat and crest ? 18 July 1536, 28 H. VIII. Barker's Grants, Stowe MS. 692, fo. 85 and 87; Harl. MS. 5846, fo. 99; Misc. Gen. et Her., i., 281; Gents. Mag., 1825, ii., 501.

SALFORD, William, gent., Clerk of the Signet, s. of John, of Derby, s. of John, of Burton-upon-Trent, and bro. of William, of London, gent., 14 May 1528, by Wriothesley and Benolte. Arundel MS. 26, S. xvi., fo. 73ᵇ.

SALKYNS, William, of London, ... ? 1586, by Cooke, Quarterly. Harl. MS. 1359, fo. 111; Add. MS. 4966, fo. 60.

SALMON, William, of Wyldheath, Cheshire, sa., three salmons hauriant or, confirmed 20 Dec. 1613, by Segar. See Thomas SALMON, by Sir R. St. George. Add. MS. 12,225, fo. 99ᵇ; Harl. MSS. 1105, fo. 11, and 6140, fo. 49.

„ Paul, of West Barsham, Norf., ... 1591, by Cooke. Harl. MS. 1422, fo. 23ᵇ.

„ Thomas, of Hackney, Middx., Citizen and merchant of London, s. of William, of Wildheath, Cheshire, etc., confirmed 23 Feb. 1621-2, by Sir R. St. George, Norr. (formerly granted by Segar). Add. MS. 14,293, fo. 7; Stowe MS. 714, fo. 178; Guil. 240; Harl. MS. 6140, fo. 66ᵇ.

SALT, William, London, ... by Ro. Cooke .... Stowe MS. 670, fo. 23.

SALTER, ... gu., 10 billets or, 4, 3, 2, 1, on a bordure engrailed arg. 9 roundles (3 each), bezants (or), hurts (az.) and torteaux (gu.), by Borough? Caius Coll. Camb. MS. 551; Guil. 36.

„ Thomas, of Oswaldstre, Salop [in the Marches of Wales], confirmed [2 May 1513] 5 H. VIII., 1513, by [Thomas] Wriothesley (and Machado) [and John Yong, Norroy] [2 G. 4, fo. 105ᵇ, 106, Her. Coll.]; allowed at Visit. of Suff. [1612, C. 15, Her. Coll.]; attested in 1623. Her. and Geneal., i., 125.

SALTERS' COMPANY, ... 1530 .... Hawley's seal, then Carlisle Herald; probably by Benolte. Her. and Geneal., i., 122. [Thomas Benolte was Clarenceux from 1516 to 1534].

SALTONSTALL, Richard, of London, ... 1588, by Cooke. Harl. MS. 1359, fo. 115; Add. MS. 4966, fo. 95ᵇ; Harl. MS. 5887, fo. 77ᵇ bis.

SAMES, John, of Wickham (of Langford in Essex [Harl. MS. 1359], fo. 99), of Wickham Bishop in Essex, 4 July 1593, 35 Q. Eliz., quarterly, by Cooke. Harl. MS. 1359, fo. 99, 112; Q's Coll. Oxf. MS. 146, fo. 473; Add. MS. 4966, fo. 20ᵇ, 93ᵇ; Stowe MS. 670, fo. 8 bis.,; Harl. MS. 5887, fo. 29ᵇ.

SAMPSON, ... crest . . . .   Barker's Grants, Harl. MS. 5846, fo. 93ᵇ ; Stowe MS. 692, fo. 83, as Norton Sampson.

SAMSON, Lady Annys, wife to Sir John Bowier, maior of London, 24 June 1545, by ? Hawley.   Add. MS. 16,940, fo. 200.

SAMPSON, Katherine, wife of Sir John Gresham, maior, 25 Oct. 1556, by Hawley, Clar.   Add. MS. 16,940, fo. 208ᵇ.

SAMUEL, George (or SAMWELL), s. of William, s. of William, of Doncaster, Yorks, arms confirmed and crest granted 20 July 1603, by Segar.   Add. MSS. 12,225, fo. 99ᵇ, and 14,295, fo. 117 ; Harl. MSS. 1359, fo. 37ᵇ, and 6140, fo. 27, 78 ; Guil. 197.

SAMUELL, William, of Northampton, ... quarterly, by Cooke.   Add. MS. 4966, fo. 53 ; Harl. MS. 1359, fo. 88ᵇ.

SANCROFT, William, D.D., preb. of Durham and Dean of York, and to his brother
  „   Thomas, ... 1663, by W. Dugdale, Norr.   (Her. Coll.)

SANCTA CILLIA, Anthony de, ... grant ? (? 45 Q. Eliz.), by William Dethick, Gart.   Stowe MS. 676, fo. 140ᵇ ; Q's Coll. Oxf. MS. 36, fo. 102, copy of grant.

SANDBACHE, Francis, or SUNBISHE, of Kent, crest 20 May 1579, by Sir G. Dethick, Gart.   Stowe MS. 676, fo. 51 ; Harl. MS. 1441, fo. 90 ; Q's Coll. Oxf. MS. 37, fo. 68, copy of grant (MS. 145, fo. 48) ; Misc. Gen. et Her., 2nd S., vol. ii., p. 1 ; Grants I., 180 ; Harl. MS. 5887, fo. 29.

SANDELL, of London, confirmed . . . . 155– to 156–.   (Harvey's Grants), Add. MS. 16,940, fo. 22.

SANDERS, Collingwood, of Caldwall, co. Derby, from Surrey, by R. St. George, Norr.   Harl. MS. 1105, fo. 9.   See SAUNDERS.

  „   Helen, d. of John Sanders and wife of Sir James Altham, Baron of the Exchequer, ... Oct. 1610, by Camden.   Harl. MSS. 1422, fo. 21ᶜ, and 6095, fo. 14.   (She was wife first to John Hyde, citizen and merchant.)

SAUNDERSON, Henry, ... quarterly . . . . by W. Dethick, Gart.   The crest is Sir Christopher Heydon's of Norfolk, but only that hee hath made the care black, which is not a sufficient difference.   Entered by R. Brooke, York Her.   Harl. MS. 1453, fo. 33ᵇ.

SANDERSON, Henry, of Brancepeth, co. Durham, ... by Segar and Sir Rich. St. George.   Add. MS. 12,225, fo. 100.

  „   John, and his brother Thomas, D.D. (rector of All Hallows, London, 1603), 1 March 1603-4, by Camden.   Harl. MSS. 1422, fo. 21, and 6095, fo. 11ᵇ.

SAUNDERSON, William, a fishmonger of London, quarterly of 4 and crest . . . . 1594, by W. Dethick, Gart., who to warrant the same hath forged a pedigree of 18 descents, wherein he hath committed the most apparent errors that ever were comitted by an[y] whatsoever.   A crest for one that had conquered the whole world.   Entered by R. Brooke, York Her.   Harl. MS. 1453, fo. 34 ; Guil. 401.

SANDWALL, Jeffrey, of Minster, Isle of Thanet, 10 May 1631, by R. St. George, Clar.   Harl. MS. 1432, fo. 328 ; Jasper in Harl. MS. 6140, fo. 24.

SANTON, Thomas, of Santon, co. Linc., set out but with one coate by William Dakins, a forged arms and ped.   Add. MS. 17,506, fo. 28 ; Le Neve's Church Notes Linc. [Her. Coll. ?].

SAPCOTS, John, of Tharfield, Herts, grant 20 Nov., 3 and 4 Philip and Mary, 1556, by Harvey.   Copy of grant in Harl. MS. 1116, fo. 51 and 57 ; Add. MS. 16,940, fo. 13, of Tharfield.

SARE (Adie, of Norton), of Kent, Counsellor-at-Law of the Inner Temple, patent 7 Feb. 1612-13, by Camden.   (Drury in margin.)   (1611 in Burke.)   Harl. MSS. 6095, fo. 32. and 1422, fo. 39ᵇ ; Guil. 229.

SAUNDERS, Collingwood, of Little Ireton, Derby, and Charlewood, Surrey, 1615, by R. St. George, Norr. : Sa., on a chev. erm. betw. three bulls' heads cabossed arg. a rose gu. ; crest, a demi-bull erased gu., on his shoulder a rose ar., maned of the last.   Harl. MS. 1105, fo. 9.

SAUNDERS, Edward, Lord Chief Baron, 17 June 1562. (Harvey's Grants), Add. MS. 16,940, fo. 40[b]; Bannerman MS., No. 9, fo. 514.

„ Robert, of London, out of Herts, Lieut.-Col. of a regt. of foot under Fairfax, grant 4 July 1648, by Bysshe. Stowe MS. 677, fo. 38; Harl. MS. 6832, fo. 413.

„ Sir Thomas, of Charlewood, Surrey, 1 March 1551-2, by T. Hawley, Clar. Add. MSS. 16,940, fo. 205, and 7098, fo. 75; Harl. MS. 1115, fo. 66[b].

SAVAGE, Sir John, coat and crest . . . . Barker's Grants, Harl. MS. 5846, fo. 97[b]; Stowe MS. 692, fo. 86[b].

„ (John) of Clifton . . . . Margaret, dau. and heir of Sir Thomas Daniers of Bradley in Appleton, commonly called Daniel, mar. to her 2nd husband, John Savage of Clifton, by whom she had a son John, to whom she granted the liberty of using her arms, *temp.* 3 Hen. V., 1415-16. Guil. Introd., p. 8; Hist. Soc. of Lanc. and Chesh., xxxi., 8.

„ Walter, of Clanfield, Oxon., 16 July 1574. Arg., on a fesse sa. betw. three pheons sa. as many roses or. Berry's Appendix.

SAVEREY als CHEROURIEE DE NORMANDIE. *See* Stowe MS. 697, fo. 111[b].

SAVOYE, Les Armes de L'hospitall de. Barker's Grants, Harl. MS. 5846, fo. 95; Stowe MS. 692, fo. 85[b]. *See* Rich. SUTTON.

SAXTON, Christopher, of Dunningley, Yorks, exemplified 1 July 1579, by Flower. MS. Ashm. 834, i., fo. 22[b], copy of grant, Bodleian Lib.; "for his services to Geography" in Guil. 352.

SAWYER, Edmond, of Kettering, Northants, 8 May 1604, by Camden. Harl. MSS. 1115, fo. 8, 2275, fo. 90, and 5839, fo. 2.

„ Anne, wife of Sir Edmund, and dau. of Sir William Whitmore of London, confirmation of arms impaling Whitmore, Houghton, an escocheon of pretence, 9 April 1627, by Segar and J. Philipot. Add. MS. 12,225, fo. 100. *See* WHITMORE.

SAYE AND SELE, James Fines, Lord, 1 Nov., 27 H. VI., 1448, dignity of Lord Say conceded by John, Lord of Clinton, together with the arms, by Charter. Harl. MS. 1178, fo. 29.

SAYER, Robert, 1615, see SYER.

„ John, H.M.'s Master Cooke, augmentation 13 Nov. 1661, by Sir E. Walker, Gart. Harl. MS. 6179, fo. 59[b]; Her. Coll., fo. 42.

SCACHT, Baldwin, Captain, of the town of Marguizevo in Boulogne, etc., arms as put up after his death in All Saints' Church, London, attested by the Herald painter. Coat only confirmed 15 April 1592, by W. Dethick, Gart. Stowe MS. 676, fo. 84[b]; Q's Coll. Oxf. MS. 36, fo. 6, copy of confirmation in Latin.

SCAMBLER, ..., of Hickling, Norfolk, ... 1591. Arg., a body heart gu., a chief sa. 1 Crest, a garb or, enriched in a ducal coronet gu. [out of a ducal coronet gu. a garb or]; 2, a garb or, banded gu. Berry.

„ Edmond, Bp. of Peterborough, 3 Sept. 1559, 1 Q. Eliz., by Sir G. Dethick. Harl. MSS. 1441, fo. 63[b], and 5847, fo. 5; Q's Coll. Oxf. MS. 145, fo. 5; (3 Dec. 1560) Grants I., 63.

„ Edmond, D.D., Bp. of Norwich, arms confirmed and crest given 20 Dec. 1585, 28 Q. Eliz., by Cooke. Harl. MS. 1359, fo. 15[b], 112[b]; Add. MS. 14,295, fo. 6[b].

SCARBURGH, Henry, John and Edmund, sons of Henry, of North Walsham, gent., coat confirmed and crest granted 10 Sept. 1614, by Segar. Add. MS. 12,225, fo. 100[b]; Harl. MS. 1422, fo. 15; Guil. 306; Grants I., 371.

SCARLETT, ..., crest, Feb. 1611-12, by Camden : arms, chequy or and gu., a lion per fess erm. and erminois, a canton az. Harl. MSS. 6095, fo. 17[b], and 1085, fo. 10 and 10[b].

SCATTERGOOD, John, of Ellaston, co. Staff., attorney-at-law, 3 June 1662, by W. Dugdale, Norr. Harl. MS. 1105, fo. 60, and Her. Coll.

SCAWEN, Robert, of Meleneck in Cornwall, 1601, assigned colours to seal, by W. Camden. Harl. MS. 1079, fo. 135ᵇ.

SCHOOLEY, Richard, of Cadwell, Bedf., confirmed 6 June 1582, by Flower. MS. Ashm. 834, fo. 54ᵇ, copy of grant, Bodleian Lib.; Guil. 360.

SCOBELL, John, of Devon, testified 11 June 1629, by Segar. Add. MS. 12,225, fo. 101, of Plymouth ; Grants II., 683.

SCOFELD, Cuthbert, of Scofeld, co. Lanc., etc. (s. of John), confirmed 6 March 1582-3, by Flower. MS. Ashm. 834, fo. 40; Guil. 151.

SCÖLÖW, Owen (also Kox or Cox), of Gottenburg, Sweden, 8 March 1660, by K. of Sweden. Le Neve MS. 472.

SCORY, John, of Risbury, co. Hereford, ... 1588, by Cooke : quarterly [1 and 4, Or, on a saltire Sable five cinquefoils of the field ; 2, Argent, a chevron between three billets Gules ; 3, Or, on a chief Azure two mullets of six points Or. Crest, out of a ducal coronet a demi-eagle displayed, all Or]. Harl. MSS. 1359, fo. 113ᵇ, and 1422, fo. 120 ; called Sylvester Skory in Stowe MS. 670, fo. 28ᵇ ; Add. MS. 4966, fo. 61ᵇ.

SCOTT, Cuthbert, Bishop of Chester, arms 15 Sept. 1556, by Hawley ? Add. MS. 16,940, fo. 208ᵇ.

„ .... Lincoln's Inn, London (and Longhurst, Kent, in Berry), ... 1590, by R. Cooke, Clar. : arg., a cross crosslet fitchée sa. ; crest, an eagle preying on a bittern ppr. Stowe MS. 670, fo. 44.

„ Thomas, Great Barr, co. Staff., 9 Dec. 1663, by W. Dugdale, Norr. Her. Coll.

SCOTTON (SCOTTOW), Richard, Alderm. of Norwich, July 1647, by Bysshe, Gart. Add. MS. 26,758, fo. 16 ; Scott in Stowe MS. 677, fo. 35 ; Scottow in Harl. MS. 6179, fo. 62.

SCOWLES, Jasper, of Charlton, par. of Wanting, Berks, grant 10 July 1613, by Segar. Add. MS. 12,225, fo. 100ᵇ ; Guil. 247 ; Harl. MSS. 5887, fo. 112, and 6140, fo. 65ᵇ.

SCRASS, Tupin, of Blechington, Sussex, s. and h. of Richard, s. of Edward, s. of Richard, s. and h. of Richard, of Hangleton, Sussex, and stiled " valettus ad corona domini Regis Edwardi 4ᵗⁱ," and sealed with a dolphin. Arms confirmed and crest granted 14 Aug. 1614, 14 Jac., by Segar. Add. MS. 12,225, fo. 101 ; Harl. MS. 1507, fo. 111, copy of grant, Brit. Mus. ; Q's Coll. Oxf. MS. 38, fo. 141, copy of grant (MS. 146, fo. 138) ; Her. and Geneal., i., 83 ; Sussex Arch. Coll., viii., 7 ; Guil. 247 ; Grants I., 281 : Scrase Family, by M. A. Lower, p. 7.

SCRIVENERS' COMPANY, of London, ... grant of supporters, crest and motto 11 Nov. 1634, by Sir R. St. George, Clar. Harl. MS. 1470, fo. 265.

SCROOPE, Annabella (nat. dau. of Emanuel, Earl of Sunderland), wife of John Grubham Howe of Langar, Notts, precedence 1 June 1663 ; exemplification 24 June 1664, by W. Dugdale, Norr. Grants III., 1ᵃ.

„ Elizabeth (nat. dau. of Emanuel, Earl of Sunderland), 1st wife of Thomas, Earl Rivers, precedence to, ? after death, 1 June 1663 ; exemplified to her issue 24 June 1664, by Walker or Bysshe. Harl. MS. 6834, fo. 178 ; Grants III., 1 and 119. Arms and supprs. 9 Nov. 1680, by [Dugdale] Gart. and [St. George] Clar. See RIVERS.

„ Mary (nat. dau. of Emanuel, Earl of Sunderland), wife 1st of Henry Carey, and 2nd of Charles, Marquis of Winchester (? precedence after death 1 June 1663), exemplified to issue 24 June 1664, by Walker or Bysshe. Harl. MS. 6834, fo. 178 ; Grants III., 119, and 1.

SCUTT, William, of Micklefield, Suff., 20 May 1664, by Sir E. Bysshe, Clar. Harl. MS. 1105, fo. 39ᵇ ; Bysshe's Grants, 31.

SEABROK, ... (mar. a dau. of Sheldrake), confirmed April 1633, by Sir R. St. George, Clar. Harl. MS. 6179, fo. 68.

SEALE, Robert, Clerk of the Cheque of Her Majesty's Guard, ? coat and crest granted 9 July 1599, by Camden. Stowe MSS. 676, fo. 114, and 706, fo. 20ᵇ; Q's Coll. Oxf. MS. 36, fo. 49, copy of grant; (called Thos. or Robert in Harl. MS. 6095, fo. 24ᵇ; called Thos. Seal in Morgan's Sphere, ii., 112; called Robert Thomas [Seal, Clerk of the chequer] in Guillim, p. 193); Harl. MS. 6140, fo. 75; Le Neve's MS. 426.

SEAMAN, Aldred, of Milverton, Somerset, 4 May 1670, ? by Sir E. Bysshe, Clar. Harl. MS. 1105, fo. 42; Crisp's Fragmenta Geneal., iii., 77.

SEARELL, Anthony (written over John), of Thanks, Cornwall, gent., and heir of that family, viz., s. of Wymond, s. of John, s. of Richard, gent., living *temp.* E. IV. at Thanks; 16 June 1602, by Camden. Cott. MS. Faust., E. 1, fo. 52, 59, as John; Guil. 234 as Searell (erroneous).

SEBONE, Richard, of Sutton, co. Heref., gent., granted 5 June, 2 and 3 Phil. and Mary, 1555-6, by Sir G. Dethick, Gart. Q's Coll. Oxf. MS. 39, fo. 70, copy of grant; Harl. MS. 1359, fo. 67; Grants I., 186.

SEBRIGHT, William, town clerke of the city of London, 1 April 1580, by Cooke; confirmed 1590, by W. Dethick. Harl. MS. 1422, fo. 122.

SEDENOVE, Richard, ... Hen. VII. .... Add. MS. 26,702, fo. 49ᵇ.

SECKFORD or SACKFORD, Thomas, of Sickford Hall, Suff., crest confirmed 1559. (Harvey's Grants), Add. MS. 16,940, fo. 42ᵇ; Sir John Seckford, quarterly, Harl. MS. 5887, fo. 14; Sackford in Harl. MS. 1116, fo. 60.

SEDDEN, Thomas, of London, gent., crest 4 Aug. 1590, by Cooke. Harl. MS. 1359, fo. 122ᵇ; Stowe MS. 677, fo. 29; Guil. 137.

SEE, Robert, of Undredown, par. of Heron (? Herne), Kent, coat and crest (12 Dec. 1536 in Lansd. MS. 260, fo. 234). Barker's Grants, Harl. MS. 5846, fo. 98; Stowe MS. 692, fo. 86ᵇ; Misc. Gen. et Her., N. S., iii., 298; Harl. MS. 5887, fo. 6.

SEGAR, ... of Wrotham, Kent: az., a cross moline, arg., a chief or, by Segar. Add. MS. 12,225, fo. 101ᵇ; Harl. MSS. 5887, fo. 107ᵇ, and 6140, fo. 81.

  „ Robert, of the Isle of Sheppey, Kent, gent., crest 10 June (or Jan.), 8 Eliz., 1568 *sic* (? 1566), by Gilb. Dethick, Gart. Q's Coll. Oxf. MSS. 38, fo. 82, copy of grant, and 39, fo. 126; Harl. MS. 1507, fo. 453, Brit. Mus., copy of grant; Harl. MS. 1359, fo. 2, and Guil. 104; Grants I., 133; Le Neve's MS. 453.

  „ Sir William, Garter, 1612: Az., a cross moline or, ? argt. Crest, on a ducal coronet or two snakes vert, entwined round a sceptre of the first, betw. two wings, the dexter or, the sinister arg. Harl. MS. 1441, fo. 154ᵇ; Berry; Harl. MS. 6140, fo. 43ᵇ, trick and motto, Arte et Ingenio.

SELBY, William, of Essex, s. of Sir John, now of Braexston, Northumberland, ... by Ro. Cooke, Clar. Stowe MS. 670, fo. 38.

SELLECK, John, D.D., Archdeacon of Bath, imployed by the Bishops into Africa to redeem the captives at Algiers, Tunis and Tripoly; 20 Feb. 1662-3, by Sir E. Walker, Gart. Her. Coll., fo. 49.

SELLECKE, William, of Plainesfeld, par. of Overstone, Somerset, s. of William, of the same, 23 Dec. 1653, by Sir E. Bysshe. Harl. MS. 1172, fo. 14, copy of grant; called Sullock of Camsfield in Add. MS. 31,896, fo. 88ᵇ.

SELWYNE, Thomas, of Freston or Friston, Sussex, 1 June 1611, by Camden. Harl. MSS. 1422, fo. 35ᵇ, and 6095, fo. 15; Guil. 289; Harl. MS. 1562, fo. 85.

SENKES, Elizabeth, dau. of William, ux. Sir Richard Ricke of Brendishe, Essex, ... by Barker, Gart. Harl. MS. 5846, fo. 87.

SEPTUANS, Christopher, als HARFLEETE, of Moland in Ashe-next-Sandwich, Kent, esq., patent 26 July 1574, 16 Q. Eliz., quarterly of 7, quarterly of 8, by Cooke. Harl. MSS. 1359, fo. 87, and 1422, fo. 119ᵇ. *See* CHEQUER and HARFLEETE. Add. MS. 4966, fo. 67ᵇ.

SERJEANT, Thomas, late of Cotes on the side of Trent in co. Staff., who married Agnes, dau. of James Coleire of Darleston, said co.; 13 Feb. 1639-40, certified unto his grandchildren, by W. Segar or W. Le Neve, Clar. Add. MS. 12,225, fo. 101b; Grants II., fo. 602, Her. Coll.; Guil. 240.

SERLE, Henry, Elseworth, co. Cambr., 1 May 1544, 36 H. VIII., by T. Hawley, Clar. Add. MSS. 16,940, fo. 200b, and 7098, fo. 76b (fo. 30).

SESSIONS or SECHION, William, of Milton, Oxon., gent., ... by Segar. Add. MS. 12,225, fo. 102.

SEWELL, Robert, of London, gent., of the Privy Chamber Extraordinary, 6 June 1667, by Sir E. Walker, Gart. Her. Coll., fo. 63.

SEYWELL, Robert, woollen draper at St. Paul's Churchyard and merchant taylor of London, by Sir E. Walker, Gart. Harl. MS. 1441, fo. 152b.

SHADWELL, Thomas, of Lynedowne, co. Staff., coat 2 June 1537. Barker's Grants, Harl. MS. 5846, fo. 99b; 1537 in Add. MS. 14,295, fo. 77; Harl. MS. 1115, fo. 3; Vis. Engn and Wales, iii., 106; Harl. MS. 1069, fo. 1b.

SHAKERLY, Sir Peter, of Holme, Cheshire, crest . . . . 1610, by R. St. George. Harl. MSS. 1422, fo. 124, and 1441, fo. 153; 1610 in Berry.

SHAKESPEARE, John, of Stratford-upon-Avon, co. Warwick, gent. (who mar. (Mary) daughter and heir of Robert Arden of Willingcot, co. Warwick), whose parents and late grandfather's antecessors for his faithful and valiant service was advanced and rewarded with lands and revenues given him by the most prudent prince Hy. VII. of famous memory, etc.; arms and crest granted 20 Oct. 1596, by W. Dethick, Gart. Q's Coll. Oxf. MS. 36, fo. 54, copy of grant; Harl. MS. 6140, fo. 45; Stowe MS. 676, fo. 116b; Misc. Gen. et Her., 2nd S., i., p. 109; Her. and Geneal., i., p. 510; Guil. 335; referred to in MS. Ashm. 846, fo. 50, 50b.

„ William, ... Harl. MS. 6140, fo. 47.

SHALCROSS, Humfrey, of London (High Sheriff, Herts, 1654), 12 May 1621, by Segar. Add. MS. 12,225, fo. 102; Stowe MS. 697, fo. 116.

SHANKE, Thomas, of Rowlsby, Norfolk, gent., 15 Aug. 1562, by Sir G. Dethick, Gart. Harl. MS. 1441, fo. 80, and Q's Coll. Oxf. MS. 145, fo. 31b.

SHAPLEIGH, Robert, of Devon, ... by Segar. Add. MS. 12,225, fo. 102b.

SHARP, John, D.D., Dean of Canterbury, after Archbp. of York,
„ Joshua, his brother,
} 16 May 1691, by T. St. George, Gart. and Clar. Stowe MS. 714, fo. 70; Grants IV., 79; Harl. MS. 1085, fo. 56.

SHARPEY, Robert [or SHARPLEIGH], of Sharpey, Kent, esq., Sept. 1595, by Lee. Harl. MS. 6140, fo. 62; Add. MS. 14,295, fo. 18; Harl. MS. 1359, fo. 16b; Stowe MS. 670, fo. 59. See the next grant.

SHARPLEIGH, Robert, Knt., receiver-general of H.M.'s rents and revenues within the counties of Kent, Sussex and Surrey, 1595, by Lee. Stowe MS. 706, fo. 10b; Harl. MSS. 1069, fo. 22, and 6140, fo. 71.

SHARROCK, Robert, of co. Hereford, confirmed . . . . 1544, 36 H. VIII., by Barker. Stowe MSS. 706, fo. 82, and 703, fo. 82.

SHAW, Edward, of city of London, a proctor of the Arches Court of Canterbury, 21 June 1698, by T. St. George, Gart. and Clar. Add. MS. 14,831, fo. 100; Grants IV., fo. 265.

„ James, of St. Saviour's, Southwark, Surrey, and for want of his issue to Joseph Williams of the same place, 28 Jan. 1668-9, by Sir E. Bysshe, Clar. Harl. MS. 1105, fo. 40; Bysshe's Grants, 33.

SHAWE, John, Clarke of the Chamber of London, ... 1586, by Cooke. Harl. MSS. 1359, fo. 89, and 1422, fo. 51b; Add. MS. 4966, fo. 34; called William in Harl. MS. 5887, fo. 84.

SHAW, Mary, d. of George, of Bristowe, gent., wife of Thomas Frear, Doctor of phissick, confirmed 12 Feb. 1602-3, by Camden. Q's Coll. Oxf. MS. 38, fo. 116, copy of grant; Harl. MSS. 6095, fo. 19, and 1395, fo. 26b.

SHELDON, Daniel (and other issue of Raphe, elder bro. of the Archbp.), of Ham Court, Surrey, nephew of Gilbert, Archbp. of Canterbury, confirmed 26 Dec. 1681, by Sir W. Dugdale, Gart., and H. St. George, Clar. Misc. Gen. et

Her., N. S., i., 371 ; Grants III., 145-7-9 ; Guil. 207, with honourable augmentation. *See* arms of his wife Judith, born Rose, widow of Diggs.

SHELDON, Gilbert, S.T.D., out of Derbyshire (Bp. of London), All Souls', Oxf., 4 Sept. 1660, by Walker. Add. MSS. 14,293, fo. 91, and 14,294, fo. 27 ; Harl. MS. 1172, fo. 71 ; Misc. Gen. et. Her., 2nd S., vol. v., pl. 8.

„   Samuel, of Upton-on-Severn, grant .... Berry.

„   William, of Arden, co. Warwick, confirmed 8 Feb., 14 Ed. IV., 1474-5, by William Hawkeslow, Clar. Guil. 75 ; Grants II., 541.

SHELLETO, Francis, of Houghton, Yorks, etc., crest 24 Jan. 1602-3, by W. Dethick, Gart. Surtees Soc., XLI., xlv ; *see also* Harl. MS. 1105, fo. 1b.

„   George, of Heth, Yorks, ... by Sir W. Segar, Gart. Harl. MS. 1105, fo. 1b.

SHELTON, Theophilus, of Wakefield, Yorks, Farley, co. Staff., and Mansfield, co. Notts, 11 Sept. 1690 .... Harl. MS. 6834, fo. 178 ; Grants IV., 65 ; Harl. MS. 1172, fo. 53b, by Gart. and Norr.

SHEPPARD, ... , of Loudon, ... by R. St. George, Clar. Harl. MS. 6140, fo. 23b.

SHEAPARD, Alexander, of Buckingham, Doctor, patent 23 Feb. 1615, by Camden. Harl. MSS. 1422, fo. 40, and 6095, fo. 33 ; called Allen Sheapard by Guil. 342.

SHEPPARD, Robert, of Pesemarsh, Sussex, grant 2 Sept. 1570, by Cooke. Her. and Geneal., i., 82.

SHEPHARD, Robert, of Peasmarsh, Sussex, esq., s. of Richard, gent., confirmed 7 May 1574, *sic*, 17 Q. Eliz., by Cooke. Harl. MSS. 1507, fo. 62b, 1422, fo. 91b, and 1359, fo. 106b ; Q's Coll. Oxf. MS. 38, fo. 92, copy of grant ; Add. MS. 4966, fo. 85.

SHEPPARD, Robert, of Kirby Bedon, Norfolk, patent .... 1598, by Camden. Harl. MS. 6095, fo. 24b ; Guil. 342.

SHERIFFE, Laurence, of Rugby, co. Warw., gent., ratified, confirmed, assigned and granted 1 Q. Eliz., 1559, by Hervey. Harl. MS. 1359, fo. 41 ; Add. MS. 16,940, fo. 68.

SHERINGTON (W.), of Gray's Inn, London, whose father died in the Charterhouse and was buried in S. Dennis, Fanchurch St. ; with his armes and crest, ... 1583, by Cooke. Add. MS. 14,295, fo. 34 ; Harl. MS. 1359, fo. 98 ; Guil. 67 ; Add. MS. 4966, fo. 36 ; Harl. MS. 5887, fo. 3b.

SHERLAND, Thomas, of Winston, Suff., ... 1592, by Ro. Cooke, Clar. Stowe MS. 670, fo. 49b.

„   .... , of Devonsh., ... 1668, by .... , arg., a fesse wavy betw. three lions ramp. az., a canton gu. charged with a naval coronet or. Crest, a sea-horse arg. charged with an anchor sa. Berry.

SHERMAN, John, of Wackton, Norfolk, gent., 16 Oct. 1576, by Robert Cooke. Grants II., 527 ; Harl. MS. 6140, fo. 43.

SHERWIN, John, of the City of Chichester, Sussex, gent., crest 27 Oct. 1571, by Cooke. Add. MS. 14,295, fo. 84b.

SHERWOOD, Sir Rowland, set out by Wm Dakins, a forger of arms and pedigrees. R. Lee's Visit. Notes, 1592 ; Add. MS. 17,506, fo. 28.

SHETHER or SCHETHER, Elizabeth, dau. of Robert, of London, wife of Robert Forth of London, *see* FORTH. Grant, coat only .... by Barker. Harl. MS. 5846, fo. 36b ; Stowe MSS. 692, fo. 42, 83, and 702, fo. 115.

SHINKELL, Bartholomew, and ⎫ brothers, from Germany, crest granted 10 Nov.
„   Comodo,   ⎭   1566, by Sir G. Dethick, Gart. Stowe MS. 676, fo. 30b ; Q's Coll. Oxf. MS. 37, fo. 45, copy of grant ; Grants I., 156.

SHIPHAM, Thomas, of Weobley, co. Hereford, s. of William, s. of Thomas ; crest granted 20 Oct. 1581, to posterity of father William, by Cooke. Harl. MS. 1359, fo. 20 ; Add. MS. 14,295, fo. 16b ; Misc. Gen. et Her., N. S., iv., 367.

SHIPMAN, Thomas, of Scarington, Notts, capt. of a foot Company in the trayned bands in the County, and to William and Gervase, his brothers, 12 May 1663, by W. Dugdale, Norr. : gu., on a bend arg., betw. six estoiles or, three pellets. Crest, a leopard sejant arg., spotted sa., reposing his dexter paw on a ship's rudder az. Dugdale's Grants, fo. 2 ; Visit. Nottinghamsh. [1662], C. 34, fo. 30 ; Berry.

SHIPPINGDALE, John, of Humberston, co. Leic., D.C.L., one of the Masters of the High Court of Chancery, s. of George, " out of Craven, co. Linc.," granted 16 May 1594, by W. Dethick, Gart. Stowe MS. 676, fo. 91, 106^b ; Q's Coll. Oxf. MS. 36, fo. 34.

SHIPWRIGHT's Co., of London, 9 Jan. 1605, by Camden. Cott. MS. Faust., E. 1, fo. 2^b.

SHIRBROOK, Michael, of Morton or Norton, ... by Cooke, Clar. Stowe MS. 670, fo. 42^b.

SHIRECLIFF, Nicholas, of Ecclesfield Hall, Yorks, s. of Nicholas, s. of Alexander, confirmed . . . . 1614, by R. St. George, Norr. Stowe MS. 706, fo. 16^b.

SHIRLEY, ..., co. Essex, ... by Cooke, Clar. Stowe MS. 670, fo. 19^b.

„ Robert, of London, arms confirmed and crest granted 10 Sept. 1609, by Segar. Add. MS. 12,225, fo. 102^b ; goldsmith in Harl. MS. 1442, fo. 14^b ; Guil. 413 ; Harl. MSS. 5887, fo. 112, and 6140, fo. 77 ; Grants II., 479, 532 ; Le Neve's MS. 465.

SHISH, John and Thos., Master Shipwrights of H.M. Dockyards at Deptford and Woolwich, Kent, s. of John, late Master of Deptford Yard, 10 June 1682, by Sir W. Dugdale, Gart. and Clar. Harl MS. 6834, fo. 178 ; Grants III., 151 ; Harl. MS. 6179, fo. 71^b.

SHOOBRIDGE, Robert, of Uckfield, Sussex, gent., grant 16 April 1662, by Sir E. Bysshe, Clar. Harl. MS. 1470, fo. 126. copy of grant, Brit. Mus. ; Harl. MSS. 1105, fo. 20, and 1172, fo. 53 ; Bysshe's Grants, fo. 17, Her. Coll. ; Guil. 260.

SHORT, ..., of Tenterden in Kent, patent . . . . Nov. 1614, by Camden, Clar. : az., a griffin passant or betw. three estoiles arg. Crest, a griffin's head or betw. two wings expanded azure, semée of estoiles argent. Harl. MS. 1422, fo. 39 ; of Kent in Harl. MS. 6095, fo. 31.

„ John, of London, merchant taylor, and ⎫ 3 June 1663. Bysshe's Grants, fo. 18,
„ Peter, ⎬ his brothers, ⎪ Her. Coll. ; Harl. MS. 1105, fo. 20 ;
„ Thomas, ⎭ ⎬ Add. MS. 14,293, fo. 7^b ; Guil.
⎭ 265 ; Harl. MS. 6179, fo. 52^b.

SHORTER, Sir John, Knt., Lord Mayor of London, 14 Oct. 1687, by Sir T. St. George, Gart. and Clar. Harl. MS. 6834, fo. 178 ; Grants III., 329 ; Lansd. MS. 867, fo. 52 ; Harl. MS. 6179, fo. 64^b bis.

SHORTRIDGE, Richard, of Shortridge, Devon, probably after the Visit. in 1620, by R. St. George, Clar. Add. MS. 14,295, fo. 102^b.

SHOVELL, Sir Cloudesley, Knt., Rear Admiral of the Blue Squadron, 6 Jan. 1691-2, by T. St. George, Gart. and Clar. Add. MS. 14,830, fo. 187 ; Grants IV., 103 ; Stowe MS. 712, fo. 1^b, 2 ; Harl. MS. 6179, fo. 83^b.

SHRAWLEY, Kenelm, of London, ... 1588, by Cooke. Harl. MSS. 1359, fo. 113, and 1422, fo. 95 : sa., a lion passant guardant betw. three mullets arg. ; Crest, a hind's head [couped] arg., holding [pierced through with] an arrow [bendways] headed and feathered arg. [or]. Called Crawley in Stowe MS. 670, fo. 23 ; Add. MS. 4966, fo. 61.

SHRUBSOLE, Richard, " sonn & heire of Robert Shrubsole of Graveny in the countie of Kent, and his brother in [blank], the 10th of October, in the 10th yeare of King James," 1612, by Camden, Clar. : " argent, three cherrey trees with fruit on them pp." Harl. MS. 6140, fo. 25^b.

SHUGER, William, utter barrister-at-law, s. of John, of Tilney in Marshland, co. Linc., s. of Thomas, s. of John, alias Hungerford, s. of William Hungerford, etc., grant 12 May 1591, by W. Dethick, Gart. Stowe MS. 676, fo. 86^b, 97^b ; Q's Coll. Oxf. MS. 36, fo. 12, copy of grant.

SHUTE, Christopher, of Giggleswick in Craven, Yorks, confirmed .... April 1616, by Camden. Harl. MSS. 1422, fo. 40ᵇ, and 6095, fo. 33ᵇ.

„ (Robert), of Okington, co. Camb., Baron of the Exchequer, s. of Christopher, of Kent, confirmation of arms .... 1579, by Sir G. Dethick, Gart. Q's Coll. Oxf. MS. 37, fo. 71, copy of confirmation in Latin. Harl. MS. 6140, fo. 42, gives a trick of the arms.—" Shutt, one of the Judges," quarterly: 1 and 4, per chevron sable and or, in chief two eaglets displayed or; 2, Arg., on a bend cotticed sable three martlets arg. ? 3, per fesse or and az., three crescents, two and one, counterchanged. Crest: described in Add. MS. 26,753, fo. 124, " and to his crest on a torce or [and] sa., A Gryffyne sedant ar., the winges volant [endorsed] or, beked and leged or, thrust thorowe the brist wᵗ a broken spere, the stafe sa., the hed ar., wonde gules, drope." Add. MS. 26,753, describes the arms: "or., on a fece p cheveru sa. two eglytes displayed or." Add. MS. 26,753, fo. 124 ; Harl. MS. 6140, fo. 42.

SHUTER, Thomas, of Winterbourne Cherburgh, Wilts, a patent July 1614, by Camden. Harl. MS. 6095, fo. 30 ; called John in Guil. 78, and in Morgan's Sphere ; William in Harl. MS. 1422, fo. 39 ; Quarterly in Harl. MS. 6140, fo. 27ᵇ.

SYDLEY, Sir William, of Southfleet, Kent, ... Jan. 1606, by Camden ; exemplified and confirmed. Morgan's Sphere, 108 ; Harl. MSS. 1422, fo. 20, and 6095, fo. 8.

SIDNEY, Visct. Henry, supporters (crest 9 April 1689) 5 March 1691-2, by T. St. George, Gart. Harl. MS. 6834, fo. 178 ; Grants IV., 106.

SIDNEY AND SUSSEX COLLEGE, Cambridge, arms of, founded by Frances, dau. of Sir William Sidney, Kt., and widow of Thos. Radcliff, Earl of Sussex, in 1595 ; grant 1675, by Walker. [Arg., a bend engrailed Sable, Radcliff, impaling or, a pheon Azure for Siduey.] Berry's Armory and Burke.

SILK THROWERS' Co., of London, arms, crest, supporters and seal .... July 1629, by Sir R. St. George (incorporated by R. letters patent 23 April, 5) [6 Chas. I., 1630]. Add. MS. 14,295, fo. 68.

SILLISDEN, Thomas, of Finchley, Essex, by Wriothesley, Gart. Harl. MS. 1441, fo. 59 ; Add. MS. 4966, fo. 45ᵇ.

SILVER, John, of Norwich, citizen, born at Whitehurst, Hants, s. of John, of Wareford in the said co., grant 28 July 1589, by W. Dethick, Gart. Stowe MS. 676, fo. 77ᵇ ; Q's Coll. Oxf. MS. 37, fo. 113, copy of grant.

SYMPSON, ... per bend nebulée sa. and or, a lion ramp. counterchanged, by Segar and R. St. George. Add. MS. 12,225, fo. 108ᵇ.

SING [sic, ? SINGE, no references given].

SINGLETON, Edward, s. of Thomas, of Broughton Tower, co. Lanc., gent., a patent of crest 20 May 1560 (2 Q. Eliz.), by Dalton. Harl. MSS. 1359, fo. 46, and 5887, fo. 3ᵇ.

„ Nicholas, see Thomas BANDE.

SITSILT, John, and Sir William Feckenham, controversy as to arms decided by Edward de Beaulile and John de Monbray, 4 June 1332, in favour of Sitsilt of Duncombe, co. Hereford, descended from Sitsilt of Beaufort (now Beaupré), co. Glam., arm. John Bossewell's Works of Armourie, 1572, p. 81 and 105, had seen the orig. writings, and Collins' Peerage, ii., 584-5 ; Harl. MS. 980, fo. 51.

SITWELL, George, of Renishaw, co. Derby, grant 1 March, 13 Chas. II., 1660-61, by Sir Ed. Walker, Gart. MS. Ashm. 858, fo. 153-4, copy of grant, Bodleian Lib., grant by Bysshe 15 Feb. 1647-8 ; Harl. MS. 1441, fo. 132 ; Reliquary, xxii., 52.

SKEGGS, John, of St. Ives, Hunts, one of the gent. sewers and surveyors to the Q.'s Majesty for Hunts, and his younger brother

„ Edward, of Bramfield, Herts, purveyor for the mouth of her Majesty ; sons of Richard Skeggs of Enesbury, Hunts, granted 29 Aug. 1568, by Sir

G. Dethick, Kt., Gart., and Cooke and Flower. Harl. MS. 1441, fo. 75; 30th Aug. in Q's Coll. Oxf. MS. 39, fo. 139, (6 Sept.) fo. 140, (29 Aug.) copies of grant (MS. 145, fo. 21ᵇ); Harl. MS. 1359, fo. 53ᵇ.

SKERES, ..., of Yorkshire, a patent . . . . Oct. 1612, by Camden. Harl. MSS. 1422, fo. 37ᵇ, and 6095, fo. 24.

SKYNNER, Anthony, of Kinwarton, co. Warwick, 15 May, "in the first yeare of Quene Mary " (1554), by T. Hawley, Clar. Add. MS. 16,940, fo. 207, and 15 March 1553-4 in Add. MS. 7098, fo. 78ᵇ (fo. 107).

[Add. MS. 7098, fo. 78ᵇ, calls him gen., and has : "he beareth sa., on a cheveron unde between 3 griffens heads erasy ar., langued gu., three flower de lyes az., upon his helme one torse ar. and sa., a serpentes head conpe vᵗ, p'fled or, langued and armed gu., about his nec his tayle rolled the end ayeringe upwards, holding in his pawe a brance of palme in its pp collour, mantled g., doubled ar, given nt supᵃ 15 mᵈch 1 Mar." No trick.]

SKINNER, Anthony, one of the Six Clerks, of London, alteration, the trefoil on the chevron taken away, Aug. 1594, by Lee. Harl. MSS. 1422, fo. 56ᵇ, and 1069, fo. 16ᵇ; Add. MS. 14,295, fo. 25ᵇ, same coat as Anthony [above]; Stowe MS. 670, fo. 57; Harl. MS. 6179, fo. (15) 38.

[Harl. MS. 1069, fo. 16, has : " Skynner. These armes were before [Sa.] a cheveron Or, inter 3 Griffins heads erased Argent, on yᵉ cheveron 3 flower de luces Azure, but now altered thus to . . . . Skynner, p. Richard Lee, Clar., in August 1594." The trick shows the above arms, without the fleurs-de-lis on the chevron, and the Crest, "a griffin's head erased [argent] holding in his beak a gauntlet [silver]." The colours are supplied from Harl. MS. 1422, fo. 56ᵇ.

Add. MS. 14,295, fo. 25ᵇ, gives the same arms, but has: "The armes was afore a chevron wavye or," etc. Stowe MS. 670, fo. 57, has the arms as before, and gives the name " Anthony Skinner of London, one of the six Clerks."]

„　Edward, of Burtons, par. of Ledbury, Herts. by Segar. Add. MS. 12,225, fo. 103; Harl. MSS. 6140, fo. 80, and 1441, fo. 161ᵇ.

SKYNNER, John, of co. Linc., Receiver of the Honour of Bolingbroke, s. and h. of Robert, of Exeter, 10 July 1557, by Hervey, Clar. Arms : erm., three lozenges sa., on each a fleur-de-lis or. Crest : a dragon's head erased arg., etc. [azure platey, on the neck two gemelles golde "]. No record in the Coll. of Arms [Burke]. Misc. Gen. et Her., N. S., i., 80; Add. MS. 16,940, fo. 21.

SKINNER, Thomas, of London, Sheriff 1587-88, grant 29 Sept. 1587, by W. Dethick, Gart. Stowe MS. 676, fo. 66ᵇ; Q's Coll. Oxf. MS. 37, fo. 93, copy of grant.

SKINNERS' Co., of London, arms, crest and supporters, 5 or 8 Oct. 1550, by Hawley. Crest and supporters, Harl. MS. 1470, fo. 227, copy of grant, Brit. Mus.; Add. MSS. 16,940, fo. 204, and 26,702, fo. 75.

SKIP, John, of Ledbury, co. Hereford, Esq., 10 May 1666, by Sir E. Bysshe, Clar. Harl. MS. 1105, fo. 40ᵇ; Bysshe's Grants, fo. 37.

SKIPPE (Robert, of Ulsted, Norfolk, or Richard, of London), az., a lion rampt. betw. three trefoils slipped arg.; grant . . . . by Sir G. Dethick, Gart. (? Alteration 24 or 29 July 1577, by Cooke, Harl. MSS. 1422, fo. 15), 1441, fo. 89, and 5847, fo. 45ᵇ; Q's Coll. Oxf. MS. 145, fo. 46ᵇ; Harl. MS. 1085, fo. 50.

SKIPWITH, William, of St. Albans, Herts, Esq., arms and crest given at London 20 May 1507, 22 H. VII, by Tho. Writhe aīs Wriothesley, Gart., and Roger Machado aīs Richmont Clar. Harl. MS. 1359, fo. 17ᵇ; Add. MSS. 14,295, fo. 19ᵇ, and 6140, fo. 71.

SKORY, see SCORY.

SKRYMSHIRE, Thomas, of Aqualate, co. Staff., confirmation 13 April 1584, by

Flower. MSS. Ashm. 834, fo. 41, and 858, fo. 120-21, copy of grant, Bodleian Lib.; Guil. 178.

SKRYNE, John, of Warleigh, par. of Strode, Som^t, 8 Nov. 1682, by Sir W. Dugdale, Gart. and Clar. Stowe MS. 677, fo. 70^b; Grants III., fo. 165.

SKUTTE, John, of Staunton, Somerset, coat and crest . . . ., Barker's Grants, Harl. MS. 5846, fo. 99; Stowe MS. 692, fo. 86^b, in a later hand (and fo. 87).

SLANEY, Stephen, Esq., Alderm. of London, arms and crest given 1 Aug. 1595, 37 Q. Eliz., by Lee. Add. MS. 14,295, fo. 17^b; Harl. MS. 1359, fo. 16^b; Stowe MS. 670, fo. 59.

SLANNYNG, Nicholas, of Bickleigh, Devon, coat and crest 155– or 156–. (Harvey's Grants) Add. MS. 16,940, fo. 41; Slanning impaling Amydas, quartering Mortimer and Wrotham, by Cooke, Stowe MS. 670, fo. 6, no crest.

SLEIGH, Gervase, of Ash, Devon (s. of Hugh, of Pilsbury), who married Elizabeth, dau. to John Cholmleigh, Esq., etc., by whom he had Samuel, of Gray's Inn, Gervase and Hugh. Arms confirmed 2 May 1626, by Segar. Add. MS. 12,225, fo. 104^b; Harl. MS. 1537, fo. 123.

SLEIGH or SLEY [Edmund], Alderm. of London, as on an achievement in Cheapside, 1657, by ? Bysshe. Harl. MS. 1441, fo. 150^b.

SLOW, Lady Elizabeth, dau. of John, of King's Norton, co. Warwick, and wife to Alex^r Avenon, Ld. Mayor of London, grant . . . . 1570, 12 Q. Eliz., by Sir G. Dethick, Cooke and Flower. Harl. MS. 1441, fo. 76; Q's Coll. Oxf. MS. 145, fo. 25^b.

SMALE, Mathew, of Paddington, Middx., s. of Nicholas, ... 1590, by Cooke, Clar. Bannerman's MS., No. 9, 447.

SMALLMAN, see also SWALMAN, Thomas, of Elton, co. Heref., 10 Oct. 1589, 30 Eliz., by Cooke, Clar. Add. MS. 14,293, fo. 122; (Harl. MS. 1359, fo. 101^b) copy of grant, Brit. Mus.

SMALPAGE, Michael, als SMALPAIS, of the Inner Temple, London, and of Yorkshire, quarterly, ... 1585, by Cooke. Harl. MSS. 1359, fo. 99^b, and 1422, fo. 119^b; Add. MS. 4966, fo. 18^b.

SMALLPEICE, Robert, of Hockering, Norfolk, gent., confirmed 20 Aug. 1568, 10 Q. Eliz., by Cooke. Stowe MS. 677, fo. 20; 1590 in Harl. MS. 1359, fo. 94, copy of patent; Grants II., 501.

SMALLWOOD, Matthew, D.D., Dean of Lichfield, and to his brother
   ,, James and Mathew sic, Chequy arg. and sa., on a canton of the 2nd a sword bendways of the first. Berry. Augmentation 15 April 1672, by W. Dugdale, Norr. (Her. Coll.), and last page of MS.

SMART, Griffith, of Calleys, 10 Dec. 1550, by ? Hawley. Add. MS. 16,940, fo. 204.
   ,, Rowland, s. of Robert, both sword bearers to the City of London, lineally descended from Sir John Smart, sometime Garter K. of Arms, confirmed 13 May 1609, 7 Jac., by Segar. Add. MS. 12,225, fo. 103^b; Guil. 334 (and ? bro. Robert); Grants I., 377; Harl. MS. 5887, fo. 105^b.

SMERT, Henry, s. of John, of North Petheram, Cornwall, 2 June 1579, by Sir G. Dethick, Gart. Harl. MS. 1441, fo. 101^b, and Q's Coll. Oxf. MS. 145, fo. 52.

SMETHWICK, William, of Smethwick, Cheshire, confirmed 9 Oct. 1579, by Dakins, Norr. Misc. Gen. et Her., 2nd S., vol. i., p. 324, copy of grant, Brit. Mus. Probably a forgery, see also RUDIARDE. [A spurious grant, Dakyns was never Norroy.]

SMYTH, ... Cheshire . . . . temp. Hen. VII.: arg., on a fesse betw. three demi-griffins couped sa., as many bezants. Crest, a demi-griffin erased sa., collared arg., collared with a fesse arg^t? Barker's Grants, Harl. MSS. 1422, fo. 29, and 5846, fo. 92^b; Add. MS. 26,702, fo. 42^b.

SMYTHE, ... (No. 1) crest, an arm in pale garnished chequy arg. and vert., the hand holding iij darts or. Barker's Grants, Harl. MS. 5846, fo. 92; Stowe MS. 692, fo. 86, of Essex.

SMYTH, ... (No. 2) crest (with the greyhound, three) dragons' heads erased
arg., spotted sa., langued and eared gu. Barker's Grants, Harl. MS. 5846,
fo. 92 ; Stowe MS. 692, fo. 86.

„ . . . . (of Stratford-on-Avon, co. Warwick), *temp.* Hen. VII. : arg., 2 or ? 3
[three] greyhounds conrant [in pale sa.], 9 cross crosslets fitchée (or crosses
patées) gu. or sa.? Crest, a griffin's head erased arg. [? sa.], pellettée
[? bezantée]. Barker's Grants, Harl. MS. 1422, fo. 28ᵇ ; Add. MS. 26,702,
fo. 42ᵇ. [? Two families, one of Stratford and another of Shirford, co.
Warw., *see* Burke's Armory.]

„ . . . ., an Innkeeper in the town of Huntingdon, 1594, by Wᵐ Dethick, Gart.
Arms, the ancient arms of Chamberlayne, entered by R. Brooke, York Her.,
arg., a chevron betw. three leopards' faces gu. Crest, a crescent, thereon
a leopard's face gu., "of Water Newton in Huntingdonshire." Harl. MSS.
1453, fo. 32ᵇ, and 3526, fo. 8ᵇ.

SMITH, ... by Cooke . . . . arg., on a chevron cottised ? betw. 3 cross crosslets gu.
as many martlets or. Harl. MS. 1359, fo. 118ᵇ ; Add. MS. 4966, fo. 101 ;
Stowe MS. 670, fo. 70.

„ . . . . of co. Glouc., confirmed . . . . Feb. 1614-15, by Camden : or, on a fesse
gu. betw. 3 saltires sa. as many fleurs-de-lis arg. Harl. MSS. 1422, fo. 38ᵇ,
and 6095, fo. 28ᵇ.

„ . . . ., of Binderton, Sussex. Add. MS. 4966, fo. 18, ... by Segar.

„ . . . ., of London, merchant, azure, two bars between three escallops or, by
R. St. George, Clar. Harl. MS. 1105, fo. 7ᵇ.

„ . . . ., of Brindley, Cheshire, azure, on a fess or between three wolves' heads
erased argent as many fleurs-de-lys sable, by R. St. George, Clar. Stowe
MS. 703, fo. 73.

„ . . . ., of Westminster, by W. Ryley, Lanc. Her. Stowe MS. 703, fo. 63.

SMYTH, ..., Alderman and Salter, of Broad St. (died at his house at Hammersmith
Oct. 1667), by Sir Ed. Bysshe. Stowe MS. 677, fo. 25ᵇ.

SMITH, Andrew, of Yateley, Hants, descended of John Smith of Thackstead, Essex,
12 Jan. 1579-80, by Sir G. Dethick, Gart. Harl. MS. 1441, fo. 90 ; Q's
Coll. Oxf. MS. 145, fo. 48ᵇ ; Harl. MS. 5887, fo. 38.

„ Anne, wife to Sir John Yorke, Sheriff of London, 1 Dec. 1549, by ? Hawley.
Add. MS. 16,940, fo. 203 ; Harl. MSS. 578, fol. 9ᵇ, and 3526, fo. 9ᵇ [which
has " Smith of London "].

„ Anthony, of Milford, Surrey, Esq., one of the band of gent. pentioners to
Chas. II., who was also servant to Chas. I., 4 June 1662, by Sir E. Walker,
Gart. Her. Coll., fo. 47.

„ Thomas, brother of Anthony, and to the heirs of Anthony their father ; new
arms 29 June 1667, by Sir E. Bysshe, Clar. Add. MS. 14,293, fo. 2 ;
Guil. 163 : argt., a bend betw. two unicorns' heads erased azure.

„ Christopher, of London, one of the proctors of the Arches, by Sir G. Dethick,
Cooke and Flower. Harl. MS. 1441, fo. 76 ; Q's Coll. Oxf. MS. 145,
fo. 25 ; Harl. MS. 5887, fo. 44.

„ Christopher, of Buckhurst, Sussex, *see under* William SMITH of Old Windsor.

„ Edmond, of Middx. (s. and h. of Peter, of Tudenham, Suff., s. and h. of
Robert, of Bury-St-Edmunds), confirmed 5 May 1561, by Hervey. Add.
MS. 16,940, fo. 21 ; Harl. MS. 1470, fo. 27, 140, copy of grant, Brit. Mus. ;
Guil. 292.

„ Edward, of London, arg., a fess vert betw. 3 ogresses, by Camden. Morgan's
Sphere, 117.

„ Edward, of London, Esq., s. of John, of Bourton-on-the-Wolds, co. Leic., s.
of Paul, of the same, 29 Oct. 1667, by Walker, Gart. Harl. MSS. 1172,
fo. 37, and 1144, fo. 37.

„ Edward, 1671 in Burke, *see* William, etc. Harl. MS. 1172, fo. 39.

„ Gawen, one of her Majesties dromers, (? crest) on the top of a pillar [ppr.]
a spear (sphere) or, 1587, by Cooke, " the engineer without Aldgate, one

of the drumsters to Queen Elizabeth." Harl. MSS. 1359, fo. 110, 587, fo. 4, and 3526, fo. 4 : Berry. Arms : arg., a saltire wavy az., an inescocheon or, guttée de sang [poix], thereon a lion rampt. sa., armed gu., *see* Add. MS. 4966, fo. 56.

SMITH, George, of London, s. of John, of Sleghill, Westmorld., gent.   23 March 1576-7 in Q's Coll. Oxf. MS. 145, fo. 42b.   *See* John.

„   Henry, of Old Stretford, co. Warwick, 20 May 1668, by Sir E. Walker, Gart. Her. Coll., fo. 73.

„   Hugh (s. of John), of Long Ashton, Somersᵗ, ratified and confirmed 1568 "by all the Kings and Heralds"; grant of crest (a griffin's head) by Hawley, 36 Hen. VIII.   C. 22 [Visit. of Somersetsh., 1623], fo. 344b, Her. Coll. ; Guil. 262 ; Harl. MS. 1116, fo. 43b.

„   Humphrey, of Charlton, par. of Vainton, s. of John, of Columpton, etc., crest 4 June 1574, by Cooke.   Stowe MS. 676, fo. 44b ; Q's Coll. Oxf. MS. 37, fo. 57, copy of grant.

„   Humfrey, s. and h. of John, of Collumpton, decᵈ, etc., 30 Mar. 1583, by Sir G. Dethick. (Justice Smith?)   Harl. MS. 1441, fo. 80 ; Q's Coll. Oxf. MS. 145, fo. 31b. Alteration.

„   Humphrey, of Farmington, co. Glouc., and William, of London, grandsons of Humfrey Smith, rector of Castle Eaton, Wilts, benefactor to the College of Arms ; Warrant 7 Oct. 1674, certified by Dugdale, Norr. : per pale erm. and erminois, an eagle displayed sa.   MS. Ashm. 858, fo. 239-40, copy of grant, Bodleian Lib.

„   Israel, eldest Capt. in Col. Ewer's regᵗ (*see* that name), 23 Feb. 1647-8, by Sir Ed. Bysshe.   Add. MS. 26,758, fo. 14b ; (Stowe MS. 677, fo. 36) copy of grant.

„   James, of London and of Bray, Berks (in Bysshe's Grants), s. of James, of Cookham, Berks, 23 Jan. 1653-4, by Bysshe, Gart.   Add. MS. 26,758, fo. 16 ; Stowe MS. 677, fo. 49b ; MS. Ashm. 858, fo. 228-9 ; Harl. MS. 6832, fo. 413b.

„   James, of New Windsor, Berks, *see* under William SMITH of Old Windsor.

„   Sir John, Knt., Alderm. and Sheriff of London, s. of James, of Bray, by Sir E. Bysshe, Clar. (Harl. MS. 1105, fo. 39) ; Bysshe's Grants, 30.

SMYTHE (John), of Bristol, lord of Stryden, co. Glouc., "quarterly, azure & golde, a fesse owndy cottessed, thereon a griffen betwene ij mulletts, upon eche quarter a Bulls head and a griffin counterchaunged of the felde ; his creste a demye griffen azure issant oute of a cressant gold, wr[eath] ar. and sa., m[antlet] g., lined ar., b. [balls or tassels ?] or."   Barker's Grants, Stowe MS. 692, fo. 84 ; Harl. MS. 5846, fo. 93 ; John, 9 May, Harl. MS. 1544 ; Add. MS. 16,940, fo. 205 [has "John Smithe of Bristowe, Somersetshire, a Pattent of armes and crest given unto him the ix of Maye in the xxxvjᵗʰ yere of Henry the VIIIᵗʰ " (1544)].

SMYTH, John, of Walden, Essex, descended of honest lineage, all his ancestors and predecessors bearing arms, but being uncertain, etc. ; arms, sa., a fesse dancettée, etc. ; crest, a demy-lion reguardant, holding in the dexter paw a spear ppr. ; 12 March 1545-6, 36 H. VIII., by Barker.   Lansd. MS. 210, fo. 79b ; Stowe MS. 692, fo. 82 ; Grants I., 211 ; by Barker, Gart., 1545, 35 H. VIII., a note in Harl. MS. 5846, fo. 93, in another hand. (His 2nd son Sir Thomas, secretary to Edw. VI. and Q. Eliz., Chancellor of the Order of the Garter, quartering Charnock and impaling the arms of Karkike and Wilford [his two wives] ; Crest, a salamander regnardant in flames proper, ducally gorged or, *see* Visitations 1552, 1558 and 1612) ; Harl. MS. 6065, fo. 41b, 42b ; Life of Sir Thomas Smith, by John Strype, app. i.

SMITH, John, of Newcastle-under-Lyme, co. Staff., gent., 17 Sept., 4 Q. Eliz., 1561, a patent of confirmation and gift of the crest by Sir G. Dethick, Gart. : barry of six erm. and gu., over all a lion ramp. gu., crowned or.   Quite a different coat allowed at the Visit. in 1583 to Ralph, s. of John.

December in Guil. 403, and Harl. MSS. 1441, fo. 102, and 1359, fo. 82 ; Add. MS. 4966, fo. 41[b].

SMYTHE, John, of Old Buckenham, Norfolk, gift . . . . 1562. (Harvey's Grants), Add. MS. 16,940, fo. 16[b] ; Visit. of Norfolk ; Harl. MS. 1552, fo. 35[b]. Arms, per chev. nebulée sa. and or, three panthers' heads counterchanged. Crest, a horse's head erased per chev. nebulée or and sa.

SMITH, John (or George), of London, gent., s. of John, of Sleghill, Westmorld., gent., 23 Mar. 1576-7, by Sir G. Dethick, Gart. Harl. MS. 1441, fo. 86 ; called George in Q's Coll. Oxf. MS. 145, fo. 42[b], and in Harl. MS. 5887, fo. 42.

  „ John, of Halesworth, Suff. [exemplified 2 Dec. 1588], ... by Cooke. Harl. MSS. 1359, fo. 95[b], and 1069 : az., billetée or, a bend erm. ; crest, on a chapeau [gu., turned up erm.] two wings az., billetée or, on each wing a bend erm. Visit. of Norfolk, 1613 ; Harl. MS. 1552, fo. 60[b].

  „ John, Craffield, Suff., 9 July 1663 (? 1633 rather), by R. St. George, Clar. Harl. MS. 1085, fo. 27[h].

  „ John (Capt.), of Willoughby, co. Linc. (descended of Smith of Cuerdly, co. Lanc.), Capt. of 250 soldiers under Henry Volda, E. of Meldritch, etc. ; grant of knighthood and arms to him by Sigismund Bathori, Count of Transylvania (Leipsic). 9 Dec. 1603 (? 1623), for services against the Turk. Granted three Turks' heads for his arms, as he had with his own sword cut off the heads of three. Registered at Heralds' College and alteration of coat 19 Aug. 1625, by Segar. Q's Coll. Oxf. MS. 38, fo. 142, copy of testimonial, etc., and Harl. MS. 1507, fo. 399 ; Add. MSS. 4304, fo. 93, and 12,225, fo. 103[b] ; Capt. John Smith's true travels, etc., 1630, p. 17 ; Guil. 251 ; see Harl. MS. 6140, fo. 54 ; for trick see Le Neve's MS. 399 ; Cotton MS. Julius, C. vii., fo. 243[b].

  „ Laurence, of Brabant, etc., addition Jan. 1663-4, by Walker, Gart. Add. MSS. 14,293, fo. 63, and 14,294. fo. 18 ; Harl. MSS. 1172, fo. 63[b], and 6179, fo. 77[b].

  „ Margaret (dau. of Thomas, of Cockermouth), wife to Edward Wilmot of Southampton, arms 15 Sept. 1552, by ? Hawley. Add. MS. 16,940, fo. 205[b] ; Harl. MSS. 578, fo. 9[b], and 3526, fo. 9[b].

  „ Mary (dau. of Cooper), ux. 1 William Tofte, 2 Rich. Smith ; she was the dau. of Dorothy Smith, late ux. John Cooper of London, esq. ; by Ro. Cooke, Clar. Stowe MS. 670, fo. 4[b].

SMYTH, Matthew, of Denby (High Sheriff), co. Derby, 10 Feb. 1684-5, by Sir W. Dugdale and Norroy : per chev. az. and or, three escallops counterchanged ; crest, an escallop per fess or and az. Harl. MS. 6834, fo. 178 ; Grants III., 253 ; Lansd. MS. 867, fo. 52.

SMITH, Miles, Bp. of Gloucester, a confirmation June 1617, by Camden. Harl. MS. 6095, fo. 35[b] ; C. 17 [Visit. Glouc., 1623], Her. Coll., and Visit. Glouc., 1623, Harl. Soc., p. 148.

SMYTH, Philip, of London, crest 16 July 1569, by Cooke. Add. MS. 14,295, fo. 49[b] ; Harl. MS. 1359, fo. 118[b] ; Add. MS. 4966, fo. 101 ; Harl. MS. 5887, fo. 75.

SMITH, Randulph, late Sheriff of Norwich, gent., 2nd son of John, s. of Randle, of Stockport, Chesh., and coz. to Sir Thos., late of Chester, father of Sir Laurence, Knt., confirmed (? a grant) 21 April 1593, by W. Dethick, Gart. Q's Coll. Oxf. MS. 36, fo. 16, copy of grant or confirmation ; Stowe MS. 676, fo. 87[b], 99.

  „ Richard, of London, 31 Jan. 1502-3, 24 H. VII., by John Wrythe or Wriothesley, Gart., and Roger Machado, Richmond Clar. Add. MS. 17,506, fo. 37 ; Le Neve's MS. 259.

  „ Richard, of London, in Bow Lane, fishmonger, 12 Nov. 1571, by Cooke. Harl. MS. 1359, fo. 87 ; date from Visit. of London, 1634 ; Add. MS. 4966, fo. 66[b].

SMITH (Richard), of the Exchequer, was of Herefordsh. (2nd s. of Thomas, of Credenhill, co. Heref.), 1590, by Cooke. Harl. MS. 1359, fo. 101ᵇ; 1590 in Harl. MS. 1545, fo. 40ᶜ, 101ᵇ; see Harl. MS. 1396, fo. 282, 293, and Visit. of Shropshire. 1623.

„ Richard, Doctor of Physic in Ord. to the Queen, born in co. Glouc.: arg., three saltires sa., on a chief gu. a lion passant or; crest, out of flames ppr. a phœnix head or; confirmed 10 Aug. 1591, by W. Dethick, Gart. Q's Coll. Oxf. MS. 36, fo. 15, copy of confirmation; (1592 in Harl. MS. 1359, fo. 16); Add. MS. 14,295, fo. 16; Stowe MS. 676, fo. 87, 98ᵇ.

„ Richard, clerk of the cheyne [cheque] of H.M.'s Yeoman of the Guard, 16 Sept. 1662, by Sir E. Walker, Gart. Her. Coll., fo. 48.

„ Robert, of London, quarterly . . . . 1581, by Cooke: 1 and 4, [sa. ?] a chev. betw. three gryphons segreant or, a chief of the last; 2 and 3, sa., a fesse and in chief three fleurs-de-lis or. Crest, a talbot passant per pale or and sable. Harl. MSS. 1359, fo. 96ᵇ, and 1422, fo. 121ᵇ.

SMYTH, Roger, of Withcocks, co. Leic. (s. of John Smyth alias Heriz), crest 16 May 1565, by Sir G. Dethick: An arm couped, the sleeve per pale or and gu., holding in the hand a griffin's head erased az., beaked or, langued, eyed and eared gu. See William HARES als SMYTH (p. 114), 8 Feb. 1499, by C. Carhill, Norr. Top. and Geneal., iii., 258, copy of grant, and of Dethick's grant, p. 259.

SMITH, Samuel, one of the clerks of the House of Lords assembled in Parlᵗ 1640, of London: an escocheon 27 July 1642, by J. Borough, Gart. Grants II., 679; Harl. MS. 1105, fo. 58.

SMYTH, Simon, of Boughton Monchelsey, Kent, confirmation 14 Sept. 1605, by Camden. Harl. MS. 6095, fo. 19ᵇ; Stowe MS. 618, fo. 104ᵇ; Guil. 77; Harl. MS. 5887, fo. 14ᵇ.

SMITH, Simon, of Westminster, co. Middx., see under William Smith of Old Windsor.

SMITH als REED, Thomas, of Norfolk, gent., 15 January 1481-2, 21 E. IV., by Thomas (Holme), Clar. See Proc. Soc. of Antiq., 1897, 2nd S., xvi., p. 345.

SMYTHE or SMITH, Thomas, of Campden, co. Glouc., esq. (Stowe MS. 692, fo. 84ᵇ, arms, sa., on a fesse betw. iij saltires or as many pellets, each charged with a fleur-de-lis of the second: Crest, ij amphibions in a Knott indorsant az., langued gu., wreathed or and az., lined arg.); dated at Bullen 4 Sept. 1540, 36 Hen. VIII., by Barker; confirmed by Gilb. Dethick, Gart. (1542 in Harl. MS. 1359, fo. 2); Harl. MS. 1507, fo. 451, and Q's Coll. Oxf. MS. 38, fo. 45, copy of grant; Harl. MS. 3526, plate or fo. 4, Nos. 3 and 4; Grants II., 15 (1544, 36 Hen. VIII.); Gwilt's Notices of Thomas and Henry Smith (1836), p. 14; Le Neve's MS. 452.

SMYTH, Thomas, of Hart place, Herts, 10 Nov. 1556, by ? Hawley. Add. MS. 16,940, fo. 208ᵇ.

SMYTHE, Thomas, of London, customer, gift 1559. (Harvey's Grants), Add. MS. 16,940, fo. 28ᵇ, per pale or and az., a chev. arg. betw. three lions passant guardant counterchanged. Father of Sir John Smythe of Ostenhanger, Kent, Visit. of Lond., 1568. Thomas, 2nd s. of John, of Corsham, Wilts, became farmer of the customs to Q. Eliz. and Q. E. ? [Q. Mary and Q. Eliz. ?].

SMITH, Thomas, of Backton, Suff., ... 1572, by Cooke. Harl. MS. 1359, fo. 106; Add. MS. 4966, fo. 93; Stowe MS. 670.

„ Thomas, s. and h. of Sir Laurence Smith of Hough, Cheshire, s. of Sir Thomas Smith, confirmed 7 July 1579, by Flower, Norr. MS. Ashm. 834, fo. 7, copy of grant, Bodleian Lib.; Guil. 184. A baronetcy conferred in 1660.

„ Thomas, of London, quarterly . . . . 1588, by Cooke. Add. MS. 4966, fo. 31; Harl. MSS. 1359, fo. 109, and 1422, fo. 120ᵇ.

SMITH, Thomas, of Credenhill, co. Hereford, ... 1590, by Cooke. Stowe MS. 670, fo. 41.

„ Thomas, of . . . ., co. Hereford, 24 Sept. 1569, by Cooke. Bannerman's MS., No. 9, 447.

„ Thomas, of Crestonhager (Westenhanger), Kent, ... 1591, by Cooke. Harl. MS. 1359, fo. 102 ; Stowe MS. 670, fo. 45ᵇ.

SMYTH, Thomas, lately elected Alderm. city of London, and now master of the Skinners' Co., 13 Aug. 1629, by Sir R. St. George, Clar. Add. MS. 14,295, fo. 67 ; Grants II., 654.

„ Thomas, of the par. of St. Mary Magdalen, Milk St., citizen and stationer of London, s. of John, of Church Lawford, co. Warwick, confirmed 18 Oct. 1633, by R. St. George, Clar., at the Visit. of London. Add. MS. 14,295, fo. 58, 97ᵇ ; C. 24 [Visit. of London, 1634], fo. 384, father of Thomas, of Westerham, Kent.

SMITH, Sir Thomas, of Burgh, Norfolk, 27 March 1672, by Sir E. Bysshe, Clar. Harl. MS. 6179, fo. 35ᵇ.

„ Thomas, see under Anthony SMITH.

SMYTH, William, als HARES, 1499, see HARES and William SMITH als HARES of Leicester.

SMITH, William, of the city of Hereford, esq., and one of the Clarks of the Privy Council, confirmed 2 July 1563, by Sir G. Dethick, Gart. Harl. MS. 1441, fo. 65 ; Q's Coll. Oxf. MS. 145, fo. 7 ; 10 May in Grants II., 562.

SMITHE, William, of Nunstanton, co. Durham, confirmed 11 Jan. 1567-8, by Flower, Gart. MS. Ashm. 834, fo. 70ᵇ, copy of grant, Bodleian Lib. ; Guil. 164.

SMITH, William, of Plumpton, Kent, by Cooke. Harl. MS. 1359, fo. 91ᵇ ; Add. MS. 4966, fo. 64ᵇ ; erm., a mullet gu. betw. three bezants, by Norroy, 1586, in Stowe MS. 670, fo. 14.

SMITH or SMYTH, William, of Luton, Beds, 20 March 1580-81, by Sir G. Dethick, Gart., yeoman of the buttery : erm., on a chev. engrailed az. three estoiles or (or three fleurs-de-lis), in chief a mullet gu. ; confirmed 25 Oct. 1583, by Cooke " I believe." Harl. MSS. 1441, fo. 90ᵇ, and 1422, fo. 22ᵇ ; Q's Coll. Oxf. MS. 145, fo. 49 ; MS. Ashm. 844, fo. 47, copy of grant, Bodleian Lib. ; Guil. 88.

SMITH, William, of the Inner Temple (s. of William, of Brailsford, co. Derby, granted . . . . 1585, by Cooke. Harl. MS. 1359, fo. 88ᵇ ; Guil. 372 ; Add. MS. 4966, fo. 52ᵇ ; Harl. MS. 5887, fo. 37.

„ William, of Axwell, co. Durham, ... 1615, by R. St. George, Norr. Stowe MS. 706, fo. 11ᵇ, 17ᵇ.

„ William, of Damagh, co. Kilkenny, Sec. to James, Earl of Ormond, ... June 1635, by Thomas Preston, Ulster K. of Arms. Kilken. Arch. Soc., i., 261, copy of grant, Brit. Mus.

„ William (called Edward by Burke), ⎫ sons of Christopher, late of Windsor, s.
 of Old Windsor, Berks,   ⎪ of Walter, granted (on the authority
„ Christopher, of Buckhurst, Sussex, ⎬ of their grandfather's seal [the
„ James, of New Windsor, Berks, and ⎪ colours assigned " untill upon dilli-
„ Simon, of Westminster, Middx., ⎭ gent serch they shall find what were
  the Originall Collers ") 21 April
1671 ; not signed, but ? by Walker. Harl. MS. 1172, fo. 39, copy of grant, Brit. Mus., " vera copia."

SMITH als HARES, William, of . . . ., co. Leic., arms 8 Feb. 1499-1500, by Chʳ Carlyl, Norr. Top. and Genl., iii., 255 ; see Visit. of London 1568, Leic. 1619 and Northamptonshire 1618-19.

SMITHES, George, of the Court of Wike, Somerset (out of Lanc.), now of London, Sheriff and Alderm., gent., grant of crest 9 March 1602-3, by W. Dethick, Gart., and Camden, Clar. Q's Coll. Oxf. MS. 36, fo. 99, copy of grant ;

Misc. Gen. et Her., ii., 96 ; Harl. MS. 6095, fo. 23 ; Stowe MS. 676 fo. 139ᵇ ; Grants 1., 349.

SMITHSBY, William, esq., servant to K. Jas., ... by Camden. Add. MS. 14,295, fo. 55ᵇ ; Camden's Grants, fo. 47ᵇ.

SMITHSON, Hugh, of London, ... by W. Ryley, Lanc. Her. Stowe MS. 703, fo. 63.

„ Sir Hugh, of Stanwick, Yorks, Knt. and Bart. (s. of Anthony, of Newsam, co. York), late citizen and merchᵗ of London, and fined for Alderman (and to his brother Bernard, of London, Apothecary), 20 Nov. 1663, by Sir E. Walker, Gart. Harl. MS. 1470, fo. 50 ; Add. MSS. 14,295, fo. 62, and 14,294, fo. 14ᵇ ; Harl. MS. 1172, fo. 63ᵇ, copy of grant ; Harl. MS. 1441, fo. 49ᵇ, copy of grant ; Geneal., vol. i., p. 137, and Hist. of Alnwick, by Geo. Tate, i., 355.

„ John, of Kent, given by patent at London 27 May 1572, 4 Q. Eliz., by Sir Gilb. Dethick. Q's Coll. Oxf. MS. 145, fo. 28ᵇ ; Harl. MS. 1441, fo. 78 ; Add. MS. 14,295, fo. 7, 24ᵇ ; 22ⁿᵈ May in Harl. MS. 1359, fo. 12ᵇ ; Harl. MS. 1441, fo. 49ᵇ, copy of grant.

SNELGRAVE alias SNELGAN, Henry, s. of Thomas, s. of William, s. of Job, of Fisherton, Delamere, Wilts, 2 Oct. 1607, by Camden, Clar. Harl. MS. 1166, fo. 87 ; Le Neve's MS. 421.

SNELLING, Charles, of East Horsley, Surrey, ... 1631, by Segar. Add. MS. 12,225, fo. 104 ; C. 21 [? C. 2], fo. 355, Her. Coll. ; Guil. 268 ; Add. MS. 46,140, fo. 63.

„ Sir George, of Portslade and West Grinstead, Sussex, Knt., s. of Richard, of West Grinstead, by Margaret, dau. to Sir Thomas May of Mayfield in the said co., ... 1611, by Segar. Add. MS. 12,225, fo. 104 ; Guil. 162.

„ Robert, of nᵣ Ipswich, Suff., gent., grant 23 April 1594, by W. Dethick, Gart. Stowe MS. 676, fo. 110ᵇ ; Q's Coll. Oxf. MS. 36, fo. 42, copy of grant ; Harl. MS. 1085, fo. 19ᵇ.

SNIGG, Sir John, Baron of the Exchequer, ... May 1610, by Camden. Harl. MSS. 1422, fo. 21, and 6095, fo. 12ᵇ ; Guil. 258 ; Harl. MSS. 5887, fo. 41ᵇ, and 6140, fo. 51ᵇ.

SNYGGE, George, of Bristol, counsellor-at-law, ... 1591, by Cooke. Harl. MS. 1422, fo. 23ᵇ.

SNODE, Mary, wife of Edward Lister, doctor in physic, Dec. 1611, by Camden. *See* FARMERY. Harl. MS. 6095, fo. 17 ; Stowe MS. 702, fo. 115.

SNOWE, Richard, of Chicksand, Beds, 15 Feb. 1545-6, by Hawley. Add. MSS. 16,940, fo. 201ᵇ, and 7098, fo. 77ᵇ (fo. 46).

SOAME, Sir Stephen (Lord Mayor of London 1598), of Suff., ... 1572 ; arms, gu., a chev. betw. three mullets [mallets ?] or ; crest. Berry.

SOAMES, Edward, of Walpole, Norfolk, ... 1587, by Cooke. Harl. MS. 1359, fo. 107.

SOANE or SOAME, Thomas, of Bodley, Suff., ... 1587, by Cooke. Harl. MSS. 1359, fo. 109ᵇ, and 1422, fo. 94 ; called Soame of Bradley, Add. MS. 4966, fo. 31ᵇ.

SODAYE or SODAGE, John, of Spayne, ... gift . . . . 1559. (Harvey's Grants), Add. MS. 16,940, fo. 14.

SOLE, Robert, of London, s. of John, of Eckington, co. Worc., gent., crest 18 June 1591, by Cooke. Harl. MSS. 1422, fo. 51, and 1359, fo. 102 ; Add. MS. 14,295, fo. 23.

SOME, Thomas, of Wanesden, Suffolk, coat and crest . . . . Barker's Grants, Harl. MS. 5846, fo. 91ᵇ ; Stowe MS. 692, fo. 87.

SOMER, ..., Salop, 17 Feb. 1651-2 : per pale vert and gu., a chev. indented erm., in chief a lion passant betw. two martlets arg. Berry.

SOMMER, John, of Newland, par. of St. Maries, Kent, 1 Dec. 1566, by Sir G. Dethick, Gart. Harl. MS. 1441, fo. 67 ; (? Ashm. 834, fo. 9ᵇ, copy of grant, Bodleian Lib., as Somer) ; Q's Coll. Oxf. MS. 145, fo. 10ᵇ.

SOMER, John, of Kent, arm., April, 17 Eliz., 1575, by Sir G. Dethick, Gart. MS. Ashm. 834, fo. 9ᵇ, copy of grant, Bodleian Lib. *See* John SOMMER, above.

„ Thomas, of Glasley, Salop, gent., 19 Oct. 1524, by T. Wriothesley, Gart., and T. Tonge (Norr.). Grants I., 1 ; (Harl. MS. 5846, fo. 98 ; Stowe MS. 692, fo. 86ᵇ, confirmed by C. Barker, Gart.) ; Harl. MS. 6179, fo. 24ᵇ.

SOMERS, Sir George, Knt., of Baron or Boxolm, Dorset, assigned, given and granted, the crest here exemplified, 2 March 1604-5, by Camden. Harl. MSS. 1422, fo. 37ᵇ, and 6095, fo. 22ᵇ ; *see* Harl. MS. 5887, fo. 90ᵇ.

„ John, Lord, Lord Chancellor, supporters 24 Dec. 1697. Grants IV., 242.

SOMESTER, William, of Penisford (? Pinesford), Devon, confirmed 14 March 1586-7, by Cooke. Harl. MSS. 1359, fo. 107, and 1422, fo. 93 ; Guil. 305 ; Add. MS. 4966, fo. 68ᵇ ; Harl. MS. 6140, fo. 69ᵇ.

SOMNER, William and John, ? SUMNER, both of Canterbury, 25 Aug. 1663. Harl. MS. 1105, fo. 19, 37ᵇ, ? by Sir E. Bysshe, Clar. ; Le Neve's MS. 510.

„ William, of Dinton, Bucks, gent., 3 March 1669-70. Harl. MS. 1105, fo. 37ᵇ, ? by Sir E. Bysshe.

SONESON, Olaus, an Ostrogoth in Sweden, augmentation and crest, letters patent, grant (Seal) 1 Dec., 26 Eliz., 1583. MS. Ashm. 834, fo. 57, copy of grant, Bodleian Lib.

SORANZO, Jacob, *see* SUPERANTIUS.

SORELL, of Ipswich, Suff. Harl. MS. 1105, fo. 38ᵇ and 39 ; Bysshe's Grants, 32.

SORREY or SERROY, George, of Midnell, Somᵗ, arms confirmed, with difference, and crest granted 5 May 1567, by Sir G. Dethick, Gart., and Flower. Q's Coll. Oxf. MS. 39, fo. 128, copy of grant.

SOUCH (or SOUTH), ..., of Dorset, confirmed *circa* 1606, by Camden (gu., ten bezants on a canton or, a lozenge vert, charged with a fleur-de-lis ar.). Called Souch in Camden's Grants and in Morgan's Sphere, 112 ; Harl. MS. 6095, fo. 21.

SOUTH, Sir Francis, of Fotherbey and of Kelsterne, co. Linc., 2nd s. of George, of Fotherbey, s. of John, s. of Thomas, of Fotherbey, crest 22 June 1605, by Camden. Harl. MSS. 6095, fo. 19, and 5887, fo. 12ᵇ.

„ John, of Fotherby and Kelsterne, co. Linc., confirmed 22 June 1602, by Camden. Guil. 101 ; Harl. MS. 5887, fo. 12ᵇ.

„ Thomas, of Swallow Cliff, Wilts, 8 Oct. 1564, 6 Eliz., by Sir G. Dethick. Harl. MS. 1441, fo. 66ᵇ, 83ᵇ ; Q's Coll. Oxf. MS. 145, fo. 9ᵇ, 38ᵇ ; Grants II., 652, and another different coat in ? 1575, but same crest ; Grants II., 652ᵇ.

SOUTHAICKE, George, citizen and merchant of London, exemplified and confirmed by Camden. Stowe MS. 712, fo. 71 ; Harl. MSS. 6179, fo. 14, and 5887, fo. 35, grocer.

SOUTHAMPTON TOWN, arms, crest and supporters 4 Aug. 1575, by Cooke. Add. MS. 14,295, fo. 85 ; Cat. Her. Exhib. Soc. of Antiq., 68.

SOUTHBY, John, of Careswell, Berks, gen., s. and h. of Richard, s. of John, exemplified 10 Feb. 1631-2, under his hand and seal of office (by Sir W. Segar, Knt., Gart.). Add. MS. 12,225, fo. 105 ; MS. Ashm. 840, fo. 406, copy of grant, Bodleian Lib.

SOUTHABY or SUTHABY, Robert, of Birdsall, Yorks, 15 Aug. 1563, by Flower. Surtees Soc., XLI., xl ; Harl. MS 1359, fo. 34ᵇ ; 5th of Aug. in Add. MS. 14,295, fo. 39 and 74 ; Harl. MS. 6140, fo. 68ᵇ.

SOUTHERNE, George, of Fitz als Twells, Salop, gen., eldest son of Gilbert, gen., etc., } 20 June 1628, by Segar. Add. MS. 12,225, fo. 104ᵇ ; C. 24 [Visit. of London, 1634], fo. 22ᵇ, and R. 22, fo. 307-8, Her. Coll.; Misc. Gen. et Her., N. S., i., 217 ; Guil. 213.

„ John, of London, 2nd son,

„ William, of London, 3rd son,

„ Reynold, of Gray's Inn, 4th son,

SOUTHERTON, Thomas, of Norwich, confirmed 1562. (Harvey's Grants), Add. MS. 16,910, fo. 13 ; Harl. MS. 5887, fo. 61.

SOUTHLAND, Sir William, of Kent, ... June 1604, by Camden. Harl. MSS. 1422, fo. 18, 1115, fo. 9, 2275, fo. 91, and 5839, fo. 3 ; Guil. 339.

SOUTHOUSE, Christopher, quarterly arms and crest . . . . by Cooke. Harl. MSS. 1359, fo. 114, and 1422, fo. 118ᵇ ; Add. MSS. 14,295, fo. 38ᵇ, and 4966, fo. 97.

SOUTHWELL, Richard, of St. Faith's, Norfolk, quarterly of 6, confirmed (a bordure for diff.) and crest granted 15 Dec. 1568, by Sir G. Dethick, Gart., Cooke and Flower. MS. Ashm. 841, fo. 1, and Q's Coll. Oxf. MS. 39, fo. 134, copy of grant (MS. 145, fo. 14ᵇ) ; Harl. MS. 1441, fo. 69ᵇ ; Guil. 290, confirmed and a crest granted 30 Nov. 1577, by Ro. Cooke, Clar. ; Q's Coll. Oxf. MS. 37, fo. 67, copy of confirmation, and Stowe MS. 676, fo. 49ᵇ.

SOUTHWOOD, ..., of London, merchant, 6 March 1646-7, by Bysshe, Gart. Harl. MS. 6140, fo. 18.

SOUTHWORTH, Sir John, of Sainsbury in Com. Lanc., Knt., s. and h. of Sir Thomas, s. and h. of Sir John, s. and h. of Sir Christopher, s. and h. of Richard, esq., s. and h. of Sir Thomas, of Sainsbury, quarterly, 3 Dec. 1560, by Dalton, Norr. Harl. MS. 1359, fo. 47ᵇ.

SOWDON, Hugh, of London, gent. and mercht., 11 July 1637, by Borough, Gart. Harl. MS. 1105, fo. 55ᵇ ; Add. MS. 26,702, fo. 90ᵇ ; Stowe MS. 606, fo. 176. copy of grant.

SPARCHFORD, John, of Sparchford, Salop, 25 Nov. 1556, by ? Hawley, Clar. Add. MS. 16,940, fo. 208ᵇ.

SPARKE or SPARKES, ..., London, 10 Aug. 1577, by Cooke (or ? G. Dethick). Harl. MSS. 1422, fo. 123ᵇ, and 6140, fo. 35ᵇ.

SPARROW, Ann, dau. of John, of London, gent., wife to Sir Robert Dymoke, Knt. and Bannᵗ, 25 June 1516, Hen. VIII., by Sir T. Wriothesley, Gart., and T. Benolt, Clar. Add. MSS. 26,702, fo. 60ᵇ, and 14,295, fo. 43ᵇ ; Q's Coll. Oxf. MS. 146, fo. 185 ; Harl. MS. 1359, fo. 35ᵇ.

„ Anthony, D.D., Bishop of Exeter, s. and h. of Samuel, of Depden, Suff., 29 May 1669. Harl. MS. 1105, fo. 21 ; Bysshe's Grants, fo. 22, Her. Coll.

„ Robert, of Ipswich, s. of John. of Somersham, Suff., by Cooke. The crest allowed by Richᵈ Lee, Clar. (20 June 1594 in Harl. MS. 1422, fo. 51) ; Harl. MS. 1359, fo. 30ᵇ ; Add. MS. 14,295, fo. 22 ; Harl. MS. 6832, fo. 131ᵇ.

SPATEMAN, John, of Rednooke, co. Derby, 2 March 1663-4, by W. Dugdale, Norr. (Her. Coll.)

SPECKART, Abraham, of London, Nov. 1611, by Camden. Harl. MSS. 1422, fo. 35ᵇ, and 6095, fo. 16 ; Guil. 182.

SPEED, John, of London, ... by Camden. Harl. MSS. 1422, fo. 20, and 6095, fo. 7ᵇ.

SPENCE, ..., of Baulkham (Balcombe), Sussex, 1623 : sa., a fesse embattled arg., quartering Cavendish, Stratton, Byron, Clayton, and Colwich, 1623, by Segar. Add. MS. 12,225, fo. 105 ; Harl. MS. 1076, fo. 107.

SPENCER, John, and ⎱ brothers, sons of . . . . Spencer of co. Warwick, gent., altered
„ Thomas, ⎰ 26 Nov., 20 Hen. VII., 1504, by Richmont Clar. ; confirmed, with crest, by W. Dethick, Gart., to Sir John Spencer. Q's Coll. Oxf. MS. 36, fo. 122, see below ; (s. of William in Add. MS. 14,295, fo. 6) ; Harl. MS. 1359, fo. 15ᵇ.

„ Sir John, s. of Sir John, of Wormleighton and Althorpe, co. Warwick, altered 20 Hen. VII., 1504 ; confirmed, etc., with crest, by W. Dethick, Gart. Q's Coll. Oxf. MS. 36, fo. 122, copy of confirmation.

„ John, of Worstold, Norfolk, gent., 10 Sept., 1 Q. Mary, 1553, by Sir G. Dethick, Gart. Grants I., 218 ; Harl. MS. 1359, fo. 63ᵇ ; ? Q's Coll. Oxf. MS. 140, 50.

„ Nicholas, of London, and to ⎱ by Cooke . . . . Harl. MSS. 1359, fo. 99, and
„ Nicholas, of Sandwich, Kent, ⎰ 1422, fo. 49 ; Add. MS. 4966, fo. 20.

SPENCER, Richard, of Chester city, crest 4 June 1573, by Flower. Harl. MSS. 1422, fo. 49, and 6140, fo. 69ᵇ ; (Thomas in Add. MS. 14,295, fo. 76ᵇ).

„ Thomas, of Everton or Everdon, Northants, gift . . . . 155- to 156-. (Harvey's Grants) Add. MS. 16,940, fo. 32.

SPICER, Nicholas, late Maior and Alderm., city of Exeter, Devon, s. of Thomas, etc., granted 16 May 1594, by W. Dethick, Gart. Stowe MS. 676, fo. 112ᵇ ; Q's Coll. Oxf. MS. 36, fo. 47, copy of grant.

SPYCER, William, of Knapton, co. Warw., ... 1591, by Cooke. Harl. MS. 1359, fo. 103ᵇ.

SPYLLER, Henry, of Kingsey, Bucks, confirmed . . . . by Camden. This was a confirmation made on a piece of vellum with his hand and seale at it, which came to my hands by chance (J. Withie), etc. Harl. MSS. 1422, fo. 38ᵇ, and 6095, fo. 29 ; Guil. 105.

SPILLER, John, of Shaftesbury, Wilts, recte Dorset, crest 15 Feb. 1575-6, by Cooke. Harl. MS. 1422, fo. 22.

SPYLER, John (? William), of Shotesbery, Dorset, gift . . . . 1557. (Harvey's Grants), Add. MS. 16,940, fo. 42ᵇ.

SPILLMAN, Thomas, of Walden, Essex, crest . . . . Barker's Grants, Harl. MS. 5846, fo. 98ᵇ ; Stowe MS. 692, fo. 87.

SPINOLA, Sir Paul Baptist, of Genoa, an augmentation (by Ed. VI.) 1 Aug. 1550. MS. Ashm. 858, fo. 18, copy of grant, Bodleian Lib.

SPONER, Thomas, of Wyck Wantford (Wickhamford), co. Worc., 1589, by Cooke. Harl. MSS. 1359, fo. 100ᵇ, and 1422, fo. 94ᵇ ; Add. MS. 4966, fo. 88ᵇ.

SPRACKLING, Robert, of the Isle of Thanet, ... 1590, by Cooke. Harl. MS. 1359, fo. 96.

SPRAGGE, Sir Edward, Kt. (s. of Lichfield Spragge, a Capt. of foot in Ireland), Vice-Admiral, 30 April 1668, by Walker, Gart. Add. MS. 14,294, fo. 29ᵇ.

SPRANGER, Sir Richard, of Canes in North Weald Bassett, Essex, and unto his uncle John, of Halley Hall, Great Amwell, Herts, D. Phys., 18 Jan. 1660-61, by Sir E. Walker, Gart. Add. MS. 31,896, fo. 30 ; Harl. MS. 1085, fo. 2ᵇ. Arms, per pale or and sa., three fleurs-de-lis counterchanged ; crest, see Armory. Harl. MSS. 6179, fo. 35, and 6065, fo. 22ᵇ.

SPRIGNALL, Sir Richard, of "Higate," Middx., 10 Sept. 1639, by Borough, Gart. Harl. MSS. 1105, fo. 56ᵇ, and 1441, fo. 58ᵇ ; Add. MS. 26,702, fo. 93 ; a Capt. of trained bands, Guil. 170.

SPRING, ..., of Pakenham, Suffolk, 2 June 1602, by Camden. See Morgan's Sphere, ii., 18 ; Caius Coll. Camb. MS. 551, fo. 29ᵇ, arg., a chev. betw. three mascles gu.

SPRINGETT, Herbert, s. of Sir Thomas, of Broyle place, Sussex, coat confirmed and crest granted 21 Nov. 1612, by Segar. Add. MS. 12,225, fo. 105ᵇ, but ent. MS. 7, A. (? Austin) ; C. 27 [Visit. of Sussex, 1633], fo. 128ᵇ, Her. Coll. ; Guil. 398 ; Harl. MS. 1562, fo. 124.

SPRINT, John,   ⎱ of . . . ., Hants ?, and his son, 1591, ? by Cooke. Harl. MS.
  „ John, D.D., ⎰   1422, fo. 12 ; 1575 in Harl. MS. 1441, fo. 46.

SPRYE . . . ., of Devon, az., two bars or, in chief a chev. of the same, 28 March 1619 (under the hand and seale of W. Segar). Add. MS. 12,225, fo. 105ᵇ.

SPYER, ..., of Walgrove [Wargrave] and Shortletts [Scarletts], Berks, ... 1560. Berry and Burke.

SPYER or SPEERE, Thomas, of Huntercombe, Oxon., confirmation of arms and crest granted 20 April 1588, by Cooke, Clar. Harl. MS. 1359, fo. 121 ; Grants I., 102.

SPURLING or SPERLING, John, of Weston, co. Heref., ... 1574, by Cooke. Harl. MSS. 1359, fo. 90ᵇ, 115ᵇ, and 1422, fo. 93 ; Add. MS. 4966, fo. 65ᵇ ; Berry gives date 1586 : az., two bars or, in chief three mascles of the last ; Crest [on a chapeau az., turned up ermine, a greyhound sejant or].

SQUIBB, Arthur, Clar., died 1651. Add. MS. 31,896, fo. 29.

SQUIRE, Dame Alice, wife of Sir Edward North of Kirtling, arg., on a chev. battelley betw. three eaglets or as many pannuses gu. and or. Barker's Grants, Stowe MS. 692, fo. 71.

  „ Scipio le, deputy Chamberlain, King's Exchequer, s. of Edmund, certified pedigree and arms 3 May 1623, by R. St. George, Clar. *See* Records of the Parish of Whitkirk, I. M. Platt and Morkill.

SQUIER, William, of London (scrivener, dwelling in Cheapside), by Cooke. Harl. MSS. 1359, fo. 116, and 5887, fo. 5ᵇ; Add. MS. 4966, fo. 63.

STACKHOUSE, Christopher, copy of grant 11 Dec. 1518; letters patent from Maximilian, Emperor of Rome and Hungary. Harl. MSS. 1172, fo. 74 (1397, fo. 32), copy of grant.

STAFFORD, ..., of Sydenham, Devon, ... by Borough, Gart. Harl. MSS. 1105, fo. 55, and 1441, fo. 57; Add. MS. 26,702, fo. 88ᵇ; Guil. 77.

STALLER, Thomas, D.D., died 14 March 1605-6, buried at St. Mary-at-Hill; patent *circa* (14 March) 1605, by Camden. Harl. MSS. 6095, fo. 20, and 5887, fo. 23ᵇ.

STAUNFORD or STAMFORD, William, of Holloway or Hadley, Middx., grant 16 May 1542, by Barker. MS. Ashm. 858, fo. 110, copy of grant, Bodleian Lib., Exhibited at Lichfield 1613, Visit. of Staffordshire; Harl. MS. 2145, fo. 111ᵇ, 112.

  „ William, of Rousley, co. Staff., coat and crest, 25 June 1544, by Barker. Harl. MS. 5846, fo. 97; Stowe MS. 692, fo. 86ᵇ; Add. MS. 26,702, fo. 19; Edwᵈ in Harl. MS. 5807, fo. 43ᵇ; Harl. MS. 2145, fo. 111ᵇ, 112.

STEMPE, Elias or Ellis, of Hampshire, 8 Jan. 1577-8, by Sir G. Dethick, Gart. Harl. MS. 1441, fo. 88ᵇ; Q's Coll. Oxf. MS. 145, fo. 45ᵇ; Harl. MS. 5887, fo. 39; "of the Chapell," called Temple in Add. MS. 26,753; Harl. MS. 1544, fo. 3.

STAMPE, Thomas, of Moulsford, Berks, quarterly . . . . by Cooke. Harl. MS. 1359. fo. 92ᵇ; Add. MS. 4966, fo. 59ᵇ.

  „ (or STOMPES), William, of Malmesbury, Wilts, gent., grant 1 Dec. 1549, by Hawley. Q's Coll. Oxf. MS. 38, fo. 55, copy of grant; called Sir James in Add. MS. 16,940, fo. 203ᵇ.

STANDON, Edmund, of East Molesey, Surrey, confirmed 155- to 156-. (Harvey's Grants), Add. MS. 16,940, fo. 56ᵇ.

STANLEY, (Edward, 3rd) Earl of Derby, Constable of England, Lord Stanley, Monthault and Man; quarterly: in the 1st quarter, Stanley, Lathom and Warren; 2nd, Man; upon all the escocheon of Monthault. The crest of Stanley is a hart silver; the crest of Lathom is the eagle and child, etc. Barker's Grants, Harl. MS. 5846, fo. 95ᵇ; Stowe MS. 692, fo. 86.

  „ Henry, of Sutton Bonington, Notts (and Anne, dau. of Richard Bradshaw, his wife), 18 Mar. 1576-7, by Cooke, Clar. Grants II., 510; Nichols' Leic., vol. iv., pt. i., 552.

  „ Richard (als STONELEY), gent., arms granted 20 Feb., 2 and 3 Philip and Mary, 1555-6, by Sir G. Dethick, Gart. Q's Coll. Oxf. MS. 39, fo. 77, copy of grant; Grants I., 232; Harl. MSS. 1359, fo. 64ᵇ, and 1116, fo. 61.

  „ Richard, als STONELEY, of Duddinghurst, Essex, crest granted 20 Nov. 1557, by Harvey, Clar. Add. MS. 16,940, fo. 28ᵇ; Grants I., 34, countersigned by Ro. Cooke.

  „ Sir Thomas, of Essex, by J. Borough, Gart. Harl. MSS. 1105, fo. 55, and 1441, fo. 57ᵇ; Add. MS. 26,702, fo. 89.

  „ Sir William, of Hutton or Hooton, coat and crest. Barker's Grants, Harl. MS. 5846, fo. 97ᵇ; Stowe MS. 692, fo. 86ᵇ.

STANNARD, William, of London, inholder, of Laxfield, Suff., gent., 10 March 1631-2, by Segar. Add. MS. 12,225, fo. 106; Visit. of London, C. 24 [1634]; Guil. 77; Le Neve's MS. 258.

STANYSBYE, Robert, of Darneton in the Bishoprick of Durham, 8 April 1543, by

I I

Christopher Barker, Gart., coat and crest. Barker's Grants, Harl. MS. 5846, fo. 98ᵇ ; Stowe MS. 692, fo. 83, 86ᵇ ; Cat. Herald. Exhib. Soc. of Antiq., 63.

STANSFIELD (Edmund), quarterly : 1 and 4, sa., three goats passant arg. ; 2 and 3, [trick, gules, four bars argent, a chief silver]. Crest, a goat arg., tusked and bearded or. Dyers coat and crest. "These arms and crest were conformed to one Stansfeild that married the Viscountess Byndon, but by whome I know not. The crest is the Earle of Bedford's without any difference ; the coate is another man's also. There is a large pedigree forged for these armes and crest, which I have seen." Entered by R. Brooke, York Herald. Harl. MS. 1453, fo. 34ᵇ.

STANSFEILD, John, of Lewes, Sussex, out of Yorks, coat and crest, ... Barker's Grants, Add. MS. 26,702, fo. 22.

STANSFIELD, John, of yᶜ Cliff, nʳ Lewes, Sussex, out of Yorks, 4 Dec. 1628, by Segar. Add. MS. 12,225, fo. 106 ; Guil. 152.

  „   Richard, of Shipley, Yorks, grant 8 April 1546, by Barker, Gart. ; confirmed 15 Nov. 1550 [4th Edw. VI.], by Harvey. Harl. MS. 5846, fo. 93 ; Stowe MS. 692, fo. 87 ; S. Kent's Banner Displayed, 674.

STAPLEY, Anthony, of Framfield, Sussex, 1 Jan. 1592-3, by Knight, Norr. Berry ; Harl. MSS. 1076, fo. 174ᵇ, and 6179, fo. 42ᵇ.

STARKEY, Roger, of London, mercer, grant 27 June 1543, 35 H. VIII., by Barker. Harl. MS. 1507, fo. 441, copy of grant, Brit. Mus. ; Q's Coll. Oxf. MSS. 38, fo. 43, 44, and 39, fo. 4, copy of grant ; 27ᵗʰ of June in Harl. MS. 1359, fo. 71 ; Grants I., fo. 11, 13 ; Grant in Record Office ; Le Neve's MS. 441 ; Misc. Gen. et Her., 3rd S., iii., 65.

STARLING, Samuel, of the hamlet of Steppesley in Luton, Bedf. (Lord Mayor 1670), 1 Sept. 1661, by Sir E. Bysshe, Clar. Add. MS. 14,293, fo. 1ᵇ ; Bysshe's Grants, fo. 1, Her. Coll. ; 5ᵗʰ Sept. in Guil. 348, and Harl. MS. 1105, fo. 16ᵇ.

STATIONERS, the Company of, of the City of London, arms 5 Sept., 4 and 5 Philip and Mary, 1557, by Sir G. Dethick, Gart. Q's Coll. Oxf. MS. 39, fo. 87, copy of grant ; Harl. MS. 1359, fo. 71.

STAUNTON, Sir Francis, of Birchmoore, par. of Woburne, Beds, confirmed 3 Jan. 1623-4, 21 K. Jac., 1633, by Sir R. St. George, Clar. Add. MS. 14,295, fo. 70ᵇ ; C. 31, fo. 56, [Visit. of] Bedfordsh. [1634] ; Harl. MS. 6179, fo. 37.

  „   John, citizen and mercht.-taylor of London, coat confirmed and crest granted 16 April 1575, by Flower. Misc. Gen. et Her., 2nd S., vol. i., p. 44, facsimile copy of grant, Brit. Mus., and Cat. Herald. Exhib. Soc. of Antiq., 68.

  „   Laurence, D.D., Dean of Lincoln, Nov. 1610, by Camden. Harl. MSS. 1422, fo. 21ᵇ, and 6095, fo. 13ᵇ.

STAVELEY, Baron, supporters . . . . by Sir E. Walker, Gart. Her. Coll.

STAWEL, Ralph, Lord, ... supporters 9 March 1682-3, by Ailesbury, Deputy Earl Marshal. Harl. MS. 6834, fo. 178 ; Grants III., 190.

STAYNINGS, Thomas, of Somerset, crest 29 Nov. 1559, by Harvey. Harl. MS. 1422, fo. 22ᵇ ; Edward in Add. MS. 16,940, fo. 48.

STEDE, William, of Harrietsham, Kent, gent., confirmed 16 Nov. 1588, by Cooke. Add. MS. 14,295, fo. 93 ; Harl. MS. 1359, fo. 102ᵇ ; Cooke's Grants, fo. 13, 23ᵇ ; crest altered, Harl. MS. 5887, fo. 51 ; Stowe MS. 670, fo. 29, 55ᵇ.

STEERE, John, of Ockley, Surrey, 6 Dec. 1662, ? by Bysshe, Clar. Harl. MS. 1105, fo. 42.

STEIBER, Lawrence, a German, of Erllstegen, born in Nuremberg, augmⁿ letters patent, dated at my Castle of Windsor 8 Oct. 1520, 12 H. VIII. ; Knighted by the King. Harl. MS. 4900, fo. 35ᵇ ; MS. Ashm. 834, fo. 73, and 858, fo. 43, copy of grant, Bodleian Lib.

STEPHENS, John, of Barton-ou-the-Hill, co. Glouc., ... 1591, by Cooke. Harl.
MS. 1359, fo. 102.

,, John, of Colchester, Essex, quarterly arms and crest given . . . . April 1592,
33 Q. Eliz., by Cooke. Harl. MSS. 1359, fo. 15, 111ᵇ, and 1422. fo. 116ᵇ;
Add. MSS. 14,295, fo. 10, and 4966, fo. 24.

STEPKIN, John, of East Smithfield, Middx., gent., allowed by Sir J. Borough, Gart.,
W. Le Neve, Clar., and H. St. George, Norr. No date. Grants I., 427;
Harl. MS. 1441, fo. 150.

STEPNETH, Alban, of Prendergast. co. Pemb., 3rd s. of Thomas, of St. Alban's,
? original grant in full in Latin 15 March 1605-6, by Camden. Harl. MS.
7025, fo. 200 ; see also quarterly coat, Harl. MS. 6095, fo. 5 ; Harl. MS.
1422, fo. 108 ; Le Neve's MS. 282, 499.

STEPNETHE, Robert, of East Hamburnells, Essex, confirmed quarterly. (Harvey's
Grants), Add. MS. 16,940, fo. 21ᵇ ; Le Neve's MS. 356.

STERMYN, William, of Wisbech, s. of John, late of the Isle of Ely, co. Camb.,
granted by the late Clar. (Cooke), and confirmed, 29 May 1593, by
W. Dethick, Gart. Stowe MS. 676, fo. 89, 102ᵇ ; Q's Coll. Oxf. MS. 36,
fo. 23, copy of grant.

STEVENS (Thomas), of Estington, co. Glouc., attorney to Hen., Prince of Wales,
confirmed 1606, Stevens quartering Lugg, by Camden. Harl. MSS. 1422,
fo. 109, and 6095, fo. 20ᵇ ; Guil. 381 ; Harl. MS. 5887, fo. 26, 48ᵇ.

,, Henry, of Culham, Berks, 3 Dec. 1694, by T. St. George, Gart. and Clar.
Grants IV., fo. 173 ; Harl. MS. 1085, fo. 58.

STEVENSON, John, Esq., of Stanton and Elton-in-the-Peak, co. Derby, [the heiress]
mar. [Holden], etc., grant 14 June 1688, by T. St. George, Clar., and
J. Dugdale, Norr. Harl. MS. 6834, fo. 49ᵇ ; Stowe MS. 714, fo. 125 ;
Grants IV., 11 ; Guil. 262.

STEWARDE, Augustine, see STYWARDE.

STEWARD, Nicholas, of Okhey (? Essex), allowed 10 March 1586-7, by Cooke. Guil.
273, and Burke.

,, Robert, of Ely, clerk, certif. of various Steward bearings, 14 Sept. 1520,
by Sir T. Wriothesley, Gart. Add. MS. 15,644, fo. 2 ; see Harl. MS. 5887,
fo. 11ᵇ, as Styward, 27 June 1543 ; by W. Harvey in Le Neve's MS.
503-4.

,, Richard, D.D., dean of H.M.'s Chapel, at Jersey 8 Feb. 1649-50, augmentation and alteration by Sir E. Walker, Gart. Her. Coll., 2.

STEWARDE, Symeon, of Lakingheott, Suff., grant 1 May 1558, by Harvey. Add.
MSS. 15,644, fo. 60ᵇ, and 16,940, fo. 31.

STEWKLEY, Thomas, of Marshe, co. Somerset, crest given 21 June 1595, 37 Q. Eliz.,
by R. Lee, Clar. Add. MS. 14,295, fo. 17 ; Harl. MSS. 1359, fo. 16, and
5887, fo. 90 ; date 1597 in Stowe MS. 670, fo. 59.

STILL, John, D.D., late Master of Trin. Coll., Camb., and Vice-Chanc. of that
Univ., Bp. of Bath and Wells, grant 10 April 1590, by W. Dethick, Gart.
Stowe MS. 676, fo. 90ᵇ, 106 ; Q's Coll. Oxf. MS. 36, fo. 31, copy of
grant.

STOCKDALE, Christopher, of Bilton Park (2nd s. of Robert Walters of Cundale,
Yorks) (assumed surname and arms of Stockdale by royal sign manual),
19 Feb. 1694-5. Grants IV., 187 ; Guil. 121, by St. George, Gart. and
Norr.

,, Robert, of Lockington, Yorks, gent., arms confirmed and crest given 28 June
1582, by Flower. MS. Ashm. 844, fo. 54, copy of grant, Bodleian Lib. ;
Harl. MS. 1359, fo. 33 ; Add. MS. 14,295, fo. 35 ; Guil. 333 ; Harl. MS.
5887, fo. 21.

STOCKWOOD, Edward, of Westm., gent., arms 10 June 1522, by T. Wriothesley and
T. Benolte. Add. MS. 14,295, fo. 97.

STONE, ..., of London, arg., three cinquefoils sa., a chief az., by W. Segar, Gart.
Add. MS. 12,225, fo. 107 ; crest, out of a ducal coronet a griffin's head

erm. betw. a pair of wings or, Harl. MS. 1422, fo. 59ᵇ. (*See* Sir Richard and William.)

STONE, ..., of London, fishmonger, gu., an eagle displayed or, gorged with a ducal crown az., by Segar. Add. MS. 12,225, fo. 107ᵇ.

„ John, of London, ... sa., a fesse betw. three tigers passant or ; crest, out of a ducal coronet a demi-peacock with wings expanded or, ... by Cooke. Harl. MSS. 1359, fo. 93, and 1422, fo. 59ᵇ ; Add. MS. 4966, fo. 37.

„ Sir Richard, of Suckling, Sheriff of Hunts, *temp.* Chas. I., confirmed . . . . 1614 ?, granted . . . . 1515, arg., three cinquefoils sa., a chief az. (Berry.)

„ Thomas, of London, merchᵗ, who mar. Elizabeth, d. and h. of William Lufkin, Stone quartering 2 Brickleston, 3 Girdler, 4 Lufkin, ... by Segar. Add. MS. 12,225, fo. 106ᵇ ; C. 24 [Visit. of London, 1634], fo. 447ᵇ, Her. Coll. ; Guil. 392 ; [Lufkin, on escutcheon of pretence in the Visit. of Lond., 1634].

„ Thomas, of Wedmore, Kent, and of Somerset, ... 1588, by Ro. Cooke, Clar. Stowe MS. 670, fo. 24ᵇ.

„ Thomas, of Framfield, Sussex, 4 Dec. 1628 (14 Dec. in Guil. 137), by Segar. Add. MS. 12,225, fo. 106ᵇ ; Harl. MS. 1422, fo. 59ᵇ ; [Visit. of] Sussex [1633], C. 27, 42, Her. Coll.

„ Thomas, the elder, of Bedingham, s. of William, of Stockton, Norf., 12 May 1681, by Sir W. Dugdale, Gart., and H. St. George, Clar. Harl. MS. 6834, fo. 178 ; Grants III., 129.

„ William, of London, granted . . . . 1583 by Cooke, confirmed 1614 by Segar : "to . . . . Stone of London." Arms, arg., three cinquefoils sa., a chief az. Crest, out of a ducal coronet or a griffin's head erm., beaked and wings displayed or. Cooke's Grants, Her. Coll., fo. 2 ; Add. MSS. 12,225, fo. 107, and 14,295, fo. 34 ; Harl. MSS. 1359, fo. 98, and 1422, fo. 59ᵇ ; Guil. 136 ; Add. MS. 4966, fo. 36. *See above.*

„ Sir William, of London, fishmonger, s. of Reginald, 2 Jan. . . . . by Segar and Camden : arms, or, on a pale az. three escallops of the first, and crest. Add. MS. 12,225, fo. 107 ; Harl. MSS. 1422, fo. 18ᵇ, 59, and 6095, fo. 4 ; Guil. 244. *See above.*

STONEHOUSE, George, of Little Peckham, Kent, gent., crest 1 or 5 Feb., 2 and 3 Philip and Mary, 1555-6, by Sir G. Dethick, Gart. Q's Coll. Oxf. MS. 39, fo. 61, copy of grant ; MSS. Ashm. 840, fo. 387, and 858, fo. 195, copy of grant, Bodleian Lib. ; 5ᵗʰ in Grants I., 226 ; Harl. MS. 1359, fo. 64.

STONER (or STOVER), John, of Essex, gift . . . . 1561, 3 Q. Eliz. Add. MS. 16,940, fo. 16, "p fece sa. & golde, a pale engrailed & counterchanged in every poinct of ye fierst, an eagle displaid of the secounde, [Crest] on a wrethe argent & sable an ounse passant azur Besantey wᵗʰ a crowne about the necke & a cheyne gold."

STONES, Christopher, D.D., Chancellor of York Cathedral, late preb. of Lowton [Langhton], etc., 26 Oct. 1666, by W. Dugdale, Norr. Stone in Her. Coll. ; Surtees Soc., XLI., liii, has Stones.

„ Thomas, of Musboro, co. Derby, 21 July 1693, by Thos. St. George, Gart. and Norr. Grants IV., 147.

STONESTREET, George, of Lewes, Sussex, gent., 11 Jan. 1662-3. Bysshe's Grants, fo. 23, Her. Coll. ; Harl. MSS. 1105, fo. 21, and 6179, fo. 54.

STONLEY, *see* STANLEY.

STONYNGS, Gregory, of Litchfield, co. Staff., arms and crest ; grant in a later hand. Barker's Grants, Stowe MS. 692, fo. 86 ; Harl. MS. 5887, fo. 9.

STONYWELL, Abbot, ... Hen. VIII. Add. MS. 26,702, fo. 53 ; Harl. MS. 1116, fo. 22ᵇ, sa., on a chev., betw. three cinquefoils [quatrefoils ?] or, pierced gu. [or s.], as many palm leaves vert, on a chief or a ducal coronet gu. betw. two blackbirds [birds sable].

STORY, John, Kineton (or Kneeton), Notts, gent., 29 Dec. 1676, by Sir W. Dugdale. Harl. MS. 6834, fo. 178 ; Grants III., 48.

STOURTON, Edward, of co. Linc., confirmed quartering 2, Cawley of Staff., and 3, Smith of co. Leic., ... 1618, by Segar. Add. MS. 12,225, fo. 107ᵇ.

STOWE, William, of Newton-next-Trent, co. Linc., gent., 14 June 1660, by Sir E. Walker, Gart. Add. MSS. 14,293, fo. 102, and 14,294, fo. 34 ; Harl. MSS. 1172, fo. 71ᵇ, and 1441, fo. 152.

STRACHY, William, of Rutlandes in Saffron Walden, Essex, grant 4 July 1587, by Cooke. Harl. MS. 1441, fo. 8ᵇ ; copy of grant, Brit. Mus., Harl. MS. 1359, fo. 107ᵇ ; Harl. MS. 1422, fo. 93ᵇ ; Add. MS. 4966, fo. 30ᵇ.

STRANGWAYS, Giles, of Stynysford, Dorset, Esq. of the body, crest 24 Jan. 1512-13, by T. Wriothesley, Gart., and Benolte, Clar. Stowe MS. 676, fo. 9 ; MS. Ashm. 834, fo. 2ᵇ, copy of grant, Bodleian Lib.

STREET, Humfry, of London, descended out of Derbyshire, by Segar. Add. MS. 12,225, fo. 108.

STRELLEY, Robert, of Bowdon, co. Leic., and one of the Privy Council to Q. Mary, 15 Dec. 1555, by W. Hervye, Clar. (Norr.). Geneal., vol. iv., p. 193 ; Rawlinson MS. (Bodleian Lib.) Misc. 116, fo. 126 ; Add. MS. 16,940, fo. 7.

STRETLEY, ... Stretley, co. Staff., ... 1583, arg., a hound passant gu.   Berry.

STREYE, ... crest ....   Barker's Grants, Harl. MS. 5846, fo. 94ᵇ ; Stowe MS. 692, fo. 84.

STREYNSHAM, Thomas, of Canterbury, confirmed 4 May 1577, by Cooke. Harl. MS. 1359, fo. 111 ; MS. Ashm. 834, fo. 16, copy of grant, Bodleian Lib. ; Harl. MS. 1422, fo. 95ᵇ ; Guil. 32 ; Add. MS. 4966, fo. 60.

STRICKLAND, William, of Boynton-on-the-Would, Yorks, gent., gift 15 April 1550, 4 Ed. VI., by Harvey. Harl. MS. 1359, fo. 33ᵇ ; Add. MSS. 14,295, fo. 36ᵇ, 74, and 16,940, fo. 7 ; Harl. MS. 6140, fo. 68ᵇ.

STRINGER, Anthony, of London, gift, ... 1557. (Harvey's Grants), Add. MS. 16,940, fo. 36ᵇ.

„   Stephen, of Goudhurst, Esq.,
„   John, of Ashford,   ⎤   8 Nov. 1664. Harl. MS. 1105, fo. 19 ;
„   Edward, ⎱ of Goudhurst in ⎰   Bysshe's Grants, fo. 14, Her. Coll.
„   Thomas, ⎰   Kent,
„   Thomas, of Bexwells, Essex, 1677, ? by Sir E. Bysshe, Clar. Harl. MS. 1105, fo. 42ᵇ.

STRIPLING, George, of London, 4 May 1663. Harl. MS. 1105, fo. 18ᵇ ; Bysshe's Grants, fo. 10, Her. Coll. ; Guil. 348 ; Harl. MS. 6179, fo. 31.

STURGEON, Roger, of Whepsted, Suff., quarterly, exemplified and confirmed to him and to his brethren by Camden. Harl. MSS. 1422, fo. 20ᵇ, and 6095, fo. 10ᵇ.

STURT, Anthony, late one of the Commissioners for victualling H.M.'s royal navy (s. of Humphrey, of Yateley, Hunts), and to Joseph and Nathaniel, his nephews, 19 Oct. 1691, by T. St. George, Gart. and Clar. Stowe MS. 714, fo. 71, 160 ; Grants IV., 91 ; Harl. MS. 1085, fo. 56.

STYDOLPH, Elizabeth, wife to John Birch, coat only, by Barker. Harl. MS. 5846, fo. 20 ; Foss' Judges, 5th S., 462, M.I. St. Giles-in-the-fields ; Stowe MS. 702, fo. 115 ; 4 quarterings in Harl. MS. 5887, fo. 87.

STYLE, ... crest ....   Barker's Grants, Harl. MS. 5846, fo. 94ᵇ ; Stowe MS. 692, fo. 84.

STILE, Humfrey, s. of John, of Bromley, Kent, 28 March 1529, 20 H. VIII., by T. Wriothesley, Gart. (Stowe MS. 714, fo. 186), who died 24 Nov. 1534.

STILEMAN, Anthony, of Steeple Aston, Wilts, confirmed 6 May 1562, by Harvey. Add. MS. 16,940, fo. 14ᵇ.

STYWARD, Augustine, s. of Symon, of Lakenheath, Suff., exemplification by Cooke, of a Charter of Chas. VI. of France granting an augmentation of arms to Alexander, s. of Andrew Stywart of Scotland, and dated at Paris 1 July 1563, 5 Eliz. ; exemplified 14 Feb. 1573-4, 6 Eliz., by Cooke. MSS. Ashm.

834, fo. 2, and 858, fo. 29, 30, copy of grant, Bodleian Lib.; *see* Le Neve's MS. 505.

STYWARD, Simon, *see* STEWARD.

SUCKLING, ... at Norwich 13 Aug. 20 Eliz., by Cooke, Clar. Harl. MS. 1441, fo. 152.

„ Sir John, crest 26 Nov. 1617, by Camden; Capt. of a troop of horse 1640. Harl. MS. 1441, fo. 152; Add. MS. 4966, fo. 44ᵇ.

SUDBURY, Town of, co. Suffolk, 20 Sept. 1576, by Cooke. Cat. Her. Exhib. Soc. of Antiq., p. 68.

SUDELL, Roger, of Preston, Lanc., } 4 May 1686, by Sir T. St. George, Gart.,
„ William, of Wanley, Yorks, } and J. Dugdale, Norr. Harl. MS. 6834, fo. 178; Grants III., fo. 299; Lansd. MS. 867, fo. 52; Harl. MS. 1085, fo. 58.

SUFFOLK, Lady Frances, late Duchess of, augmentation, letters patent, at palace of Westminster 3 Dec., 2 Q. Eliz., 1559, by G. Dethick, Gart., and Harvey. Harl. MS. 6064, fo. 49; Le Neve's MS. 427.

SUGDEN, William, of London, confirmed . . . . 1565. (Harvey's Grants), Add. MS. 16,940, fo. 11.

SUMMER ISLANDS COMPANY, of the City of London, for the plantation of the Islands, coat and supporters 4 Aug. 1635, by Borough, Gart. Stowe MS. 697, fo. 106ᵇ; Caius Coll. Camb. MS. 551.

SUMNER, *see* SOMNER.

SUPERANTIO (SORANZO), Jacobus, a patrician of Venice, grant 5 Feb. 1551-2, 6 Ed. VI. MS. Ashm. 858, fo. 21, 22, copy of grant, Bodleian Lib.; Le Neve's MS. 466.

SURGEONS' COMPY., of London, gift . . . . 155– or 156–, by (? Harvey). Add. MS. 16,940, fo. 42ᵇ; *see* Barbory and Surgery, 1451.

SUTCLIFFE, John, groome of the privy chamber to K. Chas., by Segar. ["A., an Elephant passant S." "Crest, viz¹, On a wreath a demi-man armed in antique mail O., holding in his right hand a Speare in pale of ye same, his left a Kembe [akimbo], His shoulder belt G."] Add. MS. 12,225, fo. 108; in Harl. MS. 1422, fo. 14, difference in crest [trick of Arms, A., an elephant passant sable, tusks or, and Crest, man in chain mail ppr, sword belt gules, baton in the right hand, in bend Or] (1 Sept. 1624), to John Suckliffe of Melroid, esq. of the body to K. Jas., by William Segar, Gart.; Guil. 146.

SUTTON, Richard, s. of John, of Henley, s. of William, of Eden Hall, co. Staff., by Cooke. Harl. MSS. 1359, fo. 106, and 1422, fo. 59; Add. MS. 4966, fo. 92ᵇ?; a different coat in Stowe MS. 670, fo. 46ᵇ.

„ Richard, chevalier, maistre a l' Hostell de la maison de Syon en la counte de Middlesex, crest 26 Sept., aº 16 [Hen. VIII.], 1524, by Wriothesley, Gart. Barker's Grants, Harl. MS. 5846, fo. 95; Stowe MS. 692, fo. 85ᵇ.

„ Thomas, of Over Haddon, co. Derby, crest 26 Nov. 1550, by Harvey. Harl. MS. 1422, fo. 59; Add. MSS. 14,295, fo. 32ᵇ, and 16,940, fo. 56. Another crest 24 Oct. 1566, with liberty to use either of them, by G. Dethick, Gart., Flower and Cooke. Add. MS. 14,295, fo. 32ᵇ; Harl. MSS. 1422, fo. 117ᵇ, and 1486, fo. 31.

„ William, of Maxfeld or Macclesfield, Cheshire, ... April 1575, by Flower. Harl. MSS. 1453, fo. 74, and 1535, fo. 27ᵇ.

SWALE, Francis, of Yorkshire, by R. St. George, Norr. Visitation [?].

„ Richard, of London, D.C.L., a cadet of de Swale of Kirklington, crest granted 29 March 1591 or 1592, by W. Dethick. Stowe MS. 676, fo. 84ᵇ, 94; Q's Coll. Oxf. MS. 36, fo. 5, copy of grant.

SWALLOW, Thomas, Surveyor of the Mint, 25 April 1668, by Sir E. Walker, Gart. Harl. MS. 6179, fo. 23; Her. Coll., fo. 64.

SWALMAN, William, of Canterbury, gift . . . . 1565. (Harvey's Grants), Add. MS. 16,940, fo. 56ᵇ.

SWANN, Anne, ux. 1st R. Wilcocks, 2nd of Ownerley; not a grant, 1585, by Cooke's deputy.   Stowe MS. 670, fo. 12.

,,   Francis, of Wye, in Kent, ... 1588, by Cooke.   Harl. MSS. 1359, fo. 108ᵇ, and 1422, fo. 94 : Add. MS. 4966, fo. 31.

SWAYNE, William, born in Somerset, arms 29 Jan., 39 Hen. VI. (1460-61) [by Guyan King of Armes, "that hee bears Azure, a Cheveron of golde betwene three brode arrowe heads of the same, A Chiefe gules with three maydens heads [proper] in there heare" [or].   Sketch of a broken seal bearing] On a fesse, betw. three fleurs-de-lis, as many bucks' heads and two woodmen with staves for supporters [round the edge the letters] W.R. . . . . [on one side and] G I O N [on the other]—the arms of Wickesworth, i.e., John Wrexworth, Guyan King of Arms.   Add. MS. 14,295, fo. 5ᵇ, copy of the patent ; and also Q's Coll. Oxf. MSS. 37, fo. 4, and 38, fo. 4, and in MS. 146, fo. 17 ; Harl. MSS. 1359, fo. 12, 1122, fo. 1ᵇ, 1470, fo. 154ᵇ, and 1507, fo. 10ᵇ, copy of grant, Brit. Mus., and Harl. MS. 1172, fo. 2.

,,   William (als Thomas), gent., citizen and merch. adventurer of London, who produced a grant of the said ? coat to William Swayne of Somerset, his progenitor, under the hand of Guion King of Arms, 29 Jan., 39 H. VI., 1460-61 ; confirmed 10 July 1612, by Segar and Camden.   Add. MS. 12,225, fo. 108ᵇ; Guil. 335 gives the date as 10 June 1602 ; Harl. MS. 6095, fo. 38.

SWEIT, Sir Giles, Knt., D.C.L., Dean of Arches, confirmed 10 April 1665, by Walker.   Add. MSS. 14,293, fo. 32, and 14,294, fo. 5 ; Guil. 129.

SWEETAPLE, Sir John, citizen and late Sheriff, city of London, grant 25 Aug. 1699, by T. St. George, Gart., and H. St. George, Clar.   Misc. Gen. et Her., 2nd S., vol. i., p. 133 ; Grants IV., 306.

SWETTENHAM, Lawrence, of Somerford, Cheshire, crest granted 9 Feb. 1568-9, by Sir G. Dethick, Gart., Cooke and Flower.   Q's Coll. Oxf. MS. 39, fo. 150, copy of grant (MS. 145, fo. 16ᵇ) ; MSS. Ashm. 844, fo. 5, and 858, fo. 147, copy of grant, Bodleian Lib. ; Harl. MSS. 1359, fo. 54, and 1441, fo. 71 ; Guil. 298.

SWIFTE, John, of London, one of H.M.'s auditors, ? granted 2 Feb. 1560-61, and confirmed 20 Oct. 1561, by Sir G. Dethick, Gart.   Q's Coll. Oxf. MSS. 37, fo. 39 (4 Feb.), and 39, fo. 119 (20 Oct.), copy of grant, MS. 145, fo. 12 ; and Harl. MS. 1359, fo. 61 (20 Oct.) ; Grants I., 174.

SWIFT, (Sir) Robert, Rotheram, Yorks, 10 May 1562, by Sir G. Dethick, Gart. Harl. MS. 1441, fo. 66 ; 1567 in Q's Coll. Oxf. MS. 145, fo. 8ᵇ ; Grants II., 652.

SWYNBOURNE, John, of Chopwall in the Bpk. of Durham, Esq., s. of John, nat. s. of Thomas, s. of John, of Netherton, Northumbld., confirmed 6 Sept. 1551, 6 Ed. VI., by W. Harvey, Norr.   Add. MS. 16,940, fo. 6ᵇ; Grants II., 553.

SWINGLEHURST, ..., of the East India Company, ... 1646, by E. Bysshe. Harl. MS. 6140, fo. 17ᵇ.

SWINNERTON, John, merchᵗ taylor and Sheriff of London, ... 1602, by Cooke. Ld. Mayor 1612, two crests in Berry ; Guil. 57.

SWYNOKE, Thomas, the elder, of Maidstone, Kent, exemplified by R. St. George, Clar.   Add. MS. 14,295, fo. 102; Harl. MSS. 6179, fo. 65, and 1432, fo. 327ᵇ.

SYER, Robert, of Isham, Northts., s. of Roger, etc., confirmed 11 Feb. 1614-15, by Camden.   Q's Coll. Oxf. MS. 38, fo. 123; Harl. MS. 1507, fo. 367 ?; copy of confirmation, Cains Coll. Camb. MS. 551, fo. 19ᵇ ; Harl. MSS. 5839, fo. 30ᵇ, and 6095, fo. 28ᵇ, as Sayer ; Morgan's Sphere (ii.), 114 ; Guil. 207, as Syer ; see also grant of a different coat to Adie Sare about the same date, Harl. MS. 1422, fo. 38ᵇ, as Sayre ; Le Neve's MS. 327, 367.

SYLESDEN, Thomas, of Finchamfield, Essex.   Add. MS. 26,702, fo. 76.

SYMES, William, of Chard, Somt., (6 Aug.) 1591, by Cooke. Harl. MSS. 1422, fo. 15ᵇ, and 5887, fo. 82, azure, three escallops in pale or ; Stowe MS. 670, fo. 55.

SYMMINGS or SIMINGS, John, of London, Doctor in physick, s. of William, of Coventry, and of Alice his wife, d. and h. to Owen Hall of Anglesey, and heir by her mother's side to Richard Lovett of Wyrardisbury, Bucks (grant 17 Jan. 1560-61, by Dalton), confirmed 1568, by Cooke. New coat and crest 6 July 1574, by Cooke. Harl. MS. 1359, fo. 48ᵇ, 87ᵇ ; Add. MSS. 14,295, fo. 47, and 4966, fo. 59ᵇ, 67 ; Harl. MS. 5887, fo. 60. M.B. of Bologna ; incorporated at Oxford in 1554 ; died 7 July 1588.

SYMON, Ryce, of London, ... Hen. VII. Add. MS. 26,702, fo. 60ᵇ.

SIMONS, Edward, of Marden, Kent, grant 19 Feb. 1662-3. Harl. MS. 1105, fo. 17ᵇ ; Add. MS. 14,293, fo. 3ᵇ ; Bysshe's Grants, fo. 5, Her. Coll. ; Guil. 397.

SYMONDS, Giles, s. of Thomas, of West Stafford, Dorset, gent., crest granted 24 June 1596, by W. Dethick, Gart. Stowe MS. 676, fo. 117ᵇ ; Q's Coll. Oxf. MS. 36, fo. 56, copy of grant.

SYMMANES or SYMONES, John, of London, Surveyor of the Castell, Dover, 1591, by Cooke. Harl. MSS. 1359, fo. 112ᵇ, and 1422, fo. 65ᵇ ; Stowe MS. 670, fo. 46ᵇ.

SYMONDS, Richard, of Gt. Yeldham, Essex, s. of John, of Newport, Salop, coat confirmed and crest granted 10 Jan. 1625-6, by R. St. George, Clar. Her. and Geneal., iii., 431 ; ? copy of grant, Brit. Mus.

SYMONS or SIMONS, Robert, of Wilcsford, co. Camb., Jan. 1605-6, by W. Camden : arms, az., a fess engrailed or betw. three demi-lions [? with two tails or] arg. Crest, out of a mural coronet gu. three arrows [two in saltire and one in pale] or, feathered arg., tied with a blue ribaud. Harl. MSS. 1422, fo. 18ᵇ, 6095, fo. 3ᵇ, and 1401, fo. 48ᵇ [with pedigree].

SYMONDS, William, of Lyme Regis, Dorset, ... 1587, by Cooke. Harl. MSS. 1359, fo. 107ᵇ, and 1422, fo. 65ᵇ ; Add. MS. 4966, fo. 31ᵇ.

SIMONDS, William, Thomas and Richard, of Dorset (of Exeter), 20 Q. Eliz., 1577, by Cooke. Harl. MS. 1427, fo. 75ᵇ ; Burke adds, grant of 2nd and 3rd quarterings 29 Eliz., 1587 ; Harl. MS. 6179, fo. 15ᵇ.

SYMS, Edward, of Daventry, Northts., granted .... 1592, by Cooke. Harl. MSS. 1359, fo. 104, and 1422, fo. 95 ; Guil. 91 ; Add. MS. 4966, fo. 85ᵇ.

SYSELEY, Clement, of Barrow Hall, Essex, gent., s. of Richard, s. of Francis, s. of Christopher, s. of Francis, of Founteyns, Yorks, gent., confirmed 31 Dec. 1560, by Dalton. Harl. MS. 1359, fo. 45.

T

TADLOWE, John and James, s. of William, of London, 1478, 13 Ed. IV., by Thos. (Holme), Clar. Harl. MSS. 1422, fo. 12, and 1441, fo. 46.

TAILLER, George, of Lingfield, Surrey, 23 May 1535, by Tonge, Clar. Stowe MS. 692, fo. 89ᵇ ; Harl. MS. 5846, fo. 101ᵇ, by Barker, Gart. ; Harl. MS. 5887, fo. 6.

TALBOTT, Thomas, of Wyndam, Norfolk, crest .... 1584, by Cooke. Harl. MS. 1359, fo. 116ᵇ ; Add. MS. 14,295, fo. 37 ; Guil. 190 ; Add. MS. 4966, fo. 29ᵇ.

TALCARNE, ... on "A fesse (between) iij Cornyshe chowghes theyre heades turned backe s., bekyd & membryd g., on the fesse a sheefe (garb) bet. ij [trick, ? crosses crosslet fitchée gold] or ; of Cornewall." Barker's Grants, Stowe MS. 692, fo. 90.

TALLOW CHANDLERS' COMPANY, of London, patent 24 Sept. 1456, temp. Edw. IV., by John Smert, Gart. ; confirmation of coat, correction of crest and grant of supprs. 29 Jan. 1602-3, by Camden and Segar. In French, Add. MSS.

14,295, fo. 20^b, and 12,225, fo. 27 ; Harl. MS. 1359, fo. 72 ; Her. and
Geneal., i., 120, 123 ; Cat. Heraldic Exhib. Soc. of Antiq., p. 60.

TATTON, ... quartering Mereton and crest, by Cooke. Stowe MS. 670, fo. 82.

TAVERNER, Francis, of Hexton, co. Herts, s. of Peter, of Hexton, s. of Richard, of
Wooder, Oxon., 1st s. of John, of North Ellingham, Norfolk, brother to
Roger, of Upminster, Essex : a patent . . . . Feb. 1614-15, ? crest by
Camden. Harl. MSS. 1422, fo. 38^b, and 6095, fo. 29 ; Guil. 371.

„   Roger, of Upminster, Essex, surveyor to Q. Eliz., crest 3 May 1570, by Sir
G. Dethick, Gart. Add. MS. 14,293, fo. 21 ; confirmed . . . . May 1575,
17 Q. Eliz., Harl. MS. 1441, fo. 82 ; Q's Coll. Oxf. MS. 145, fo. 36.

TAWE, John, of the Inner Temple and of Hadley, Middx., coat and crest 30 April,
37 H. VIII., 1546, by Barker. Harl. MS. 5846, fo. 102^b ; Stowe MS. 692,
fo. 89^b (37 H. VIII.) ; Harl. MS. 5887, fo. 8.

TAYLOUR, ... of Parkhouse, Kent, ... 1588. Berry. Altered by R. St. George,
Norr., Feb. 1605. Harl. MS. 5887, fo. 37^b.

TAYLOR, ..., of Lane and Lindon, 24 Dec. 1674, erm., on a chief endented sa.
three escallops or ; crest, a demi-lion rampant sa. holding betw. his paws
a ducal coronet or. Berry.

TAYLER (Edward, Guil. 290), of Girdlers' Hall, London [descended from that name
and family in the North] : or, on a chev. sa. three annulets of the field, in
chief two lyons passant of the second ; certified by Segar, Gart. Add. MS.
12,225, fo. 109 ; C. 24 [Visit. of London, 1634], fo. 148^b, Her. Coll. ;
Guil. 290 ; Harl. MS. 6140, fo. 76 ; see Harl. MS. 5887, fo. 37^b.

TAYLOR, George, of Chesterfield, co. Derby, Esq., Justice of the peace, late merchant
of the East India Co., London, 6 Dec. 1662, by W. Dugdale, Norr. Harl.
MS. 1105, fo. 60, and Her. Coll. ; Harl. MS. 1441, fo. 131^b.

„   James, of Gomersall, Yorks, D.D., crest confirmed 27 Feb. 1606-7, by R. St.
George, Norr. Add. MS. 14,295, fo. 54.

„   . . . ., Or, on a chevron sable three mullets argt., in chief two lyons rampant
of the second. Altered by R. St. George, Norr., Feb. 1605, the mullets
being taken off the chevron and a lozenge sable added in the base. Harl.
MS. 5887, fo. 37^b.

„   John, als BARKER, of Gloucester, gent., 20 July, 5 E. VI., 1551, granted by
Sir G. Dethick, Gart. Q's Coll. Oxf. MS. 39, fo. 36, copy of grant ; MS.
Ashm. 858, fo. 18, copy of grant, Bodleian Lib. ; Harl. MSS. 1359, fo. 61,
and 1422, fo. 13 ; Grants I., 137 ; Harl. MSS. 6140, fo. 62, and 1116,
fo. 51^b.

TAYLER, John, of Thurnham, Kent, ... 1589, by Cooke. Harl. MSS. 1359,
fo. 96, and 1422, fo. 87^b.

TAYLOUR, John, of London, 11 Sept. 1592, by Cooke. Harl. MSS. 1359, fo. 111^b,
and 1422, fo. 87^b ; Add. MS. 4966, fo. 93^b.

TAYLOR, John, of London : Taylor quartering Bemler and Seley, by Cooke. Harl.
MS. 1359, fo. 118 ; Add. MS. 4966, fo. 100^b ; Harl. MS. 5887, fo. 72.

„   John, of Easton, Bedf., 4th s. of John, of Brekerton, Yorks, 12 April 1635,
by Sir R. St. George, Clar. An esquire to Henry, Lord Clifford, made
K.B. at the creation of Henry, Prince of Wales. Surtees Soc., XLI., li.

TAYLOUR, John, of London, ... by W. Ryley, Lanc. Her. Stowe MS. 703,
fo. 64.

TAYLOR, Richard, of Grimsbury, par. of Bolnhurst, Bedf., a Bencher of Linc. Inn,
s. of Thomas, s. of Thomas, etc., arms confirmed, with a difference, and
crest granted 15 July 1624, by Sir R. St. George, Clar. Harl. MS. 1507,
fo. 395 ; Q's Coll. Oxf. MS. 38, fo. 140, copy of grant ; Harl. MS. 1105,
fo. 7 ; Le Neve's MS. 395.

„   Richard, of Wallingwells, Notts, 8 Nov. 1682, by Sir W. Dugdale and Norroy.
Harl. MS. 6834, fo. 178 ; Grants III., fo. 170.

„   Robert, of London, 1st s. of Thomas, of Cumberld., gent., crest 20 Mar.
1565-6, 8 Q. Eliz., by Sir G. Dethick. Cott. MS. Faust., E. 1, 19.

K K

TAYLOR, Robert, of London, Sheriff, ... 1592, by Cooke. Harl. MSS. 1359, fo. 87ᵇ, and 1422, fo. 87ᵇ ; Add. MS. 4966, fo. 92ᵇ.

TAYLOUR, Robert, of Steventon, Bedf., Nov. 1610, by Camden. Harl. MSS. 1422, fo. 21ᵇ, and 6095, fo. 14 ; Stowe MS. 706, fo. 39ᵇ ; Guil. 162.

TAYLOR, Roger, s. of Thomas, s. of Roger, of London, Esq., arms confirmed and crest granted 27 Dec. 1614, ? 1632, by Segar. Add. MS. 12,225, fo. 109 ; Guil. 244. Bur. in St. Botolph's, Aldersgate, London. Harl. MS. 1441, fo. 161 ; Le Neve's MS. 255.

„ Thomas, of Battersey, Surrey, Cumberland in the grant, gent., s. of John, of Heseldon Grange, co. Glouc., etc., 16 Dec. 1600, with reversion to the posterity of his father, by Camden, Clar. Stowe MS. 714, fo. 127 ; Grants II., 632 ; Proc. Soc. of Antiq., 1897, 2nd S., xvi., p. 353.

„ Thomas, of Thurnham, Kent, quarterly, by Cooke's deputy. Stowe MS. 670, fo. 38.

TEDCASTELL, John, of London, ... 1590, by Cooke (and Elizabeth May, his wife, see). Harl. MSS. 1359, fo. 94, and 1422, fo. 115ᵇ.

TEMPLE, John, of Stowe, Bucks, ... 1593, by Cooke. Stowe MS. 670, fo. 56.

„ Peter, of Burton Dassett, co. Warw., granted 8 Feb. 1569-70, by Sir G. Dethick, Cooke and Flower. Harl. MSS. 1441, fo. 72, and 1359, fo. 55ᵇ ; 18ᵗʰ Feb. in MS. Ashm. 844, fo. 42 (copy of grant, Bodleian Lib.) ; Guil. 231 ; Q's Coll. Oxf. MS. 39, fo. 161, copy of grant ; (MS. 145, fo. 24). Confirmation of arms and gift of crest by patent 10 Nov. 1576, by Cooke. Harl. MSS. 1359, fo. 82, and 1422, fo. 52 ; Add. MS. 14,295, fo. 23ᵇ ; Grants I., 14 ; Harl. MS. 5889, fo. 44.

„ Sir Richard, Knt. of the Bath and Bart., of Stowe, Bucks, exemplified 25 July 1686, by H. St. George, Clar. Stowe MSS. 714. fo. 129ᵇ, 130, and 716, fo. 51ᵇ ; Grants IV., fo. 13.

TEMYS, William, of London, quarterly, confirmed . . . . 1561, 4 Q. Eliz. (Harvey's Grants), Add. MS. 16,940, fo. 32 ; Harl. MS. 5887, fo. 10ᵇ.

TENACRE, Elizabeth, dau. of William, s. and h. of Henry, of Halling, Kent, wife to John Thurston, late Sheriff and Alderm. of London, coat only, by Barker. Harl. MS. 5846, fo. 103 ; Stowe MSS. 692, fo. 90, and 702, fo. 115.

TENANT, John, of Scotton, nᵉ Richmond, Yorks, exemplified 1 April 1613, by R. St. George, Norr. MS. Ashm. 858, fo. 223-5, copy of grant, Bodleian Lib. ; Surtees Soc., XLI., xlvii.

TENCHE, Nicholas, of Salop, allowed 1 July 1628, by Segar. Add. MS. 12,225, fo. 109ᵇ ; Visit. London, 1634, C. 24, 318ᵇ ; Guil. 187 ; Harl. MS. 6197, fo. 86ᵇ.

TENISON, Philip, D.D. (rector of Hethersett [co. Norfolk]), Archdeacon of Norfolk, 1 Dec. 1660, by Walker. Harl. MS. 1172, fo. 75 ; Misc. Gen. et Her., 3rd S., vol. i., p. 225 ; Stowe MS. 670, fo. 82ᵇ.

TERREY, William, of London, draper, confirmed . . . . 1615, by Camden. Tirrey in Harl. MS. 1422, fo. 40 ; Harl. MS. 6095, fo. 39ᵇ ; field ermine with different crest in Harl. MS. 6140, fo. 26 ; Le Neve's MS. 346.

TERRICK, John, of Clayton Griffith, co. Staff., c. 1596. Harl. MS. 1096, fo. 38ᵇ.

TESH, Tristram, of co. Yorks, coat and crest. Barker's Grants, Harl. MS. 5846, fo. 104.

TEWYDALL, Nicholas, of Staines, Middx., confirmed 155- or 156-. (Harvey's Grants), Add. MS. 16,940, fo. 33.

TEY, John, of West Bromwich, co. Staff., out of Essex, confirmed or granted 28 Aug. (1595 in Guil. 229), by W. Dethick, Gart. Q's Coll. Oxf. MS. 36, fo. 118, copy of grant.

THACKER, Thomas, of Highedge in Derbyshire, 1 May 1538, by W. Fellows, Norr. Egerton MS. 996, fo. 79ᵇ ; Harl. MS. 6104, fo. 110 ; Reliquary, xxii., 50.

THAYRE, ... of London and of Yorks, ... by Sir R. St. George. Harl. MS. 6179, fo. 59ᵇ.

THEKESTONE, Richard, of Thekestone, Yorkshire, confirmed 21 Feb. 1587-8, by Flower. MS. Ashm. 844, fo. 73, copy of grant, Bodleian Lib. ; Guil. 409.

THELWALL, John, of Bathawarne Park, co. Denbigh, 26 June 1608, by Sir R. St. George, Esq. [Norr.]. Harl. MS. 2586, fo. 124 ; Add. MS. 14,295, fo. 60 ; Welsh Pedigrees, Flintsh., p. 124, Her. Coll. ; 17th of June in Harl. MS. 6179, fo. 13b.

THEOBALD, Stephen, of Seale, Kent, Esq., arms quarterly, confirmed and crest given .... 1583, by Cooke. Harl. MSS. 1359, fo. 120, and 1422, fo. 118, of Seale ; Add. MS. 14,295, fo. 34b ; Guil. 74.

„   .... of Barking, Suff., ... 1631, by R. St. George, Clar. Harl. MS. 1085, fo. 16b.

THISTLEWAYTE, Alexander, s. of Giles, of Winterslowe, Wilts, arms confirmed and crest granted 29 April 1607, by Segar. Add. MS. 12,225, fo. 109b ; Guil. 334.

THOMAS, ... of London, ... Feb. 1606-7, by Camden. Harl. MSS. 1422, fo. 20, and 6095, fo. 8b.

„   Edmund, als HARPWAYE, of Gwenvoe Castle in Wales, allyed to many honble. and worthy families as appears by his pedigrees ; arms confirmed and crest granted .... by Segar. Add. MS. 12,225, fo. 110b.

„   Richard, of Clifford's Inn, London, gent., a filazer of the Court of Common Pleas, ... July 1609, by Camden. Harl. MSS. 1422, fo. 20b, and 6095, fo. 10b ; Guil. 226.

„   Robert, of Wrotham, Kent, 12 May 1574, by Sir G. Dethick, Gart. Harl. MSS. 5823, fo. 34b, and 1441, fo. 140 ; Q's Coll. Oxf. MS. 145, fo. 34b ; Stowe MS. 703, fo. 35.

„   Robert, seal clerk of the Exchequer, temp. Q. Eliz., assigned 9 July 1599, by Camden. Guil. 193. Apparently an error for Robert Seale, clerk, etc. : argt., a fesse az. betw. three wolves' heads erased sa., and a crescent for difference.

„   William, of Llan Thomas, co. Brecon, gent., granted 1 Feb., 6 Ed. VI., 1551-2, by Hawley. Harl. MSS. 1470, fo. 189, and 1507, fo. 435, copy of grant, Brit. Mus. ; Harl. MS. 1359, fo. 4b ; Q's Coll. Oxf. MSS. 38, fo. 58, and 39, fo. 34, 37, copies also of grant ; Grants II., 442 ; Guil. 267 ; Le Neve's MS. 435.

„   William, of Lewes, Sussex, descended out of the principality of Wales, grant 14 May 1608, by Segar. Add. MSS. 12,225, fo. 110, and 12,442, fo. 9 ; 1628 in Guil. 96 [? misprint for 1608].

„   William, of Selling, Kent (mar. Bridget, dau. of Stephen Worley of Scuthington, par. of Thong, Kent), s. of Robert, of Wrotham, s. of John, of the same ; confirmed 17 July 1622, by Segar. Add. MS. 12,225, fo. 110 ; June in Guil. 226.

TOMPSON, Allen, of London, 1599, by W. Dethick, Gart. Harl. MS. 6140, fo. 35.

TOMSON, ... crest .... Barker's Grants, Harl. MS. 5846, fo. 103b ; Stowe MS. 692, fo. 90.

„   Henry, of Esholt, Yorks, gent., one of the Kinges Majesties gent. at armes at Boleigne, gift 15 April 1559, 1 Q. Eliz., by Dalton. Harl. MSS. 1394, fo. 337, and 1359, fo. 41b ; Add. MS. 14,295, fo. 74.

THOMSON, Humfrey, of Richmondshire, gift .... 1553 (Harvey, Norr.). Add. MS. 16,940, fo. 6.

„   John, one of the Queen's Majesties Auditors, pedigree 1 March 1562-3, with arms and crest subscribed by W. Harvey (decd 1573) ; certified, confirmed and allowed, 12 Feb. 1572-3, by Sir Gilb. Dethick, Gart. : " of right ought to have 4 coats & 3 crests," depicted above (for Thompson, Chudworth, Glover and Smythe), by Cooke. (Dorothy Gilbert, his wife, see.) Harl. MSS. 1115, fo. 16, 1359, fo. 11b, 1422, fo. 3b, and 1116, fo. 62 ; Add. MS. 16,940, fo. 22b, name only ; Q's Coll. Oxf. MS. 146, fo. 23 ; see Lincolnshire Peds. [Harl. Soc.].

THOMPSON, Rowland, of Thorp Market, Norfolk, 12 Jan. 1602-3, by Camden.
(Berry.) [Confirmed to Rowland Tompson, son of Mathew Tompson " of
the auntient familie of Thompson of Tinmouth Castle in Northumberland,"
12 January or 12 June 1602-3.]
  ,,   Samuel, ... by Cooke. Harl. MSS. 1359, fo. 104, and 1422, fo. 43 ; Add.
MS. 4966, fo. 92.
THOMSON, Thomas, of Kenfield, par. of Petham, Kent. gent., s. of Thomas, of
Sandwich, Kent, confirmed 3 Jan. 1600-1, and to the posterity of his
father, by W. Dethick, Gart., and Camden. Stowe MS. 676, fo. 134ᵇ ;
Q's Coll. Oxf. MS. 36, fo. 88, copy of grant ; Allen in Harl. MS. 6140,
fo. 35, in the year 1599.
THOMPSON, Thomas, of Warmsfield, Yorks, s. of Thomas, ... 1612, by R. St.
George, Norr. Harl. MS. 1422, fo. 43 ; Stowe MS. 706, fo. 17 ; Harl. MS.
1085, fo. 37.
THORNE, Robert, of Bristow and Bristow port, 3 H. VIII., 1511-12, by Wriothesley,
Gart., and Benolte, Clar. Harl. MS. 1116, fo. 41.
THORNDYKE, Francis, of Great Carleton, co. Linc., s. of Nicholas, of the same, decᵈ,
grant .... by Segar : arg., six guttes de sang, 3, 2, 1, on a chief of the
last three leopards' faces or. Crest, a damask rose ppr., leaves, thorns and
stalk vert, at the foot of the stalk a beetle or, scarabee ppr., which is killed
by the rose, they being of heterogeneous natures. Add. MS. 12,225,
fo. 110ᵇ.
THORNEDIKE, Francis, of Burnell, co. Linc., and brother ⎫ augmentation and new
  ,,   Herbert, of Greenfield, same co.   ⎭ crest 20 Nov. 1616,
                                       by Camden : sa., a
cross erm. betw. four leopards' faces or. Crest, a demi-lion or holding
a wreath ppr. Harl. MS. 1507, fo. 418, copy of grant, Brit. Mus. ; Harl.
MS. 6095, fo. 34ᵇ ; Q's Coll. Oxf. MS. 38, fo. 130, copy of grant ;
Grants II., 568 ; Le Neve's MS. 339 and 418.
THORNEHOLME als CHORLEY, ... 1594, by W. Dethick, Gart. ; entered by Brooke,
York Her. Harl. MSS. 1453, fo. 33, and 3526, fo. 142ᵇ.
THORNEHOLME, John, of Hasthorpe, Yorks, gent., arms confirmed and crest given
at Carthorpe 6 Sept. 1563, by Flower. Harl. MS. 1359, fo. 32ᵇ ; 11ᵗʰ Sept.
in Add. MS. 14,295, fo. 31, 74 ; Harl. MS. 6140, fo. 68.
THORNEY, Peter, of London, chirurgeon, s. of John, ont of Notts, coat confirmed
and crest granted 10 Dec. 1615, by Segar. Add. MS. 12,225, fo. 111 ;
Harl. MS. 1470, fo. 34, copy of grant, Brit. Mus. ; "surgeon" in Guil.
374 ; Harl. MS. 6140, fo. 75.
THORNEHURST, Stephen, of city of Canterbury, gent., crest 11 Feb. 1575-6, by
Cooke. Called Thorneyhurst in MS. Ashm. 834, fo. 4, copy of grant,
Bodleian Lib. ; Guil. 258.
THORNHAUGH, John, of Fenton, Notts, confirmed 4 Feb. 1582-3, by Flower. MS.
Ashm. 834, fo. 56, copy of grant, Bodleian Lib. ; Add. MS. 14,295,
fo. 92ᵇ ; Reliquary, v. xviii., p. 16, and xxii., 244 ; Grants II., 625 ;
Guil. 289.
THORNHILL, Robert, of Walkrimyham, Notts, Esq., crest 14 June, 2 Ed. VI., 1548,
by Gilb. Dethick, Norr. Q's Coll. Oxf. MS. 39, fo. 20 ; Harl. MS. 1507,
fo. 452, copies of grant (Brit. Mus.) ; Harl. MS. 1359, fo. 2 ; Grants I.,
318 ; Le Neve's MS. 452.
THORNECROFT, Edward, of Thornecroft, exemplified 10 Sept. 1651, by W. Ryley,
Norr. MS. Ashm. 858, fo. 183, copy of exemplification, Bodleian Lib.
THORNICROFT, Edward, of Thornicroft, Cheshire, and   ⎫ brothers, grant 29 Oct.
  ,,   John, of St. Andrew's, Holborn, London, bar.-at-law, ⎭ 1687, by Sir T. St.
                                           George, Gart., Clar.
and Norr. Vert., a mascle or betw. four crosslets arg. Crest, on a mural
crown gu. a falcon volant ppr., jessed, membered and beaked or, betw. two
palm branches of the last. (On 26 Nov. 1692 this grant of 1687 was

declared to be a confirmation.) Harl. MS. 6834, fo. 178 ; Grants III.,
327 ; Lansd. MS. 867, fo. 52 ; Berry ; Grants IV., fo. 139 ; Stowe MS.
716, fo. 37ᵇ.

THORNLEY, Stephen, citizen and goldsmith of London, 8 Dec. 1655, by Sir Ed.
Bysshe. Copy of grant, Add. MS. 26,758, fo. 15 ; Misc. Gen. et Her.,
2nd S., ii., p. 294 ; out of Cheshire in Stowe MS. 677, fo. 56 ; Harl. MS.
6832, fo. 414.

THORNTON. . . . ., of Birdforth, Yorks, crest 1 July 1612, by R. St. George, Norr.
Stowe MS. 706, fo. 15 ; Harl. MS. 6140, fo. 72ᵇ.

„   John, Alderm. of Hull, Yorks, *circa* 1563, by Flower. Harl. MSS. 1453,
fo. 74, and 6140, fo. 70.

„   Robert, of East Newton [Yorks], confirmed 4 Oct. 1563, by W. Flower, Norr.
Surtees Soc., XLI., xl [*see*], LXII., 359 ; Harl. MS. 1359, fo. 43 ; Grants
II., 589.

„   Thomas, of Grendon, Middx.,   ⎫ 12 March 1595-6, subscribed by
„   Thomas, D.D., preb. of Ch. Ch., Oxon., ⎭ Lee, Clar. Harl. MS. 6179, fo.
15ᵇ, differenced with a martlet,
12 March 1595-6, by Lee, Clar. ; Add. MS. 14,295, fo. 29 ; Harl. MSS.
1359, fo. 32, and 1422, fo. 57ᵇ ; Berry.

THOROLD, George, of Boston, co. Linc., 10 Nov. 1631, alteration in arms and crest
granted by Sir R. St. George, Clar. Harl. MS. 1470, fo. 24, 27, 88, 89 ;
Guil. 152.

„   Thomas, of Marston, co. Linc., quarterly of 4, confirmed 9 April 1574, by
Sir G. Dethick. Harl. MS. 1441, fo. 81ᵇ ; Q's Coll. Oxf. MS. 145,
fo. 33ᵇ.

THOROTON, Robert, of Car Colston, Notts, gent., D. Phys., 12 May 1663, by
W. Dugdale, Norr. Her. Coll.

THOROWGOOD, Elizabeth, d. and h. of Thomas, of Hoddesdon, ux. Marmaduke
Rawdon of London [*see* RAWDON], confirmed . . . . by Camden. Stowe
MS. 706, fo. 66 ; Harl. MS. 5839, fo. 40 ; Stowe MS. 702, fo. 115.

„   Nicholas, ... 1594 . . . . *see* TROOGOOD.

„   Thomas, of Hoddesdon, Herts, crest . . . . 1573, by Cooke. Harl. MS. 1422,
fo. 23ᵇ.

THROWGOOD, William, of London, draper, ... by Cooke. Harl. MS. 1359, fo. 87 ;
Add. MS. 4966, fo. 58ᵇ.

THORPE, Richard, of Aldborough, Yorks, ... 1612, by R. St. George, Norr. Add.
MS. 14,295, fo. 59ᵇ.

„   William, of Southampton in Hampshire ; of Thorpe, Notts, coat and crest
. . . . Barker's Grants, Harl. MS. 5846, fo. 102 ; Stowe MS. 692, fo. 89ᵇ.
Az., a fesse arg. betw. three lyonceaux ramp. or, langued gu. Crest,
a falcon or.

THRUSTON, John, of Haxne, Suff., gent., grant 5 May 1573, by G. Dethick : " being
now (10 Feb. 1586-7) stept in yeares, of old age." W. Dethick confirmed
to him another coat and crest as descended from Thruston of Anderton,
co. Lanc. (Harl. MS. 1085, fo. 27ᵇ) ; Q's Coll. Oxf. MS. 37, fo. 53 and
97 ; Stowe MS. 676, fo. 42, 68ᵇ, copies of grants.

THRUXTON, Thomas, of Thruxton, co. Worc., gent., s. of John, s. of William, s. of
Thomas, who was lineally descended of Henry Thruxton of Thruxton, that
married the dau. and heir of Oliver Pypart, Kt., living *temp.* Ed. IV.
Crest, 12 Oct. 1595, Thruxton and Pypart quarterly, and to the descendants
of his father John, by Cooke, Clar. Add. MS. 14,295, fo. 76, 94 ; Harl.
MSS. 1359, fo. 13, and 1422, fo. 116.

THURLEY, John, gent., Nov. 164- . . . . by William Ryley, Norr. Add. MS. 26,699,
fo. 6ᵇ, copy of grant, Brit. Mus.

THURLOW, John, Lord of the manor of Burnham Oveny, Norf., 19 Nov. 1664,
16 Ch. II. Harl. MS. 1105, fo. 18, 15ᵇ ; Bysshe's Grants, fo. 8, Her.
Coll. ; Guil. 302 ; Add. MS. 14,293, fo. 1ᵇ.

THURSTON, John (late Sheriff and Alderm. of London, *see* TENACRE), coat. Barker's Grants, Harl. MS. 5846, fo. 102[b], crest fo. 103 ; Stowe MS. 692, fo. 90.

THWAITES, John, of Marston, Yorks, Esq., arms confirmed and crest given 30 Jan. 1564-5, by Flower. Harl. MSS. 1441, fo. 160, and 6140, fo. 68 ; Add. MS. 14,295, fo. 37[b] ; Harl. MS. 1359, fo. 34 and 40[b] ; Guil. 88 ; Add. MS. 4966, fo. 41.

„   William, Alderm. of London, 22 Oct. 1598, by [Dethick and ?] W. Camden. Camden's Grants, 38, Her. Coll. ; Thomas in Morgan's Sphere, ii., 118, az., a plain cross sa. fretty or, in the dexter quarter a lis gu. *See* William TWAYTZ, 1592, the same coat.

THYNNE, John, of Longelete, Wilts, coat and crest 10 June 1550, and a Knt. Add. MS. 16,940, fo. 206 ; Barker's Grants, Harl. MS. 5846, fo. 104 ; Stowe MS. 692, fo. 90.

„   Thomas, Visct. Weymouth, *see* WEYMOUTH.

TIBBETT, Beryn, of Dundry, Somerset, Coroner of the county, by Sir E. Bysshe, Clar., 30 Aug. 1672. Harl. MS. 1105, fo. 38 ; Bysshe's Grants, 35.

TICHBORNE, ..., of Tichborne, Hants, confirmed arms, crest and supporters, by Segar, R. St. George, and Camden. Add. MS. 12,225, fo. 111.

TIDCOMBE, Col. John, of Escott, Wilts, 15 Feb. 1692-3, by T. St. George, Gart. and Clar. Harl. MS. 6834, fo. 178 ; Grants IV., fo. 137 ; Harl. MSS. 1085, fo. 57, and 6179, fo. 89[b].

TILDEN, John, of Wye, Kent, ..., by Segar and Sir R. St. George, confirmed after. Add. MS. 12,225, fo. 111[b].

„   Robert, of Brenchley, Kent, exemplified quarterly, by Segar. Add. MS. 12,225, fo. 111[b] ; Richard in Harl. MS. 6140, fo. 64.

TYLDESLEY, Thurston [of Wardley ?], co. Lanc., crest confirmed . . . . 1560 (by L. Dalton, Norr.). Add. MS. 16,940, fo. 48 ; Harl. MS. 1116, fo. 65.

TILLESLEY, William, of Borneham, Bucks, and now of Pele in the par. of Hilton [Hulton], co. Lanc., coat and crest . . . ., by Barker. Barker's Grants, 1526—49, Harl. MS. 5846, fo. 102 ; Stowe MS. 692, fo. 89[b] ; Harl. MSS. 1116, fo. 42, and 6179, fo. 17 ; Add. MS. 26,702, fo. 19.

TILERS AND BRICKLAYERS of the city and suburbs of London, arms and crest, 3 Jan. or Feb. 1569-70, by Sir G. Dethick, Cooke and Flower. Q's Coll. Oxf. MS. 39, fo. 160 ; copy of grant (MS. 145, fo. 23[b]) ; Add. MS. 26,702, fo. 88[b] ; Harl. MS. 1441, fo. 71[b] ; Stowe MS. 703, fo. 27.

TILLOTT, James, of Ipswich, and one of the company of the twelve portmen of the said townmen descended from Tillott of Rougham, Suff., by Segar, Gart. (procured by me, R. Mundy). Stowe MS. 677, fo. 7[b].

TILNEY, Richard, of Rotherwick, Hants, s. of Robert, of East Tuddenham, Norfolk, gent., dec[d], exemplified 14 May 1632 by consent and certificate of Philip Tilney of Shelleigh, Suff., Esq., by R. St. George, Clar. Add. MS. 14,295, fo. 113 ; Grants I., fo. 32 ; Le Neve's MS. 455.

TILSON, Henry, Bp. of Elphin, 2 s. of Henry, of Highroyd, par. of Heptonstall, Yorks, 4 Sept. 1639, by Thomas Preston, Ulster K. of Arms. Stowe MS. 714, fo. 144 ; Grants II., 671 ; certificate in Harl. MS. 1441. fo. 55[b].

„   Ralph, of Huxleigh, Cheshire, confirmed 28 Aug. 1580, by Flower. MS. Ashm. 844, fo. 57, copy of grant, Bodleian Lib. ; Guil. 125.

TINDALL, Jane, dau. of Edmond Tindall, and ux. William Russell, Esq., one of the gentlemen of the Queen's Majesties Chamber, grant 10 Jan. 2 and 3 Philip and Mary, 1555-6, by Sir G. Dethick. Harl. MS. 1359, fo. 164[b] ; Q's Coll. Oxf. MS. 39, fo. 67, copy of grant ; Grants I., 230.

„   John, of Dickleborough, Norfolk, s. of John, of Barham, s. of John, of New Buckenham, Norf., ... July 1611, by Camden (arms of Boteler of London, wife of Tindall). Harl. MSS. 1422, fo. 35, and 6095, fo. 15[b] ; Grants II., 597[b] ; Guil. 375 ; Stowe MS. 702, fo. 115.

TINDALL, Thomas, of Sussex, ..., by Cooke. Harl. MSS. 1359, fo. 97, and 1422, fo. 94ᵇ; Add. MS. 4966, fo. 89ᵇ; Sir John, *see* Harl. MS. 6140, fo. 53.

TIPPETS, John, Esq., a Commissioner of the Navy, 24 March 1669-70, by Sir E. Walker, Gart. Her. Coll., fo. 67 ; Cat. Her. Exhib. Soc. of Antiq., 73.

TIPPING, Thomas, of Draycott, Oxon, ... 1574, arg., on a bend engrailed vert, three pheons of the field. Crest, out of a ducal coronet or, an antelope's head vert, attired and maned gold (Berry). Stowe MS. 670, fo. 62.

TIPTOFT, ..., Earl of Worcester, arg., a saltire engrailed gu., ... 1450 (Berry).

TIRREY, William, of London, goldsmith, s. of Anthony, of Marden, co. Hereford, confirmation, arms and crest granted 13 June 1616, by Segar. Add. MS. 12,225, fo. 112 ; Harl. MS. 1441, fo. 53ᵇ ; (Guil. 104); copy of grant, Harl. MS. 6140, fo. 64ᵇ.

TITUS, Sir Silus (Silas or Siluis), one of the grooms of H.M.'s bedchamber, Royal Warrant for arms, augmentation and crest, 1 June 1665, by Walker. Add. MS. 14,294, fo. 29 ; Clutterbuck Herts, i., 315.

TOCKNELL, Walter, of Bristol, 19 Dec. 1668, by Sir E. Walker, Gart. Her. Coll., fo. 65.

TOKE, George, of co. Worcester, gent., served at Musselborough, grant, 6 Oct., 1 Ed. VI., 1547, at Newcastle-upon-Tyne, by G. Dethick, Norr. Q's Coll. Oxf. MS. 38, fo. 47, copy of grant ; Grants I., 340 ; Harl. MS. 1116, fo. 39ᵇ.

TOLL, ..., sergeant at armes, with crest, Hen. VIII., ... Add. MS. 26,702, fo. 53.

„ Cecyle, wife to William Cowper (*see*) of Thurgarton, of London, arms, 1 Jan. 1549-50, by ? Hawley. Add. MS. 16,940, fo. 201ᵇ.

TOLLEY, Thomas, of Ramsey, with crest, Hen. VIII., ... Add. MS. 26,702, fo. 49.

TOLSON, *see* TOUNSON.

THOMLINSON, Thomas, of London, ..., 1590, by Cooke. Harl. MSS. 1359, fo. 97ᵇ, and 1422, fo. 94ᵇ ; Add. MS. 4966, fo. 87ᵇ.

TOMLINSON, William, by Cooke, Clar., ..., 1560, argent, three greyhounds sable. Nichols's Leic., IV., pt. I., 304.

TONGE, William, of the Middle Temple, ⎫ sons of William Tonge of Tunstall, co.
„ James, of Tunstall, co. Kent, ⎪ Kent, gent., no date, by W. Segar,
„ John, of Bredgar, co. Kent, ⎬ Gart. Visit. of Kent, 1619, ed. by
„ Nicholas, of Bredgar, co. Kent, ⎪ J. J. Howard, p. 66, from Arch. Cant.,
„ Richard, of Borden, co. Kent, ⎭ vol. vi., 255 (Her. Coll. R. 21, p. 278) ; ? copy of grant, Brit. Mus.

„ Thomas, Clar., and Susan White [his wife, gilt copper Plate, with Arms], 1554. *See* Cat. Her. Exhib. Soc. of Antiq. [p. 30,] late XII.].

TOOKE, James, of London, mar. Dorothy, dau. to John Gray of Gray's Inn, Tooke quartering Haule, Tooke, Gray, by Segar. Add. MS. 12,225, fo. 112 ; C. 24 [Visit. of London, 1634], fo. 442ᵇ, Her. Coll. ; Guil. 395.

„ William, of Goodnestone, Kent, gent. (auditor of the Courts of Wards and liveries), Crest, 3 April 1546, 37 Hen. VIII., by Barker. Harl. MSS. 1359, fo. 18, 25, and 5846, fo. 103ᵇ ; Stowe MS. 692, fo. 90 ; 8ᵗʰ of April in Add. MS. 14,295, fo. 10 ; Q's Coll. Oxf. MS. 146, fo. 31, copy of grant.

„ Walter (s. of William, of Goodneston, genl. auditor), of the manor of Popes als Holbaches, par. of Bishop Hatfield, Herts, Esq., also genl. auditor of wards and liveries, arms exemplified and crest altered, 17 April 1600, by Camden. Add. MS. 14,295, fo. 111 ; Harl. MS. 1359, fo. 25 ; Q's Coll. Oxf. MS. 146, fo. 31, copy of exemplification.

TOOKER, Giles, of Madington, Wilts, gent., 21 Feb. 1572-3, by Sir G. Dethick. Harl. MS. 1441, fo. 84ᵇ ; Q's Coll. Oxf. MS. 145, fo. 39ᵇ.

TOOTHILL, Geffrey, of Peamore, Devon, confirmed 1563.   (Harvey's Grants), Add.
    MS. 16,940, fo. 33.
TORLESSE, Adam, s. of William, of Whatcombe, Berks, confirmed or granted
    26 June 1637, by Borough.   Harl. MSS. 1105, fo. 55, and 1441, fo. 57^b;
    Add. MS. 26,702, fo. 89^b, and Guil. 181.
TORNER or TURNER, John, of Tablehurst, Sussex, 3rd s. of Thomas, of Reading,
    Berks, confirmed 27 June 1579, by Cooke.   Guil. 386;   Harl. MS. 1076,
    fo. 120^b.
TORPORLEY, ... by Cooke, Clar., ...   Stowe MS. 670, fo. 33^b.
TORRINGTON, Earl of (Herbert), supporters 13 June 1689, by T. St. George, Gart.
    Harl. MS. 6834, fo. 178;   Grants IV., fo. 41.
TOTELL or TOTHILL (Richard), of London, printer, ... by Cooke.   Harl. MS.
    1359, fo. 116, publisher of Gerard Leigh's Accedence and Bossewell's
    Workes on Armorie;   Add. MS. 4966, fo. 28^b.
TOUNSON, Robert, Bishop of Salisbury, a patent .... by Camden.   Tolson in Cott.
    MS. Faustina, E. 1, fo. 61^b, 62;   Harl. MSS. 6095, fo. 37^b, and 1422,
    fo. 43.
TOURNER, Oliver, of Essex, crest .... by Cooke.   Add. MS. 26,702, fo. 44^b;
    Harl. MS. 1422, fo. 55, coat of Tourner of Salop, *temp.* Hen. VII., confirmed
    to him.
TOWERS, ..., Northants, gent., arms given and allowed 1584, by Cooke.   Harl.
    MS. 1359, fo. 120^b;   Add. MS. 14,295, fo. 41, arms only, arg., a tower gu.;
    Stowe MS. 670, fo. 4.   *See* Samuel TOWERS.
    „   ...., descended out of Lanc.: sa., on a chev. betw. three towers arg. as
    many pellets, a mullet for difference, ... by Segar.   Add. MS. 12,225,
    fo. 112^b;   C. 24 [Visit. of London, 1634], fo. 192^b, Her. Coll.;   Guil.
    361.
    „   Samuel, of the Cliff n^r Lewes, co. Sussex, upon good proofes made at the time
    of the Visitation of that county, 1634, were registered and entered in the
    office: az., a tower or, a mullet of five points for diff.   Stowe MS. 670,
    fo. 4, crest, a griffin statant per pale or and az., a mullet sa. for diff., by
    J. Philipott, deputy for Sir J. Borough.
TOWERSON, William, citizen and merch^t of London, as well adventurer of the
    Societies of Muscovy, Spaine, Portugal and the East partes;   a younger
    brother of Towerson of Coupland, Cumberland;   augmentation 24 Jan.
    1581-2, by Flower.   MS. Ashm. 834, fo. 53, copy of patent, Bodleian Lib.,
    and full account of services;   Morgan's Sphere of Gentry (lib. iii.) 111, and
    Principal Historical and Allusive Arms, by an Antiquary (Col. de la Motte),
    107.
TOWNROWE or TOWNRAWE, William (s. of John, s. of Henry, of co. Derby),
    confirmed 20 May 1562, by W. Flower.   Harl. MS. 1359, fo. 115;   MS.
    Ashm. 834, fo. 21^b, copy of grant, Bodleian Lib.;   Guil. 363;   Add. MS.
    4966, fo. 95;   Reliquary, xxii., 245.
TOWNESEND, J., ... Hen. VI. ....   Add. MS. 26,702, fo. 30^b.
TOWNSEND als AGBOROUGH, Sir Robert, his father-in-law Aurelius Townsend, near
    kinsman to Horatio, Lord Townsend;   took name and arms of Townsend
    by consent of Horatio, Lord Townsend, 12 March 1662-3;   grant 29 May
    1663, by Walker.   Guil. 245;   Genealogist, i., 151.
TOWNESEND, Steven, of Surrey, 4 May 1564, by Sir G. Dethick, Gart.   Harl. MS.
    1441, fo. 87;   Q's Coll. Oxf. MS. 145, fo. 43^b;   Harl. MS. 5887, fo. 41.
    „   Thomas, gent., deputy to the Earl of Sandwich and master of the Great
    Wardrobe, 16 Dec. 1661, by Sir E. Walker, Gart.   Her. Coll., fo. 44.
TRADESMEN AND ARTIFICERS, Company of, granted 10 July 1637, by Borough,
    Gart.   Harl. MS. 1410, fo. 11.
TRAFFLES, Edward, of Winchester, registrar to the Archdeacon of Winchester and
    deputy reg^r to the Lord Bishop, 25 June 1672, by Walker, Gart.   Add.
    MS. 14,293, fo. 66;   Harl. MS. 1172, fo. 64^b, copy of grant.

TRAFFORD, ..., of Essex, exemplified . . . . arg., a gryphon ramp. segreant gu., and 13 quarterings, by Segar. Add. MS. 12,225, fo. 112ᵇ.

TRANT, Patrick, a commissioner and manager of H.M. revenue of Hearth money ; living in Russell St., par. of St. Giles in Fields ; 30 Dec. 1682, by Sir W. Dugdale, Gart., and Sir H. St. George, Clar. Add. MS. 14,831, fo. 112 ; Grants III., 183 ; Harl. MS. 6179, fo. 61.

TRAPPS, Robert, gent., citizen and goldsmith of London, grant 1 June 1559, by Harvey. Q's Coll. Oxf. MS. 38, fo. 73, 78, and MS. 39, fo. 98, and Harl. MS. 1507, fo. 443, for copies of grant (Brit. Mus.) ; Add. MS. 16,940, fo. 27 ; Harl. MS. 1359, fo. 3ᵇ ; Grants II., fo. 545-7 (see arms to wife Joan Crispe) ; Le Neve's MS. 443.

„ . . . . of Theydon, Essex, 1570, by R. Cooke, Clar. Harl. MSS. 1441, fo. 145, and 1116, fo. 40ᵇ.

TRAVELL, Henry, of Coventry, grandson of Richard, of Northants, 16 Feb. 1516-17, 8 Hen. VIII., by Wriothesley, Gart., and Benolte, Clar. Harl. MS. 1422, fo. 69ᵇ, and Berry's Armory ; Harl. MS. 1167, fo. 161ᵇ.

„ Thomas, of Jermyn Street, London, 27 Nov. 1683, by Sir W. Dugdale and Clar. Harl. MS. 6834, fo. 178 ; Grants III., fo. 212.

TRAYTON, see TRETON.

TREGONNELL, John, of Bodmin, Cornwall, coat and crest. Barker's Grants, Harl. MS. 5846, fo. 101ᵇ ; Stowe MS. 692, fo. 89ᵇ ; Harl. MS. 5887, fo. 3.

TREHERON, John, gentleman porter of the house to Q. Eliz. and K. Jas., coat and crest exemplified and ratified 14 Nov. 1616, by Camden. Camden's Grants, fo. 42ᵇ ; Harl. MSS. 6059, fo. 36ᵇ, and 1359, fo. 40ᵇ ; Add. MS. 14,295, fo. 56ᵇ.

TRESWALLEN, ..., of St. Creed, Cornwall, ... 1558, by Harvey. Berry.

„ . . . . co. Middx., by W. Ryley, Lanc. Her. Stowe MS. 703, fo. 63.

TRETON, Thomas, als TRAYTON, of Lewes, Sussex, 10 June 1606, by Segar, Camden and R. St. George, quartering Vinal, Savil, Gotley and Martin. Add. MS. 12,225, fo. 113 ; C. 27, fo. 21, Her. Coll. ; Guil. 345, which see, s. of Thomas, etc. ; Harl. MSS. 1562, fo. 60ᵇ, and 6140, fo. 52.

TRINDER, John, of Westwell, Oxon. (s. of John, of Hollwell, par. of Broadwell, Ox.), and to his brothers Charles, Henry and William, 3 Dec. 1663, by Walker. Add. MSS. 14,293, fo. 48, and 14,294, fo. 16ᵇ ; Harl. MS. 1172, fo. 55 ; Guil. 157.

TRINITY HALL, Cambridge, 17 Sept. 1575, by Cooke, Clar. Add. MS. 5822.

TRIPP, ..., on an ancient escocheon the following : " This Atchievement was given unto my lord Howard's 5ᵗʰ Son at ye Seige of Bullogne, King Harry ye 5ᵗʰ being there asked how they tooke ye Town and Castle. Howard answered, ' I Tripp'd up ye Walls.' Saith ye King, ' Tripp shall be thy name and no longer Howard,' and honoured him with ye scaling ladder for his bend." Burke's Armory.

„ Charles, of the Middle Temple, gu., a chev. betw. three horses heads erased or, bridled gu., by Camden. Harl. MSS. 1422, fo. 40, and 6059, fo. 33.

TROLLOP, Thomas, of Durham, an attorney, 27 July 1639, by Borough. Surtees' Durham, i., 91 ; Harl. MSS. 1105, fo. 56ᵇ, and 1441, fo. 92 ; Add. MS. 26,702, fo. 58, akin to John, of the Bpk. of Durham, see letter 8 May 1639, Surtees' Durham, i., 91 ; Add. MS. 4966, fo. 33ᵇ.

TRISTRAM, Matthew, Nativity of St. John Baptist 1467, by Romeryck, King of Arms of the Holy Roman Empire. Le Neve's MS. 512.

TROOGOOD, Nicholas, of Thornhall, Northts., gent., ..., 1594, by R. Lee, Clar. Add. MS. 14,295, fo. 18ᵇ ; Harl. MS. 1359, fo. 17.

TROTMAN, Edward, onter Barrister of yᵉ Inner Temple, and of Cam, co. Glouc., Esq., s. of Richard, of the same, grant 20 or 27 Nov. 1616, 14 Jac., by Segar. Add. MS. 12,225, fo. 113, and (20ᵗʰ Nov.) Grants I., 373 ; Misc. Gen. et Her., N. S., iv., 188 ; Guil. 121 ; Harl. MS. 6140, fo. 23ᵇ.

L L

Trotman, Samuel, of Bristol, B.D., 29 May 1663, ? by Bysshe, Clar. Harl. MS.
1105, fo. 42.

Trott, ..., by Edward Norgate, Windsor Her. Stowe MS. 703, fo. 71.

.. John [als] Guylemyn, of Awgill, Wales, 1 Nov. 1553, by ? Hawley. Add.
MS. 16,940, fo. 206ᵇ.

„ John, of the city of London, assigned . . . . 1574, by Flower. MS. Ashm.
844, fo. 75 (*see* Cartwright), copy of grant, Bodleian Lib. ; Guil. 404.

Trotter, Robert, of Skelton Castle, Yorks, confirmed 16 Feb. 1587, by Flower,
Norr. Harl. MS. 1422, fo. 22ᵇ ; MS. Ashm. 844, fo. 75, copy of grant,
Bodleian Lib. ; Guil. 177 ; " & it hath noe hande thereunto, patent dated
1587, 30 Q. Eliz. ; William Flower, Norroy, mentioned on the patent " in
Harl. MS. 1359, fo. 9ᵇ.

Troughton, ..., of Troughton, co. Worc., ..., by Cooke. Stowe MS. 670,
fo. 75 ; Add. MS. 4966, fo. 66.

„ Christopher, of Great Lynford, Bucks, granted 30 Oct. 1566, by Hervey.
Grants II., 216 m ; Guil. 361 ; confirmed by Segar, Add. MS. 12,225,
fo. 113ᵇ, sa., on a chev. betw. three swans' necks erased arg. gorged with
coronets or, as many pellets.

Troutbeck, Sir William, coat and crest . . . ., Barker's Grants ; Harl. MS. 5846,
fo. 101 ; Stowe MS. 692, fo. 89.

Trowte, Alan, native of Westmorld., grant 8 Nov. 1376, 16 Ed. III. [Novr. 1376
was the 50th Edw. III. ; the 16th was 1342], by Thomas Tronte, Norr.
(a forgery) ; copy of grant, *see* Lower's Curiosities of Heraldry, 315 ; Q's
Coll. Oxf. MS. 38, fo. 2, copy of grant, and MS. 39, fo. 1 ; Harl. MS. 1507,
fo. 447, copy of grant, Brit. Mus. ; Harl. MS. 1359, fo. 2ᵇ ; Grants II.,
fo. 619, in French ; Le Neve's MS. 447.

Troute, Thomas, of Devon, 1 Oct. 1588, by Cooke. Harl. MS. 1052, fo. 15,
copy of grant, Brit. Mus. ; Harl. MSS. 1359, fo. 109, and 1422, fo. 94 ;
Add. MS. 4966, fo. 57.

Trowvedale or Trowsedale, William, of Hundon, co. Linc., Ar., confirmed . . . . .
1562 (Harvey's Grants). Add. MS. 16,940, fo. 12ᵇ.

Troys, ..., crest, a ragged stokke, *i.e.*, staffe or stick, arg., out of the which
a branch of oak in his kinde. Barker's Grants, Harl. MS. 5846,
fo. 99ᵇ.

Trubshaw, Charles, of Gray's Inn, Middx., 31 Oct. 1688, by T. St. George, Gart.
and Clar. Add. MS. 14,831, fo. 23 ; Grants, vol. iv., fo. 24 ; Stowe MS.
714, fo. 131 ; Guil. 385.

Trumbull, William, of Easthampstead, Berks, grant 10 Oct. 1662, by Walker.
MS. Ashm. 858, fo. 189, 190, copy of grant, Bodleian Lib. ; Harl. MS.
6179, fo. 23ᵇ.

Tryon, Peter, of London (& of Harringworth [co. Northampton ?]), 1 July 1610,
by Camden. Harl. MS. 1105, fo. 38, copy of grant, Brit. Mus. ; Morgan's
Sphere (lib. ii.), 106 ; Harl. MSS. 6095, fo. 13, and 1422, fo. 21ᵇ, has
1620 for the date of the grant ; Guil. 89.

Tubb, George, of Evengoff, or Tringoff, Cornwall, Esq., 8 Nov. 1571, by Sir G.
Dethick, Gart. Harl. MS. 1441, fo. 76ᵇ ; Q's Coll. Oxf. MS. 145, fo. 26 ;
Harl. MS. 1079, fo. 196ᵇ.

Tucker, *see* Tooker.

Tucker, ..., by W. Segar, Gart., ... Harl. MSS. 6140, fo. 48, and
1105, fo. 6ᵇ.

Tuckfield, John, of Fulford, Devon, and brothers Walter and Roger Tuckfield of
Raddon Court, Kent, 4 April 1666, by Sir E. Bysshe, Clar. Bysshe's
Grants, 41.

Tudor, Lady Mary, natˡ dau. of Chas. II., Roy. Warrant 4ᵗʰ, and E. Marshal's
Warrant, 15 Aug. 1687. Harl. MS. 6834, fo. 63 ; Genealogist, iii., 280.

Tufton or Tuston, John, of Northiam, Sussex, gent., 15 May, 1 Q. Mary, 1554,
by Sir Gilb. Dethick, Gart. (? Tuston in) Q's Coll. Oxf. MS. 37, fo. 32,

and MS. 39, fo. 52, copy of grant ; 16th May in Grants I., 244 ; Harl. MS.
1359, fo. 62b ; Add. MS. 35,336, fo. 4b, 63.

TUFTON, Sir Nicholas, Knt. and Bart., Baron of Tufton and Earl of Thanet, quarterly
of 6, alteration in coat and grant of supporters, 22 Oct. 1628, by Segar,
Achievment, 5 quarterings. Add. MS. 12,225, fo. 113b ; Harl. MS. 1470,
fo. 199, copy of grant, Brit. Mus. ; Q's Coll. Oxf. MS. 38, fo. 144, copy of
grant.

TUPHOLME, William, of Boston, co. Linc., quarterly, confirmed 26 Oct. 1562.
(Harvey's Grants), Add. MS. 16,940, fo. 37 ; (26 Oct. in Burke as
Cupholme).

TURBUTT, William, s. and h. of Richard, grant 20 March 1628-9, 4 Car., by Segar.
Surtees Soc., XLI., xlix. ; Add. MS. 12,225, fo. 113, of York city.

TURFOOTE, Edward, of London, grant 10 May 1576, by Cooke. Harl. MS. 1422,
fo. 22.

TURNER (see also TORNER and TOURNER), (. . . .), of Blechingley, Surrey, . . . ,
Nov. 1604, by Camden. Harl. MSS. 6059, fo. 2, and 1422, fo. 18 ; Guil.
133.

„ (. . . .), of London, by Barker, Gart. Harl. MS. 6179, fo. 15.

„ Edmond, of Saffron Walden, Essex, 22 Feb. 1629-30, by Sir R. St. George.
Add. MS. 14,295, fo. 70 ; C. 21, 166 [Visit. of] Essex [1634].

„ John, of Kirk Leatham, Yorks, Esq., Justice of the peace and bencher of the
Inner Temple, 30 April 1661, by W. Dugdale, Norr. Her. Coll.

TURNER (or TOWMER), Richard, of Keymer, Sussex, 26 July 1671. Harl. MS.
1105, fo. 42b ; Bysshe's Grants, fo. 9, 21, Her. Coll.

„ (Sir) Thomas, of Kelmscott, Oxon, s. of Thomas, of Hall place, by Ann
Deane of Oxon, 4 Jan. 1664-5. Harl. MS. 1105, fo. 20b ; Bysshe's Grants,
fo. 21, Her. Coll.

„ Sir William, Kt., Alderm. of London, 30 April 1661. Harl. MS. 1105,
fo. 18 ; Bysshe's Grants, fo. 9, Her. Coll.

TURPYN, Sir George, of Knaptofte, co. Leic., crest, 1 April 1552, by ? Hawley.
Add. MS. 16,940, fo. 205b.

TURTON, William, of West Bromwich, co. Staff., and his brother,⎤

„ Richard, sons of William, late of West Bromwich, decd., │ 1 July 1660, by
and to ⎱ Wm. Dugdale,
„ William, of Alrewas, and his ⎱ these two differenced ⎰ Norr.,   Her.
brother ⎰ with a canton. │ Coll.
„ John, s. of John, late of West ⎰ ⎦
Bromwich, decd,

TURVEY, Thomas, of Walm, co. Warwick, High Sheriff, and to his brother

„ Richard, 2 Feb. 1656-7, by Sir E. Bysshe, Gart. Harl. MS. 1441, fo. 151b ;
perhaps written Turvey in Harl. MS. 2275, fo. 40 ; Harl. MS. 1466,
fo. 24b.

TUSTON, see TUFTON.

TUTE (or TWYTE of Ireland), John, porter unto the Great Wardrobe in Carter
Lane, quarterly, gules and argent. Harl. MS. 6140, fo. 26b.

TUZERD (TUSSER), Clement, of Ryvenhall, Essex, confirmation 1 Feb. 1560-1.
(Harvey's Grants), Add. MS. 16,940, fo. 60b.

TWAYTZ, William, Esq., sometime Alderm. of London, 24 Feb. 1591-2, by
W. Dethick, Gart., and Camden. Add. MS. 14,295, fo. 63 ; (I. 9, 19b,
Her. Coll.). See THWAITES.

THWAITES, William, 22 Oct. 1598, Her. Coll. ; called Thos. Thwaites, Alderm., in
Morgan's Sphere, ii., 116.

TWEDY, Richard, of Stoke, Essex, crest, 1 Jan. 1548-9, by ? Hawley, Clar. Add.
MS. 16,940, fo. 201b.

TWISLETON, George, of Barley, Yorks, Esq., s. of Christopher, s. and h. of John,
sometime Alderm. of London, coat confirmed and crest granted 22 Nov.
1602, by Segar. Add. MS. 12,225, fo. 113 ; Harl. MS. 1359, fo. 9 ;

Guil. 199; "of London, but now alderm. of York," in Harl. MS. 1422, fo. 52; Harl. MS. 6140, fo. 67[b].

TWYFORD, Roger, of Sawston, co. Camb., Esq., crest 16 Dec., 4 and 5 Philip and Mary, 1557, by Sir G. Dethick, Gart. Q's Coll. Oxf. MS. 39, fo. 93, copy of grant; Grants I., 158; called Robert in Harl. MSS. 1359, fo. 71[b], and 6179. fo. 24[b].

TWYNE, John, of Preston, Kent, confirmed 21 Nov. 1571, by Cooke; attested by R. Glover, Somerset. MSS. Ashm. 834, fo. 32, and 844, fo. 21, copy of grant, Bodleian Lib.; Guil. 87.

TWYTE, see TUTE.

TYAS, Robert, of London, ... by Cooke. Harl. MSS. 1359, fo. 99[b], and 6179, fo. 14[b]; Add. MS. 4966, fo. 53[b].

TYDUR als MOWSSE, Anthony, 6 Oct. 1633, by R. St. George, Clar. Harl. MS. 1105, fo. 2[b].

TYLER, Sir William, Knighted at Milford Haven, Hen. VII. Add. MS. 26,702, fo. 61[b].

TYSSEN, Francis, of London, Alderm. and Sheriff, 24 Nov. 1687, by Sir T. St. George, Gart., and H. St. George, Clar. Misc. Gen. et Her., N. S., iii., 379-380; Grants III., 332; Lansd. MS. 867, fo. 52; Harl. MS. 6179, fo. 75.

U

UMBLE, ? HUMBLE, ..., vintner at ye bull in Southwark, by Camden. Harl. MS. 1422, fo. 15; Peter in Le Neve's MS. 357.

UNWYN, William, of Chatterley, co. Staff., confirmed 18 Nov. 1581, by Flower. MS. Ashm. 844, fo. 50, copy of grant, Bodleian Lib.; Guil. 132.

UPHOLDERS' COMPANY, of London, 11 Dec. 1465, by W. Hawkesloe, Clar. Her. and Geneal., 120, and Sylv. Morgan's Sphere of Gentry, 1661, lib. ii., fo. 94, copy of grant.

UPTON, William, of Ore, Sussex, s. of Henry, s. of Thomas (of the house of Lupton in Devonshire), crest granted 9 or 28 April 1569, by Sir G. Dethick, Gart., Cooke and Flower. Harl. MSS. 1359, fo. 56, and 1441, fo. 73; Misc. Gen. et Her., 2nd S., vol. v., p. 296, facsimile; Q's Coll. Oxf. MS. 39, fo. 151, copy of grant (MS. 145, fo. 19); MSS. Ashm. 834, fo. 27, and 844, fo. 29, copies of grant, Bodleian Lib.

URMESTON, Robert, als DICONSON, of Abington, confirmed 3 Oct. 1555, by ? Hawley. Add. MS. 16,940, fo. 207[b].

URREN als CURRANCE, Allan, Esq., the late Sheriff of Radnor in Wales, 27 Feb. 1619-20, by Segar. Add. MS. 12,225, fo. 114; Harl. MS. 1422, fo. 13[b], as Utren; Stowe MS. 714, fo. 96; Guil. 262.

USBORNE, see OSBORNE.

UTBER, Thomas, of Hoo, n[r] East Dereham, Norfolk, patent 25 Aug. 1613, by Camden. Harl. MS. 6095, fo. 38[b] (1441, fo. 152[b], has the year 1615, of Norwich); Harl. MSS. 1055, fo. 43, and 5887, fo. 110.

V

VAN ALDENNE, Gawin, born at Cologne, grant Oct., by G. Dethick, Gart.; Q's Coll. Oxf. MS. 36, fo. 125, copy of grant in Latin; Grants I., 95.

VANE, Christopher, Lord Barnard, grant of supporters 27 Feb. 1724-5, with achievement, copy of grant, Harl. MS. 6832, fo. 236.

„ Ralph, of Hadlow, Kent, coat and crest, Barker's Grants. Harl. MS. 5846, fo. 115.

„ Sir Thomas, of Badsell, Kent, Kt., 15 May 1574, by Sir G. Dethick, Gart.

Harl. MSS. 5823, fo. 34ᵇ, and 1441, fo. 140 ; Q's Coll. Oxf. MS. 145, fo. 34ᵇ ; Stowe MS. 703, fo. 35.

VANHESSE, Jo(hn), augmentation (*temp.* Jas. I., Feb. 1621-2), by letters patent, by Sir Ed. Walker's Collection. MS. Ashm. 858, fo. 88, copy of grant, Bodleian Lib. ; Add. MS. 6297, fo. 309.

VANNAM, William, citizen and fishmonger of London, 1 June 1661, by Sir E. Walker, Gart. Her. Coll. 40.

VANSITTART, Peter, of London, mercht., a native of Dantzic, 8 Nov. 1697, by T. St. George, Gart. and Clar. Add. MS. 14,830, fo. 61 ; Grants IV., fo. 231, Her. Coll.

VAN WILDER, Philip, of Little Braddow [Little Bredy ?], Dorset, Esq., coat and crest, grant, Barker's Grants, Harl. MS. 5846, fo. 113 ; Stowe MS. 692, fo. 95.

VAUGHAN, ..., of Wales, ... 1491, ... per pale, az. and purp., a fish hauriant or ; crest. [a man erect ppr. with arms extended, habited in a jacket arg. breeches sa. hair flotant, in the dexter hand a large knife of the second. Burke]. Berry.

„ Edward, of Talgarth in Wales, his crest, Barker's Grants. Harl. MS. 5846, fo. 113 ; Stowe MS. 692, fo. 95.

„ Hugh, gent., a native of the principality of Wales, and gent. Usher to the King, gift of arms, crest and guydon, 4 Oct., 6 H. VII., 1490. (The day of St. Andrew [30 Nov.] 1491, 7 H. VII., fo. 13), by John Writhe [reference to MS. at Her. Coll. ?].

„ Sir Hugh, of the King's Privy Council, (arms), crest and supporters, 27 March 1508, 24 H. VII. A marginal note in Harl. MS. 4900, fo. 17ᵇ (No. XXII.), says, "*vide* p crista (MSS.), Wriothesley & Benolt 1514, Hugoni Vaughan, Sʳ Tho : Shirley's Book, pag. 78." [Le Neve's MS.] in J. Foster's Collection.

„ Sir Hugh, of Littleton, Middx., Kt., new crest and standard 4 May 1514, 6 Hen. VIII., by Wriothesley, Gart., and Benolte. Harl. MSS. 4900, fo. 17ᵇ, and 5815, fo. 42ᵇ, 43ᵇ ; Add. MS. 14,295, fo. 12ᵇ, 13ᵇ, 14 ; Q's Coll. Oxf. MS. 146, fo. 32, 33, 34 ; Misc. Gen. et Her., 3 s., vol. i., p. 33, copies of grant. [The three Hugh Vaughan's are bracketed together as if they were one person.]

„ Sir John, of Whitland, of Wales, 1 Oct. 1551, by ? Hawley. Add. MS. 16,940, fo. 204ᵇ ; Harl. MS. 1105, fo. 3.

„ Mary, dau. of Huntingden, confirmed . . . . 1558. (Harvey's Grants), Add. MS. 16,940, fo. 15.

„ Richard, of Corsigedall, co. Merioneth, Esq., crest 12 Dec. 1583, 26 Eliz., by Sir G. Dethick. Harl. MSS. 1441, fo. 68ᵇ, and 1422, fo. 22ᵇ ; Q's Coll. Oxf. MS. 145, fo. 13.

„ Sir Ro., of Byland Abbey, Yorks, Knt., confirmed 31 July 1604, by R. St. George, Norr. Add. MS. 14,295, fo. 58ᵇ ; B. 21, 133 [Her. Coll.] ; C. 13 [Visit. of Yorks 1612, Her. Coll.], 133 ; ? Harl. MS. 6140, fo. 54 ["Sʳ Henry Vaughan of Sutton upon Darwin in Yorkshire"].

„ Stephen, of London, coat and crest (14 April 1509). Barker's Grants, Harl. MSS. 1422, fo. 221, and 5846, fo. 111ᵇ ; Stowe MS. 692, fo. 94ᵇ ; Harl. MSS. 1476, fo. 175, and 5887, fo. 3.

„ Thomas, Bailiff of Dover, Kent, coat and crest, Barker's Grants, 1526—49. Harl. MS. 5846, fo. 108 ; Stowe MS. 692, fo. 93ᵇ.

„ William, of Payans Castle in Wales, Doctor of Civil Laws, arms 12 June 1527, 19 Hen. VIII., by T. Wriothesley, Gart. Add. MS. 26,702, fo. 53ᵈ ; Harl. MS. 1359, fo. 28 ; Q's Coll. Oxf. MS. 146, fo. 461.

VAUX, Edward, Marshal of the King's household, descended of the House of Vaux of Caterline, coat and crest. Barker's Grants, Harl. MS. 5846, fo. 108ᵇ ; Stowe MS. 692, fo. 93ᵇ.

LE VAUX, Sir Theodore, of Thisleworth, Middx., Knt., 2 July 1678, by

W. Dugdale, Gart., and Sir H. St. George, Norr.   Stowe MS. 714, fo. 122 ;
  Harl. MS. 6179, fo. 87ᵇ ; Grants III., p. 176.
VENABLES, Bertie Montague, Lord Norreys, *see* name and arms 24 Nov. 1687, by
  Sir T. St. George. Grants III., 333, by Clar. and Norr.
   „   Sir Thomas, of Golborne, Cheshire, etc., Baron of Kinderton, confirmed
       30 Oct. 1560, by Dalton, quarterly of 6 : 1 and 6, Venables ; 2; Golborne ;
       3, Augmentation ; 4, Eleston [Eccleston] ; 5, Colton [Cotton] ; augmen-
       tation to coat and grant of crest. Called Thomas Venables of Golborne, etc.,
       in copy of grant, Q's Coll. Oxf. MS. 37, fo. 36, and in MS. 146, fo. 24 ;
       2 Nov. in MS. Ashm. 840, 388 g., 858. fo. 169, 172, copy of grant,
       Bodleian Lib.; Harl. MS. 1359, fo. 46ᵇ; Stowe MS. 676, fo. 25ᵇ ;
       Harl. MS. 1106, fo. 32.
VERE, Robert de, Earl of Oxford, and "Marqui" of Dublin, letters patent at
  Westmʳ, 3 Jan. 1385-6. Stowe MS. 840, fo. 55, P.R., 9 R. II.,
  pt. 1, m. 1.
VERMUYDEN, Sir Cornelius, ..., by Sir J. Borough, Gart. Add. MS. 4966,
  fo. 32.
VERNEY, Sir Richard, of Belton, Rutland, confirmed 9 Feb. 1698-9, by T. St. George.
  Grants IV., 317. *See* WILLOUGHBY DE BROKE.
VERNON, John, out of Cheshire, confirmed 8 June 1583, by Flower. MS. Ashm.
  834, p. 40ᵇ, copy of grant, Bodleian Lib. ; Guil. 5, 125.
   „   (? John, s. of William, s. of William), of Little Beligh, Essex, by Cooke.
       Harl. MSS. 1083, fo. 60ᵇ, 1137, fo. 65, 126ᵇ, 1422, fo. 122ᵇ, 1541, fo. 8ᵇ,
       and 1542, fo. 138.
VERRE, John, of Blakenham, Suff., ..., 1584, by Cooke. Harl. MS. 1359,
  fo. 96ᵇ.
VICARY, Richard, of Drinkswell, Devon, gent., 4 Feb. 1559-60, by Sir G. Dethick,
  Gart. Harl. MS. 1441, fo. 140ᵇ : Q's Coll. Oxf. MS. 145, fo. 35ᵇ ;
  Vicaris in Harl. MS. 6179, fo. 33ᵇ.
VIDIAN, Andrew, of Halfe Yoake, par. of Maidstone, Kent (s. of Andrew, of Cliff,
  Knt.), Clerk of the Papers. Court of King's Bench, 3 Sept. 1664, by
  Walker. Add. MSS. 14,293, fo. 50, and 14,294, fo. 9ᵇ ; Harl. MS. 1172,
  fo. 53 ; Guil. 120.
VILETT, John, of London, gent., ..., 1572, by Cooke, Clar., ar., on a chev. gu.
  three castles of the field, on a canton az. a fleur-de-lis or ; Crest, a tiger's
  head, erased, erm. ducally gorged or. (Berry.)
[VILLETT *alias* VIOLET, Argent, on a chevron gules three towers triple towered of
  the field, on a canton azure a fleur-de-lis or ; Crest, a tiger's head erased
  ermine, ducally gorged and tufted or. Henry Villett *alias* Violett of
  London, now of Kent. Visit. of London, 1568, p. 73.]
VILLERS, ..., crest, ... Barker's Grants, Harl. MS. 5846, fo. 114ᵇ.
VILLIERS, Edward, Visct., supporters, 7 Dec. 1691, by T. St. George, Gart. Harl.
  MS. 6834, fo. 178 ; Grants IV., fo. 101.
VINALL, John, of Kingstone, Sussex, ? Essex, s. of John, s. of William, s. of
  William, 10 Dec. 1657, by Sir E. Bysshe, Gart., and 22 Nov. 1661,
  13 Chas. II., by Bysshe, Clar. Harl. MSS. 1172, fo. 21, 38ᵇ, and 1105,
  fo. 19ᵇ ; Bysshe's Grants, fo. 15, Her. Coll., copy of grant.
VINCENT, ..., descended from Vincent Lovell, whose son called himself a
  Vincent, *see* MS. [Visit. of London, 1634], az., a chev. betw. three
  quatrefoils arg., on their stalks a crescent for diff., ..., by Segar, Gart.,
  and Nich. Charles, Lanc. Herald. Add. MS. 12,225, fo. 113 (*see* next
  grant*) ; C. 24 [Visit. of London, 1634], Her. Coll. ; Guil. 135.
   „   Augustin *alias* Rouge Croix, 3 s. of William, of Thingdon, Northts., 2 s. of
       Richard, s. of William, s. of William, of Stamford Baron, receiver of the
       Abbey of Crowland, etc. (a bordure added 8 May 1504 by Roger Machado,
       Richmont Clar., and confirmed to William Vincent of Stamford Baron, and
       again to Joan Mulsho 10 Nov. 1587, by W. Dethick, Gart. Q's Coll. Oxf.

MS. 38, fo. 133, and Harl. MS. 1470, fo. 19 and 39, copy of grant (Brit. Mus.) ; Add. MS. 12,225, fo. 113ᵃ). A grant of an altered coat, this practically a new one, and crest for a difference of lineage, 1 Jan. 1621-2, by Segar, Camden, and R. St. George, Norr. Add. MS. 12,225, fo. 113ᵇ; Nicolas life of Vincent, p. 102 ; Harl. MS. 6140, fo. 77 ; pedigree, *see* Le Neve's MS. 369 ; copy of grant, 390.

VINCENT, Joane (ux. Robert Mulsho, of Thingdon, Northants), dau. and sole heir of Francis Vincent of the same, s. of Richard, s. of William, s. of William by Anne his wife, d. and h. of Godfrey Dene of Stamford Baron, Northts., etc., confirmed quarterly of 6 at London 10 Nov. 1587, 29 Q. Eliz., by W. Dethick, Gart. Q's Coll. Oxf. MS. 38, fo. 109, copy of grant ; Harl. MSS. 1359, fo. 21, 1470, fo. 259, 1507, fo. 75, 368, and 1422, fo. 115 ; Le Neve's MS. 368, 359.

„   Philip, clerk, A.M., of Stoke D'Abernon, Surrey, then sailing to Gniana : confirmed of his genealogy and descent, etc., *see* MS. grant of the coat of Cowleby of Great Smeton, who bore arg., a cross sarceles in pale and formée in fess sa., the old crest of the Northern Vincents . . . . by Segar. Add. MS. 12,225, fo. 114 ; Harl. MS. 5887, fo. 31ᵇ, gives a trick of the arms and crest as Sir Thomas Vincent of Surrey, and also the arms of his wife.

   [Add. MS. 12,225, fo. 14, reads :—

      " Vincent, 45 E. [III., ? 1371], O., a Cross Sarcelee in
            pale & formée in Fess G.

   " To Philip Vincent, Clerk, A.M., of Stoke D'Abernon in Com. Surr., then sailing to Gniana, Confirm. of his Genealogy & descent And yᵗ he was borne at Frisby in yᵉ parish of Coningburgh, in Com. Ebor., son of Richard V[incent], son of another Richard [Vincent], who served in ye French warrs & was a Younger Brother of ye Vincents of Braywell near Frisby yᵗ bore for Arms, A., two barrs b., & on a Canton G. a flour de luce O., a Cadet of yᵉ Vincents of Great Smeaton whose arms were a trefoil on a Canton, which Smeton Line enjoyed yᵗ place by intermarriage with yᵉ daughter & heir of Cowleby of Great Smeaton who bore A. a cross sarcelié in pale & forme in fess [G.]. Grant of yᵉ sᵈ Cross in a field, called Crux Colbeiana, & Crest, vizt., The old Crest of yᵉ Northerne Vincents, vizt., a beares head issuing out of a Crowne."]

„   William, of Northants, descended from Vincent of co. Leicester, devised, ordained and assigned 8 May 1504, by Roger Machado als Richmont Clar. March in Add. MS. 14,295, fo. 77ᵇ ; Harl. MS. 1359, fo. 29.

VINTNERS' COMPANY, of London [by W. Hawkeslowe, Clar., 17 Sept. 1447 ; confirmed by T. Benolte, Clar., 22 Oct., 22 Hen. VIII., 1550]. Add. MS. 26,702, fo. 74ᵇ.

VIRGINIA, Seal, 9 Aug. 1662, by Sir E. Walker, Gart. Her. Coll., fo. 5.

„   College of Divinity, 14 May 1694, by T. St. George, Gart. and Clar. Grants IV., 158 and 284.

VIVIAN, John, of St. Colomb, Cornwall, ... by Borough, Gart. Harl. MSS. 1105, fo. 55ᵇ, and 1441, fo. 57 ; Add. MS. 26,702, fo. 89ᵇ ; Guil. 187.

VYVYAN alias WANNYWORTH, Thomas, Bp. and Prior of Bodmin in Cornwall (3 April 1507). Add. MS. 26,702, fo. 71 ; Harl. MS. 1079, fo. 121.

VOWELL, ..., servant to my Lord Treasurer, ... by Cooke, Clar. Stowe MS. 670, fo. 50ᵇ.

VOYSEY, John, Bp. of Exeter (1519—51, alias HARMAN). Add. MS. 26,702, fo. 50ᵇ.

VYELL, Abraham and John, of London, 1629, certified and pedigree by ? R. St. George, Clar. C. 24, Visit. of London [1634] ; Add. MS. 14,295, fo. 57.

VYNAR, Henry, "of Castelle in Com. Wiltshire, a gift Aᵒ 1558." (Harvey's
Grants), Add. MS. 16,940, fo. 47ᵇ [which adds: "Azur, a bend golde, on
a chief argent a saulter eng gules betw. 2 cornyshe chowys sables in thir
proper conler, on a wrethe golde and azur an armyd arme argent, garnyshed
golde, holding a gold ryng with a dyamond."]

W

WADE, Armigell, a native of the northern parts of England, granted 1 Nov.,
1 Ed. VI., 1547, by G. Dethick, Norr. Q's Coll. Oxf. MS. 37, fo. 14, and
MS. 39, fo. 7 ; Harl. MS. 1507, fo. 436, copy of grant in French (Brit.
Mus.) ; Harl. MS. 1359, fo. 4ᵇ ; Grants I., 119 ; Le Neve's MS. 436.
„   John, of Coventry, gent., grant 20 Feb., 34 Hen. VIII., 1542-3, by T. Hawley,
Clar. Harl. MS. 1507, fo. 405, and Q's Coll. Oxf. MS. 38, fo. 41, copy of
grant ; (Add. MS. 16,940, fo. 201, 16 Jan. 1539-40, 31 Hen. VIII.). *See*
WARDE.
„   William, of Gray's Inn, s. of Armigel of Hampstead, Esq., etc., 6 April 1574,
by Sir G. Dethick. Harl. MSS. 1441, fo. 81ᵇ ; Q's Coll. Oxf. MS. 145,
fo. 34, all being quarterly, the 1 and 4 being the 2 and 3 quarters in Stowe
MS. 670, fo. 37ᵇ ; then of Belsize in Hampstead, Clerk of the Council.
„   William (s. of William, s. of William, s. of Robert), of Bildeston, Suff.,
confirmed 8 Nov. 1604, by Camden. Harl. MS. 1470, fo. 16 and 49, copy
of grant, Brit. Mus. ; Grants II., 574 ; Guil. 248.
WADESON, John, of Yafforth, Yorks, 18 Nov. 1612, by R. St. George, Norr. Add.
MS. 14,295, fo. 59ᵇ ; B. 12, fo. 207 [Her. Coll.] ; C. 13 [Visit. of Yorks,
1612], fo. 207 ; Robert in Guil. 213.
WADMAN, John, of Brooke, Wilts, 20 May 1667, by Sir E. Walker, Gart. Her.
Coll., fo. 64.
WAGSTAFF, Anthony, of Hasel end, co. Derby, granted . . . . Aug. 1611, by
R. St. George, Norr. Guil. 63 ; Harl. MS. 6179, fo. 13.
WAGSTAFFE, Thomas, of Warwick, gent., descended from Wagstaffe of Cheshire ;
a confirmation Feb. 1616, by Camden. Harl. MSS. 6059, fo. 35ᵇ, and
5887, fo. 93ᵇ.
WAINEWRIGHT or WAYNEWRIGHT, ..., 1647, by Bysshe, Gart. Add. MS.
26,758, fo. 16 ; Stowe MS. 677, fo. 34 ; Harl. MS. 6832, fo. 413.
WAKE, William, of Blandford and Wareham, Dorset, certified by Sir William Wake
of Piddington Grange, Northants, in 1676. Grants IV., 162-3. ? Father
of the Archbp. next named.
„   William, of Gray's Inn, D.D., rector of St. James, Westminster (after Archbp.
of Canterbury), s. of William, of Shapwick, confirmed 16 May 1694, by
T. St. George, Gart. Grants IV., 185. ? Per E. Marshal's Warrant.
WAKEHAM, John, of Borough, Devon, an attorney of Court of Com. Pleas and an
ancient of Lyon's Inn, granted . . . . 1638, by Borough. Harl. MSS. 1105,
fo. 55ᵇ, and 1441, fo. 59 ; Add. MS. 26,702, fo. 90 ; Guil. 397.
„   Richard, of Bedford, co. Gloucester, ... 1586, by Cooke. Harl. MSS. 1359,
fo. 89, and 1422, fo. 51ᵇ ; Add. MS. 4966, fo. 35ᵇ.
„   Robert, of Bere Ferris, Devon, D.D., patent 16 May 1616, by Camden. Add.
MS. 14,295, fo. 63ᵇ ; Camden's Grants 35 ; and C. 1 [Visit. of Devon,
1620], fo. 159, Her. Coll. ; Harl. MSS. 6059, fo. 34, and 1422, fo. 40ᵇ.
WALDEGRAVE, Henry, Lord, supporters 3 June 1686, by Sir T. St. George, Gart.,
and Sir J. Dugdale, Norr. Harl. MS. 6834, fo. 178 ; Grants III., fo. 295 ;
Lansd. MS. 867, fo. 52.
WALDEN, Sir Richard, of Kent, Knt., *temp.* Hen. VI., coat and crest. Barker's
Grants, Harl. MS. 5846, fo. 109 ; Stowe MS. 692, fo. 94.
WALKEDEN, Geoffrey, of Stone, co. Staff., gift . . . . 1558. (Harvey's Grants), Add.
MSS. 16,940, fo. 55, and 5887, fo. 54.

WALKAERT, Sir Abraham, from Brabant, given at Oxford (4) May 1645, by Walker. Add. MS. 14,294, fo. 28. (*See* next entry.)

WALKER, Abraham, of the Hague, by Walker, Gart. Jeweller unto the princess Royal. Augmentation and crest at Oxford May 1645. (*See* last entry.) Her. Coll., 28; (arg., on a chev. ringed at the point, betw. three crescents sa., a star or, Berry).

„ Anthony, of Yorks, gent., granted 11 March 1553-4, by Sir G. Dethick, Gart.; confirmed 12 June 1563, by Harvey, Clar.; "m^d neither Garter nor Clar. ought to have given theis arms but only M^r (W. Flower) Norroy." Q's Coll. Oxf. MS. 37, fo. 41, and MS. 39, fo. 47, copy of grant (MS. 146, fo. 22); Add. MS. 14,295, fo. 75^b; Harl. MS. 1359, fo. 8, 76^b; Grants I., 405.

„ Christopher, of the Inner Temple, ? by Sir E. Bysshe, Gart. Harl. MS. 1105, fo. 15. Bencher 1652; died 12 Jan. 1655-6.

„ Sir Edward, Garter, principal K. of Arms, clerk of the Council and receiver-general of H.M.'s money, granted at Jersey 8 Feb. 1649-50; alteration of crest and augmentation, arg., on a cross of St. George gu. five leopards' faces or, quartering arg., a chev. betw. three crescents sa., by Walker, Gart. Her. Coll., fo. 3; Harl. MSS. 1052, fo. 211^b, and 1105, fo. 12^b. *See* Agnes REEVE, his wife.

„ Francis, of Bringwood, co. Hereford, a zealous Royalist, 20 Dec. 1660, by Walker. Add. MSS. 14,293, fo. 27, and 14,294, fo. 2^b; MS. Ashm. 858, fo. 131-2, copy of grant, Bodleian Lib.; Harl. MS. 1172, fo. 50; Guil. 187; Gu., a cross raguly betw. four lions' heads erased ar., crowned or.

„ George, of Cambridge, Esq., confirmed . . . . by Cooke : sa., three tigers passant regardant [in pale ?] ermine; [Crest] out of a clump of trees a lion issuant, all ppr. Stowe MS. 706, fo. 52.

„ Henry, of Kington, co. Hereford, arms, on a chevron [trick, ? arched] at the point betw. three crescents sa. two plates . . . . all within a bordure invackted of the 2nd, by Camden. Cains Coll. Camb. MS. 551, fo. 30; " Camden's Guifts," of " Kinton."

„ John, of Hillingdon, Middx. (s. of William, of Wakefield, Yorks, etc.), assistant to the clerk of the parliaments Lords, 10 Sept. 1663, by Walker : arg., a fesse embattled counter embattled betw. three crescents sa. Add. MS. 14,294, fo. 14.

„ Thomas, High Sheriff, Surrey, March 1657, by Sir E. Bysshe, Gart. Harl. MS. 1172, fo. 23, copy of grant.

„ Thomas, D.D., Master Univ. Coll., Oxon.; died 5 Oct. 1665; arms assigned to his ex'ors by Walker. Guil. 96.

„ Walter, Bachelor of Law and Commissary of the Court at Bedford . . . . by Sir H. St. George, patent or confirmation. Harl. MS. 6179, fo. 58^b.

„ William, of Bushey, Herts, Doctor of the laws and Judge Advocate, by Segar. Add. MS. 12,225, fo. 114^b.

„ William, B.D., descended out of Lancashire, arg., on a chev. sa. betw. three pellets as many crescents of the first, testified by Segar. Add. MS. 12,225, fo. 114^b; C. 28, fo. 44^b, 2nd Index, Her. Coll.; Guil. 361; Harl. MSS. 6140, fo. 78^b, and 1440, fo. 161.

WALL (Thomas), of Cryche in Darbishire, Norroy King of Arms, coat and crest. Barker's Grants, Harl. MS. 5846, fo. 105^b; Stowe MS. 692, fo. 92^b.

„ Humfrey, of Leominster, co. Hereford, gent., confirmation of arms and gift of crest 8 July, 36 Q. Eliz., 1594, by Lee, Clar. Stowe MS. 670, fo. 58^b; Harl. MS. 1359, fo. 31; of Lutwidge in Harl. MS. 1422, fo. 56^b; 7th of July in Add. MS. 14,295, fo. 26^b, which adds " the arms were John's, his father an officer under Hen. VIII., E. VI., Q. Mary and Q. Eliz. in the buttrie, who died the xith of Feb. 1564, bur. in St. Margaret's, Westminster"; Harl. MS. 6179, fo. 15.

„ William, of Hogesdon, Middx., a patent . . . . April 1613, by Camden. Harl.

MS. 6059, fo. 26^b; Guil. 380; erroneously called Hall in Morgan's Sphere,
ii., 113, and Le Neve's MS. 320.

WALLES or WALLIS, Lewis, als DART, of Barnstaple, Devon, ... 1590, by Cooke.
Harl. MS. 1359, fo. 96^b; Wallis in Harl. MS. 1079, fo. 160, and Stowe
MS. 670, fo. 39^b.

WALLEY, Thomas, s. of Thomas, of Stonepitt, Kent, and sometime of Somerset,
. . . . . 1591, by Cooke, Clar. Stowe MS. 670, fo. 45^b.

WALMSLEY, Thomas, of Dukenhalgh, co. Lanc., Esq., quarterly of 8, 10 Aug.
1548, by Sir G. Dethick. Harl. MS. 1441, fo. 86; confirmed 20 Aug.
1560, by G. D[ethick]; Q's Coll. Oxf. MS. 145, fo. 42; quarterly of 6,
Harl. MS. 6140, fo. 28, 53^b.

WALLPOOLE, Sir John, of Dunster, co. Linc., cornet of the King's troops, augmen-
tation 1 June 1646 at Oxford, by Walker. Harl. MS. 1105, fo. 12^b;
Genealogist, vol. i., 101; Her. Coll., fo. 27, copy of grant, Brit. Mus.;
Harl. MS. 1052, fo. 211.

WALPOLE, Robert, of Pinchbeck, co. Linc., ar., confirmed . . . . 1561 (Harvey's
Grants). Add. MS. 16,940, fo. 16^b.

WALTER, ..., of Kent, a patent 4 May 1613, by Camden. Harl. MSS. 6059,
fo. 27, and 1548, fo. 188^b.

   „ Edmond, of London, gent., 15 March 1545-6, by Barker. Stowe MS. 677,
fo. 10. *See* William below.

   „ Henry, of Stebenheath, Middx., gent., s. of John, etc., confirmed, but more
probably a grant, 20 March 1571-2, by Cooke. Stowe MS. 676, fo. 39;
Q's Coll. Oxf. MS. 37, fo. 51, copy of grant.

   „ (Sir) Robert, Lord Mayor of York, at the entrance of K. James into
England, confirmed 1 Oct. 1603, by Segar. Add. MS. 12,225, fo. 115;
Harl. MSS. 1422, fo. 52, and 1359, fo. 9; Guil. 322; Knighted by the
King on his way south, Harl. MS. 6140, fo. 67^b.

   „ William, of Crowden, co. Camb., and } grant, coat and crest 15 March 1545-6.
   „ Edmund, of London,   } *See* Edm^d above. Barker's Grants,
Harl. MSS. 5846, fo. 112, and
1422, fo. 72^b; Stowe MS. 692, fo. 94^b.

WALTHAM als MASON, who was master Mason to Hen. VIII., by Cooke, ...
Harl. MS. 1422, fo. 15^b.

WALTHEW or WALTHOW, Robert, of Deptford, Kent, "serviens confectionarius"
to K. James, patent 10 June 1611, by Camden. Harl. MS. 6059, fo. 25;
Jan. in Guil. 285, and 20 Jan. in Harl. MS. 1172, fo. 41, copy of grant.

WANDESFORD, Richard, of Upper Sapey, co. Hereford, coat . . . ., Barker's Grants.
Harl. MS. 5846, fo. 111; Stowe MS. 692, fo. 94^b.

WANKFORD, Robert, of Barwick Hall in Topsfield, in Essex, 14 May 1663. Harl.
MSS. 1085, fo. 4, and 1105, fo. 18^b; Bysshe's Grants, fo. 10, Her. Coll.,
and a new coat, etc., 18 Sept. 1664, fo. 13; Guil. 359.

WANTON, Thomas, of London, gent., grant 6 Nov., 5 and 6 Philip and Mary, 1558,
by Sir G. Dethick, Gart. Q's Coll. Oxf. MS. 39, fo. 89, copy of grant;
Grants I., 160: Harl. MS. 1359, fo. 71.

WAPPAM, Elizabeth, wife to Sir William Locke, Maior of London (out of Sussex),
1 Aug. 1550, by ? Hawley. Add. MS. 16,940, fo. 203^b.

WARBLETON, John, s. and h. of John de, arms claimed by Theobald, s. of Sir
.Theobald Russell, formerly Gorges, given in favour of John Warbleton, by
Henry, Earl of Lancaster, Derby and Leicester, and Steward of England,
1347. Stowe MS. 840, fo. 57.

WARBURTON, Peter, of co. pal. Chester, Sergeant at law, grant 25 Feb. 1593-4, by
W. Dethick, Gart. Stowe MS. 676, fo. 109^b; Q's Coll. Oxf. MS. 36,
fo. 40, copy of grant, Quarterly, "Warberton, who is illegitimate, &
therefore not to bear the armes of Dutton with the difference of an ermyn,
but with their great prejudice which they have complayned of. Garter had
for it 20^{li}," entered by R. Brooke, York Her. Harl. MS. 1453, fo. 31.

WARBURTON, Piers, of Northwich, Cheshire, s. of Thos., s. of John, 4 s. of Geoffrey, of Chesh., 19 Sept. 1580, 22 Eliz., by Flower, in French.   MS. Ashm. 844, fo. 49, copy of patent, Bodleian Lib.

WARD, ..., of Birmingham, co. Warw. . . . . 1575, ..., ? visitation.   (Berry.)

„   (George), of Brooke, Norfolk, 10 Aug. 1576, by Cooke.   Harl. MS. 1085, fo. 39, Berry.   Thomas in Add. MS. 14,294, fo. 79, copy of grant, Brit. Mus.

WARDE, Edward, late of Postwick, now of Bixley, Norfolk, gent., s. of Henry, s. of Robert, gent., 22 Nov. 1575, by Sir G. Dethick.   Harl. MS. 1441, fo. 84 ; Q's Coll. Oxf. MS. 145, fo. 39ᵇ.

„   Giles. of London, ..., by Cooke.   Harl. MS. 1422, fo. 44ᵇ.   Arms, az., a cross patonce or, charged with a crescent gu. ; Crest, a wolf's head and neck couped or, charged with a fesse ermine.

„   John, of Coventry, quarterly, coat confirmed and crest granted 20 Feb. 1542-3, by Hawley, Clar.   Le Neve's MS. 405.   (See WADE.)

„   John, of Great Ilford, Essex, out of Yorks, quarterly of 4, certificate, by Segar.   Add. MS. 12,225, fo. 115ᵇ ; Grants I., 387.

„   Leonard, of Lincolns Inn, ..., by W. Ryley, Lanc. Herald.   Stowe MS. 703, fo. 64.

„   Richard, of Gorleston, Suff. (12 July) 1593, by Cooke.   Harl. MSS. 1359, fo. 105ᵇ, and 1422, fo. 44ᵇ ; 12 July in Edmondson's Armory ; Add. MS. 4966, fo. 24ᵇ.

„   William and ⎱ sons of William, of Pilton, Devon, confirmed coat and crest
„   Richard,   ⎰   granted 21 or 27 July 1614, by Segar.   Add. MS. 12,225, fo. 115 ; Harl. MS. 1470, fo. 171, copy of grant ; C. 24 [Visit. of London, 1634], fo. 104ᵇ, Her. Coll.; Guil. 231 ; 21ˢᵗ July in Harl. MS. 1359, fo. 65, copy of patent in Brit. Mus.

WARD, William, of Houghton Parva, Northants, and to sisters Mary and Dorothy, 31 May 1695, by T. St. George, Gart. and Clar.   Stowe MS. 714, fo. 121 ; Grants IV., 206 ; Guil. 229.

WARDELL, Ann, of Caen, Normandy, descended of John, who was the first that came into Normandy, confirmed by Ro. Cooke, 1584, arg., a chev. betw. 3 boars' heads couped sa. on a chief vert 3 bezants.   Berry.   Stowe MS. 670, fo. 6 ; Add. MSS. 14,297, fo. 6, and 12,474, fo. 54ᵇ.

WARDMAN, Anthony, of London, ..., by Ro. Cooke.   Stowe MS. 670, fo. 49ᵇ.

WARDOUR, Chideock, coz. and heir of John, of Westbury, Wilts, confirmed . . . . 1585, by Cooke.   Harl. MSS. 1359, fo. 99ᵇ, and 1052, fo. 18 ; Guil. 196 ; Add. MS. 4966, fo. 19 ; Harl. MS. 5887, fo. 20ᵇ.

WARHAM, Hugh (de), of Malshanger, Hants (bro. of the Archbp.), coat and crest, allowed ? Hants Visit.   Harl. MS. 1544, fo. 32ᵇ ; Barker's Grants, Harl. MS. 5846, fo. 108ᵇ ; Stowe MS. 692, fo. 93ᵇ.

WARLEY, William, of London, gent., patent 9 April, 33 Q. Eliz., 1591, by Cooke.   Harl. MSS. 1359, fo. 118ᵇ, and 5887, fo. 88ᵇ.

WARME, see WORME.

WARMINGTON, Francis (or WARRINGTON), arg., on a bend sa. three eaglets displayed regardant or ; Crest, out of a ducal coronet az. a demi eagle as in the arms.   Caius Coll. Camb. MS. 551, fo. 31, Camden's Guifts ; Harl. MS. 1441, fo. 151ᵇ, as Winnington.

WARNE, William, of Southampton, gent., grant 6 Feb. 1657, by E. Bysshe, Gart.   Harl. MSS. 1441, fo. 52, copy of grant, and 1105, fo. 15ᵇ.

WARNER, ..., of Essex, crest June 1609, by Camden, must be a sarisones head in this manner : this crest was given to one Warner, of Sussex, altered to Suffolk.   Harl. MSS. 6059, fo. 9, and 1422, fo. 20.

„   . . . . of Kent . . . . 1616, attestation, arms and quarterings.   Quarterly : 1 and 4, per pale indented arg. and sa.; 2, az., a fleur-de-lis or ; 3, vert, a cross engrailed arg. . . . . by Segar.   Add. MS. 12,225, fo. 121ᵇ ; see also Visit. of Kent, 1666, by Bysshe, ? as Warne.

WARNER, Mark, of Strowde, Middx., gent., s. and h. of Robert, of Strowd, s. and h. of John, of London, Alderm., 20 June 1573, 15 Q. Eliz., by Cooke. Harl. MS. 1359, fo. 82ᵇ, 1577 crest; Harl. MS. 1422, fo. 123, quartering 2 Vavasour, 3 Hariot. Mem. that these were no heires.

„   Thomas, of London, a Spanish mercht., ... 1579, by Sir G. Dethick, Gart. Berry.

WARNESCOMBE, Thomas, of Lugwardine, co. Hereford, coat and crest. Barker's Grants, Harl. MS. 5846, fo. 113ᵇ ; Stowe MS. 692, fo. 95, as John.

WARRE (LAWARD), Richard, of Hestercombe, Somerset, Esq., confirmed 10 July 1576, by G. Dethick, Gart. Q's Coll. Oxf. MS. 145, fo. 41 ; Add. MS. 18,582, fo. 43.

WARREN, ..., of Newton, Suff., ... 1589 : Arg., a fesse chequey or and az. betw. three talbots sa. Crest. [No reference.]

„   . . . ., London and Walterstaff, Devon, 14 March 1623 : Crest, a greyhound sa. seizing a hare ppr. Arms, arg., three mascles sa. betw. two bars countercompony or and az., on a canton of the second three ducal crowns or, all within a bordure gu. charged with eight bezants. Berry.

WARRYN, Francis, of Rutland, 18 November 1511, by Carlyle, Norr. Harl. MS. 1116, fo. 39ᵇ.

WARREN, Gregory, of Horden, s. of Gregory, of St. Peter's in St. Albans, Herts, ... by Camden. Harl. MSS. 1422, fo. 47ᵇ, and 1441, fo. 51.

„   Jasper, of Great Thurlow, s. of Thomas, of Long Melford, Suff., ... 1538, by Hawley. Harl. MS. 1422, fo. 16.

„   John, of London, ... by Cooke. Add. MS. 14,295, fo. 94, 95 ; Harl. MS. 1422, fo. 23.

„   John, of London, 15 Sept. 1555, by ? Hawley. Add. MS. 16,940, fo. 207ᵇ.

„   John, of London, ... 1613, by Camden. Morgan's Sphere, 118.

WARYN, Laurence, of Herts : arms, arg., a fesse, a pile in pale pierced of the field betw. iiij leopards' heads gu. Crest, a scorpion party per pale gu. and az., flamed arg. 10 May 1552, 6 Ed. VI. Add. MS. 16,940, fo. 205ᵇ ; Stowe MS. 692, fo. 94ᵇ ; (Barker's Grants) rather Hawley.

WARRYN, Rauffe, of London (gent.), coat . . . . Barker's Grants, Harl. MS. 5846, fo. 107ᵇ ; Stowe MS. 692, fo. 93.

WARYNE, Robert, of London resident, but of Long Melford, Suff., grant 28 June 1538, by Hawley. Harl. MS. 1820, fo. 5ᵇ.

WARREN, { Roger, of Suff., gift . . . . 1560. (Harvey's Grants), Add. MS. 16,940, fo. 18ᵇ.

„   { Thomas, of Newberry, Suff., new crest 1589 at request of Drury, deputy to Cooke, Clar. Stowe MS. 670, fo. 35 ; Add. MS. 14,297, fo. 33.

WARTON, ... crest . . . . Barker's Grants, Harl. MS. 5846, fo. 110 ; Stowe MS. 692, fo. 94.

WASHINGTON, Laurence, of Sulgrave, Northants, ... by Cooke, 1592. Harl. MS. 1422, fo. 13ᵇ. 71ᵇ ; Washingle in Stowe MS. 670, fo. 50.

WASSE, John, of London, gent., crest granted 1 Feb., 3 Q. Eliz., 1560-61, by Sir Gilb. Dethick, Gart. Q's Coll. Oxf. MS. 39, fo. 118, copy of grant; Grants I., 282 ; Harl. MSS. 1359, fo. 81, and 5887, fo. 5ᵇ ; copy of grant, Harl. MS. 1116, fo. 51.

WASTELL, ... prior . . . . Hen. VII. Add. MS. 26,702, fo. 44ᵇ.

WATERHOUSE, John, of Hemel Hempsted, Herts, gent., grant 10 June, 25 Hen. VIII., ? 1533, by Hawley, Clar. (? Tonge, Clar.). 1528 in Harl. MS. 1507, fo. 40ᵇ ; Add. MS. 16,940, fo. 9ᵇ ; 1533 in Q's Coll. Oxf. MS. 38, fo. 34, copy of grant ; of Berkhampsted, Harl. MS. 1116, fo. 57ᵇ, as Harvey ; Le Neve's MS. 406.

„   Robert, of Halifax, Yorks, late escheator and Justice of the peace in said county, patent granted 7 April 1561, by Dalton. Harl. MS. 1359, fo. 49ᵇ.

„   Robert, of Halifax, Yorks, 9 Oct. 1573, by Sir G. Dethick, Gart. Harl. MS. 1441, fo. 80ᵇ ; Q's Coll. Oxf. MS. 145, fo. 32 ; Harl. MS. 5887, fo. 43.

WATERS, Robert, of Royton, Kent, gift .... 1564. (Harvey's Grants), Add. MS. 16,940, fo. 31.

WATKINS, Humfrey, of Hall Wall, Somerset. s. of Thomas, of Yorks, confirmed 2 Jan. 1560-61, by Dalton. Harl. MS. 1359, fo. 49.

WATKINSON, Henry, Doctor of law (out of Yorkshire), 16 Oct. 1664, by Walker. Add. MS. 14,294, fo. 8 ; Surtees Soc., XLI., liii.

WATMOUGH, Francis, s. of Richard, s. of William, of Micklehead, co. Lanc., crest 17 Jan. 1602-3, by Segar. Stowe MS. 677, fo. 15ᵇ ; Harl. MS. 1115, fo. 67, copy of grant. Brit. Mus.

WATSON, ... crest .... Barker's Grants, Harl. MS. 5846, fo. 110ᵇ ; Stowe MS. 692, fo. 94.

„ Anthony, D.D., of Chicham, Surrey, Bp. of Chichester and Almoner to Q. Eliz., s. of Edward, s. of William, both of Thorpe Thewlesse, co. Durham, gift 8 Sept. 1596, 38 Q. Eliz., by Lee. Harl. MSS. 1069, fo. 10ᵇ, and 1359, fo. 18 ; 7ᵗʰ Sept. in Add. MS. 14,295, fo. 11.

„ Edward, of Lidington, Rutland, coat and crest. Barker's Grants, Harl. MS. 5846, fo. 107ᵇ ; Stowe MS. 692, fo. 93, again after.

„ Rowland, of White Webbs, par. of Enfield, Middx., 3rd s. of William, of Newport, Salop, s. of Thomas, 2. s. of William, of Gisboro, Yorks, Esq., which Thomas was bro. and heir to Robert, of Gisboro aforesaid (arms, or, on a chief vert, three martlets of the field), gift ; Crest, an ermine passant or, collared, ringed and lined or, ... by Cooke. Harl. MSS. 1052, fo. 14ᵇ, and 1359, fo. 88 ; Add. MS. 4966, fo. 52.

„ Thomas, Bp. of Lincoln, arms 2 (Dec.) 1556, by ? Hawley. Add. MS. 16,940, fo. 208ᵇ.

„ Thomas, of Halstead (or Hasted, Kent), and his wife, 22 July 1613, by Camden. (Harl. MSS. 1422, fo. 14ᵇ, and 5839, fo. 42ᵇ, different crests) ; styled a Knight in Caius Coll. Camb. MS. 551, fo. 31ᵇ.

WATTE, ..., of Kent and Somst., ... 1591 .... arg., on a cross sa. five lions rampant or. Crest, a cubit arm erect in coat of mail, holding in the hand a pistol, all ppr. Berry.

WATT, ... of Leominster, co. Hereford, 7 July 1594 .... Berry.

WATTE, Richard, of Rochester, Kent, 1 April 1552, by ? Hawley. Add. MS. 16,940, fo. 205ᵇ.

WATTS, ..., of Norfolk, ... May 1610, by Camden. Harl. MSS. 1422, fo. 21, and 6059, fo. 12.

„ ...., of Norwich, ... 18 Jan. 1664-5, by Bysshe, Clar. Berry.

„ Edward, of Blakesley, Northts., and bro. } sons of William, s. of Thos. of
„ Montague, of Lincoln's Inn, Esq.,   } London, etc., crest granted 15 Feb. 1614-15, by Camden. Q's Coll. Oxf. MS. 38, fo. 127, copy of grant ; Harl. MSS. 1507, fo. 378, 6059, fo. 39ᵇ, and 1422, fo. 40 ; Stowe MS. 714, fo. 84 ; Le Neve's MS. 348, 378.

WATTES, Hugh, of Shanks, par. of Cuckling, Somerset, s. of William, 10 July 1616, by Segar. Add. MS. 12,225, fo. 115ᵇ; C. 22 [Visit. of Somerset, 1623], fo. 363, Her. Coll. ; Grants I., 376 (10 July) ; Guil. 332.

WATTS, John, of London, Alderm., gift 2 July 1596, by R. Lee. Harl. MSS. 1359, fo. 32, and 1422, fo. 58ᵇ ; Add. MS. 14,295, fo. 29ᵇ.

WATTYS, Robert, and } of Berks, confirmed 27 Sept. 1503, by (R. Machado) Rich-
„ John,   } mond Clar. MS. Ashm. 834, fo. 10, copy of grant, Bodleian Lib. ; Harl. MS. 1422, fo. 108ᵇ ; Guil. 223 ; Harl. MS. 6140, fo. 71.

WAXCHANDLERS, Company of, of London, granted 3 Feb. 1484-5, 2 R. III., by Sir Thomas Holme, Clar. ; confirmed 11 Oct. 1530 (1523 in Her. and Geneal., i., 121), 22 Hen. VIII., by T. Benolt. (Alteration 12 Oct. 1536, by Hawley, Harl. MSS. 1052, fo. 205) and 1052, fo. 202, 203, 205, copy of grant, Brit. Mus. ; MSS. Ashm. 858, fo. 40, and 834, fo. 62, copy of grant, Bodleian Lib. ; Cat. Her. Exhib. Soc. of Antiq., 61.

WAYE, Thomas, Master of the Marshalsea, quarterly, by Cooke ; the crest given 24 March 1674 (? 1574). Harl. MS. 1359, fo. 118 ; called May in Harl. MS. 1422, fo. 121 ; Stowe MS. 670, fo. 69ᵇ ; Harl. MS. 5887, fo. 68ᵇ ; Add. MS. 4966, fo. 100ᵇ ; Harl. MS. 5887, fo. 68.

WAYLTON, Gregory, confirmed .... 1560. (Hervey's Grants), Add. MS. 16,940, fo. 9.

WAYTE, Thomas, H.M.'s receiver of cos. Warwick and Leic., a patent .... June 1612, by Camden. Harl. MSS. 1422, fo. 37, and 6059, fo. 23ᵇ ; Guil. 316.

WEAVERS' GUILD, 4 Aug. 1490, by Sir T. Holme, Clar. ; confirmed 11 Oct. 1530, by Benolte ; supporters 10 Aug. 1616, by Segar. Her. and Geneal., i., 121, 123 ; Add. MS. 12,225, fo. 116 ; 10 Aug. in Bishop's MS. in Puttick's Sale, April 15, 1898.

WEBBE, Emma, dau. of Henry, of Kimbolton, Hants, wife to John Cordall of Long Melford, Suff., 10 April 1554, by ? Hawley. Add. MS. 16,940, fo. 206ᵇ.

WEBB, Henry, of London, gent., one of the King's gent. ushers, and chief porter Tower of London, grant 20 Feb. 1543-4, and a new coat and crest 10 Sept., 4 Ed. VI., 1550, by Hawley. Q's Coll. Oxf. MS. 38, fo. 38, 57, copies of grants ; Misc. Gen. et Her., 3ʳᵈ S., vol. ii., p. 156 ; Grants II., 458 ; Guil. 395 ; Le Neve's MS. 411.

„ Henry, of Harrow (on the) Hill, Middx., ... 1587, by Cooke. Harl. MSS. 1359, fo. 108, and 1422, fo. 61ᵇ ; Add. MS. 4966, fo. 57ᵇ.

WEBBE, Robert, of Cliffords, Somerset, ... 1591, by Cooke. Harl. MSS. 1359, fo. 121ᵇ, and 1422, fo. 23ᵇ.

„ ....., gules a fess between three owls or, June 1627, by R. St. George, Clar. Harl. MS. 1105, fo. 7.

„ Thomas, of London, ..., by Cooke. Harl. MSS. 1359, fo. 87ᵇ, 1422, fo. 61ᵇ, and 5887, fo. 66 ; Add. MS. 4966, fo. 58.

WEBB, Thomas, of Gillingham, Kent, s. of John, s. of John, s. of Bernard, of the same, granted ...., by Cooke. Cooke's Grants, fo. 4, Her. Coll. ; Guil. 221 ; (Ardolfe quartered by Webbe, of Kent, 1584 ; Cott. MS. Faustina E. 2, fo. 232) ; (Stowe MS. 670, fo. 3ᵇ).

„ William, of Motcombe, Dorset (2 s. of William, of New Sarum, Wilts, etc., and of Katherine his wife, dau. and h. of John Aborough, Esq.), and to his wife Katherine, dau. and coh. of Geo. Tourney, gent., s. and h. of William Tourney and Anne, dau. and coh. of Stephen Payn, Esq., s. and h. of, etc., quarterly of 4, and an escocheon of pretence, quarterly of 9, 17 June 1577, by Cooke. The patent was surrendered to Robert Cooke, the cross altered to a plain one, and the arms allowed to William Webb and John, his brother ; at the suyte of one .... Wyatt of the Inner Temple, 26 March 1586 (fo. 63ᵇ). MS. Ashm. 844, fo. 63, copy of grant, Bodleian Lib. ; Cooke's Grants, fo. 46ᵇ, Her. Coll. ; Guil. 221 ; Harl. MS. 5887, fo. 37 ; Stowe MS. 670, fo. 58.

WEBLEY or WEBLIN(CKE), Wessell, of Upthall in Essex, s. of John, s. of John, s. of Garret, born in Westphalia under the Empire, 9 Feb. 1606-7, by Camden. Harl. MSS. 1422, fo. 19ᵇ, and 6059, fo. 6ᵇ ; (1604-5 in Add. MS. 14,293, fo. 21ᵇ), az., a saltire, flurtée, etc., a gryphon passant in chief or, by Segar ; Gu., a saltire flurtée or, in chief a lyon passant of the same, and of Southwark, brewer, in Add. MS. 12,225, fo. 116.

WEBSTER, George, Master Cooke, gift .... 1559 (Harvey's Grants). Add. MS. 16,940, fo. 28 ; Harl. MS. 6140, fo. 31ᵇ.

WECKHERLIN, see WICKHERLIN.

WEDDALL, John, of Stebenheath, als Stepney, Middx., Capt. of the Rainbow, a principall Ship in the King's Navy, took the castle of Kochmay in the gulf of Persia, etc., grant 2 May 1627, by Segar. Add. MS. 12,225, fo. 116ᵇ ; 3ʳᵈ of May in Guil. 330 ; Harl. MS. 6140, fo. 76ᵇ.

WEDGWOOD, John, of Harkles, co. Staff., confirmed 20 Nov. 1576, 19 Eliz., by Cooke. MS. Ashm. 858, fo. 119 (copy of grant, Bodleian Lib.) ; 1576, 19 Q. Eliz. in Harl. MS. 1359, fo. 121.

WEDNESTER, Charles, of Bromyard, co. Hereford, Esq., s. of John, s. of John, crest granted 30 Nov. 1588, by Cooke. Q's Coll. Oxf. MS. 37, fo. 114, copy of grant ; Grants II., 487 ; Harl. MS. 1359, fo. 95ᵇ ; Guil. 212 ; Stowe MS. 676, fo. 76, says given by W. Dethick.

WELBY, Richard, of Halstead, co. Line., coat confirmed and crest granted 21 March 1562-3. Add. MS. 16,940, fo. 12ᵇ ; Grants II., 594, as 16ᵗʰ March, and Wilbe ; by Harvey, Her. and Geneal., i., 82 ; Misc. Gen. et Her., i., 249.

WELBY or WOLBY, Robert, of Billesby, co. Line., Esq., s. of Vincent, of Thorpe in the said co., who mar. Margaret, dau. and one of the heirs of Laurence Mears of Kirton, Esq., ..., by Segar. Add. MS. 12,225, fo. 122.

WELCHE, Sir John, of Gloucester, coat and crest. Barker's Grants, Harl. MS. 5846, fo. 104ᵇ ; Stowe MS. 692, fo. 92.

WELCOME, William, of Market Stanton, co. Line., gent., 1 Jan. 1581-2, by Sir G. Dethick, Gart. Q's Coll. Oxf. MS. 145, fo. 43 ; Harl. MS. 1441, fo. 86ᵇ ; Add. MS. 17,506, fo. 7 and 26, 23 Eliz., i.e., 1580-1, Le Neve's MS. 251.

WELD, Sir Humphrey, Mayor of London, a confirmation 30 Aug. 1606, by Camden, quarterly, Weld, Grants als Buttall and Fitz Hugh. Harl. MS. 1441, fo. 97 (no bordure) ; Harl. MSS. 1422, fo. 110. and 6059, fo. 21ᵇ ; Berry's Appendix ; Harl. MS. 5887, fo. 48ᵇ.

„ John, of Eton, Cheshire, s. of John, etc., crest 10 April 1552, by Sir G. Dethick, Gart. Misc. Gen. et Her., i., 10 ; Q's Coll. Oxf. MS. 145, fo. 1 ; Harl. MS. 1441, fo. 61 (and a diff. crest ermine, fo. 68ᵇ, 23 Jan.) ; Harl. MS. 5887, fo. 46.

„ John, gent. and haberdasher, of London, s. of John, of Eton, Cheshire, s. of John, of Eton, s. of Edward, of Eton, descended of worshipful lineage (assigned, ratified, confirmed and set forth), confirmed (within a bordure) 28 Jan. 1559, by Sir G. Dethick, Gart. Harl. MS. 1441, fo. 68ᵇ ; Q's Coll. Oxf. MS. 38, fo. 75, copy of grant (and MS. 145, fo. 12ᵇ) ; Grants I., 128 ; Harl. MSS. 1359, fo. 53, and 5887, fo. 46 ; Stowe MS. 703, fo. 4.

WELDON, Edward, crest 14 Feb., 4 and 5 Philip and Mary, 1557-8, by Sir G. Dethick, Gart. Q's Coll. Oxf. MS. 39, fo. 92, copy of grant in Latin ; Grants I., 23 ; Harl. MS. 1359, fo. 71ᵇ ; see quarterly coat, Harl. MS. 6140, fo. 44ᵇ.

WELDYSHE, William, of Lynton in Kent, vert, iii running hounds, ar., on a chief arg., a fox passant gu. ; Crest, a demi fox ppr. erased gu. (Granted 19 March 1542-3, Harl. MS. 5524, fo. 28ᵇ) ; Barker's Grants, Stowe MS. 692, fo. 95ᵇ ; see Harl. MS. 5887, fo. 22.

WELLER, Richard, B.D., rector of Warbilton, Sussex, grant 3 May 1672, by Sir Edw. Bysshe, Clar. Her. and Geneal., i., 83 ; Harl. MS. 1105, fo. 89ᵇ ; (as David), Bysshe's Grants, 30.

WELLS, Barnard, of Holme, co. Derby, grant 14 Nov. 1634, by St. George, Clar. MS. Ashm. 858, fo. 162, copy of grant, Bodleian Lib. ; Reliquary, xxii., 51. See WEBB.

WELLES, George or Thomas, of Kese College in Cambridge, patent Nov. 1614, by Camden. Harl. MSS. 6059, fo. 31, and 1422, fo. 39ᵇ.

„ Jon, gent., Anglois de Houborne, a fief and seigneury in ye par. of Bucksted, Sussex, s. of Jan, s. of Jan, s. of Jan Welles als Atwells, etc., ensign to Capt. Mich. Wood's Compy. in the regt. of Sir Horace Vere in service of the state, ..., by Segar. Add. MS. 12,225, fo. 116ᵇ.

WELLES, Richard, of Ware, Herts, confirmed . . . . 1550. (Harvey's Grants), Add. MS. 16,940, fo. 15ᵇ.

WENDOVER, Edward, of the city of Salisbury, confirmed quarterly, 16 June 1615, by Segar. Add. MS. 12,225, fo. 117 ; Harl. MS. 6140, fo. 77 : 14ᵗʰ June in Guil. 185.

WENHAM, John, of Morehall, Sussex, by Cooke, Clar.   Stowe MS. 670, fo. 76ᵇ.

WENMAN (WEYNMAN), Richard, of Whitney, Oxon., gent., grant 20 Sept. 1509, by Thos. Writhe or Wriothesley, Gart., and Roger Machado a̅s Richmont Clar.   Q's Coll. Oxf. MS. 38, fo. 25, copy of grant in French ; Harl. MS. 1359, fo. 8, Grant in Record Office.

„   Sir Richard, of Tame Park, Oxon., Knt., created Baron Wenman of Kill-mainham in Dublin, and Visct. Wenman of Tuam, co. Galway, 25 July 1628, confirmation of coat and quartering, and supporters granted 17 June 1630, by Segar.   Add. MS. 12,225, fo. 118ᵇ.

WENTWORTH, John, of Somerton, Suff., 11 Oct. 1576, by Cooke.   Coat and crest, Harl. MS. 1359, fo. 85ᵇ : Thomas in Harl. MS. 5887, fo. 14.

„   Thomas, Lord, Baron Wentworth of Woodhouse and Visct. Wentworth, confirmed grant of supporters by Segar.   Add. MS. 12,225, fo. 119.

WEOLEY, Thomas, of Camden, co. Gloucs., gent., s. and h. of Christopher and of Alice his wife, d. of William Swetenham of Swettenham in Cheshire, gent., which Christopher was s. of Richard and Margaret his wife, dau. of Walter Aylworth, of Aylworth Hall, co. Glouc., gent., which Richard was s. of Thomas Weoley and Alice his wife, d. of Compton of Compton, co. Warw., which Thomas was s. of William Weoley and of Alice his wife, dau. of William Bovy of Campden aforesᵈ, which William, s. of John, s. of Henry, of Campden, co. Glouc. ; grant of crest to Thomas and the descendants of his father Christopher 25 April 1580, by Cooke.   Harl. MS. 1470, fo. 201, copy of grant, Brit. Mus., and in 1359, fo. 84, and 1441, fo. 12 ; (Guil. 101) ; Crisp's Frag. Geneal., v., 1.

WERGG, Thomas, vintner in Aldersgate St., London, fined for Sheriff, patent circa 1670, by Sir Edw. Bysshe.   Harl. MS. 6179, fo. 59.

WESLID, John, of Winthorpe, co. Linc., 1 or 5 Aug. 1590, by Cooke.   Grants II., 505 ; Harl. MS. 1550, fo. 132ᵇ, for pedigree.

WEST, ..., of London, draper, arg., a fesse dancettée sa. betw. three pellets . . . . by Segar.   Add. MS. 12,225, fo. 117.

„   Francis, of Mincing Lane, London, and Rotherham, Yorks, 1634, ? Visit. : arg., a fesse dancettée betw. three leopards' heads sa.   Crest, etc., out of a mural crown or a griffin's head arg., charged with a fesse dancettée sa. Berry.

„   John, of London, s. of William, s. of John, of Flynt Castle, 15 Oct. 1600, by Camden.   Grants II., 572 ; Misc. Gen. et Her., 3rd S., vol. ii., p. 177, copy of grant, Brit. Mus.

„   Nicholas, of Great Hamden, Buck, quarterly, confirmed 13 Feb. 1560-61 (Harvey's Grants) in a note altered by Cooke, Clar., 12 June 1573.   Add. MS. 16,940, fo. 19 ; Berry.

„   Reynold, co. Brastwick, co. Yorks, who was s. of William, s. of John, of Twynsted, Essex, etc., 23 July 1446, by John Guyon and Roger Legh [Rogier Lygh], Clar., and Roger Durroit, Lancʳ Herald, King of the North of England, Herald to John Dike of Lancaster [" Rogier Durroit antre-ment dit Lancastre Roy de North Dangleterre herault a Johan Duke de Lancastre "].   Cott. MS. Faustina, E. 1, fo. 11, copy of grant, Brit. Mus.; by Wrexworth in Grants II., 639 ; see Harl. MSS. 6140, fo. 47ᵇ [has of West Awchton in com. Yorks], and 1105, fo. 9 [has, with a trick of arms and crest, " Mʳ Fran. West of London, grocer, 4ᵗʰ son of Anthony West of Bolton in Craven in com. Yorke, gent. ; died 23 Jan. and buried in the Church of All Hallows in Bread Street 5 Feb. 1623."]

„   Sir William, of Amberden Hall, Essex, s. of Thomas, descended from West of

Aughton, Yorks, augmentation of coat and gift of crest 1 March 1535-6, 16 Hen. VIII., by Hawley. Harl. MSS. 1069, fo. 12, and 1359, fo. 20ᵇ; Surtees Soc., XLI., p. xxxix; Add. MS. 14,295, fo. 14; Harl. MS. 1116, fo. 16ᵇ, copy of grant.

WEST, William, Esq., and Eleanor his wife, of the family of Ashton of Lever, co. Lanc., father and mother to John West, Esq., and of the bedchamber to K. Chas.; certif. (impaling Ashton) quarterly of four and two crests, 5 Nov. 1633, by Segar. Add. MS. 12,225, fo. 117ᵇ; C. 24 [Visit. of London, 1634], Her. Coll.; Grants I., 365; Guil. 41.

WESTBUREY, Robert, Abbot . . . . by Wriothesley, Gart. Add. MS. 26,702, fo. 57ᵇ, sa., a cross botonnée betw. four leopards' faces or, on a bordure engrailed arg. ten torteaux.

WESTBYE, John, late of Westeby, Yorks, now of Mowbreak, co. Lanc., quarterly. The crest given under the hand and seale of Dalton 20 May 1560. Harl. MSS. 1359, fo. 46, and 5887, fo. 35.

WESTCOMBE, ... of City of Yorke, D. Phys., and Westcombe of Devon and Somersetsh., by W. Ryley. Harl. MS. 6179, fo. 60, trick of arms and crest: Or, two bars Sable, a canton ermine, "quere quarter." Crest, out of a mural crown or a griffin's head argent, beaked sa.

WESTFALLING, Herbert, of Oxford, D.D., 1 March 1575-76, by Cooke. Misc. Gen. et Her., N. S., ii., 55; Harl. MS. 1359, fo. 99ᵇ; Cat. Her. Exhib. Soc. of Antiq., 68.

WESTFIELD, Thomas, D.D., preacher at S. Bartholomew the Great, London, by R. St. George, Clar. Harl. MS. 1105, fo. 10.

WESTMINSTER, City of, 1 Oct. 1601, by Camden. Cott. MS. Faustina, E. 1, 14ᵇ; 1 Oct. 1601, by W. Dethick, Add. MS. 5533, fo. 12ᵇ.

WESTON, John, ... or, an eagle displayed reguardant sa. (same as Richd. Weston of Rugeley), by Segar. Add. MS. 12,225, fo. 118; Harl. MS. 6140, fo. 78.

,, Richard, of Rugeley, co. Staff., Esq., quarterly . . . . by Segar. Add. MS. 12,225, fo. 117ᵇ; Harl. MS. 6140, fo. 78.

,, Sir Richard, elected Baron Weston of Neyland, arms and crest as John Weston and grant of supporters 16 May 1629, by Segar. Add. MS. 12,225, fo. 118.

WESTROW, Thomas, of London, grocer, s. of John, patent 24 (29) March or April 1613, by Camden. Harl. MS. 6059, fo. 26ᵇ; Guil. 95 has 24ᵗʰ of March; Sheriff of London 1625, died 31 Dec. 1625 in Harl. MS. 1422, fo. 13ᵇ, trick of arms and crest.

WESTWOOD, Humphrey, s. of Simon, of co. Worc., confirmation of coat and crest granted 24 Nov. 1602, 45 Eliz., by Segar. Add. MS. 12,225, fo. 118ᵇ; Guil. 102; Harl. MS. 5887, fo. 77ᵇ.

WETHIS, William Thomas, of Lauvenith in the principality of Wales, descended from William, s. of Thomas, s. of Griffith, s. of William Wethis de Langathbyn, gent., by Thomas Writhe or Wriothesley, Gart. Harl. MS. 1359, fo. 57.

WEYMOUTH, (Thomas Thynne) Visct., quartering and supporters 23 Dec. 1682, by Sir W. Dugdale. Harl. MS. 6834, fo. 178; Grants III., fo. 179.

WEYMOUTH TOWN AND MELCOMBE REGIS, co. Dorset, 1 May 1592, by Cooke. G. A. Ellis' Weymouth, 1829, 8vo, p. 198, copy of grant, Brit. Mus.

WEYNS, Jacob, a Belgian, s. of Jacob, s. of Peter, confirmed . . . . Oct. 1573, by W. Dethick, York Herald. Stowe MS. 676, fo. 42ᵇ; Q's Coll. Oxf. MS. 37, fo. 54, copy of grant in Latin.

WHADCOCK, Humphrey, of Buckley (or Birchley) Place, par. of Corley, co. Warw., 11 May 1699, by T. St. George, Gart. and Clar., vert, a chev. arg. betw. 3 pheasant cocks or, combed and wattled gu.: Crest, a dragon's head per pale or, guttee de sang and vert, erased gu. Grants IV., fo. 291.

WHALLEY, Edmond or Edward, Abbott of our Lady at York (1521—9), [Argent,

N N

on a chev. betw. three whales' heads erased, lying fessways Sable, as many birds volant of the field], Whaley, on a chief or betw. 2 lions passant, a cinquefoil [rose ?] gu. Add. MS. 26,702. fo. 54.

WHARTON, Sir Thomas, Kt., Lord Wharton of Wharton, co. Westmorland, arms and crest confirmed (? grant of supporters). Barker's Grants, Harl. MS. 5846, fo. 112ᵇ ; Stowe MS. 692, fo. 95.

„ Thomas, Lord, augmentation for services against " our ancient enemies the Scots," St. Katharine's Eve, 34 Hen. VIII., 1542, by Roy. Warrant *temp.* Ed. VI. to Harvey, Norr. (1550-3); MSS. Ashm. 834, fo. 42, and 858, fo. 40, copies of grants, Bodleian Lib. ; *see also* Harl. MS. 5846, fo. 112ᵇ, and Stowe MS. 692, fo. 95.

WHEELER, ..., of London, goldsmith, who came out of Worcestershire, quarterly, by Cooke. Harl. MS. 1359, fo. 86, same as the next entry; Add. MS. 4966, fo. 91ᵇ ; Harl. MS. 1172, fo. 2.

„ . . . ., of Burbury, co. Warwick, formerly of co. Worc., 1585, Visitation ? . . . ., or, a chev. betw. 3 leopards' heads [faces] sa. ; 1, crest, on a ducal coronet or, an eagle displayed gu. ; 2, on a five-leaved coronet or, an eagle displayed sa. Le Neve's MS. 122. Berry.

„ George, of Martin, co. Worc., ... 1585, by Cooke's Deputy. Stowe MS. 670, fo. 11ᵇ.

WHELLER, Henry, ..., Wilts, ... (Harvey's Grants), Add. MS. 16,940, fo. 9.

WHEELER, Humphrey, of London, ..., by Cooke. Harl. MS. 1422, fo. 77ᵇ.

„ Nicholas, of London, ..., by Cooke. Stowe MS. 670, fo. 12. *See* Edith Parry.

WHEELAR, Richard, of Lincoln's Inn, Esq., ... 1584, by Cooke. Add. MS. 14,295, fo. 39ᵇ ; Harl. MS. 1359, fo. 117 ; Add. MS. 4966, fo. 20ᵇ.

WHELAR, Thomas, of London, ... 1568, by Cooke, erm. on a chief sa. three lions rampant guardant arg. ; no crest. Harl. MS. 1359, fo. 88 ; Add. MS. 4966, fo. 19ᵇ.

WHETLEY, William, of South Creke, Norfolk, confirmed . . . . 1562. (Harvey's Grants), Add. MS. 16,940, fo. 16 ; Harl. MS. 5887, fo. 28.

WHETSTONE, Bernard, Augmentation for [" his valiant service on horseback upon the enemy nere Zutphen the 22 Sept. 1586 "] from Robert, Earl of Leicester, 30 Sept. 1586 at Zutphen. Harl. MS. 7017, fo. 177 ; Whitestone in Stowe MS. 677, fo. 55 ; Le Neve's MS. 507.

WHYDDON, Sir John, of Devon, Kt., confirmed 12 Nov. 1564. (Harvey's Grants), Add. MS. 16,940, fo. 19, and Berry.

WHISTLER, ..., of co. Cambridge, ..., ? by W. Segar. Harl. MS. 1105, fo. 30.

WHITACKERS, Stephen, of Westbury under the playne, Wilts, gent. (16 March 1560-1 in Q's Coll. Oxf. MS. 145, fo. 42ᵇ, and Berry), and ? again 17 March 1574-5, 20 Eliz., by Sir G. Dethick, sa., three mascles arg., two and one ; Crest, a horse passant or. Harl. MSS. 1441, fo. 86ᵇ, and 5887, fo. 42.

WHITBROKE, Hugh, of Bridgnorth, Shropshire, attested 1563, by Harvey, Clar. Harl. MS. 1116, fo. 55.

WHITBY, *see* WILBY.

WHITCOMBE, ... (? Somerset), arg., 3 pales sa., thereon 3 eagletts displayed of the first, by Sir G. Dethick, Gart. Add. MS. 26,753, fo. 122.

WHITE, ..., of South Warnborough, Hants, crest [Stowe MS. 692, fo. 94, has] (a hawk's head vert, etc. [" betwene ij wings, the first or, the other argent holding in his becke a braunche purple, the flowres silver the leves vert "]), Arms, arg., a chev. gu. betw. three parrots [popinjays] all vert. [Harl. MS. 5846, fo. 109ᵇ, has the same crest without the word purple, and adds, " The coat is more auntient then this Creast as appeareth by old monuments in South Warnborne Church, being argent, a cheveron gules between 3 parrots all vert beaked & legged gules all wᵗʰin a bordure

azur besante."]   Barker's Grants, Harl. MS. 5846, fo. 109ᵇ ; Stowe MS.
692, fo. 94 ; Harl. MS. 5887, fo. 32 [has a trick of the arms and crest as
in Harl. MS. 5846].

WHITE, Edmund, citizen and haberdasher, of London, s. of William (John in
Guil. 399), of Mickleton, co. Glonc., testified arms and crest 10 April
1616, by Segar.   Add. MS. 12,225, fo. 119 ; see Harl. MS. 6140,
fo. 63.

„   James, of Exeter, see under Walter WHITE.

WHYTE, John, of Southwick in Hampshire, gent., grant 29 May, 35 Hen. VIII.,
1543, by Hawley (Add. MS. 7098, fo. 76ᵇ).   Add. MS. 7098, fo. 75, 76ᵇ ;
Stowe MS. 692, fo. 95ᵇ ; Harl. MS. 5846, fo. 113ᵇ, among Barker's
Grants ; Az., a cross quarterly ermine and or, etc.

[Add. MS. 7098, fo. 75, has "The Armes & Crest of John Whyte of
Southwyke in the county of Southt. gent. he beareth azure a playne crosse
ferminge the field ermynes and gold quarterly inte'changed between 4
falcons silver, becked & membered gold, about every legg a bell of the
same, chessed gules, upon the crosse a frett between 4 fuscalx gules, upon
his helme soe issuing forth of a cronall gold and gules pty p. pale a camells
head azure langued & oreiled gold, about his neck a ga[r]land of roses
genles & silver stalked & leaved vert, manteled azure, doubled silver, given
by the said Clarencienlx by patent dat. 29 May A. 35. H. 8."]

WHYT or WHITE, John, Bp. of Lincoln, 1553—6, Patent, arms, 5 April, 1 of Q.
Mary (1554), by ? Hawley.   Add. MS. 16,940, fo. 206ᵇ.

[The arms granted by Thomas Hawley, Clar., were : " Silver & genles
embateled p chevron three Roses entrechainged of the felde, stalked and
leved Vert.   Geven and graunted by me Thomas Hawley als Clarenseulx
Kyng of Armes the flyfte day of Aprill in the first yere of the Reyne of our
Sonreyne Quene Mary."   The Arms are ensigned with a mitre, based
probably on the seal used by the Bishop, which bore the arms, three roses
stalked and leaved, on the fesse point a trefoil slipped (or cinquefoil).]

Bp. of Winchester 1556—60, 5 Jan., 3 and 4 Philip and Mary,
1556-7, [confirmed], by Sir G. Dethick, Gart.   Q's Coll. Oxf. MS. 39,
fo. 81, copy of grant ; Grants I., 87 ; Harl. MS. 1359, fo. 68ᵇ ; Arms :
Per chevron embattled [or and gu.], three roses [counterchanged]
slipped, etc.

[The above arms were confirmed by a patent in Latin by Sir Gilbert
Dethick, Garter, 5 Jan., 3 and 4 of Philip and Mary, with the addition of
a chief gules charged with three hour glasses argent, framed or.   The arms
ensigned with a mitre.

Riland Bedford (Blazon of Episcopacy, p. 123) says that the Bishop's
monument bore the above arms, with a lion passant-guardant on the chief.
This alteration in his arms has not been traced.

The Bishop was buried in Winchester Cathedral, and whilst Warden of
the College there in 1555 had a brass engraved and laid down in the
College Chapel for his own monumental memorial.   At each angle or
corner of the stone was a shield of arms bearing the same coat [Azure,
three plates each charged with three bars wavy vert], with a mullet for
difference, as noted by Anthony à Wood, who visited the College in
February 1684.   " At each corner his arms, viz., a mullet between three
fountains."   (Her. and Geneal., iv., p. 114 n.)

The arms, with the lion of England on the chief, are attributed on a
vellum painting in Vincent's Hampsh., fo. 158, to " Richard Whyte
utriusque Juris Dr A° 1574," of Basingstoke, per chevron embattled
argent and gules, three roses counterchanged, on a chief gules a lion of
England, all within a bordure ermine.   Supporters, two dragons Argent.
Crest, a heron (?) resting his dexter foot on an honr glass.   No authority
for these Arms has been found.]

WHYT, John, erm., on a bend sa. 3 peacocks' heads rased or ; Crest, a peacock's head rased or, by ? Sir G. Dethick, Gart. Add. MS. 26,753, fo. 122^b.

WHITE, John, of Ashtead, Surrey, ... 1586, by Cooke. Stowe MS. 670, fo. 81 ; Ald. MS. 4966, fo. 87.

„ John, of London, chiefest governor of Virginia, quarterly of 8, crest granted, by W. Dethick, Gart. Q's Coll. Oxf. MS. 36, fo. 120, copy of grant ; 1, coat of augmentation ; 2, arg., a chev. betw. three goats' heads erased, etc. ; 3, Wymarke ; 4, Wyat ; 5, Killyowe ; 6, Gaker ; 7, Buddyen ; 8, Butler. [See Additions and Corrections.]

„ John, of London, quarterly of 4 [1586—1588 ?], by Cooke. Harl. MS. 1359, fo. 92 ; Add. MS. 4966, fo. 58^b ; [1], or, a chev. vert betw. 3 goats' heads erased sa., a crescent for diff. [White] ; [2, A., on a bend. betw. two cottices azure, 3 escutcheons ar.], Wymarke ; [3, gu., 2 bars gemelles betw. 3 martlets A.], Wyatt ; [4, A. (or), a chevron betw. 2 cinquefoils in chief and a mullet of six points in base all sable], Williowe [Killiowe].

„ John, of Tuxford, Notts, ... by Cooke. Harl. MSS. 1359, fo. 93, and 1422, fo. 62^b, gu., a chev. vair (argt. and az.) between three lions rampant or ; Add. MS. 4966, fo. 37.

„ John, of Dorchester, Oxon., ... 1645, by W. Ryley, Lanc. Her. Stowe MS. 703, fo. 63. Same arms as John, of Southwick, 1543, above.

„ Mary, dau. of .... ; Foster and Bradley quartered, by Cooke. Harl. MS. 1359, fo. 98 ; Stowe MS. 670, fo. 79 ; Add. MS. 4966, fo. 36.

WHYTE, Robert, of Denham, Bucks, ... 1593, by Cooke. Harl. MSS. 1359, fo. 106, and 1422, fo. 62^b ; Add. MS. 4966, fo. 92^b.

WHITE, Stephen, of London, ... 1646, by W. Ryley, Lanc. Her. Stowe MS. 703, fo. 64.

WHYTE, Thomas, of London (Maior 1 Q. Mary, 1553-4), coat and crest. Harl. MS. 5846, fo. 114 ; Barker's Grants.

„ Thomas, of the manor of Fytleford, Dorset, esq. (devised, ordained and assigned, given and) granted 12 June 1559, 1 Q. Eliz., by Harvey. Q's Coll. Oxf. MS. 38, fo. 74, copy of grant ; Harl. MS. 1359, fo. 6 ; Grants II., 551 ; Add. MS. 16,940, fo. 28 ; Harl. MS. 1441, fo. 139^b.

WHITE, Thomas, Bp. of Peterborough, arms only 29 Jan. 1685-6, by Sir W. Dugdale, Gart., and H. St. George, Clar. Harl. MS. 6834, fo. 178 ; Grants III., fo. 293 ; Lansd. MS. 867, fo. 52.

„ Walter, High Sheriff of Exeter, and } sons of Richard, late of Newton, Devon,
„ James, of Exeter,   } 24 March 1641-2, by J. Borough, Gart. Harl. MS. 1105, fo. 58 ; Guil. 104 ; (23 May 1642 in Grants II., 556).

„ William, ... , 1 March 1467, sa., on a chev. erm. betw. three flagons with spouts ar. as many martlets gu. Berry.

„ William, of Duffield, co. Derby, confirmed .... 1602, by Camden. Morgan's Sphere ; Guil. 152 : gules, a chevron betw. three goats' heads erased argt. (B') [Bart. ?].

WHITEBROOKE, Hugh, of Bridgnorth, Salop, gen., 20 Mar. 1559-60, by Sir G. Dethick. Harl. MS. 1441, fo. 64 ; Q's Coll. Oxf. MS. 115, fo. 6, as Whitbroke ; Harl. MS. 1116, fo. 55 ; see also Harl. MS. 1116, fo. 55, Katherine Jacob.

WHITEHALGH, Joseph, of Whitehalgh, co. Staff., crest 16 July 1634, by Sir H. St. George, Norr. MS. Ashm. 858, fo. 161, copy of grant, Bodleian Lib.

WHITEHEAD or WHITHED, Robert, of Gilden-Sutton, Chesh., ... July 1613, by R. St. George, Norr. Harl. MS. 1422, fo. 14 ; Add. MS. 14,295, fo. 75^b.

WHITESTONES (see WHETSTONE), ... 22 Sept. 1586, arg., a lion rampant sa., with augmentation of a rose on a canton ermine. Berry.

WHITFIELD, Ralph, of Whitfield, Northumbld., crest 1 June 1591, by Ed. Knight, Norr. Harl. MS. 1069, fo. 17 ; Add. MS. 14,295, fo. 27^b.

„ Thomas, of Mortlake, Surrey, s. of Robert, of the same ; Whitfield quartering

Whetley, ... 1616, by Segar and Camden. Add. MS. 12,225, fo. 119ᵇ; 1606 in Guil. 62.

WHITGIFT, John, Bp. of Worcester, confirmed 2 May 1577, by Sir G. Dethick. Harl. MS. 1441, fo. 61ᵇ; Q's Coll. Oxf. MS. 145, fo. 1ᵇ; Stowe MS. 703, fo. 4ᵇ.

„ John, Archbp. of Canterbury, s. of Henry, late of Grimsby, co. Linc., s. of John, of Yorks. . . . . 1588, by Cooke. Harl. MSS. 1359, fo. 108ᵇ, and 1422, fo. 94; confirmation (grant) 22 Jan. 1598-9, by Wᵐ Dethick, Gart., and Camden. Stowe MS. 676, fo. 124; Q's Coll. Oxf. MS. 36, fo. 68, copy of grant; Add. MS. 4966, fo. 57ᵇ.

WHITGREVE, Robert (one of the compters of the Exchequer), grant in French 13 Aug. 1442 (20 Hen. VI.), by Humphrey, Earl of Stafford. (? Staff. Visit., 1614, fo. 82ᵇ [William Salt Soc., reprint, p. 309]); MS. Ashm. 858, fo. 93 (copy of grant, Bodleian Lib.); Guil. Intro., p. 7, gives 26 Hen. VI.; Camden's Remains, 217, 1st Ed.; Le Neve's MS. 506.

WHITHERE, Christopher, of Aldersham, Sussex, s. of John, of Newsars, Wilts, descended from a younger branch of the family settled at Wallop, Hants; grant Feb. 1593-4, by W. Dethick, Gart. Stowe MSS. 676, fo. 91ᵇ, and 108, fo. 113ᵇ; Q's Coll. Oxf. MS. 36, fo. 37, 44, copies of grant.

WHITLEY, Col. Roger, gent. Usher of the Privy Chamber, augmentation at Brussels July 1659, by Walker, Gart. Her. Coll., 4.

WHITLOCK, Richard, gent., s. of Richard, gent., grant quarterly coat and crest 20 April 1592, by W. Dethick, Gart. Stowe MS. 676, fo. 87ᵇ, 99ᵇ; Q's Coll. Oxf. MS. 36, fo. 17, copy of grant.

WHITMORE, Anne (dau. of Sir William Whitmore of London), Lady Anne Sawyer, wife of Sir Edmund Sawyer and daughter of Whitmore, descended from Humfry Houghton of Manchester in Lancashire, her great Grandfather, and from Moseley and Aldersey. Confirmation of Sawyer arms [blason in English, Latin and French: " B. a fess checquy O. S. between 3 Seapyes A. bequed & membred G.,"] impaling Whitmore [" viz', V. frette 8 pieces O. a mullet difference & bearing "], Houghton (in an escocheon of pretence) [" Houghton in pretence upon Whitmore, viz., S. 3 barrs A. in chief two Mullets O."], " Aprill 9 Anno Dom. 1627, Segar, J. Philipot, Somerset [Her.], 2 Whitmore, 3 Haughton." Add. MS. 12,225, fo. 100.

„ John, a haberdasher of London, arms and crest 1594, by W. Dethick, Gart., for which [he had] £6 13s. 4d. Arms of Whitmore of Cheshire, differenced with a canton or, thereon a cinquefoil az.; entered by R. Brooke, York Herald. Harl. MS. 1453, fo. 32.

„ William, of Rotherham, Yorks, crest 4 Feb., 7 Eliz., 1564-5, by Flower. MS. Ashm. 858, fo. 156, copy of grant, Bodleian Lib.

„ William, late citizen and merchant of London (s. of William, out of Lanc.): died 7 Aug. 1593; granted 13 Nov. 1593 for him and his three sons, by W. Dethick, Gart. Stowe MS. 676, fo. 91; Harl. MS. 1115, fo. 2ᵇ; Q's Coll. Oxf. MS. 36, fo. 33, copy of grant, and MS. 146, fo. 136.

WHITTINGHAM, Timothy, s. of William, Dean of Durham, by W. Dethick. Caius Coll. Camb. MS. 551; Harl. MS. 6140, fo. 23.

„ William, of Balkes, Yorks, out of Cheshire, confirmed at Durham 5 or 10 Sept. 1575, by Flower. Harl. MS. 1453, fo. 74, where styled Dean of Durham; MS. Ashm. 834, fo. 14, copy of grant, Bodleian Lib.; Stowe MS. 676, fo. 47ᵇ; Q's Coll. Oxf. MS. 37, fo. 62, copy of confirmation in Latin; Grants II., fo. 621; Guil. 246.

WHITINGTON or WHITTINGTON, Capt. Luke, royalist, ratified and confirmed 12 Sept. 1660, by Sir Edw. Walker, Gart. Add. MSS. 14,293, fo. 104, and 14,294, fo. 35; Harl. MS. 1172, fo. 71ᵇ; Guil. 412, gu., a fesse checquy or and az. betw. six martlets argt.; Harl. MS. 1172, fo. 71ᵇ, perhaps by Bysshe.

WHITTINGTON, Matthew, of Louth, co. Linc., gent., descended of the house of

WITTINGTON, of Norbury, co. Staff., confirmed 25 May 1587. by Cooke. Add. MS. 17,506, fo. 36ᵇ; Harl. MS. 1359, fo. 107ᵇ; Q's Coll. [Oxf. ?] MS. 146, fo. 472; Add. MS. 4966, fo. 30.

WHITTLE, Dame Elizabeth, dau. of William (s. of Nicholas), late of co. pal. of Lanc., decᵈ, and now wife of the Hon. Sir Stephen Fox, Knt., 1ˢᵗ clerk of the green cloth and a lord of the Treasnry, etc., 13 Sept. 1688, by T. St. George, Gart. and Clar. Harl. MS. 6834, fo. 67; Grants IV., fo. 15, "chevron vair"; Alteration 24 May 1694, by Sir T. St. George. Stowe MS. 677, fo. 79; Grants IV., fo. 164-5, "chevron fimbriated"; Harl. MS. 1085, fo. 57.

WHYTTELL, William, of London, gu., a chev. erm. betw. 3 talbots' heads erased or, ... 1587, by Cooke. Harl. MSS. 1359, fo. 108, and 1422, fo. 94; Burke says Whettell of Thetford and Ampton, Suff.; Add. MS. 4966, fo. 64.

WHITWICK, Francis, of Whitwick, co. Staff., gent., s. of Humphrey, s. of John, exemplified 22 Dec. 1612, by Camden. Harl. MS. 6059, fo. 25ᵇ; Grants II., 524, and allowed 16 April 1613, Harl. MS. 6059, fo. 26ᵇ; Guil. 333; quarterly in Harl. MS. 6140, fo. 31ᵇ.

WICHELALSH (WICHALSE), Nicholas, of Cheudley, Devon, crest 10 Aug. 1545, by ? Hawley. Add. MS. 16,940, fo. 201.

WICKERLIN or WECKHERLIN, George Rudolphus, a Swede, confirmed 24 April 1639, 15 Chas. I., by Borough. Add. MS. 14,295, fo. 96.

WICKHAM, William, Bp. of Lincoln (1 s. of John, of Walden, Essex, confirmed 8 Dec. 1584, by Cooke. Harl. MS. 1359, fo. 99; MS. Ashm. 844, fo. 59, copy of grant, Bodleian Lib.; Guil. 107; Add. MS. 4966, fo. 20ᵇ.

WICKINS (Robert in Guil. 396), of Stoke Bruern, Northants, 23 May 1642, by Borough. Harl. MS. 1105, fo. 58; Robert, 1640, in Berry.

WICKLIFF, Francis, of Richmondshire, Yorks, ... 1575, by Flower and Glover, Somerset Her. Add. MS. 14,295, fo. 74ᵇ (47ᵇ).

WICKS, Henry, esq., late paymaster of his majesties works over all England, 20 Feb. 1649-50, by Arthur Squibb, Clar. Add. MS. 26,758, fo. 16ᵇ, az., a fesse wavy betw. three towers 2 and 1 ....; Weekes in Harl. MS. 6832, fo. 413ᵇ.

WICKSTEED, John, of Wicksteed, Cheshire, crest 13 Nov. 1607, by R. St. George, Norr.; MS. Ashm. 858, fo. 142-3, copy of grant, Bodleian Lib.

WIDNALL, William, of Tandridge, Surrey, 23 Nov. 1575, by Cooke. Harl. MS. 1359, fo. 87; Add. MS. 4966, fo. 66; Harl. MS. 1561, fo. 161.

WYDNAM, ..., of Sussex, ..., by Cooke. Harl. MS. 1359, fo. 92.

WIDSON or WIELDSON, Bartholomew, of Loudham, Notts, gent., 10 Aug. 1574, by Sir G. Dethiek. Harl. MS. 1441, fo. 80ᵇ; Q's Coll. Oxf. MS. 145, fo. 32ᵇ.

WIGFALL, Zachary, s. of George, of co. Derby, confirmed ...., by Segar. Add. MS. 12,225, fo. 119ᵇ; ? the original in Harl. MS. 1410, fo. 46, 2 escallops in chief added by Sir Wᵐ Dugdale. Harl. MS. 1441, fo. 160ᵇ.

WIGHT, ..., of Barkingwood, Essex, 1 July 1656. Harl. MSS. 6179, fo. 49ᵇ, and 6140, fo. 65.

„ John, of London, "now of great age," grant 2 Feb. 1587-8, 30 Eliz., by W. Dethick, Gart. Stowe MS. 676, fo. 74ᵇ; Q's Coll. Oxf. MS. 37, fo. 108, copy of grant; see Harl. MS. 5887, fo. 67ʰ.

WIGHTMAN, William, of Harrow Hill, Middx., confirmation (grant 14 July) 1562. (Harvey's Grants), Add. MS. 16,940, fo. 35. See BURKE.

WIGHTWICK, see WHITWICK.

WIGLEY, Thomas, of Midleton, co. Derby, crest 22 June 1611, by Sir R. St. George, Norr. MS. Ashm. 858, fo. 161, copy of grant, Bodleian Lib.; Add. MS. 14,295, fo. 80ᵇ; Grants I., 380; Reliquary xxii., 244; John in Harl. MS. 6179, fo. 13; Thomas in Harl. MS. 6140, fo. 41, 71ᵇ.

WIGMORE, Thomas, of Shobdon, co. Hereford, ... 1586, by Cooke's deputy. Stowe MS. 670, fo. 15ᵇ. Berry.

WIGSTEN, ..., ermene et ermilie (incomplete). Barker's Grants, Harl. MS. 5846, fo. 105 ; Add. MS. 26,702, fo. 35ᵇ ; crest. [? Arms, per chev. erm. and ermines on a chevron per chev. sa. and ar. three estoiles or ; Crest, a lion's head erased per pale gu. and az. guttée d'or].

WILBRAHAM, Thomas, of Woodhay, Chesb., confirmed 28 July 1580, by Flower. MS. Ashm. 834, fo. 147, copy of grant, Bodleian Lib. ; Guil. 192.

WILBY, ..., Mayor of Chester in the yeare of the Visitation 1613, confirmed 1613, by R. St. George, Norr. Stowe MS. 706, fo. 19ᵇ ; called Whitby in Harl. MS. 6179, fo. 14.

WILCOCKS, Henry, Archdeacon of Leics., ... Add. MS. 26,702, fo. 60.

„ Roger (impaling Swann, see SWANN), at funerall, by Cooke's deputy. Stowe MS. 670, fo. 12.

WILCOCKES, Thomas, of Leicestershire, ... 1590, by Cooke. Harl. MS. 1359, fo. 101ᵇ.

WILDE, John, of Kettleworth, Notts, by Cooke, Clar. Stowe MS. 670, fo. 54ᵇ ; Harl. MS. 1555, fo. 155.

„ Thomas, of Canterbury, crest by Drury, Dep. to Cooke, Clar. Stowe MS. 670, fo. 47ᵇ.

WYLDEGOSE, John, of Saltherst, Sussex, gift .... 1558. (Harvey's Grants), Add. MS. 16,940, fo. 54ᵇ.

WYLDGOS, John, of Iridge, Sussex, Esq., ... 1586, by Cooke. Harl. MSS. 1359, fo. 110ᵇ, and 1422, fo. 93ᵇ ; Guil. 289 ; Add. MS. 4966, fo. 68ᵇ.

WILFORD, John, of the manor of Elsings als Norys Hall in par. of Enfield, Middx., coat and crest. Barker's Grants, Harl. MS. 5846, fo. 109 ; Stowe MS. 692, fo. 94.

WYLFORD, John, of Enfield, Middx., gent., an old patent confirmed to him 1586, by Cooke. Harl. MS. 1359, fo. 91 ; 1580 in Harl. MS. 1422, fo. 93 ; Add. MS. 4966, fo. 69ᵇ.

WILKES, ..., Clerk of the Council, ... by Cooke. Stowe MS. 670, fo. 9 ; Harl. MS. 5887, fo. 1.

„ Alice (dau. of Thomas or John, of London), ux. Judge Owen ; first mar. to Alderm. Elkyn ; arms and crest granted 4 Dec. 1595, by Lee. Add. MS. 14,295, fo. 22ᵇ ; Q's Coll. Oxf. MS. 146, fo. 185 ; Harl. MSS. 1069, fo. 14ᵇ, and 1438, fo. 15ᵇ ; Stowe MS. 702, fo. 115.

„ John, of Leighton Buzzard, Beds, by J. Borough, Gart. Harl. MSS. 1105, fo. 56, and 1441, fo. 58 ; Add. MS. 26,702, fo. 91 ; Harl. MS. 6179, fo. 46.

WILKS, Luke, chief yeoman of H.M.'s removing wardrobe, also Mathew and Mark, his elder brothers, and Joan, their sister, being children of Edward Wilks of Layton Beaudesert (Leighton Buzzard), Bucks, decᵈ, 22 June 1670, by Walker. Add. MSS. 14,293, fo. 75, and 14,294, fo. 22ᵇ ; Harl. MS. 1172, fo. 61ᵇ ; Guil. 403.

WILKINS, John, of Cole Orton, co. Leic., 10 Dec. 1685, by Sir W. Dugdale, Gart. and Clar. Harl. MS. 6834, fo. 178 ; Grants III., 280 ; Lansd. MS. 867, fo. 52.

WYLKYNS, John, of Stoke, Kent, gent.. 16 Oct., 5 and 6 Philip and Mary, 1558, by Sir G. Dethick, Gart. Add. MS. 16,940, fo. 25ᵇ ; confirmed for that it was Dalton's gift, Grants I., 151 ; Harl. MS. 1359, fo. 76ᵇ.

WILKINSON, Edward, of Charlton, Kent, Yeoman of the Mouth to our late sovereign Lord of famous memory Hen. VIII. and Q. Anne his wife, and also to late Ed. VI. his son, and at the present Maister Cooke of the Household to our most dread Sovereign Lady Q. Eliz., etc., for 30 years ; granted at London 20 April 1559, by Hervey, Clar. Harl. MSS. 1359, fo. 66, and 1470, fo. 269, copy of grant, Brit. Mus. ; Add. MS. 16,940, fo. 11ᵇ ; Guil. 380.

WILKINSON, Hugh, of Old Buckenham, Norfolk, gift 13 Sept. 1564. (? Harvey's Grants), Add. MS. 16,940, fo. 54ᵇ.

WILKINSON alias HARLYN, John, of London, 3 Aug. 1519, by Wriothesley and Benolte. (By Sir C. Barker in Stowe MS. 702); Misc. Gen. et Her., 2nd S., vol. ii., p. 200, facsimile ; Harl. MS. 5846, fo. 107 ; Stowe MS. 692, fo. 93 ; Add. MS. 26,702, fo. 38.

WILKINSON, John, of Havering atte Bower, Essex, quarterly, confirmed .... 1562 .... (Harvey's Grants), Add. MS. 16,940, fo. 29ᵇ.

„ Richard, of Wateringbury, Kent, one of the six clarks of the Chancery, confirmation 14 Sept. 1605, by Camden. Harl. MS. 6059, fo. 19ᵇ ; Guil. 163 ; Harl. MS. 5887, fo. 16ᵇ.

„ William, of Dorrington, co. Durham, 18 or 28 Sept. 1538, by Hawley : gu., a fesse (another a chev.) vair betw. three unicorns erm. Berry ; Edmondson's Armory ; Fragments Fam. Hist., by Sus. P. Flory, 1896, plate a.

„ William, of Bolton upon Dearne, Yorks, gent., arms confirmed and crest given 13 Sept., 6 Q. Eliz., 1564, by Flower. Add. MS. 14,295, fo. 33ᵇ ; Harl. MS. 1359, fo. 32ᵇ ; John in Harl. MS. 6104, fo. 69.

WILLAN, James, s. of Leonard, of Kingston on Hull, confirmed 1 May 1617, on the warrant of the Scottish Herald 25 April 1617, by R. St. George, Norr. Misc. Gen. et Her., 3rd S., vol. i., p. 60 ; Stowe MS. 714, fo. 177 ; Harl. MS. 1470, fo. 3, copy of grant, Brit. Mus. ; Grants II., 599ᵇ ; Guil. 363 ; Harl. MS. 5887, fo. 95ᵇ, and 6140, fo. 73ᵇ.

WILLETT, Thomas, of Waltham Stowe, ... by Cooke. Harl. MS. 1359, fo. 93 ; Add. MS. 4966, fo. 36ᵇ.

WILLEY, John, s. of Ralph, of Houghton in the Bpk. of Durham, 18 May 1615, by R. St. George. Surtees Soc., XLI., xlviii.

WYLLEY, Nicholas, of Monmouth, ... 1558, by .... Harl. MS. 1116, fo. 58.

WILLIAMS, Sir Abraham, "anciently of Tredare in Wales but now of Westminster," attested Williams ["Parti per pale B. & S. 3 flower de luces O." Blason in English, Latin and French in Add. MS. 12,225, fo. 120 : Williams "quartering G. 3 Castles triple towered, ports ouvert A. and impaling his wife S. 3 dexter hands erect & couped at yᵉ wrist A. Motto, Me flos Virtutis adornat." Harl. MS. 6140, fo. 81ᵇ, calls the impalement Hanchell] quartering Hanchett and impaling .... by Segar. Add. MS. 12,225, fo. 120 ; Harl. MS. 6140, fo. 81ᵇ.

„ Adam, of Sloford, Devon, grant 20 Nov. 1538, by Hawley, Clar. Add. MS. 16,399, fo. 76ᵇ (and 90), copy of grant, Brit. Mus.

„ Sir James, of Tallowcrowthe (Telacconth), co. Carmarthen, coat and crest. Barker's Grants, Harl. MS. 5846, fo. 111ᵇ ; Stowe MS. 692, fo. 94ᵇ.

WILLIAMS alias BYLLESDON, John, gent., 25 Sept., 13 Ed. IV. (1473), by W. Hawkeslowe, Clar. Add. MS. 17,506, fo. 37.

WILLIAMS, John, of Hadenham, co. Camb., by Cooke. Stowe MS. 670, fo. 33.

„ John, D.D., Chaplain in ordinary, preb. of Canterbury, and rector of St. Mildred's, London, etc. (died Bp. of Chichester), 28 Oct. 1696, by T. St. George, Gart. and Clar. Grants IV., fo. 233.

„ Joseph, of Southwark, Surrey, in remainder to the arms James Shaw of the same, if his line becomes extinct, 28 Jan. 1668-9, by Sir E. Bysshe. Harl. MS. 1105, fo. 40 ; Bysshe's Grants, 33.

WILLIAMS alias CROMWELL, Richard, of London, gent., 17 July 1534, by Tonge, Clar. Add. MS. 14,295, fo. 92.

WILLIAMS, Roger, of Langibbie Castle. co. Monmouth, Esq., 16 March 1575-6, 18 Q. Eliz., by Cooke. Harl. MS. 1470, fo. 188, copy of grant, Brit. Mus., and also in Harl. MS. 1359, fo. 83ᵇ ; Guil. 391, who says also by Flower, Norr. ; copy of grant (Brit. Mus.), Add. MS. 5524, fo. 192.

WILLIAMSON, Joseph, keeper of H.M.'s paper office for matters of state and council, Whitehall, and Clerk of P.C. extraordinary, etc., alteration 9 Feb. 1670-1, by Walker. Add. MSS. 14,293, fo. 81, and 14,294, fo. 24 ; Harl.

MS. 1172, fo. 69ᵇ; Stowe MS. 714, fo. 129, says 23ʳᵈ Feb.; Guil. 133 says 1ˢᵗ, and of Melbeck Hall, Cumberland; Le Neve's MS. 457, coat of augmentation and supporters, letters patent 1 March 1682-3.

WILLIAMSON, Nicholas, of Northts., gift . . . . 1557. (Harvey's Grants), Add. MS. 16,940, fo. 8ᵇ.

„   Nicholas, of Tisemore (Tusemore), Oxon., ... 1595, by Lee. Harl. MS. 1422, fo. 124.

„   Richard, of Gainsborough, co. Linc., ... 1602, by Camden. Morgan's Sphere, 118; rather to Giles, of Marksha [?], Notts. 7 May 1602, Harl. MSS. 6140, fo. 35, and 6179, fo. 11ᵇ.

„   Thomas, of Scarborough, Yorks, crest, gift 14 Feb. 1557, by Harvey, confirmed . . . . 1565, 8 Q. Eliz., by Flower (a knight, and one of the bayliffes of the town, Add. MS. 14,295, fo. 39ᵇ, 74). Harl. MSS. 1069, fo. 27, 1359, fo. 34ᵇ, and 6140, fo. 68ᵇ; Add. MS. 16,940, fo. 8ᵇ; Guil. 134; see Harl. MS. 6140, fo. 68ᵇ to 75.

„   ? Sir Thomas, of Gt. Markham, Bart., testified 30 March 1633, by John Borough. MS. Ashm. 858, fo. 160, copy of grant, Bodleian Lib.; Harl. MS. 6140, fo. 35.

WILLINGHAM, ..., a vellum scocheon only subscribed, by Cooke. Stowe MS. 670, fo. 62ᵇ.

WILLIS, Thomas, D. Med. Oxon., Sedley prof. Nat. phil., fellow of Coll. of Med., London, and of the Royal Socy., etc., 10 May 1670, by Walker. Add. MSS. 14,293, to. 76, and 14,294, fo. 22; Harl. MSS. 1172, fo. 61ᵇ, 71, and 6179, fo. 78ᵇ.

WILLMER als WULFMERE, Thomas, of Rnyton, co. Warwick, 16 Feb. 1582-3, 25 Q. Eliz., by Cooke. Harl. MS. 1359, fo. 121ᵇ; MS. Ashm. 834, fo. 23, copy of grant, Bodleian Lib.; Guil. 213; Bannerman MS., No. 9, 517.

WILMOT or WILLYMOTT, James, of Kelshall, Herts, H. Sheriff, colours assigned to coat and crest 18 June 1681, by Sir H. St. George, Clar. Grants III., fo. 245; Lansd. MS. 867, fo. 52.

WILMOT, Edward, of Southampton, Hants, 17 Aug. 1552, by ? Hawley, and his wife, see M. Smith. ? Add. MS. 16,940, fo. 205ᵇ.

WILMOTT, Edward, of Newent, co. Glouc., gent., granted 15 April, 2 and 3 Philip and Mary, 1556, by Sir G. Dethick, Gart. Q's Coll. Oxf. MS. 39, fo. 63, copy of grant; Stowe MS. 714, fo. 73ᵇ; Grants I., 234; Harl. MSS. 1359, fo. 67, and 5887, fo. 7.

WILMOTE, George, of Letcombe, Berks, exemplified 10 Feb. 1627-8, by Segar. MSS. Ashm. 858, fo. 193-5, and 840, fo. 419-20, copy of grant, Bodleian Lib.; Add. MS. 12,225, fo. 120; Guil. 216; Harl. MS. 6140, fo. 62ᵇ.

WILLIMOT, Nicholas, of Osmaston, co. Derby, J.P., now a Bencher of Gray's Inn, 3 Feb. 1662-3, with remainder to his cousins german Robert and Edward, of Chaddesden, co. Derby, brethren, with a canton, etc., for their diff. ["as also to Robert Willimot of Chaddeston in the said County, and Edward his brother, cosen germans to the said Nicolas. The said Robert & Edward to beare these armes wᵗʰ a canton Varry ermine & gules, and about the Eagles neck [in the Crest] a Crown murali sable." The Arms are, sable on a fesse or, between three falcons' (?) heads couped ar., as many escallop shells sable. Crest, an eagle's head couped ar. holding in the beak an escallop shell gules] by W. Dugdale, Norr. Dugdale's Grants, fo. 1ᵇ, Her. Coll.; and Berry.

WILLOUGHBY DE BROKE, Lord (Richard Verney), supporters 1 April 1699, by Sir T. St. George, Gart. Grants IV., fo. 319; confirmation of arms 9 Feb. 1698-9 (fo. 317).

WILSON, ..., of Herts, sa., a wolf rampant or, in chief 3 etoiles arg., by Segar. Add. MS. 12,225, fo. 121.

„   Thomas, of Kendal, Westmorland, quartering Osye, an Italian, 1586, by

Cooke. Harl. MS. 1359, fo. 110^b; Q's Coll. Oxf. MS. 146, fo. 472; Add.
MS. 4966, fo. 68.

WILSONN, William, of Welborne, co. Linc., s. of William, of Penrith, Cumberld.,
arms confirmed and crest given 24 (29 March in Harl. MS. 1422, fo. 52)
March 1586, 29 Q. Eliz., by Flower. MS. Ashm. 834, fo. 31, copy of
grant, Bodleian Lib.; Harl. MS. 1359, fo. 31; Guil. 394; he or his son
preb. of Windsor 1594, *see* Add. MS. 14,295, fo. 24^b.

WILTON, Dame Cecilia (dau. of Sir Richd., Kt.), late wife of Sir John Brewes of
Norfolk, Kt., ? grant confirmed 6 Dec. 1587, by W. Dethick, Gart. Stowe
MS. 676, fo. 74; Q's Coll. Oxf. MS. 37, fo. 107, copy of grant.

WYMBERLEY, ..., of co. Linc., ..., az., two bars and 3 bucks' heads caboshed
in chief or, attested with pedigree . . . ., by Segar. Add. MS. 12,225,
fo. 121.

   „   Thomas, of Bitchfield, co. Linc., gent., arms confirmed and crest given
16 May, 30 Q. Eliz., 1588, by Cooke. Harl. MS. 1359, fo. 12^b; Add. MS.
14,295, fo. 7.

WYNCHE, Robert, of Woodford in Essex, ... by Cooke. Harl. MSS. 1359,
fo. 102^b, and 6140, fo. 24.

WYNCHECOMBE, John, of Newbery, Berks, coat and crest 26 Oct. 1549. Harl. MS.
1441, fo. 53, copy of grant, and MS. Ashm. 858, fo. 72, 73, copy of grant,
Bodleian Lib.; Barker's Grants, Harl. MS. 5846, fo. 105^b; Stowe MS.
692, fo. 92^b.

WINCHESTER, Dean and Canons of the Cathedral Church, 1 June 1541, by Barker,
Gart. Add. MS. 14,295, fo. 89.

WINDELOWE, James, now called Windelove of Notley, Bucks, gent., gift of crest
1596, by Lee. Add. MS. 14,295, fo. 122; Harl. MS. 1359, fo. 89^b.

WINDOW, William, of the city of Gloucester, gent., 29 Aug. 1660, by Walker.
Add. MSS. 14,293, fo. 89, and 14,294, fo. 26^b; Harl. MS. 1172, fo. 71;
20th Aug. in Guil. 189.

WYNDOWTE or WINDOWER, Bartholomew, of Radyswell, co. Hertford, coat and
crest. Barker's Grants, Harl. MS. 5846, fo. 108; Stowe MS. 694, fo. 93^b,
and Berry.

WINDIE, Thomas, of Cambridgeshire, coat and crest. Barker's Grants . . . . Harl.
MS. 5846, fo. 114; Stowe MS. 692, fo. 95^b, as Wyndye.

WYNDYBANK, Sir Richard, Kt. (Knight Marshal at Bullone), grant, coat and crest.
Barker's Grants, Harl. MS. 5846, fo. 112; Stowe MS. 692, fo. 94^b.

WYNGATE, ..., of Harlington, Beds, ... by Cooke. Harl. MS. 1359, fo. 115;
Add. MS. 4966, fo. 95^b.

WINGATE, Roger, of Flamburgh, Yorks, (? confirmed) 4 July 1609, by R. St. George,
Norr. Add. MS. 14,295, fo. 54.

WINN, George, Esq., late servant and draper to Q. Eliz., exemplified . . . . by Segar.
Add. MS. 12,225, fo. 120^b; Guil. 213; Harl. MSS. 6140, fo. 80, and 1441,
fo. 161.

WYN, Thomas, of Duffryn Alyd at Llansannon, co. Denbigh, gent., arms quarterly
of 6 confirmed and crest granted 12 Feb. 1590-91, by W. Dethick, Gart.
Stowe MS. 676, fo. 79; Q's Coll. Oxf. MS. 37, fo. 116.

WYNINGTON, ..., of the Middle Temple, London, and Hermitage and Offerton,
Cheshire, granted 1675: arg., an orle betw. [within] eight martlets [in
orle] sa. Crest, a still arg. Berry; a different crest in Harl. MS. 5887,
fo. 67.

WYNSTON, ..., arms quarterly of 6: 1, parti per pale gu. and az., a lion rampant
arg. sustaining a tree erect and eradicated vert, by Segar. Add. MS.
12,225, fo. 125^b; quarterly in Harl. MSS. 5887, fo. 26, and 1476, fo. 167^b.

WYNTER, John, preby. of Canterbury, 6 March 1610, by Camden. Harl. MS. 6059,
fo. 13; Winter in Harl. MS. 1422, fo. 21^b.

WINTER, Thomas, dean of Cathedral Church of Wells, archdeacon of York and
Richmond, Chancellor of the Cathedral of Sarum, Preb. of St. John's,

Beverley, Lincoln, and Southwell, rector of St. Matthews, Ipswich, 26 Mar. 1526, 17 Hen. VIII., by Wriothesley, Gart., Benolt and Tonge.   Harl. MS. 4900, fo. 19.

WYNTHROPE, John, s. of Adam, of Groton, Suff., gent., grant 24 June 1592, by W. Dethick, Gart.   Stowe MS. 676, fo. 86ᵇ, 97 ;   Q's Coll. Oxf. MS. 36, fo. 11, copy of grant.

WYNTHORP, ..., of Suffolk, ... 1594, by W. Dethick ; entered by R. Brooke, York Herald.   Harl. MS. 1453, fo. 33.

WIRDNAM (WARDNAM, WORDNAM), William, of Charlton, Berks, grant 31 March 1561, by Harvey.   Stowe MS. 677, fo. 63 ; Add. MS. 16,940, fo. 12.

WYSSE, Thomas, of Warminster, Wilts, 5 June 1554, by ? Hawley.   Add. MS. 16,940, fo. 207.

WISEMAN, impaled by EVERARD, see.   (Another impalement, Harl. MS. 6140, fo. 45).

WYSEMAN, John, of Felsted, Essex, gent., grant 1 July 1542, 34 Hen. VIII., by Hawley (fo. 20).   Add. MS. 7098, fo. 75ᵇ.

WISEMAN, John, of Canfeld, Essex, confirmed .... 1562.   (Harvey's Grants), Add. MS. 16,940, fo. 30.

„   Richard, one of H.M.'s surgeons in ordinary, royalist, 24 April 1671 ; coat and crest by consent of his kinsman Sir Richard Wiseman, Kt., H.M.'s advocate, by Walker.   Add. MSS. 14,293, fo. 84, and 14,294, fo. 25 ; Harl. MS. 1172, fo. 69ᵇ ; Guil. 310.   Augmentation.

„   Thomas, of Waltham, Essex, 23 May 1572, by Sir G. Dethick.   Harl. MS. 1441, fo. 77ᵇ ; Q's Coll. Oxf. MS. 145, fo. 27ᵇ.

„   Thomas, of Felsted, Essex, gent., s. and h. of John, of the same, esq., 22 Feb. 1574-5, by Cooke.   Harl. MSS. 1359, fo. 11, and 1115, fo. 15.

„   Thomas, 3rd s. of John, of Canfield, Essex, ... by Cooke.   Harl. MSS. 1359, fo. 90, and 1422, fo. 51ᵇ ; Add. MS. 4966, fo. 35.

WYTHERS, Robert, of London, coat and crest, ...   Barker's Grants, Harl. MS. 5846, fo. 115.

WITHENS or WYTHENS, ..., of Wantage, Berks, Eltham, Kent, and London, ... 1649 [? misprint for 1594].   Berry.

„   Robert, of London, merchᵗ [Vintner] and sheriff, decᵈ (fined 22 Oct. 1593), s. of William, of Cheshire, grant 10 Jan. 159? [1594-95 ?], by W. Dethick, Gart.   Stowe MS. 676, fo. 111ᵇ, confirmed ; Q's Coll. Oxf. MS. 36, fo. 45 copy of grant ; Caius Coll. Camb. MS. 528, fo. 4 ; Add. MS. 14,295, fo. 75ᵇ.   See Margaret PARKE, his wife, (? the same as).

„   Robert, a vyntner, of London, by W. Dethick, Gart., after his death, for which the said Garter had ten pounds.   [Margaret, dau. of Thomas Park of Bassingham, co. Lincoln, and] wife of [Robert Wythens], a vintner, of London, by W. Dethick, Gart., 1597, in Harl. MS. 1453, fo. 34, entered by R. Brooke, York Her.   Harl. MS. 1453, fo. 34 bis.   [Harl. MS. 1453, fo. 34, gives a trick of the arms as entered by Brooke : Gules, a chevron embattled counter embattled ermine between three martlets or.   Crest, in a ducal coronet per pale or and gu. an ounce sejant ermine, holding in the dexter paw a ring of rope or chain azure.   "This Armes is past to the wife of one Wythens A Vintner of London by Garter that now is 1597."   Trick : A., on a fesse Sable three escallops of the field, a canton ermines.]

[WYTHENS, William, of Cheshire, by W. Dethick, Gart., 10 Jan. 1593 : "gules, a cheuron crenelle between 3 martletts or, his Crest a Lyon seiant ermyne gorged with a crowne and thereto a chayne."   A very rough trick partly in ink and partly in pencil, Add. MS. 14,295, fo. 71ᵇ.]

WITHERING, Edward, descended from John, of Overton, Salop, testified .... by Segar.   C. 24 [Visit. of London, 1634], fo. 516, Her. Coll. ; Guil. 359.

„   John, gent., sewer to K. James, descended from John Withering of co. Staff., ..., by Segar.   Harl. MS. 1105, fo. 3ᵇ ; Add. MS. 12,225, fo. 120ᵇ.

WITHERNEWYKE, John, of Claxby, co. Linc., assigned and granted 26 March 1562, by Harvey. Add. MSS. 17,506, fo. 33ᵇ, and 16,940, fo. 54 ; Le Neve's Notes, 258.

WITHIE, John, of Wolton Bassett, Wilts, gent., s. of John, of Berry Narbor, Devon, gent., crest granted 12 June 1615, by Camden. Q's Coll. Oxf. MS. 38, fo. 126, copy of grant ; 1611 in Harl. MS. 1115, fo. 30, 31ᵇ ; Morgan's Sphere, 115 ; Le Neve's MS. 311.

„   John, of London, Painter Stainer, *see* preceding entry (confirmed 1612 or 1615, coat and crest), by Sir R. St. George, Clar. Berry's Appx.; Harl. MS. 1105, fo. 5.

WYTTON, Thomas, of London, scrivener, confirmed 1551. (Harvey's Grants), Add. MS. 16,940, fo. 10ᵇ ; Harl. MS. 5887, fo. 57, quarterly arms.

WODESON, Elizabeth, d. and coh. of Reynold Wodeson and wife unto Robert Benne of London, gent., confirmed .... 1573, by Cooke. Add. MS. 14,295, fo. 50.

WODINGTON, Thomas, Doctor of Decrees, official of the Court of Canterbury, Dean of the Arches, also Canon of Landaff, ... Barker's Grants, Stowe MS. 692, fo. 98ᵇ ; arms in Add. MS. 26,702, fo. 50ᵇ. *See* WOODINGTON.

WOLFE, Francis, of Madeley, Salop, and his son Francis, augmentation (by the King's Warrant 2 July, 13 Chas. II.) in consideration of their protection of his person after the battle of Worcester, Augmentation 4 July 1661, by Walker. MS. Ashm. 858, fo. 128-9, copy of grant, Bodleian Lib. ; Misc. Gen. et Her., N. S., ii., 475 ; Harl. MS. 6179, fo. 25ᵇ.

WOLLACOMBE, ..., of Devonshire, ... Feb. 1611-12, by Camden. Harl. MS. 6059, fo. 17ᵇ ; Guil. 66, with 6 quarterings ; Harl. MS. 6140, fo. 39ᵇ.

WOLLASTON, Henry, of London, draper, s. of Henry, of Perton, co. Staff., crest 10 July 1616, by Camden. Morgan's Sphere (iii.), 118 ; Nichols's Leic. IV., pt. 2, p. 541.

WOLMES or WOLMER, Gregory, of Swynstead, co. Linc., crest confirmed 1562. Harvey's Grants, Add. MS. 16,940, fo. 47.

WOLSEY, Edmond, of Norfolk, gift .... 1564. (Harvey's Grants), Add. MS. 16,940, fo. 22ᵇ.

WOLSTENHOLME, John (s. of John), of Dronfield, co. Derby, confirmed coat and grant of crest 10 Aug. 1604, by Camden and Segar. Add. MS. 12,225, fo. 121ᵇ ; Grants II., fo. 576 ; Guil. 335 ; Harl. MS. 6140, fo. 29ᵇ, 51.

WOMBWELL, William, of Northfleete, Kent, coat confirmed and crest granted 10 Sept. 1574, by Cooke. Q's Coll. Oxf. MS. 38, fo. 89. (MS. 146, fo. 461), and Harl. MS. 1507, fo. 98, copies of grant (Brit. Mus). Harl. MS. 1359, fo. 26ᵇ ; Add. MS. 4966, fo. 95.

WOMERTON, ..., of Womerton, co. Worc., and Hatton, Salop and London, ... 1571, by Cooke, or, 3 escocheons sa., each charged with an eagle displayed of the field. Berry.

WOOD, Sir John, of Stapleford, Essex, descended out of the house of Wood of Snodland, Kent, impaling Barthram, by Cooke. Harl. MS. 1359, fo. 114 ; Add. MS. 4966, fo. 97ᵇ ; Harl. MS. 5887, fo. 7ᵇ.

„   .... of Enfield, Middx., and Colwick and Lamley, Notts, and of London, quarterly of 4, by Segar, yᵉ canton in augmentation for taking a Frenchman prisoner. Add. MS. 12,225, fo. 122ᵇ [gives the blazon in English, Latin and French. " G. semi de Cross crosslets fichee A, 3 demi Savages with clubbs elevated ppr., a canton sinister of France & a flower de luce difference, quartering 2ᵈ a Pelican in her Piety in her nest S. 3ᵈ, G. on a fess A., three Crosses pattée of ye first. 4ᵗʰ, G., three fusills in fess A., in chief two cinquefoils O., & Crest, vizᵗ on a Wreath, a Mount V. thereon an Oak pp. fructed O., 2, Cantrell, 3, Story, 4, Colwich, N.B. yᵉ Canton an augmentation for taking a Frenchman prisoner "].

„   Anthony, M.A. of Merton College, Oxf., and to the issue of Thomas, his

father, dec^d, 1 May 1661, by .... Harl. MS. 1105, fo. 21^b ; Bysshe's
Grants, fo. 24, Her. Coll.

WOOD, Edmond, of the city of Norwich, Norfolk, gent., Grant 10 Dec. (1 Ed. VI.)
1547, by Hawley. Copy of grant, Q's Coll. Oxf. MSS. 37, fo. 1 and 16
(Edmond or Edward), and 39, fo. 10 : Add. MS. 16,940, fo. 202^b ;
Harl. MS. 1359, fo. 6 ; (Edward in Stowe MS. 676, fo. 16^b) ; Grants II.,
482.

„ Edward, of Sandwich, Kent, crest 20 Nov. 1574, by Cooke, arms, sa., on a
chev. betw. 3 oak trees eradicated or, as many martlets of the field ; Crest,
an arm embowed, habited in green leaves, the hand and elbow ppr.
holding a spear broken in 3 pieces, one in pale and two in saltire ppr.
Berry.

„ Henry, of London, and of Watering- ⎫ certif., by Segar. Add. MS. 12,225,
bury, Kent, and ⎬ fo. 122^b ; C. 24 [Visit. London,
„ Robert, his brother, ⎭ 1634], fo. 507^b, Her. Coll. ;
Grants I., 385 ; Guil. 128.

„ James, of Staple Inn, Middx., gent., out of Kent, grant 6 May 1613, by
Segar. Add. MS. 12,225, fo. 122 ; Harl. MS. 1422, fo. 37 ; Q's Coll. Oxf.
MS. 38, fo. 124, and Harl. MS. 1507, fo. 121, copy of grant (Brit. Mus.) ;
Misc. Gen. et Her., 3 S., vol. i., 46 ; Guil. 132 ; Harl. MS. 1441,
fo. 154^b.

WODE, John, of Harstone, Devon, confirmed 6 Feb. 1532-3, by Benolte. Misc.
Gen. et Her., 2 S., vol. iii., p. 206, facsimile, copy of grant, Brit. Mus.

WOOD, John, of Kings Nympton, Devon, Esq., and a captain employed by sea and
land in the Q.'s service, 1 Feb. 1602-3, by W. Dethick, Gart. Add. MS.
19,815, fo. 18 ; Harl. MS. 1545, fo. 33^b.

„ Lancelot, B.A., Sidney Coll., Camb., now of Gray's Inn, and to the issue of
Richard, his father, sometime Mayor of Hull, decd., 20 Nov. 1670, by Sir
E. Bysshe, Clar. Harl. MS. 1172, fo. 46, copy of grant ; Harl. MS. 1105,
fo. 21^b ; Bysshe's Grants, fo. 25, Her. Coll.

„ Richard, of Islington (out of Lanc.), granted to his eldest brother ...., crest
granted .... 1582, by Flower. Guil. 192.

„ Richard, of the city of London, surgeon, a traveller, ?7 Nov. 1595, by
W. Dethick, Gart. Grants I., 346 ; Harl. MS. 5887, fo. 47^b.

„ Richard, of Brokthorp, co. and city of Glouc., Esq., circa 1606, by Camden.
Harl. MSS. 6059, fo. 20^b, and 1422, fo. 37.

„ Roger, of Islington, Middx., Sergt. at arms, Feb. 1606, by Camden. Harl.
MSS. 1422, fo. 20, and 6095, fo. 8 ; Guil. 191.

WOODE, Thomas, of London, gift .... 1559. (Harvey's Grants), Add. MS.
16,940, fo. 26.

WOODD, Thomas, of Woodend, Berks, gift .... 1560. (Harvey's Grants), Add.
MS. 16,940, fo. 54.

WOOD, Thomas, of Kilnwick, Yorks, arms confirmed and crest given 6 May 1578,
by Flower. (5th May in Harl. MS. 1422, fo. 37) ; Harl. MS. 1359,
fo. 34 ; Add. MS. 14,295, fo. 38 ; Harl. MS. 6140, fo. 68.

„ Thomas, of Suffolk, gent., D. of phys., coat confirmed and crest granted
8 Jan. 1592-3, by Cooke. Harl. MSS. 1359, fo. 111^b, (1441, fo. 11^b, copy
of grant, Brit. Mus.), 1422, fo. 37, and 5887, fo. 7^b ; Add. MS. 4966,
fo. 24.

„ Thomas, of Hackney, Middx., s. and h. of Henry, of Hackney, servant to
Q. Eliz., s. of Thomas, of Burnley, co. Lanc., s. of Barney, of the same,
s. of Thomas, descended from Le Sieur de Boys, Dauphin of France,
28 June 1634, by Sir R. St. George, Clar. Harl. MS. 1485, fo. 3^a ; Add.
MS. 14,295, fo. 104 ; Grants II., 664, Her. Coll. ; Guil. 178.

„ Thobey, of Lincoln, ... June 1586, by Cooke. Harl. MSS. 1359, fo. 91,
and 1422, fo. 37 ; " of Lincoln's Inn " according to Add. MS. 4966, fo. 69,
and Harl. MS. 5887, fo. 38, High Sheriff of Middx. 1605. [Toby Wood

of London, gen., son and heir of Toby Wood, arm., bencher, adm. 10 Nov. 1606, Linc. Inn Register.]

WOOD, William, of Snodland, Kent, s. of Allen, s. of John, of Norfolk, 20 Nov. 1570, by Cooke or G. Dethick. Harl. MSS. 1422, fo. 37, and 1548, fo. 99ᵇ, for ped. ; Harl. MSS. 1541, fo. 209ᵇ, and 6140, fo. 74ᵇ.

„ William, of Warden, par. of Aston, co. Warwick, Esq., 1 May 1663. Harl. MS. 1105, fo. 19 ; Bysshe's Grants, fo. 11, Her. Coll.

WOODHALL, William, of Walden or Walton, Essex, Esq., s. of John, s. of John, of Ullocke, Cumberld., arms quarterly confirmed and crest granted 2 June 1592, by Cooke. Q's Coll. Oxf. MS. 38, fo. 111, and Harl. MS. 1507, fo. 381 (Brit. Mus.), copies of grant ; Harl. MS. 1359, fo. 112 ; Q's Coll. Oxf. MS. 146, fo. 473 ; Add. MS. 4966, fo. 93ᵇ.

WOODHOUSE, Luke, of Kimberley, Norfolk, ... by Segar. Add. MS. 12,225, fo. 123 ; Harl. MS. 6140, fo. 79ᵇ ; 17 Aug. 1611, Robert in Reliquary, xxii., 49.

WOODINGTON (? WODINGTON), Thomas, dean of the Arches, ... Hen. VII. Add. MS. 26,702, fo. 50ᵇ. See WODINGTON.

WOODMONGERS' COMPANY, of London, incorporated 1605, arms and crest allowed [? granted] 1 Oct. 1605, 3 Jas. I., by Camden. [Harl. MS. 1098, fo. 59 ; Cotton MS. Tib., D. x., fo. 360ᵇ] ; Add. MS. 14,295, fo. 118 ; Harl. MSS. 1359, fo. 76, and 2220, fo. 11.

WOODDROFF, David, Alderm. of London, 15 May 1554, by T. Hawley ; Add. MS. 16,940, fo. 207 ; Harl. MS. 5887, fo. 6ᵇ.

WOODS, ..., of Norwich, 2 July 1664, by E. Bysshe, Clar. Berry.

WOODWARD, ..., of Dean, co. Glouc., ... 1420, temp. Hen. V. Berry.

„ George, of Upton, Bucks, gent., a gift at London 26 April 1527, 19 Hen. VIII., ? by Wriothesley, Gart., and Benolte. Q's Coll. Oxf. MS. 146, fo. 464 ; Harl. MS. 1359, fo. 31 ; John in Add. MS. 26,702, fo. 46 ; and Dec. in Add. MS. 14,295, fo. 23, but same arms in both.

„ John, of Avon Dassett, co. Warwick, ... by Cooke. Harl. MSS. 1359, fo. 96, and 1422, fo. 87.

„ John and Richard, of London, brethren, patent 13 Feb. 1578-9, by Cooke. Harl. MSS. 1359, fo. 27, and 1422, fo. 87 ; Add. MS. 4966, fo. 95.

WOOLHOUSE, Anthony, of Glapwell, co. Derby, confirmed 17 Aug. 1611, by R. St. George, Norr. MS. Ashm. 858, fo. 160, copy of grant, Bodleian Lib. ; Wolhouse in Harl. MS. 1422, fo. 15ᵇ ; to Robert, s. of Anthony, 9 Feb. 1611-12, Harl. MS. 1537, fo. 104 ; Harl. MS. 6140, fo. 71ᵇ.

WOORKESLEY [or WORSLEY], Sir Robert, of Woorkesley, co. Lanc., Kt., crest given 25 Nov. 1561 (by ? Dalton). Harl. MS. 1359, fo. 51.

WORLEY, Richard, Sergt at arms, confirmed . . . . 1557. (Harvey's Grants), Add. MS. 16,940, fo. 47.

„ Thomas, of London, gent., s. of John, s. of Henry, sometime Alderm. of London, crest granted 6 May 1567, by Sir Gilb. Dethick, Gart., and Flower. Q's Coll. Oxf. MS. 39, fo. 129, copy of grant ; Harl. MS. 1359, fo. 6 and 56ᵇ. Quarterly, 1 and 4, erm., a lion rampant gu. crowned, for Worley, though said to be the arms of Turberville (vide D. 28 [Visit. of Dorset, 1677], and C. 22 [Visit. of Dorset, 1623], fo. 126ᵇ) ; 2, erm., a fesse chequy or and az. ; 3, az., a lion rampant sa., collared gu., holding a quill arg., and 1564 in Grants I., 129. See William Worley in Add. MS. 4966, fo. 101.

WORLICHE, Charles, of Cawling, Suff., ... 1587 in Harl. MS. 1422, fo. 93, by Cooke. Harl. MS. 1359, fo. 90ᵇ ; Add. MS. 4966, fo. 65ᵇ.

„ Charles, of Sussex, ..., by Cooke. Harl. MS. 1359, fo. 92ᵇ ; Add. MS. 4966, fo. 59, different coats and crest to the first named ; Sir William in Harl. MS. 6887, fo. 12.

WORME, Richard, of Peterborough, Northants, ... 1583, by Cooke. Harl. MSS. 1422, fo. 15ᵇ, and 1359, fo. 93ᵇ ; Add. MS. 4966, fo. 37.

WORMELAYTON, Ralfe, of Leicestershire, crest, 1 Dec. 1610 or March 1611, by
Camden. Harl. MS. 1422, fo. 35ᵇ, and 6059, fo. 14ᵇ; Guil. 215;
Le Neve's MS. 490, *see*.

WORSELEY, Ralph, of Bricket, Cheshire, Esq., coat and crest .... Barker's
Grants, Harl. MS. 5846, fo. 114ᵇ; Stowe MS. 692, fo. 95ᵇ.

WOTTON, Charles Kirkhoven, Lord, supporters at the Hague 26 May 1660, by
Sir E. Walker. Her. Coll., fo. 13.

„ Edward, of Kent, Quarterly of 9, Pickering, on an inescocheon, 18 March
1580-1, by Cooke. MS. Ashm. 844, fo. 41, copy of grant, Bodleian Lib.;
? this rather a grant of arms for wife Hester Pickering, Guil. 59.

WRAGG, Thomas, of Sparrow Hawk in Tolshunt Darcy, Essex, grant, certificate
2 July 1649, by Squibb, Clar. Harl. MS. 1105, fo. 10ᵇ.

WRAY, Sir Christopher, of Wrentham, co. Linc., Chief Justice King's Bench,
Feb., 29 Eliz., 1586-7, by Cooke. MS. Ashm. 834, fo. 66, 67, copy
of grant, Bodleian Lib. [1 and 4, Azure, on a chief Or, three martlets
Gules], quartering 2 and 3, Arg., on a chev. sa. betw. 3 sheldrakes'
[heads] erased, as many cinquefoils of the field [Crest, an ostrich Or],
13 Feb. 1592-3 (*sic*) in Harl. MS. 1422, fo. 123; Le Neve's MS. 371.

„ Leonard, of Adwicke, Yorks, "fratri suo seniori" de Chʳ Wray, C. J. Com.
Pleas, exemplification 21 May 1587, by Flower. Harl. MS. 1509, fo. 369,
copy of grant, Brit. Mus., in Latin; MS. Ashm. 844, fo. 1, copy of grant,
Bodleian Lib., and Q's Coll. Oxf. MS. 38, fo. 110, copy of grant in Latin;
Le Neve's MS. 367.

„ Thomas, of St. Nicholas, Richmond, Yorks, brother german of Sir Christopher
Wray, Chief Justice of the Common Pleas, exemplified 21 May 1587, by
Flower. Harl. MS. 1507, fo. 369.

„ Sir Thomas, alteration granted, by Barker, Gart. Stowe MS. 692, fo. 93, in
a later hand; Harl. MS. 6179, fo. 12ᵇ.

WRENCH, Thomas, of Hadenham, Isle of Ely, co. Camb., ..., gu., three cross-
crosslets in bend or. Stowe MS. 670, fo. 33.

WRENNE, Charles, of the Bishoprick of Durham, crest ? April 1607, by R. St.
George, Norr. Add. MS. 14,295, fo. 79 (fo. 276).

WRIGHT (. . . .), of Kent, afterwards one of yᵉ Stable, party per pale or and sa., a
bend counterchanged, assigned by Segar. Add. MS. 12,225, fo. 123; Guil.
392.

„ (Nicholas), of Hampshire, Haberdasher of London, ..., by Cooke, Clar.
Stowe MS. 670.

„ Edmond, of Sutton Hall, Suff., ... 1559..... (Harvey's Grants), Add.
MS. 16,940, fo. 40ᵇ; chevron engrailed in Bannerman's MS. No. 9, 454.

„ George, of Gray's Inn, gent., s. of Thomas, etc., confirmed 1593,
by W. Dethick, Gart. Stowe MS. 676, fo. 90ᵇ, 105ᵇ; Q's Coll. Oxf. MS.
36, fo. 30, and Caius Coll. Camb. MS. 528, fo. 8, copy of confirmation in
Latin; Grants I., 24; Le Neve's MS. 256.

„ John, of Ashted, Surrey, ... 1588, by Cooke. Harl. MSS. 1359, fo. 97, and
1422, fo. 62ᵇ.

„ John, of Wrightsbridge in Hornechurch als Havering atte Bower, 20 June
1590, ... Harl. MS. 1422, fo. 56; Add. MS. 14,295, fo. 25ᵇ.

„ Nicholas, gent., s. of Robert, of co. Southants, gent., descended from Wright,
of the North, crest 15 May 1580, 22 Q. Eliz., by Cooke. Add. MS. 7098,
fo. 105ᵇ, 106, copy of grant; (Harl. MSS. 1422, fo. 15ᵇ, and 1359, fo. 119ᵇ,
have "of London, haberdasher"); Stowe MS. 670, fo. 67ᵇ; Add. MS.
4966, fo. 61.

„ Richard, sergᵗ at arms (s. of John, of Bickley, Chesh.), allowed and confirmed
18 Dec. 1583, by Flower. MS. Ashm. 844, fo. 50, copy of grant, Bodleian
Lib.; Guil. 262.

„ Richard, of Bickley, Cheshire, 1 July 1612, by R. St. George, Norr. Harl.
MS. 1422, fo. 124; Add. MS. 14,295, fo. 76; Harl. MS. 4199, fo. 102ᵇ.

WRIGHT, Richard, of London, 25 Oct. 1587, crest, by Cooke.   Harl. MSS. 1359, fo. 110, and 1422, fo. 56 ; Add. MSS. 4966, fo. 56, and 1433, fo. 101.

„   Robert, of Plowland, Yorks, s. of John and Alice, d. and coh. of John Ryther of Alfordwell, gift of coat and crest and confirmation of quarterings, by Flower.   Harl. MSS. 1359, fo. 34, and 1422, fo. 118 ; Add. MS. 14,295, fo. 38.

„   Thomas, of Mile End, Middx., Purveyor to the Navy, 28 Feb. 1697-8, by T. St. George, Gart. and Clar.   Grants IV., 247.

„   William, of Oxford, 11 Feb. 1686-7, by T. St. George, Gart. and Clar., arg., two [three] bars gemelles gn. [on a chief az.] three leopards' heads [faces] or ; [Crest, out of a mural crown, chequy gold and gules, a dragon's head Vert, purfled ar. scaled or, gorged on the neck with three leopards' faces also gold between two bars gemelles silver], certif. for Sir Benj. Wright, Bart.   Harl. MS. 6834, fo. 178 ; Lansd. MS. 867 [Schedule of Grants entered in the Earl Marshal's Book and delivered to his Grace 10 March 1687], fo. 52 ; Grants III., 307 ; Harl. MS. 1085, fo. 58.

WRIGHTSON, Michael, of Osbaston, co. Leic., 23 April 1695, by T. St. George, Gart. and Clar.   Grants IV., 192.

WRIGLEY, ..., coat confirmed and crest granted, by Bysshe, Gart.   Harl. MS. 6179, fo. 89b.

WROTH, ..., of Enfield, crest . . . .   Barker's Grants, Harl. MS. 5846, fo. 110 [" a Lyons head erased & crowned or eared and langued g̃ betweene two winges bendie of foure peaces argent and s. w[reath] or and b."] ; Stowe MS. 692, fo. 94 [has the same blazon of the crest, and adds (wr or b.) Wriothesley or Benolte ?] ; ? Sir Robert Wroth, quarterly of 6, Harl. MS. 5887, fo. 20b.   [" Sr Robert Wrothe of Midellsex & of London," a trick of Arms, 1 and 6, Arg., on a bend Sable, three lions' heads erased Argent, crowned Or ; 2, Az., two bars indented Or, on a chief Arg. a crescent Sable for difference ; 3, Or, three roses gules, two and one, barbed Vert ; 4, Az., six lions rampant, 2, 3 and 1 [so tricked] [Argent] on a canton Or a mullet Gules ; 5, Arg., two chevrons Az., a bordure engrailed Gules.   Crest, a lion's head erased Arg., crowned Or, betw. two wings expanded, bendy of four pieces Silver and Sable ; " his wyfe was a Sydney."]

WYBARNE, John, s. of Thomas, of Kent, 13 May, 3 Ed. VI., 1463, by J. Wrexworth, Guyon K. of Arms.   Grants II., 676.

WICHE or WYCHE, Thomas, of Davenham, Cheshire, gent., s. of Richard, s. of Richard, s. of William, grant or exemplification 28 July 1587, by Flower, confirmed with alteration (15) Aug. 1590, 32 Q. Eliz., by W. Dethick, Gart.   Q's Coll. Oxf. MS. 37, fo. 121, copy of grant, etc. ; MSS. Ashm. 844, fo. 69*, and 858, fo. 181-2, copy of grant, Bodleian Lib. ; Stowe MS. 676, fo. 81b ; Hugh in Add. MS. 14,295, fo. 76 ; Gnil. 47.

WYDOP, John, of the Court, Jan. 1572-3, by Flower.   Harl. MSS. 1422, fo. 46, and 6140, fo. 69b.

WYOTT, Henry, of Alyston, Kent, 16 Jan. 1507-8, by Wriothesley, Gart., and R. Machado, Clar.   MS. Ashm. 858, fo. 28, copy of grant, Bodleian Lib.

WYETT, Sir Henry, coat and impalement, ...   Barker's Grants, Harl. MS. 5846, fo. 107 ; Stowe MS. 692, fo. 93.

WYGGES, Thomas, of London, gent., exemplified . . . . 1589, by W. Dethick, Gart.   Harl. MS. 1422, fo. 113b.

WYLD, see WELD, ..., haberdasher of Hatts and Capps, ..., az., a fess undée or, in chief 3 crescents ermine, by Segar.   Add. MS. 12,225, fo. 123b ; Vincent MS. 154, Her. Coll. ; Guil. 94.

WILDE, George, of the Inner Temple, 2 s. of Thomas, Crest, a martlett, by Cooke, 1585, altered to a lyon . . . . 1587, quarterly coat.   Harl. MSS. 1359, fo. 32b, 98b, and 1422, fo. 117 ; Add. MS. 14,295, fo. 32, as Wylde.   Add. MS. 4966, fo. 62.

WILDE, George, Bp. of Londonderry, 10 Nov. 1660, by Walker, Gart. Her. Coll. 34.

WILD, Marmaduke, of Hunton, Yorks, 29 Aug. 1612, by R. St. George, Norr. Stowe MS. 706, fo. 14 ; Harl. MS. 6179, fo. 13[b].

WYLDE (or WILD), Thomas, of the city of Canterbury, ... 1583 ; arg., a chev. sa., on a chief of the second three martlets of the first. Berry ; called Thomas Weld in Harl. MS. 1422, fo. 84.

WYLD, William, of Nettleworth, Notts, granted 16 Oct. 1561, (Harl. MS. 1359) 3 Eliz. ; confirmed 10 June 1567 in grant, 9 Eliz. ; grant of a new coat, the former one to be in the 2nd quarter (15 June 1575, 17 Eliz., in Berry ?), all by G. Dethick, Gart. Q's Coll. Oxf. MSS. 37, fo. 48 (1561), copies of grants, and 39, fo. 121 (1561) ; Harl. MS. 1359, fo. 60[b] ; Stowe MS. 676, fo. 32[b] ; Grants I., 262.

WYMON, John, of Greenehall, Sussex, ... 1586, by Cooke. Harl. MSS. 1359, fo. 91[b], and 1422, fo. 93 ; Add. MS. 4966, fo. 64[b].

WYNYARD, George, of London, gent., 2 Jan. 1579-80, by Cooke. Grants I., 36, Her. Coll. ; see Harl. MS. 5887, fo. 63[b].

WYRLEY, Roger de, to adopt the arms of Sir John de Heronyle, Kt., by consent, 30 Jan. (Tuesday before 2 Feb.), 38 Rich. III., 1363-4. Harl. MS. 1116, fo. 43, and Berry ; reprinted by J. Gray Bell.

WYRRALL, WYRALL or WETHERALL, Gervase, of Loversall, Yorks, crest 1537, 29 Hen. VIII., by Barker. Harl. MS. 1359, fo. 8[b] ; Add. MS. 14,295, fo. 74[b] ; Harl. MS. 6140, fo. 69.

WYTHE, John, of Droitwiche, co. Worc., and } crest, 27 Nov. 1581, by
  ,, Robert, of the Inner Temple, Esq., his brother, } Cooke ; confirmed quarterly of 4. Stowe MSS.

    714, fo. 147, and 677, fo. 76 ; Harl. MS. 6179, fo. 39[b].

WYTHENS, see WITHENS.

Y

YALDWIN, William, the elder, of Blackdowne, Sussex, 15 Mar. 1651-2, by E. Bysshe, Gart. Harl. MS. 1105, fo. 15 ; Stowe MS. 703, fo. 70 ; Guil. 363.

YALLOP, Sir Robert, of Bowthrop, Norfolk, and to } sons of Robert ; Yaldwin and
  ,, Edward,   } Giles quarterly, 10 Nov.
  ,, George,   } 1664. Bysshe's Grants, fo.
  ,, Giles,   } 20, Her. Coll. ; Harl. MS. 1105, fo. 20[b].

YARWAY, Robert, of London, a captain, granted 15 Aug. 1652 and confirmed 18 Sept. 1664, by E. Bysshe, Esq., Clar. Harl. MS. 1105, fo. 15[b] ; Add. MS. 14,293, fo. 6 ; Bysshe's Grants, fo. 10, Her. Coll.

YATE, ..., "of Gloucestershire and Barkley." quarterly, by Cooke. Harl. MS. 1359, fo. 93 ; Add. MS. 4966, fo. 36[b] ; Harl. MS. 5887, fo. 27, Thomas, of Arlingham.

YAXLEY, Francis, of Yaxley, Suff., gent., crest . . . . (Harvey's Grants), Add. MS. 16,940, fo. 8.

YEOMAN, William, gent., ... 29 March, 16 Ed. IV., 1476, by W. Hawkeslow, Clar. Stowe MS. 1047, fo. 219.

YONGE, Doctor . . . ., of Oxon. and Berks, Hen. VIII. Add. MS. 26,702, fo. 49.
  ,, ..., crest, a demi-squirrell . . . .? of Oxford. (? If this is a crest to the coat of Henry Young, see Harl. MS. 1422, fo. 32[b], and Add. MS. 26,702, fo. 69[b].) Harl. MS. 5846, fo. 60 ; Stowe MS. 692, fo. 58[b] ; Barker's Grants, 1526—49, see Stowe MS. 702.

YOUNG, ... of Colliton, Devon, from Bassingbourne, Berks [?], granted . . . . 1583, by Cooke. C. 1 [Visit. Devon, 1620], 107, Her. Coll. ; Guil. 268.

YONG, ..., of Dornford, Wilts, ... 1572, by Cooke : vair, on a chief gu. three lions ramp. regnardant or.   Crest, a demi-greyhound erased arg. (or).   The same coat Yong of Wilts.   Caius Coll. Camb. MS. 551, fo. 31ᵇ; Harl. MS. 1422, fo. 44, but *see* Harl. MS. 1441, fo. 149ᵇ.

YONG, Sir George, of city of York, ... 1612, by St. George, Norr.   Harl. MSS. 1422, fo. 44, and 6140, fo. 73.

YOUNG, Gregory, of Yorkshire, 10 Nov. 1609, by Segar.   Add. MS. 12,225, fo. 124ᵇ; Harl. MS. 5887, fo. 66ᵇ.

„ Henry, ..., Arg., a chevron chequy sa. and or, betw. 3 griffins' heads erased gu., on a chief vert a ducal coronet arg. betw. 2 bezants; no crest. (*See* crest, a demi-squirrel, Harl. MS. 5846, fo. 60; Stowe MS. 692, fo. 58ᵇ); Harl. MS. 1422, fo. 32ᵇ; Add. MS. 26,702, fo. 69ᵇ.

„ Henry, of Poulton-cum-Seacomb, Cheshire, s. of Richard, of the same, s. of Maurice, of Flints., 10 June 1625, by Segar.   Add. MS. 12,225, fo. 124; Guil. 385; Harl. MS. 6140, fo. 65.

YONGE (John, of Bristowe, esquire for the body of K. Hen. VIII., Stowe MS. 692, fo. 96), coat lozengy arg. and vert, a bend az., thereon an annulet, etc., crest, an Ibex head.   Barker's Grants, Harl. MS. 5846, fo. 115ᵇ; Stowe MS. 692, fo. 96.

YOUNG, John, D.D., Bp. of Rochester, 7 April 1578, by Sir G. Dethick, Gart. Harl. MSS. 1441, fo. 88ᵇ, and 1422, fo. 20; Q's Coll. Oxf. MS. 145, fo. 46.

YOUNGE, John, of Axminster, Devon, ..., by Cooke.   Harl. MSS. 1359, fo. 93ᵇ, and 1422, fo. 44; Add. MS. 4966, fo. 36ᵇ.

YOUNG, John, of Roxwell, Essex, gift 12 March 1607-8, by Camden.   Harl. MSS. 1359, fo. 24ᵇ, and 1422, fo. 44; Add. MS. 14,295, fo. 52.

YOUNGE, John, s. and h. of John, Bp. of Rochester, coat granted, by G. Dethick, Gart., crest, Feb. 1609, by Camden.   Harl. MSS. 1422, fo. 20, and 6059, fo. 9.

„ John, of London (who mar. Ann, dau. of Thomas Garway), s. of George, of Draycott, co. Staff., s. of Robert, of the same, quarterly ...., by Segar. C. 24 [Visit. of London, 1634], fo. 375ᵇ, Her. Coll.; Guil. 320.

„ Lancelot, the Queen's glasier, ..., by Cooke's Deputy.   Stowe MS. 670, fo. 34.

YONGE, Robert, a fishmonger of London, arms given by W. Dethick, Gart., after Yonge was dead, being his wife's father, entered by R. Brooke, York Herald.   Harl. MS. 1453, fo. 33.

YOUNG, Lionel, of London, gen., 8 May 1558, by Ro. Cooke, Clar.   Proc. Soc. of Antiq., 1897, 2nd S., xvi., 349; *see* Le Neve's MS. 515.   [Foster marks this grant " ? forgery."   Is the date wrong ?   Cooke became Clarenceux in 1567.]

„ Thomas, then at Florence in Italy, testified the antiquity of his family, and that he was born in the north of England, gu., a fesse betw. 3 lions ramp. or, ..., by Segar.   Add. MS. 12,225, fo. 125.

„ William, of Ternt (Trent), Somerset, Esq., being descended from Young, of Wilts, confirmed April 1615, by Camden.   Harl. MSS. 1422, fo. 39ᵇ, and 6059, fo. 32; Guil. 119.

„ William, of Kettleston, Norfolk, 1664, an escotcheon, by Camden.   Harl. MS. 1085, fo. 44.

„ William, of Balleston (Basildon), Berks, Esq., attested by Camden and approved 1607, by Segar.   Guil. 361; Add. MS. 12,225, fo. 124; Harl. MS. 6140, fo. 46ᵇ.

YONGER, Capt. Henry, Comptroller gent. of H.M.'s trayne of Artillery, augmentation ...., by Walker.   Add. MS. 14,294, fo. 31; at Oxford 10 May 1645, Her. Coll., fo. 25.

Report for the Year 1914.

THE Council have to report that at and since the Annual General Meeting, held on the 21st day of February 1914, eight new Subscribers have joined the Society, of whom two are Subscribers to the Register Section.

During the same period the Society has lost one Subscriber by death.

The number on the Roll on the 31st of December 1914 is two hundred and fifty-four, of whom one hundred and sixty-four are Subscribers to the Register Section.

A Volume of Middlesex Pedigrees, as collected by RICHARD MUNDY in Harl. MS. 1551, edited by SIR GEORGE JOHN ARMYTAGE, Bart., F.S.A., Chairman of the Council, forming the sixty-fifth volume of the Publications, has been issued to the Subscribers for 1914.

A Volume containing a list of " Grantees of Arms to the end of the Seventeenth Century," compiled by JOSEPH FOSTER, Hon. M.A., Oxon, Brit. Mus. Add. MS. 37,147, now being transcribed, to be edited by W. H. RYLANDS, Esq., F.S.A., Vice-Chairman of the Council, will be issued to the Subscribers for 1915.

Part I. of the Registers of St. Mary le Bow with Allhallows, Honey Lane, and St. Pancras, Soper Lane, E.C., containing the Baptisms and Burials, edited by the SECRETARY, forming the forty-fourth volume of the Registers, has been issued to the Subscribers to the Register Section for 1914, and—

Part II. of the same Registers, containing the Marriages and an Index to both parts, forming the forty-fifth volume of the Registers, has been issued to the Subscribers for 1915.

Part I. of the Marriage Registers of St. Mary le Bone, Middlesex, commencing in 1668, edited by the Secretary, is in the press.

The Balance Sheet for the year, duly audited, is appended to the Report.

By Order of the Council,

W. BRUCE BANNERMAN,

Secretary.

The Harleian Society.

FOUNDED 1869.   INCORPORATED 1902.

ACCOUNTS FOR THE YEAR ENDING 31ST DECEMBER, 1914.

ORDINARY ACCOUNT.

Dr.

		£	s.	d.		£	s.	d.
Balance to 31st December 1913............						95	10	3
Subscriptions	1912	£4	4	0				
	1913	52	10	0				
	1914	234	13	6				
	1915	1	1	0				
						292	8	6
Books purchased by Subscribers						13	8	10
Dividend, 3 per cent. Stock. Lancashire and York- shire Railway (£500)						14	2	2
						£415	**9**	**9**

Cr.

	£	s.	d.
Messrs. Mitchell Hughes & Clarke:—			
Balance of account for printing the Visitations of Hampshire and the Isle of Wight	82	3	3
Paid for Blocks	27	4	11
Balance of cost of Transcript..........	11	6	0
Messrs. Mitchell Hughes & Clarke:—			
For printing Middlesex Pedigrees..........	183	15	5
H. Soane. Account for drawing Arms for blocks as per estimate	20	0	0
Messrs. Mitchell Hughes & Clarke:—			
General Account	20	0	6
Fire Insurance	6	5	0
Commission on Cheques and Cheque Book		4	1
Auditor's Fee	1	1	0
Balance..........	63	9	7
	£415	**9**	**9**

REGISTER SECTION.

Dr.	£ s. d.		Cr.	£ s. d.
Balance to 31st December, 1913	118 0 8		Messrs. Mitchell Hughes & Clarke:—	
Subscriptions 1912 £1 1 0			On account of printing Registers of St. Mary le Bow, Allhallows, Honey Lane, and St. Pancras, Soper Lane, E.C.	150 0 0
1913 37 16 0			Paid for Transcript	25 0 0
1914 162 15 10			Gratuity to Verger	1 1 0
	201 12 10		Paid for Transcript of Registers of St. Stephen, Walbrook, and St. Bennet Sherehog	18 0 0
Book purchased by Subscribers	3 15 8		Secretary and Treasurer	30 0 0
			Balance	99 8 2
	£323 9 2			£323 9 2

GENERAL BALANCE.

1914.	£ s. d.		1914.	£ s. d.
To Balance, Ordinary Section	63 9 7		Dec. 31. By Balance in the Bank	162 17 9
Register Section	99 8 2			
	£162 17 9			£162 17 9

Examined and approved,

M. W. KER, *Auditor*

29th January 1915.

W. BRUCE BANNERMAN, *Treasurer.*

www.armorial-register.com

www.ingramcontent.com/pod-product-compliance
Lightning Source LLC
Chambersburg PA
CBHW060327100426
42812CB00003B/908